Frommer's®

by D   n

e

WILEY

John Wiley & Sons, Inc.

ABOUT THE AUTHORS

As a team of veteran travel writers, **Darwin Porter** and **Danforth Prince** have produced various titles for Frommer's. A film critic, columnist, and broadcaster, Porter is also a Hollywood biographer. His recent releases include *Brando Unzipped,* documenting the private life of Marlon Brando, and *Jacko: His Rise and Fall,* the first complete biography ever written on the tumultuous life of Michael Jackson. Prince was formerly employed by the Paris bureau of *The New York Times* and is today the president of Blood Moon Productions.

Published by:

JOHN WILEY & SONS, INC.

111 River St.
Hoboken, NJ 07030-5774

ISBN 978-1-118-08605-6 (paper); ISBN 978-1-118-22337-6 (ebk); ISBN 978-1-118-23671-0 (ebk); ISBN 978-1-118-26165-1 (ebk)

Editors: Naomi P. Kraus and Jennifer Moore
Production Editor: Lindsay Conner
Cartographer: Roberta Stockwell
Photo Editor: Richard Fox
Production by Wiley Indianapolis Composition Services

Front Cover Photo: View to the arches at Marinha beach in Lagoa, Alvor, Portimao Algarve © Joel Santos / Aurora Images.

Back Cover Photo: St Vincent statue and Sao Vicente de Fora church Alfama Lisbon, Portugal © Simon Reddy / Alamy Images.

For information on our other products and services or to obtain technical support, please contact our Customer Care Department within the U.S. at 877/762-2974, outside the U.S. at 317/572-3993 or fax 317/572-4002.

Wiley also publishes its books in a variety of electronic formats. Some content that appears in print may not be available in electronic formats.

Manufactured in the United States of America

5   4   3   2   1

CONTENTS

14 MADEIRA & PORTO SANTO 367

15 PLANNING YOUR TRIP TO PORTUGAL 402

Index 425

LIST OF MAPS

HOW TO CONTACT US

In researching this book, we discovered many wonderful places—hotels, restaurants, shops, and more. We're sure you'll find others. Please tell us about them, so we can share the information with your fellow travelers in upcoming editions. If you were disappointed with a recommendation, we'd love to know that, too. Please write to:

Frommer's Portugal, 22nd Edition
John Wiley & Sons, Inc. • 111 River St. • Hoboken, NJ 07030-5774
frommersfeedback@wiley.com

AN ADDITIONAL NOTE

Please be advised that travel information is subject to change at any time—and this is especially true of prices. We therefore suggest that you write or call ahead for confirmation when making your travel plans. The authors, editors, and publisher cannot be held responsible for the experiences of readers while traveling. Your safety is important to us, however, so we encourage you to stay alert and be aware of your surroundings. Keep a close eye on cameras, purses, and wallets, all favorite targets of thieves and pickpockets.

FROMMER'S STAR RATINGS, ICONS & ABBREVIATIONS

Every hotel, restaurant, and attraction listing in this guide has been ranked for quality, value, service, amenities, and special features using a **star-rating system.** In country, state, and regional guides, we also rate towns and regions to help you narrow down your choices and budget your time accordingly. Hotels and restaurants are rated on a scale of zero (recommended) to three stars (exceptional). Attractions, shopping, nightlife, towns, and regions are rated according to the following scale: zero stars (recommended), one star (highly recommended), two stars (very highly recommended), and three stars (must-see).

In addition to the star-rating system, we also use **seven feature icons** that point you to the great deals, in-the-know advice, and unique experiences that separate travelers from tourists. Throughout the book, look for:

special finds—those places only insiders know about

fun facts—details that make travelers more informed and their trips more fun

kids—best bets for kids and advice for the whole family

special moments—those experiences that memories are made of

overrated—places or experiences not worth your time or money

insider tips—great ways to save time and money

great values—where to get the best deals

The following abbreviations are used for credit cards:

AE	American Express	DISC	Discover	V	Visa
DC	Diners Club	MC	MasterCard		

TRAVEL RESOURCES AT FROMMERS.COM

Frommer's travel resources don't end with this guide. Frommer's website, **www.frommers. com**, has travel information on more than 4,000 destinations. We update features regularly, giving you access to the most current trip-planning information and the best airfare, lodging, and car-rental bargains. You can also listen to podcasts, connect with other Frommers. com members through our active-reader forums, share your travel photos, read blogs from guidebook editors and fellow travelers, and much more.

THE BEST OF PORTUGAL

S wept by the winds of the Atlantic Ocean, seafaring Portugal is a study in contrasts. In Lisbon's historic Alfama, cows are walked house to house to provide fresh milk for the varinas (fishwives). Only blocks away computers process data from around the globe. Meanwhile, in the country giant stone castles and tiny red-roofed villas of the east give way to verdant mountains and vineyards in the west. Street markets, unique architecture, and festivals are a magnet for both visitors and locals.

CITIES Spread across seven famous hills, vibrant **Lisbon** still revels in relics from its 15th-century Golden Age. One of the most talked about cities of Europe, Portugal's capital is cutting edge in fashion, art, music, chic night clubs, and fado cafes. **Porto** in the north is a modern metropolis of stunning buildings and monuments to its glory of yesterday. Savor its port wine in one of the Left Bank "caves."

COUNTRYSIDE The sound of Portugal's most authentic fado lures visitors with its siren call to **Coimbra,** one of Europe's most historic cities and site of its oldest university. Explore the vast, sparsely inhabited **Alentejo** in the desert-like east, with its crumbling castles, cork trees, and hilltop towns, anchored at medieval **Évora.** Find a spot on the beach at the resort-studded **Algarve** in the south where glitz, glamour, almond blossoms, and fun in the sun prevail. Beaches, hidden lagoons, haunted forests, and mountain peaks dot the central **Beiras.**

EATING AND DRINKING The exotic tastes and smells of a far-flung and majestic former empire, stretching from Angola to Macoa, converge in Portugal's varied cuisine, enlivened with virgin olive oil, fresh garlic, and aromatic herbs. Sizzling from the grill, the fresh seafood of **Lisbon** spreads its wafting aromas. From the ranches and arid plains of **Alentejo** comes succulent beef and acorn-sweetened pork.

COAST From boat trips to water parks, both children and adults squeal with delight on the miles of sandy beaches at southern tier **Algarve** resorts. The sands of the **Costa do Sol** north of Lisbon attract everyone from deposed royals to fashion models to its glamorous sands. Coastal fishing villages of central **Estremadura** are bordered by golden sands. With its hundreds of peppermint-striped tents, the traditional village of **Nazaré** joins fishing boats with European chic.

FROMMER'S favorite
PORTUGAL EXPERIENCES

o **Hiking in the Algarve:** Portugal's incredible physical beauty makes it a spectacular place for outdoor activities. In the southern Algarve region's low-lying lagoons and rocky highlands, the panoramas extend for miles over the nearby ocean. Especially rewarding is trekking through the territory near Sagres, which has retained its mystical hold on journeyers since it was known as the end of the world. Other worthwhile hikes include the footpaths around the villages of Silves and Monchique, where eroded river valleys have changed little since the Moorish occupation. See chapter 9.

o **Pousada-Hopping:** After World War II, the Portuguese government recognized that the patrimony of its great past was desperately in need of renovation. It transformed dozens of monasteries, palaces, and convents into hotels, honoring the historical authenticity of their architectural cores. Today's travelers can intimately experience some of Portugal's greatest architecture by staying in a pousada, part of a chain of state-owned and -operated hotels. The rooms are often far from opulent, and the government-appointed staffs will probably be more bureaucratic than you'd like. Nonetheless, pousada-hopping rewards with insights into the Portugal of long ago.

o **Playing Golf by the Sea:** British merchants trading in Portugal's excellent wines imported the sport of golf around 1890. Until the 1960s, it remained a diversion only for the very wealthy. Then an explosion of interest from abroad led to the creation of at least 30 major courses. Many courses lie near Estoril and in the southern Algarve. The combination of great weather, verdant fairways, and azure seas and skies is almost addictive (as if golf fanatics needed additional motivation).

o **Swooning to Fado:** After soccer, fado (which translates as "fate") music is the national obsession. A lyrical homage to the bruised or broken heart, fado assumes forms that are as old as the troubadours. Its four-line stanzas of unrhymed verse, performed by such legendary stars as Amália Rodriguez, capture the nation's collective unconscious. Hearing the lament of the *fadistas* (fado singers) in clubs is the best way to appreciate the melancholy dignity of Iberia's western edge.

o **Finding a Solitary Beach:** Portugal has long been famous for the glamour and style of the beaches near Estoril, Cascais, Setúbal, and Sesimbra. More recently, the Algarve, with its 200km (124 miles) of tawny sands, gorgeous blue-green waters, and rocky coves, has captivated the imagination of northern Europeans. While the most famous beaches are likely to be very crowded, you can find solitude on the sands if you stop beside lonely expanses of any coastal road in northern Portugal.

o **Fishing in Rich Coastal Waters:** Portugal's position on the Atlantic, its (largely) unpolluted waters, and its flowing rivers encourage concentrations of fish. You won't be the first to plumb these waters—Portugal fed itself for hundreds of generations using nets and lines, and its maritime and fishing traditions are among the most entrenched in Europe. The mild weather allows fishing year-round for more than 200 species, including varieties not seen anywhere else (such as the 2m-long/6½-ft. scabbard). The country's rivers and lakes produce three species of trout, as well as black bass and salmon; the cold Atlantic abounds in sea bass, shark, tope, grouper, skate, and swordfish.

o **Trekking to the End of the World:** For medieval Europeans, the southwestern tip of Portugal represented the final frontier of human security and power. Beyond that point, the oceans were dark and fearful, filled with demons waiting to devour the bodies and souls of mariners foolhardy enough to sail upon them. Adding Sagres and its peninsula to the Portuguese nation cost thousands of lives in battle against the Moors, and getting there required weeks of travel over rocky deserts. Making a pilgrimage to this outpost is one of the loneliest and most majestic experiences in Portugal. Come here to pay your respects to the navigators who embarked from Sagres on journeys to death or glory. Half a millennium later, the excitement of those long-ago voyages still permeates this lonely corner. See chapter 9.

o **Losing It at a Spa:** Compared to the sybaritic luxury of spas in Germany and France, Portuguese spas are underaccessorized, and by California's frenetic standards, they're positively sleepy. Still, central and northern Portugal share about half a dozen spas whose sulfur-rich waters have been considered therapeutic since the days of the ancient Romans. Luso, Monte Real, and Cúria are the country's most famous spas, followed closely by Caldas do Gerês, Vimeiro, and São Pedro do Sul. Don't expect the latest in choreographed aerobics and spinning classes; instead, sink into communion with nature, rid your body of the toxins of urban life, and retire early every night for recuperative sleep.

o **Tasting & Touring in Port Wine Country:** Across the Rio Douro from the heart of the northern city of Porto lies Vila Nova de Gaia, the headquarters of the port-wine trade since the 1600s. From vineyards along the Douro, wine is transported to "lodges" (warehouses), where it is matured, bottled, and eventually shipped around the world. More than 25 companies, including such well-known names as Sandeman, maintain port-wine lodges here. Each offers free guided tours, always ending with a tasting of one or two of the house wines. The tourist office in Porto will provide you with a map if you'd like to drive along the Douro to see the vineyards. See chapter 12.

THE best TOWNS TO VISIT

o **Sintra:** Since the Moorish occupation, Portuguese kings and nobles have recognized this town's irresistible charm. You'll find a denser concentration of beautiful villas and gardens here than anywhere else in Portugal. At least five major palaces and convents are tucked amid the lush vegetation. See p. 163.

o **Óbidos:** This town is the most perfectly preserved 13th-century village in central Portugal. Its historical authenticity is the primary concern of the population of more than 5,000. For 600 years, Óbidos was the personal property of Portuguese queens, a symbolic love offering from their adoring husbands. Óbidos has always breathed romance. See p. 190.

o **Nazaré:** This folkloric fishing village in central Portugal produces wonderful handicrafts. The town has a strong sense of traditional culture that's distinctly different from that of nearby communities. See p. 201.

o **Fátima:** In 1913, an apparition of the Virgin Mary appeared to three shepherd children from Fátima, who were called upon to spread a message of peace. Their story was at first discounted and then embraced by a church hierarchy under assault by the ravages of World War I. Later, 70,000 people who were assembled on the site claimed to witness miracles. Today Fátima is the most-visited pilgrimage site in Iberia, home to dozens of imposing churches and monuments. See p. 206.

o **Évora:** This is one of the country's most perfectly preserved architectural gems. A well-preserved ancient Roman temple rises across the street from convents and monasteries that flourished when the kings of Portugal used this town as their capital in the 12th century. These buildings combine with remnants of the Moorish occupation to form one of the most alluring, if not largest, architectural medleys in Europe. See p. 268.

o **Tomar:** Beginning in the 12th century, the Knights Templar and later the Knights of Christ (two warlike and semimonastic sects) designated Tomar as their Portuguese headquarters. They lavished the town with adornments over the centuries until it looked, as it does today, like a living monument to the architecture of medieval Portugal. See p. 259.

o **Coimbra:** The country's academic center, this town boasts a university with roots in the Middle Ages, a rich historic core, and a tradition of troubadour-style singing that's one of the most vital in Iberia. See p. 284.

o **Porto:** The second city of Portugal, Porto has rich associations with the port-wine trade. Entrepreneurs who returned home after making their fortunes in Brazil built some of the town's most imposing villas here in the late 19th century. But as Portugal's economic center, Porto has also moved into the 21st century, with new office buildings; modern apartment complexes; fashionable shops and restaurants in its commercial heart; and such stunning developments as the Fundação Serralves, the National Museum of Modern Art, set in a 18-hectare (44-acre) park in the western part of the city. See p. 308.

o **Guimarães:** The birthplace of the country's first king, Afonso Henríques, and the core from which the country expanded, Guimarães is the cradle of Portugal and was designated the European Capital of Culture for 2012. Its medieval section is one of the most authentic anywhere. The town was also the birthplace of Gil Vicente (1465–1537), a playwright referred to as the Shakespeare of Portugal. See p. 342.

o **Viana do Castelo:** This northern town with strong folkloric traditions is noted for pottery, women's regional dresses, abundant rainfall, and a collection of distinctive and dignified public buildings. Its heyday was in the 1500s, when fleets departed from here to fish for cod as far away as Newfoundland. Profits from their activities helped pay for the town's handsome collection of Manueline buildings. See p. 354.

o **Guincho:** On the Estoril Coast, 9km (5⅔ miles) northwest of Cascais, this is the westernmost point in continental Europe. It's a dramatic, spectacular site where waves crash against three sides of a restored 17th-century fortress (now the Hotel do Guincho, one of the most unusual, luxurious hotels in Europe). Balconies—best shared with a loved one—overlook the panoramic scene, with beaches on both sides. The crashing surf makes good background music for a torrid affair straight out of a romance novel. See p. 158.

o **Serra de Arrábida:** This whale-shaped ridge never exceeds 1,525m (5,003 ft.) in height. The masses of wildflowers that flank its sides are among the most colorful and varied in Iberia. The Serra lies between Sesimbra and Setúbal, across the estuary of the Tagus from Lisbon. En route from Lisbon, you'll find crowded and secluded beaches, a medieval Capuchin monastery (the Convento Novo), and a smattering of good restaurants. The town of Sesimbra, with its historic, sleepy main square and ruined fortresses, offers bars, restaurants, and insight into the Iberia of a bygone era. See p. 182.

THE best BEACHES

o **Costa do Sol:** Sometimes called the Estoril Coast, this stretch of seafront extends 32km (20 miles) west of Lisbon. Its two major resorts are Estoril and Cascais.

Once the playground of the wintering wealthy, the area now attracts throngs of tourists, mainly from northern Europe. See chapter 6.

o **The Algarve:** This region at the southern tip of Portugal gained its place on world tourist maps because of its string of beautiful, clean, sandy beaches. Lovely coves, caves, and grottos—some accessible only by boat—add to the region's allure. Albufeira and Praia da Rocha are set against a backdrop of towering rock formations; the best cove beach is at Lagos, a former Moorish town with a deepwater harbor and wide bay. See chapter 9.

o **The Beiras:** In central Portugal, north of Lisbon, some of the finest beaches in Europe open onto the Atlantic. Like gems in a necklace, good, sandy beaches stretch from Praia de Leirosa north to Praia de Espinho. The surf can be heavy and the undertow strong. Major resorts include Figueira da Foz and nearby Buarcos. The beaches between Praia de Mira and Costa Nova are more secluded. See chapter 11.

o **Costa Verde:** As the northern coastline approaches Galicia in Spain, the Atlantic waters grow colder, and even in summer they're likely to be windswept. But on certain days they're among the most dramatic in Europe. We like the wide, sandy beach at Ponte de Lima, but there are many others. Notable destinations are the resort of Espinho, south of Porto, and other beach meccas, including Póvoa do Varzim and Ofir, which have some of the best hotels, restaurants, and watersports equipment in the country. See chapter 12.

THE best HOTELS

o **Pestana Palace** (Lisbon; ✆ 21/361-56-00; www.pestana.com): One of the grandest hotels to open in Portugal in years, this hotel lies in an upscale residential section 5km (3 miles) from the historic center. It was carved out of a villa built in 1907. It's a stunning example of the Romantic Revival architectural style. See p. 81.

o **Four Seasons Hotel Ritz Lisbon** (Lisbon; ✆ 800/819-5053 in the U.S., or 21/381-14-00; www.fourseasons.com): Built in the 1950s and host to a roster that reads like a who's who of international glamour, the Ritz is one of Portugal's legendary hotels. Everywhere in the hotel, you'll get the impression that a swanky reception is about to begin. See p. 68.

o **York House Hotel** (Lisbon; ✆ 21/396-24-35; www.yorkhouselisboa.com): A former 17th-century convent and private home, York House is *the* place to stay in Lisbon. It abounds with climbing vines, antiques, four-poster beds, and Oriental carpeting—fittings and furnishings that maintain the building's historical character without flattening your wallet. See p. 75.

o **Albatroz** (Cascais; ✆ 21/484-73-80; www.albatrozhotels.com): In a garden overlooking the Atlantic, this inn was originally built as the summer residence of the dukes of Loulé. Since its transformation into a stylish hotel, its aristocratic elegance has drawn guests from throughout Europe. Service is impeccable. See p. 151.

o **Palácio Estoril** (Estoril; ✆ 21/465-86-00; www.palacioestorilhotel.com): The Palácio enjoyed its heyday during the 1950s and 1960s, when every deposed monarch of Europe seemed to disappear into the Art Deco hotel's sumptuous suites. The result: the curious survival in Estoril of the royal ambience of a Europe gone by. Today "the Palace" maintains a staff whose old-timers are among the best in Europe at offering royal treatment to guests. See p. 145.

o **Tivoli Palácio de Seteais** (Sintra; ✆ **21/923-32-00;** www.tivolihotels.com): One of the most elegant hotels in Portugal bears one of the country's most ironic names. In 1807, a treaty ending the Napoleonic campaign in Portugal was signed here, with terms so humiliating to the Portuguese that they labeled the building the Palace of the Seven Sighs. Any sighing you're likely to do today will be from pleasure—at the setting, the lavish gardens, and the reminders of an old-world way of life. See p. 168.

o **Dona Filipa Hotel** (Almancil; ✆ **28/935-72-23;** www.donafilipahotel.com): Rising above the sea, this hotel is comfortable, modern, well designed, and sophisticated, but the most stunning feature is the 180 hectares (445 acres) surrounding it. Part of the land is devoted to a superb golf course. Don't let the severe exterior fool you—the inside is richly appointed with Chinese and Portuguese accessories, many of them antique. See p. 245.

o **Monte do Casal** (Estói; ✆ **28/999-15-03;** www.montedocasal.com): An 18th-century country house on the Algarve converted into one of the most charming and tranquil places along the coast, Monte do Casal is set on 3 hectares (7½ acres) of flowering trees. It offers a chance to escape from the curse of the high-rise sea resort hotels and into an inn of style that captures some of the spirit of the region itself. See p. 254.

o **Bussaco Palace Hotel** (Buçaco; ✆ **23/193-79-70;** www.almeidahotels.com): This palace, built between 1888 and 1907 as a sylvan refuge for the royal family, saw tragedy early. A year after its completion, the king and his oldest son were assassinated, leaving Queen Amélia to grieve within its *azulejo*-sheathed walls. In 1910, the palace's enterprising Swiss chef persuaded the government to allow him to transform the place into an upscale hotel. Bittersweet memories of its royal past still seem to linger within the thick walls. See p. 294.

o **HF Ipanema Park** (Porto; ✆ **22/532-21-00;** www.hfhotels.com): One of the leading hotels in the north of Portugal offers 15 floors of grand comfort with the largest roster of facilities in the city, including an outdoor pool with a panoramic view on the 15th floor. This bastion of good taste and luxury is as popular with tourists as it is with its business clients. See p. 321.

o **Hotel Infante Sagres** (Porto; ✆ **22/339-85-00;** www.hotelinfantesagres.pt): A textile magnate built this hotel in 1951 in the style of a Portuguese manor house. Its elegant detailing makes it appear much older than it is. It's the most nostalgic, elegant, and ornate hotel in Porto. The managers began their careers here as teenage bellboys, and the staff members take obvious pride in their hotel. See p. 321.

o **Reid's Palace** (Funchal; ✆ **800/223-6800** in the U.S., or 29/171-71-71; www.reidspalace.com): For more than a century (it was founded in 1891 and enlarged in 1968), Reid's has fulfilled the colonial fantasies of every British imperialist abroad. Set on a rocky promontory, it serves tea promptly at 4pm, contains English antiques that the Portuguese staff waxes once a week, and plays chimes to announce the beginning of the dinner service. It also features terraced gardens spilling down to the sea and a very correct clientele that once included Winston Churchill. See p. 376.

o **Praia D'El Rey Marriott Golf & Beach Resort** (Amoreira; ✆ **26/290-51-00;** www.marriott.com/lisdr): Devotees of modern luxury should head to one of the most spectacular resorts north of Lisbon, 16km (10 miles) west of the romantic walled city of Óbidos. It opens onto a sandy beach and boasts an 18-hole golf course on 243 hectares (600 acres) of oceanfront property. Its facilities include a spa, health club, tennis courts, and a choice of three first-class restaurants. See p. 193.

THE best POUSADAS

- **Pousada de Setúbal, São Filipe** (Setúbal; ✆ 26/555-00-70; www.pousadas.pt): During the 1500s, this structure served as a defensive link in a chain of fortresses surrounding Lisbon. Today it boasts antique *azulejos* (glazed earthenware tiles), panoramic views of the town, and a keen sense of Portuguese history. The rooms are simple (some might say monastic) but comfortable and tidy. See p. 185.

- **Pousada de Óbidos, Castelo de Óbidos** (Óbidos; ✆ 26/295-50-80; www. pousadas.pt): This pousada lies in a wing of the castle that protects one of the most perfectly preserved medieval towns in Portugal. In 1285, King Dinis offered the castle—along with the entire village—to his beloved Queen Isabel. Inside, the medieval aesthetic coexists with improved plumbing, electricity, and unobtrusive contemporary comforts. See p. 193.

- **Pousada de Elvas, Santa Luzia** (Elvas; ✆ 26/863-74-70; www.pousadas.pt): This pousada opened in 1942 during the most horrible days of World War II, near the strategic border crossing between neutral Portugal and fascist Spain. Vaguely Moorish in design, with two low-slung stories, it was most recently renovated in 1992. It offers comfortable, colorful lodgings. See p. 267.

- **Pousada de Estremoz, Rainha Santa Isabel** (Estremoz; ✆ 26/833-20-75; www. pousadas.pt): Housed in a structure built during the Middle Ages, the Santa Isabel is the most lavish pousada in Portugal. Reproductions of 17th-century antiques, about .5 hectares (1¼ acres) of gleaming marble, and elaborately detailed tapestries create one of the most authentic old-fashioned decors in the region. Guests have included Vasco da Gama, who was received here by Dom Manuel before the explorer's departure for India. See p. 265.

- **Pousada de Évora, Lóios** (Évora; ✆ 26/673-00-70; www.pousadas.pt): This pousada was conceived as a monastery and rebuilt in 1485 adjacent to the town's ancient Roman temple. The purity of its design and the absence of exterior encroachments from the modern world contribute to one of the most aesthetically thrilling experiences in Portugal. Inside there are no traces left of its original austerity—everything is luxurious and comfortable. See p. 272.

THE best RESTAURANTS

- **Clara Restaurante** (Lisbon; ✆ 21/885-30-53; www.lisboa-clara.pt): This elegant citadel, with a refined dining room playing soft piano music and serving a remarkable Portuguese and international cuisine, is a favorite among serious palates. The chefs take special care with all their ingredients, and we sing their praises year after year for their impeccable offerings. See p. 85.

- **Gambrinus** (Lisbon; ✆ 21/342-14-66; www.gambrinuslisboa.com): It isn't as upscale as some of its competitors or the preferred rendezvous of the country's most distinguished aristocrats. Nonetheless, this is one of the hippest, best-managed seafood restaurants in Lisbon; the stand-up bar proffers an astonishing array of shellfish. Enjoy a glass of dry white port accompanied by some of the most exotic seafood in the Atlantic. See p. 86.

- **Casa da Comida** (Lisbon; ✆ 21/388-53-76; www.casadacomida.pt): This restaurant is probably at its best on foggy evenings, when roaring fireplaces remove the damp chill from the air. Don't let the prosaic name fool you—some visitors prefer its Portuguese-French cuisine over the food at any other restaurant in Lisbon. Portions are ample, and the ambience is bracing and healthful. See p. 85.

- **Cozinha Velha** (Queluz; ✆ **21/435-61-58**): During the 1700s, food for the monarchy's most lavish banquets was prepared here (the name means "old kitchen"). Today the high-ceilinged kitchens serve an unusual restaurant, whose cuisine reflects the old days of Portuguese royalty. Dishes include *cataplana*, a savory fish stew with clams, shrimp, and monkfish. Equally outstanding is soufflélike *bacalhau espiritual* (codfish), which takes 45 minutes to prepare and should be ordered when you make your reservation. The restaurant is celebrated for its desserts, many of which are based on ancient convent recipes. See p. 162.
- **Porto de Santa Maria** (Guincho; ✆ **21/487-10-36** or 21/487-02-40; www.porto santamaria.com): The understated beige-and-white decor highlights this restaurant's bubbling aquarium and sea view. The menu lists nearly every conceivable kind of shellfish, served in the freshest possible combinations in a justifiably popular dining room. See p. 160.
- **Four Seasons** (in the Palácio Estoril, Estoril; ✆ **21/464-80-00**): This tranquil restaurant, with its rich colors and artful accents, has been a fixture in Estoril since the days when deposed European monarchs assembled here with their entourages. High glamour, old-world service, and impeccably prepared international cuisine are this place's hallmarks. See p. 147.
- **Casa Velha Restaurante** (Quinta do Lago, near Almancil; ✆ **28/939-49-83**; www.restaurante-casavelha.com): On a rocky hilltop above the modern resort of Quinta do Lago (with which it is not associated), this restaurant occupies a century-old farmhouse, with kitchens modernized for the preparation of gourmet food. The sophisticated cuisine includes preparations of upscale French and Portuguese recipes. See p. 246.
- **Churrascão do Mar** (Porto; ✆ **22/609-63-82**): Porto's most elegant restaurant, serving Brazilian cuisine, is housed in a 19th-century antique manor restored to its Belle Epoque glory. The town's finest chefs turn out a savory cuisine specializing in grilled seafood. See p. 327.
- **Don Tonho** (Porto; ✆ **22/200-43-07**; www.dtonho.com): Visiting celebrities are usually directed to this citadel of fine cuisine (both European and Portuguese) in the eastern end of this port city. The setting perfectly suits the bracing cuisine that often features freshly caught fish from the Atlantic. The prices are surprisingly affordable for such deluxe dishes. See p. 328.

THE best PALACES & CASTLES

- **Castelo de São Jorge** (the Alfama, Lisbon; ✆ **21/880-06-20**; www.castelode saojorge.pt): This hilltop has long been valued as a fortification to protect settlements along the Tagus. Today the bulky castle crowns one of the most densely populated medieval neighborhoods of Lisbon, the Alfama. It encompasses a nostalgic collection of thick stone walls, medieval battlements, Catholic and feudal iconography, verdant landscaping, and sweeping views of one of Europe's greatest harbors. See p. 104.
- **Palácio Nacional de Queluz** (near Lisbon; ✆ **21/434-38-60**; www.pnqueluz. imc-ip.pt): Designed for the presentation of music and royal receptions in the 1700s, this castle was modeled as a more intimate version of Versailles. It's a symmetrical building ringed with gardens, fountains, and sculptures of mythical heroes and maidens. Although gilt, crystal, and frescoes fill its interior, most Portuguese are proudest of the *azulejos* room, where hand-painted blue-and-white tiles depict day-to-day life in the Portuguese colonies of Macao and Brazil. See p. 162.

- **Palácio Nacional da Pena** (Sintra; ℂ 21/910-53-40; www.cm-sintra.pt): Only a cosmopolitan 19th-century courtier could have produced this eclectic, expensive mélange of architectural styles. Set in a 200-hectare (494-acre) walled park, it was commissioned by the German-born consort of the Portuguese queen; it reminds some visitors of the Bavarian castles of Mad King Ludwig. Appointed with heavy furnishings and rich ornamentation, it's a symbol of the Portuguese monarchs at their most aesthetically decadent stages. See p. 166.

- **Castelo dos Mouros** (Sintra; ℂ 21/923-73-00; www.parquesdesintra.pt): In the 19th century, the monarchs ordered that this castle, evocative of the Moorish occupation of Portugal, remain as a ruined ornament to embellish their sprawling parks and gardens. Set near the much larger, much more ornate Pena palace (see above), the squat, thick-walled fortress was begun around A.D. 750 by the Moors and captured with the help of Scandinavian Crusaders in 1147. It retains its jagged battlements, a quartet of eroded towers, and a ruined Romanesque chapel erected by the Portuguese as a symbol of their domination of former Moorish territories. See p. 164.

- **Bussaco Palace Hotel** (Buçaco; ℂ 23/193-79-70; www.almeidahotels.com): Of all the buildings in this list, the Palace of Buçaco is the most important national icon. Completed in 1907, it's also the only one that operates as a hotel, allowing visitors to sleep within the walls of a former royal palace. Constructed from marble, bronze, stained glass, and exotic hardwoods, and inspired by the greatest buildings in the empire, it represents more poignantly than any other Portuguese palace the final days of the country's doomed aristocracy. See p. 294.

THE best MUSEUMS

- **Museu da Fundação Calouste Gulbenkian** (Lisbon; ℂ 21/782-30-00; www.museu.gulbenkian.pt): Its namesake was an Armenian oil czar, Calouste Gulbenkian (1869–1955), whose fortune derived from a 5% royalty on most of the oil pumped out of Iraq. His eclectic collections of Asian and European sculpture, paintings, antique coins, carpets, and furniture are on display in a modern compound in a lush garden. See p. 110.

- **Museu Nacional dos Coches** (Lisbon; ℂ 21/361-08-50; http://en.museu doscoches.pt): Founded by Queen Amélia in 1904, when the horse-drawn buggy was becoming obsolete, this museum is located on the premises of the riding school of the Palácio do Belém (the official home of the Portuguese president). It contains dozens of magnificent state carriages, some decorated with depictions of Portugal's maritime discoveries. See p. 109.

- **Museu Nacional de Arte Antiga** (Lisbon; ℂ 21/391-28-00; www.mnarteantiga-ipmuseus.pt): In the 1830s, the power of many of Portugal's fabulously wealthy monasteries was violently curbed. Many of the monasteries' art treasures, including the country's best collection of Portuguese primitives, as well as gold and silver plates crafted from raw materials mined in India, are displayed at the 17th-century palace of the counts of Alvor. See p. 112.

- **Museu de Marinha** (Lisbon; ℂ 21/362-00-19; http://museu.marinha.pt): The most important maritime museum in the world—a rich tribute to Portugal's Age of Exploration—is in the west wing of the Jerónimos Monastery. The thousands of displays include royal galleons dripping with gilt and ringed with depictions of saltwater dragons and sea serpents. See p. 109.

THE best CHURCHES & ABBEYS

o **Mosteiro dos Jerónimos** (Belém; ✆ 21/362-00-34; www.mosteirojeronimos.pt): More than any other ecclesiastical building in Portugal, this complex represents the wealth that poured into Lisbon from the colonies during the Age of Discovery. Begun in 1502 in Belém, the seaport near the gates of Lisbon, it's the world's most distinctive Manueline church. Richly ornate and unlike any other building in Europe, it has, among other features, columns carved in patterns inspired by the rigging of Portuguese caravels laden with riches from Brazil and India. See p. 106.

o **Palácio Nacional de Mafra** (Mafra; ✆ 26/181-75-50; www.cm-mafra.pt/turismo/palacio.asp): This convent was originally intended to house only about a dozen monks, but after the king of Portugal was blessed with an heir, he became obsessed with its architecture and vastly augmented its scale. Construction began in 1717, and funding came from gold imported from Portuguese settlements in Brazil. Some 50,000 laborers toiled more than 13 years to complete the convent. Today the buildings alone cover 4 hectares (10 acres) and include a royal palace as well as accommodations for 300 monks. A park whose outer wall measures 19km (12 miles) surrounds the complex. See p. 173.

o **Mosteiro de Santa Maria** (Alcobaça; ✆ 26/250-51-20): More closely associated with the Portuguese wars against the Moors than almost any other site in Iberia, this monastery was a gift from the first Portuguese king (Afonso Henríques) to the Cistercians in 1153. As part of one of the most dramatic land-improvement projects in Portuguese history, a community of ascetic monks cleared the surrounding forests, planted crops, dug irrigation ditches, and built a soaring church (completed in 1253) that critics cite as one of the purest and most artfully simple in Europe. See p. 200.

o **Mosteiro de Santa Maria da Vitória** (Batalha; ✆ 24/476-54-97): In 1385, the Castilian Spaniards and the Portuguese, led by a youth who had been crowned king only a week before, fought one of the most crucial battles in Iberian history. The outcome ensured Portugal's independence for another 200 years. It was celebrated with the construction of the monastery at Batalha, whose style is a triumph of the Manueline and Flamboyant Gothic styles. See p. 205.

o **Convento da Ordem de Cristo** (Tomar; ✆ 24/931-34-81; www.conventocristo.pt): Built in 1160 along the most hotly contested Muslim-Christian border in Iberia, this convent was originally intended as a monastic fortress. Successive building programs lasted half a millennium, ultimately creating a museum of diverse architectural styles. Some of the interior windows, adorned with stone carvings of ropes, coral, frigate masts, seaweed, cables, and cork trees, are the most splendid examples of Manueline decoration in the world. See p. 260.

THE best SHOPPING

Here's a list of some of the more enchanting artifacts and handicrafts produced in Portugal:

o **Arraiolos Carpets:** The Moorish traditions that once prevailed in the town of Arraiolos, where the carpets are still manufactured, inspired their intricate stitching. Teams of embroiderers and weavers work for many days, using pure wool in combinations of petit point with more widely spaced ponto largo cross-stitches. The resulting depictions of garlands of fruit and flowers (a loose interpretation of French Aubusson carpets) and animals scampering around idealized gardens (a theme vaguely inspired by carpets from Persia and Turkey) are some of the most charming items for sale in Portugal. The size of the piece and the intricacy of the design determine the price, which is often less than half what you'd pay in North America. If you can't make it to Arraiolos, you'll find the carpets for sale at outlets in Lisbon.

o **Ceramics & Tiles:** Early in Portugal's history, builders learned to compensate for the lack of lumber by perfecting the arts of masonry, stuccoing, and ceramics. All were used to construct the country's sturdy, termite-proof buildings. After the ouster of the Moors, their aesthetic endured in the designs painted on tiles and ceramic plates, vessels, and jugs. Later, styles from Holland, England, and China combined to influence a rich tradition of pottery-making. The most prevalent of these appear as the blue-and-white *azulejos* (tiles), each with an individual design, which adorn thousands of indoor and outdoor walls throughout the country. Equally charming are the thousands of plates, wine and water jugs, and vases adorned with sylvan landscapes populated with mythical creatures. New and (to a lesser extent) antique samples of any of these items can be acquired at outlets throughout Portugal.

o **Jewelry:** In Portugal, any piece of jewelry advertised as "gold" must contain at least 19.2 karats. This purity allows thousands of jewelers to spin the shining stuff into delicate filigree work with astounding detail. Whether you opt for a simple brooch or for a depiction in gold or filigreed silver of an 18th-century caravel in full four-masted sail, Portugal produces jewelry worthy of an infanta's dowry at prices more reasonable than you might expect. The country abounds in jewelry stores.

o **Handicrafts:** For centuries, the design and fabrication of lace, rugs, hand-knit clothing, woodcarvings, and embroidered linens have evolved in homes and work-shops throughout Portugal. Although some of the cruder objects available for sale are a bit clunky, the best can be called art. From the north to the south, store after store offers regional handicrafts.

o **Leather Goods:** Iberia has always been a land of animal husbandry, bullfighting, and cattle breeding, and the Portuguese leather-making industry is known through-out the world. Its products include jackets, shoes, pocketbooks, and wallets, all of which sell for prices much more reasonable than those outside Portugal. The best stores are concentrated in Lisbon.

THE best OFFBEAT TRIPS

o **Horseback Riding Along the Coast:** Seeing this beautiful country from the back of a well-trained, even-tempered Lusitano is a rewarding experience, but some of the best opportunities can be had along the Atlantic Ocean beach. Some of the best tours are available through the American company Equitour. In addition to beach riding, the company offers trekking through olive groves, vineyards, pine forests, and lagoons. For more details, see chapter 2.

o **Appreciating Manueline Architecture:** Manuelino—as it's known in Portu-guese—marked a dramatic artistic shift from the late Gothic style prevalent during the reign of King Dom Manuel. It mixes Christian motifs with shells, ropes, and strange aquatic shapes and is usually crowned with heraldic or religious symbols.

The best example is the grand Mosteiro dos Jerónimos (Jerónimos Monastery) in Belém, outside Lisbon, dating from the 16th century (p. 106). Another towering example is the mysterious and astrologic visions of the famous window of the Convento da Ordem de Cristo (Convent of Christ) in Tomar, the bastion of the Knights Templar in days gone by. See p. 260.

o **Visiting the Lost Continent of Atlantis:** One of the most offbeat travel experiences in Europe is a trip to the Azores. Mythologists believe the remote Portuguese islands in the mid-Atlantic are the only remnants of the lost continent of Atlantis. For hundreds of years they were considered the end of the earth, the outer limits of the European sphere of influence, beyond which ships could not go. Even today they're a verdant but lonely archipelago where the winds of the ocean meet, cyclones call on each other, and urbanites can lose themselves in fog-bound contact with the sea. See p. 398 for info.

o **Paying a Call on Berlenga Island:** Berlenga is a granite island 11km (6¾ miles) west of the Portuguese coastline. The island has always been the first line of defense against invaders from the sea. In 1666, 28 Portuguese tried to withstand 1,500 Spaniards who bombarded the site from 15 ships. A medieval fortress demolished in the battle was rebuilt several decades later and today houses a no-frills hostel. The entire island and the rocky, uninhabited archipelago that surrounds it are a designated nature reserve whose flora and fauna—both above and below the surface of the sea—are protected from development and destruction. Boat transport departs from the Peniche Peninsula, about 92km (57 miles) north of Lisbon. See chapter 8.

o **Heading "Beyond the Mountains":** The northernmost district of Trás-os-Montes is a wild, rugged land whose name means "beyond the mountains." Exploring this region provides a glimpse into a Portugal infrequently seen by outsiders. Most of the population lives in deep valleys, often in traditional houses built of shale or granite, and speaks a dialect of Galician similar to that spoken just across the border in northwestern Spain. Much of the plateau is arid and rocky, but swift rivers and streams provide water for irrigation, and thermal springs have bubbled out of the earth since at least Roman times. You can drive through these savage landscapes, but don't expect superhighways. What you'll find are ruins of pre-Roman fortresses, dolmens, and cromlechs erected by prehistoric Celts, and decaying old churches. See chapter 13.

PORTUGAL
IN DEPTH

Portugal, positioned at what was once thought to be the edge of the Earth, has long been a seafaring nation. At the dawn of the Age of Exploration, mariners believed that two-headed, fork-tongued monsters as big as houses lurked across the Sea of Darkness, waiting to chew up a caravel and gulp its debris down their fire-lined throats.

In spite of these paralyzing fears, the Portuguese launched legendary caravels on explorations that changed the fundamental perceptions of humankind: Vasco da Gama sailed to India, Magellan circumnavigated the globe, and Dias rounded the Cape of Good Hope. In time, Portuguese navigators explored two-thirds of the earth, opening the globe to trade and colonization and expanding the intellectual horizons of Western civilization for all time.

Despite its former global influence, Portugal has long suffered from one of the most widespread misconceptions in European travel—that it's simply "another Spain," and a poorer version, at that. But for those who know it well, Portugal is charming and uniquely sophisticated, with art, music, and a history of architecture that's uniquely different from that of its Iberian neighbor. And generations of exposure to other cultures within its far-flung empire has made it more cosmopolitan than you'd ever have expected, Before its European political and economic integration in 1986, some dared to call it "the last foreign country of Europe."

PORTUGAL TODAY

Only a few years ago, there was a prevailing sense of optimism as Portugal moved deeper and deeper into the 21st century. But today the people of Portugal are holding their breath, waiting to see what is going to happen next.

Like Greece and other nations, their economy is floundering and their deficit is rising. The country is struggling with a record unemployment rate of 11.2%. And in direct contrast to the favorable economic prospects that dominated the country's economic sector at the turn of the millennium, Experts within the EU as well as officials within the Bank of Portugal have predicted an actual shrinking of the country's economy throughout the lifetime of this edition. In May of 2011, Portugal became the third country in the Euro zone to accept public funds, as did Greece and Ireland. Thousands upon thousands of Portuguese have taken to the streets to protest government austerity measures, sometimes disturbing public transit and government services with strikes. The best way to deal with future events that even the savviest of commentators find hard to predict involves keeping a sense of humor and, preferably, a sense of charity for the hardships that the average citizen will face during the potential for social unrest to come.

Even in these dire economic times, Lisbon's sidewalks are still crowded in the evening, and strollers still climb the hilly, cobbled streets of this moody city on the Atlantic Ocean. Even in good times, there has always been a lingering melancholy in Lisbon, once the seat of a former world empire. This nostalgia is reflected in their music, the sad laments of fado, speaking of lost love and lost glory.

The brave little country struggles into what is hoped will be a brighter future. After the turn of the millennium, this windswept Atlantic nation began to reduce its dependence on imported fossil fuels. The government embarked on a renewable energy project that harnessed the country's wind and hydropower, but also its sunlight and ocean waves.

Today nearly 45% of the electricity in Portugal's grid comes from renewable sources, up 17% from just five years ago. This is an amazing achievement in such a short time.

LOOKING BACK: PORTUGAL HISTORY

THE ROMANS ARRIVE Starting in 210 B.C., the Romans colonized most of Iberia. They met great resistance from the Celtiberian people of the interior. The Lusitanian (ancient Portugal was known as Lusitania) leader, Viriatus, looms large in Portuguese history as a freedom fighter who held up the Roman advance; he died about 139 B.C. The Romans were ultimately unstoppable, however, and by the time of Julius Caesar, Portugal had been integrated into the Roman Empire. The Roman colonies included Olisipo (now Lisbon).

Christianity arrived in Portugal near the end of the 1st century A.D. By the 3rd century, bishoprics had been established at Lisbon, Braga, and elsewhere. Following

DATELINE

210 B.C. The Romans invade the peninsula, meeting fierce resistance from the Celtiberian people.

60 B.C. During the reign of Julius Caesar, Portugal is fully integrated into the Roman Empire.

409 A.D. Invaders from across the Pyrenees arrive, establishing a Visigothic empire that endures for some 2 centuries.

711 Moorish warriors arrive in Iberia and conquer Portugal within 7 years.

1065 Ferdinand, king of León and Castile, sets about reorganizing his western territories into what is now modern Portugal.

1143 Afonso Henríques is proclaimed the first king of Portugal and begins to drive the Moors out of the Algarve.

1249 Afonso III completes the Reconquista of the Algarve, as Christians drive out the Moors.

1279–1325 Reign of Dinis, the Poet King. Castile recognizes Portugal's borders.

the decline of the Roman Empire, invaders crossed the Pyrenees into Spain in 409 and eventually made their way to Portugal. The Visigothic Empire dominated the peninsula for some 2 centuries.

THE MOORS INVADE & RETREAT   In 711, a force of Moors arrived in Iberia and quickly advanced to Portugal. They erected settlements in the south. The Christian Reconquest—known as the Reconquista—to seize the land from Moorish control is believed to have begun in 718.

In the 11th century, Ferdinand the Great, king of León and Castile, took much of northern Portugal from the Moors. Before his death in 1065, Ferdinand set about reorganizing his western territories into Portucale.

Portuguese, a Romance language, evolved mainly from a dialect spoken when Portugal was a province of the Spanish kingdom of León and Castile. The language developed separately from other Romance dialects.

PORTUGAL IS BORN   Ferdinand handed over Portugal to his illegitimate daughter, Teresa. (At that time, the Moors still held the land south of the Tagus.) Unknowingly, the king of Spain had launched a course of events that was to lead to Portugal's development into a distinct nation.

Teresa was firmly bound in marriage to Henry, a count of Burgundy. Henry accepted his father-in-law's gift of Portugal as his wife's dowry, but upon the king's death, he coveted Spanish territory as well. His death cut short his dreams of expansion.

Following Henry's death, Teresa ruled Portugal; she cast a disdainful eye on, and an interfering nose into, her legitimate sister's kingdom in Spain. Teresa lost no time mourning Henry and took a Galician count, Fernão Peres, as her lover. Teresa's refusal to conceal her affair with Peres and stay out of everyone else's affairs led to open strife with León.

Teresa's son, Afonso Henríques, was incensed by his mother's actions. Their armies met at São Mamede in 1128. Teresa lost, and she and her lover were banished.

Afonso Henríques went on to become Portugal's founding father. In 1143, he was proclaimed its first king, and official recognition eventually came from the Vatican in 1178. Once his enemies in Spain were temporarily quieted, Afonso turned his eye

1383	Battle of Aljubarrota. João de Avis defeats the Castilians and founds the House of Avis to rule Portugal.		(1495–1521). Portugal's Golden Age begins.
1415	Henry the Navigator sets up a school of navigation in Sagres. Madeira is discovered in 1419; the Azores are discovered in 1427.	1521	Portugal becomes the first of the great maritime world empires, dominating access to the Indian Ocean.
1488	Bartolomeu Dias rounds the Cape of Good Hope.	1521–57	Reign of João III, ushering in Jesuits and the Inquisition.
1497–98	Vasco da Gama rounds India's west coast, opening up trade between the West and the East.	1578	João's son, Dom Sebastião, disappears in the battle of Morocco, leaving Portugal without an heir.
1500	Brazil is discovered. Peak of the reign of Manuel the Fortunate	1580–1640	Philip II of Spain brings Habsburg rule to Portugal.
		1640	Following a nationalist revolution, João IV restores independence

continues

toward the Moorish territory in the south of Portugal. Supported by crusaders from the north, the Portuguese conquered Santarém and Lisbon in 1147. Afonso died in 1185. His son and heir, Sancho I, continued his father's work of consolidating the new nation.

Successive generations waged war against the Moors until Afonso III, who ruled from 1248 to 1279, wrested the Algarve from Moorish control. The country's capital moved from Coimbra to Lisbon. After Portugal became independent in the 11th century, its borders expanded southward to the sea.

The Moors left a permanent impression on Portugal. The language called Mozarabic, spoken by Christians living as Moorish subjects, was integrated into the Portuguese dialect. The basic language of today, both oral and written, was later solidified and perfected in Lisbon and Coimbra.

Castile did not recognize Portugal's borders until the reign of Pedro Dinis (1279–1325). Known as the Poet King or the Farmer King (because of his interest in agriculture), he founded a university in Lisbon in about 1290; it later moved to Coimbra. Dinis married Isabella, a princess of Aragon who was later canonized. Isabella was especially interested in the poor. Legend has it that she was once smuggling bread out of the palace to feed them when her husband spotted her and asked what she was concealing. When she showed him, the bread miraculously turned into roses.

Their son, Afonso IV, is remembered today for ordering the murder of his son Pedro's mistress. During Pedro's reign (1357–67), an influential representative body called the Cortes (an assembly of clergy, nobility, and commoners) began to gain ascendancy. The majority of the clergy, greedy for power, fought the sovereign's reform measures, which worked to ally the people more strongly with the crown. During the reign of Pedro's son, Ferdinand I (1367–73), Castilian forces invaded Portugal, Lisbon was besieged, and the dynasty faced demise.

In 1383, rather than submit to Spanish rule, the Portuguese people chose the illegitimate son of Pedro as regent. That established the House of Avis. João de Avis (reigned 1383–1433), which secured Portuguese independence by defeating Castilian forces at Aljubarrota in 1385. João's union with Philippa of Lancaster, the

and launches the House of Bragança.

1755 A great earthquake destroys Lisbon and parts of Alentejo and the Algarve.

1822 Portugal declares Brazil independent.

1908 Carlos I, the Painter King, and his son, the crown prince, are assassinated in Lisbon.

1910 The monarchy is ousted and the Portuguese Republic is established.

1916 Portugal enters World War I on the side of the Allies.

1926 The Republic collapses and a military dictatorship under Gomes da Costa is established.

1932–68 António de Oliveira Salazar keeps a tight hold on the government during his long reign as dictator. Portugal is officially neutral in World War II, but Salazar grants the Allies bases in the Azores.

1955 Portugal joins the United Nations.

1974 The April "flower revolution" topples the dictatorship; Portugal collapses into near anarchy.

1976–83 Sixteen provisional governments reign over a Portugal in chaos.

granddaughter of Edward III of England, produced a son, Prince Henry the Navigator, who oversaw the emergence of Portugal as an empire.

HENRY BUILDS A MARITIME EMPIRE Henry's demand for geographical accuracy and his hunger for the East's legendary gold, ivory, slaves, and spices drove him to exploration. To promote Christianity, he joined the fabled Christian kingdom of Prester John to drive the Muslims out of North Africa.

To develop navigational and cartographic techniques, Henry established a community of scholars at Sagres, on the south coast of Portugal. He was responsible for the discovery of Madeira, the Azores, Cape Verde, Senegal, and Sierra Leone, and he provided the blueprint for continued exploration during the rest of the century. In 1482, Portuguese ships explored the mouth of the Congo, and in 1488, Bartolomeu Dias rounded the Cape of Good Hope. In 1497, Vasco da Gama reached Calicut (Kozhikode), on India's west coast, clearing the way for trade in spices, porcelain, silk, ivory, and slaves.

The Treaty of Tordesillas, negotiated by João II in 1494, ensured that Portugal's eventual occupation of Brazil (beginning in 1500), would bring the new colony firmly into the Portuguese orbit. Using the wealth of the whole empire, Manuel I (the Fortunate; reigned 1495–1521) inspired great monuments of art and architecture whose style now bears his name. His reign inspired Portugal's Golden Age. By 1521, the country had begun to tap into Brazil's natural resources and had broken Venice's spice-trade monopoly. As the first of the great maritime world empires, Portugal dominated access to the Indian Ocean.

João III (reigned 1521–57) ushered in the Jesuits and the Inquisition. His son, Sebastião, disappeared in battle in Morocco in 1578, leaving Portugal without an heir. Philip II of Spain claimed the Portuguese throne and began 60 years of Spanish domination. In the East, Dutch and English traders undermined Portugal's strength.

THE HOUSE OF BRAGANÇA A nationalist revolution in 1640 brought a descendant of João I to the throne as João IV. That began the House of Bragança,

1986 Portugal joins the European Union. Mário Soares is elected president.

1989 Privatization of state-owned companies begins.

1991 Soares is reelected.

1992 Portugal holds the presidency of the European Union.

1995 Portugal is designated the cultural capital of Europe.

1998 Millions flock to Lisbon for EXPO '98, celebrating the heritage of the oceans.

1999 Portugal officially adopts the euro as its soon-to-be standard currency.

2002 Portugal abandons the escudo and switches to the euro.

2001–05 Under a Socialist government, Portugal continues to carry out modern reforms.

2006 Portugal sets aside its southwest coast as a natural park; Aníbal Cavaco Silva becomes president.

2008–2009 Portugal legalizes abortion but upholds ban on gay marriage.

2011 Portugal faces dire economic crises; the ban on same-sex marriages is lifted.

THE NAVIGATORS WHO CHANGED world maps

From 1415 to 1580 Portugal gave birth to some of the greatest navigators of all time. They set out on a Golden Age of imperial expansion, rewriting the maps of the world.

Henry the Navigator (1394–1460) was the third son of John I and his English-born queen, Philippa of Lancaster. *Henrique o Navegador* became one of the most imposing visionaries in Portuguese history. Serving much of his life as governor of the Algarve, he was never crowned king (leaving that honor to his older brother, Edward), he organized Portuguese expeditions into uncharted regions of Africa long before those of any other European power and established in Sagres an observatory and school of navigation that eventually became the envy of Europe. Influenced by legends of rivers of gold and the existence of isolated Christian empires within central Africa, Henry improved methods of navigation and shipbuilding, compiled the world's best library on the navigational observations of long-dead sailors, and focused the dreams of many generations of Portuguese colonists, explorers, and conquistadores. Although he never physically participated in any of the voyages, the discoveries and colonizations that ensued during his lifetime (Madeira, the Azores, Cape Verde, Senegal, and Sierra Leone) brought unprecedented wealth to Portugal, leading to the eventual foundation of the colonial empire.

Bartolomeo Dias (ca. 1450–1500) was the navigator chosen by King John in 1487 to lead an exploration into uncharted waters around the tip of Africa. This he accomplished in 1488, thus making him the first-known European to sail into the Indian Ocean. The name he gave the southern tip of Africa, Cabo Tormentoso (Cape of Storms), was later changed by King John to *Cabo da Boa Esperança* (Cape of Good Hope). His other discoveries included the mouth of the Congo River. Dias died when the ship he was commanding foundered in a tropical storm on its way to Brazil.

Christopher Columbus and his "lunatic plans of discovery" didn't impress the Portuguese kings, yet they funded some of the world's most momentous voyages in the Golden Age.

The great **Vasco da Gama** (ca. 1460–1524) was born at Sines in the former province of Alentejo. Little is known of his early life, but his discovery of the sea route to India, which opened commerce between the West and East, gave him an honored place in the history books. This towering Portuguese navigator made the first voyage from Western Europe around Africa by way of the Cape of Good Hope to the East. This voyage is the subject of the Portuguese epic *Os Lusíadas* by Camões. On a second journey (1502–3), da Gama established colonies at Sofala and

which lasted into the 20th century. João IV forged an English alliance by arranging his daughter's marriage to Charles II. For her dowry, he "threw in" Bombay and Tangier. In 1668, Spain recognized Portugal's independence with the Treaty of Lisbon.

On All Saints' Day in 1755, a great earthquake destroyed virtually all of Lisbon. In 6 minutes, 15,000 people were killed. The Marquês de Pombal, adviser to King José (reigned 1750–77), later reconstructed Lisbon as a safer and more beautiful city. Pombal was an exponent of absolutism, and his expulsion of the Jesuits in 1759 earned him powerful enemies throughout Europe. He curbed the power of the Inquisition

Mozambique and was named viceroy of Portuguese Asia in 1524, the last year of his life.

Vasco da Gama died at Cochin (part of modern India) on December 24, 1524; his tomb can be visited at the Mosteiro dos Jerónimos in Bélem outside Lisbon (see p. 106).

In the wake of da Gama's sailing the ocean blue came **Pedro Alvars Cabral** (1467 or 1468-1520). Prompted by the maritime success of Vasco da Gama, Manuel I sent Cabral with 13 ships to establish trade with India in 1500. Cabral headed the ships westward in an attempt to avoid the coast of Africa (and thinking the world was much smaller than it actually is), but the expedition was carried by ocean currents and prevailing winds to the coast of Brazil (April 22, 1500). After claiming Brazil for Portugal, Cabral continued his ship toward India, lost four of his ships off the southern tip of South America, and eventually reached Calcutta and Cochin, where he established trading posts on India's uncharted northeastern edge. He returned to Portugal with only four ships. Cabral is an explorer who history has credited as the European colonizer of Brazil and Eastern India.

One of the greatest feats of navigation occurred during the rule of **Dom Manuel I the Fortunate** (1495-1521), who was called "the King of Gold," because of all the riches pouring into Portugal.

Ferdinand Magellan (Fernan de Magilhaes/Fernando de Magallanes; ca. 1480-1521) was an explorer and navigator. He served in Portuguese expeditions to Malacca and India (1505-12) and to Azamor (1513-14). When no further expeditions were forthcoming for him from Portugal, he offered his services to Spain. In 1517, he received funding from Charles V for an exploration of the Spice Islands (the Moluccas) via the unexplored western route. Two years later, he left Spain with five ships on one of the most celebrated maritime explorations in history. His stops included the La Plata River estuary of Argentina, after which his crew mutinied rather than continue around the stormy tip of South America. (This Magellan suppressed.) Between October and November 1520, he maneuvered around the endless islets and blind channels at the bottom of South America, eventually discovering the channel that led into the open waters of the Pacific. The following March, he discovered Guam, then the Philippines, where he was killed by a treacherous native chief with whom he had made an alliance. The much-diminished expedition, captained after Magellan's death by Masque-born Juan de Elcano, continued from the Philippines around the tip of Africa and back to Spain; it arrived there in 1522 after completing the first circumnavigation of the globe.

and reorganized and expanded industry, agriculture, education, and the military. Upon the death of his patron, King José, he was exiled from court.

In 1793, Portugal joined a coalition with England and Spain against Napoleon. An insane queen, Maria I (reigned 1777–1816), and an exiled royal family facilitated an overthrow by a military junta. A constitution was drawn up, and Maria's son, João VI (reigned 1816–26), accepted the position of constitutional monarch in 1821. João's son, Pedro, declared independence for Brazil in 1822 and became a champion of liberalism in Portugal.

FROM REPUBLIC TO DICTATORSHIP   Between 1853 and 1908, republican movements assaulted the very existence of the monarchists. In 1908, Carlos I (reigned 1889–1908), the Painter King, and the crown prince were assassinated at Praça do Comércio in Lisbon. Carlos's successor was overthrown in an outright revolution on October 5, 1910, ending the Portuguese monarchy and making the country a republic.

Instability was the watchword of the newly proclaimed republic, and revolutions and uprisings were a regular occurrence. Portugal's attempt to remain neutral in World War I failed when—influenced by its old ally, England—Portugal commandeered German ships in the Lisbon harbor. This action promptly brought a declaration of war from Germany, and Portugal entered World War I on the side of the Allies.

The republic's precarious foundations collapsed in 1926, when a military revolt established a dictatorship, headed by Gomes da Costa. His successor, António Óscar de Fragoso Carmona, remained president until 1951, but only as a figurehead. António de Oliveira Salazar became finance minister in 1928 and rescued the country from a morass of economic difficulties. He went on to become the first minister, acting as (but never officially becoming) head of state. He was declared premier of Portugal in 1932, and he rewrote the Portuguese Constitution along Fascist lines in 1933.

In World War II, Salazar asserted his country's neutrality, although he allowed British and American troops to establish bases in the Azores in 1943. After Carmona's death in 1951, Salazar became dictator, living more or less ascetically and suppressing all opposition. He worked in cooperation with his contemporary, the Spanish dictator Francisco Franco.

In 1955, Portugal joined the United Nations. Salazar suffered a stroke in 1968 and died in 1970. He is buried in the Panteão Nacional in Lisbon.

MODERN PORTUGAL WRESTLES WITH DEMOCRACY   In 1968, Dr. Marcelo Caetano replaced Salazar. Discontent in Portugal's African colonies of Mozambique and Angola had been brewing since around 1960, and shortly after Caetano's rise to power, revolution broke out, a conflict which eventually spread back to the Portuguese mainland. The dictatorship was overthrown on April 25, 1974, in a military coup dubbed the "flower revolution" because the soldiers wore red carnations instead of carrying guns. After the revolution, Portugal drifted into near anarchy. Finally, after several years of turmoil and the failures of 16 provisional governments from 1976 to 1983, a revised constitution came into force in the 1980s.

In 1976, Portugal loosened its grasp on its once-extensive territorial possessions. The Azores and Madeira gained partial autonomy. All the Portuguese territories in Africa—Angola, Cape Verde, Portuguese Guinea, Mozambique, and São Tomé and Príncipe (islands in the Gulf of Guinea)—became independent countries. Portugal also released the colony of East Timor, which Indonesia immediately seized.

From the time of the revolution until 1987, Portuguese governments rose and fell much too quickly for the country to maintain political stability. Moderates elected General Ramalho Eanes as president in the wake of the revolution, and he was reelected in 1980. He brought the military under control, allaying fears of a right-wing coup to prevent a Socialist takeover. However, Eanes appointed a Socialist, Mário Soares, prime minister three times.

In the 1985 elections, the left-wing vote was divided three ways, and the Socialists lost their vanguard position to the Social Democratic Party. Their leader, Dr. Aníbal Cavaco Silva, was elected prime minister. In January 1986, Eanes was forced to resign the presidency. He was replaced by Soares, the former Socialist prime minister, who became the first civilian president in 60 years.

THE LADY IN THE tutti-frutti HAT

She was called "The Brazilian Bombshell." In the 1940s, one critic labeled her Brazil's most famous export. Ah, but there's a secret here: The great Carmen Miranda, the star of all those big Hollywood musicals in the 1940s and 1950s, was actually Portuguese. In 1909 she was born Maria do Carmo Miranda da Cunha, in the little village of Marco de Canavezes, in the north of Portugal.

Costumed garishly, with bowls of fruit perched on her head, she wriggled outrageously through such kitschy numbers as "Tico Tico," in such 20th Century Fox films as *Downstairs Argentine Way* and *The Gang's All Here.* Although she appeared with a number of other stars, fans most remember her for her appearance with co-stars Cesar Romero and Alice Faye. Today an entirely new generation of young people is discovering this Latin bombshell as her old hits are revived on TV.

In 1911, she moved with her family to Rio de Janeiro, where in time she learned to make outrageous hats for wealthy customers. One of them asked her to sing at a party. With her sambas and tangos, she was an immediate hit. At age 19, she made her first record on the RCA Victor label. Called *Taí,* it sold a record-breaking (for the era) 35,000 copies. Her career was launched, eventually leading to 140 records and six films produced in Brazil.

The United States soon discovered her and she was lured to Hollywood, where her career soared. By 1943, she (along with Barbara Stanwyck and Bing Crosby) was one of the highest-paid performers in the United States. Her act captured the fantasy of drag queens around the world (and still does!). With her colored dresses, stylized bananas, turbans, outrageous platform shoes that made Joan Crawford look flat-heeled, dangling earrings, and a shimmering dance step, Carmen Miranda emerged as an ambassador of the Portuguese world like no star before or since.

Although a hit with American audiences, she did not always meet with approval in her native Latin world. Many Latin Americans objected to the stereotype she projected—that of an oversexed, vivacious, and clownish cartoon of a Brazilian woman.

Regrettably, her career also degenerated into caricature. After a failed marriage and a severe bout of depression, she ended up making farcical appearances in the 1950s. She made appearances on TV with Milton Berle (also dressed in Carmen Miranda drag). On August 5, 1955, she collapsed on the set of "The Jimmy Durante Show" and died of a heart attack shortly after.

Today, decades after her death, the memory of this Portuguese-Brazilian legend is kept alive by her legions of impassioned fans. A biography, *Carmen Miranda,* by Cássio Emmanuel Barsante, has been published, with 900 photos and illustrations, the result of 20 years of exhaustive research. A film was made of her life, *Bananas Is My Business.* Even the Film Forum in New York has honored her with retrospectives.

Coveted, adored, ridiculed, and eulogized, Carmen Miranda will no doubt remain a legend as long as there's a late show on TV.

Although his administration had its share of political scandal, President Soares won a landslide victory in the January 1991 elections. With the elections of 1995, constitutional limitations forced Soares to step down. He was replaced by Jorge Sampaio, the former Socialist mayor of Lisbon.

As president, Sampaio didn't make great waves, focusing on moderation. He did oversee the return of the Portuguese island of Macau to China in December 1999, and he also championed the cause of independence for East Timor, another former Portuguese colony. Most editorial writers in Lisbon called the presidency of Sampaio "remarkably uneventful."

That said, Portugal took a major leap in 1999 when it became part of the euro community, adopting a single currency, along with other European nations such as Spain, Italy, Germany, and France. On February 28, 2002, the nation of Portugal formally assigned its longtime currency, the escudo, to permanent mothballs and started trading in euros. This officially launched Portugal, along with 11 other European nations, into the European Monetary Union.

PORTUGAL TODAY In 2006, Sampaio was succeeded in office by Aníbal Cavaco Silva, the politician he defeated in 1996. In office, the eco-friendly Silva stressed the environment, not only protecting it in his own country but in all E.U. countries as well. In 2006, Portugal's sleepy southwestern shore became Europe's latest coastal preserve, as 80,937 unspoiled hectares (200,000 acres) were set aside for the enjoyment of future generations. Southwest Alentejo and Costa Vicentina Natural Park, farmland since Roman times, is now under severe building restrictions which will maintain its pristine beauty. The area begins in the town of Sines, a 2-hour drive south of Lisbon, and stretches for 91km (57 miles) of dunes, beaches, and black basalt cliffs.

Since taking office in 2006, Silva has also positioned himself as a firm believer in globalization and counterterrorism and has worked to promote economic growth and to deal with unemployment in Portugal.

Although elected as a center Right candidate, Silva has disappointed many of his backers. He is a practicing Roman Catholic and a self-described believer in the Fátima apparitions, yet, critics claim, he has not vetoed legislation proposed by the Left. For example, he signed into law a bill legalizing abortion within the first 10 weeks of pregnancy. With low voter turnout in 2008—58% did not vote—abortion was legalized.

In the election of January 2011 Silva was reelected for a second five-year term; he trounced five other candidates and swept to an easy victory with about 53% of the vote. His nearest competitor, Manuel Alegre, captured less than 20% of the vote. Silva is now presiding over a debt-laden Portugal.

ART & ARCHITECTURE

Although not as rich in art and architecture as neighboring Spain, tiny Portugal made its own artistic statement and developed its own style.

FROM ROMAN TO ROMANESQUE Most of the ancient Roman buildings of Portugal were destroyed by a series of invaders who swept over the country.

One of the greatest Roman monuments, **Templo de Diana** (p. 270) stands in Évora. It dates from either the 1st or 2nd century A.D. Its 14 granite Corinthian columns are still intact, more or less, showing the harmony of classical architecture in Portugal.

Portugal's greatest Roman remains are found at **Conímbriga,** 16km (10 miles) southwest of the university city of Coimbra. See p. 293 for details about visiting this ancient setting.

It really wasn't until the 11th century, when Portugal became a separate kingdom, that architecture took on a national identity. Portuguese art began with the Burgundy dynasty when Romanesque architecture and sculpture were in its heyday.

The architecture was heavily influenced by France but took on characteristics of its own. This architecture in the north of Portugal, bordering Galicia, would survive until the 15th century. Most of the churches built during that time were modeled after the great pilgrimage center of Santiago de Compostela, which lies north of the Portuguese border.

One of the greatest examples of architecture from this period is the **cathedral,** or **Sé** (p. 347), in the city of Braga, dating from the 12th century. It was originally constructed to replace a church destroyed by the Moors in the 8th century. Major rebuilding in the 16th to the 18th century has destroyed much of the 12th-century structure. The most significant remains of the Middle Ages are in the south portal with its six pillars crowned by capitals and ornamented with sculptured monsters and geometric traceries.

By 1185, Afonso Henríques, "The Conqueror," had vastly increased Portugal's territories. Monastic orders moved into the former territories controlled by the Moors. Great monasteries arose, especially the **Mosteiro de Santa Maria** (p. 200) at Alcobaça, which dates from the 12th century and was founded by Cistercian monks. At the city of Tomar, the **Convento da Ordem de Cristo** (p. 260), was built by **the Knights Templar.**

Of all the Romanesque churches erected at this time, the classic one is **Sé Velha** (p. 286) standing in the university city of Coimbra, which Afonso Henríques had made his capital. The cathedral evokes a fortified castle, and merges French Romanesque with Peninsula architectural styles.

An even more awe-inspiring church from the Romanesque era is the **Sé,** or **cathedral,** at Évora (p. 270), dating from 1186. Built in the shape of a Latin cross, it is a blend of Romanesque and Gothic.

THE GOTHIC & RENAISSANCE ERAS Winning the battle against invading Castile in 1385, João I came to the throne. As the first monarch of the House of Avis, he presided over a flowering of Portuguese art and architecture. This era, with Manueline influences (see below), would survive for 2 centuries, until 1580, when Portugal fell under the Spanish crown for 60 years.

While the Italian Renaissance style was sweeping parts of Europe, Portugal seemed stuck in the Gothic period.

Begun in the late 14th century, the **Mosteiro de Santa Maria da Vitória** (p. 205) at Alcobaça remains a glorious monument to this time. It is arguably the most outstanding example of Gothic architecture in Portugal.

When Renaissance architectural styles and art arrived in Portugal, it was most often incorporated into Gothic art, leading to a medley of styles. Gothic sculpture was mainly developed for the adornment of tombs such as the Royal Cloister at Batalha. The royal chapel arches built here were in the original late-Gothic style, but the masonry rising above them show the intricacies of the newly emerging Manueline style.

Portugal was never a leader in art in its earliest centuries, but a primitive painter, Nuno Gonçalves, rose up through the ranks to become celebrated for his **polyptych,** which he created between 1460 and 1470, depicting 60 portraits of the leading figures in Portuguese history. His masterpiece hangs today in the **Museu Nacional de Arte Antiga** (p. 112) in Lisbon.

Very little is known about this mysterious artist, not even his exact birth or death dates. However, he was active between 1450 and 1490. He is depicted, among several other historic figures, on the Padrão dos Descobrimentos, or Monument of the Discoveries, in Belém near Lisbon.

PORTUGAL'S UNIQUE MANUELINE STYLE   The style known as Manueline or Manuelino is unique to Portugal. It predominated between 1490 and 1520, and remains one of the most memorable art forms to have emerged from the country. It's named for Manuel I, who reigned from 1495 to 1521. When Dom Manuel I inaugurated the style, Manueline architecture was shockingly modern, a farsighted departure from the rigidity of medieval models. It originally decorated portals, porches, and interiors, mostly adorning old rather than new structures. The style marked a transition from the Gothic to the Renaissance in Portugal.

Old-timers claim that Manuelino, also called Atlantic Gothic, derived from the sea, although some modern-day observers detect a surrealism that foreshadowed Salvador Dalí's style. Everything about Manueline art is a celebration of seafaring ways. In Manuelino works, Christian iconography combines with shells, ropes, branches of coral, heraldic coats of arms, religious symbols, and imaginative waterborne shapes, as well as with Moorish themes.

Many monuments throughout the country—notably the Monastery of Jerónimos in Belém, outside Lisbon—offer examples of this style. Others are in the Azores and Madeira. Sometimes Manuelino is combined with the famous tile panels, as in Sintra National Palace. The first Manueline building in Portugal was the classic Church of Jesus at Setúbal, south of Lisbon. Large pillars in the interior twist in spirals to support a flamboyant ribbed ceiling.

Although it's mainly an architectural style, Manuelino affected other artistic fields as well. In sculpture, Manuelino was usually decorative. Employed over doorways, rose windows, balustrades, and lintels, it featured everything from a corncob to a stalk of cardoon. Manuelino also affected painting; brilliant gemlike colors characterize works influenced by the style. The best-known Manueline painter was Grão Vasco (also called Vasco Fernandes). His most famous works include several panels, now on exhibition in the Grão Vasco museum, that were originally intended for the Cathedral of Viseu. The most renowned of these panels are *Calvary* and *St. Peter,* both dating from 1530.

"The Great Vasco" was but one of a series of Manueline painters who flourished between 1505 and 1550. These men created a true Portuguese School of Painting, with life-size human figures.

Another leading artist was Jorge Afonso, court painter from 1508 to 1540 and a native of Brazil. He was the leader of the so-called Lisbon School of Painting. No existing works can be definitely attributed to him, however.

Gil Vicente (1465–1537) achieved success as a goldsmith, using precious metals shipped back from South America. He was actually a Renaissance man, also excelling as a playwright, poet, and musician.

Portuguese art declined during the 60-year reign of Spain beginning in 1580. The new Spanish rulers suppressed the unique Manueline style and restored classical motifs from Italy.

Even when the Portuguese took back their country, with the reign of João IV, an artistic revival did not occur until decades later.

BAROQUE ART (LATE 17TH-18TH CENTURY) The baroque style of art and architecture comes from the Portuguese word *barroco*. Under the reign of King João V (1706–50), the **Monastery of Mafra** was constructed outside Lisbon between 1713 and 1730. It is Portugal's answer to the more famous Escorial outside Madrid. Rather severe in its lines, the monastery is neoclassical, except for spired cupolas on its cubic towers.

Obviously, extensive rebuilding had to follow the devastating earthquake that destroyed much of Lisbon in 1755. As a result of this earthquake, the **Terreiro do Paço** was created, and it remains today one of the great squares of the world, forming the official entrance to the city of Lisbon.

A royal palace at **Queluz** (p. 161) was constructed in 1787 and is similar to the palace of Versailles outside Paris. Rococo art, coming in the wake of the baroque, found few adherents in Portugal.

A great sculptor rose out of the 18th century, **Joaquim Machado de Castro** (1732–1822). He cultivated terra-cotta relief, and did so with great delicacy and restraint.

LATE 18TH TO THE 19TH CENTURY Political upheavals dominated this period. Portuguese architects worked in a medley of styles, their buildings having no national identity. The conservative taste of both the people and the government ruled the day, although **Ventura Terra,** who died in 1889, was a forerunner of the 20th-century international style.

The artist of the day was **António de Sequeira** (1768–1837), who was court painter in Lisbon in 1802. He drifted into Romanticism, and was mainly concerned with man's personality and purpose. He was also an artist of great perception, and evolved into a master of chiaroscuro, balancing light and shade in a painting.

In sculpture, **Teixeira Lopes** (1866–1918) became a dominant figure. Born in Porto, he is known for his monument to the novelist Eça de Queirós, which stands in Lisbon.

Among painters, **Columbano Bordalo Pinheir** (1856–1929), achieved renown with his portraits and still lifes. A sense of French Romanticism prevailed in his paintings. He often posed his subject in a dramatic light against a cloudy background.

20TH CENTURY In the first decades of the 20th century, Art Nouveau and Art Deco began to occupy the architects of Portugal, especially in the cities of Coimbra, Leiria, and Lisbon. The **Museu Gulbenkian** (p. 110) in Lisbon definitely moved Portugal into the foreground of modern architecture.

From the Porto School of Architecture emerged Álvaro Siza, who was commissioned to restore the Chiado quarter in Lisbon, which was devastated by a fire in 1988. In the 1980s Tomás Taviera distinguished himself by constructing in Lisbon a postmodern **Torre das Amoreiras.**

In sculpture, the towering figure of the 20th century was **Francisco Franco** (1885–1955), who designed many commemorative monuments to the dictator Salazar.

No giant figure arose in painting, although many Portuguese modern artists have distinguished themselves, including **Almada Negreiros** (1889–1970), who was influenced by Cubism, as well as **Maria Helena Vieira da Silva** (1908–1920), who was influenced by the Portuguese *azulejos* (tiles) in her works, especially the color in her paintings. **Amadeo de Souza Cardoso** (1887–1918) found his motif in the development of Cubism and shows the influence of his friend Modigliani.

Lourdes de Castro, José de Guimarães, and Júlio Pomar are among some of the leading contemporary painters of the 20th century.

PORTUGAL IN POP CULTURE

Books

GENERAL

The Portuguese: The Land and Its People, by Marion Kaplan (Viking, 2006), is one of the best surveys of the country. The work covers Portuguese history all the way from the country's Moorish origins to its maritime empire and into the chaotic 20th century. It also gives travel information and discusses politics, the economy, literature, art, and architecture.

A towering achievement, *Journey to Portugal: In Pursuit of Portugal's History and Culture,* is a compelling work by the Nobel Prize–winner José Saramago. Saramago traveled across his homeland to get a "new way" of feeling about Portugal's history and culture. From that personal quest, he created this monumental work.

HISTORY

A Concise History of Portugal, by David Birmingham is far too short at 209 pages to capture the full sweep of Portuguese history, but it is nonetheless a very readable history for those who like at least a brief preview of a country's past before landing there.

Another version of the same subject is *Portugal: A Companion History,* by José H. Saraiva. It provides a sweeping saga of the land you're about to visit.

Portugal's role abroad is best presented in Charles Ralph Boxer's *Portuguese Seaborne Empire.* Since its initial publication in 1969, this frequently reprinted book has been the best volume for explaining how an unimportant kingdom in western Europe managed to build an empire stretching from China to Brazil.

FICTION & BIOGRAPHY

The epic poem of Portugal, *Os Lusíadas,* written in 1572 by the premier Portuguese poet Luís Vaz de Camões, celebrates the Portuguese Age of Discovery. In 1987, Penguin rereleased this timeless classic. The best biography on Camões himself remains Aubrey Bell's *Luis de Camões.*

One of Portugal's most beloved writers, Eça de Queirós, wrote in the late 19th century. Several of his best-known narratives have been translated into English, notably *The Maias, The Illustrious House of Ramires* (New Directions Publishing, 1994), *The Mandarin and Other Stories, The City and the Mountains, The Relic, The Sin of Father Amaro,* and *Dragon's Teeth.* Queirós (1845–1900) was the most realistic Portuguese novelist of his time, and his works were much admired by Emile Zola in France. *The Maias* is the best known and the best of his works.

The great poet Fernando Pessoa (1888–1935) is second only to Camões in the list of illustrious Portuguese writers. Some of his works have been translated into English. Pessoa is still beloved by the Portuguese, and for decades he appeared on the 100-escudo note before it went out of circulation in 2002.

The Return of the Caravels, by António Lobo Antunes, is an unusual novel set in 1974. It brings back Portugal's history as an imperial power by "collective memory," as Vasco da Gama, Cabral, and other explorers return to Lisbon, anchoring their small but significant vessels alongside the giant tankers of today.

THE shakespeares OF PORTUGAL

Some of Portugal's greatest writers have been translated into English.

During the Renaissance, Portuguese literature flourished, especially under the pen of **Luís de Camões** (1524-1580), who celebrated Vasco da Gama's sea voyages to India in Portugal's greatest epic, *The Lusiads*, 1572. This epic was modeled on the *Aeneid*.

His masterpiece is today the national epic of Portugal. Ironically, Vasco da Gama died the year Camões was born. The poet was the son of impoverished aristocrats. His early life is undocumented but the subject of legend, some historians claiming he was born in Morocco.

In addition to his epic, he wrote odes, elegies, satires, epigrams, comedies, and sonnets, including *Filodemo* and *Amphitriões*. He developed Portuguese lyric to its highest point and had an everlasting influence on national drama. He is buried at the Mosteiro dos Jerónimos in Bélem (see p. 106).

Gil Vicente (1470-1536) is known as the Portuguese Shakespeare. Vicente was court dramatist to Manuel I and John III. He produced 44 extant plays, some in Portuguese, some in Castilian, and some in a quirky combination of languages and medieval dialects. His works show a powerful lyricism as well as strong talents for comedy. They range from the courtly tragedy *Don Duardos* to the comedic *Farsa de Inés Pereira* and include solemn religious pageants, low farces, and witty comedies.

Joao Batista da Silva Leitão de Almeida Garrett (1800-54) is the greatest of the Portuguese Romantics. He successfully mingled the spirit and pathos of European romanticism with the lyricism and realism of the Portuguese psyche. His best-known dramas include the heavily politicized *Frei Luis de Sousa* (1844). His favorite poems are *Romanceiro* (*Songbook*, 1850) and *Folhas caídas* (*Fallen Leaves*, 1853), which are considered the greatest collection of love poems in the Portuguese repertoire. Equally well received were *Camões* and *Dona branca* (*The White Lady*), both released in 1828, and a historical novel set in the 14th century, *O arco de Sant' Ana*.

José Maria Eça de Queiros (1845-1900) is the greatest Portuguese novelist. He was a member of the "Generation of '70" group of intellectuals whose passion was the promulgation of realism within art. Containing prose that has been called muscular, satirical, and vibrant, his surprisingly modern works include *O crime do padro Amaro (Father Amaro's Crime)*, *O primo Basilio (Cousin Basil)*, and *Maya*. When not writing, he served as the Portuguese consul in Havana (1972-74), London (1874-88), and Paris (1888-1900). Today, his works are required reading for every educated Portuguese.

José Saramago, winner of the Nobel Prize for Literature (see "General," above), remains one of the best novelists of modern-day Portugal. His ***Baltasar and Blimunda*** is a magical account of a flying machine and the construction of Mafra Palace—it's a delightful read.

The work ***New Portuguese Letters*** by the "Three Marias" (Maria Isabel Barreno, Maria Teresa Horta, and Maria Fátima Velho da Costa), first published in Portugal in 1972, is available in English. The Portuguese government banned and confiscated all copies and arrested its authors on a charge of "outrage to public decency." They were acquitted 2 years later, and the case became a cause célèbre for feminist organizations around the world.

WINES

The finest book on the most famous of Portuguese fortified wines, port, is Richard Mayson's ***Port and the Douro.*** This is a comprehensive, articulate, and intriguing work. You learn the history of port from the 4th century up through modern methods of bottling the wine today.

Music

Arguably the oldest urban folk music in the world, **fado** remains the soul music of Portugal. From the 1940s until her death in 1999, **Amália Rodrigues** was the top diva *fadista* in Portugal. No one in the post-millennium has dethroned her.

A current sensation, **Ana Laíns,** takes a much more contemporary approach to fado than did Amália. Her first album, *Sentidos,* was released in 2006 and scored an international success. Her songs blend introspective themes with simple lullaby melodies remembered from her childhood.

The greatest guitar player in Portugal is **Antonio Chainho.** His voice plays "second fiddle" to his guitar, whose music he makes the focal point of his concerts and recordings.

After the release of his solo album, *O Mesmo Fado,* **António Zambujo** has been hailed as "best new fado singer" in the Lisbon press. As a *fadistic,* Zambujo is a lover of tradition—that is, classical fado.

Another respected *fadista* is **Cristina Branco,** who preferred jazz, blues, or bossa nova until she discovered the "passion and emotion of fado." Her unique interpretation of fado is heard on her latest album, *Murmúrios.*

One of the most promising of today's young male *fadistas* is **Durate;** another new-generation *fadistic* is **Joana Amendoeiraq,** who is known for her sensuous and moving harmonies, which have gained her an international following.

Ever since she released her first album, *Mafalda,* in 1999, **Mafalda Arnauth** has become an important voice of fado, not only in Portugal but abroad as well.

Mariza was singing fado before she could read. Her first CD, *Fado em Mim,* offers six of the most classic fado songs and six original compositions. In all of them she "tugs at the heart and soul," in the words of one music critic.

Groups that are current favorites in the Portuguese music world include **Ala Dos Namorados,** known for their innovative repertoire that ranges from rhythms of Cape Verde to re-creations of medieval voices.

You can purchase music by all of the singers mentioned above at **Valentim de Carvalho** (Rua do Carmo; ✆ **21/324-15-70**), the best music store in Lisbon.

Films

The Portuguese film industry is barely drawing a breath, but occasionally a flick will come along of worldwide interest.

Before you go you might pick up a DVD of *Fados,* a 2007 documentary about the soul music of the Portuguese working class. The film comes at an opportune time as fado music is enjoying a renewed vogue in the nightclubs of Portugal, with the best and most prolific number of dives located in Lisbon.

The film, written and directed by Carlos Saura, traces the birth of fado in the slums of Lisbon in the 1820s. Originally, the music expressed the longing for the homelands of the immigrants who had settled into Lisbon from far-flung Portuguese colonies. Fado also sang of lost loves and unfulfilled hopes. The film pays particular homage to the late Amália Rodrigues, greatest of all *fadistas.*

EATING & DRINKING IN PORTUGAL

In her book *Invitation to Portugal,* Mary Jean Kempner gets to the heart of the Portuguese diet: "The best Portuguese food is provincial, indigenous, eccentric, and proud—a reflection of the chauvinism of this complex people. It takes no sides, assumes no airs, makes no concessions or bows to Brillat-Savarin—and usually tastes wonderful."

DINING CUSTOMS   Much Portuguese cooking is based on olive oil and the generous use of garlic. If you select anything prepared to order, you can request that it be *sem alho* (without garlic).

It's customary in most establishments to order soup (invariably a big bowl filled to the brim), followed by a fish and a meat course. Potatoes and rice are likely to accompany both the meat and fish platters. In many restaurants, the chef features at least one *prato do dia* (plate of the day). These dishes are prepared fresh that day and often are cheaper than the regular offerings.

CUISINE   *Couverts* are little appetizers, often brought to your table the moment you sit down. These can include bread, cheese, and olives. In many restaurants they are free; in others you are charged extra. It's a good idea to ask your waiter about extra costs. In many places, the charge for these extras is per person. **Remember:** Not everything served at the beginning of the meal is free.

Another way to begin your meal is to select from *acepipes variados* (hors d'oeuvres), which might include everything from swordfish to olives and tuna. From the soup kitchen, the most popular selection is *caldo verde* (green broth). Made from cabbage, sausage, potatoes, and olive oil, it's common in the north. Another ubiquitous soup is *sopa alentejana,* simmered with garlic and bread, among other ingredients. Portuguese cooks wring every last morsel of nutrition from their fish, meat, and vegetables. The fishers make *sopa de mariscos* by boiling the shells of various shellfish and then richly flavoring the stock and lacing it with white wine.

The first main dish you're likely to encounter on any menu is *bacalhau* (salted codfish), faithful friend of the Portuguese. As you drive through fishing villages in the north, you'll see racks and racks of the fish drying in the sun. Foreigners might not wax rhapsodic about *bacalhau,* although it's prepared in imaginative ways. Common ways of serving it include *bacalhau cozido* (boiled with such vegetables as carrots, cabbage, and spinach, and then baked), *bacalhau à Bras* (fried in olive oil with onions and potatoes, and flavored with garlic), *bacalhau à Gomes de Sá* (stewed with black olives, potatoes, and onions, and then baked and topped with a sliced boiled egg), and *bacalhau no churrasco* (barbecued).

Aside from codfish, the classic national dish is *caldeirada,* the Portuguese version of bouillabaisse. Prepared at home, it's a pungent stew containing bits and pieces of the latest catch.

Next on the platter is the Portuguese sardine. Found off the Atlantic coasts of Iberia as well as France, the country's 6- to 8-inch-long sardines also come from Setúbal. As you stroll through the alleys of the Alfama or pass the main streets of small villages throughout Portugal, you'll sometimes see women kneeling in front of braziers on their front doorsteps grilling the large sardines. Grilled, they're called *sardinhas assadas*.

Shellfish is one of the great delicacies of the Portuguese table. Its scarcity and the demand of foreign markets, however, have led to astronomical price tags. The price of lobsters and crabs changes every day, depending on the market. On menus, you'll see the abbreviation *Preço V.*, meaning "variable price." When the waiter brings a shellfish dish to your table, always ask the price.

Many of these creatures from the deep, such as king-size crabs, are cooked and then displayed in restaurant windows. If you do decide to splurge, demand that you be served only fresh shellfish. You can be deceived, as can even the experts, but at least you'll have demanded that your fish be fresh and not left over from the previous day's window display. When fresh, *santola* (crab) is a delicacy. *Santola recheada* (stuffed crab) might be too pungent for unaccustomed Western palates, though; *amêijoas* (baby clams) are a safer choice. *Lagosta* is translated as "lobster" but is, in fact, crayfish; it's best when served without adornment.

The variety of good-tasting, inexpensive fish served here includes *salmonette* (red mullet) from Setúbal, *robalo* (bass), *lenguado* (sole), and sweet-tasting *pescada* (hake). Less appealing to the average diner, but preferred by many discriminating palates, are *eiros* (eels), *polvo* (octopus), and *lampreas* (lampreys, a seasonal food in the northern Minho district).

Piri-piri is a sauce made of hot pepper from Angola. Jennings Parrott once wrote: "After tasting it you will understand why Angola wanted to get it out of the country." Unless you're extremely brave, consider ordering something else. Travelers accustomed to hot, peppery food, however, might like it.

Porto residents are known as tripe eaters. The local specialty is *dobrada* (tripe with beans), a favorite of workers. The *cozido á portuguesa* is another popular dish. This stew often features both beef and pork, along with fresh vegetables and sausages. The chief offering of the beer tavern is *bife na frigideira* (beef in mustard sauce), usually served piping hot in a brown ceramic dish with a fried egg on top. Thinly sliced *iscas* (calves' livers) are usually well prepared and sautéed with onion.

Portuguese meat, especially beef and veal, is less satisfying. The best meat in Portugal is *porco* (pork), usually tender and juicy. Especially good is *porco alentejano* (fried pork in a succulent sauce with baby clams), often cooked with herb-flavored onions and tomatoes. *Cabrito* (roast kid) is another treat, flavored with herbs and garlic. Chicken tends to be hit-or-miss and is perhaps best when *frango no espeto,* or spit-roasted golden brown. In season, game is good, especially *perdiz* (partridge) and *codorniz estufada* (pan-roasted quail).

Queijo (cheese) is usually eaten separately and not with fruit. The most common varieties of Portuguese cheese are made from sheep or goat's milk. A popular variety is *queijo da serra* (literally, cheese from the hills). Other well-liked cheeses are *queijo do Alentejo* and *queijo de Azeitao.* Many prefer *queijo Flamengo* (similar to Dutch Gouda).

While locked away in isolated convents and monasteries, Portuguese nuns and monks have created some original sweet concoctions. Many of these desserts are sold in little pastry shops throughout Portugal. In Lisbon, Porto, and a few other cities, you can visit a *salão de chá* (tea salon) at 4pm to sample these delicacies. Regrettably, too few restaurants feature regional desserts.

The most typical dessert is *arroz doce*, cinnamon-flavored rice pudding. Flan, or caramel custard, appears on all menus. If you're in Portugal in summer, ask for a peach from Alcobaça. One of these juicy, succulent yellow fruits will spoil you forever for all other peaches. Sintra is known for its strawberries, Setúbal for its orange groves, the Algarve for its almonds and figs, Elvas for its plums, the Azores for their pineapples, and Madeira for its passion fruit. Some people believe that if you eat too much of the latter, you'll go insane.

Portugal doesn't offer many egg dishes, except for omelets. However, eggs are used extensively in many sweets. Although egg yolks cooked in sugar might not sound appealing, you might want to try some of the more original offerings. The best known are *ovos moles* (soft eggs sold in colorful barrels) that originate in Aveiro. From the same district capital comes *ovos de fio* (shirred eggs).

WINE   For generations, much of what the English-speaking world knew about Portugal came from the reports that wine merchants brought back to Britain from the wineries of the Douro Valley. Today Portugal is famous throughout the world for its port wines, and many parts of central and northern Portugal are covered with well-tended vines sprouting from intricately laid-out terraces.

o **Port:** Known for decades as the Englishman's wine, port was once the drink uncorked for toasting in England. In gentlemen's clubs, vintage port (only 1% of all port made) was dispensed from a crystal decanter. Later, when the English working classes started drinking less superior port in Midland mill towns, they often spiked it with lemon. Today the French consume almost three times the amount of port that the British do.

   Some 40 varieties of grape go into making port. Made from grapes grown in rich lava soil, port today is either single vintage or blended, and ranges from whites to full-bodied tawnies and reds. The latter is often consumed at the end of a meal with cheese, fruit, or nuts. You can visit a port-wine lodge to learn more about port—and, more important, to taste it. The best lodges to visit are concentrated in Vila Nova de Gaia, a suburb of Porto across the Douro from Porto's commercial center.

o **Vinhos Verdes** (pronounced *veen*-yosh *vair*-desh): These "green wines" are more lemony in color. Many come from the Minho district in northwest Portugal, which, like Galicia in the north of Spain, gets an abundance of rain. Cultivated in a humid atmosphere, the grapes are picked while young. Some wine aficionados don't consider this wine serious, finding it too light. With its fruity flavor, it's said to suggest the cool breezes of summer. It's often served with fish, and many Portuguese use it as a thirst quencher in the way an American might consume a soft drink. The finest *vinhos verdes* are from Monção, just south of the river Minho. Those from Amarante are also praised.

o **Dão:** Dão is produced from grapes grown just south of the Douro in the north's mountainous heartland. "Our vines have tender grapes" goes the saying throughout the valleys of Mondego and Dão, each split by a river. Summers are fiery hot and winters wet and often bitter cold. A lot of Dão wine is red, notably the *vinhos maduros,* matured in oak casks for nearly 2 years before being bottled. The wine is velvety in texture and often accompanies roasts. At almost every restaurant in Portugal, you'll encounter either *branco* (white) or Dão *tinto* (red). The best bottles of red Dão wine are the reserve (RESERVA is printed on the label). Other names to look for include Porta dos Cavaleiros and Terras Altas. (No one seems to agree on how to pronounce the word *Dão—daw*-ng, *da*-ow, or, least flattering, *dung.*)

PORTUGUESE: THE softer sister OF SPANISH

Today Portuguese is the world's sixth most spoken language, mostly in Portugal itself, but also in Brazil, Angola, and Mozambique. It's also heard from Macau in China to Goa in India. Portuguese unites more than 200 million people worldwide.

Portuguese is a Romance language that evolved mainly from a dialect spoken when Portugal was a province of the Spanish kingdom of León and Castile. Portuguese has developed separately from other Romance dialects, such as those that evolved into Spanish. After Portugal became independent in the 11th century, its borders expanded southward to the sea, and the country took in areas previously governed by Muslim Moors. The language called *Mozarabic*, spoken by the Christians living as Moorish subjects, was integrated into the Portuguese dialect, which created the language of Portugal. The basic language of today, both oral and written, was solidified and perfected in Lisbon, the capital, and Coimbra, the ancient university city. There are, of course, regional variations and pronunciations.

One writer suggested that Portuguese has "the hiss and rush of surf crashing against the bleak rocks of Sagres." If you don't speak it, you'll find French, Spanish, and English commonly spoken in Lisbon, along the Costa do Sol, and in Porto, as well as in many parts of the Algarve. In small villages and towns, hotel staffs and guides usually speak English. The Portuguese people are helpful and patient, and gestures often suffice.

o **Madeira:** Grown from grapes rooted in the island's volcanic soil, this wine traces its origins to 1419. Its history is similar to that of port, in that it was highly prized by aristocratic British families. George Washington was among the wine's early admirers, although the Madeira he consumed little resembled the product bottled today. Modern Madeira wines are lighter and drier than the thick, sweet kinds favored by generations past.

The wine, which is fortified and blended, includes such varieties as Malmsey, Malvasia, and Boal—sweet, heavy wines usually served with dessert or at the end of a meal. The less sweet Verdelho is often consumed as a light drink between meals, in much the same way that a Spaniard downs a glass of sherry. Dry and light, Sercial is best as an aperitif and is often served in Portugal with toasted and salted almonds. None of these wines is likely to be consumed with the main dish at dinner.

BEER *Cerveja* (beer) is gaining new followers yearly. One of the best of the local brews is sold under the name Sagres, honoring the town in the Algarve that enjoyed associations with Henry the Navigator.

WHEN TO GO

Because of its coastline and its beaches, summer is the most popular season. It is also the most overcrowded, especially in July and August. You get better deals if you go in September and June, when the weather is still good, and you avoid the crowds.

As an Atlantic country, winters in Portugal can be cold, windy, and rainy. But, to the delight of the locals and visitors, the country can experience many glorious days of sunshine even in February.

Weather

"We didn't know we had an April," one Lisbon resident said, "until that song came out." As a song and a season, "April in Portugal" is famous. Summer might be the most popular time to visit, but for the traveler who can chart his or her own course, spring and autumn are the best seasons to visit.

To use a North American analogy, the climate of Portugal most closely parallels that of California. There are only slight fluctuations in temperature between summer and winter; the overall mean ranges from 77°F (25°C) in summer to about 58°F (14°C) in winter. The rainy season begins in November and usually lasts through January. Because of the Gulf Stream, Portugal's northernmost area, Minho, enjoys mild (albeit very rainy) winters, even though it's at approximately the same latitude as New York City.

Snow brings many skiing enthusiasts to the Serra de Estrela in north-central Portugal. For the most part, however, winter means only some rain and lower temperatures in other regions. The Algarve and especially Madeira enjoy temperate winters. Madeira, in fact, basks in its high season in winter. The Algarve, too, is somewhat of a winter Riviera that attracts sun worshipers from North America and Europe. Summers in both tend to be long, hot, clear, and dry.

Lisbon and Estoril enjoy 46°F (8°C) to 65°F (18°C) temperatures in winter and temperatures between 60°F (16°C) and 82°F (28°C) in summer.

Average Daytime Temperature (°F & °C) & Monthly Rainfall (Inches) in Lisbon

	JAN	FEB	MAR	APR	MAY	JUNE	JULY	AUG	SEPT	OCT	NOV	DEC
Temp.(°F)	57	59	63	67	71	77	81	82	79	72	63	58
Temp.(°C)	14	15	17	19	22	25	27	28	26	22	17	14
Rainfall	4.3	3.0	4.2	2.1	1.7	0.6	0.1	0.2	1.3	2.4	3.7	4.1

Holidays

Watch for these public holidays, and adjust your banking needs accordingly: **New Year's Day** and **Universal Brotherhood Day** (Jan 1); **Carnaval** (Feb or early Mar— dates vary); **Good Friday** (Mar or Apr—dates vary); **Liberty Day,** anniversary of the revolution (Apr 25); **Labor Day** (May 1); **Corpus Christi** (May or June—dates vary); **Portugal Day** (June 10); **Feast of the Assumption** (Aug 15); **Proclamation of the Republic** (Oct 5); **All Saints' Day** (Nov 1); **Restoration of Independence** (Dec 1); **Feast of the Immaculate Conception** (Dec 8); and **Christmas Day** (Dec 25). The **Feast Day of St. Anthony** (June 13) is a public holiday in Lisbon, and the **Feast Day of St. John the Baptist** (June 24) is a public holiday in Porto.

Calendar of Events

Verify the dates below with a tourist office because they can vary greatly from year to year. Sometimes last-minute adjustments are made because of scheduling problems.

For an exhaustive list of events beyond those listed here, check http://events.frommers. com, where you'll find a searchable, up-to-the-minute roster of what's happening in cities all over the world.

JANUARY

Festa de São Gonçalo e São Cristovão, Vila Nova de Gaia, across the river from Porto. These resemble fertility rites and are two of the most attended religious festivals in Portugal. An image of São Gonçalo is paraded through the narrow streets as merrymakers beat drums. Boatmen along the Douro ferry a figure of São Cristovão with a huge head down the river. Much port wine is drunk, and cakes baked into phallic shapes are consumed by all. Call ℭ **22/ 339-34-72** for more information. Early January.

FEBRUARY TO APRIL

Carnaval (Mardi Gras), throughout the country, notably in Nazaré, Ovar, Loulé, and Funchal (Madeira). Each town has its unique way of celebrating this final festival before Lent. Masked marchers, flower-bedecked floats, and satirically decorated vehicles mark the occasion. Food and wine are consumed in abundance. For more details, check with the Portuguese National Tourist Office (see "Visitor Information" under "Fast Facts" in chapter 15). February or March.

Easter, all over Portugal. Some of the most noteworthy festivities take place at Póvoa de Varzim, Ovar, and especially the town of Braga, where Holy Week processions feature masked marchers and bejeweled floats along with fireworks, folk dancing, and torch parades. For more details, check with the Portuguese National Tourist Office (see "Visitor Information" under "Fast Facts" chapter 15). March or April.

MAY

Festas das Cruzes, Barcelos, on the river Cávado, near Braga. Since 1504, this festival has been celebrated with a Miracle of the Cross procession centered on a carpet made of millions of flower petals. Women in colorful regional dress adorn themselves with large gold chains. A giant fireworks display on the river signals the festival's end. Call ℭ **25/381-18-82** for more information. Early May.

First pilgrimage of the year to Fátima. In 1930, the bishop of Leiria authorized pilgrimages to this site. Today people from all over the world flock here to commemorate the first apparition of the Virgin to the little shepherd children in 1917. The year's last pilgrimage is in October (see below). Make hotel reservations months in advance, or plan to stay in a neighboring town. For more information, call the Fátima tourist office (ℭ **24/484-87-70;** www.rt-leiria fatima.pt). Mid-May.

JUNE

Feira Nacional da Agricultura (also known as the Feira do Ribatejo), Santarém, north of Lisbon on the river Tagus. This is the most important agricultural fair in Portugal. The best horses and cattle from all provinces are on display, and horse shows and bullfights enliven the festival. Food pavilions feature various regional cuisines. For more information, call ℭ **24/330-03-00.** Early June.

Festas dos Santos Populares, throughout Lisbon. Celebrations begin on June 13 and 14 in the Alfama, with feasts honoring Saint Anthony. Parades commemorating the city's patron saint feature *marchas* (parading groups of singers and musicians) along Avenida da Liberdade, and there is plenty of singing, dancing, drinking of wine, and eating of grilled sardines. On June 23 and 24, for the Feast of St. John the Baptist, bonfires brighten the night and participants jump over them. The night of the final celebration is the Feast of St. Peter on June 29. The Lisbon tourist office (ℭ **21/ 031-27-00;** www.visitlisboa.com) supplies details about where some of the events are staged, although much of the action is spontaneous. Mid-June to June 30.

Feast of St. John, Porto, home of the famous port wine. Honoring São João (St. John), this colorful festival features bonfires, all-night singing and dancing, and processions of locals in colorful costumes. Call ℭ **22/339-34-72** (www.portoturismo. pt) for more information. June 23 and 24.

Festas do São Pedro, Montijo, near Lisbon. This festival honoring St. Peter has been held since medieval times. The final day features a blessing of the boats and a colorful procession. Grilled sardines are the main item on the menu. Bull breeders bring their beasts into town and release them through the streets to chase foolish young men, who are often permanently injured or killed. There are also bullfights. On the final night, participants observe the pagan rite of setting a skiff afire and offering it as a sacrifice to the river Tagus. Call ℭ **21/031-27-00** for more information. Late June.

JULY

Colete Encarnado (Red Waistcoat), Vila Franca de Xira, north of Lisbon on the river Tagus. Like the more famous *feria* in Pamplona, Spain, this festival involves bulls running through narrow streets, followed by sensational bullfights in what aficionados consider the best bullring in Portugal. Fandango dancing and rodeo-style competition among the *Ribatejo campinos* (cowboys) mark the event. For more information, call ✆ **26/328-56-00** (www.coleteencarnado. no.sapo.pt). First or second Sunday in July.

Estoril Festival. Outside Lisbon at the seaside resort of Estoril, this festival of classical music occupies two concert halls that were built for the 500th anniversary of Columbus's first voyage to the New World. For information, write **Associação Internacional de Música da Costa do Estoril,** Galerias Estoril, Rua de Lisboa, 5 Lj. 12, 2765-240 Estoril (✆ **21/468-51-99;** fax 21/468-56-07; www.estorilfestival.net). Early July to first week in August (dates vary).

AUGUST

Feast of Our Lady of Monte, Madeira. On Assumption Eve and Day (Aug 14–15), the island's most important religious festival begins with devout worship and climaxes in an outburst of fun. Music, dancing, eating, and general drinking and carousing last until dawn. For more information, call ✆ **29/121-19-00.**

Festas da Senhora da Agonia, Viana do Castelo, at the mouth of the river Lima, north of Porto. The most spectacular festival in the north honors Our Lady of Suffering. A replica of the Virgin is carried through the streets over carpets of flowers. The bishop directs a procession of fishers to the sea to bless the boats. Float-filled parades mark the 5-day-and-night event as a time of revelry and celebration. A blaze of fireworks ends the festival. Call the tourist office (✆ **25/880-93-94**) for exact dates, which vary from year to year. Reserve hotel rooms well in advance or be prepared to stay in a neighboring town. Mid-August.

SEPTEMBER

Romaria da Nossa Senhora de Nazaré, Nazaré, Portugal's most famed fishing village. The event (Our Lady of Nazaré Festival) includes folk dancing, singing, and bullfights. The big attraction is the procession carrying the image of Nossa Senhora de Nazaré down to the sea. For more information, call ✆ **26/256-11-94.** Early to mid-September.

OCTOBER

Last Pilgrimage of the Year to Fátima, brings thousands of pilgrims from all over the world, who descend on Fátima to mark the occasion of the last apparition of the Virgin, which is said to have occurred on October 12, 1917. Call ✆ **24/484-87-71** for more information.

THE LAY OF THE LAND

Portugal has a coastline stretching some 800km (498 miles). It's bounded on the south and west by the Atlantic Ocean and on the north and east by Spain. Continental Portugal totals some 88,060 sq. km (34,000 sq. miles); its Atlantic islands, including Madeira and the Azores, extend the size of the country by another 3,108 sq. km (1,200 sq. miles). The Azores lie some 1,127km (700 miles) west of Lisbon (Lisboa), the capital of the country.

Portugal has four major rivers—the Minho, in the north, which separates the country from Spain; the Douro, also in the north, known for vineyards producing port wine; the Tagus, which flows into the Atlantic at Lisbon; and the Guadiana, in the southeast. Part of the Guadiana forms an eastern frontier with Spain.

The topography of Portugal is made up of a high plain of uneven height split by deep valleys. In the south the landscape is lower and less rugged than the north. Mountains are few on the Algarve, except for the Serra de Monchique or the Serra de São Mamede near the Spanish border.

The north has a series of mountain chains with high massifs such as the Serra do Marão rising to some 1,219m (4,000 ft.). The Tagus River forms a natural border between north and south.

Flora and fauna differ between the north and south of Portugal, because of the climatic differences. In the south, you find plant species indigenous to Africa and the Atlantic islands, whereas in the north the species are those found in European and Mediterranean zones. Along the coast, the maritime pine tree predominates.

The climate is temperate and usually mild, with dry summers, especially in the north. Because of the influence of the Atlantic, dry spells don't last for long periods. In fact, the ocean gives Portugal one of the highest rainfalls in Europe. However, in the extreme southern point of the Algarve rainfall annually might be lower than 16 inches.

The capital, Lisbon, of course has the densest concentration of people, followed by the second city of Porto in the north. Lisbon lies on the Tagus, Porto on the Douro River.

The other leading cities are few. Braga, which was Portugal's first capital, lies between the Cávado and Este rivers, dominating the valley of the Minho. Braga is followed by the university city of Coimbra, which lies on the right bank of the Mondego River. Setúbal, to the south of Lisbon, lies on the wide Sado estuary on the shores of the Bay of Setúbal and is sheltered by Cape Espichel, a part of the Serra da Arrábida mountain range.

More than half of the country is under cultivation. Soil in the south tends to be poor, but in the north it is rich and ideal for cultivation. Sea products represent about one-fifth of the nation's exports. Sardines are the major catch, followed by tuna.

RESPONSIBLE TRAVEL

Portugal may have been slow in coming around to environmentalism, but it is beginning to take hold in this beautiful land. Many places are overbuilt, especially along the seacoast. But other areas, especially in the interior, are being preserved and set aside for future generations to enjoy.

Portugal's major national park is **Peneda-Gerês,** in the Minho district, north of the city of Braga, close to the Spanish border. Most of the nature reserves are in the mountainous regions, including Montesinho, near Bragança; Alvão, near Vile Real Amarante; and Serra dos Candeeiros, near Fátima.

In recent years, the government has also declared some of Portugal's coastal areas as protected landscapes, rescuing them from developers. These areas include the resorts of Esposende; Sintra-Cascais; and southeast Alentejo, near Cabo de São Vicente.

If you'd like to find lodging in Portugal's protected areas, check out **Turismo da Natureza em Portugal** at Av. Eng. Arantes e Oliveira No. 13, 4B, 1900-221 Lisboa (www.icat.fc.ul.pt).

For a list of eco-friendly accommodations in Portugal, search www.itsagreengreen world.com. You can choose from homesteads, *quintas,* and villas, ranging from the Algarve north to the Minho.

Another good site to peruse for ecotourism is www.ecoclub.com, listing members and activities that center around ecotourism. For example, you might hook up with **Nature Meetings** on the island of Madeira, the first company on that island to provide in-depth walking experiences. You might also link yourself to an eco-friendly yurt holiday in the mountains of Portugal near the ancient university town of Coimbra, or else an ecological estate in the famous Serra da Estrela Nature Park, where you can stay on the banks of the River Mondego at a large granite-built farmhouse with a private pool.

Responsible Travel (www.responsibletravel.com) contains a great source of sustainable travel ideas run by a spokesperson for responsible tourism in the travel industry. **Sustainable Travel International** (www.sustainabletravelinternational.org) promotes responsible tourism practices and issues an annual Green Gear & Gift Guide.

You can find eco-friendly travel tips, statistics, and touring companies and associations—listed by destination under "Travel Choice"—at the TIES website, www. ecotourism.org. Also check out **Conservation International** (www.conservation. org)—which, with *National Geographic Traveler,* annually presents **World Legacy Awards** (www.nationalgeographic.com) to those travel tour operators, businesses, organizations, and places that have made a significant contribution to sustainable tourism. **Ecotravel.com** is part online magazine and part ecodirectory that lets you search for touring companies in several categories (water-based, land-based, spiritually oriented, and so on).

In the U.K., **Tourism Concern** (www.tourismconcern.org.uk) works to reduce social and environmental problems connected to tourism and find ways of improving tourism so that local benefits are increased.

The **Association of British Travel Agents** (**ABTA;** www.abta.com) acts as a focal point for the U.K. travel industry and is one of the leading groups spearheading responsible tourism to Portugal.

The **Association of Independent Tour Operators** (**AITO;** www.aito.co.uk) is a group of specialist operators leading the field in making Portuguese holidays sustainable.

In addition to the resources for Portugal listed above, see www.frommers.com/planning for more tips on responsible travel.

THE ACTIVE VACATION PLANNER

BULLFIGHTS No discussion of Portuguese recreation would be complete without a reference to *la tourada* (bullfighting). Unlike the rituals in Spain and parts of South America, in Portuguese bullfighting the bull is not killed at the end of the event, but is released to a life of grazing and stud duties. The *cavaleiros* (horsemen) dress in 18th-century costumes, which include silk jackets, tricornered hats, and tan riding breeches. Bullfights are held regularly in Lisbon's Campo Pequeno area, across the Tagus in the working-class city of Santarém, throughout the south-central plains, and in the Azores.

FISHING The northern section of Portugal receives abundant rainfall and contains rugged hills and some of the best-stocked streams in Iberia. Most noteworthy are the Rio Minho, the Rio Vouga, the Rio Lima, and the creeks and lakes of the Serra de Estrela. For fishing in the area in and around Lisbon, contact the **Clube dos Amadores de Pesca de Lisboa,** Travessa do Adro 12, 1800 Lisbon, or the **Clube Desportivo e Cultural de Amadores de Pesca da Costa do Sol,** Rua das Fontainhas 8, 2750 Cascais (© **21/484-16-91**). For information about fishing elsewhere in the country, contact regional tourist offices.

Fishing in inland waters is limited compared to fishing along the 800km (498 miles) of coastline. Deep-sea fishing, in waters richly stocked with fish swept toward Europe on northeast-flowing ocean currents, yields abundant catches. Fishing boats can be rented, with and sometimes without a crew, all along the Algarve as well.

FOOTBALL   Football—called soccer in the United States—is the most popular sport in Portugal. It's taken so seriously that on Sunday afternoons during important matches (with Spain or Brazil, for example), the country seems to come almost to a standstill. Notices about the venues of upcoming matches are prominently posted with hotel concierges, in newspapers, and on bulletin boards throughout various cities. One of the most-watched teams is that of Porto, which won the European Cup in 1987. The loyalty of Lisbon fans seems equally divided between the two hometown teams, Benfica and Sporting Club.

GOLF   With its sun-flooded expanses of underused land and its cultural links to Britain, Portugal has developed a passion for golf. Most of the nation's finest courses date from the late 1970s. The most important ones are in the Algarve; many are world-class. Others have been developed near Lisbon and Estoril, near Porto, and even on Madeira and the Azores. Usually within sight of the sea, most courses incorporate dramatic topography, and such famed golf-course designers as Robert Trent Jones (Sr. and Jr.), Henry Cotton, and Frank Pennink conceived most. For more information and an overview, contact the **Federação Portuguesa de Golfe (Portuguese Golf Federation)**, Av. Das Túlipas 6, Edificio Miraflores, 1495-161 Algés (✆ **21/412-37-80;** www.fpg.pt).

HORSEBACK RIDING   The Portuguese have prided themselves on their equestrian skills since their earliest battles against Roman invaders. Most of the resorts along the Algarve, plus a few in Cascais, maintain stables stocked with horses for long trail rides over hills, along beaches, and through ancient sun-baked villages. For more information, contact the **Federação Equestre Portuguesa (Portuguese Equestrian Federation)**, Av. Manuel Maia 26, 1000-201 Lisboa (✆ **21/847-87-74;** www.fep.pt).

The best offering available from **Equitour,** P.O. Box 807, 10 Stalnaker St., Dubois, WY 82513 (✆ **800/545-0019** or 307/455-3363; www.ridingtours.com), is a program of 8 days and 7 nights, with Lisbon as a meeting point. The price is $1,740 to $1,995 per person, and the weight limit is 185 pounds. Accommodations and special transfers are included in this tour, "The Blue Coast Ride." The rides go across some of the most scenic parts of Portugal, through valleys, along passes, and past waterfalls.

NATURE WATCHING   Hiking in Portugal is great for bird-watchers. The westernmost tip of continental Europe lies along the main migration routes between the warm wetlands of Africa and the cooler breeding grounds of northern Europe. The moist, rugged terrain of northern Portugal is especially suited for nature watching, particularly around Peneda-Gerês, where wild boar, wild horses, and wolves still roam through hills and forests.

WATERSPORTS   With much of its national identity connected to the sea, Portugal offers a variety of watersports. Outside the Algarve, few activities are highly organized, although the country's 800km (498 miles) of Atlantic coastline are richly peppered with secluded beaches and fishing hamlets. A recent development, especially in the Algarve, is the construction of a series of water parks, with large swimming pools, wave-making machines, waterslides, and fun fountains.

Sailing on well-designed oceangoing craft can be arranged at the Cascais Yacht Club, at any of the marinas in the Tagus, near Lisbon, or along the Algarve—particularly near the marina at Vilamoura. The surfing along the sun-blasted, wind-swept coast at Guincho has attracted fans from throughout Europe. For information about sailing and water events, contact the **Associação Naval de Lisboa (Naval Association of Lisbon)**, Doca de Belém, 1400-038 Lisboa (© **21/361-94-80**; www.anl.pt); the **Federação Portuguesa de Vela (Portuguese Sailing Federation)**, Doca de Belém, 1300-038 Lisboa (© **21/365-85-00**; www.fpvela.pt); or the **Federação Portuguesa de Actividades Subaquáticas (Portuguese Underwater Sports Federation)**, Rua José Falcão 4, 1170-193 Lisboa (© **21/191-08-68**; www.fpas.pt).

TOURS & SPECIALTY TRAVEL
Archaeology Tours

You might have read about archaeology tours, but most permit you only to look at the sites, not actually dig. A notable and much-respected exception is **Earthwatch Institute,** 114 Western Ave., Boston, MA 01754 (© **978/461-0081**; www.earth watch.org). It offers more than 150 programs designed and supervised by well-qualified academic and ecological authorities. At any time, at least 50 programs welcome participants for hands-on experience in preserving or documenting historical, archaeological, or ecological phenomena of interest to the global community. Projects in Portugal have included digs that uncovered a string of ancient and medieval hill forts across the country.

Cultural Exchanges

Servas ("to serve" in Esperanto), 1125 16 St., Ste. 201, Arcata, CA 95521 (© **707/ 825-1714**; www.usservas.org) is a nonprofit, nongovernmental, international, interfaith network of travelers and hosts. Its goal is to help build world peace, goodwill, and understanding by providing opportunities for deeper, more personal contacts among people of diverse cultural and political backgrounds. Servas travelers share living space, without charge, with members of communities worldwide. Visits last a maximum of 2 nights. Visitors fill out an application and are interviewed for suitability; if approved, they receive a directory listing the names and addresses of prospective hosts.

Cycling Tours

Cycling tours are a good way to see the back roads of a country and stretch your limbs. Although dozens of companies in Britain offer guided cycling tours on foreign turf, only a handful offer itineraries through Portugal. One is the **Cyclists' Tourist Club,** Parklands, Railton Road, Guildford, Surrey GU2 9JX (© **0844/736-8454**; www.ctc.org.uk). It charges £36 a year for membership, which includes information and suggested cycling routes through Portugal and dozens of other countries.

In the United States, bicyclists can contact **Backroads,** 801 Cedar St., Berkeley, CA 94710 (© **800/GO-ACTIVE** [462-2848] in the U.S.; www.backroads.com). Another outfitter arranging bike tours in Portugal is **Uniquely Europe,** a division of Europe Express, 3303 Monte Villa Parkway, Ste. 200, Bothell, WA 98021 (© **800/ 927-3876**; www.europeexpress.com).

Shipping Tips

Many stores in Portugal will crate and ship bulky objects. Any especially large item, such as a piece of furniture, should be sent by ship. Every antiques dealer in Lisbon has lists of reputable maritime shippers. For most small and medium-size shipments, air freight isn't much more expensive than sending the items by ship. TAP, the Portuguese airline, has a separate toll-free U.S. number for cargo inquiries (✆ **800/221-7890**). Once in Lisbon, you can contact TAP to make air-shipping arrangements for larger purchases by calling the Lisbon cargo department offices at ✆ **21/841-63-36.** It's open Monday through Friday from 9am to 6:30pm.

Remember that all your air-cargo shipments will need to clear Customs in the United States, Canada, or your home country. This involves some additional paperwork and perhaps a trip to the airport near where you live. It's usually best to hire a commercial Customs broker to do the work for you.

See the "Taxes" info on p. 422 for info on value-added tax rules here.

Escorted General-Interest Tours

Escorted tours are structured group tours with a group leader. The price usually includes everything from airfare to hotels, meals, tours, admission costs, and local transportation.

There are many escorted tour companies to choose from, each offering transportation to and within Portugal, prearranged hotel space, and such extras as bilingual tour guides and lectures. Many tours to Portugal include excursions to Spain.

Some of the best escorted tours to Portugal are offered by **Blue Danube Holidays** (✆ **800/268-4155** or 416/362-5000; www.bluedanubeholidays.com in the U.S.), a long-established company. It offers a Grand Tour of Portugal along with any number of beach holidays (from Madeira to the Algarve), and even city tours of Lisbon.

Some of the most expensive and luxurious tours are run by **Abercrombie & Kent International** (✆ **800/554-7016;** www.abercrombiekent.com), including deluxe 15-day tours of the Iberian Peninsula by train. Guests stay in some of the country's finest hotels.

Alternative Travel Group Ltd. (✆ **018/6531-5678;** www.atg-oxford.co.uk) is a British firm that organizes walking and cycling vacations in Portugal and Spain. Tours explore the scenic countryside and medieval towns of each country. To request a brochure outlining the tours, call ✆ **018/6531-5665.**

Petrabax Tours (✆ **800/634-1188** in the U.S.; www.petrabax.com) attracts those who prefer to see Portugal by bus, although the company also offers fly/drive packages. A number of city packages are also available, plus trips that try to capture the essence of Portugal and Spain.

Golf Tours

The best golf tours (usually in the Algarve) are arranged by **Golf International,** 14 E. 260 Fifth Ave., New York, NY 10001 (✆ **800/833-1389** or 212/986-9176; www.golfinternational.com).

shopping TIPS

Regardless of where it's made—from the Azores to the remote northeast province of Trás-os-Montes—merchandise from all over Portugal ends up in Lisbon stores. But if you're going to a particular province, try to shop locally, where prices are often about 20% less than those in Lisbon. A general exception is the fabled handmade **embroideries** from Madeira; prices there are about the same as in Lisbon.

Pottery is one of the best buys in Portugal, and pottery covered with brightly colored roosters from Barcelos is legendary. In fact, the rooster has become the virtual symbol of Portugal. Blue-and-white pottery is made in Coimbra and often in Alcobaça. Our favorite items come from Caldas da Rainha. They include yellow-and-green dishes in the shape of vegetables (especially cabbage), fruit, animals, and even leaves. Vila Real is known for its black pottery, and Aceiro is known for polychrome pottery. Some red-clay pots from the Alentejo region in the southeast are based on designs that go back to the Etruscans. **Atlantis crystal** is another good buy. **Suede** and **leather,** as in Spain, are also good buys. In the Algarve, handsome **lanterns, fire screens,** and even **outdoor furniture** are constructed from metal—mainly copper, brass, and tin.

The best buy in Portugal, **gold,** is strictly regulated by the government. Jewelers must put a minimum of 19.2 karats into the jewelry they sell. **Filigree jewelry** in gold and silver is popular in Lisbon and elsewhere in Portugal. The art of ornamental openwork made of fine gold or silver wire dates to ancient times. The most expensive items—often objets d'art—are fashioned from 19¼-karat gold. Filigree is often used in depictions of caravels. Less expensive trinkets are often made of sterling silver, sometimes dipped in 24-karat gold.

Products made of **cork,** which range from place mats to cigarette boxes, are good buys. Collectors seek out **decorative glazed tiles.** You also might find good buys in Lisbon in **porcelain** and **china,** in **fishermen's sweaters** from the north, and in **fado recordings.**

Intricately woven lightweight **baskets** make attractive, practical gifts. It's best to shop for handmade **lace** in Vila do Conde, outside Porto, where you get a better buy; many Lisbon outlets carry the lace as well.

Language Classes

The National Registration Center for Study Abroad (NRCSA), P.O. Box 1393, Milwaukee, WI 53201 (© **414/278-0631;** www.nrcsa.com), allows you to experience Portugal by living and learning the language. The NRCSA has helped people of all ages and backgrounds participate in foreign travel and cultural programs since 1968. Contact the NRCSA for details about the courses and their costs.

Walking Tours

With its historic sights and beautiful countryside, Portugal is an appealing place for hill climbing and hiking. In the United Kingdom, **Exodus,** 1311 63rd St., Ste. 200, Emeryville, CA 94608 (© **800/843-4272;** www.exodus.co.uk), offers 7- and 14-day walking tours through Portugal several times a year. **Sherpa Expeditions,** 131a Heston Rd., Hounslow, Middlesex TW5 0RF (© **020/8577-2717;** www.sherpa expeditions.com), offers trips through off-the-beaten-track regions of the world, which include the Portuguese island of Madeira.

SUGGESTED PORTUGAL ITINERARIES

If you have unlimited time, one of Europe's greatest pleasures is getting "lost" on the dusty plains of Alentejo or in
the little hidden coves of the Algarve. It's fun to wander
about Portugal at random, making new discoveries off the
beaten path, finding enchanting towns you've never heard of or read about
in a guidebook, places like Vila Real, the remote capital of Trás-os-Montes,
Portugal's least explored province.

But few of us have such a generous amount of time in the speeded-up
21st century. Vacations are getting shorter, and a "lean-and-mean" schedule is called for if you want to experience the best of Portugal in a ridicu-
lously short amount of time.

If you're such a time-pressed traveler, as most of us are, you may find
"Portugal in 1 Week" or "Portugal in 2 Weeks" below most helpful for
skimming the highlights. If you've been to Portugal before, exploring such
well-trodden tourist meccas as Lisbon and Sintra, you may want to discover a different area of the country this time. See, for example, "The
Algarve in 1 Week," later in this chapter. This is the southernmost province of Portugal, and it has much to discover. Many visitors who have gone
to North Africa feel that the Algarve is the European version of that strip
of Arabic land.

You might also want to refer to chapter 1 to see what experiences or
sights appeal to you, and adjust the itineraries to suit your particular travel
desires.

If you stick to the main highways, Portugal has fine and well-maintained roads. But when you wander off the beaten trail, you may find less
than desirable driving conditions. At any rate, when driving in Portugal
you'll encounter (hopefully not face-to-face) some of Europe's most reckless drivers. The country has an alarming vehicular accident rate, so be
duly cautious and drive defensively. Many Europeans refer to the Portuguese as "cowboys of the road."

Portugal is blessed with a fast and efficient rail system to transport you
to the highlights. Where the train ends, a bus is usually waiting to take
you the rest of the way.

The itineraries that follow take you to some of the major attractions
such as Lisbon but also direct you to more secluded villages such as the

picture-postcard-perfect hamlet of Óbidos. The pace may be a bit breathless for some visitors, so skip a town or sight occasionally to have some chill-out time—after all, you're on vacation.

The Regions in Brief

Here is Portugal in a nutshell, a tantalizing preview of what the country has to offer, and from which you can make choices about where you'd like to go.

Lisbon & the Costa do Sol Portugal's capital is on hilly terrain beside one of the finest harbors in Europe—the estuary of the Tagus (Tejo) River. Within a few miles of the city limits, the beaches of the Costa do Sol cater to residents of the capital, who easily reach them by bus and train. Until the development of beaches in the Algarve, those on the Costa do Sol were among the most crowded and glamorous in the country. The best-known resorts include Estoril and Cascais, long playgrounds of the wintering wealthy.

Estremadura The name translates as "the extremity," but it has radically different connotations from those associated with the harsh landscapes of Estremadura in neighboring Spain. Early in the development of the Portuguese nation, rulers based in the country's north-central region coined the term to refer to the Moorish territories to the south that the Portuguese eyed enviously. Technically, those territories included Nazaré, Óbidos, and Fátima; in many cases, the word is now used to include the territory around Lisbon as well. Estremadura's coastline is flanked by some of the country's richest fishing banks.

The Algarve Encompassing the extreme southwestern tip of Europe, the Algarve boasts a 161km (100-mile) coastline with some of the best beaches in Europe. It's permeated with memories of the long-ago Moorish occupation, when the region was called Al-Gharb. The garden of Portugal, this naturally arid district is laced with large-scale irrigation projects. Except for the massive development of beach resorts since the late 1960s, the landscape in many ways resembles the coast of nearby Morocco, with which it has much in common.

Alentejo & Ribatejo East and southeast of Lisbon, these regions form the agrarian heartland of Portugal. Underpopulated but fertile, and marked mostly by fields and grasslands, these are horse- and bull-breeding territories, with some of the most idyllic landscapes in Iberia. Their medieval cities, including Évora, Tomar, Beja, Elvas, and Estremoz, contain famous examples of Roman and Manueline architecture.

Coimbra & The Beiras Between two of the country's most vital rivers, the Beiras were incorporated into the medieval kingdom of Portugal earlier than the territories farther south, including Lisbon. Given their history, they're among the most traditional Portuguese areas in the country. The medieval university town of Coimbra is the highlight of the region; a cluster of spas and the legendary forest of Buçaco also draw visitors. The region technically consists of three districts: Coastal Beira (Beira Litoral), Low Beira (Beira Baixa), and High Beira (Beira Alta). The Beiras contain the country's highest peaks—the Serra de Estrela—and the Mondela River.

Porto & The Douro Porto, Portugal's second-largest city, has thrived as a mercantile center since English traders used it as a base for the export of port, London's favorite drink during the Regency. The river that feeds it, the Douro, flows through some of the world's richest vineyards before emptying into the Atlantic in Porto's harbor. Porto abounds with the 19th-century mansions of merchants who grew wealthy from growing wine grapes or through investments in such colonies as Brazil. The most popular resort in the region is the once-sleepy former fishing village of Póvoa de Varzim.

The Minho This is the northernmost region of Portugal, an isolated, idiosyncratic area with a population descended more or less directly from Celtic ancestors.

The local tongue is a tricky dialect that more closely resembles that of Galicia (in northwestern Spain) than it does Portuguese. The Minho is almost a land unto itself; with most of the population centered in Viana do Castelo, Guimarães, and Braga. Ardently provincial and suspicious of outsiders, the district figured prominently in the development of medieval Portugal as a kingdom separate from Spain, producing early kings who moved south in their conquest of territories, which were held, until then, by the Moors.

Trás-os-Montes   This far northeastern and least visited corner of Portugal is a wild, rugged land whose name translates literally as "beyond the mountains." Aggressively provincial, the region nevertheless has strong ties to its neighbor, the Minho. Local granite dominates the architecture. The district stretches from Lamego and the Upper Douro to the Spanish border. Vila Real is the largest town.

Madeira   Near the coast of Africa, 855km (531 miles) southwest of Portugal, Madeira is the much-eroded peak of a volcanic mass. Wintering English gentry first discovered the island's recreational charms; today it's one of the world's most famous islands, known for the abundant beauty of its gardens. Only 57km (35 miles) long and about 21km (13 miles) across at its widest point, the island is an autonomous region of Portugal and has a year-round population of 255,000.

The Azores   This island chain is one of the most isolated in the Atlantic Ocean. It constitutes an autonomous region and has some 240,000 year-round occupants who live amid rocky, moss-covered landscapes closely tied to the sea. The archipelago spans more than 800km (497 miles) that stretch from the southeastern tip of Santa Maria to the northwestern extremity of the island of Corvo. The chain's largest island is São Miguel, which lies a third of the way across the Atlantic, about 1,200km (746 miles) west of Portugal and 3,400km (2,113 miles) east of New York. Today the Azores are widely known within yachting circles as the final destination for annual sailboat races from Newport and Bermuda.

PORTUGAL IN 1 WEEK

The very title of this tour is a misnomer. You can't possibly see all of Portugal in 1 week, merely a few of its highlights. But you can have a memorable vacation in Portugal if you budget your time carefully. Use the following itinerary to make the most out of a week in Portugal, but feel free to drop a place or two to save a day to relax.

Days 1 to 3: Lisbon: Gateway to Portugal ★★★

Lisbon is the highlight of Portugal, as befits a capital city, and it also happens to be the arrival point for most rail, plane, and bus trips. Try to arrive in Lisbon as early as possible in the morning to get in a full round of the city's attractions.

After checking into a hotel, head for the **Alfama,** climaxed by a visit to the **Castelo de São Jorge** (**St. George's Castle;** p. 104), where you'll also be treated to the most panoramic view in all of Lisbon. Wander around the narrow streets of the Alfama for 2 hours.

In the afternoon, head for the suburb of **Belém,** where you can visit the **Mosteiro dos Jerónimos** (p. 106), **Torre de Belém** (p. 110), and later the **Museu Nacional dos Coches** (**National Coach Museum;** p. 109). Spend the night going to a fado club where you not only can enjoy a regional dinner but also listen to some of the country's favorite songs.

Best Portugal Itineraries

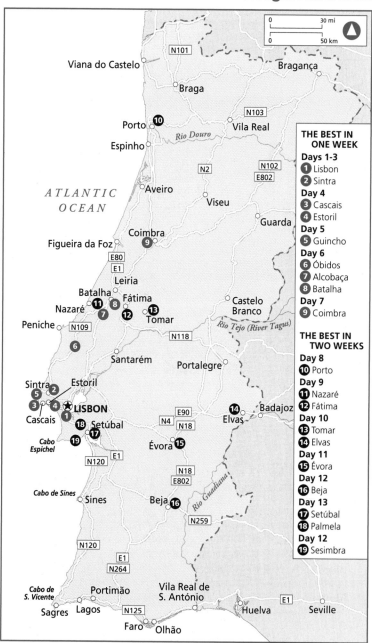

THE BEST IN ONE WEEK

Days 1-3
1 Lisbon
2 Sintra
Day 4
3 Cascais
4 Estoril
Day 5
5 Guincho
Day 6
6 Óbidos
7 Alcobaça
8 Batalha
Day 7
9 Coimbra

THE BEST IN TWO WEEKS

Day 8
10 Porto
Day 9
11 Nazaré
12 Fátima
Day 10
13 Tomar
14 Elvas
Day 11
15 Évora
Day 12
16 Beja
Day 13
17 Setúbal
18 Palmela
Day 12
19 Sesimbra

On Day 2, travel outside Lisbon to glorious **Sintra,** the single most beautiful town in all of Portugal—Lord Byron likened it to Eden. You can spend an entire day here wandering about, losing yourself in its quaint streets. However, allow enough time to visit its two major attractions, **Palácio Nacional de Sintra** (p. 166) and **Palácio Nacional da Pena** (p. 166). Return to Lisbon for the night.

On the morning of Day 3, mop up the major attractions of Lisbon you didn't have time to see on Day 1. Among these is the **Museu da Fundação Calouste Gulbenkian** (p. 110), one of the world's finest private art collections, assembled by the tycoon Calouste Gulbenkian, and now beefed up by new bequests. Allow an hour and a half for a visit. Follow this with a late morning visit to the **Museu Nacional de Arte Antiga** (p. 112), which will take up at least another 1½ hours. This is the country's most distinguished museum and a showcase for its national treasures, which include some of Europe's grandest old master paintings.

In the afternoon, after lunch in a typical Lisboan tavern, take our walking tour of Baixa, the center of Lisbon, and the **Chiado** (p. 117). This will take up to 3 hours of your afternoon. If time remains, get in some shopping by walking such streets as **Rua Áurea** or **Rua de Prata** (for a list of our suggestions, coverage begins on p. 127).

Days 4 & 5: Costa do Sol: Lisbon's Riviera ★★★

Leave Lisbon in the morning and head west along its Riviera, the Costa do Sol. The best place here for overnighting is the former fishing village of **Cascais** (p. 149), now a major beach resort. You can stop off and explore **Estoril** (p. 144) in the morning, as it lies only 24km (15 miles) west of Lisbon. In this former stamping ground of royalty, walk through the **Parque Estoril** in the center of town and maybe spend an hour or two on the beach if time allows.

Continue on to **Cascais,** 6.5km (4 miles) west of Estoril, for the night. You can arrive early enough in the day for a seafood lunch, which you can enjoy after you check into a hotel. Spend the rest of the day wandering the village's narrow streets, shopping, and sightseeing. Although the city has museums, none is more intriguing than the streets of the town itself. In summer, make hotel reservations way in advance. If you skipped beach time in Estoril, you can head for the sands at Cascais.

If you want to take an afternoon excursion, make it to the **Boca do Inferno** (**Mouth of Hell;** p. 150) to see its thundering waves from the Atlantic.

On Day 5, after time on the beach in the morning, devote the rest of the day to nearby excursions. Numero uno is the **Palácio Nacional de Queluz** (p. 162), the most brilliant example of the rococo style of architecture in Portugal. After spending an hour and a half exploring the royal palace, dine at the **Cozinha Velha** (**The Old Kitchen;** p. 162), one of the most evocative in the area and the former kitchen of the old palace.

Later that afternoon head for **Guincho** (p. 158) to take in the treacherous ocean scenery, some of the most dramatic in Europe. Return to Cascais for the night.

Day 6: Óbidos ★★, Alcobaça ★★ & Batalha ★★★

If you can't visit all of these attractions in 1 day, make it to **Óbidos** and **Alcobaça** on Day 6, and stop off at **Batalha** en route to Coimbra on Day 7. To see the most enchanting medieval town in all of Portugal, continue north from Lisbon for 93km (58 miles) to Óbidos, or a shorter distance if you spent the night in Cascais.

If you leave the Greater Lisbon area early enough, you can be in Óbidos in time for 2 hours of sightseeing, followed by lunch at the **Castelo de Óbidos** (p. 200), the most famous restaurant—and justifiably so—in Portugal.

Leave Óbidos after lunch and drive to Alcobaça, 38km (24 miles) northeast of Óbidos. Once here, you can spend an hour visiting the **Mosteiro de Santa Maria** (p. 205), once one of the richest and most prestigious monasteries in Europe, dating from 1178. Seek out, in particular, its lavish Gothic tombs.

After a visit, continue northeast to Batalha, spending an hour and a half exploring its **Mosteiro de Santa Maria da Vitória** (p. 205). Still celebrated for its royal cloisters to this day, in the 14th century this was the most luxurious and grandest monastery in all of Portugal—and much of its former glory remains.

Accommodations are limited in both Alcobaça and Batalha. If you didn't make reservations in advance in summer, you might have to continue to our final stop, the city of Coimbra, for the night (see below).

Day 7: Coimbra: The University City ★★

Outside of Lisbon and the second city of Porto, Portugal's most romantic and historic city is Coimbra, lying 198km (123 miles) north of Lisbon. You can easily reach it from Óbidos, Alcobaça, or Batalha, if you stopped at either of these places on Day 6.

In 1 full day of sightseeing, you can take in Coimbra's major monuments, including **Sé Velha,** the old cathedral (p. 286), and **Universidade de Coimbra** (p. 287), the university that was founded here in 1537. Also of interest are the **Biblioteca Geral da Universidade,** the university library (p. 287), established in 1716, and **Igreja e Mosteiro da Santa Cruz** (p. 286), dating from the 12th century.

Overnight in Coimbra before making the 1½-hour drive to Lisbon in the morning for transportation back home.

PORTUGAL IN 2 WEEKS

With 2 weeks to explore the country, you aren't as rushed, of course, as you might have been with the agenda proposed above. With more breathing time, you can visit the second city of Portugal, Porto, as well as some of the more intriguing destinations in the plains, especially the historic city of Évora.

Days 1 to 7

Refer to the 1-week itinerary outlined above.

Day 8: Porto: Port Wine & the Gateway to the North ★★★

After leaving Coimbra, continue north to the city of **Porto,** a distance of 116km (72 miles). Plan on arriving in the late morning, so you'll have time to take our walking tour (p. 318) of the inner core of this old city on the water.

Porto is known, of course, as the main distribution center of port wine. Sampling port and touring the wine lodges is the main reason to come here. If you have time to visit only one lodge, we recommend **Ramos Pinto** (p. 316), one of the most famous and one of the best. If you have time left over for a second visit to a lodge, we suggest **Porto Sandeman** (p. 316).

After touring some lodges, plan a festive dinner at one of the city's highly rated restaurants, such as **Restaurante Portucale** (p. 328). If that's beyond your budget, you'll find plenty of local taverns serving good-tasting and affordable fare.

Day 9: Nazaré ★★ & Fátima

If you have another week, the north of Portugal, lying above Porto, awaits you. But if you have to confine your schedule to 2 weeks, we suggest a return south to hit the highlights before driving back to Lisbon.

On the morning of Day 9, you face a choice: Either drive to the fishing port of **Nazaré** (coverage begins on p. 201), a distance of 217km (135 miles) south of Porto, or, especially if you're Catholic, head south to **Fátima** (coverage begins on p. 206), a distance of 191km (119 miles) from Porto. Nazaré and Fátima are two completely different experiences.

Nazaré is the most famous fishing village in the country, and it also has some of Portugal's best beaches. You can make a day of it wandering this ancient port and watching the fishing boats come in with their catch, or lounging on the sands. Be sure to budget some time to shop for some of the famous Nazaré fishermen's sweaters, too.

Conversely, if your interests are more religious than secular, descend on Fátima, world famous as a pilgrimage site because the Virgin Mary was said to have appeared here in the early 20th century. The faithful from all over the world flock here to see the **Chapel of the Apparitions** (p. 208).

Day 10: Tomar ★★ & Elvas ★★

Depending on your base for the previous night, either Nazaré or Fátima, you can begin Day 10 by driving to the southeast of Fátima to explore the old city of **Tomar,** a distance of 39km (24 miles). Tomar was the former headquarters of the Knights Templar, and you can explore its attractions, mainly **Convento da Ordem de Cristo** (p. 260), in 2 hours. You might stay in Tomar for lunch before heading on, striking out this time to the southeast to visit the city of **Elvas,** a distance of 229km (142 miles). You should arrive in the midafternoon. After checking into a hotel for the night, set out on foot to explore the attractions of Elvas (coverage begins on p. 266), wandering its narrow, cobblestone streets. Elvas boasts a good pousada and some fine *estalagems* (inns) for overnighting.

Day 11: Évora: Capital of Alto Alentejo ★★★

On the morning of Day 11, drive southwest from Elvas to the city of **Évora,** a distance of 85km (53 miles). This city of bubbling fountains, whitewashed houses, and cobblestoned streets will be the highlight of your tour of the Portuguese plains. After checking into a hotel for the night, set out to explore the main attractions, which include the **Templo de Diana** (p. 270); the **Sé,** or cathedral (p. 270); and the **Igreja de São João Evangelista** (p. 270). In spite of the charm of these particular sites, the real allure of Évora is the beautiful city itself. It is filled with monuments from the 14th to the 16th centuries, and most of these can be enjoyed simply by strolling its streets. Évora also boasts the best and most atmospheric accommodations in this part of western Portugal. Our favorite place to stay here is **Pousada de Évora, Lóios** (p. 272), a historical monument from the 15th century that nonetheless contains modern conveniences.

Day 12: Beja: Capital of Baixo Alentejo ★

Leave Évora in the morning and drive 76km (47 miles) south to the ancient city of **Beja,** which, it is said, was founded by Julius Caesar. After checking into a hotel, you can spend the rest of the morning wandering its colorful streets. After a typical lunch in a local restaurant, visit the **Museu Rainha Dona Leonor** (p. 275) in the afternoon, followed by a trip to the 14th-century ruins of **Castelo de Beja** (p. 275). If time remains, shop for handicrafts along **Rua Capital João Francisco de Sousa** in the town center.

Day 13: Setúbal ★ & Palmela

On the morning of Day 13, leave Beja and head northwest to the old city of **Setúbal,** a distance of 144km (89 miles). At Setúbal, you'll be only 40km (25 miles) southeast of Lisbon. After checking into a hotel here, we suggest you drive to **Palmela,** a distance of 8km (5 miles) north of Setúbal for lunch in the **Castelo de Palmela Pousada** (p. 188), one of the best government-run country inns in Portugal. You can also overnight here if you prefer not to spend the night in Setúbal.

After lunch, return to Setúbal for your exploration of this old city, said to have been founded by a grandson of Noah. Its chief attraction is the **Convento de Jesús** (p. 184), a stellar example of 15th-century Manueline architecture. You can also visit **Museu da Setúbal** (p. 184) in the afternoon, and perhaps shop for local handicrafts (our suggestions begin on p. 185). Factory tours are available in the environs of Setúbal for those who want to make the trek.

Day 14: Sesimbra on Your Return to Lisbon

Spend a leisurely Day 14 by driving back along the coast south of the Tagus to Lisbon, where you can overnight before departing Portugal. After leaving Setúbal in the morning, drive west along the southern coast, enjoying the mountain scenery of the **Serra de Arrábida.** The fishing village of **Portinho da Arrábida** makes a good luncheon stopover if you got a late start from Setúbal—its coastal road features lots of sandy coves, perfect for exploring if the weather's nice.

Your major stopover for the day can be the little resort and fishing village of **Sesimbra** (p. 179), lying 26km (16 miles) southwest of Setúbal and 43km (27 miles) south of Lisbon. You can spend at least 2 hours wandering its harbor and exploring its streets, including a walk along the ruined battlements of the ancient **Castle of Sesimbra** (p. 180). Afterward, you can make the half-hour drive north to Lisbon.

PORTUGAL FOR FAMILIES

The trick to planning an itinerary for your family is choosing attractions that'll amuse young ones, but balancing those with some museum hopping and church going (kids might just marvel at the art and architecture). Below are some suggestions on how to achieve that happy balance between so-called adult attractions and amusements for kids.

Day 1: Lisbon: Gateway to Portugal ★★★

Arrive early in the morning, if possible, for a full day of sightseeing. After checking into a family-friendly hotel, head for **Castelo de São Jorge** (p. 104), crowning the historic Alfama with its narrow, winding streets. Allow at least an hour to visit the castle (which might remind your kids of the one at Disney), followed by another hour walking around the district—perhaps even getting momentarily lost in the narrow streets of the old Alfama.

After lunch, take your kids by train to the suburb of **Belém** where the entire family should be fascinated by the flamboyant **Mosteiro dos Jerónimos** (p. 106). Allow an hour. This can be followed by two kid-pleasing attractions, **Museu de Marinha,** the maritime museum (p. 109), and **Museu Nacional dos Coches,** the national coach museum (p. 109), which will hold fascination for adults as well. Return to your hotel in the heart of Lisbon for the night.

Day 2: Sintra: Glorious Eden ★★★

For a change of pace, take the train to Sintra, only 29km (18 miles) northwest of Lisbon where the very town itself, with its parks, palaces, and gardens, is a treat for people of all ages. In the morning, visit the **Palácio Nacional de Sintra** (p. 166), where kids should delight in wandering around the former palace of the Moorish sultans.

Later in the afternoon, visit **Castelo dos Mouros** (p. 164), a former Moorish stronghold dating from the 8th century. Return to Lisbon for the night.

Day 3: Another Day in Lisbon

In one very busy day you can visit the **Jardim Zoológico de Lisboa** (p. 118) in the morning, with its 2,000 animals roaming a 26-hectare (64-acre) setting. You can also rent a rowboat for an hour or so and take your kids for a ride across the lake. Later, you can visit the **Oceanário de Lisboa** (p. 117), the second-largest aquarium in the world. Kids delight in coming within arm's length of such critters as penguins, sharks, or playful sea otters. The Oceanário lies within the **Parque das Nações,** which is a virtual playground for children, with rides, an interactive science museum, and fairgrounds.

In the afternoon you can visit the **Planetário Calouste Gulbenkian** (p. 118), with astronomical shows throughout the day that should appeal to the entire family. You can spend the rest of the afternoon at **Jardim da Estrela,** which is perfect for a family outing. It boasts duck ponds and lush flora, as well as playgrounds for children.

Day 4: Beach Fun along Costa do Sol

While still based in Lisbon, you can plan Day 4 at the beach along Lisbon's Riviera. Sunny days are almost guaranteed here in July and August. A train from Estação Cais do Sodré will put you in Estoril in only 30 minutes, with continuing service to the former fishing village (now resort) of Cascais.

You can get off the train in **Estoril** and wander its **Parque Estoril** in the center of town before descending on the beach for 2 hours or so.

After time on the sands, take the train's continuing service to **Cascais,** where you can have a seafood lunch in one of the town's affordable taverns. Cascais is a far more architecturally intriguing town to explore than Estoril, and parents and their children can spend at least 2 hours traversing its narrow streets and

Portugal for Families

taking walks along the harborfront where fishing boats bob. Kids will also be fascinated by the **Museu do Mar** (p. 150), with its marine artifacts and model boats.

Later in the day, you can rent a car to **Cabo da Roca** (p. 158), at nearby **Guincho,** to see some of the most turbulent and dramatic Atlantic Ocean scenery in Portugal. After a day of sightseeing, you can drive back to Lisbon for the night.

Day 5: Óbidos ★★, Alcobaça ★★ & Nazaré ★★

On the morning of Day 5, leave Lisbon and drive north to Portugal's most enchanting village, the walled town of **Óbidos,** a distance of 93km (58 miles). Again your child may think this medieval city, with its golden towers, crenellated battlements, and ramparts, a creation of Disney. Spend 2 hours exploring the town, climaxed by a lunch at the **Castelo de Óbidos** (p. 193).

After lunch, continue northeast to **Alcobaça,** a distance of 38km (24 miles). Although it's one of Portugal's grandest monuments, and is certainly an adult attraction, kids often stand in awe as they wander through **Mosteiro de Santa Maria** (p. 200), one of the most impressive Gothic monasteries in the country. Allow an hour to explore it.

Afterward, head 13km (8 miles) northwest to the fishing village of **Nazaré.** Nazaré isn't blessed with a lot of family-friendly inns; your best possibility is **Hotel Praia** (p. 203), rising six floors and overlooking the port's best beach.

Spend some time on the harborfront, watching the fishing boats pull in for the evening with the day's catch; or head to the **Sítio,** the upper town, to wander through its narrow streets. By early nightfall, a family seafood dinner is in order.

Day 6: Coimbra: Youthful Exuberance ★★

The crown jewel of the three Beiras, Coimbra is a city peopled in part by backpackers and students (many of whom appear in medieval costumes on the street at night as singing "tuna," as their groups are called). From Nazaré, it's an easy drive to the northeast, a distance of 110km (68 miles) to Coimbra. Plan to overnight here, perhaps at the moderately priced **Hotel Astória** (p. 289).

You can walk with your kids through the **Universidade de Coimbra** (p. 287), and duck into the **Igreja e Mosteiro da Santa Cruz** (p. 286), but they'll probably be most interested in **Portugal dos Pequenitos** (p. 288). This is "Portugal for the Little Ones," a re-creation of buildings from every province in miniature, including everything from windmills to castles and palaces, even an Indian temple.

Day 7: Porto: City on the Douro River ★★★

In the morning of Day 7, leave Coimbra and continue north for 116km (72 miles) until you reach the city of Porto. Then take the family on our **walking tour** of town (p. 318). After you finish, have lunch in one of the local taverns (most serve seafood).

After lunch, visit **Torre dos Clérigos** (p. 315), dating from 1754 and rising to a height of 76m (249 ft.). You can climb the 225 steps to the top for one of the finest views of a cityscape in the north of Portugal.

You can fly back to Lisbon in the early evening (returning your rental car, of course), or you can overnight in Porto and fly back to Lisbon the next morning for an onward connection. Flight time is about 40 minutes.

THE ALGARVE IN 1 WEEK

Rocky coves and long, sandy beaches characterize the southern tier of Portugal, the former stronghold of the Moors during their occupation of the country. Though uncontrolled tourist development has destroyed much of the old charm of this part of Portugal, much remains to enchant. Not all the towns of interest lie along the water, as many are inland, including such scattered attractions as the Roman ruins at **Estói** (north of Faro) or the old Moorish town of Silves, within easy reach of Portimão.

You can rent a car in Lisbon and make the 280km (174-mile) drive to **Sagres,** the so-called "end of the world" in the western Algarve to begin this tour. Those on a more rushed schedule can fly to **Faro,** capital of the Algarve, and rent a car there. If you choose the latter option, use Faro as a base for 2 days, so that you'll have time to explore the environs, and then head west to Sagres—basically you'll be doing this tour in reverse.

Day 1: Sagres: The Southwestern Corner of Europe ★

This is the port where Henry the Navigator launched Portugal upon its era of exploration, which led to colonies around the world. After checking into a hotel or local pousada, set out to explore the surrounding cape, which ancient people thought marked the end of the world. After spending 30 minutes or so at the **Fortaleza de Sagres** (p. 214), drive 5km (3 miles) to the promontory of **Cabo de São Vicente** (p. 215). It was from this cape that Vasco de Gama launched his caravels to discover the world. You can spend 2 hours or so exploring the cape and its dramatic ocean scenery with wind-tossed waves. (One good way to discover the cape is by biking.) If time remains in the day, you can take in some beach action. Our favorite is **Mareta,** but countless other beaches dot the peninsula around Sagres. See chapter 9.

Days 2 & 3: Lagos ★ & Portimão

On Day 2, leave Sagres in the morning and drive 34km (21 miles) east to reach the ancient port city of **Lagos.** Historically a port of call for the sailors of Admiral Nelson's fleet, Lagos can be visited in 2 hours. In the town itself, its single major attraction is **Igreja de Santo António** (p. 218), dating from the 18th century and containing remarkable baroque gilt carvings. Allow 30 minutes for a visit. Spend another hour or so wandering the streets of the old town, poking into courtyards and ducking into shops looking for handicrafts. The Old Customs House, **Antigo Mercado de Escravos** (p. 218), was the site of the arcaded slave market, the largest in Portugal. Before leaving the area, drive 2km (1¼ miles) to **Ponta da Piedade** (p. 217), one of the most beautiful spots of the western Algarve.

Enjoy a lunch in Lagos at **Restaurante D. Sebastião** (p. 220), then continue east toward the bustling fishing port of **Portimão,** lying 18km (11 miles) to the east of Lagos. Frugal travelers can seek affordable lodgings in Portimão itself, and others can stay at one of the surrounding beach resorts such as **Praia da Rocha,** which has the most options.

After checking into a hotel, you can explore Portimão itself or spend the afternoon at **Praia da Rocha's beach** (p. 222), 3km (1¾ miles) from the center of Portimão. If you'd rather play golf, you'll find some good courses here (see "Golf," p. 224).

On the morning of Day 3, while still based in the Portimão area, set out on a voyage of exploration of your own. Our favorite excursion is to the mountain range of **Monchique** (coverage begins on p. 228). After a morning of driving through the mountains, have lunch at the **Estalagem Abrigo de Montanha** (p. 228).

In the afternoon, you can head for **Silves** (coverage begins on p. 229) for 3 hours of wandering about. Lying inland, Silves is reached after an 18km (11-mile) drive to the northeast of Portimão. Its chief attractions are the red-sandstone **Castelo dos Mouros** (p. 230) and the 13th-century **Cathedral of Silves** (p. 230). Because Silves was the capital of the Moorish kings and is an ancient site, we suggest spending ample time—at least 1½ hours—poking about its streets. Return to Portimão or Praia da Rocha for the night.

Day 4: Albufeira: The St. Tropez of Portugal ★

On the morning of Day 4, leave the Portimão area and drive 28km (17 miles) east to the cliffside town and old fishing village of **Albufeira** (p. 231). Resembling a village in North Africa, Albufeira is at the center of one of the great beachside tourist developments in all of Portugal. Your choice of hotel for the night can be in Albufeira itself or in **Quarteira** (p. 239) farther on, or perhaps around **Almancil** (p. 244), with its dramatic resorts Vale do Lobo and Quinta do Lago.

Of course, you may decide never to leave Albufeira itself, as it offers some of the best beaches in the Algarve, notably **Falésia.** Golfers can get in a game at **Pine Cliffs** (p. 232) or drive over to one of the courses outside Quarteira. Especially good are **Vila Sol** (p. 240) and **Oceanico Old Course** (p. 240). The finest concentration of restaurants in all of the Algarve is also found in this area, especially if you want to dine deluxe.

Days 5 & 6: Faro: Capital of the Algarve ★

On the morning of Day 5, leave the Albufeira area, driving 38km (24 miles) east to **Faro.** Here you can check into a hotel for 2 nights as you set out to discover not only Faro itself but a number of colorful satellite towns. After leaving your hotel, you can go on a 2-hour walk through the ancient streets of Faro, taking in the **Capela dos Ossos** or Chapel of Bones (p. 249) and the old **Sé** (or cathedral; p. 249). Faro's museums are of only minor interest but it's worth exploring the town's major shopping streets, **Rua Santo António** and **Rua Francisco Gomes,** and stopping at the **Mercado de Faro** (p. 250), the town's best market. After lunch in Faro, perhaps at the Dois Irmãos (p. 250), head for **Praia de Faro,** Faro's major beach, in the afternoon.

While still based in Faro, head out on a driving tour in the morning of Day 6. The best road-trip possibilities include a stopover in the old market town of **Loulé,** lying 15km (9⅓ miles) north of Faro and in the heart of the Algarve's

The Algarve in 1 Week

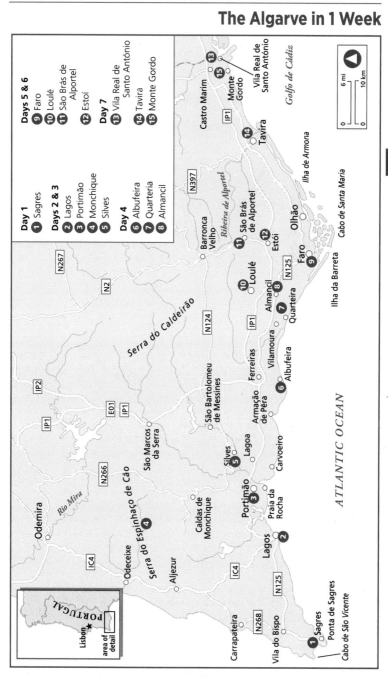

Day 1
1. Sagres

Days 2 & 3
2. Lagos
3. Portimão
4. Monchique
5. Silves

Day 4
6. Albufeira
7. Quarteria
8. Almancil

Days 5 & 6
9. Faro
10. Loulé
11. São Brás de Alportel
12. Estói

Day 7
13. Vila Real de Santo António
14. Tavira
15. Monte Gordo

chimney district. Fret-cut plaster towers rise from many of this town's cottages and houses. These are our favorite chimneys in all of Europe, and you can purchase miniatures of them as souvenirs. The town also features two worthy attractions, the **Igreja de São Clemente, Matriz de Loulé** (p. 252) and the ruins of its old **Moorish castelo** (p. 252).

En route back to Faro for the night, stop off in the little town of **Estói** (p. 253) where you can explore the grounds of the baroque **Palácio do Visconde de Estói** (p. 253). The drive back to Faro is 8km (5 miles) to the south, heading toward the coast.

Day 7: Vila Real de Santo António

On the morning of Day 7, leave Faro and plan to drive 85km (53 miles) east to the border town of **Vila Real,** adjoining the Spanish frontier. En route here, you can make two stopovers—first, at **Olhão,** a distance of 10km (6¼ miles) east of Faro. Beloved by painters, this is the famous cubist town of the Algarve, so called because its homes are stacked like white blocks one upon the other. You can easily spend 2 hours wandering its ancient streets, which are very evocative of North Africa.

After a visit, continue east toward **Tavira,** a distance of 31km (19 miles) east of Faro. On the banks of the Ségua and Gilão rivers, you can spend another 1½ hours wandering the streets of this town. Because of its many canals, the town is likened to Venice, but that, of course, is a gross exaggeration. You can see a seven-arched Roman bridge and many arches, as well as flamboyant chimney decorations. Wander also to the fruit and vegetable market along the river esplanade.

After lunch here, drive on to **Vila Real de Santo António** (p. 254) for the night, a distance of 23km (14 miles). After checking into a hotel, set out to explore the streets of the town, good examples of 18th-century town planning. Then try to visit the castle-fortress of **Castro Marim** (p. 255). If you have time remaining in the day, you can head southwest of Vila Real to check out the beaches of **Monte Gordo** (p. 255), lying 4km (2½ miles) to the southwest of Vila Real at the mouth of the Guadiana River.

Return to Vila Real for the night, and depart for Lisbon the following morning.

SETTLING INTO LISBON

B athed in pure Atlantic light, crowned by the story-book St. George's Castle and straddling seven hills, Lisbon is one of Europe's most visually striking capitals. Looks aside, the city will surely win you over with its genuine friendliness and blissfully laid-back pace. At once nostalgic and progressive, Lisbon's charm shines through in everyday life—listening to the mournful fado songs in the Moorish Alfama's alleys, indulging in custard tarts in gilded Art Nouveau patisseries and living it up at a Bairro Alto street party.

4

THINGS TO DO   Nothing says Lisbon like a ride on century-old **tram 28,** which trundles past stately plazas, **Estrela Basilica's** graceful dome and the Romanesque **Sé (cathedral).** Jump off at hilltop **St George's Castle** for a rampart stroll and views reaching to the Tagus River. Just steps away, the Moorish **Alfama** quarter's mazy lanes are full of laundry billowing, neighbors gossiping and melancholic fado songs. Down by the river, **Jerónimos Monastery's** fantastically ornate Manueline cloisters whisk you back to Portugal's Age of Discovery.

SHOPPING   Kid leather gloves, tawny port, tinned fish—you'll find it all in the specialty stores lining **Pombaline Baixa, Rossio** and **Chiado.** Compare purchases over a *bica* (espresso) on the terrace of Art Deco **A Brasileira** cafe. Young Lisboetas combine bar crawling with late-night shopping in the **Bairro Alto,** where boutiques stock vintage fashion and the sassy collections of Portuguese style icons Lena Aires and Fátima Lopes. **Avenida da Liberdade** is Lisbon's catwalk of big-name designers.

RESTAURANTS & DINING   Arrive before the crowds at the famous **Antiga Confeitaria de Belém** to devour crisp, cinnamon-dusted custard tarts hot from the oven. Lisboetas make the most of warm nights by dining alfresco on fresh fish in the Alfama's lantern-lit lanes and world flavors on pavement terraces in the buzzy Bairro Alto. The ornately tiled monastery-turned-beer hall **Cervejaria da Trindade** pairs cold beers with local specialties like *bacalhau com natas* (cod with cream). Go north of the city center to the stylish Michelin-starred restaurant **Eleven.**

NIGHTLIFE & ENTERTAINMENT   Join locals for sunset shots of *ginjinha* (cherry liqueur) on the cobbles in front of hole-in-the-wall **A Ginjinha,** going strong since the 1840s. Lisbon's unrivaled hot spot is the bar-lined **Bairro Alto,** where revelers hit the street to chat, drink, and dance before heading to riverside mega club **Lux.** The mood is more

Lisbon

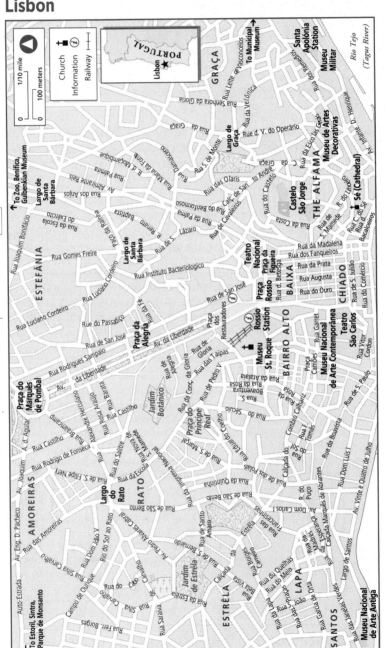

relaxed in the lantern-lit **Alfama,** where fado songs recalling lost love and destiny fill the atmospheric vaults of **Clube de Fado.**

LISBON YESTERDAY & TODAY

In its golden age, Lisbon gained a reputation as the eighth wonder of the world. Travelers returning from the city boasted that its riches rivaled those of Venice. As one of the greatest maritime centers in history, the Portuguese capital imported exotic wares from the far-flung corners of its empire.

Treasures from Asia—including porcelain, luxurious silks, rubies, pearls, and other rare gems—arrived at Indian seaports on Chinese junks and eventually found their way to Lisbon. The abundance and variety of spices from the East, such as turmeric, ginger, pepper, cumin, and betel, rivaled even Keats's vision of "silken Samarkand."

From the Americas came red dyewood (brazilwood), coffee, gold, diamonds, and other gemstones. The extensive contact signaled a new era in world trade, and Lisbon sat at the center of a great maritime empire, a hub of commerce for Europe, Africa, and Asia.

In the second decade of the new millennium, and after a slumber that lasted for most of the 20th century, there is a new Lisbon awaiting you today. Some of that is good news and some of it isn't—at least for traditionalists. Although some medieval facades and old palaces have been restored, others have given way to modern office blocks and more impersonal structures, which have replaced many of the 19th-century Art Nouveau buildings that were so much a part of the cityscape. Some of the famous old trams from years ago are still seen on the streets, but they are gradually being replaced by newer, more streamlined, and much faster trams.

A Bit of Background

Many Lisboans claim unabashedly that Ulysses founded their city. Others, with perhaps a more scholarly bent, maintain that the Phoenicians or the Carthaginians were the original settlers.

The Romans settled in Lisbon in about 205 B.C., later building a fortification on the site of what is now St. George's Castle. The Visigoths captured the city in the 5th century A.D.; in 714, centuries of Moorish domination began. The first king of Portugal, Afonso Henríques, captured Lisbon from the Moors in 1147. But it wasn't until 1256 that Afonso III moved the capital here, deserting Coimbra, now the country's major university city.

The Great Earthquake occurred at 9:40am on All Saints' Day, November 1, 1755. "From Scotland to Asia Minor, people ran out of doors and looked at the sky, and fearfully waited. It was, of course, an earthquake," chronicled *Holiday* magazine. Tidal waves 15m (49 ft.) high swept over Algeciras, Spain. The capitals of Europe shook. Some 22 aftershocks followed. Roofs caved in; hospitals (with more than 1,000 patients), prisons, public buildings, royal palaces, aristocratic town houses, fishers' cottages, churches, and houses of prostitution all were toppled. Overturned candles helped ignite a fire that consumed the once-proud capital in just 6 days, leaving it in gutted, charred shambles. Voltaire described the destruction in *Candide*: "The sea boiled up in the harbor and smashed the vessels lying at anchor. Whirlwinds of flame and ashes covered the streets and squares, houses collapsed, roofs were thrown onto foundations and the foundations crumbled." All told, 30,000 inhabitants were crushed beneath the tumbling debris.

When the survivors of the initial shocks ran from their burning homes toward the mighty Tagus, they were met with walls of water 12m (39 ft.) high. Estimates vary, but approximately 60,000 drowned or died in the 6-day holocaust.

After the ashes had settled, the Marquês de Pombal, the prime minister, ordered that the dead be buried and the city rebuilt at once. To accomplish that ambitious plan, the king gave him virtually dictatorial powers.

What Pombal ordered constructed was a city of wide, symmetrical boulevards leading into handsome squares dominated by fountains and statuary. Bordering these wide avenues would be black-and-white mosaic sidewalks, the most celebrated in Europe. Today, the mixture of old and "new" (post-earthquake) here is so harmonious that travelers consider Lisbon one of the most beautiful cities on earth. Fountains abound; one, the *Samaritan,* dates from the 16th century. The boulevards flank new high-rise apartment houses, while in other quarters, laundry hanging from 18th-century houses flaps in the wind.

The Tagus, the river flowing through Lisbon, has been called the city's eternal lover—and in many ways it is the most vital part of the city. From the Bairro Alto (Upper City), cable cars run down to the waterfront, where boats from Africa unload their freight. This is also a city that gives nicknames to everything, from its districts to its kings. Fernando, who built one of the most characteristic walls around Lisbon, was honored with the appellation "the Beautiful." Streets bear colorful names or designations, such as Rua do Açúcar (Street of Sugar). Praça do Comércio, the bull's-eye center of the Lisbon waterfront, is also known as Black Horse Square.

Many who have never been to Lisbon know it well from watching World War II spy movies on TV. In the classic film *Casablanca,* Lisbon embodied the passage point to the Americas for refugees stranded in northern Africa. During the war, Lisbon, officially neutral, was a hotbed of intrigue and espionage. It was also a haven for thousands of refugees, including deposed royalty.

Lisbon Today

No longer the provincial town it was as late as the 1970s, post-millennium Lisbon has blossomed into a cosmopolitan city often beset with construction pains. Many of its old structures are simply falling apart and must be either restored or replaced. Some of the formerly clogged streets of the Baixa have been turned into cobblestone pedestrian malls.

Lisbon is growing and evolving, and the city is considerably more sophisticated than it once was, no doubt due in part to Portugal's joining the European Union (E.U.). The smallest capital of Europe is no longer a backwater at the far corner of Iberia. Some 1.9 million people now live in Lisbon, and many of its citizens, having drifted in from the far corners of the world, don't even speak Portuguese. Textiles, shoes, clothing, china, and earthenware are among its leading industries.

Sections along Avenida da Liberdade, the main street of Lisbon, at times evoke thoughts of Paris. As in Paris, sidewalk portrait painters will sketch your likeness, and artisans will offer you jewelry claiming that it's gold (when you both know it isn't). Handicrafts, from embroidery to leatherwork, are peddled right on the streets as they are in New York.

Consider an off-season visit, especially in the spring or fall, when the city enjoys glorious weather. The city isn't overrun with visitors then, and you can wander about and take in its attractions without being trampled or broiled during the hot, humid weather of July and August.

ORIENTATION
Arriving

BY PLANE   Foreign and domestic flights land at Lisbon's **Aeroporto de Lisboa** (℗ 21/841-35-00; www.ana-aeroportos.pt), about 6.5km (4 miles) from the heart of the city. An AERO-BUS runs between the airport and the Cais do Sodré train station every 20 minutes from 7:45am to 8:15pm. The fare is 3.50€. It makes 10 intermediate stops, including Praça dos Restauradores and Praça do Comércio. There's no charge for luggage. Taxi passengers line up in a usually well-organized queue at the sidewalk in front of the airport, or you can call **Rádio Táxi** at ℗ **21/811-90-00.** The average taxi fare from the airport to central Lisbon is 12€. Each piece of luggage is 1.60€ extra.

For ticket sales, flight reservations, and information about the city and the country, you can get in touch with the Lisboa personnel of **TAP Air Portugal,** Aeroporto de Lisboa (℗ **70/720-57-00** for reservations; www.tap-airportugal.pt).

BY TRAIN   Most international rail passengers from Madrid and Paris arrive at the **Estação da Santa Apolónia,** Avenida Infante Dom Henrique, the major terminal. It's by the Tagus near the Alfama district. Two daily trains make the 10-hour run from Madrid to Lisbon. Rail lines from northern and eastern Portugal also arrive at this station. Connected to the Metro system and opened in time for EXPO '98, the newer and modern **Gare de Oriente at Expo Urbe** is the hub for some long-distance and suburban trains, including service to such destinations as Porto, Sintra, the Beiras, Minho, and the Douro. At the **Estação do Rossio,** between Praça dos Restauradores and Praça de Dom Pedro IV, you can get trains to Sintra. The **Estação do Cais do Sodré,** just beyond the south end of Rua Alecrim, east of Praça do Comércio, handles trains to Cascais and Estoril on the Costa do Sol. Finally, you can catch a ferry at **Sul e Sueste,** next to the Praça do Comércio. It runs across the Tagus to the suburb of Barreiro; at the station there, **Estação do Barreiro,** you can catch a train for the Algarve and Alentejo. For all rail information regarding any of the terminals above, call ℗ **80/820-82-08** (www.cp.pt) between 7am and 11pm daily.

BY BUS   Buses from all over Portugal, including the Algarve, arrive at the **Rodoviária da Sete Rios** (℗ 21/358-14-72; www.rede-expressos.pt). If your hotel is in Estoril or Cascais, you can take bus no. 1, which goes on to the Cais do Sodré. At least six buses a day leave for Lagos, a gateway to the Algarve, and nine buses head north every day to Porto. There are 14 daily buses to Coimbra, the university city to the north. One-way fare from Lagos to Lisbon is 20€.

BY CAR   International motorists must arrive through Spain, the only nation connected to Portugal by road. You'll have to cross Spanish border points, which usually pose no great difficulty. The roads are moderately well maintained. From Madrid, if you head west, the main road (N620) from Tordesillas goes southwest by way of Salamanca and Ciudad Rodrigo and reaches the Portuguese frontier at Fuentes de Onoro. Most of the country's 15 border crossings are open daily from 7am to midnight. See "Getting Around" below for info on car-rental agencies in the city.

Visitor Information

The main **tourist office** in Lisbon is at the Palácio da Foz, Praça dos Restauradores (℗ **21/120-50-50;** www.visitportugal.com), at the Baixa end of Avenida da Liberdade. Open daily from 9am to 8pm (Metro: Restauradores), it sells the **Lisbon**

Card, which provides free city transportation and entrance fees to museums and other attractions, plus discounts on admission to events. For adults, a 1-day pass costs 17€, a 2-day pass costs 29€, and a 3-day pass costs 35€. Children 5 to 11 pay 10€ for a 1-day pass, 15€ for a 2-day pass, and 18€ for a 3-day pass. Another tourist office is located across from the general post office in Lisbon on Rua do Arsenal 15, 1100-038 Lisbon (*©* **21/031-27-00;** www.visitlisboa.com). This tourist office is open daily from 9am to 7pm.

City Layout

MAIN STREETS & SQUARES Lisbon is the westernmost capital of continental Europe. According to legend, it spreads across seven hills, like Rome. That statement has long been outdated—Lisbon now sprawls across more hills than that. Most of the city lies on the north bank of the Tagus.

No one ever claimed that getting around Lisbon was a breeze. Streets rise and fall across the hills, at times dwindling into mere alleyways. Exploring the city, however, is well worth the effort.

Lisbon is best approached through its gateway, **Praça do Comércio (Commerce Square),** bordering the Tagus. It's one of the most perfectly planned squares in Europe, rivaled only by the Piazza dell'Unità d'Italia in Trieste, Italy. Before the 1755 earthquake, Praça do Comércio was known as Terreiro do Paço, the Palace Grounds, because the king and his court lived in now-destroyed buildings on that site. To confuse matters further, English-speaking residents often refer to it as Black Horse Square because of its statue (actually a bronze-green color) of José I.

Today the square is the site of the Stock Exchange and various government ministries. Its center is used as a parking lot, which destroys some of its harmony. In 1908, Carlos I and his elder son, Luís Filipe, were fatally shot here by an assassin. The monarchy held on for another 2 years, but the House of Bragança effectively came to an end that day.

Directly west of the square stands the City Hall, fronting Praça do Município. The building, erected in the late 19th century, was designed by the architect Domingos Parente.

Heading north from Black Horse or Commerce Square, you enter the hustle and bustle of **Praça de Dom Pedro IV,** popularly known as the Rossio. The "drunken" undulation of the sidewalks, with their arabesques of black and white, have led to the appellation "the dizzy praça." Here you can sit sipping strong unblended coffee from the former Portuguese provinces in Africa. The statue on the square is that of the Portuguese-born emperor of Brazil.

Opening onto the Rossio is the **Teatro Nacional de Dona Maria II,** a freestanding building whose facade has been preserved. From 1967 to 1970, workers gutted the interior to rebuild it completely. If you arrive by train, you'll enter the **Estação do Rossio,** whose exuberant Manueline architecture is worth seeing.

Separating the Rossio from Avenida da Liberdade is **Praça dos Restauradores,** named in honor of the Restoration, when the Portuguese chose their own king and freed themselves of 60 years of Spanish rule. An obelisk commemorates the event.

Lisbon's main avenue is **Avenida da Liberdade (Avenue of Liberty).** The handsomely laid-out street dates from 1880. Avenida da Liberdade is like a 1.5km-long (1-mile) park, with shade trees, gardens, and center walks for the promenading crowds. Flanking it are fine shops, the headquarters of many major airlines, travel agents, coffeehouses with sidewalk tables, and hotels. The comparable street in Paris is the Champs-Elysées; in Rome, it's Via Vittorio Veneto.

At the top of the avenue is Praça do Marquês de Pombal, with a statue erected in honor of the 18th-century prime minister credited with Lisbon's reconstruction in the aftermath of the earthquake.

Proceeding north, you'll enter Parque Eduardo VII, named in honor of the son of Queen Victoria, who paid a state visit to Lisbon. In the park is the Estufa Fria, a greenhouse well worth a visit.

FINDING AN ADDRESS Finding an address in the old quarters of Lisbon is difficult because street numbering at times follows no predictable pattern. When trying to locate an address, always ask for the nearest cross street before setting out. Addresses consist of a street name followed by a number. Sometimes the floor of the building is given as well. For example, Av. Casal Ribeiro 18 3 means that the building is at number 18 and the address is on the third floor. See p. 411 in chapter 15 for more tips on addresses.

STREET MAPS Arm yourself with a good city map before setting out. Maps with complete indexes of streets are available at most newsstands and kiosks. Those given away by tourist offices and hotels aren't adequate because they don't show the maze of little streets.

Neighborhoods in Brief

Baixa The business district of Lisbon, Baixa contains much Pombaline-style architecture. (The term refers to the prime minister who rebuilt Lisbon following the earthquake.) Many major Portuguese banks are headquartered here. Running south, the main street of Baixa separates Praça do Comércio from the Rossio. A triumphal arch leads from the square to Rua Augusta, lined with many clothing stores. The two most important streets of Baixa are **Rua da Prata (Street of Silver)** and **Rua Áurea,** formerly called Rua do Oro (Street of Gold). Silversmiths and goldsmiths are located on these streets.

Chiado If you head west from Baixa, you'll enter this shopping district. From its perch on a hill, it's traversed by **Rua Garrett,** named for the noted romantic writer João Batista de Almeida Garrett (1799–1854). Many of the finest shops in the city, such as the Vista Alegre, a china and porcelain house, are here. One coffeehouse in particular, **A Brasileira,** has been a traditional gathering spot for the Portuguese literati.

Bairro Alto Continuing your ascent, you'll arrive at the Bairro Alto (Upper City). This sector, reached by trolley car, occupies one of the legendary seven hills of Lisbon. Many of its buildings were left fairly intact by the 1755 earthquake. Containing much of the charm and color of the Alfama, it's the location of some of the finest fado (meaning "fate" and describing a type of music) clubs in Lisbon, as well as excellent restaurants and bars. There are also antiques shops. Regrettably, many of the side streets at night are peopled with drug dealers and addicts, so be duly warned.

Santos This waterfront district is one of the emerging new neighborhoods of Lisbon, attracting artists, designers, architects, and other creative people. Big development plans are underway to add a vast array of studios, restaurants, bars, design outlets, and galleries. The area still has many 19th-century warehouses with wrought-iron balconies that are being recycled for 21st-century use. The neighborhood of Bairro Alto lies next door, and locals go there for their nightlife, but Santos is beginning to develop its own after-dark diversions.

The Alfama East of Praça do Comércio lies the city's oldest district, the Alfama.

Saved only in part from the devastation of the 1755 earthquake, the Alfama was the Moorish section of the capital. Nowadays it's home in some parts to stevedores, fishermen, and *varinas* (fishwives). Overlooking the Alfama is **Castelo São Jorge,** or St. George's Castle, a Visigothic fortification that was later used by the Romans. On the way to the Alfama, on Rua dos Bacalhoeiros, stands another landmark, the **Casa dos Bicos (House of the Pointed Stones),** an early-16th-century town house whose facade is studded with diamond-shape stones. Be careful of muggers in parts of the Alfama at night.

Belém   In the west, on the coastal road to Estoril, the suburb of Belém contains some of the finest monuments in Portugal, several built during the Age of Discovery, near the point where the caravels set out to conquer new worlds. (At Belém, the Tagus reaches the sea.) At one time, before the earthquake, Belém was an aristocratic sector filled with elegant town houses.

Two of the country's principal attractions stand here: the **Mosteiro dos Jerónimos,** a Manueline structure erected in the 16th century, and the **Museu Nacional dos Coches,** the National Coach Museum, the

finest of its kind in the world. Belém is Lisbon's land of museums—it also contains the Museu de Arte Popular and the Museu de Marinha.

Cacilhas   On the south side of the Tagus, where puce-colored smoke billows from factory stacks, is the left-bank settlement of Cacilhas. Inhabited mainly by the working class, it's often visited by right-bank residents who come here for the seafood restaurants. You can reach the settlement by way of a bridge or a ferryboat from Praça do Comércio.

The most dramatic way to cross the Tagus is on the **Ponte do 25 de Abril.** Completed in 1966, the bridge helped open Portugal south of the Tagus. The bridge is 2.2km (1⅜ miles) long, and its towers are 190m (623 ft.) high. The longest suspension bridge in Europe (it stretches for 16km/10 miles), **Ponte Vasco da Gama,** also spans the Tagus here. It's made areas from the north of the country and the southern Algarve, to the east across the Alentejo plain to southern Spain, more accessible. Standing guard on the left bank is a monumental statue of Jesus with arms outstretched.

GETTING AROUND

Central Lisbon is relatively compact and, because of heavy traffic, it's best explored by foot. That's virtually the only way to see such districts as the Alfama. However, when you venture farther afield, such as to Belém, you'll need to depend on public transportation like trams, which are inexpensive but often slow. Considering the hilly terrain and the fact that many of the streets were designed for donkey carts, though, the tram system works well.

As one Frommer's reader wrote, "In the 15 years since my last visit there, Lisbon has become one of the noisiest cities I've ever visited. Traffic is outrageous; driving is difficult because of the speed and the tendency of the natives to ride 6 inches from your rear bumper. The buses, of which there are a great many, are very noisy, and produce volumes of smoke. Honking of car horns seems to be a national pastime." Her description is, unfortunately, apt. Even the most skilled chauffeurs have been known to scrape the fenders of their clients' rented limousines while maneuvering through the city's narrow alleyways.

By Public Transportation

CARRIS (*©* **21/361-30-00;** www.carris.pt) operates the network of funiculars, trains, subways, and buses in Lisbon. The company sells a *bilhete de assinatura* *turístico* (tourist ticket). A 1-day pass goes for 3.80€. Passes are sold in CARRIS booths, open from 8am to 8pm daily, in most Metro stations and network train stations. You must show a passport to buy a pass.

METRO   Lisbon's Metro stations are designated by large м signs. A single ticket costs .90€, a day pass 4€. One of the most popular trips—and likely to be jampacked on *corrida* (bullfight) days—is from Avenida da República to Campo Pequeno, the brick building away from the center of the city. Service runs daily from 6:30am to 1am. For more information, call ✆ **21/350-01-15** (www.metrolisboa.pt).

Surprisingly, riding the Lisbon Metro is like visiting an impressive art collection. Paintings, glazed tiles, and sculptures make for an underground museum. You'll see interesting collections of contemporary art, including some works by famous Portuguese artists such as Maria Keil and Maria Helena Vieira da Silva. Stations that display some of the finest art include Cais do Sodré, Baixa/Chiado, Campo Grande, and Marquês de Pombal.

BUS & TRAM   Lisbon's buses and trams are among the cheapest in Europe. The *eléctricos* (trolley cars, or trams) make the steep run up to the Bairro Alto. The double-decker buses come from London and look as if they need Big Ben in the background to complete the picture. If you're trying to stand on the platform at the back of a jammed bus, you'll need both hands free to hold on.

The basic fare on a bus or *eléctrico* is 1.45€ if you buy the ticket from the driver (✆ **21/361-30-00**; www.carris.pt). The transportation system within the city limits is divided into zones ranging from one to five. The fare depends on how many zones you traverse. Buses and *eléctricos* run daily from 6am to 1am.

At the foot of the Santa Justa Elevator, on Rua Áurea, there's a stand with schedules pinpointing the zigzagging tram and bus routes. Your hotel concierge should have information.

The antediluvian *eléctricos,* much like San Francisco's cable cars, have become a major tourist attraction. Beginning in 1903, the *eléctricos* replaced horse-drawn trams. The most interesting ride for sightseers is on *eléctrico* no. 28, which takes you on a fascinating trip through the most history-rich part of Lisbon.

ELECTRIC TRAIN   A smooth-running, modern electric train system connects Lisbon to all the towns and villages along the Portuguese Riviera. There's only one class of seat, and the rides are cheap and generally comfortable. You can board the train at the waterfront Cais do Sodré Station in Lisbon and head up the coast all the way to Cascais.

The electric train does not run to Sintra. For Sintra, you must go to the Estação do Rossio station, opening onto Praça de Dom Pedro IV, or the Rossio, where frequent connections can be made. The one-way fare from Lisbon to Cascais, Estoril, or Sintra is 2€ to 5€ per person (✆ **21/261-30-00**; www.carris.pt).

FUNICULARS   Lisbon has a trio of funiculars: the **Glória,** which goes from Praça dos Restauradores to Rua São Pedro de Alcântara; the **Bica,** from the Calçada do Combro to Rua da Boavista; and the **Lavra,** from the eastern side of Avenida da Liberdade to Campo Mártires da Pátria. A one-way ticket on any of these costs 1.45€ (✆ **21/261-30-00**; www.carris.pt).

FERRY   Long before the bridges across the Tagus were built, reliable ferryboats chugged across the river, connecting the left bank with the right. They still do, and have been rebuilt and remotorized so they're no longer noisy. Many Portuguese who live on the bank opposite Lisbon take the ferry to avoid the heavy bridge traffic during rush hour.

Most boats leave from Cais de Alfândega (Praça do Comércio) and Cais do Sodré, heading for Cacilhas. The trip is worth it for the scenic views alone. Arrivals are at the Estação do Barreiro, where trains leave about every 30 minutes for the Costa Azul and the Algarve. Ferries depart Lisbon throughout the day about every 15 to 20 minutes; trip time across the Tagus is 15 minutes. The cost of the continuing train ticket includes the ferry. The separate ferry fare from the center of Lisbon to Cacilhas is 1€ (© **80/820-30-50**; www.transtejo.pt).

By Taxi

Taxis in Lisbon tend to be inexpensive and are a popular means of transport for all but the most economy-minded tourists. They usually are diesel-engine Mercedes and can be hailed on the street or at designated stands. The basic fare is 2.50€ for the first 153m (502 ft.), .20€ for each extra 162m (531 ft.), plus 20% from 10pm to 6am. The law allows drivers to tack on another 50% to your bill if your luggage weighs more than 66 pounds. Portuguese tip about 20% of the modest fare. For a Rádio Táxi, call © **21/811-90-00** (www.retalis.pt).

Many visitors stay at a Costa do Sol resort hotel, such as the Palácio in Estoril or the Cidadela in Cascais. If you stay there, you'll probably find taxi connections from Lisbon prohibitively expensive. Far preferable for Costa do Sol visitors is the electric train system (see above).

By Car

In congested Lisbon, driving is extremely difficult and potentially dangerous—the city has an alarmingly high accident rate. It always feels like rush hour in Lisbon. (Theoretically, rush hours are Mon–Fri 8–10am, 1–2pm, and 4–6pm.) Parking is seemingly impossible. Wait to rent a car until you're making excursions from the capital. If you drive into Lisbon from another town or city, call ahead and ask at your hotel for the nearest garage or other place to park. Leave your vehicle there until you're ready to depart.

CAR RENTALS The major international car-rental companies are represented in Lisbon. There are kiosks at the airport and offices in the city center. They include **Avis,** Av. Praia da Vitória 12C (© **21/351-45-60**; www.avis.com), open daily from 8am to 7pm; and **Hertz,** Rua Castilho 72 (© **21/381-24-30**; www.hertz.com), open Monday to Friday 8am to 7pm, Saturday 9am to 1pm and 2 to 7pm, and Sunday 9am to 1pm and 3 to 7pm; **Budget,** Rua Castillo 167B (© **21/386-05-16**; www.budget.com), is open Monday to Friday 9am to 6pm and Saturday 9am to 1pm.

[FastFACTS] LISBON

Your hotel's concierge usually is a reliable source of information. See also "Fast Facts" on p. 411.

Babysitters Most first-class hotels can provide babysitters from lists the

concierge keeps. At small establishments, the sitter is likely to be a relative of the proprietor. Babysitters charge between 11€ and 14€ per hour in Lisbon. Rates vary within this range

based on whatever deal the individual sitter demands; 12€ an hour is fairly standard. Remember to request a babysitter early—no later than the morning if you're planning on going out that evening. Also request a sitter with at least a minimum knowledge of English. If your sitter is fluent in English, count yourself lucky.

Currency Exchange
Currency-exchange booths at Santa Apolónia station and at the airport are both open 24 hours a day. ATMs offer the best exchange rates. They pepper the streets of the central Baixa district and are also found less frequently in other parts of the city. The post office (see "Mail," below) will exchange money as well.

Dentists
The reception staff at most hotels maintains lists of local, usually English-speaking dentists who are available for dental emergencies. Some of them will contact a well-recommended dental clinic, **Clinica Medica e Dentaria da Praça d'Espanha,** Rua Dom Luís de Noronha 32 (☏ **21/796-74-57**). Some of the staff members speak English.

Doctors
See "Hospitals," below.

Drugstores
Farmácia Valmor, Av. Visconde Valmor 60B (☏ **21/781-97-43**), is centrally located and well stocked.

Emergencies
To call the police or an ambulance, telephone ☏ **112.**

Hospitals
In case of a medical emergency, ask at your hotel or call your embassy and ask the staff there to recommend an English-speaking physician. Or try the **British Hospital,** Rua Saraiva de Carvalho 49

(☏ **21/394-31-00**), where the telephone operator, staff, and doctors speak English.

Hot Lines
The drug abuse hot line is ☏ **1414.** The number for the Lisbon office of Alcoholics Anonymous is ☏ **21/716-29-69.**

Internet Access
You can check your e-mail at **Cyber.bica,** Duques de Bragança 7 (☏ **21/322-50-04;** www.cyberbica.com), in the Chiado district (Metro: Baixa-Chiado). It's open Monday to Friday 11am to midnight.

Laundry
Keeping your clothes clean can be a problem if you're not staying long in Lisbon. For a self-service laundry, try **Lavatax,** Rua Francisco Sanches 65A (☏ **21/812-33-92**).

Lost Property
For items lost on public transportation, inquire at **Secção de Achados da PSP,** Olivais Sul, Praça Cidade de Salazar Lote 180 (☏ **21/853-54-03**), which is open Monday to Friday 9am to 12:30pm and from 1:30 to 5pm.

Luggage Storage & Lockers
These can be found at the **Estação da Santa Apolónia** (☏ **80/820-82-08**), by the river near the Alfama. Lockers cost 4€ for up to 48 hours.

Mail
While in Portugal, you can have your mail directed to your hotel (or hotels), to the American Express representative, or to Poste Restante (General Delivery) in Lisbon. You must present your passport to pick up mail. The main

post office, Correio Geral, in Lisbon is at Praça do Restauradores, 1100 Lisboa (☏ **21/323-89-71**). It's open Monday to Friday 8am to 10pm, and Saturday and Sunday 9am to 6pm.

Police
Call ☏ **112.**

Safety
Lisbon used to be one of the safest capitals of Europe, but that hasn't been true for a long time. It's now quite dangerous to walk around at night. Many travelers report being held up at knifepoint. Some bandits operate in pairs or in trios. Not only do they take your money but they demand your ATM code. One of the robbers holds a victim captive while another withdraws money. (If the number proves to be fake, the robber might return and harm the victim.) During the day, pickpockets galore prey on tourists, aiming for wallets, purses, and cameras. Congested areas are particularly hazardous. Avoid walking at night, especially if you're alone.

Taxes
Lisbon imposes no city taxes. However, the national value-added tax (VAT) applies to purchases and services (see "Taxes" under "Fast Facts," p. 422).

Telephone
You can make a local call in Lisbon in one of the many telephone booths. For most long-distance telephone calls, particularly transatlantic calls, go to the central post office (see "Mail," above). Give an assistant the number, and he or she will make the call for you,

billing you at the end. Some phones are equipped for using calling cards, including American Express and Visa. You can also purchase phone cards. See "Telephones" in chapter 15 for more info. Lisbon's city code is ☎ 01.

Time For the local time in Lisbon, phone ☎ **12151,** the "Speaking Clock."

Transit Information
For airport information, call ☎ **21/841-35-00.** For train information, dial ☎ **80/820-82-08.** Call **TAP Air Portugal** at ☎ **70/720-57-00.**

WHERE TO STAY

Lisbon has a much wider range of accommodations than ever before. Once hotels here were so cheap that they were reason alone to travel to Lisbon. Unfortunately, that's no longer the case. Today hotels such as the Four Seasons Hotel Ritz Lisbon and the Tivoli Lisboa charge virtually the same prices as first-class hotels in other high-priced European capitals.

Most visitors in Lisbon have to decide whether to stay in a hotel in the city proper or at a resort in the neighboring towns of Estoril and Cascais (see chapter 6). Much will depend on your interests. If it's summer and you'd like to have a sea-resort vacation while experiencing Lisbon's cultural attractions, a beach resort might be ideal, even though you'd have to commute into Lisbon. Electric trains run about every 20 minutes, so it's entirely possible to stay on the Costa do Sol and still go sightseeing in Lisbon.

If you're primarily interested in seeing Lisbon's attractions and are pressed for time, opting to stay in the city is a better bet. Also, the off season (Nov–Mar) is not ideal for a sea-resort vacation.

If you can't afford to stay in Lisbon's world-class hotels, a good alternative is the city's reasonably priced guesthouses—called *pensãos* (pensions). Most of these are no-frills accommodations. Often you'll have to share a bathroom, although many have hot and cold running water in a sink in your room. Some of the pensions in Lisbon are centrally located and are a good way to see the sights day and night without shelling out a lot of money for accommodations.

If you arrive without a reservation, begin your search for a room as early in the day as possible. If you arrive late at night, you might have to take what you can get, and pay more than you expected.

In the Center
VERY EXPENSIVE

Four Seasons Hotel Ritz Lisbon ★★★ The 10-floor Ritz, built by the dictator Salazar in the late 1950s on one of Lisbon's seven hills, is now operated by Four Seasons. Its suites boast the finest decoration you'll see in any major Portuguese hotel: slender mahogany canopied beds with fringed swags, marquetry desks, satinwood dressing tables, and plush carpeting. Some of the soundproof, spacious, modern rooms have terraces opening onto Edward VII Park; each boasts a marble bathroom. The least desirable rooms are the even-numbered ones facing the street. The odd-numbered accommodations, opening onto views of the park, are the best. Some studios with double beds are rented as singles, attracting business travelers.

Rua Rodrigo de Fonseca 88, 1099-039 Lisboa. www.fourseasons.com. ☎ **800/819-5053** in the U.S., or 21/381-14-00. Fax 21/383-17-83. 282 units. 405€–510€ double; from 1,165€ suite. AE, DC, MC, V. Free parking. Metro: Marquês de Pombal. Bus: 1, 2, 9, or 32. **Amenities:** Restaurant; bar; babysitting; concierge; exercise room; indoor heated pool; room service; spa. *In room:* A/C, TV/DVD, CD player, hair dryer, minibar, Wi-Fi (20€ per 24 hr.).

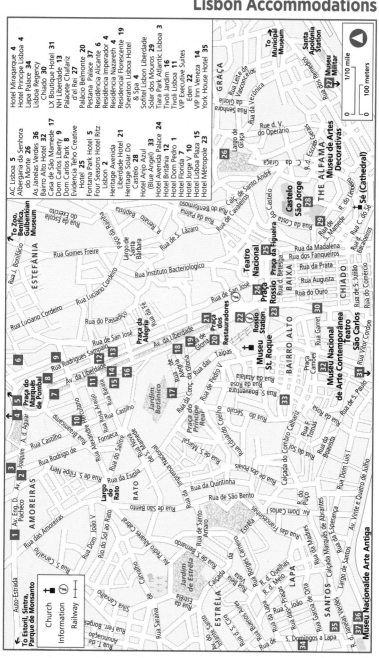

AC Lisboa **5**
Albergaria da Senhora
  do Monte **26**
As Janelas Verdes **36**
Bairro Alto Hotel **32**
Casa de São Mamede **17**
Dom Carlos Liberty **9**
Dom Carlos Park **8**
Evidencia Teho Creative
  Hotel **25**
Fontana Park Hotel **5**
Four Seasons Hotel Ritz
  Lisbon **2**
Heritage Avenida
  Liberdade Hotel **21**
Heritage Solar Do
  Castelo **28**
Hotel Anjo Azul
  (Blue Angel) **33**
Hotel Avenida Palace **24**
Hotel Britânia **12**
Hotel Dom Pedro **1**
Hotel Florida **7**
Hotel Jorge V **10**
Hotel Lisboa Plaza **15**
Hotel Métropole **23**

Hotel Miraparque **4**
Hotel Príncipe Lisboa **4**
Lapa Palace **34**
Lisboa Regency
  Chiado **30**
LX Boutique Hotel **31**
NH Liberdade **13**
Palacete Chafariz
  d'el Rei **27**
Palácio Belmonte **20**
Pestana Palace **37**
Residência Alicante **6**
Residência Imperador **4**
Residência Nazareth **4**
Residencial Florescente **19**
Sheraton Lisboa Hotel
  & Spa **4**
Sofitel Lisbon Liberdade **29**
Solar dos Mouros **29**
Tiara Park Atlantic Lisboa **3**
Tivoli Jardim **16**
Tivoli Lisboa **11**
VIP Executive Suites
  Eden **22**
VIP Inn Veneza **14**
York House Hotel **35**

Hotel Dom Pedro ★★   Rated five stars by the Portuguese government and associated with some of the most glamorous hotels of the Algarve and Madeira, this bastion of luxury is in the central Amoreiras district, across from one of the city's biggest shopping centers. A hypermodern sheathing of reflective glass covers its 21 stories. The interior is as conservative and rich-looking as the exterior is futuristic. The good-size guest rooms are richly furnished, usually with heraldic symbols or medallions woven subtly through the fabrics and wallpapers.

Av. Engenheiro Duarte Pacheco 24, 1070-109 Lisboa. www.dompedro.com. © **21/389-66-00.** Fax 21/389-66-01. 263 units. 106€–395€ double; 186€–630€ suite. AE, DC, MC, V. Parking 19€. Metro: Marquês de Pombal. **Amenities:** 2 restaurants; 2 bars; airport transfers (35€); babysitting; concierge; room service; spa; Wi-Fi (free, in lobby). *In room:* A/C, TV, hair dryer, minibar.

Lapa Palace ★★★ ☺   In a palace built in 1870 for the count of Valença, this government-rated five-star hotel, purchased by Orient Express in 1998, is the most talked-about accommodation in Lisbon and the city's premier address. In 1910, the de Valença family sold the villa and its enormous gardens to a wealthy, untitled family that retained it until 1988. Its lushly manicured gardens lie close to the Tagus, south of the city center. All but about 20 of the rooms are in a modern six-story wing. The spacious guest rooms in both sections contain amply proportioned marble surfaces, reproductions of French and English furniture, and a classic design inspired by a late-18th-century model. The marble bathrooms are among the city's most elegant, often adorned with bas-reliefs. Each unit opens onto a balcony. The older rooms have more charm and grace; many of the newer ones open onto panoramic vistas of Lisbon. The public areas have multicolored ceiling frescoes and richly patterned marble floors.

Rua do Pau da Bandeira 4, 1249-021 Lisboa. www.lapapalace.com. © **21/394-94-94.** Fax 21/395-06-65. 109 units. 370€–675€ double; from 1,300€ suite. Rates include buffet breakfast. AE, DC, MC, V. Free parking. Bus: 13 or 27. **Amenities:** 2 restaurants; bar; babysitting; children's center; concierge; exercise room; 2 pools (1 heated indoors); room service; spa; Wi-Fi (15€ per 24 hr., in lobby). *In room:* A/C, TV, hair dryer, minibar.

Sheraton Lisboa Hotel & Spa ★★   Built in 1972, and completely restored in 2007, this deluxe hotel is sheltered in a 25-floor skyscraper lying at a traffic-clogged intersection a bit removed from the center of the action, a few blocks north of Praça do Marquês de Pombal. The impressive pink-marble lobby features chandeliers and fancy carpeting. The guest rooms are small to midsize for the most part, but have been given a trendy look with modern furnishings. The most desirable rooms are in the tower, opening onto views of the Vasco da Gama Bridge, the Tagus, or the city. There's also a private lounge and bar where you can mingle with other hotel guests (many of whom are business travelers), as well as a bar on the 26th floor, with a panoramic view of Lisbon and dancing to live music nightly.

Rua Latino Coelho 1, 1069-025 Lisboa. www.sheratonlisboa.com. © **800/325-3535** in the U.S., or 21/312-00-00. Fax 21/354-71-64. 366 units. 138€–249€ double; from 445€ suite. AE, DC, MC, V. Parking 19€. Bus: 1, 36, 44, or 45. **Amenities:** Restaurant; 2 bars; babysitting; concierge; exercise room; outdoor pool; room service; spa. *In room:* A/C, TV, hair dryer, minibar, Wi-Fi (19€ per 24 hr.).

EXPENSIVE

Fontana Park Hotel ★   Possessing one of the most striking minimalist chic designs in Lisbon, this hotel is northeast of Parque Eduardo VII, within walking distance of the Marquês de Pombal, a landmark square at the top of Avenida da Liberdade. Its interior car park rises five floors, the best parking garage in central Lisbon.

Bedrooms are in a sleek, tasteful contemporary design, with panoramic windows, advanced modern lighting, and Philippe Starck deep white Duravit bathtubs that twinkle with lights of their own. The most desirable accommodations are on the seventh floor, with their sleek, angular black surfaces and panoramic viewing terraces. Drawing an international clientele, the very black Bonsai Restaurant serves a Japanese cuisine. DJ-spun music and *caipirinhas* lure visitors to the also black Fontana Bar.

Rua Engenheiro Vieira da Silva 2, 1050-105 Lisboa. www.fontanapark-hotel.com. ℂ **21/357-62-12.** Fax 21/357-92-44. 139 units. 105€–290€ double. AE, DC, MC, V. Parking 20€. Metro: Parque. **Amenities:** Restaurant; bar; airport transfers (29€); room service. *In room:* A/C, TV, hair dryer, minibar, Wi-Fi (10€ per 24 hr.).

Heritage Avenida Liberdade Hotel ★   Right on the main street of Lisbon, this sleekly modern hotel in a restored late-18th-century palace opened its doors in 2006. It's already considered one of Lisbon's best hotels, partly because the decor was created by famed architect Miguel Câncio Martins, known for such landmarks as the Buddha Bar in Paris. His designs combine traditional architectural features with the most modern of technology, a winning combination the way he does it. Though the 18th-century exterior was retained, the interior was virtually re-created to fit modern living standards. Rooms range from midsize to spacious, and are glamorously laid out. The six-floor hotel also boasts the sort of personalized service you'd expect from a small property.

Av. da Liberdade 28, 1250-145 Lisboa. www.heritage.pt. ℂ **21/340-40-40.** Fax 21/340-40-44. 42 units. 139€–340€ double. Children under 12 stay free in parent's room. AE, DC, MC, V. Parking nearby 30€. Metro: Restauradores. **Amenities:** Bar; babysitting; concierge; exercise room; indoor heated pool; room service. *In room:* A/C, TV/DVD, CD player, hair dryer, minibar, Wi-Fi (free).

Hotel Avenida Palace ★★   Built in 1892, Hotel Avenida Palace is the most distinguished old-fashioned hotel in Lisbon, an antiques-filled link to the past. Its extremely convenient location right at the Rossio is terribly noisy, but inside, it is another world entirely. Still the grand dame of Lisbon hotels, it retains its 19th-century aura and elegance, with a marble staircase, beautiful salons, and silk brocades. The Belle Epoque–style Palace offers all the modern comforts, especially in its restored guest rooms, which are soundproof and elegantly furnished, often in 17th- or 18th-century style.

Rua 1er Dezembro 123, 1200-359 Lisboa. www.hotelavenidapalace.pt. ℂ **21/321-81-00.** Fax 21/342-28-84. 82 units. 176€–450€ double; 198€–550€ junior suite. Rates include buffet breakfast. AE, DC, MC, V. Free parking. Metro: Restauradores. Tram: 35. **Amenities:** Bar; babysitting; concierge; exercise room; room service. *In room:* A/C, TV, hair dryer, minibar, Wi-Fi (6€ per hour).

Hotel Florida ★   Although this central hotel opened only in 2008 (it's the latest reincarnation of an establishment that dates from 1941), it's like a throwback to the 1950s. You get that impression when you see life-size photos of those *Sabrina* stars, Humphrey Bogart and Audrey Hepburn, staring back at you in the elevator. On some of the walls are famous American film quotations. Even the restaurant evokes an American diner from the '50s. Bedrooms are comfortably furnished, and also extend the movie kitsch, taking names of Tinseltown's favorite classic stars, everybody from Robert De Niro to Jack Nicholson. We searched for the Marilyn Monroe room or the James Dean room but they must have been occupied.

Rua Duque de Pamela 34, 1250-098 Lisboa. www.hotel-florida.pt. ℂ **21/357-61-45.** 72 units. 120€–220€ double; from 160€ junior suite. Rates include buffet breakfast. AE, DC, MC, V. Metro: Marquês de Pombal. **Amenities:** Bar; concierge; room service. *In room:* A/C, TV, hair dryer, minibar, Wi-Fi (20€ per day).

Hotel Lisboa Plaza ★★ Hotel Lisboa Plaza, in the heart of the city, is a charmer of a boutique hotel. A family-owned and -operated government-rated four-star hotel, it has many appealing Art Nouveau touches, including the facade. The hotel was built in 1953 and has been frequently overhauled and modernized since. A well-known Portuguese designer, Graça Viterbo, decorated it in contemporary classic style. The midsize guest rooms—with well-stocked marble bathrooms and double-glazed windows—are well styled and comfortable. Try for a unit in the rear, looking out over the botanical gardens.

Travessa do Salitre 7, Av. da Liberdade, 1269-066 Lisboa. www.heritage.pt. ✆ **21/321-82-18.** Fax 21/347-16-30. 106 units. 99€–385€ double; 270€–625€ suite. Children under 12 stay free in parent's room. AE, DC, MC, V. Parking nearby 10€. Metro: Avenida. Bus: 1, 2, 36, or 44. **Amenities:** Restaurant; bar; babysitting; concierge; exercise room; room service. *In room:* A/C, TV/DVD, CD player, hair dryer, minibar, Wi-Fi (free).

Lisboa Regency Chiado ★ Opened in 2000, this hotel occupies several floors of an eight-story shopping center that's otherwise devoted to such merchandizing giants as FNAC. It was designed by prestigious Portugal-born designer Siza Vieira. You'll register within a street-level lobby and then be ushered upstairs to one of the artfully minimalist bedrooms. The best of these have private terraces on a rooftop that blooms with bougainvillea vines and brightly colored wildflowers and afford wonderful views. The standard bedrooms are midsize, each well furnished in a tasteful, modern style with a well-organized private bathroom. Of special note is the hotel's bar, a postmodern oasis of soaring vertical lines, copies of 18th-century antiques, and theatrical panoramas over St. George's Castle.

Rua Nova do Almada 114, 1200-290 Lisboa. www.lisboaregencychiado.com. ✆ **21/325-61-00.** Fax 21/325-61-61. 40 units. 130€–290€ double; 294€–400€ suite. Free parking. AE, DC, MC, V. Metro: Baixa Chiado. **Amenities:** Bar; airport transfers (30€); room service. *In room:* A/C, TV, hair dryer, minibar, Wi-Fi (free).

Lisbon Marriott ★ A favorite of business travelers, this Marriott outpost, a 10-minute taxi ride north of the historic core in the vicinity of the airport and the Gulbenkian Museum, was built in the 1970s, but now sports the chain's trademark conservatively modern and international decor. It occupies a panoramic site atop a hill overlooking the city. The Marriott compares favorably with the Sofitel Lisboa (see below). The primary difference between the two is location. The Marriott is less convenient to the major sights of Lisbon, but it is in a quieter, more tranquil environment. It has better facilities, including an outdoor pool set in a garden and a health club. The hotel also lies closer to sports facilities, including a full spa, beaches, snorkeling, and golf.

Av. dos Combatentes 45, 1600-042 Lisboa. www.marriott.com. ✆ **21/723-54-00.** Fax 21/726-42-81. 577 units. 95€–260€ double; from 215€ suite. Parking 15€. AE, DC, MC, V. Metro: Ciudad Universitária or Laranjeiras. **Amenities:** Restaurant; bar; babysitting; concierge; exercise room; outdoor pool; room service; Wi-Fi (20€ per 24 hr., in lobby). *In room:* A/C, TV, hair dryer, minibar.

NH Liberdade ★ This hotel is conveniently located in the center of town in a sector that bridges the gap between the historic old town and the newer commercial sections of Lisbon. With its rooftop swimming pool and its chic black-and-cream motif, it has quickly become a hip address. The developers (the Liberdade is the latest project of the Heritage hotel chain, and like the Heritage Avenida Liberdade Hotel, was designed by the Portuguese architect Miguel Martins) took a late-18th-century building and retained the facade and some original architecture features;

otherwise, they created a hotel of contemporary comfort and extreme modernity. The lobby of the hotel balances whimsical and modern aspects—note the faux fur lamp—with the traditional (the architecture evokes a Lisbon manor home). There are 83 stylish rooms, of which 25 are suites, with minimalist furnishings. Some rooms have terraces with good city views.

Av. da Liberdade 180B, 1250-146 Lisboa. www.nh-hotels.com. © **21/351-40-60.** Fax 21/314-36-74. 83 units. 123€–180€ double; from 250€ suite. Parking 17€. AE, DC, MC, V. Metro: Avenida. **Amenities:** Restaurant; bar; babysitting; concierge; access to nearby exercise room; outdoor pool; room service. *In room:* A/C, TV, hair dryer, minibar, Wi-Fi (17€ per 24 hr.).

Sofitel Lisbon Liberdade ★   One of the capital's major deluxe hotels, the Sofitel sports a great location on one of Lisbon's showcase boulevards. Though it has a high-tech edge to its design, the hotel still features touches of intimacy. The comfortably appointed and good-size guest rooms offer the standard extras, and accommodations on each of the building's nine floors are outfitted with a different color scheme. Special rooms for business travelers offer extra luxuries. The major difference between the Sofitel and the Marriott (see above), which is of equal rank, is location. The Sofitel is located in the heart of Lisbon on its most prestigious boulevard, which puts you closer to the most important shops and major attractions of the city—and also puts you in a noisy, congested area. But if you will be spending most of your time in the city and aren't too interested in outdoor activities, opt for this property over the Marriott.

Av. da Liberdade 127, 1269-038 Lisboa. www.sofitel.com. © **21/322-83-00.** Fax 21/322-83-10. 171 units. 90€–315€ double; from 280€ suite. Parking 20€. AE, DC, MC, V. Metro: Avenida. Free parking. **Amenities:** Restaurant; bar; babysitting; exercise room; room service. *In room:* A/C, TV, hair dryer, minibar, Wi-Fi (5€ per hour).

Tiara Park Atlantic Lisboa ★   One of the most dramatic major hotels in Lisbon, this hotel, which opened in 1985, lies in an 18-floor tower of concrete and mirrored glass. It's across the street from the superior Four Seasons Hotel Ritz Lisbon. The lobby has lost some of its early glitter, but it's still impressive, with white marble, polished chromium, and mirrors. A symmetrical entrance frames the tile-bottomed fountains, whose splashing water rises to the top of the sunlit atrium. The small to midsize guest rooms are soundproof and tastefully decorated with business travelers in mind.

Rua Castilho 149, 1099-034 Lisboa. www.tiara-hotels.com. © **21/381-87-00.** Fax 21/389-05-05. 331 units. 90€–300€ double; from 375€ suite. AE, DC, MC, V. Parking 16€. Metro: Marquês de Pombal. Bus: 1, 2, 9, or 32. **Amenities:** Restaurant; bar; airport transfers (100€); babysitting; concierge; exercise room; room service; sauna; Wi-Fi (free, in lobby). *In room:* A/C, TV, CD player, hair dryer, minibar.

Tivoli Jardim ★ 🔥   Under the same ownership as its neighbor, the Tivoli Lisboa (see below), the Jardim is not nearly as prestigious, but is a most worthy, good-value choice; guests of the Jardim share the same facilities as the higher-rated neighbor, but pay less. And because the Jardim is set behind its more famous namesake, it avoids the traffic noise along Avenida da Liberdade. The modern structure from 1968 is adorned with "cliff-hanging" balconies, two shafts of elevators, and well-styled and attractively furnished midsize bedrooms. The public lounges—set in a cathedral-high lobby—are popular with Portuguese businesspeople.

Rua Julio Cesar Machado, 1250-135 Lisboa. www.tivolihotels.com. © **21/359-10-00.** Fax 21/359-12-45. 119 units. 140€–270€ double. Rates include buffet breakfast. AE, DC, MC, V. Parking 15€. Metro: Avenida. Bus: 1, 2, 9, 44, or 45. **Amenities:** 2 restaurants; bar; babysitting; concierge; outdoor heated pool; room service; Wi-Fi (18€ per 24 hr.). *In room:* A/C, TV, hair dryer, minibar, MP3 docking station.

Tivoli Lisboa ★★   In spite of increased competition among upscale hotels, this enduring favorite continues to hold its own, luring guests with such enticing features as the only hotel pool in central Lisbon. Right on the main boulevard, it has extensive facilities, but its prices are not extravagant, considering the luxuries. The two-story reception lobby has an encircling mezzanine lounge that's almost arena-size, with comfortable islands of furniture arranged on Oriental rugs. Adjoining the O Terraço restaurant is a homey salon with a wood-burning fireplace. The guest rooms contain a mixture of modern and traditional furniture. The larger and best rooms face the front, although those in the rear are quieter; rooms ending in the number 50 have the most spacious bathrooms.

Av. da Liberdade 185, 1269-050 Lisboa Codex. www.tivolihotels.com. ℂ **21/319-89-00.** Fax 21/319-89-50. 329 units. 162€–510€ double; from 372€ suite. Rates include continental breakfast. AE, DC, MC, V. Garage 18€. Metro: Avenida. Bus: 1, 2, 9, or 32. **Amenities:** 2 restaurants; 2 bars; babysitting; concierge; exercise room; outdoor heated pool; room service; outdoor tennis court (lit). *In room:* A/C, TV, hair dryer, minibar, Wi-Fi (18€ per 24 hr.).

MODERATE

AC Lisboa   If you're seeking Old Lisbon, check into the Hotel Avenida Palace (see above). But if you want a completely comfortable and up-to-date address, with mid-size to spacious bedrooms, consider AC Lisboa. Next to the heartbeat Praça Marquês de Pombal and Sottomayor Palace, this hotel rises in the commercial district of Lisbon but still manages to stay affordable. Rooms are modern and functional, with well-maintained bathrooms. Though the on-site restaurant and cafe aren't amazing, that shouldn't be an issue considering how many restaurants are nearby.

Largo de Andaluz 13 B, 1050-121 Lisboa. www.ac-hotels.com. ℂ **21/005-09-30.** Fax 21/005-09-31. 83 units. 85€–155€ double; 94€–178€ superior double. Parking 17€. AE, DC, MC, V. Metro: Marquês de Pombal. **Amenities:** Restaurant; bar; babysitting; concierge; exercise room; room service; sauna. *In room:* A/C, TV, hair dryer, minibar, Wi-Fi (13€ per 24 hr.).

As Janelas Verdes ★★ 📱   Although York House Hotel (see below) is still the most atmospheric—and certainly the most famous in its category—in Lisbon, this hotel is giving it serious competition and is almost its equal. In fact, it used to be an annex to York House Hotel but broke away and is becoming known as a historic hotel in its own right. Located near the Museum of Ancient Art, it was the former house of the Portuguese novelist Eça de Queirós. Though it's modern, its traditional past has been respected. Rooms are luxurious with comfortable furniture, style, and abundant closet space. The red lounge evokes turn-of-the-20th-century Lisbon. Other special features include a small but beautiful garden and two honor bars as well as a top-floor library and terrace.

Rua das Janelas Verdes 47, 1200-690 Lisboa. www.asjanelasverdes.com. ℂ **21/396-81-43.** Fax 21/396-81-44. 29 units. 135€–295€ double; 225€–380€ triple. Parking 10€. AE, DC, MC, V. Bus: 27, 40, 49, or 60. **Amenities:** Bar; babysitting; concierge; room service. *In room:* A/C, TV/DVD, CD player, hair dryer, Wi-Fi (free).

Dom Carlos Park 📱   This central hotel is just off Praça do Marquês de Pombal but charges only a fraction of what its rivals in the neighborhood do. The curvy facade is all glass, lending an outdoorsy feeling reinforced by trees and beds of orange and red canna. The good-size guest rooms are paneled in reddish Portuguese wood; even so, they're rather uninspired and functional. An occasional hand-carved cherub softens the Nordic-inspired furnishings. The hotel faces a triangular park dedicated to

Camilo Castelo Branco, a 19th-century poet. The lobby lounge is satisfactory; more inviting is the mezzanine salon, where sofas and chairs face the park.

Av. Duque de Loulé 121, 1050-089 Lisboa. www.domcarlospark.com. ℂ **21/351-25-90.** Fax 21/352-07-28. 76 units. 138€–170€ double; from 196€ junior suite. Rates include buffet breakfast. AE, DC, MC, V. Parking 12€. Metro: Marquês de Pombal. Bus: 1, 36, 44, or 45. **Amenities:** Restaurant; bar; babysitting; room service; Wi-Fi (free, in lobby). *In room:* A/C, TV, hair dryer, minibar.

Hotel Britânia ★   Designed in 1942 by the well-known Portuguese architect Vassiano Branco, this boutique hotel is the only surviving original Art Deco inn in Lisbon. Located about a block from the Liberdade, it boasts great service, a loyal clientele, and much of its original decor, including murals in the bar and candelabra in the public lounge. A former town house, it originally housed studio apartments, which explains why the bedrooms are much larger than most other competitors in Lisbon. Yearly maintenance and upgrading on an as-needed basis keep it looking good. Many of the old Art Deco touches are still intact, including a lavish use of marble and "porthole" windows as on a ship.

Rua Rodrigues Sampaio 17, 1150-278 Lisboa. www.heritage.pt. ℂ **21/315-50-16.** Fax 21/315-50-21. 32 units. 130€–285€ double. Parking 15€. AE, DC, MC, V. Metro: Avenida. Bus: 1, 2, 11, or 21. **Amenities:** Bar; concierge; room service. *In room:* A/C, TV/DVD, CD player, hair dryer, minibar, Wi-Fi (free).

Hotel Métropole   Originally built around 1900, this is the most centrally located hotel in town, ideal for theater, sightseeing, dining, or business. A narrow flight of marble stairs runs to the lobby. Many 1920s Art Deco appointments adorn the public rooms. The cozy guest rooms, which vary greatly in size, contain reproductions of traditional furniture, and come equipped with neatly kept bathrooms. Those in front overlook the noisy, animated square; the rooms in back overlook the congestion of the Bairro Alto.

Praça de Dom Pedro IV 30 (Rossio), 1100-200 Lisboa. www.almeidahotels.com. ℂ **21/346-91-64.** Fax 21/346-91-66. 36 units. 152€–173€ double. Rates include buffet breakfast. AE, DC, MC, V. No parking available at the hotel. Metro: Rossio. **Amenities:** Bar; babysitting; concierge; room service; Wi-Fi (free, in lobby). *In room:* A/C, TV, hair dryer, minibar.

VIP Inn Veneza ★ 🎒   Although this palace stands in the center of Lisbon, you could pass it by and not even know that it's a hotel. It's like a beautiful, old-fashioned hideaway waiting to be discovered, and it offers a rare chance to live in a palace that was once occupied by the wealthy Portuguese of the 19th century. A grand staircase leads to the three upper floors. Although this hotel is modernized, you'll feel you're stepping back into another time inside its walls. Rooms are midsize for the most part and tastefully and comfortably furnished with tile bathrooms. Guests gather in the bar for drinks or breakfast. The hotel has old-fashioned charm and style but is lean on amenities. The staff solves that problem by granting its guests access to the facilities of the well-equipped Tivoli Lisboa (see above).

Av. da Liberdade 189, 1250-141 Lisboa. www.viphotels.com. ℂ **21/352-26-18.** Fax 21/352-66-78. 37 units. 43€–110€ double. AE, DC, MC, V. Parking 11€. Metro: Avenida. **Amenities:** Bar; room service. *In room:* A/C, TV, hair dryer, minibar, Wi-Fi (10€ per 24 hr.).

York House Hotel ★★   Once a 17th-century convent, this boutique hotel is outside the center of traffic-filled Lisbon, and so attracts those who desire peace and tranquillity. It has long been known to the English and to diplomats, artists, writers, poets, and professors. Book well in advance. Near the National Art Gallery, it sits high on a hillside overlooking the Tagus and is surrounded by a garden. A distinguished Lisbon designer selected the tasteful furnishings. About five of the rooms here are outfitted with antiques and early-20th-century bric-a-brac; the others are contemporary in their styling. The public rooms boast inlaid chests, coats of armor, carved ecclesiastical figures, and ornate ceramics. The former monks' dining hall has deep-set windows, large niches for antiques, and—best of all—French-Portuguese cuisine.

Rua das Janelas Verdes 32, 1200-691 Lisboa. www.yorkhouselisboa.com. © **21/396-24-35.** Fax 21/397-27-93. 32 units. 60€–300€ double. AE, DC, MC, V. Parking nearby 10€. Bus: 27, 40, 49, 54, or 60. **Amenities:** Restaurant; bar; babysitting; concierge; room service. *In room:* A/C, TV, hair dryer, Wi-Fi (free).

INEXPENSIVE

Casa de São Mamede ★ 🏨   Built in the 1800s as a private villa for the count of Coruche, this building lies behind the botanical gardens—it's an oasis of tranquillity in an otherwise noisy city. Managed today by the Marquês family, it became a hotel back in 1945. Although renovated, the high-ceilinged rooms retain an aura of their original, slightly dowdy, somewhat frayed charm. All units are well kept and have private bathrooms with tub/shower combinations. Breakfast is served in a sunny second-floor dining room decorated with antique tiles. Service is friendly and attentive.

Rua da Escola Politécnica 159, 1250-100 Lisboa. www.casadesaomamede.com. © **21/396-31-66.** Fax 21/395-18-96. 28 units. 90€–120€ double; 140€ triple. Rates include continental breakfast. MC, V. No parking available at the hotel. Tram: 24. Bus: 22, 49, or 58. *In room:* A/C, TV.

Dom Carlos Liberty ☺   This establishment, set on a busy corner near Avenida da Liberdade, doesn't deserve a spectacular rating, but it's a decent place to spend the night. Built in the late 1960s, it's recommended for families because the management will add an extra bed to any room for 30€ to 35€. The guest rooms are small and nicely laid out, each with a built-in chestnut headboard, bed lights, a tiled bathroom, and even a valet stand. The modest-size reception lounges are on three levels, connected by wide marble steps.

Rua Alexandre Herculano 13, 1150-005 Lisboa. www.domcarlosliberty.com. © **21/351-25-28.** Fax 21/352-02-72. 49 units. 138€–170€ double. Rates include buffet breakfast. Parking nearby 12€. AE, DC, MC, V. Metro: Marquês de Pombal. Bus: 1, 36, 44, or 45. **Amenities:** Bar; babysitting; exercise room; Wi-Fi (free, in lobby). *In room:* A/C, TV, hair dryer, minibar.

Evidencia Tejo Creative Hotel ◢   In the ancient quarter of Baixa stands this modern and completely restored hotel that is one of the better bargains in the area. Talented Portuguese architects and designers lent their creativity to designing a relaxing atmosphere with stylish, comfortable bedrooms. Accommodations are available as doubles or twins (the same price), and there are also three luxurious suites that are still bargains. It's in a busy section of Lisbon, but soundproofing on the windows protects your ears.

Rua dos Condes de Monsanto 2, 1100-159 Lisboa. www.evidenciatejohotel-lisbon.com. © **21/886-61-82.** Fax 21/886-51-63. 58 units. 110€ double, 150€ suite. AE, MC, V. Metro: Restauradores. **Amenities:** Breakfast room; room service; Wi-Fi (free). *In room:* A/C, TV, hair dryer, minibar.

Hotel Jorge V   The Jorge V is a neat little hotel with a 1960s design. It boasts a choice location a block off the noisy Avenida da Liberdade. Its facade contains rows of balconies roomy enough for guests to have breakfast or afternoon refreshments. A tiny elevator runs to a variety of aging rooms, which aren't generous in size but are comfortable; all have small tile bathrooms. A highlight is the regional-style combination bar and breakfast room.

Rua Mouzinho da Silveira 3, 1250-165 Lisboa. www.hoteljorgev.com. ☎ **21/356-25-25.** Fax 21/315-03-19. 49 units. 54€–111€ double; 64€–135€ suite. Rates include continental breakfast. AE, DC, MC, V. Free parking. Metro: Avenida or Marquês de Pombal. **Amenities:** Bar; room service. *In room:* A/C, TV, hair dryer, minibar.

Hotel Miraparque
Miraparque lies on a secluded, quiet street opposite Edward VII Park (some rooms offer views of the pretty park). The small guest rooms haven't been called modern since the 1960s, but are well maintained. The hotel is a little worn but still recommendable because of its central location and low prices. The wood-paneled lounges are furnished in simulated brown leather.

Av. Sidónio Pais 12, 1050-214 Lisboa. www.miraparque.com. ☎ **21/352-42-86.** Fax 21/357-89-20. 100 units. 60€–150€ double; 80€–180€ triple. Rates include buffet breakfast. AE, DC, MC, V. Parking (in nearby lot) 15€. Metro: Parque. Bus: 91. **Amenities:** Restaurant; bar; babysitting; room service. *In room:* A/C, TV, hair dryer, minibar, Wi-Fi (3€ per hour).

Hotel Príncipe Lisboa ☺
Built in 1961, this nondescript place is a favorite with visiting Spanish and Portuguese matadors. Most guest rooms are spacious, and most open onto their own balconies. The matadors seem to like the Príncipe's dining room and bar. The hotel's eight floors are accessible by two elevators. Though hotels in central Lisbon are not particularly oriented for families with small children, this one tries by providing some of the best babysitters in town and an on-site guest laundry so families can catch up on the family wash.

Av. Duque d'Ávila 201, 1050-082 Lisboa. www.hotelprincipelisboa.com. ☎ **21/359-20-50.** Fax 21/359-20-55. 70 units. 45€–85€ double. Rates include continental breakfast. Children 4 and younger stay free in parent's room. Parking 6€. AE, DC, MC, V. Metro: São Sebastião. Tram: 20. Bus: 41 or 46. **Amenities:** Bar; babysitting; room service. *In room:* A/C, TV, hair dryer, Wi-Fi (10€ per 24 hr.).

LX Boutique Hotel ★ 👔
Launched in 2010, this quirky hotel is outside the center of Lisbon, convenient to Belém and the beaches of Costa do Sol. Its motto is "five floors, five themes—one Lisbon." That means that each floor is dedicated to a particular aspect of the city, including one that covers the Tejo (Tagus) River with nautical artifacts and (naturally) has river views. Another floor is devoted to one of Lisbon's greatest poets, Fernando Pessoa (1888–1935); and yet another, "The Fado Floor," is filled with drawings and musical instruments evoking the sound of fado. Bedrooms are well furnished but tend to be small. The most desirable accommodation is the Xplendid Suite, with a retracting glass roof. The on-site restaurant specializes in sushi, and you can relax over a glass of port wine in the stylish bar.

Rua do Alecrim 12, Cais do Sodré, 1200-017 Lisboa. www.lxboutiquehotel.com. ☎ **21/347-43-94.** Fax 21/347-31-82. 45 units. 100€–145€ double; from 300€ suite. AE, DC, MC, V. Metro: Cais do Sodré. **Amenities:** Restaurant; bar; concierge; room service. *In room:* A/C, TV, fridge, Wi-Fi (free).

Residência Alicante
This hotel's postwar facade curves around a quiet residential corner in an undistinguished neighborhood. The Alicante is welcoming and safe. You register on the street level with kindly staff members who speak little or no English; a small elevator runs to the four upper floors. Furnishings and room sizes vary, but most budget-minded visitors find the Alicante an acceptable place to stay. The quieter accommodations overlook an interior courtyard.

Av. Duque de Loulé 20, 1050-090 Lisboa. www.residenciaalicante.com. ☎ **21/353-05-14.** Fax 21/352-02-50. 50 units. 55€–65€ double. Rates include buffet breakfast. AE, DC, MC, V. Parking 10€. Metro: Picoas or Marquês de Pombal. Bus: 32, 36, 44, or 45. **Amenities:** Bar; babysitting. *In room:* A/C, TV, hair dryer, Wi-Fi (4€ per hour).

Residência Imperador The Portuguese-pinewood entrance of the Residência Imperador is small, even claustrophobic. However, the rooms and the upper lounge are adequate in size. The units are neatly planned, with comfortable beds and simple lines. The decor, though bland, uncontroversial, and neutrally international, is comfortable. On the top floor are a public room and a terrace with a glass front, where breakfast is served.

Av. 5 de Outubro 55, 1050-048 Lisboa. www.imperador.com.pt. ✆ **21/352-48-84.** Fax 21/352-65-37. 42 units. 45€–70€ double; 50€–80€ triple. Rates include continental breakfast. AE, DC, MC, V. Parking (in nearby lot) 13€. Metro: Saldanha. Bus: 44, 45, or 90. **Amenities:** Bar; Internet lounge; room service. *In room:* A/C, TV, hair dryer, Wi-Fi (in some, free).

Residêncial Florescente ★ 🍴 Centrally located in the Baixa district, this is one of the best budget bets in central Lisbon. On a bustling street, with many restaurants and bars nearby, this is a well-run establishment with a welcoming staff who takes care of your needs. The bedrooms are simply furnished, a bit like a roadside motel, but well kept and comfortable. Some of the rooms with three beds are suitable for families.

Rua das Portas de Santo Antão 99, 1150-266 Lisboa. www.residencialflorescente.com. ✆ **21/343-66-09.** Fax 21/342-77-33. 68 units. 45€–80€ double; 65€–95€ triple. Rates include breakfast. AE, MC, V. Parking 15€. Metro: Rossio. *In room:* A/C, TV, Wi-Fi (free).

Residência Nazareth The only part of this hotel that evokes Old Portugal is the vaulted ceiling in the cellar-level bar and an occasional view of exposed original stonework. Otherwise, everything inside has been efficiently modernized into a bland and basic international format whose main allure derives from relatively low rates and a staff that shows occasional touches of humor. Some of the guest rooms contain platforms, requiring guests to step up or down to either the bathrooms or to the simple but comfortable beds.

Av. António Augusto de Aguiar 25, 1050-102 Lisboa. www.residencianazareth.com. ✆ **21/354-20-16.** Fax 21/356-08-36. 32 units. 50€–65€ double. Rates include continental breakfast. AE, DC, MC, V. Free parking. Metro: São Sebastião or Parque. Bus: 46. *In room:* A/C, TV, hair dryer, Wi-Fi (5€ per hr.).

VIP Executive Suítes Éden ★ ☺ One of the most unusual conversions in central Lisbon, this hotel occupies the site of the former Eden Theater, a landmark Art Deco building whose enviable location puts its occupants close to the center of virtually everything. At least some of its clients are in town for business, making use of each unit's kitchenette during company-sponsored stays of a month or more. Since its opening, however, units have suffered a bit and in some cases might benefit from a decorative overhaul. But if you don't mind their need of some updating, you might find the place appropriate because of its location, its panoramic rooftop terrace and swimming pool (whose views extend out over the core of antique Lisbon but whose opening hours seem to change with the whim of the staff), and a sense that its developers made good use of the site's original Art Deco design and framework.

Praça dos Restauradores 24, 1250-187 Lisboa. www.edenaparthotelvip.com. ✆ **21/321-66-00.** Fax 21/321-66-66. 134 units. 62€–97€ studio; 88€–144€ apartment. AE, DC, MC, V. Parking not available at the hotel. Metro: Restauradores. Bus: 2, 11, 32, 36, 44, 45, or 91. **Amenities:** Bar; babysitting; outdoor pool. *In room:* A/C, TV, hair dryer, kitchen, Wi-Fi (3€ per hour).

In the Alfama
EXPENSIVE

Heritage Solar Do Castelo ★★ 🎁 A stay at this historic building is one of the city's highlights. Set inside the walls of the formidable 18th-century St. George's

Castle (Lisbon's first royal palace), this boutique hotel is reached only on foot because vehicles are off-limits. Some of the medieval architecture remains, such as an old cistern that was part of the original palace. Although the building is antique, the bedrooms are of a high-quality contemporary design, mixing old elements such as original stone fortifications with contemporary fabrics and furnishings. Each room comes with a balcony overlooking a picture-perfect courtyard.

Rua das Cozinhas 2, 1100-181 Lisboa. www.solardocastelo.com. ☎ **21/880-60-50.** Fax 21/887-09-07. 14 units. 149€–340€ double. AE, DC, MC, V. Parking not available at the hotel. Metro: Rossio. Bus: 37. **Amenities:** Bar; babysitting; concierge; room service. *In room:* A/C, TV/DVD, CD player, hair dryer, Wi-Fi (free).

Palacete Chafariz d'el Rei ★★★ 🎒 This is the true insider's special address in Lisbon, a restored Brazilian Art Nouveau mansion on the edge of the ancient district of the Alfama. Returning to his native Lisbon after striking it rich in Brazil, João Antonio Santos erected this stunning mansion with stained glass windows. Over the past decades, the micro hotel fell into disrepair, until lovingly restored by a Spaniard and his Portuguese partner. Today everyone from Barcelona architects to English filmmakers to Berlin fashionistas occupy the lavish suites, which come with a Brazilian butler. The stunning suites open onto views of the Tagus and the Alfama. Elaborate moldings and antiques are found throughout, especially in the ground-floor public rooms. Our favorite is the Suite Amaya, which is spacious, glamorous, and even sensual with vintage decorations. There's even embroidery work on the ceiling. A special delight is the private terrace garden filled with the aroma of flowering plants.

Chafariz del Rei 6, 1100-140 Lisboa. www.chafarizdelrei.com. ☎ **91/897-33-76.** 6 units. 180€–360€. AE, MC, V. Tram: 28. **Amenities:** Breakfast room. *In room:* A/C, TV, hair dryer, minibar, Wi-Fi (free).

Palácio Belmonte ★★★ 🎒 Deep in the heart of the Alfama lies this romantic hideaway found outside the walls of Castelo de São Jorge. When the hotel was launched at the dawn of the millennium, *Condé Nast Traveler* called it one of the "21 coolest hotels in the world." Each accommodation is a luxuriously furnished suite named after a towering figure in Portuguese arts and letters, including, for example, Gil Vicente. The inn is imbued with antique art, Portuguese tiles, antiques, and works of art, and it has a 4,000-tome library. Its special feature is a swimming pool lined in black marble. Our favorite is the Fernão Magalhães Suite, named after the maritime explorer who circumnavigated the globe for the first time. It lies in the western Muslim tower and has a luxe marble bathroom.

Páteo Dom Fradique 14, 1100-624 Lisboa. www.palaciobelmonte.com. ☎ **21/881-66-00.** Fax 21/881-66-09. 11 suites. 600€–1,200€. AE, MC, V. Free parking. Tram: 28. **Amenities:** Bar; outdoor pool; room service. *In room:* A/C, TV, hair dryer, minibar, Wi-Fi (free).

MODERATE

Solar dos Mouros ★ 🎒 One of the most stylish small hotels in Lisbon occupies a tangerine-colored, steeply vertical antique building on a quiet street that runs parallel to the base of St. George's Castle. All of the rooms have a starkly modern minimalist decor that might remind you of a photo set from *Architectural Digest*. Each contains at least one boldly abstract painting; some pieces are the work of the hotel's owner, Luis Memos. Rooms have hardwood floors, cutting-edge furniture, and lots of space; all of them open onto a starkly contemporary staircase. The location in the heart of the Alfama means you'll be amid some of the city's hippest and most avant-garde attractions. Breakfast is the only meal served.

Rua Milagre de Santo António 6, 1100-351 Lisboa. www.solardosmouros.com. ✆ **21/885-49-40.** Fax 21/885-49-45. 12 units. 119€–320€ double. AE, DC, MC, V. No parking available at the hotel. Tram: 28. **Amenities:** Bar; concierge; room service. *In room:* A/C, TV, CD player, minibar, Wi-Fi (free).

In the Bairro Alto

EXPENSIVE

Bairro Alto Hotel ★★★   With a location that's unmatched for its association with literary, historic, and Romantic-era Portugal, this 2005 reincarnation of Lisbon's oldest hotel sits within an ocher-colored six-story baroque building within a few steps of the square (Praça Luís de Camões) that commemorates Portugal's most important literary patriarch. It originated in 1845 when it was rebuilt from the rubble of Lisbon's Great Earthquake less than a century before as the Hotel de l'Europe, then the capital's most visible hotel. Huge effort was taken to blend the historic with the cutting edge here, from the ample use of thousands of feet of exotic hardwoods, to the presence of all the electronic accessories that the post-millennium generation would expect. Bedrooms and their furnishings are rich with references to Portugal's imperial past, yet updated with a sense of upscale minimalism and with lots of postmodern amenities. There's also a sophisticated bar, a rooftop terrace with a splendid panorama, and a gem-size restaurant (p. 95).

Praça Luís de Camões 8, 1200-243 Lisboa. www.bairroaltohotel.com. ✆ **21/340-82-88.** Fax 21/340-82-00. 55 units. 385€–530€ double; 530€–650€ suites. Rates include buffet breakfast. Parking 15€. AE, DC, MC, V. Metro: Baixa/Chiado. **Amenities:** Restaurant; bar; babysitting; concierge; exercise room; room service. *In room:* A/C, TV/DVD, hair dryer, minibar, Wi-Fi (5€ per hour).

INEXPENSIVE

Hotel Anjo Azul (Blue Angel) 🏳️‍🌈   This is the only hotel in Lisbon that markets itself to a gay clientele, although heterosexual clients also check in and are welcome. Set on a narrow street in the Bairro Alto, a short walk from such well-recommended gay or mixed bars as Portas Largas and Frágil, it occupies a narrow, much-renovated 18th-century town house that retains many of its original blue-and-white tiles. Don't expect luxury or even an elevator—just clean but small and exceptionally simple rooms, and a thoughtful and helpful staff well versed in the advantages of the surrounding neighborhood. No meals of any kind are served and there's no bar on-site, but the attractive, international, and worldly clientele, many of whom return for second and third visits, don't really seem to mind.

Rua Luz Soriano 75, 1200-246 Lisboa. www.anjoazul.com. ✆/fax **21/347-80-69.** 20 units, 7 with private bathroom. 40€–50€ double without bathroom; 50€–85€ double with bathroom. AE, MC, V. No parking available at the hotel. Metro: Baixa Chiado. Tram: 28. *In room:* TV/DVD, hair dryer.

In the Graça District

MODERATE

Albergaria da Senhora do Monte ★ 🏳️‍🌈   This unique little hilltop hotel is perched near a belvedere, the Miradouro Senhora do Monte, in a seldom visited part of the city. It has a memorable nighttime view of the city, the Castle of St. George, and the Tagus. The intimate lounge evokes the feel of a living room in an upscale home and features large tufted sofas and oversize tables and lamps. Multilevel corridors lead to the excellent guest rooms, all of which have verandas. The rooms reveal a decorator's touch, especially the gilt-edged door panels, the grass-cloth walls, and the tile bathrooms.

Calçada do Monte 39, 1170-250 Lisboa. www.albergariasenhoradomonte.com. ℂ **21/886-60-02.** Fax 21/887-77-83. 28 units. 70€–145€ double; 120€–175€ suite. Rates include continental breakfast. Free parking nearby. AE, DC, MC, V. Metro: Socorro. Tram: 28. Bus: 12, 17, or 35. **Amenities:** Bar; babysitting; room service; Wi-Fi (4€ per hour). *In room:* A/C, TV, hair dryer.

In the Alcântara

MODERATE

Hotel Vila Galé Ópera   In the Alcântara district (next to the Ponte do 25 de Abril bridge), this modern hotel successfully blends the traditional and modern—but with less flair than the Bairro Alto (see above). Still, if you want a good location, a comfortable but affordable room, and a well-run hotel with a hospitable staff, consider checking in here. Bedrooms range from midsize to spacious, and are of a high standard, with sleek contemporary bathrooms. Most of the rooms open onto views of the Tagus River and the bustling dockland area. Befitting the operatic name, the interior decoration is musically inspired, and its restaurant is named in honor of Falstaff. Though this is a rather sprawling hotel, personal service isn't overlooked.

Travessa do Conde da Ponte, 1300-141 Lisboa. www.vilagale.pt. ℂ **21/360-54-00.** Fax 21/360-54-50. 259 units. 80€–160€ double; 104€–230€ suite. AE, DC, MC, V. Parking 7.50€. Metro: Cais do Sodré. **Amenities:** Restaurant; bar; babysitting; exercise room; indoor heated pool; room service; sauna; Wi-Fi (3€ per hour). *In room:* A/C, TV, hair dryer, minibar.

In Alto de Santo Amaro

VERY EXPENSIVE

Pestana Palace ★★★   Set within an upscale residential neighborhood known as Santo Amaro-Ajuda, about 5km (3 miles) west of the commercial core of Lisbon and about 1.5km (1 mile) north of the Alcântara Railway Station, this grand, imperial-looking hotel occupies a villa that was originally built in 1907 by a Portuguese mogul. The award-winning hotel's core is one of the best examples of Romantic Revival architecture in Portugal, combining at least four distinct architectural styles (including what the Portuguese refer to as *rocaille baroque* and Doña Maria revival) into one shimmering whole. The Pestana hotel chain added two rambling wings and state-of-the-art kitchens and security systems. Only four of the bedrooms—each a high-ceilinged suite—lie within the original villa. Most accommodations are elegantly modern, with hardwood trim, *trompe l'oeil* detailing, upholstered headboards, and hints of the Romantic Revivalism that permeates the hotel's original core. The hotel offers its guests four-times-per-day shuttle service, without charge, from the hotel to predesignated points in central Lisbon, a boon to anyone unwilling to navigate the traffic and congested parking of the city center.

Rua Jau 54, 1300-314 Lisboa. www.pestana.com. ℂ **21/361-56-00.** Fax 21/361-56-01. 190 units. 180€–375€ double; 630€–3,000€ suite. Parking 17€. AE, DC, MC, V. Tram: 28. **Amenities:** Restaurant; bar; babysitting; concierge; exercise room; Jacuzzi; heated indoor and outdoor pool; room service; sauna. *In room:* A/C, TV, hair dryer, minibar, Wi-Fi (18€ per 24 hr.).

At Parque Das Nações

EXPENSIVE

Tivoli Oriente ★   Lisbon's third Tivoli hotel is close to the Vasco de Gama shopping center and about a 5-minute taxi ride from the airport. The Estação do Oriente, a major transportation hub for Lisbon, is just a 2-minute walk away. Opened in 2001, the hotel has quickly become a landmark in this evolving residential and business neighborhood. Bedrooms are midsize, for the most part, and comfortably and traditionally furnished (though some renovated rooms boast a more modern decor). The room selection is wide ranging, from smaller single rooms to large suites. The hotel is also one of the best equipped in the area and has many winning features, such as a 16th-floor gourmet restaurant offering a panoramic view over Lisbon and the Tagus River.

Av. D. João II, Parque das Nações, 1990-083 Lisboa. www.tivolihotels.com. ✆ **21/891-51-00.** Fax 21/891-53-45. 279 units. 80€–330€ double; 415€ suite. Rates include buffet breakfast. AE, MC, V. Parking 13€. Metro: Oriente. Bus: 28. **Amenities:** 2 restaurants; bar; babysitting; concierge; exercise room; Jacuzzi; indoor heated pool; room service; sauna; Wi-Fi (5€ per hour, in lobby). *In room:* A/C, TV, hair dryer, minibar.

Near Jardim Zoológico
MODERATE
Corinthia Hotel Lisbon ★ ☺   This government-rated five-star hotel is one of the largest in the city and is equipped with the latest technology, including recreational facilities. In the heart of the financial district, it's a 5-minute taxi ride from the historic center. We prefer the top floors because of the panoramic views. The most personalized service is in the Executive Club; guests here also get to enjoy the Sky Lounge on the 24th floor. Bedrooms come in a wide range from standard doubles to spacious suites. In spite of the size of this hotel, the decor in the rooms is rather cozy, and the tiled bathrooms are spotless. The hotel is also known for its national and international buffets. On Sundays, the hotel stages a brunch for kids and their parents, complete with games.

Av. Columbano Bordalo Pinheiro, 1099-031 Lisboa. www.corinthiahotels.com. ✆ **21/723-63-63.** Fax 21/723-63-64. 518 units. 125€–320€ double; 605€ suite. Rates include buffet breakfast. Children under 12 stay free in parent's room. AE, DC, MC, V. Parking 18€. Metro: Jardim Zoológico. **Amenities:** 2 restaurants; bar; babysitting; concierge; health club & spa; outdoor heated pool; room service; Wi-Fi (18€ per 24 hr., in lobby). *In room:* A/C, TV, hair dryer, minibar.

In Entre Campos
MODERATE
Hotel Villa Rica ★   Forsaking a concept of traditional Portuguese architecture, this sleekly modern high-rise was constructed in Entre Campos, the city's financial district. As such, it attracts mainly commercial travelers in Lisbon on business trips. The hotel is so sleek and modern that its public rooms almost evoke a recently constructed airport. You don't get cozy comfort here, but are offered midsize bedrooms that are comfortable, though furnished in an almost minimalist style that evokes some hotels in Japan. The cuisine in the trio of restaurants here is international, and the hotel is one of the best in the area for facilities, ranging from a spa to an indoor pool.

Av. 5 de Outubro 301–319, 1600-035 Lisboa. www.hotelvillaricalisboa.com. ✆ **21/004-30-00.** Fax 21/004-43-33. 171 units. 71€–243€ double. Parking 20€. AE, DC, MC, V. Metro: Entre Campos. Bus: 32 or 83. **Amenities:** 3 restaurants; 2 bars; concierge; health club; indoor heated pool; sauna. *In room:* A/C, TV, hair dryer, minibar.

In Belém
EXPENSIVE
Altis Belém ★★   This chain hotel has moved into ancient Belém, with its maritime associations, and has opened at a waterfront location close to the landmark

Tower of Belém. For its decorative theme it draws upon Portugal's Golden Age when it sent its ship captains around the world to capture new territories for their homeland; because they went to nearly every continent of the world, each wing is decorated to represent a different land mass. The decor inside is sleekly modern and minimalist; the good-sized rooms have white walls and wooden floors. Carpeting, furnishings, and wall panels are tasteful and stylish. The hotel also has one of the best spas in the area, with all sorts of treatments such as Tibetan massages or Japanese shiatsu. The crowning glory of the hotel is its rooftop swimming pool opening onto panoramic views of the city of Lisbon. Each suite comes with a terrace and a Jacuzzi overlooking the water. Even the regular rooms have such features as small espresso machines. Depending on their location, rooms come in a wide range of prices, from the relatively moderate to the very expensive.

Doca do Bom Sucesso, Belém, 1400-038 Lisboa. www.altisbelemhotel.com. ✆ **21/040-02-00.** 50 units. 150€–570€ double; from 650€ suite. AE, DC, MC, V. Bus: 28 or 43. **Amenities:** Restaurant; bar; concierge; exercise room; 2 pools (outdoor); room service. *In room:* A/C, TV, hair dryer, minibar (in some), Wi-Fi (free).

Jerónimos 8 ★ 🏆   Many discerning guests prefer this little discovery in Belém away from the congestion of Lisbon. This sleek, modern hotel lies close to the Jerónimos Monastery and a few steps from the Tagus riverfront. The hotel is housed in a traditional but restored Portuguese building from the 1940s. Each of the midsize bedrooms is individually designed and flooded with natural light, most of them opening onto panoramas of the monument-loaded district. Pristine white walls, tasteful furnishings, and lavish marble bathrooms characterize the rooms, some of which contain private Zen-inspired terraces with green bamboo. The Bussaco Wine Bar, in a hip red-and-white theme, is the only bar in Lisbon that serves wines from the legendary Buçaco Reserve in the north.

Rua dos Jerónimos 8, 1400-211 Lisboa. www.almeidahotels.com. ✆ **21/360-09-00.** Fax 21/360-09-08. 65 units. 135€–270€ double; 325€ suite. AE, DC, MC, V. Parking (in nearby lot) 25€. Tram: 15. **Amenities:** Bar; room service. *In room:* A/C, TV, hair dryer, minibar, Wi-Fi (free).

WHERE TO EAT

The explosion of restaurants in Lisbon in the early 21st century indicates that the Portuguese regard dining just as seriously as Spaniards. High prices have not suppressed their appetites, and residents of the capital are dining out more frequently than in the past.

Plenty of restaurants serve the usual fish and shellfish, and many erstwhile Portuguese colonials from Brazil, and even Mozambique and Goa, have opened restaurants in the capital. The menus in the top establishments remain on par with those of Europe's leading restaurants. In Lisbon, you'll encounter the best of Portuguese cooking mixed with Continental classics.

You needn't pay exorbitant prices for top-quality food, though. Restaurants featuring Portuguese and foreign fare—from beer-and-steak taverns to formal town-house dining rooms to cliffside restaurants with panoramic views—suit all budgets. For the best value, look for the "tourist," or fixed-price menu, which usually includes two or three courses, and sometimes wine, for far less than ordering a la carte. You might also want to consider an evening meal at a fado cafe (see chapter 5). Lisboans tend to eat much later than most American, Canadian, and British visitors, although not

Lisbon Restaurants

A Góndola 7
Adega da Tia Matilde 9
Alcântara Café 16
António 7
Aqui Há Peixe 29
Bica do Sapato 47
Bota Alta 30
Café Martinho da Arcada 41
Casa da Comida 3
Casa do Leão 44
Casa Nostra 31
Cervejaria Trindade 39
Chafariz do Vinho 13
Clara Restaurante 11
Comida de Santo 14
Eleven 6
Espalha Brasas 16
Faz Figura 48
Flores 33
Gambrinus 27
Hard Rock Café 26
Il Gattopardo Restaurant 1
KAIS 37
La Paparrucha 28
Largo 38
Marisqueira de Santa Maria 10

Martinho da Arcada 42
Mezzaluna 2
O Cantinho da Paz 22
O FUNIL 9
Olivier Avenida 12
100 Maneiras 24
Panorama Restaurant 8
Pap' Açorda 32
Pastelaria Versailles 9
Restaurant/Cafeteria Teatro Nacional de São Carlos 36
Restaurant d'Avis 47
Restaurant 33 4
Restaurante Valle Flor 19
Restaurante a Colmeia 34
Restaurante Doca Peixe 15
Restaurante Lapa 18
Restaurante Pabe 5
Restaurante Sancho 25
Restô do Chapitô 45
Royale Café 35
Sacramento do Chiado 40
Solar dos Bicos 43
Tasaquinha d'Adelaide 17
Telheiro 7
Terra 23
Tromba Rija 20
Via Graça 46
Yasmin 21

as late as their Spanish neighbors. Some restaurants (including Gambrinus, Bachus, and Cervejaria Trindade) stay open very late.

In the Center

VERY EXPENSIVE

Casa da Comida ★★★ FRENCH/TRADITIONAL PORTUGUESE Local gourmets tout Casa da Comida as offering some of the finest food in Lisbon. The dining room is handsomely decorated, the bar is done in the French Empire style, and there's a charming walled garden. Specialties include lobster with vegetables, roast kid with herbs, a medley of shellfish, and *faisão à convento de Alcântara* (stewed pheasant marinated in port wine for a day). The cellar contains an excellent selection of wines. The food is often more imaginative here than at some of the other top-rated choices. The chef is extraordinarily attentive to the quality of his ingredients, and the menu never fails to deliver some delightful surprises.

Travessa de Amoreiras 1 (close to Jardim de Las Amoreiras). 𝄐 **21/388-53-76.** www.casadacomida.pt. Reservations required. Main courses 32€–45€; menu degustation 40€; fixed-price menu 35€. AE, DC, MC, V. Tues-Fri 1-4pm; Mon-Sat 8–11pm. Metro: Rato.

Clara Restaurante ★★ INTERNATIONAL/PORTUGUESE On a hillside amid decaying villas and city squares, this green-tile house owned by Célia Pimpista contains an elegant restaurant with a number of different seating areas. You can enjoy a drink under the ornate ceiling of the bar or grab a seat in the indoor dining room—perhaps near the large marble fireplace, in range of the soft music played during dinner; during lunch, you can sit near the garden terrace's plants and fountain. Specialties include tournedos Clara, stuffed rabbit with red-wine sauce, four kinds of pasta, codfish Clara, filet of sole with orange, pheasant with grapes, and Valencian paella. Again, as in too many of Lisbon's top-rated restaurants, these dishes aren't innovative in any way, but they're often prepared flawlessly. As one of the staff told us, "When a dish has stood the test of time, why change it?" Perhaps you'll agree.

Campo dos Mártires da Pátria 49. 𝄐 **21/885-30-53.** www.lisboa-clara.pt. Reservations required. Main courses 24€–46€. AE, DC, MC, V. Mon-Fri 12:30-3pm; Mon-Sat 7:30-11:30pm. Closed Aug 1-15. Metro: Avenida.

Eleven ★★★ MEDITERRANEAN/MODERN PORTUGUESE Housed in an avant-garde building, Eleven is the only restaurant in Lisbon to win the coveted Michelin star. Filled with contemporary art, it opens onto a panoramic view across Lisbon, including the port. The restaurant is named for 11 friends who banded together because of their love of good food and their desire to see a world-class restaurant open in Lisbon. The location is just above Parque Eduardo VII, next to the Amália Rodrigues Gardens. You will wax poetic after feasting here on chef Joachim

4

SETTLING INTO LISBON | Where to Eat

Koerper's specialties, each based on market-fresh ingredients in harmony with the seasons. He uses locally grown, fresh, and natural produce, creating a luminous elegant, and innovative cuisine. Starters include a foie gras terrine with banana chutney or scallops carpaccio with black truffles, followed by such fish selections as sea bass with beetroot or roasted lobster with butter beans. Meat main courses range from Challans duck with stuffed baby pumpkin to lamb in a lemon crust with a chestnut parfait.

Rua Marquês de Fronteira. ℰ **21/386-22-11.** www.restauranteleven.com. Reservations required. Main courses 35€–55€; tasting menu 79€. MC, V. Mon–Sat 12:30–3pm and 7:30–11pm. Metro: Parque.

Gambrinus ★ REGIONAL PORTUGUESE/SEAFOOD   One of the city's premier restaurants, Gambrinus is the top choice for fish and shellfish. It's in the congested heart of the city, off the Rossio, near the rail station, on a little square behind the National Theater. The dining room is resolutely macho, with leather chairs under a beamed cathedral ceiling, but you can also select a little table beside a fireplace on the raised end of the room. Gambrinus offers a diverse a la carte menu and specialties of the day. The shades and nuances of the cuisine definitely appeal to the cultivated palate. The soups, especially the shellfish bisque, are good. The most expensive items are shrimp and lobster dishes. However, you might try conch with shellfish thermidor or sea bass *minhota,* cooked in tomato sauce with onions, white wine, and ham. If you don't fancy fish but do like your dishes hot, ask for chicken *piri-piri* (served with blazing chilies).

Rua das Portas de Santo Antão 23. ℰ **21/342-14-66.** www.gambrinuslisboa.com. Reservations recommended. Main courses 20€–36€. AE, MC, V. Daily noon–1:30am. Metro: Rossio or Restauradores.

EXPENSIVE

KAIS ★ INTERNATIONAL   At the docks, this bar and restaurant opens onto an esplanade by the river. It's installed in a late-19th-century warehouse, which has been amazingly converted into one of the most beautiful restaurants in Lisbon. Against a backdrop of Frank Lloyd Wright–inspired furniture, you can select from a dazzling array of fresh foodstuffs deftly handled by the skilled chefs in the kitchen. Shrimp in a champagne sauce is just one of the many tempting dishes that await you.

Rua da Cintura-Santos. ℰ **21/393-29-30.** www.kais-k.com. Reservations recommended. Main courses 25€–37€. Mon–Thurs 8pm–midnight; Fri–Sat 8pm–1am. AE, DC, MC, V. Closed first 2 weeks in Aug. Tram: 15.

100 Maneiras ★★★ INTERNATIONAL   Bosnian-born chef Ljubomir Stanisic is hailed by the local press as one of the most creative culinary artists in Lisbon, and we concur. The name of the restaurant translates as "100 ways of preparation." It's tucked away in a little section of the Chiado and may be hard to find. The setting is intimate, the welcome warm. Arguably, the chef offers the best tasting menu in town, nine wonderful courses, and you can also order a matching wine-tasting menu as well. Stanisic puts together lovely impromptu menus bursting with freshness and originality. There are many artful touches—your pieces of cod arrive at table hanging from clothespins. All the ingredients are fresh from the city's Ribeira market and the chef is constantly changing the menu. You might encounter a Brazilian rump steak, tender to the fork and full of flavor. He also does a great Brazilian *feijoada* or bean stew. Not unexpectedly, there are Serbian dishes on the menu, but for the most part he explores the kitchens of the world for his inspiration.

Rua do Teixeira 35. ℰ **21/099-04-75.** www.restaurante100maneiras.com. Reservations required. Tasting menu 75€; 18€–28€. AE, DC, MC, V. Mon–Fri noon–2pm; Mon–Sat 7pm–2am. Metro: Baixa-Chiado.

Panorama Restaurant ★★ INTERNATIONAL/PORTUGUESE For a restaurant and bar with a view, consider this spot in the 25-story Sheraton Lisboa Hotel & Spa. It's a celestial setting at night as you survey the twinkling lights of Lisbon. Dull, international hotel cuisine is eschewed in favor of sublime taste sensations created with market-fresh ingredients. The chef is always creating some new dish to tantalize diners, perhaps a salad of dried fruits and fresh papaya sprinkled with cheese from a sheep. His filet of cod is served in a savory ragout of fresh clams. Some of his dessert concoctions are pure poetry, especially the Belgian chocolate fondant with ginger ice cream.

Rua Latino Coelho 1. ☎ **21/312-00-00.** www.sheratonlisboa.com. Reservations required. Fixed-price menus 30€–39€. AE, DC, MC, V. Daily 12:30–3pm and 7:30–11:30pm. Bus: 1, 36, 44, or 45.

Restaurante Lapa INTERNATIONAL/ITALIAN/PORTUGUESE This is the most upscale and most highly recommended restaurant in the luxe Lapa Palace hotel (p. 70) and is a favorite of diplomats from the many embassies and consulates nearby. The dignified, elegant dining room has a view of one of the most lavish gardens in this exclusive neighborhood. A la carte items available at lunch and dinner vary with the season. They might include fresh salmon fried with sage, lamb chops with mint sauce, a succulent version of a traditional Portuguese *feijoada* (meat stew), and perfectly prepared duck breast baked with pears. This is a perfect spot to retreat to when you want an elegant meal in a refined atmosphere.

In the Lapa Palace hotel, Rua do Pau de Bandeira 4. ☎ **21/394-94-01.** www.lapapalace.com. Reservations recommended. Main courses 24€–38€. AE, DC, MC, V. Daily 12:30–3pm and 7:30–10:30pm. Closed for lunch in summer. Tram: 15.

MODERATE

Adega da Tia Matilde PORTUGUESE The Portuguese love this large, busy place in the Praça de Espanha area—foreign visitors are rare. We once overhead a Portuguese father here telling his son, "Food like this will make a man out of you." Indeed, it's a great place to sample the savory and hearty specialties of Ribatejo, including *cabrito assado* (roast mountain goat), *arroz de frango* (chicken with rice), and pungent *caldeirada* (fish stew).

Rua da Beneficência 77. ☎ **21/797-21-72.** www.adegatiamatilde.com. Main courses 11€–28€. AE, DC, MC, V. Mon–Sat noon–4pm; Mon–Fri 7:30–11pm. Metro: Praça d'Espanha. Bus: 31.

A Gôndola ★ INTERNATIONAL/ITALIAN Although its decor isn't particularly inspired, the good food at A Gôndola—including some of the finest Italian specialties in town—makes the restaurant worth the trip out of the city center. The price makes a full dinner quite a buy, considering what you get. A first-course selection might be Chaves ham with melon and figs, followed by filet of sole meunière or grilled sardines with pimientos. Yet another course—ravioli or cannelloni Roman style or veal cutlet Milanese—follows. The banquet might conclude with fruit or dessert. The Italian dishes don't compare with the best in Italy, but they're competent and professionally served. The restaurant is convenient to the Gulbenkian Museum. Courtyard seating is available.

Av. de Berna 64. ☎ **21/797-04-26.** www.restaurantegondola.com. Reservations recommended. Main courses 16€–27€; fixed-price lunch 28€. AE, DC, MC, V. Daily noon–3pm and 7:30–11pm. Metro: Praça de Espanha. Bus: 16, 26, 31, or 46.

Il Gattopardo Restaurant ITALIAN The most appealing and stylish Italian restaurant in Lisbon is distinctly different from the pasta and pizza joints that have

4

filled that niche until now. On the third floor of the Hotel Dom Pedro, it has a soothing color scheme of beiges, browns, exposed hardwoods, and leopard skin. Virtually everything is imported from Italy, including many staff members, who prepare ultrafresh seafood and pastas, among other dishes. We're mad for pappardelle seasoned with cubed zucchini and saffron. Risotto with cuttlefish is another winner, as are sea wolf coated with bread crumbs and sautéed grilled swordfish steak in parsley sauce, and roasted veal cooked in heady Barolo wine. The chef is adept at preparing tender duck breast flavored with honey and vinegar sauce. An outdoor terrace ringed with potted shrubs and vines provides sweeping views over the surrounding district.

In the Hotel Dom Pedro, Av. Engenheiro, Duarte Pacheco. ℂ **21/389-66-00.** www.dompedro.com. Reservations recommended. Main courses 17€–39€. AE, DC, MC, V. Mon–Fri 12:30-3pm and 8-11pm. Metro: Marquês de Pombal.

Marisqueira de Santa Marta ☺ PORTUGUESE   Two blocks from the landmark Avenida da Liberdade, this is the kind of family-friendly fish and shellfish house that maîtres d'hôtel throughout this prosperous neighborhood recommend to their hotel clients as a bustling, fairly priced emporium of uncontroversial Portuguese food and wine. Designed as an Iberian tavern, with pinewood chairs, tables, and paper tablecloths, it's lined with cheerful Portuguese blue-and-yellow tiles, and remains an aggressively unpretentious, brightly lit place with good food but not a lot of potential for romance. The menu lists dishes that include codfish prepared "our way" (with onions and fried potatoes); a shellfish platter for two; oysters with lemon sauce; smoked ham omelets; mixed grills; grilled pork spareribs; grilled sea bass; and grilled filets of pork.

Travessa do Enviado da Inglaterra 1. ℂ **21/352-56-38.** www.marisqueirasantamarta.pt.vu. Reservations recommended for dinner. Main courses 9€–19€. AE, DC, MC, V. Daily 9am–midnight. Metro: Avenida or Marquês de Pombal.

Martinho da Arcada PORTUGUESE   In its way, the Martinho is one of the city's most famous restaurants, thanks to its age (it was established in 1782) and its association with Portugal's beloved poet Fernando Pessoa, whose photos hang on the wall, just above the table and chair he used to compose some of his most famous works. There are three distinct sections to this place, so it pays to wander a bit before concluding that you've seen everything. There's a cafe section, for drinks and sandwiches; an outdoor terrace, where the menu is less complete than what you'll find inside; and an inside dining room, with antecedents that go back more to the 18th century. The menu here is long and varied, but if you ask for what the kitchen is proudest of, a staff member will talk about the house-style cod (a thick "tenderloin" of cod served with twice-cooked onions and fried potatoes) and house-style filet steak served with coffee sauce and fresh vegetables.

Praça do Comércio. ℂ **21/887-92-59.** Reservations recommended for dinner. Main courses 12€–22€. AE, DC, MC, V. Mon–Sat 8am-11pm. Metro: Terreiro do Paço.

Mezzaluna ★ ITALIAN   One of the best bets for your Italian fix is this restaurant slightly north of the center near Praça Marquês de Pombal. The owner-chef, Michael Guerrieri, is a Neapolitan who once owned a restaurant in New York before moving to Lisbon. He claims his is the most authentic Italian restaurant in the city—and he may be right. He has many of his products flown in daily from Italy. His cooking is traditional, including savory homemade pastas. The vegetarian dishes are so delectable that you can dine well without even ordering meat or fish—though both of these items are well flavored and often grilled just right. The menu is backed up by a reasonably priced wine list. The English-speaking staff is most helpful in guiding you to the best recommendations of the day.

Rua da Artilharia 1. ℰ **21/387-99-44.** www.mezzalunalisboa.com. Reservations required. Main courses 14€–18€. AE, DC, MC, V. Mon–Fri 12:30–3pm; Mon–Sat 7:30–11pm. Metro: Rato.

O FUNIL 🍴 PORTUGUESE O Funil (The Funnel) does *cozinha Portuguesa* (Portuguese cuisine) so well and so inexpensively that a line forms at the door; it's often hard to get a table. The owners serve their own *vinho da casa* (house wine)—try the red Alijó. The kitchen buys good-quality meats and fish fresh daily. The menu offers an array of excellent choices, including filet of fresh fish with rice, strips of cooked codfish flavored with herbs, roast goat with vegetables and roast potatoes, tiger shrimp in a picante sauce, and clams in wine sauce.

Av. Elias Garcia 82A. ℰ **21/796-60-07.** www.ofunil.com. Reservations recommended. Main courses 13€–23€. AE, MC, V. Daily noon–3:30pm; Tues–Sat 7–10:30pm. Metro: Campo Pequeno. Bus: 1, 32, 36, 38, 44, or 45.

Olivier Avenida INTERNATIONAL To escape from the often heavy Portuguese cuisine, you may want to drop into this chic rendezvous that specializes in much lighter fare. In a luxurious cosmopolitan setting, you can dine under chandeliers with light streaming in through the large windows. Light luncheon fare is featured, as well as snacks, though you can also drop in for a full-service dinner. The list of starters is one of the most varied and tastiest in the area, ranging from octopus carpaccio with sweet peppers to game sausage with a quail egg. The chef also specializes in Caesar salads, including one with grilled scallops. Try the stone bass filet on the grill or medallions of veal with fresh morels and white truffles, finishing with such desserts as cheesecake with guava jelly.

At the Tivoli Jardim, Rua Julio César Machado. ℰ **21/317-41-05.** www.restaurante-olivier.com. Reservations recommended. Main courses 16€–30€. MC, V. Daily 12:30–3pm and 8pm–midnight. Metro: Avenida.

Restaurante Doca Peixe ★★ SEAFOOD This restaurant, whose Portuguese name means "Fish Dock," stands virtually under the Ponte do 25 de Abril. The best views of the Tagus are from the tables upstairs. The fresh fish served here is among the best quality offered in the markets of Lisbon. Every variety of fish and shellfish seems to be swimming in the small aquarium at the entrance. If you don't want your fish chargrilled, you can order it cooked in salt or baked. Codfish is a specialty, appearing cooked with clams and flavored with fresh coriander (cilantro), or you can order the grilled platter of shellfish, a true delight. For carnivores, succulent sirloin steaks are among several winning choices.

Doca de Santo Amaro, Armazém 14. ℰ **21/397-35-65.** www.docapeixe.com. Reservations recommended. Main courses 17€–39€. AE, MC, V. Tues–Sun noon–3pm and 9:30pm–1am. Bus: 15 or 38.

Restaurante Pabe INTERNATIONAL/PORTUGUESE Convenient to Praça do Marquês de Pombal, this cozy pub does its best to emulate English establishments. There's soft carpeting, mugs hanging over the long bar, a beamed ceiling, coats of arms, and engravings of hunting scenes around the walls. Two saloon-type doors lead into a wood-paneled dining room, where you can dine on meat specially imported—not from England, but the United States. Chateaubriand for two is among the fanciest dishes. If you prefer local fare, start with shrimp cocktail and then try

Portuguese veal liver or *supremo de galinha* (chicken breast with mushrooms). The crowd tends to be a well-groomed Portuguese set, in addition to resident Americans and Brits.

Rua Duque de Palmela 27A. ℂ **21/353-74-84.** www.restaurantepabe.com.pt. Reservations required. Main courses 16€–26€. AE, DC, MC, V. Bar daily noon–1am. Restaurant daily noon–3pm and 7pm–midnight. Metro: Marquês de Pombal.

Restaurant 33 ★ INTERNATIONAL   Decorated in a style evocative of an English hunting lodge, Restaurant 33 is a real treasure with a great location near many recommended hotels. It specializes in succulent seafood dishes, including shellfish rice served in a crab shell, smoked salmon, and lobster Tour d'Argent; it also features tender, well-flavored pepper steak. One reader told us she found her meal here "flawless." A pianist performs during dinner. You can enjoy a glass of port in the small bar at the entrance or in the private garden.

Rua Alexandre Herculano 33A. ℂ **21/354-60-79.** Reservations recommended. Main courses 17€–30€. AE, DC, MC, V. Mon–Fri 12:30–3pm and 8–10:30pm; Sat 8–10pm. Metro: Marquês de Pombal. Bus: 6 or 9.

INEXPENSIVE

António INTERNATIONAL/PORTUGUESE   Portuguese businesspeople flock to António for its relaxing ambience and good food. It's a refreshing oasis of blue-and-white glazed earthenware tiles, a free-form blue ceiling, and white tablecloths topped with blue linen. The menu is printed in English. You can start with an excellent shellfish soup. Fish dishes garnished with vegetables include filets with tomato sauce, and baked sole. *Polvo à lagareiro* (octopus with broiled potatoes, olive oil, and garlic) is a justifiably popular specialty. If you prefer fowl or meat, try *frango na prata* (chicken broiled in foil with potatoes) or pork with clams Alentejana-style. The owner-manager recommends *açorda de marisco,* a stewlike breaded shellfish-and-egg dish. The dessert list is extensive, even listing a banana split. The chefs still cook exactly as their parents and grandparents did, and that seems to please the mainly local clientele.

Rua Tomás Ribeiro 63. ℂ **21/353-87-80.** Main courses 9€–18€. MC, V. Mon–Sat 8am–11pm. Metro: Picoas. Bus: 36, 45, 90, or 101.

Cervejaria Trindade PORTUGUESE   Cervejaria Trindade is a combination German beer hall and Portuguese tavern. In operation since 1836, it's the oldest tavern in Lisbon, owned by the brewers of Sagres beer. It was built on the foundations of the 13th-century Convento dos Frades Tinos, which was destroyed by the 1755 earthquake. Surrounded by walls tiled with Portuguese scenes, you can order tasty little steaks and heaps of crisp french-fried potatoes. Many Portuguese diners prefer the *bife na frigideira* (steak with mustard sauce and a fried egg, served in a clay frying pan). But the tavern also features shellfish; the house specialties are *amêijoas* (clams) *à Trindade* and giant prawns. For dessert, try a slice of *queijo da serra* (cheese from the mountains) and coffee. Meals are served in the inner courtyard on sunny days.

Rua Nova de Trindade 20C. ℂ **21/342-35-06.** www.cervejariatrindade.pt. Main courses 10€–33€. AE, DC, MC, V. Daily noon–2am. Metro: Chiado. Bus: 15, 20, 51, or 100.

Hard Rock Cafe AMERICAN   Set on two floors of a historic 18th-century palace, this is one of approximately 140 branches of one of the world's most visible restaurant franchises. Because it's at the lower end of the Avenida da Liberdade, in a neighborhood jammed with cheaper, more colorful, and more aggressively ethnic Portuguese restaurants, you may want to skip it. The cafe contains a collection of "museum quality" rock-'n'-roll memorabilia—in this case, clothing worn by Elton John, Madonna, David Bowie, and some of The Beatles—stiff drinks and juicy burgers, a vintage American Cadillac suspended surrealistically from the ceiling, and most endearing of all, a youthful and enthusiastic Portuguese staff who seem genuinely interested in whether you have a good time. Menu items that seem to never go out of style are the Tupelo chicken tenders, Santa Fe spring rolls, and Hard Rock nachos. A DJ spins danceable tunes every Friday and Saturday 11pm until 1am, and there's live music from local Portuguese bands every Sunday and Monday 11pm to 1am.

Av. da Liberdade 2. ✆ **21/324-52-80.** www.hardrock.com. Reservations not accepted except for parties of 6 or more. Burgers, salads, and main courses 8.50€–22€. AE, DC, MC, V. Daily noon–2am. Bar open until at least 2am. Metro: Rossio or Restauradores.

Pastelaria Versailles ★ CAFE/PASTRIES   This is the most famous teahouse in Lisbon, and it has been declared part of the "national patrimony." Some patrons reputedly have been coming here since it opened in 1932. In older days, the specialty was *licungo,* the famed black tea of Mozambique; you can still order it, but nowadays many drinkers enjoy English brands. (The Portuguese claim that they introduced the custom of tea-drinking to the English court after Catherine of Bragança married Charles II in 1662.) The decor is rich, with chandeliers, gilt mirrors, stained-glass windows, tall stucco ceilings, and black-and-white marble floors. You can also order milkshakes, mineral water, and fresh orange juice, along with beer and liquor. The wide variety of snacks includes codfish balls and toasted ham-and-cheese sandwiches. A limited array of platters of simple but wholesome Portuguese fare is on offer, too.

Av. da República 15A. ✆ **21/354-63-40.** www.pastelariaversailles.com. Sandwiches 3€; pastries 1€; plats du jour 9.50€–22€. AE, MC, V. Daily 7:30am–10pm. Metro: Saldanha.

Restaurante a Colmeia VEGETARIAN   There's no elevator to haul you up to the third floor of the 17th-century building that houses this restaurant, but most of the regular clients consider that part of the healthy vibe of this place. One of the few macrobiotic, all-vegetarian restaurants in Lisbon, with a commitment to serving only produce raised without chemical fertilizers or pesticides, it consists of a series of glass display counters that were inspired by an American-style cafeteria, and a trio of high-ceilinged dining rooms painted pink, blue, and orange, respectively. Various preparations of tofu and wheat gluten, flavored differently every day, are enduringly popular, as are different dishes of collard greens, kelp, squash, and spinach, as well as salads, spinach cakes, and "vegetable flans."

Rua da Emenda 110. ✆ **21/347-05-00.** Main courses 7€–10€. No credit cards. Mon–Fri noon–3pm. Metro: Baixa Chiado. Tram: 28. Bus: 58 or 100.

Restaurante Sancho INTERNATIONAL/PORTUGUESE   Sancho is a cozy rustic-style restaurant with classic Iberian decor—beamed ceiling, fireplace, leather-and-wood chairs, and stucco walls. In summer, it has air-conditioning. Fish gratinée soup is a classic way to begin. Shellfish, always expensive, is the specialty. Main dishes are likely to include the chef's special hake or pan-broiled Portuguese steak. If your palate is fireproof, order *churrasco de cabrito ao piri-piri* (goat with pepper sauce). For dessert, sample the crêpes suzette or perhaps chocolate mousse. This is a longtime (since 1962) local favorite, and the recipes never change. As a waiter explained, "As long as we can keep the dining room full every night, why change?"

Travessa da Glória 14 (just off Av. da Liberdade, near Praça dos Restauradores). © **21/346-97-80.** www.restaurantesancho.com.pt. Reservations recommended. Main courses 14€–26€. AE, DC, MC, V. Mon–Fri noon–3pm and 7pm–midnight; Sat 7pm–midnight. Metro: Avenida or Restauradores.

Telheiro PORTUGUESE The kitchen at Telheiro (Portuguese for "the roof") makes little concession to "lily-livered" (the words of one waiter here) foreign tastes, which makes this bistrolike place not far from the Sheraton Hotel all the more authentic. Under beamed ceilings, diners sit on wooden chairs with heart shapes carved out of their backs. Many staff members are from the former Portuguese colony of Angola. Different robust, hearty specialties are featured every day, including gazpacho, cabbage-and-potato soup, mussels, suckling pig, grilled fresh sea bass or sole, and seafood with rice in a casserole. For dessert, try fresh Portuguese fruit.

Rua Latino Coelho 10A. © **21/353-40-07.** Reservations recommended. Main courses 9€–22€. AE, MC, V. Daily noon–3pm and 7–11pm (closed Sat July–Sept). Bus: 30.

In the Bairro Alto

EXPENSIVE

La Paparrucha ★ ARGENTINE Some of the best steaks in Lisbon are served at this restaurant in the Bairro Alto section of town—the quality of the meats is as first-rate as what you'd be served in Buenos Aires. Choice cuts include *lomo* (filet) or *vacio* (flank steak), or else you can order a mixed grill of meats. These often come on a charcoal hotplate. The most desired seating is on the large wooden deck out back or, in colder weather, by one of the large picture windows opening onto panoramic views of the city. Most of the appetizers are made without meat, usually vegetables. Fresh bread comes with your main courses, which you can use to sop up the juices. The typical dessert choice is *dulce de leite,* a milk-based delight.

Rua D. Pedro V, 18–20. © **21/342-53-33.** www.lapaparrucha.com. Reservations recommended. Main courses 21€–29€. AE, DC, MC, V. Daily 7:30–11pm. Metro: Avenida.

Tasquinha d'Adelaide ★ 🍴 REGIONAL PORTUGUESE At the western edge of the Bairro Alto, about 2 blocks northeast of the Alcântara subway station and 2 blocks west of the Basilica da Estrela, this small restaurant is cramped and convivial. It's known for the culinary specialties of Trás-os-Montes, a rugged province in northeast Portugal, and for its homey, unpretentious warmth. Robust specialties include *alheiras fritas com arroz de grelos* (tripe with collard greens and rice) and *lulas grelhadas* (grilled squid served in a black clay casserole). To finish, try Dona Adelaide's *charcade de ovos* (a secret recipe made with egg yolks). Although we like this hearty cooking, the flavors might be too pungent for some palates.

Rua do Patrocínio 70–74. © **21/396-22-39.** Reservations recommended. Main courses 16€–30€. AE, DC, MC, V. Mon–Sat 12:30–4pm and 8pm–2am. Metro: Rato. Tram: 25, 28, or 30. Bus: 9, 15, or 28.

Tromba Rija ★ PORTUGUESE A five-minute walk from the Cais do Sodre railway station, this is the newest branch of a three-member restaurant chain whose original setting, in the northern city of Leira, is famous throughout Portugal. Located south of the center of Lisbon in what functioned in the 1960s as a warehouse and marketplace for fish, this venue is devoted exclusively to buffets. Thanks to an impressive selection of vegetable, meat, and fish dishes, all of them arranged on enormous platters that a staff keeps constantly replenished, it has become a favorite of families. Various menu stations are devoted, respectively, to salads (tuna, octopus, vegetarian, and country recipes made from every conceivable part of a pig); fried foods (onion rings, fried cauliflower florets, and various croquettes), and a staggering number of traditional Portuguese-inspired fish and meat platters. The waitstaff will seat you and bring you your drinks, but other than that, you'll select everything else yourself.

Rua Cintura do Porto de Lisboa, Edificio 254. Tel. 21/397-1507 www.trombarija.com. Reservations recommended. Set per person price 32€ Mon-Fri, 35€ Sat-Sun. AE, MC, V. Mon-Fri 12:30-3:30pm and 8-10:30pm; Sat-Sun 1-4pm and 8-11pm. Metro: Cais do Sodre.

MODERATE

Bota Alta PORTUGUESE   Bota Alta, at the top of a steep street in the Bairro Alto, boasts a faithful clientele that eagerly crams into its two dining rooms and sometimes stands at the bar waiting for a table. It contains rustic artifacts and lots of original art and photographs. Meals—some familiar to 19th-century diners—might include beefsteak Bota Alta; several preparations of codfish, including *bacalhau real* (fried codfish with port wine and cognac); and a frequently changing array of daily specials, including Hungarian goulash. We still aren't sure why *bacalhau* is so popular—the Portuguese claim to have as many fish off their coast as there are days on the calendar—but don't leave Portugal without sampling it at least once.

Travessa da Queimada 35-37. ℭ **21/342-79-59.** Reservations required. Main courses 12€-24€. AE, DC, MC, V. Mon-Fri noon-2:30pm; Mon-Sat 7-10:45pm. Metro: Chiado. Bus: 58 or 100.

Comida de Santo 🖼 BRAZILIAN   Opening in the early 1980s, this was the first all-Brazilian restaurant in Lisbon. At the edge of the Bairro Alto, in a century-old former private house, it has only 12 tables. Recorded Brazilian music plays softly from the bar, lending a New World flavor, and a quintet of oversize panels depicts huge, idealized jungle scenes. The appropriate beginning of any meal is a deceptively potent *caipirinha* (aguardiente cocktail with limes and sugar). Main courses include spicy versions of *feijoada* (meat-and-bean stew), *picanha* (boiled Brazilian beef with salt), *vatapá* (peppery shrimp), and several versions of succulent grilled fish. The place is incredibly popular; reservations are very important.

Calçada Engenheiro Miguel Pais 39. ℭ **21/396-33-39.** www.comidadesanto.pt. Reservations recommended. Main courses 15€-18€; tasting menu 38€. AE, DC, MC, V. Daily 12:30-3:30pm and 7:30pm-1am. Metro: Rato. Bus: 58.

Pap' Açorda PORTUGUESE   The facade of this restaurant, set on a narrow medieval street in the Bairro Alto, was originally conceived for a bakery. Today it's high on the list of hip, perpetually fashionable restaurants for the counterculture and media crowd; as such, competition for an available table is stiff. It welcomes one of Lisbon's most colorful collections of people into its dimly lit seashell-pink-and-cream interior. Most visitors order a before-dinner drink at the long, marble-topped bar, which dominates the front of the restaurant. Prospective diners jockey for the attentions of the somewhat blasé maître d'hôtel. If you ever get around to dining (and some clients actually prefer to linger at the bar as a social ritual unto itself), you'll be treated to delectable cuisine that includes Spanish-style mussels, shellfish rice, sirloin steak with mushrooms, and a wide array of fish and shellfish dishes. The house specialty, *açorda,* is a traditional dish with coriander, bread, seafood, eggs, garlic, and olive oil.

Rua da Atalaia 57-59. ℭ **21/346-48-11.** Reservations required. Main courses 16€-33€. AE, DC, MC, V. Tues-Sat noon-2:30pm and 8-11:30pm. Metro: Chiado.

INEXPENSIVE

Café Martinho da Arcada PORTUGUESE   In the Baixa district, this is the oldest cafe in Lisbon, opening in 1782 (other sources claim 1778). It was once frequented by modernist poet Fernando Pessoa and a table is still laid for him as if the staff expects him to drop in at any time (he died in 1935). You can patronize the place as a cafe or a full-service restaurant. Coffee drinkers come here to enjoy the scrumptious pastries baked fresh daily. A specialty is *pastéis de nata* or cream cake. The cookery in the wood-paneled dining room is robustly regional, including *cataplana* (clam stew), various platters of codfish, and *cabrito* (baby goat).

Praça do Comércio 3. *(©* **21/887-92-59.** Reservations not required. Main courses 12€–22€. AE, DC, MC, V. Mon–Sat 8am–10pm. Metro: Baixa-Chiado.

Casa Nostra ★ 🏠 ITALIAN   Maria Paola Porru, a movie sound engineer whose travels have exposed her to cinematic circles across Europe, rules this hip postmodern hideaway. Behind a century-old, deliberately understated facade, the setting is simple, stylish, and informal. All pastas are homemade on the premises. Accomplished menu items include *fettuccine al mascarpone* (fettuccine with cream cheese), lasagna, spaghetti with Portuguese clams, and several versions of grilled meat. A favorite dessert is Sicilian-style tiramisu, a rich dessert made with ladyfingers, coffee, and mascarpone cream.

Rua de Rosa 84–90 (enter at Travessa do Poço da Cidade 60). *(©* **21/342-59-31.** www.restaurante casanostra.com. Reservations recommended. Main courses 11€–19€. AE, MC, V. Tues–Fri 12:30–2:30pm; Tues–Sat 8–11pm; Sun 1–2:30pm. Metro: Chiado. Tram: 28 or 28B.

O Cantinho da Paz INDIAN   This restaurant honors the cuisine of the lost colony of Goa, which the government of India took over in 1961. Many Portuguese Goans brought their spicy cuisine to Lisbon and set up dining rooms, and this is the best of the lot. The curries draw discerning diners, who are richly rewarded with spices and flavors. Our favorite is shrimp curry flavored with coconut and laced with cream. But you might opt for a fiery version made with lamb, fish, or poultry. Veal stew comes with different types and levels of spiciness, and succulent medallions of pork are richly flavored with ginger and garlic. The helpful owners speak English. There is also live music from Thursday to Sunday.

Rua da Paz 4 (off Rua dos Poiais de São Bento). *(©* **21/396-96-98.** www.lxrestaurantes.com. Reservations required. Main courses 10€–25€. AE, MC, V. Tues–Sat 12:30–2:30pm and 7:30–11pm. Tram: 28. Bus: 6 or 49. Metro: Chiado.

Terra VEGETARIAN   Vegetarians do not have to forego tasty treats in Lisbon—even nonvegetarians are likely to be enthralled with the rich flavors served by the Mediterranean kitchen here. In a restored 18th-century house with a private garden, you can enjoy their daily changing buffet. Regularly featured is an array of curries, tempura dishes, burritos, and kebabs. The chef claims that for his salads he finds inspirations on all the continents of the world, including classics such as a Greek salad or a Waldorf salad. Some of the combinations are unexpected and delicious. Desserts range from a delectable chocolate brownie to a rice pudding based on a medieval recipe. There is also a classic tiramisu. The restaurant also serves the first kosher wines to be produced in Portugal in 500 years.

Rua da Palmeira 15. *(©* **70/710-81-08.** www.restauranteterra.pt. Reservations recommended Sat–Sun. Buffet 20€. AE, DC, MC, V. Tues–Sun 12:30–3pm and 7:30–10:30pm. Metro: Avenida.

In the Chiado District

EXPENSIVE

Largo ★★ MEDITERRANEAN   Formerly of the celebrated Buddha Bar in Paris, chef Miguel Castro e Silva has brought his creative specialties to the Chiado. The setting itself is elegant, with a main floor plus a mezzanine, all in a medley of architectural styles, including stone arches and pillars, mixed with a sleek contemporary design in such colors as lettuce green or fuchsia. The main restaurant was converted from the old Convent of the Cloisters of the Church of the Martyrs. The cooking is original and highly personalized with market-fresh ingredients. Vigorous flavors appear in perfectly balanced dishes. Try such fish dishes as grilled sea bass in an orange fennel sauce, or sautéed squid with shrimp in a beurre blanc sauce. Filet steak appears with a sautéed foie gras in a wine sauce, or else you can sample a delightful duck magret with a truffled risotto. Starters might include a cold almond and fennel cream soup or else smoked codfish in a pine nut vinaigrette.

Rua Serpa Pinto 10A. ☎ **21/347-72-25.** www.largo.pt. Reservations required. Main courses 25€–30€. AE, DC, MC, V. Mon–Fri 12:30–3pm; Sat 7:30pm–midnight. Metro: Baixa/Chiado.

MODERATE

Aqui Há Peixe SEAFOOD   In Portuguese the name of this stylish restaurant translates as "There is fish here." And so there is, quite a lot of it, most of it caught off the coast only that night or in the early morning. The focus is on natural flavors, capturing the sunny tastes of Portugal. The chef shows his real skill in his seafood, bringing out the natural taste of the fish and not burying it under unnecessary adornments such as heavy sauces. Begin with freshly shucked oysters or "duck clams," perhaps a savory fish soup. The garlic prawns are a real delicacy, and the tuna steak sautéed with peppercorns wins a bravo. Vegetables accompanying the main dishes are always fresh and gathered that morning at the local market. Most in-the-know diners select a light *vinho verde* to go with their seafood.

Rua da Trindade 18A. ☎ **21/343-21-54.** www.aquihapeixe.pt. Reservations recommended. Main courses 14€–22€. DC, MC, V. Tues–Sun 7pm–2am. Metro: Rossio.

Flores ★ FUSION/MEDITERRANEAN/PORTUGUESE   A meal within this manicured, impeccably correct hotel dining room is a very far cry from any of the city's larger and more mass-market dining options. Small-scale and personalized, and ringed with tilework in the Hispano-Moorish style, it's the equivalent of a meal within the homes of (wealthy) Portuguese hipsters. A uniformed staff will show you to one of only 32 seats, within a room that reeks of the baroque age with an updated sense of the 21st-century arts in the form of photographs by Rui Calçada Bastos. Cuisine, as conceived by chef Luís Rodriguez, includes fresh seasonal ingredients from local markets, with a goodly number of vegetarian specialties. Look for cream of mushroom soup with ham; a risotto made from Swiss chard, eggplant, and fresh tomatoes; a medley of grouper, potatoes, and anchovies with boletus mushrooms; a tartare of salmon with fresh herbs; and a confit of fresh hake with sweet potato cannelloni.

In the Hotel Bairro Alto, Praça Luís de Camões 8. ☎ **21/340-82-52.** www.bairroaltohotel.com. Reservations recommended. Lunch main courses 12€–19€; dinner main courses 18€–28€. AE, DC, MC, V. Daily noon–3pm and 7:30–10:30pm. Metro: Chiado.

Sacramento do Chiado ★ 🍴 INTERNATIONAL/PORTUGUESE   This place has emerged as the virtual symbol of the new and trendy Chiado district. If you opt for a meal here, get ready for access to a labyrinth of inner chambers loaded with intriguingly carved arts and crafts, some of them from Indonesia, and much of them, based on this place's self-definition as an "emporium," for sale. Beginning around 8pm, you're likely to find a hip mixture of Brazilian and Portuguese night owls scattered throughout the various bars and dining areas associated with this place. Steak tartare, tenderloin steak, pork tenderloin with prunes, stuffed breast of chicken with ratatouille, and de-boned filet of cod "Sacramento," with potatoes and garlic, are each well prepared and flavorful.

Calçada do Sacramento 44. *C* **21/342-05-72.** www.sacramentodochiado.com. Main courses 9€–32€. AE, DC, MC, V. Tues–Sat noon–3pm; Sun 7:30pm–midnight. Metro: Chiado.

INEXPENSIVE

Restaurant/Cafeteria Teatro Nacional de São Carlos ★ CONTINENTAL Just after the turn of the millennium, one of the formal "showcase" salons within Lisbon's Opera House, originally built in 1765, was transformed into this restaurant. Today it's the kind of airy, appealingly formal venue where sparkling wine might be served with fresh fish, and where you'll overhear diners relating the plot of an upcoming or past opera performance. The staff will draw your attention to the similarities of this elegant small-scale venue with the neoclassicism of La Scala in Milan, and indeed, there's something Italian and rococo about the place, especially when the opera being presented on the stage inside is broadcast onto the wide screen in the plaza outside. Excellent menu items include a cod with pesto sauce and a red cabbage risotto; magret of duck with green peppers; and grilled beef with three different kinds of Portuguese cheese.

Largo São Carlos. *C* **21/346-80-82.** www.screstauracao.com. Salads, pastas, and risottos 9€–16€; main courses 15€–28€. AE, DC, MC, V. Mon–Sat noon–midnight. Metro: Chiado.

Royale Café ★ INTERNATIONAL When this cafe first opened, it seemed to attract fashion-conscious young women and cool gay guys. When word got out about its appeal, it broadened its client base considerably. In the chic Chiado district, it is known for its creative, imaginative food, fare that lies definitely in the 21st century, not the past. A specialty is veal carpaccio with arugula, coriander-laced pesto, fresh artichokes, and cheese from the Azores. The house salad is called Royale, a mixed-leaf bowl with arugula, mozzarella on corn bread, and strawberries and pesto. A tenderloin of deer is topped with bacon and comes with pears in a syrup of Porto. For lunch, the sandwiches are the best in Chiado, largely because of the homemade organic breads, including spelt bread, a wild wheat bread that existed in Europe before the agricultural revolution. The grains of spelt are still ground in millstones.

Largo Rafael Bordalo Pinheiro. *C* **21/346-91-25.** www.royalecafe.com. Reservations not required. Main courses 9€–14€. MC, V. Mon–Sat 10am–midnight; Sun 10am–8pm. Metro: Baixa/Chiado.

In the Avenida District

EXPENSIVE

Chafariz do Vinho ★ PORTUGUESE/WINE Our favorite *enoteca* boasts not only one of the more varied and affordable wine *cartes* in Lisbon but also features good-tasting dishes, both a tasting menu and a selection of tapas. The setting is also unique, installed in an 18th-century stone-built aqueduct that once brought fresh water from the hills into Lisbon. The *enoteca* offers wines from relatively small, unknown producers of the grape, charging most reasonable prices. You can consume this *vinho* with delectable tapas such as smoked sausage with cabbage, smoked codfish with fresh grapes, or shrimp with mushrooms. The tasting menu pairs a different wine with every course, featuring such starters as mussels in sauce or dates with bacon, followed by goat cheese on toast or fresh pasta with spinach. For a main, you are likely to be served a platter of mixed smoked meats or a carpaccio of smoked duck followed by the fresh dessert of the day.

Chafariz da Mãe d'Água a Praça da Alegria. ℭ **21/342-20-79.** www.chafarizdovinho.com. Reservations recommended. Tasting menu 35€; tapas 3.50€–9€. MC, V. Tues–Sun 6pm–2am. Metro: Avenida.

In the Graça District
MODERATE
Faz Figura ★ INTERNATIONAL/PORTUGUESE   This is one of the best and most attractively decorated dining rooms in Lisbon—decked out in 19th-century style with pretty antique tiles and wall prints of city scenes—and the service is faultless. When reserving a table, ask to be seated on the veranda, overlooking the Tagus. You can stop for a before-dinner drink in the "international cocktail bar." The cuisine, including such specialties as *feijoada de marisco* (shellfish stew) and *cataplana* (a cooking pot) of fish and seafood, is generally very flavorful and occasionally spicy.

Rua do Paraíso 15B. ℭ **21/886-89-81.** www.fazfigura.com. Reservations recommended. Main courses 16€–32€. AE, DC, MC, V. Mon–Fri 12:30–3pm and 7:30–11pm; Sat 7:30–11pm. Bus: 12, 39, or 46.

Via Graça PORTUGUESE   In the residential Graça district, a few blocks northeast of the fortifications surrounding Castelo de São Jorge, this restaurant boasts a panoramic view that encompasses the castelo and the Basilica da Estrela. Flickering candles and attentive service enhance the romantic setting. Dishes aren't inventive, but they're savory and appealing to traditionalists who prefer hearty fare. Specialties of the house include such traditional Portuguese dishes as *pato assado com moscatel* (roast duck with wine from the region of Setúbal) and *linguado com recheio de camarão* (stuffed filet of sole served with shrimp).

Rua Damasceno Monteiro 9B. ℭ **21/887-08-30.** www.restauranteviagraca.com. Reservations recommended. Main courses 16€–30€. AE, DC, MC, V. Mon–Fri 12:30–3pm and 7:30–11pm; Sat–Sun 7:30–11pm. Tram: 28.

INEXPENSIVE
Restaurant d'Avis PORTUGUESE   This simple but pleasing restaurant is not associated with the Restaurante Aviz, once an important culinary citadel on Rua Serpa Pinto. This humbler, less expensive competitor was established in the late 1980s as a purveyor of the cuisine of Alentejo to cost-conscious diners. It serves regional dishes such as roast pork with clams, roast baby goat, steaming bowls of *caldo verde* (a fortifying soup made from high-fiber greens and potatoes), and perfectly prepared fresh fish. Don't expect a luxurious setting or anything even vaguely formal—the rustic venue is deliberately unpretentious, and few members of the staff speak English.

Rua do Grilo 98. ℭ **21/868-13-54.** www.davis.com.pt. Reservations recommended. Main courses 7€–18€. AE, DC, MC, V. Mon–Sat noon–4pm and 7:30–10:30pm. Bus: 18, 38, 39, 42, 59, or 105. Metro: Rossio.

In the Belém District
MODERATE
Vela Latina INTERNATIONAL/PORTUGUESE   In a verdant park close to the Tagus and the Tower of Belém, this inviting, high-ceilinged restaurant offers

well-prepared food, lots of greenery, big windows, and peace. Many visitors opt for lunch here after a visit to the nearby Jerónimos Monastery or the Coach Museum. Specialties include a wide array of classic, well-prepared Portuguese dishes, such as lobster-filled crepes, platters of fresh fish, quail salad, lamb cutlets, and filet of hake with rice. Dessert might be flan, fruit tart, or ice cream. The price of some shellfish dishes can soar above what's quoted below.

Doca do Bom Sucesso. ℭ **21/301-71-18.** www.velalatina.pt. Main courses 18€–37€; fixed-price menus 28€–60€. AE, DC, MC, V. Mon–Sat 12:30–3pm and 8–11:30pm. Kitchen closes 10pm. Bus: 12, 39, or 46.

In the Alfama
MODERATE

Casa do Leão INTERNATIONAL/PORTUGUESE   Stop for a midday meal at this restaurant, in a low-slung stone building inside the walls of Saint George's Castle. In the spacious dining room, you'll enjoy a panoramic view of the Alfama and the legendary hills of Lisbon. Your lunch might include roast duck with oranges or grapes, pork chops Saint George–style, codfish with cream, or smoked swordfish from Sesimbra. The chefs cook with the international visitor in mind, but what they prepare can be very satisfying. Menus change with the season. We'd like the service to be more attentive, but the hardworking waiters might already be moving at peak capacity.

Castelo de São Jorge. ℭ **21/887-59-62.** Reservations recommended. Main courses 13€–22€. AE, DC, MC, V. Daily 12:30–3:30pm and 8–10:30pm. Bus: 37. Metro: Rossio.

Solar dos Bicos PORTUGUESE   Near Praça do Comércio in the Alfama, this restaurant is beautifully decorated with antiques from the 16th and 18th centuries in an old building graced with stone arches. There are two dining rooms with a large terrace facing a famous landmark building, Casa dos Bicos. Fado musicians and singers are often provided to entertain you. The chef prepares any number of meat dishes, but specializes in what the sea harvested that day. Many recipes for the Portuguese dishes come from the Minho region in the north of Portugal. Start perhaps with codfish croquettes or smoked Chaves ham, or else a seafood cream soup. Squid and shrimp are grilled on the spit, or else you can order freshly grilled sardines. The chef's specialty is a *caldeirada* (Portuguese fish stew) served to two persons. Some of the best meat dishes are a mixed grill on the spit and a house specialty—chicken stew with rice to which a dash of vinegar is added. You can also order a veal sirloin steak.

Rua dos Bacalhoeiros 8-A. ℭ **21/886-94-47.** www.solardosbicos.pt. Main courses 18€–28€. AE, DC, MC, V. Tues–Sun 8pm–midnight. Tram: 28.

INEXPENSIVE

Restô do Chapitô 👥 INTERNATIONAL   This funky all-purpose rendezvous point occupies the steeply sloping premises of what was built in the 17th century as a women's prison and which functions today as a state-funded school for circus entertainers. Its location, perched on a ledge just below St. George's Castle in the Alfama, encompasses views over all of Lisbon. Bruno, the Belgian-born owner, is nonchalant about what the place is exactly. It includes a cafe and bar, a separate tapas bar, at least two different dining areas, and a venue that's conducive to drinks that are consumed in anticipation of moving on to other nocturnal adventures. Menu items are simple, full of flavor, and straightforward, and include steak with a gratin of potatoes and mushroom sauce, breast of duck with orange sauce, smoked salmon, grilled octopus salad, and mango-flavored ice cream.

Rua Costa do Castelo 7. ☎ **21/886-73-34.** www.chapito.org. Fixed-price menus 18€. No credit cards. Tues-Fri noon-2am whenever school is in session; btw. mid-July and mid-Sept, and during other school closings, Tues-Fri 7:30pm-2am and Sat-Sun 10am-2am. Tram: 28.

Santa Antonio de Alfama MEDITERRANEAN   One of the best bargains in the Alfama is this modest restaurant serving good food. It is decorated with black-and-white photographs of film stars. Because it's open late, you can even dine here after going to one of the fado clubs nearby. In summer try for a table on the adjoining leafy terrace. The chef has a clever way of cooking duck with steamed vegetables, and the pastas are also good, especially one made with smoked ham and fresh mushrooms. The catch of the day is always served, as well as Portuguese steaks cooked as you like them. For an appetizer, try the sautéed, batter-coated whitebait.

Beco de São Miguel 7. ☎ **21/888-13-28.** www.siteantonio.com. Reservations recommended. Main courses 7€-18€. DC, MC, V. Wed-Mon 12:30-7pm and 8pm-2am. Metro: Santa Apolónia.

In the Santos District
INEXPENSIVE
Yasmin ★ 🎁 PORTUGUESE   The waterfront Santos quarter of Lisbon was once where only shady characters went at night. But it is emerging as a splashy new venue after night. Once a dreary industrial area, it's fast becoming a favorite haunt for dining and drinking, and it also has a number of museums. A crowd of up-and-coming young professionals have adopted Yasmin as their favorite place. With a contemporary decor that is often called "sexy," you can dine while sitting in a Saarinen chair fashionably placed on a polished concrete floor. Surprising tastes and combinations greet you. Ever had a mango-tomato-avocado-honey vinaigrette? It's served with grilled cheeses from the Azores. For your main course, opt for the cod confit with garlic-laced sautéed spinach or perhaps loin of deer with grilled shiitake mushrooms and a corn foam. The kitchen shuts down at 12:20am, but the club stays open later.

Rua da Moeda 1A. ☎ **21/393-00-74.** www.yasmin-lx.com. Reservations required. Main courses 13€-21€. Tues-Sat noon-3pm and 7:30pm-2am. AE, MC, V. Metro: Cais do Sodré.

In the Alcântara
Alcântara Café INTERNATIONAL/PORTUGUESE   Established in 1989, this is one of the city's most enjoyable dining-and-entertainment complexes. Entertainment is provided by some of the best DJs in Portugal. It lies within the solid walls of a 600-year-old timber warehouse and attracts a hip, attractive, fun-loving young crowd. Today the vast building has forest-green and Bordeaux walls, exposed marble, ceiling fans, plants, and simple wooden tables and chairs. The varied clientele includes resident Brazilian, British, and American expatriates. Chefs make the most of regional foodstuffs and prepare hearty fare that is filled with flavor and plenty of spices—maybe too much for some palates. Menu items include rillettes of salmon, fresh fish, lacquered duck, steak tartare, and a Portuguese platter of the day, which might include fried *bacalhau* (codfish) or a hearty *feijoada*, a bean-and-meat stew inspired by the traditions of Trás-os-Montes.

Rua Maria Luisa Holstein 15. ☎ **21/362-12-26.** www.alcantaracafe.com. Reservations recommended. Main courses 16€-36€. AE, DC, MC, V. Daily 8pm-1am. Bar daily 9pm-3am. Bus: 12 or 18.

Espalha Brasas 🎁 PORTUGUESE/TAPAS   This is our favorite of the many shoulder-to-shoulder restaurants lined up at the Alcântara Docks, although part of your evening's entertainment will involve picking whichever of the 20 or so cheek-by-jowl restaurants you actually prefer. You'll enter a high-ceilinged room whose centerpiece is a weather-beaten wooden statue of a nude male beside stairs leading to an upstairs balcony with additional tables. The setting is comfortably cluttered and amiable, with candlelit tables and a display of whatever fresh seafood and meats can be grilled to your preference. The finest menu items include every imaginable kind of meat or fish, grilled the way you prefer, as well as daily specials that include rice studded with either turbot and prawns or marinated duck meat, baked haunch of pork, and codfish stuffed with prawns and spinach.

Doca de Santa Amaro, Armazém 12. Alcântara. ℂ **21/396-20-59.** www.espalhabrasas.eu. Reservations recommended for dinner Fri–Sat nights only. Main courses 11€–27€. AE, MC, V. Tues–Sun noon–2am. Bus: 57. Tram: 15 or 18.

In Lapa

Nariz de Vinho Tinto ★ 🎁 PORTUGUESE   This is one of our favorite restaurants in Lisbon—and known only to the most discerning of palates—so don't tell anyone about it. In the elegant Lapa district, the restaurant—"Red Wine Nose" in English—is owned by Antonio Ignacio. He gives equal attention to his wines as he does to his market-fresh produce. In two small dining rooms, decorated with cookbooks and wine bottles, he serves a cuisine that raises many dishes to gastronomic heights for Lisbon. His *pata negra* ham, for example, coming from the black-hoofed pig, is the single best platter of this dish we've ever tasted in Lisbon. Try his deeply smoky "game sausage" with its crackly skin and tantalizing filling, or else his cod roasted with ham fat (don't tell your doctor). Even the turnip tops cooked here are a savory treat and super green.

Rua do Conde 75. ℂ **21/395-30-35.** www.narizvinhotinto.com. Reservations required. Main courses 13€–30€. AE, DC, MC, V. Tues–Fri 12:30–3pm; Tues–Sun 7:45–11pm. Metro: Rato. Bus: 7 or 27.

In Alto de Santo Amaro

Restaurant Valle Flor ★★ PORTUGUESE   This is the most elegant hotel dining room in Lisbon, with a battalion of uniformed staff members and a physical setting that's revered as a national monument. It was designed as part of a cocoa mogul's private villa in 1907, and it contains a pair of dining rooms, each elaborately frescoed, gilded, and adorned with the finest Romantic Revival accessories of their day. Come here for an immersion into old-world glamour and protocol, and for food items that are impeccably presented and prepared. The best examples include baby snails nestled inside a potato shell; home-smoked Scottish salmon marinated in port with vermicelli and a lemon-flavored saffron sauce; a casserole of sea bass, turbot, and prawns in a white-wine sauce; and roasted quail stuffed with white sausage and sautéed turnip greens.

In the Pestana Carlton Palace Hotel, Rua Jau 54. ℂ **21/361-56-00.** www.pestana.com. Reservations recommended. Main courses 24€–35€; fixed-price menus 25€–29€. AE, DC, MC, V. Daily 6:30–10:30am, 12:30–3pm, and 7–10:30pm. Tram: 28.

In Santa Apolónia

Bica do Sapato ★★ 🎁 MODERN PORTUGUESE   This hip restaurant has a retro-minimalist decor that's calculated to attract what a local commentator described as "the scene-savvy, design-obsessed jet set." Actor John Malkovich, along with four other partners (the most visible of whom is restaurant pro Fernando Fernandes), transformed what had once functioned as a boat factory into a three-part restaurant that packs in enthusiastic scene-setters virtually every night. A sushi bar is set one floor above ground level, and a "cafeteria" shares its space on street level with the establishment's gastronomic citadel, the restaurant, which is the place we heartily recommend above the other two. Its decor evokes the waiting lounge at a 1960s international airport, but the food takes brilliant liberties with traditional Portuguese cuisine. Stellar examples include seafood broth with grilled red prawns and Asian vegetables; codfish salad in olive oil, served with chickpea ice cream; and veal knuckle browned in olive oil, with garlic, sautéed potatoes, and bay leaves.

Av. Infante Dom Henrique, Armazém (Warehouse) 8, Cais da Pedra à Bica do Sapato. ℭ **21/881-03-20.** www.bicadosapato.com. Reservations recommended. Main courses and platters 21€–32€ in restaurant; 9€–20€ in cafeteria; 6€–50€ in sushi bar. AE, MC, V. Restaurant Tues–Sun 12:30–2:30pm and 8–11:30pm, Mon 8–11:30pm; cafeteria Tues–Sun 12–3:30pm and 7:30pm–1am, Mon 5pm–1am; sushi bar Mon–Sat 7:30pm–1am. Bus: 9, 35, 39, 46, 59, 104, or 105.

In Madragoa

A TRAVESSA ★ 🏠 PORTUGUESE   Your taxi—the best way to reach the place— will deposit you within a warren of narrow, cobble-covered alleyways, and point you toward what was built in the 17th century as a convent. Today, three of the convent's largest rooms, and part of its arcade-ringed courtyard, house this restaurant. At least part of your meal might arrive unannounced from a communal platter wielded by the restaurant's congenial owner, Antonio, who might dish a portion of duck-liver stew, or perhaps scrambled eggs with exotic black trumpet mushrooms, onto your plate as an *amuse-gueule* before your meal. We enjoy the best-prepared John Dory in saffron sauce we've ever had in Portugal. Other options include filet of wild boar in port-wine sauce; escalopes of foie gras with muscatel; and at least four different preparations of steak.

Travessa do Convento das Bernardas 12. ℭ **21/390-20-34.** www.atravessa.com. Reservations recommended. Main courses 17€–29€. AE, DC, MC, V. Mon–Fri 12:30–4pm and 8pm–midnight; Sat 8pm–midnight.

At Parque Das Nações

EXPENSIVE

Sr. Peixe ★ SEAFOOD   This restaurant, "Mr. Fish" in English, lies in the Parque das Nações district at the northern tip of the site for Expo 98, beyond the mammoth Pavilhão Atlântico. Most of the catch of the day, often from the port of Setúbal to the south of Lisbon, is charcoal grilled. Fish is generally sold by weight and can be quite expensive if you opt for the lobster or some other shellfish dishes. You might begin with a fresh octopus salad or else shrimp in garlic. The anchovies and sardines are cooked fresh. The chef also makes an excellent shellfish soup as a starter. A specialty is a simmering pot of *caldeirada,* a fish stew, or else "lobster rice." If you're a carnivore dining out with fish fanciers, you'll have to settle for one of the chef's steaks. Vegetables with the meal are market fresh, and there are some tempting desserts to round out the menu.

Rua da Pimenta, Parque das Nações. ℭ **21/895-58-92.** www.cidiarte.pt/senhorpeixe. Reservations required. Main courses 18€–28€. AE, DC, MC, V. Tues–Sun noon–3:30pm and 7–10:30pm. Metro: Estação do Oriente.

EXPLORING LISBON

M any visitors use Lisbon as a base for exploring nearby sites, but they often neglect the cultural gems tucked away in the Portuguese capital. One reason Lisbon gets overlooked is that visitors don't budget enough time for it. You need at least 5 days to do justice to the city and its environs. In addition, even Lisbon's principal attractions remain relatively unknown, a blessing for travelers tired of fighting their way to overrun sights elsewhere in Europe.

This chapter guides you to the unknown treasures of the capital. If your time is limited, explore the **National Coach Museum,** the **Jerónimos Monastery,** and the **Alfama** and the **Castle of St. George.** At least two art museums, although not of the caliber of Madrid's Prado, merit attention: the **Museu Nacional de Arte Antiga** and the **Museu Calouste Gulbenkian.**

If you have time, visit the **Fundação Ricardo do Espírito Santo Silva** and watch reproductions of antiques being made or books being gold-leafed. You could also spend time seeing the gilded royal galleys at the **Naval Museum,** wandering through the fish market, visiting Lisbon's new **aquarium,** or exploring the arts and crafts of Belém's Folk Art Museum.

SUGGESTED ITINERARIES

For more extended itineraries, not only of Lisbon, but Portugal itself, refer to chapter 3.

If You Have 1 Day

Take a stroll through the Alfama (see "Walking Tour 1," later in this chapter), the most interesting district of Lisbon. Visit the 12th-century **Sé** (cathedral), and take in a view of the city and the river Tagus from the **Miradouro Santa Luzia Belvedere.** Climb up to the **Castelo de São Jorge (St. George's Castle).** Take a taxi or bus to Belém to see the **Mosteiro dos Jerónimos (Jerónimos Monastery)** and the **Torre de Belém.** While in Belém, explore one of the major sights of Lisbon, the **Museu Nacional dos Coches (National Coach Museum).**

Up, Up & Away

For a splendid rooftop view of Lisbon, take the **Santa Justa elevator,** on Rua de Santa Justa. The ornate concoction was built by a Portuguese engineer, Raul Mesnier de Ponsard, born to French immigrants in Porto in 1849. The elevator goes from Rua Áurea, in the center of the shopping district near Rossio Square, to the panoramic viewing platform. It operates daily from 9am to 9pm. A ticket costs 1.45€, and children under 4 ride free (© **21/361-30-00;** www.carris.pt). Metro: Rossio.

If You Have 2 Days

On Day 2, head for **Sintra** (p. 163), the single most visited sight in the environs of Lisbon—Byron called it "glorious Eden." You can spend the day exploring the castle and other palaces in the stunning area. Try at least to visit the **Palácio Nacional de Sintra** and the **Palácio Nacional da Pena.** Return to Lisbon for a night at a fado cafe.

If You Have 3 Days

On Day 3, spend a morning at the **Museu Calouste Gulbenkian,** one of Europe's artistic treasure-troves. Have lunch in the Bairro Alto. In the afternoon, see the **Fundação Ricardo do Espírito Santo Silva (Museum of Decorative Art)** and the **Museu Nacional de Arte Antiga (National Museum of Ancient Art).** At day's end, wander through Parque Eduardo VII.

If You Have 4 Days

On Day 4, take an excursion from Lisbon. (For convenience, consider an organized tour—see listings later in this chapter.) Visit the fishing village of **Nazaré** and the walled city of **Óbidos.** Those interested in Roman Catholic sights might also want to include a visit to the shrine at **Fátima,** although seeing this on the same day would be hectic. See chapter 8.

If You Have 5 Days

On the final day, slow your pace a bit with a morning at the beach at **Estoril** on Portugal's Costa do Sol. Then continue along the coast to **Cascais** (both in chapter 6) for lunch. After lunch, wander around the old fishing village, now a major resort. Go to **Guincho,** 6.5km (4 miles) along the coast from Cascais, which is near the westernmost point on the European continent and has panoramic views.

THE TOP ATTRACTIONS: THE ALFAMA, BELÉM & MUSEUMS

The Lisbon of bygone days lives on in the **Alfama ★★**, the most emblematic quarter of the city. The wall built by the Visigoths and incorporated into some of the old houses is a reminder of its ancient past. In east Lisbon, the Alfama was the Saracen sector centuries before its conquest by the Christians.

The devastating 1755 earthquake spared some of the buildings here, and the Alfama has retained much of its original charm. You'll see narrow cobblestone streets, cages of canaries, strings of garlic and pepper adorning old taverns, and street markets. Houses are so close together that in many places it's impossible to stretch your arms wide. The poet Frederico de Brito dramatically expressed that proximity: "Your house is so close to mine! In the starry night's bliss, to exchange a tender kiss, our lips easily meet, high across the narrow street."

Stevedores, fishmongers, and sailors still occupy the Alfama. In the street markets, you can wander in a maze of brightly colored vegetables from the countryside, bananas from Madeira, pineapples from the Azores, and assorted fish. Armies of cats prowl in search of rats. Occasionally, a black-shawled widow, stooping over a brazier, grilling sardines in front of her house, will toss a fish head to a passing feline.

Aristocrats once lived in the Alfama; a handful still do, but their memory is perpetuated mostly by the noble coats of arms fading on the fronts of some 16th-century houses. The best-known aristocratic mansion is the one formerly occupied by the count of Arcos, the last viceroy of Brazil. Constructed in the 16th century and spared, in part, from the earthquake, it lies on Largo da Salvador.

As you explore, you'll be rewarded with a perspective of the contrasting styles of the Alfama, from a simple tile-roofed fishmonger's abode to a festively decorated baroque church. One of the best views is from the belvedere of **Largo das Portas do Sol,** near the Museum of Decorative Art. It's a balcony opening onto the sea, overlooking the typical houses as they sweep down to the Tagus.

One of the oldest churches in Lisbon is **Santo Estêvão (St. Stephen),** on Largo de Santo Estêvão, originally constructed in the 13th century. The present marble structure dates from the 1700s. One of the most dramatic **views ★** of the Alfama is possible from the southwestern corner of Largo de Santo Estêvão. Also of medieval origin is the **Church of São Miguel (St. Michael),** on Largo de São Miguel, deep in the Alfama on a palm-tree-shaded square. Reconstructed after the 1755 earthquake, the interior is richly decorated with 18th-century gilt and *trompe l'oeil* walls.

Rua da Judiaria is another poignant reminder of the past. It was settled largely by Jewish refugees fleeing Spain to escape the Inquisition.

For specific routes through the Alfama, refer to the walking tour later in this chapter. The Alfama is best explored by day; it can be dangerous to wander around the area at night, when the neighborhood's spirit changes. Although the Bairro Alto is the city's traditional fado quarter, the cafes of the Alfama also reverberate with these nostalgic sounds until the early morning hours.

Castelo de São Jorge ★★ Locals speak of Saint George's Castle as the cradle of their city, and it might have been where the Portuguese capital began. Its occupation is believed to have predated the Romans—the hilltop was used as a fortress to guard the Tagus and its settlement below. Beginning in the 5th century A.D., the site was a Visigothic fortification; it fell to the Saracens in the early 8th century. Many of the existing walls were erected during the centuries of Moorish domination. The Moors held power until 1147, the year Afonso Henríques chased them out and extended his kingdom south. Even before Lisbon became the capital of the newly emerging nation, the site was used as a royal palace.

For the finest **view ★★** of the Tagus and the Alfama, walk the esplanades and climb the ramparts of the old castle. The castle's name commemorates an Anglo-Portuguese pact dating from as early as 1371. (George is the patron saint of England.)

Portugal and England have been traditional allies, although their relationship was strained in 1961, when India, a member of the Commonwealth of Nations, seized the Portuguese overseas territories of Goa, Diu, and Damão.

Huddling close to the protection of the moated castle is a sector that appears almost medieval. At the entrance, visitors pause at the Castle Belvedere. The Portuguese refer to this spot as their "ancient window." It overlooks the Alfama, the mountains of Monsanto and Sintra, Ponte do 25 de Abril, Praça do Comércio, and the tile roofs of the Portuguese capital. In the square stands a heroic statue—sword in one hand, shield in the other—of the first king, Afonso Henríques.

Rua da Costa do Castelo. © **21/880-06-20.** www.castelodesaojorge.pt. Admission 7€ adults, free for children under 10. Mar–Oct daily 9am–9pm; Nov–Feb daily 9am–6pm. Bus: 37. Tram: 12 or 28.

Igreja de Santo António   St. Anthony of Padua, an itinerant Franciscan monk who became the patron saint of Portugal, was born in 1195 in a house that once stood here. The 1755 earthquake destroyed the original church, and Mateus Vicente de Oliveira designed the present building in 1812.

In the crypt, a guide will show you the spot where the saint was reputedly born. (He's buried in Padua, Italy.) The devout come to this little church to light candles under his picture. He's known as a protector of young brides and has a special connection with the children of Lisbon. To raise money to erect the altar at the church, the children of the Alfama built miniature altars with a representation of the patron saint. June 12 is St. Anthony's Day, a time of merrymaking, heavy eating, and drinking. In the morning there are street fires and singing, followed by St. Anthony's Feast on the following day.

Largo de Santo António de Sé. © **21/886-91-45.** Admission 1.20€ adults, free for children. Tues–Sun 10am–1pm and 2–6pm. Metro: Rossio. Bus: 37. Tram 28.

Sé de Lisboa ★   Even official tourist brochures admit that this cathedral is not very rich. Characterized by twin towers flanking its entrance, it represents an architectural wedding of Romanesque and Gothic style. The facade is severe enough to resemble a medieval fortress. At one point, the Saracens reportedly used the site of the present Sé as a mosque. When the city was captured early in the 12th century by Christian crusaders, led by Portugal's first king, Afonso Henríques, the structure was rebuilt. The Sé then became the first church in Lisbon. The earthquakes of 1344 and 1755 damaged the structure.

Beyond the rough exterior are many treasures, including the font where St. Anthony of Padua is said to have been christened in 1195. A notable feature is the 14th-century Gothic chapel of Bartolomeu Joanes. Other items of interest are a crib by Machado de Castro (the 18th-c. Portuguese sculptor responsible for the equestrian statue on Praça do Comércio), the 14th-century sarcophagus of Lopo Fernandes Pacheco, and the original nave and aisles.

A visit to the sacristy and cloister requires a guide. The cloister, built in the 14th century by King Dinis, is of ogival construction, with garlands, a **Romanesque wrought-iron grill ★**, and tombs with inscription stones. In the sacristy are marbles, relics, valuable images, and pieces of ecclesiastical treasure from the 15th and 16th centuries. In the morning, the stained-glass reflections on the floor evoke a Monet painting.

Largo da Sé. © **21/886-67-52.** Admission: Cathedral free; cloister 2.50€. Daily 9am–7pm; holidays 9am–5pm. Tram: 28 (Graça). Bus: 37.

Belém ★★

At Belém, where the Tagus (*Tejo* in Portuguese) meets the sea, the Portuguese cara-vels that charted the areas unknown to the Western world set out: Vasco da Gama to India, Ferdinand Magellan to circumnavigate the globe, and Bartolomeu Dias to round the Cape of Good Hope.

Belém emerged from the Restelo, the point of land from which the ships set sail across the so-called Sea of Darkness. The district flourished as riches, especially spices, poured into Portugal. Great monuments, including the **Tower of Belém** and **Jerónimos Monastery,** were built and embellished in the Manueline style.

In time, the royal family established a summer palace here. Much of the district's character emerged when wealthy Lisboans began moving out of the city center and building town houses here. For many years, Belém was a separate municipality. Even-tually it was incorporated into Lisbon as a parish. Nowadays it's a magnet for visitors to its many museums. For most visitors, the primary sight is the Torre de Belém.

To reach the attractions previewed below, board tram no. 15 leaving from Praça do Comércio in the center of Lisbon (trip time: 15 min.). Bus no. 28 or 43 departs from Praça da Figueira, again taking 15 minutes. You can also take a suburban train leaving from Estação Cais do Sodré, taking only 10 minutes. All these fares are 1.40€. If you selected the tram or bus, get off at the stop marked Mosteiro dos Jerónimos, which is the next station after the stop called Belém. Once at the train station, walk (with care) across the tracks and then cross the street turning to the left. Mosteiro dos Jerónimos is to the right, reached after a walk through public gardens. Padrão dos Descobrimentos fronts the water. It lies across the highway to your left (take the underpass).

Centro Cultural de Belém ★★

This center occasionally functions as a show-case for temporary exhibitions of Portuguese art. Although it is mostly devoted to conventions, the center also functions at least part of the time as a concert hall, a temporary art museum, or a catchall venue. Events staged here, widely publicized in local newspapers, might include classical concerts and film festivals, in addition to industrial conventions. An inexpensive cafeteria and a handful of shops are on the premises. The building was constructed in the early 1990s as a convention hall for the meetings that brought Portugal membership in the European Union. The center is also the home of the Museu Colecção Berardo (see below).

Praça do Império. © **21/361-24-00.** www.ccb.pt. Free admission to center; 4€ adults, 2€ children for temporary exhibitions. Daily 10am–7pm.

Mosteiro dos Jerónimos ★★

In an expansive mood, Manuel I, the Fortunate, ordered this monastery built to commemorate Vasco da Gama's voyage to India and to give thanks to the Virgin Mary for its success. Manueline, the style of architecture that bears the king's name, combines flamboyant Gothic and Moorish influences with elements of the nascent Renaissance. Prince Henry the Navigator originally built a small chapel dedicated to St. Mary on this spot. Today this former chapel is the Gothic and Renaissance **Igreja de Santa Maria ★★**, marked by a statue of Henry. The church is known for its deeply carved stonework depicting such scenes as the life of St. Jerome. The church's interior is rich in beautiful stonework, particularly evocative in its **network vaulting ★** over the nave and aisles.

The west door of the church leads to the **Cloisters ★★★**, which represent the apex of Manueline art. The stone sculpture here is fantastically intricate. The two-story cloisters have groined vaulting on their ground level. The recessed upper floor

Belém Attractions

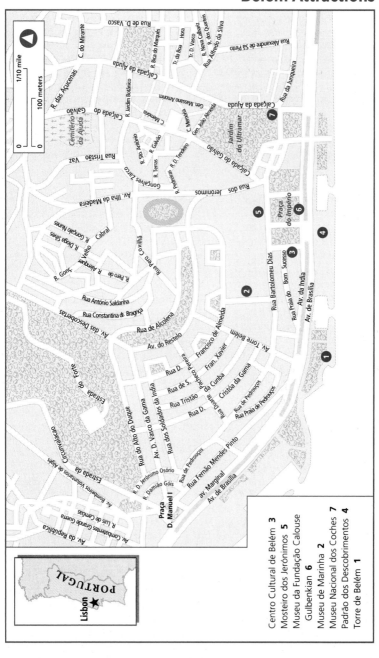

Centro Cultural de Belém **3**
Mosteiro dos Jerónimos **5**
Museu da Fundação Calouse
  Gulbenkian **6**
Museu de Marinha **2**
Museu Nacional dos Coches **7**
Padrão dos Descobrimentos **4**
Torre de Belém **1**

The Famous Custard Cream Tarts of Belém

While you're in Belém visiting the Mosteiro dos Jerónimos, drop in at **Pasteis de Belém,** Rua de Belém 84 (✆ 21/363-74-23), to sample the best custard cream tart you are likely to taste in your life. They come with a slightly burnt crust on top and a flaky edge, over which cinnamon is sprinkled. You can devour them on the spot or take them away with you in nicely packaged tubes.

When the monasteries were closed in 1834, the clergy had to eat so they started selling these sweet pastries. They were so tasty, they attracted visitors from Lisbon who savored them. Over the years, the recipe for these pastries has been passed on to the master confectioners who handcraft them in "a secret room." The recipe has come down unchanged. The pastry shop is open daily from 8am to 11pm.

is not as exuberant but is more delicate and lacelike in character. The monastery was founded in 1502, partially financed by the spice trade that grew following the discovery of the route to India. The 1755 earthquake damaged but didn't destroy the monastery. It has undergone extensive restoration, some of it ill-conceived.

The church encloses a trio of naves noted for their fragile-looking pillars. Some of the ceilings, like those in the monks' refectory, have a ribbed barrel vault. The "palm tree" in the sacristy is also exceptional.

Many of the greatest figures in Portuguese history are said to be entombed at the monastery; the most famous is Vasco da Gama. The Portuguese also maintain that Luís Vaz de Camões, author of the epic *Os Lusíadas* (The Lusiads), in which he glorified the triumphs of his compatriots, is buried here. Both tombs rest on the backs of lions. Camões's epic poetry is said to have inspired a young Portuguese king, Sebastião, to dreams of glory. The foolish king—devoutly, even fanatically, religious—was killed at Alcácer-Kibir, Morocco, in a 1578 crusade against the Muslims. Those refusing to believe that the king was dead formed a cult known as Sebastianism; it rose to minor influence, and four men tried to assert their claim to the Portuguese throne. Each maintained steadfastly, even to death, that he was King Sebastião. Sebastião's remains were reputedly entombed in a 16th-century marble shrine built in the Mannerist style. The romantic poet Herculano (1800–54) is also buried at Jerónimos, as is the famed poet Fernando Pessoa.

Praça do Império. ✆ **21/362-00-34.** www.mosteirojeronimos.pt. Admission: Church free; cloisters 7€ adults, free for those under 14. Those over 65 pay 3.50€. May-Sept Tues-Sun 10am-6pm; Oct-Apr Tues-Sun 10am-5pm.

Museu Colecção Berardo ★★   Housed in the Belém Cultural Center (see above), this is Portugal's most avant-garde showcase of modern art. It is a major treasure-trove, imbued with the works of modern masters such as Pablo Picasso, Salvador Dalí, Max Ernst, Francis Bacon, and Jackson Pollock. The museum displays some 1,000 works of art by rotation. You're never quite sure what's going to be on display at the time of your visit.

The collection is strong in European and American art, encompassing the 20th century and the beginning of the 21st century. In addition to modern art, the museum also displays one of the largest private collections of ceramic tiles, spanning some 500 years of what would become the most quintessential Portuguese art form.

Attractions: The Alfama, Belém & Museums

EXPLORING LISBON

There is still a growing collection of more than 400 pieces of beautiful and exemplary Art Deco furniture and interior decorative objects. The surprise of the museum is its unusual collection of Victorian and Edwardian chamber pots.

Praça do Império. © **21/361-28-78.** www.museuberardo.com. Free admission (subject to change). Mon–Fri 10am–6:30pm; Sat 10am–9:30pm.

Museu de Marinha (Maritime Museum) ★★ The Maritime Museum, one of the best in Europe, evokes the glory that characterized Portugal's domination of the high seas. Appropriately, it's installed in the west wing of the Mosteiro dos Jerónimos. These royal galleys re-create an age of opulence that never shied away from excess. Dragons' heads drip with gilt; sea monsters coil with abandon. Assembling a large crew was no problem for kings and queens in those days. Queen Maria I ordered a magnificent galley built for the 1785 marriage of her son and successor, Crown Prince João, to the Spanish Princess Carlota Joaquina Bourbon. Eighty dummy oarsmen, elaborately attired in scarlet-and-mustard-colored waistcoats, represent the crew.

The museum contains hundreds of models of 15th- to 19th-century sailing ships, 20th-century warships, merchant marine vessels, fishing boats, river craft, and pleasure boats. In a section devoted to the East is a pearl-inlaid replica of a dragon boat used in maritime and fluvial corteges. A full range of Portuguese naval uniforms is on display, from one worn at a Mozambique military outpost in 1896 to a uniform worn as recently as 1961. In a special room is a model of the queen's stateroom on the royal yacht of Carlos I, the Bragança king who was assassinated at Praça do Comércio in 1908. It was on this craft that his son, Manuel II; his wife; and the queen mother, Amélia, escaped to Gibraltar following the collapse of the Portuguese monarchy in 1910. The Maritime Museum also honors some early Portuguese aviators.

Praça do Império. © **21/362-00-19.** http://museu.marinha.pt. Admission 4€ adults, 2€ students and children ages 6–17, free for seniors 65 and over and children under 5. May–Sept Tues–Sun 10am–6pm; Oct–Apr Tues–Sun 10am–5pm; closed holidays.

Museu Nacional dos Coches (National Coach Museum) ★★ The most visited attraction in Lisbon, the National Coach Museum is the finest of its type in the world. Founded by Amélia, wife of Carlos I, it's housed in a former 18th-century riding academy connected to the Belém Royal Palace. The coaches stand in a former horse ring; most date from the 17th to the 19th centuries. Drawing the most interest is a trio of opulently gilded baroque carriages used by the Portuguese ambassador to the Vatican at the time of Pope Clement XI (1716). Also on display is a 17th-century coach in which the Spanish Habsburg king, Phillip II, journeyed from Madrid to Lisbon to see his new possession.

Praça de Afonso de Albuquerque. © **21/361-08-50.** http://en.museudoscoches.pt. Admission 5€, 2.50€ ages 14–25, free for children under 14. Tues–Sun 10am–6pm; closed holidays. Bus: 28, 714, 727, 729, or 751.

Padrão dos Descobrimentos ★ Like the prow of a caravel from the Age of Discovery, the Monument to the Discoveries stands on the Tagus, looking ready to strike out across the Sea of Darkness. Notable explorers, chiefly Vasco da Gama, are immortalized in stone along the ramps.

At the point where the two ramps meet is a representation of Henry the Navigator, whose genius opened up new worlds. The memorial was unveiled in 1960, and one of the stone figures is that of a kneeling Philippa of Lancaster, Henry's English mother. Other figures in the frieze symbolize the crusaders (represented by a man

Attractions: The Alfama, Belém & Museums

holding a flag with a cross), navigators, monks, cartographers, and cosmographers. At the top of the prow is the coat of arms of Portugal at the time of Manuel the Fortunate. On the floor in front of the memorial lies a map of the world in multicolored marble, with the dates of the discoveries set in metal.

Praça da Boa Esperança, Av. de Brasília. ℂ **21/303-19-50.** www.padraodescobrimentos.egeac.pt. Admission 2.50€. May–Sept Tues–Sun 10am–7pm; Oct–Apr Tues–Sun 10am–6pm.

Torre de Belém ★★   The quadrangular Tower of Belém is a monument to Portugal's Age of Discovery. Erected between 1515 and 1520, the Manueline-style tower is Portugal's classic landmark and often serves as a symbol of the country. A monument to Portugal's great military and naval past, the tower stands on or near the spot where the caravels once set out across the sea.

Its architect, Francisco de Arruda, blended Gothic and Moorish elements, using such architectural details as twisting ropes carved of stone. The coat of arms of Manuel I rests above the loggia, and balconies grace three sides of the monument. Along the balustrade of the loggias, stone crosses represent the Portuguese crusaders.

The richness of the facade fades once you cross the drawbridge and enter the Renaissance-style doorway. Gothic severity reigns. A few antiques can be seen, including a 16th-century throne graced with finials and an inset paneled with pierced Gothic tracery. If you scale the steps leading to the ramparts, you'll be rewarded with a panorama of boats along the Tagus and pastel-washed, tile-roofed old villas in the hills beyond.

Facing the Tower of Belém is a monument commemorating the first Portuguese to cross the Atlantic by airplane (not nonstop). The date was March 30, 1922, and the flight took pilot Gago Coutinho and navigator Sacadura Cabral from Lisbon to Rio de Janeiro.

At the center of Praça do Império at Belém is the Fonte Luminosa (the Luminous Fountain). The patterns of the water jets, estimated at more than 70 original designs, make an evening show lasting nearly an hour.

Praça do Império, Av. de Brasília. ℂ **21/362-00-34.** www.mosteirojeronimos.pt. Admission 5€ adults, 2€ ages 15–25 years, free for children under 14 and for seniors 65 and over; free for all Sun until 2pm. Oct–Apr Tues–Sun 10am–5pm; May–Sept Tues–Sun 10am–6pm.

Two More Top Museums

Most major Lisbon museums are at Belém, but two major attractions are in the city proper: the National Art Gallery and the Gulbenkian Center for Arts and Culture.

Museu Calouste Gulbenkian ★★★   Opened in 1969, this museum, part of the Fundação Calouste Gulbenkian, houses what one critic called one of the world's finest private art collections. It belonged to the Armenian oil tycoon Calouste Gulbenkian, who died in 1955. The modern, multimillion-dollar center is in a former private estate that belonged to the count of Vilalva.

The places below provide a view of Lisbon not often seen by the casual visitors passing through the city.

The Market   The big market of **Ribeira Nova** (☎ 21/324-49-80; www.espacoribeira.pt) is as close as you can get to the heart of Lisbon. Behind the Cais do Sodré train station, an enormous roof shelters a collection of stalls offering the produce used in Lisbon's fine restaurants. Foodstuffs arrive each morning in wicker baskets bulging with oversize carrots, cabbages big enough to be shrubbery, and stalks of bananas. Some of the freshly plucked produce arrives by donkey, some by truck, and some balanced on the heads of Lisboan women in the Mediterranean fashion. The rich soil produces the juiciest peaches and the most aromatic tomatoes.

At the market, women festively clad in voluminous skirts and calico aprons preside over the mounds of vegetables, fruit, and fish. On cue, the vendors begin howling about the value of their wares, stopping only to pose for an occasional snapshot. Fishing boats dock at dawn with their catch. The fishermen deposit the cod, squid, bass, hake, and swordfish on long marble counters. The *varinas* (fishwives) balance wicker baskets of the fresh catch on their heads and climb the cobblestone streets of the Alfama or the Bairro Alto to sell fish from door to door. It's open Monday to Saturday from 5am to 2pm. Bus: 14, 32, or 40. Tram: 15 or 28.

Estufa Fria (The Greenhouse)   The Estufa Fria (☎ 21/388-22-78) is in the handsome Parque Eduardo VII, named after Queen Victoria's son to commemorate his three trips to Lisbon. Against a background of streams and rocks, tropical plants grow in such profusion that the place resembles a rainforest. The park lies at the top of Avenida da Liberdade, crowned by a statue of the Marquês de Pombal with his "house pet," a lion. There's a 1.20€ fee to enter the greenhouse, which is usually open daily 9am to 5:30pm. *Warning:* At press time it was closed for renovations but should be open at the time of your visit. Metro: Parque or Marquês de Pombal. Bus: 2, 11, 12, 27, 32, 38, 44, 45, or 83.

Cemitério dos Ingleses (British Cemetery)   The British Cemetery lies up Rua da Estrela at one end of the Estrela Gardens. It's famous as the burial place of Henry Fielding, the novelist and dramatist who's best known for *Tom Jones.* Fielding went to Lisbon in 1754 to try to recover his health; his posthumous tract *Journal of a Voyage to Lisbon* tells the story of that trip. He reached Lisbon in August and died 2 months later. A monument honoring him was erected in 1830. Open daily 8am to 2pm; ring the bell for entry. Bus: 9, 20, 27, or 38.

Jardim Botânico (Botanical Garden) ★   On Rua da Escola Politécnica 58, Principe Real (no phone), near the Bairro Alto, this garden sprawls over 4 hectares (10 acres) that were laid out in the mid-19th century, and was heralded a century ago as the best botanical garden in southern Europe. Today, somewhat dusty and somewhat undermaintained, it's still Lisbon's most beautiful botanical garden. It's open daily from 9am to 8pm (till 6pm Oct–Apr). Admission is 1.50€ and free for children under 14. It's free to all Sunday until 2pm. Metro: Rato.

5

EXPLORING LISBON

Attractions: The Alfama, Belém & Museums

The collection covers Egyptian, Greek, and Roman antiquities; a remarkable assemblage of Islamic art, including ceramics and textiles from Turkey and Persia; Syrian glass, books, bindings, and miniatures; and Chinese vases, Japanese prints, and lacquerware. The European displays include **medieval illuminated manuscripts and** ivories ★, 15th- to 19th-century paintings and sculpture, Renaissance tapestries and medals, important collections of 18th-century French decorative works, French Impressionist paintings, René Lalique jewelry, and glassware.

In a move requiring great skill in negotiation, Gulbenkian managed to buy art from the Hermitage in St. Petersburg. Among his most notable acquisitions are two Rembrandts: *Portrait of an Old Man* and *Alexander the Great.* Two other well-known paintings are *Portrait of Hélène Fourment,* by Peter Paul Rubens, and *Portrait of Madame Claude Monet,* by Pierre-Auguste Renoir. In addition, we suggest that you seek out Mary Cassatt's *The Stocking.* The French sculptor Jean-Antoine Houdon is represented by a statue of Diana. Silver made by François-Thomas Germain, once used by Catherine the Great, is also here, as is one piece by Thomas Germain, the father.

As a cultural center, the Gulbenkian Foundation sponsors plays, films, ballets, and concerts, as well as a rotating exhibition of works by leading modern Portuguese and foreign artists.

Av. de Berna 45. ℂ **21/782-30-00.** www.museu.gulbenkian.pt. Admission 4€; free for seniors 65 and over, students, and teachers; free for all Sun. Tues–Sun 10am–5:45pm. Metro: Sebastião or Praça de Espanha. Bus: 16, 26, 31, 41, 46, or 56.

Museu Nacional de Arte Antiga ★★★ The National Museum of Ancient Art houses the country's greatest collection of paintings. It occupies two connected buildings—a 17th-century palace and an added edifice that was built on the site of the old Carmelite Convent of Santo Alberto. The convent's chapel was preserved and is a good example of the integration of ornamental arts, with gilded carved wood, glazed tiles, and sculpture of the 17th and 18th centuries.

The museum has many notable paintings, including the **polyptych ★★★** from St. Vincent's monastery attributed to Nuno Gonçalves between 1460 and 1470. There are 60 portraits of leading figures of Portuguese history. Other outstanding works are Hieronymus Bosch's triptych *The Temptation of St. Anthony* ★★★, Hans Memling's *Mother and Child,* Albrecht Dürer's *St. Jerome,* and paintings by Velázquez, Poussin, and Courbet. Especially noteworthy is the *12 Apostles,* by Zurbarán. Paintings from the 15th through the 19th centuries trace the development of Portuguese art.

The museum also exhibits a remarkable collection of gold- and silversmiths' works, both Portuguese and foreign. Among these is a cross from Alcobaça and the monstrance of Belém, constructed with the first gold brought from India by Vasco da Gama. Another exceptional example is the 18th-century French silver tableware ordered by José I. Diverse objects from Benin, India, Persia, China, and Japan were culled from the proceeds of Portuguese expansion overseas. Two excellent pairs of **screens ★★** depict the Portuguese relationship with Japan in the 17th century. Flemish tapestries, a rich assemblage of church vestments, Italian polychrome ceramics, and sculptures are also on display.

Rua das Janelas Verdes 95. ℂ **21/391-28-00.** www.mnarteantiga-ipmuseus.pt. Admission 5€ adults, free for students and children under 14. Tues 2–6pm; Wed–Sun 10am–6pm. Tram: 15 or 18. Bus: 27, 49, 51, or 60.

MORE ATTRACTIONS
The Bairro Alto ★★

Like the Alfama, the Bairro Alto (Upper City) preserves the characteristics of the Lisbon of yore. In location and population, it once was the heart of the city. Many of

The Bairro Alto

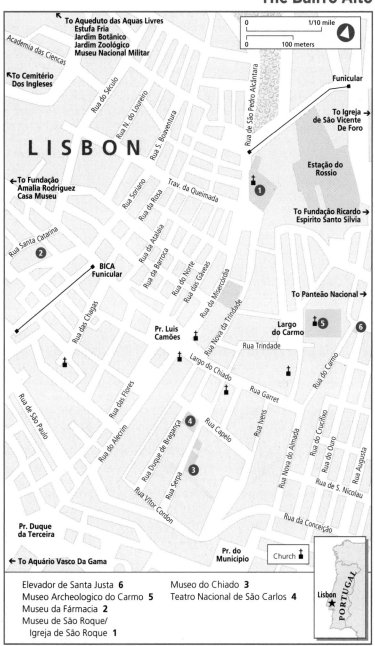

To Aqueduto das Aquas Livres
Estufa Fria
Jardim Botãnico
Jardim Zoológico
Museu Nacional Militar

Academia das Ciencas

To Cemitério
Dos Ingleses

Rua do Século

Rua N. do Loureiro

Rua de São Pedro Alcântara

Funicular

To Igreja →
de Sâo Vicente
De Foro

LISBON

Rua S. Boaventura

← To Fundação
Amalia Rodriguez
Casa Museu

Estação do
Rossio

Rua Soriano

Trav. da Queimada

Rua da Rosa

To Fundação Ricardo →
Espirito Santo Silvia

Rua Santa Catarina

Rua da Atalaia

Rua da Baroca

Rua do Norte

Rua das Gaveas

Rua da Misercórdia

To Panteão Nacional →

BICA
Funicular

Rua das Chagas

Rua Nova da Trindade

Largo
do Carmo

Rua do Carmo

Pr. Luis
Camões

Rua Trindade

Largo do Chiado

Rua Garret

Rua das Flores

Rua de São Paulo

Rua do Alecrim

Rua Duque de Bragança

Rua Capelo

Rua Ivens

Rua Nova da Almada

Rua do Crucifixo

Rua do Ouro

Rua Augusta

Museo do Chiado 3

Rua Serpa

Rua Vitor Cordon

Rua de S. Nicolau

Rua da Conceição

Pr. Duque
da Terceira

Pr. do
Município

Church †

← To Aquário Vasco Da Gama

Elevador de Santa Justa 6
Museo Archeologico do Carmo 5
Museu da Fármacia 2
Museu de São Roque/
   Igreja de São Roque 1

Museo do Chiado 3
Teatro Nacional de São Carlos 4

Lisbon

PORTUGAL

0   1/10 mile
0   100 meters

its buildings survived the 1755 earthquake. Today it's home to some of the finest fado cafes in Lisbon, making it a center of nightlife. It's also a fascinating place to visit during the day, when its charming, narrow cobblestone streets and alleys lined with ancient buildings can be appreciated in the warm light coming off the sea.

Originally called Vila Nova de Andrade, the area was started in 1513 when the Andrade family bought part of the huge Santa Catarina and then sold the land as construction plots. Early buyers were carpenters, merchants, and ship caulkers. Some of them immediately resold their land to aristocrats, and little by little noble families moved to the quarter. The Jesuits followed, moving from their modest College of Mouraria to new headquarters at the Monastery of São Roque, where the *Misericórdia* (social assistance to the poor) of Lisbon proceeds today. The Bairro Alto gradually became a working-class section. Today the quarter is also the domain of journalists—most of the big newspapers' plants are here. Other writers and artists have been drawn here to live and work, attracted by the ambience and the good local cuisine.

This area is resoundingly colorful. From the windows and balconies, streamers of laundry hang out to dry, and canaries, parrots, parakeets, and other birds sing in their cages. In the morning, housewives hit the food markets, following the cries of the *varinas* (fishmongers) and other vendors. Women lounge in doorways or lean on windowsills to watch the world go by. But everything comes most alive at night, when the area lures visitors and natives with its fado spots, restaurants, dance clubs, and small bars (called *tascas*).

Churches

"If you want to see all of the churches of Lisbon, you'd better be prepared to stay here for a few months," a guide once told us. True enough, the string of churches seems endless. What follows is a selection of the most interesting.

Igreja da São Vicente de Fora   In this Renaissance church, the greatest names and some forgotten wives of the House of Bragança were laid to rest. It's more like a pantheon than a church. Originally a 12th-century convent, the church was erected between 1582 and 1627. At that time, it lay outside the walls of Lisbon (hence the name St. Vincent Outside the Walls). On the morning of the 1755 earthquake, the cupola fell in.

The Braganças assumed power in 1640 and ruled until 1910, when the Portuguese monarchy collapsed and Manuel II and the queen mother, Amélia, fled to England. Manuel II died in 1932, and his body was returned to Portugal for burial. Amélia, the last queen of Portugal, died in 1951 and is entombed here, as are her husband, Carlos I (the painter king), and her son, Prince Luís Felipe; both were killed by an assassin at Praça do Comércio in 1908.

Aside from the royal tombs, one of the most important reasons for visiting St. Vincent is to see its spectacular tiles, some of which illustrate the fables of La Fontaine. While we suspect that no one has officially counted them, their number is placed at one million. Look for the curious ivory statue of Jesus, carved in the former Portuguese province of Goa in the 18th century.

Largo de São Vicente. ✆ **21/882-44-00.** Free admission. Mon–Sat 9am–6pm; Sun 9am–12:30pm and 3–5pm. Tram: 28. Bus: 12 or 28.

Panteão Nacional   When a builder starts to work on a Portuguese house, the owner will often say, "Don't take as long as St. Engrácia." Construction on this Portuguese baroque church, Igreja de Santa Engrácia, began in 1682; it resisted the 1755 earthquake but wasn't completed until 1966. The building, with its four square towers, is pristine and cold, and the state has fittingly turned it into a neoclassical National Pantheon containing memorial tombs to heads of state.

Memorials honor Henry the Navigator; Luís Vaz de Camões, the country's greatest poet; Pedro Álvares Cabral, "discoverer" of Brazil; Afonso de Albuquerque, viceroy of India; Nuno Álvares Pereira, warrior and saint; and, of course, Vasco da Gama. Entombed in the National Pantheon are presidents of Portugal and several writers: Almeida Garrett, the 19th-century literary figure; João de Deus, a lyric poet; and Guerra Junqueiro, also a poet.

Ask the guards to take you to the terrace for a beautiful view of the river. A visit to the pantheon can be combined with a shopping trip to the Flea Market (walk down Campo de Santa Clara, heading toward the river).

Largo de Santa Clara. ✆ **21/885-48-20.** Admission 3€ adults, 1.50€ ages 15–25, free for children under 14; free for all Sun after 2pm. Tues–Sun 10am–5pm; closed holidays. Tram: 28. Bus: 9, 39, or 46.

Museums & an Aquarium

Centro de Arte Moderna ★   Around the corner from the entrance to the Calouste Gulbenkian Museum (p. 110), the Center of Modern Art is Lisbon's first major permanent exhibition center of modern Portuguese art. The center shares parklike grounds with the Gulbenkian Foundation and was, like the Gulbenkian Museum, a legacy of the late Armenian oil magnate.

It's housed in a British-designed complex of clean lines and dramatically proportioned geometric forms with a Henry Moore sculpture in front. The museum owns some 10,000 items, including the works of such modern Portuguese artists as Souza-Cardoso, Almada, Paula Rego, João Cutileiro, Costa Pinheiro, and Vieira da Silva.

Rua Dr. Nicolau de Bettencourt. ✆ **21/782-34-74.** www.camjap.gulbenkian.org. Admission 4€ adults, free for children and students; free for all Sun. Tues–Sun 10am–6pm. Metro: Praça d'Espanha or Sao Sebastião. Bus: 16, 18, 26, 31, 41, 42, 46, or 56.

Fundação Amália Rodriguez Casa Museu 🎐   Fado diva Amália Rodriguez (1920–99) is credited more than any other singer in history with touching the nerve endings of greater numbers of Portuguese than any other popular singer in the nation's history. Born in Lisbon into a large and very poor family, her musical expressions of *saudade* (nostalgia provoked by a sense of loss) have been defined as the musical expression of the Portuguese soul. Hers is the music most likely to be heard in traditional bars, and hers is the voice most immediately recognizable to most Portuguese. After her death, which was considered a national tragedy, her body was buried with pomp and circumstance in the National Pantheon alongside the country's most prominent statesmen and writers. Today, on the street where she used to live (Rua São Bento), you'll see hundreds of stencils proclaiming it as Rua Amália.

Her ocher-color town house, not far from the Portuguese Parliament, is the headquarters of a charitable foundation established in her name. In July 2001, it was reconfigured as a testimonial to her life and accomplishments, and instantly became a pilgrimage site for her fans, evoking huge controversies about how she would (and should) be remembered within Portuguese history. You'll be issued a number when you first arrive and then be escorted on a multilingual (Portuguese, French, and English) guided tour of what used to be her home. Come here for a view of videotapes of some of her performances, especially those from the 1950s and 1960s. Tours last about 30 minutes each.

Rua de São Bento 193. ✆ **21/397-18-96.** Admission 5€ per person, free for children under 5. Tues–Sun 10am–1pm and 2–6pm. Metro: Rato. Bus: 6, 49, or 74.

Fundação Ricardo do Espírito Santo Silva ★★ 🏛   Few other sites in Lisbon offer as comprehensive an overview of the 18th-century Portuguese aesthetic as this one. The setting is the 17th-century Azurara Palace, which was acquired in 1947 by the museum's namesake and benefactor. In 1953, his collection was bequeathed to a private foundation that, after his death, continued to amass hundreds of the country's finest antiques, art objects, silverware, and paintings. These are proudly displayed over four floors of the stately looking building within a labyrinth of rooms and hallways that evoke 18th-century life in a hyper-upscale home. A bookstore and coffee shop are on the premises, and a battalion of attentive guards protect the lavish art objects inside as if they were their own. Anyone interested in the decorative arts in general and the Portuguese Empire in particular will find this collection fascinating.

Largo das Portas do Sol 2. ✆ **21/881-46-00.** www.fress.pt. Admission 4€ adults, 2€ seniors, free for children under 12. Tues–Sun 10am–5pm. Tram: 12 or 28. Bus: 37.

MUDE   A cultural highlight of the Baixa district, this museum opened in 2009 in the Palácio Verride, a former palace at the Santa Catarina viewing point. *Mude* means change in Portuguese, and that is what this Museum of Design and Fashion is all about. The museum is the venue for ever-changing temporary exhibitions, but it also has a permanent collection, including some 1,200 couture pieces. Designs are by such luminaries as the famed architect Frank O. Gehry or else André Arbus. You never know what's going to be on display. Are you old enough to remember the swimsuit by Rudi Gernreich? Perhaps the miniskirt by André Courrèges? From more recent times, perhaps couture by London's Vivienne Westwood.

Rua Augusta 24. ✆ **21/888-61-17.** www.mude.pt. Free admission (subject to change). Tues–Thurs and Sun 10am–8pm; Fri–Sat 10am–10pm. Metro: Baixa/Chiado.

Museu Archeologico do Carmo   No other Lisbon museum so well conveys the sensation that you've wandered into a living relic and witness to history. Here, the ruined nave of a church, originally built in 1389, stands in a state of partial collapse—a victim of damages wrought during the great earthquake of 1755 when many parishioners died inside. Some back rooms contain a dusty collection of exhibits, such as historic *azulejos* (glazed tiles), but the star of the museum is the church itself. Unlike several nearby monuments, the church was not rebuilt but somehow survived despite further indignities inflicted upon it over the years, including vandalisms by French soldiers occupying Lisbon during the Napoleonic wars. To many Lisboans, it's the most visible symbol of the 1755 earthquake, the single monument that most aggressively piques their sense of history and sense of loss.

Largo do Carmo. ✆ **21/346-04-73.** www.museuarqueologicodocarmo.pt. Admission 3€ adults; 1.50€ students, free for children under 14. Apr–Sept daily 10am–6pm; Oct–Mar daily 10am–5pm. Metro: Chiado.

Museu da Farmácia   Founded in 1996 in a former palace, this pharmacy museum covers more than 5,000 years of pharmaceutical history, from practices in 3600 B.C. to modern techniques developed for upcoming voyages to Mars. Four pharmacies from the 18th to the 20th centuries have been reconstructed here. There are antique exhibits that go back to ancient Egypt or Mesopotamia. One exhibit shows off a 19th-century Chinese drugstore from Portugal's former territory of Macao, off the coast of China.

Rua Maréchal Saldanha. ✆ **21/340-06-80.** Admission 5€ adults, 3.50€ students and seniors, free for children 2 and under. Mon–Fri 10am–6pm. Metro: Cais do Sodré.

Museu de São Roque/Igreja de São Roque ★   The Jesuits, who at one time were so powerful they virtually governed Portugal, founded St. Roque Church in the late 16th century. Beneath its painted wood ceiling, the church contains a celebrated chapel by Luigi Vanvitelli honoring John the Baptist. The chapel, ordered by the Bragança king João V in 1741, was assembled in Rome from such precious materials as alabaster and lapis lazuli, and then dismantled, shipped to Lisbon, and reassembled. The marble mosaics look like a painting. You can also visit the sacristy, rich in paintings illustrating scenes from the lives of saints pertaining to the Society of Jesus.

The St. Roque Museum inside the church merits a visit chiefly for its collection of baroque silver. A pair of bronze-and-silver torch holders, weighing about 380 kilograms (838 lbs.), is among the most elaborate in Europe. The 18th-century gold embroidery is a rare treasure, as are the vestments. The paintings, mainly from the 16th century, include one of a double-chinned Catherine of Austria and another of the wedding ceremony of Manuel I. Look for a remarkable 15th-century Virgin (with Child) of the Plague and a polished 18th-century conch shell that served as a baptismal font.

Largo Trindade Coelho. ✆ **21/323-53-80.** www.museudesaoroque.com. Admission 2.50€ adults, free for children under 14. Tues–Sun 10am–5pm. Metro: Chiado. Bus: 28.

Museu do Chiado   Housed in the former Convento de São Francisco, the Chiado Museum (also known as the Museum of Contemporary Art, or Museu Nacional de Arte Contemporânea) was designed by the French architect Jean-Michel Wilmotte. The permanent collection of post-1850 art and sculpture extends to 1950 and crosses the artistic bridge from Romanticism to Postnaturalism. Some excellent examples of modernism in Portugal are on display. The museum also houses frequently changing contemporary exhibitions devoted to art, sculpture, photography, and mixed media.

Rua Serpa Pinto 4. ✆ **21/343-21-48.** www.museudochiado-ipmuseus.pt. Admission 4€ adults, 2€ students and seniors, free for children under 14. Tues–Sun 10am–6pm. Metro: Baixa-Chiado. Tram: 28. Bus: 60 or 208.

Museu Militar   The Military Museum sits in front of the Santa Apolónia Station, not far from Terreiro do Paço and Castelo de São Jorge. It's on the site of a shipyard built during the reign of Manuel I (1495–1521). During the reign of João III, a new foundry for artillery was erected; it was also used for making gunpowder and storing arms to equip the Portuguese fleet. A fire damaged the buildings in 1726, and the 1755 earthquake destroyed them completely. Rebuilt on the orders of José I, the complex was designated as the Royal Army Arsenal. The museum, originally called the Artillery Museum, was created in 1851. Today the facility exhibits not only arms, but also paintings, sculpture, tiles, and examples of architecture.

The museum boasts one of the world's best collections of historical artillery. Bronze cannons of various periods include one from Diu, weighing 20 tons and bearing Arabic inscriptions. Some iron pieces date from the 14th century. Light weapons, such as guns, pistols, and swords, are displayed in cases.

Largo do Museu de Artilharia. ✆ **21/884-25-69.** www.geira.pt/mmilitar. Admission 3€ adults, 1.50€ children 2–8, free for children under 2. Tues–Sun 10am–5pm. Bus: 9, 12, 25, 28, 35, 39, 46, 104, 105, or 107.

Oceanário de Lisboa ★★   This world-class aquarium is the most enduring and impressive achievement of EXPO '98. Marketed as the second-biggest aquarium in the world (the largest is in Osaka, Japan), it's in a stone-and-glass building whose centerpiece is a 5-million-liter (1.3-million-gal.) holding tank. Its waters consist of four distinct ecosystems that replicate the Atlantic, Pacific, Indian, and Antarctic oceans. Each is supplemented with aboveground portions on which birds, amphibians, and reptiles flourish. Look for otters in the Pacific waters, penguins in the Antarctic section, trees and flowers that might remind you of Polynesia in the Indian Ocean division, and puffins, terns, and seagulls in the Atlantic subdivision. Don't underestimate the national pride associated with this huge facility: Most Portuguese view it as a latter-day reminder of their former mastery of the seas.

Esplanada d. Carlos I. ℰ **21/891-70-02.** www.oceanario.pt. Admission 12€ adults, 6€ students and children under 13. Summer daily 10am–8pm; winter daily 10am–7pm. Metro: Estação do Oriente. Pedestrians should turn right after leaving the metro station and go along Av. Dom João II where you'll see a signpost directing you left and to the water for the attraction itself.

ESPECIALLY FOR KIDS

From the winding, narrow streets of Alfama to the "dragon ships" of the Maritime Museum at Belém, much of Lisbon evokes a movie set for kids. Each new day brings something new for kids to do—an aquarium, a zoo, a planetarium—it's all here.

Aquário Vasco da Gama The Vasco da Gama Aquarium, on N6, near Algés on the Cascais railway line, has been in operation since 1898. Live exhibits include the eared seals pavilion and a vast number of tanks that hold fish and other sea creatures from all over the world. A large portion of the exhibits consist of zoological material brought back from oceanographic expeditions by Carlos I. They include preserved marine invertebrates, water birds, fish, mammals, and some of the king's laboratory equipment.

Rua Direita do Dafundo. ℰ **21/419-63-37.** Admission 3€ adults, 1.50€ children 7–17, free for children under 7. Daily 10am–6pm. Metro: Algés. Bus: 29 or 51.

Jardim Zoológico de Lisboa ★★ The Zoological Garden, with a collection of some 2,000 animals, occupies a flower-filled setting in the 26-hectare (64-acre) Park of Laranjeiras. It's about a 10-minute subway ride from the Rossio. It also has a small tram and rowboats.

Estrada de Benfica 58. ℰ **21/723-29-00.** www.zoolisboa.pt. Admission 17€, 13€ children 3–11, free for children 2 and under. Daily 10am–8pm. Metro: Jardim Zoológico. Bus: 15, 16, 16C, 26, 31, 46, 58, 63, or 68.

Planetário Calouste Gulbenkian An annex of the Maritime Museum, the Calouste Gulbenkian Planetarium is open to the public all year, with astronomical shows throughout the day (check with the planetarium for current schedules).

Praça do Império, Belém. ℰ **21/362-00-02.** Admission 5€ adults, 2.50€ children 10–18, free for seniors and children 6–9. Children under 6 not admitted (except for Sun morning). Tues–Sun 10am–6pm. Bus: 29, 43, or 49.

CITY STROLLS

Lisbon is a walker's delight; the city's principal neighborhoods abound with major sights and quiet glimpses into daily life.

WALKING TOUR 1: **THE ALFAMA**

START:	**Praça do Comércio.**
FINISH:	**Castelo de São Jorge.**
TIME:	**2 hours, more if you add sightseeing time.**
BEST TIMES:	**Any sunny day.**
WORST TIMES:	**Twilight or after dark.**

Walking Tour: The Alfama

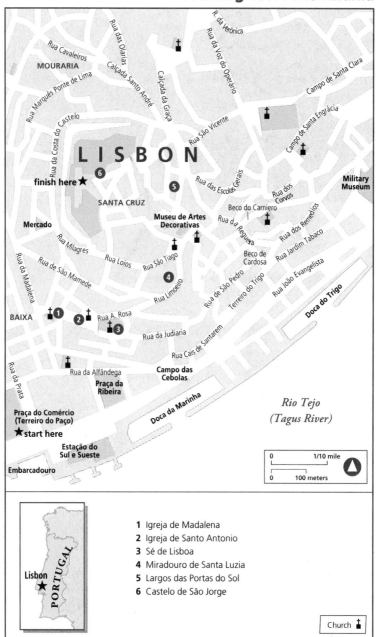

1 Igreja de Madalena
2 Igreja de Santo Antonio
3 Sé de Lisboa
4 Miradouro de Santa Luzia
5 Largos das Portas do Sol
6 Castelo de São Jorge

Church

The streets of the Alfama are best traversed on foot; but at times you must walk up steep stone stairs. Once aristocratic, this fabled section has fallen into decay. (Be aware that the Alfama can be dangerous at night.) Parts of it still allow the visitor a rare opportunity to wander back in time, though.

From Praça do Comércio, opening onto the water at the foot of Rua Augusta, which splits the center of midtown Lisbon, head east along Rua da Alfândega, which links Lower Baixa to the southern tier of the Alfama. When you reach the intersection with Rua de Madalena, head north, or left, to the Largo da Madalena. The square is dominated by:

1 Igreja de Madalena
This church dates from 1783 and incorporates the Manueline portico of a previous church that was built on this site.

Take Rua de Santo António da Sé, following the tram tracks to the small:

2 Igreja de Santo António
Opening onto Largo de Santo António de Sé, this church is from 1812, and was built over the beloved saint's alleged birthplace. For a full description, see p. 105.

A few steps higher, and to the immediate southeast, stands:

3 Sé de Lisboa
This is the cathedral of Lisbon, opening onto the tiny Largo da Sé. One would think that the cathedral of a major European capital would be graced with a more impressive edifice, but what you see is what you get. For a complete description, see p. 105.

Continuing east into the Alfama, go along Rua Augusto Rosa which becomes Rua do Limoeiro. You'll soon be at:

4 Miradouro de Santa Luzia
This belvedere is the most famous in the Alfama. From this viewpoint, you can look down over the jumble of antique houses as they seemingly pile into the Tagus River. The once impressive church, Igreja de Santa Luzia, that opens onto this square has seen better days. The fine glazed tiles that once adorned the exterior have been carted off, leaving the church a rather sorry sight and the victim of graffiti.

Continue northeast into the:

5 Largo das Portas do Sol
On this square stands the Fundação Ricardo do Espírito Santo Silva, a museum of decorative art (p. 116).

6 Take a Break 🍺
At the Miradouro de Santa Luzia are several tiny cafes and bars with outside seating. Visitors from all over the world come here to order coffee and refreshments and take in the view of the shipping activity on the Tagus. These establishments are virtually all the same, but we recommend **Cerca Moura**, Largo das Portas do Sol 4 (📞 21/887-48-59), which offers the finest menu of snacks and drinks in the area and affords a breathtaking view.

A short but steep climb from Largo das Portas do Sol via Travessa de Santa Luzia brings you to:

7 Castelo de São Jorge

The remains of this once grand fortification have been gussied up for tourists, but it's still the reason most visitors trek through the Alfama. The views alone are worth the effort to reach it, as they offer the greatest panoramas over Lisbon and the Tagus. See p. 104 for a more complete description.

WALKING TOUR 2: BAIXA, THE CENTER & THE CHIADO

START:	**Praça do Comércio.**
FINISH:	**Elevador de Santa Justa.**
TIME:	**3 hours.**
BEST TIMES:	**Any sunny day except Sunday.**
WORST TIMES:	**Monday to Saturday from 7:30 to 9am and 5 to 7pm; Sunday, when shops are closed.**

The best place to begin this tour is:

1 Praça do Comércio (also known as Terreiro do Paço)

The House of Bragança ended here at the waterfront end of Baixa with the assassination of Carlos I and his elder son, Luís Filipe, in 1908. Regrettably, employees in the surrounding government buildings now use the Praça as a parking lot. The Marquês de Pombal designed the square when he rebuilt Lisbon following the 1755 earthquake. The equestrian statue is of Dom José, the Portuguese king at the time of the earthquake.

Before you start walking, especially if it's a hot day, you might need to:

2 Take a Break 🍽

Café Martinho da Arcada, Praça do Comércio 3 (© 21/887-92-59), has been the haunt of the literati since 1782, attracting such greats as the Portuguese poet Fernando Pessoa. The old restaurant has gone upscale, but it adjoins a cafe and bar, often called the best cafe in Portugal. If you're here for lunch, ask for a savory kettle of fish, called *cataplana*, or clam stew served in the style of the Algarve. It's open Monday to Saturday 7am to 11pm.

After dining, head north along:

3 Rua Augusta

This is one of Baixa's best-known shopping streets. Leather stores and bookshops, embroidery outlets, and even home-furnishings stores line the bustling street. Many of the cross streets are closed to traffic, making window-shopping more enjoyable. The glittering jewelry stores you'll see often have some good buys in gold and silver. The many delis display vast offerings of Portuguese wine and cheese, along with endless arrays of the pastries Lisboans are so fond of.

The western part of this grid of streets is known as the **Chiado.** It's the city's most sophisticated shopping district. In 1988, a devastating fire swept the area, destroying many shops, particularly those on the periphery of Rua Garrett. The area has bounced back with vigor.

Rua Augusta leads into the:

4 Rossio (formally called Praça de Dom Pedro IV)

The principal square of Baixa, the Rossio dates from the 1200s. During the Inquisition, it was the setting of many an auto-da-fé, during which Lisboans turned out to witness the torture and death of an "infidel," often a Jew. This was the heart of Pombaline Lisbon as the marquês rebuilt it following the 1755 earthquake. Neoclassical buildings from the 1700s and 1800s line the square, which has an array of cafes and souvenir shops. The 1840 Teatro Nacional de Dona Maria II sits on the north side of the square, occupying the former Palace of the Inquisition. The statue on its facade is of Gil Vicente, the Shakespeare of Portugal, credited with the creation of the Portuguese theater.

Crowds cluster around two baroque fountains at either end of the Rossio. The bronze statue on a column is of Pedro IV, for whom the square is named. (He was also crowned king of Brazil as Pedro I.) Dozens of flower stalls soften the square's tawdry, overly commercial atmosphere.

5 Take a Break 🍴

Café Nicola, Praça de Dom Pedro IV 18 (📞 21/346-05-79), dates from 1777. It gained fame as a gathering place of the Portuguese literati in the 19th century. Though somewhat short on charm, it's the most popular cafe in Lisbon. Pastries, endless cups of coffee, and meals can be consumed indoors or out. It's open Monday to Friday 8am to 10pm, Saturday 9am to 10pm, and Sunday 10am to 7:30pm.

From the Rossio, proceed to the northwest corner of the square and walk onto the satellite square, Praça da Câmara. If you continue north, you'll reach the beginning of:

6 Avenida da Liberdade

This is Lisbon's main thoroughfare, laid out in 1879. More than 90m (295 ft.) wide, the avenue runs north for 1.5km (1 mile), cutting through the heart of the city. It has long been hailed as the most splendid boulevard of Lisbon, although many of the Art Deco and Belle Epoque mansions that once lined it are gone. Its sidewalks are tessellated in black and white. This is the heart of Lisbon's cinema district; you'll also pass airline offices, travel agencies, and other businesses.

An open-air esplanade lies in the center. Almost immediately you come to:

7 Praça dos Restauradores

This square was named for the men who, in 1640, revolted against the Spanish reign. The event led to the reestablishment of Portugal's independence. An obelisk in the center of the square commemorates the uprising. The deep-red Palácio Foz, now the Ministry of Information, is also on the square.

West of the square is the:

8 Estação do Rossio

This is the city's main rail terminus. Built in mock Manueline style to resemble a lavishly adorned palace, this is one of the strangest architectural complexes housing a rail terminal in Europe. Trains from Sintra and the Estremadura pull right into the heart of the city and leave from a platform that's an escalator ride

Walking Tour: Baixa, the Center & the Chiado

1 Praça do Comércio
  (Terreiro do Paço)
2 Rua Augusta
3 Rossio
4 Avenida da Liberdade
5 Praça dos Restauradores
6 Estação do Rossio
7 Elevador de Santa Justa

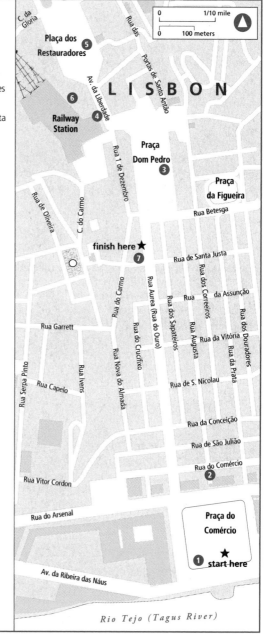

above the street-level entrances. The bustling station abounds with businesses, including souvenir shops and currency-exchange offices.

A possible detour: At this point, you can walk 1.5km (1 mile) along Avenida da Liberdade all the way to Praça do Marquês de Pombal, with its monument to the prime minister who rebuilt Lisbon. North of the square, you can stroll through Parque Eduardo VII. If you'd like to see more of the heart of Lisbon, continue south from Praça dos Restauradores.

If you choose to walk south again along Avenida da Liberdade, retrace your steps to Praça de Dom João da Câmara. Instead of returning to Rossio, continue south along Rua do 1 de Dezembro, which will become Rua do Carmo. This street will lead you to the:

9 Elevador de Santa Justa

This elevator, built in 1902, is in a Gothic-style tower at the junction of Rua Áurea and Rua de Santa Justa. It is often falsely attributed to Alexandre-Gustave Eiffel, who designed the fabled tower of Paris. In no more than a minute, it whisks you from Baixa to the Bairro Alto. There, you'll be rewarded with one of the city's grandest panoramas.

ORGANIZED TOURS

The best tours of Lisbon are offered by **Lisboasightseeing,** Rua Pascoal de Melo 3 (© **96/708-65-36;** www.lisboasightseeing.com). The half-day tour of Lisbon, costing 34€, is the most popular, taking in the highlights of the Alfama and visiting the major monuments, including Jerónimos Monastery and other attractions of Belém. It even goes over the bridge spanning the Tagus, for a panoramic view. Both morning and afternoon tours leave daily throughout the year.

The most recommended tour of the environs of Lisbon is a daily full-day tour costing 82€ and taking in all the highlights, concentrating on Sintra, Cascais, and Estoril. There's also a full-day (and jampacked) tour offered daily of the highlights north of Lisbon—Fátima, Batalha, Nazaré, and Óbidos. This tour costs 86€. Many other tours are offered that might be more suited for your desires—check with the agency for the current agenda.

If you want a more personalized tour, check out the offerings of **Inside Lisbon Tours,** Av. Forças Armadas 95 (© **96/841-26-12;** www.insidelisbon.com). Patrons are transported around in small vans and then taken on different walking tours through the most colorful and historical zones of Lisbon. A popular summer addition is a twice-weekly pub crawl. The tours are given in English and enough free time is provided to explore each district in some depth. Only eight people at a time are taken on a tour. The labyrinths of the Alfama are the most desirable and intriguing of the tours.

OUTDOOR & RECREATIONAL ACTIVITIES

Lisbon itself has very few sports facilities. Most outdoor activities, such as watersports, fishing, and scuba diving, take place on the Costa do Sol, north of the city.

If you want to lie on the beach, you can take the train from Lisbon to the Costa do Sol; the main resorts there are Estoril and Cascais (see chapter 6).

FISHING   Head for Sesimbra (p. 179), south of Lisbon, where local fishers take visitors out on boats looking for "the big one." Fees can be negotiated.

FITNESS CENTERS   Some hotels recommended in chapter 4 allow nonguests to use their health clubs for a fee. It's always best to call in advance. Outside of the hotels, a worthwhile fitness club is **Ginásio Keep Fit,** Av. João Crisóstomo 6 (© **21/793-15-36**), costing 18€ for one-time use of its facilities. It's open Monday to Friday 8am to 10pm, and Saturday 10am to 2pm (bus no. 58). Metro: Saldanha.

GOLF   The best courses lie along the Costa do Sol and Estoril Coast. The closest course to Lisbon (but not the best) is at the **Lisbon Sports Club,** Casal da Carregueira, near Belas (© **21/431-00-77**; www.lisbonclub.com). It's about a 25-minute drive from the center; allow more time if traffic is heavy. A former playground of royalty, the **Atlantic Golf Course** lies at Quinta de Penha Longa at Linho, outside Sintra (© **21/924-90-31**; www.penhalonga.com), part of the Penha Longa Hotel Spa & Golf Resort. Ranked in the top 30 courses of continental Europe, the 18-hole, par-72 championship course was designed by Robert Trent Jones, Jr. The course opens onto panoramic views of the Atlantic and has been host to numerous international competitions, including the Portuguese Open. An adjacent course, the 9-hole, par-35 **Monastery Course** spreads around the core of the resort, often attracting late arrivals who want a round of golf before the sun sets. For the Atlântico Course of 18 holes, greens fees range from 45€ to 120€. For the Mosteiro Course of 9 holes, greens fees range from 15€ to 35€.

JOGGING   We used to recommend Parque Eduardo VII as the best place for jogging, but joggers there have recently been the victims of muggings. Daytime jogging in the park is risky enough, but nighttime jogging is unwise. Some joggers head for the Estádio Nacional (National Stadium), on the northern outskirts of the city on the road to Estoril. A track worn smooth by joggers winds through pine woods. It is also unsafe at night. You might prefer to jog along the Tagus between Ponte do 25 de Abril (the major suspension bridge) and Belém, heading north. Another possibility (but likely to be congested) is the median strip of the main street of Lisbon, Avenida da Liberdade, from Praça do Marquês de Pombal toward Baixa.

TENNIS   Public tennis courts are available at **Campo Grande Estádio do 1 de Maio,** at Alvalade. To reserve a court and find out schedule info, inquire at the main tourist office in Lisbon (p. 61). Real tennis buffs head for either the **Club de Tenis do Estoril,** in Estoril, or the **Quinta da Marinha** in Cascais.

SPECTATOR SPORTS

The following activities are all accessible from the city center.

BULLFIGHTING   Bullfighting was once the sport of Portuguese noblemen. Unlike in neighboring Spain, the bull is not killed—a prohibition the Marquês de Pombal instituted in the 18th century, after the son of the duke of Arcos was killed in the sport. Much ceremony and pageantry attend the drama: The major actors are elegantly costumed *cavaleiros,* who charge the bull on horseback, and *maços de forçado,* who grapple with the bull. Many find this face-to-face combat the most exciting component of the bullfight.

Warning: Bullfights are not spectacles fit for every taste. Even though the animal is not killed, many spectators find the event nauseating and object to the notion that it's a beautiful art form. The spears that jab the bull's neck draw blood, of course, making the animal visibly weaker. One reader wrote to us, "The animals are frightened, confused, and badgered before they are mercifully allowed to exit. What sport!"

The bullfighting season in Lisbon runs from Easter until mid-July. Lisbon's 8,500-seat **Campo Pequeno,** Avenida da República (© **21/782-05-75;** www.campo pequeno.com; Metro: Campo Pequeno), is the largest ring in the country. Bullfight aficionados may also commute to Montijo, an industrial town on the Setúbal peninsula, across the Tagus from Lisbon. Here, in Montijo, bullfights on a much smaller scale are presented on a somewhat erratic basis with the **Praça de Toiros Montijo** (© **21/231-06-32**).

The details of each *tourada* and the names of the stars who will appear are usually announced well in advance of each event. Your hotel concierge can usually help you arrange tickets, or try **Agência de Bilhetes para Espectáculos Públicos,** Praça dos Restauradores (© **21/347-58-24**). Tickets generally cost 20€ to 65€, depending on whether they're in the sun or the shade.

SOCCER   The Portuguese love football (known to Americans as soccer). Nothing—not even politics, boiled codfish, or fado—excites them more. When favorite teams are playing, soccer has a following of startling passion and hysteria. "It's better than sex," one fan told us, although his wife disagreed. It's also a way for pickpockets to earn a living. They work the intent crowds, lifting wallets during intense moments.

Lisbon has a trio of teams that play almost every Sunday, but the season stretches only from September to May. You'll miss out if you visit in the summer. Try to arrive at least an hour before the match is scheduled to begin; pregame entertainment ranges from marching bands to fireworks.

The best-known team is Benfica, which holds matches in northwest Lisbon at the new and gigantic **Estádio da Luz,** Avenida General Norton Matos (© **21/721-95-00;** Metro: Colégio Militar/Luz or Alto dos Moinhos). One of the largest sports stadiums in Europe, it evokes memories of the legendary Eusébio, who led his team to five European championship finals in the 1960s. All young soccer players in Lisbon grow up with dreams of becoming the next Eusébio.

The **Sporting Clube de Portugal** plays at the **Estádio do José Alvalade** (no phone), in the north of the city, near Campo Grande. The third team is Belém's **Belenenses,** which plays at the Estádio do Restelo (© **21/301-04-61**). The team might not be as good or nearly as famous as Benfica, but don't tell that to a loyal fan during the heat of the game.

Tickets vary in price depending on the event but average 25€ to 80€. You can buy them on the day of the game at all three stadiums. However, when Benfica plays Sporting, tickets usually sell out; buy them in advance at the booth in Praça dos Restauradores. Tickets also go fast when FC Porto, from the northern city of Porto, Lisbon's main rival, is in town to play Benfica or Sporting.

LISBON SHOPPING: FROM ANTIQUES TO WINE

Portuguese handicrafts often exhibit exotic influences, in large part because of the artisans' versatility and their skill in absorbing other styles. Portugal's vast history as a seafaring nation also surely has something to do with it. The best place to see their work is in Lisbon, where shopkeepers and their buyers hunt out unusual items from all over Portugal, including the Madeira Islands and the Azores.

SHOPPING AREAS Shops operate all over the city, but **Baixa,** in downtown Lisbon, is the major area for browsing. **Rua Áurea** (Street of Gold, the location of the major jewelry shops), **Rua da Prata** (Street of Silver), and **Rua Augusta** are Lisbon's three principal shopping streets. The Baixa shopping district lies between the Rossio and the river Tagus.

Rua Garrett, in the Chiado, is where you'll find many of the more upmarket shops. A major fire in 1988 destroyed many shops, but new ones have arisen.

Antiques lovers gravitate to **Rua Dom Pedro V** in the Bairro Alto. Other streets with antiques stores include Rua da Misericórdia, Rua de São Pedro de Alcântara, Rua da Escola Politécnica, and Rua do Alecrim.

Shopping A to Z

Shops are open, in general, Monday through Friday from 9am to 1pm and from 3 to 7pm, and Saturday from 9am to 1pm.

ANTIQUES

Along both sides of the narrow **Rua de São José** in the Graça District are treasure-troves of shops packed with antiques from all over the world. Antiques dealers from the United States come here to survey the wares. You'll find ornate spool and carved beds, high-back chairs, tables, wardrobes with ornate carvings, brass plaques, copper pans, silver candelabra, crystal sconces, chandeliers, and a wide selection of wooden figures, silver boxes, porcelain plates, and bowls. Don't, however, count on getting spectacular bargains.

Cavalo de Pau Set across the street from the Portuguese Parliament, on the street where fado diva Amália Rodriguez used to live, this is a genuinely charming store that's loaded with antiques from Portugal and art objects from around the world. Look for elaborate baskets, sculptures, antique furniture, and gift items handcrafted in places such as Brazil, Indonesia, Mozambique, and France, with an articulate sales staff that's ready, willing, and able to describe the provenance of each piece. Rua de São Bento 164. ✆ **21/396-66-05.** www.cavalopau.no.sapo.pt. Tram: 28.

M. Murteira Antiguidades ★★ The artistic achievements of yesterday live on in this showcase of sculpture, paintings, and antiques that date back, in some cases, from the 1600s. Sometimes leaders of American churches come here to purchase antique religious art, although there are some works from the 20th century as well. Manuel Murteira Martins has pulled together this tasteful, well-chosen collection of the best of past centuries that was worth preserving and collecting for the modern buyer. The showcase is one of the shopping highlights for those store-hopping in Lisbon's Baixa district. Rua Augusto Rosa 19. ✆ **21/886-38-51.** www.murteira-antiguidades.com. Tram: 35.

Santos & Marcos, Lda, Antiguidades This shop, a few steps from the Praça do Principe Real, stocks a noteworthy collection of 18th- and 19th-century paintings, furniture, and sculpture, some of it ecclesiastical in nature and some of it very unusual. The best pieces require permission from a government agency to leave the country; other less-valuable pieces can be exported without hindrance. Rua Dom Pedro V 59. ✆ **21/342-63-67.** Metro: Rato or Chiado. Tram: 28.

ART GALLERIES

Chiado 8 Arte Contemporaneo Proud of its survival within an environment where some of its competitors have, during Portugal's economic woes, gone out of business, this place functions as a central exhibition point within the arts-conscious Chiado district. Within a warren of white, artfully illuminated exhibition spaces, you'll find a changing series of expositions by artists from Iberia and the rest of Europe. Exhibitions change every two months, new ones being prefaced by wine and cheese parties. Largo do Chiado 8 ℂ 21/323-7225. www.culturgest.pt. Metro: Baixa Chiado.

Galeria Jorge Shirley ★ This avant-garde gallery, one of Lisbon's most respected, lies directly north of the Praça do Príncipe Real (not the safest place to be at night) and directly south of the Jardim Botânico. It was founded in 1999 in the city of Porto but moved to Lisbon in 2003 where it found immediate success. Its changing array of art is spread over two floors of open space. Emerging new artists, both Portuguese and foreign, are represented here. Jorge Shirley has partnerships with galleries in Italy and Spain. Rua da Escola Politécnica 21-23. ℂ **21/386-84-97.** www.jorgeshirley.com. Metro: Rato.

Galeria 111 Operated by Manuel and Arlete de Brito since 1964, Galeria 111 is one of Lisbon's major art galleries. The wide-ranging exhibitions of sculpture, painting, and graphics include work by leading contemporary Portuguese artists. The gallery also sells drawings, etchings, silk screens, lithographs, art books, and postcards. It's closed August 4 to September 4. Campo Grande 113. ℂ **21/797-74-18.** www.111.pt. Metro: Entre Campus. Bus: 1, 36, 38, or 88.

Galeria Yela This showcase near the Four Seasons Hotel Ritz Lisbon prides itself on its cutting-edge expositions of emerging Iberian artists. The Euroarte gallery (see above) is its only rival on the contemporary-art scene. Look for acrylics, drawings, and engravings, most of them avant-garde in their focus and inspiration. Rua Rodrigo de Fonseca 103B. ℂ **21/388-03-99.** Metro: Marquês de Pombal.

BASKETS

One of the best selections of Portuguese baskets is at the **Feira da Ladra** (see "Markets," below).

BOOKS

Bertrand Livreiros Stop here for a selection of books ranging from the latest bestsellers (Grisham and the like) to some English-language magazines, travel guides, and maps of Lisbon and Portugal. Rua Garrett 73. ℂ **21/347-61-22.** www.bertrand.pt. Metro: Chiado.

Fabula Urbis Many English-language editions on the art, literature, music, history, architecture, and gastronomy of Lisbon are found here in the historic Alfama district near the Cathedral and the Castle of St. George. The upper floor of the book shop is used for monthly exhibitions of paintings and an occasional recital. It's also a good place to drop in for tea during a walking tour of the Alfama district. Open daily 9am to 5pm. Rua de Augusto Rosa 27. ℂ **21/888-50-32.** www.fabula-urbis.pt. Trams: 12 or 28. Bus: 37.

Tabacaria Mónaco This narrow *tabacaria* (magazine and tobacco shop) opened in 1893 and has kept its original Art Nouveau look. Tiles from Rafael Bordalo Pinheiro and an adobe painting by Rosendo Carvalheira adorn the interior. You'll find a selection of international periodicals, guidebooks, and maps. Praça Dom Pedro IV 21. ℂ **21/346-81-91.** Metro: Rossio. Tram: 12, 20, or 28.

CANDLES

Caza das Vellas Loreto   A century ago, dozens of candlemakers flourished within this neighborhood, close to the Praça Luís de Camões. Today, this is one of the very few candlemakers still surviving within Portugal, and the only one in Lisbon. The smell of beeswax permeates a 19th-century setting where customers don't proceed beyond a point of a few feet from the front door. Members of a polite staff will bring you samples of what's available. Depending on your tastes, candles contain the scent of fruit, apples, and entire bouquets of seasonal flowers. And chances are good that if a religious festival is scheduled for anytime within the next several upcoming months, this shop will have a candle to commemorate the event. Rua do Loreto 53-55. ℰ **21/046-88-02.** www.cazavellasloreto.pai.pt. Metro: Chiado.

CHINA & GLASSWARE

JAO ★   This is one of the best shops for ceramics, displaying a choice selection from Vista Alegre as well as Atlantis glassware and the works of other Portuguese and Continental manufacturers. Customers have found that the shop's Vista Alegre display of tableware is sometimes fuller than that company's own retail branches. If you don't see what you want, know that there is a large inventory warehouse at the rear of this two-floor outlet. Praça de Figueira 11C. ℰ **21/886-61-61.** Metro: Rossio.

Vista Alegre ★★   This company, founded in 1824, turns out some of the finest porcelain dinner services in the country. It also carries objets d'art and limited editions for collectors, and a range of practical day-to-day tableware. The government presents Vista Alegre pieces to European heads of state when they visit. Largo do Chiado 23. ℰ **21/346-14-01.** www.vistaalegre.pt. Metro: Chiado. Tram: 15.

CHOCOLATES

Claudio Corallo Cioccolato e Caffè ★★   This is a chocoholic's dream shop. There is no place in Portugal like it. In 2008, it burst onto the scene, the creation of Bettina and Ricciarda Corallo. Their family owns coffee plantations and cocoa fields on São Tome and Príncipe, two West African islands. The chocolates are so pure, they don't need any additives; and they are the only chocolates in the world that contain a distillate (liqueur) that is extracted from cocoa pulp. Some tiny coffee beans are coated in chocolate, and natural ginger or orange peel are sometimes added. Rua Cecilio da Sousa 85. ℰ **21/386-21-58.** www.claudiocorallo.com. Metro: Rato.

CRYSTAL

Depósito da Mairnha Grande   This unpretentious store offers glass items created in the century-old Marinha Grande factory. The merchandise includes traditional service glasses, dishes, water pitchers, and salt and pepper shakers, as well as modern colored glass services. Other items include Atlantis crystal services and Vista Alegre porcelain. Atlantis crystal from Marinha Grande is renowned in Portugal, and there are some good buys here. You can purchase full services or individual pieces. Another branch is down the road at Rua de São Bento 418–420 (ℰ **21/396-30-96**). Rua de São Bento 234-242. ℰ **21/396-32-34.** www.dmg.com.pt. Metro: Rato. Bus: 6, 49, or 100.

DEPARTMENT STORES

El Corte Inglés ★★   If you're not planning to include Spain as a stop on your trip to Iberia, you can shop here, a major outlet for the largest department store chain in Spain. From fashion to handicrafts, you'll find a vast array of merchandise, including damascene steelwork from Toledo, flamenco dolls, and embroidered shawls. Many foreign visitors find the best buys in clothing for men, women, and children. Btw. Avs. Antonio Augusto e Aguiar and Marquês de Fronteira e Sidónio Pais. ☎ **21/371-17-00.** www.elcorte ingles.pt. Metro: São Sebastião.

EMBROIDERY

Madeira House ★★ Madeira House specializes in high-quality regional cottons, linens, and gift items. Rua Augusta 131-133. ☎ **21/342-68-13.** www.madeira-house.com. Metro: Chiado. Tram: 28.

Príncipe Real ★★★ Príncipe Real specializes in linens elegant enough to grace the tables of monarchs, including that of the late Princess Grace of Monaco. Owned by Cristina Castro and her son, Victor Castro, this store is one of the last that does artistic manual embroidery by order. It produces some of Europe's finest tablecloths and sheets in cotton, linen, and organdy. The owner-designer sells to famous names (the Rockefellers, Michael Douglas, the Kennedys, and many members of European royalty), but the merchandise is not beyond the means of the middle-class tourist. The shop's factory handles custom orders quickly and professionally. It employs 80 skilled workers, who can execute a linen pattern to match a client's favorite porcelain or one of Cristina Castro's original designs. Rua da Escola Politécnica 12-14. ☎ **21/346-59-45.** www.principereal.com. Metro: Rato or Chiado. Bus: 58.

Teresa Alecrim This store bears the name of the owner, who creates refined embroideries in the style of Laura Ashley. You'll see sheets, pillowcases, towels, and bedcovers in plain and patterned cotton, plus monogrammed damask cotton hand towels. Amoreiras Shopping Center, Shop 1116. ☎ **21/383-18-70.** www.teresaalecrim.com. Metro: Rato or Marquês de Pombal. Bus: 11, 48, or 83.

FASHION

Ana Salazar ★★ An internationally known name in fashion, Ana Salazar is the most avant-garde Portuguese designer of women's clothes. Known for her stretch fabrics, Salazar designs clothes that critics have called "body-conscious yet wearable." In addition to her main store, she has a branch at Av. de Roma 16E. Rua do Carmo 87. ☎ **21/347-22-89.** www.anasalazar.pt. Metro: Rossio or Chiado. Bus: 21.

A Outra Face da Lua ★★ This Baixa shop is a fashion atelier for designer Carla Belchior. Her vintage and period clothing is the best in the country, and she often sells or rents wardrobe to film, TV, and theater people. If you want to look like flapper Clara Bow in the 1920s, head here. Carla also creates her own original styles in clothing. As an oddity, she sells rare wallpaper and even tin toys. A blast from the past. Even if you prefer your clothing new, you might still drop in for an hour or so as you make your way shopping and sightseeing in the center of Lisbon. There is a lovely little tearoom, and even a summer terrace for drinking and people-watching. A tasty selection of freshly made sandwiches and salads is offered, along with "psychoactive teas," as they are called here. Teas are described on the menu—Damiana tea, for example, is said to not only make you euphoric but is alleged to be an aphrodisiac as well. Rua da Assunção 22. ☎ **21/886-34-30.** www.aoutrafacedalua.com. Metro: Baixa-Chiado. Tram: 28.

Camisaria Pitta ★★ In the Baixa district, this is Lisbon's oldest—and best—shirt-maker for men. If Prince Charles were in town, he'd no doubt stop in for a dozen of these superbly made shirts, which come in many colors and styles. The expert tailors here will also design a suit for you. Rua Augusta 195. ☎ **21/342-75-26.** Metro: Baixa-Chiado.

Laurenço y Santos One of Lisbon's most prominent menswear stores, Laurenço y Santos is a place where a concierge at a grand hotel might refer a well-dressed guest who needs to augment his wardrobe with anything from a business suit to a golf outfit. Praça dos Restauradores 47. ✆ **21/346-25-70.** Metro: Restauradores.

Rosa e Teixeira   This is another prominent Lisbon store, similar to Laurenço y Santos, with a variety of men's clothing. Although the quality of clothing here is on the same level as Laurenço y Santos, prices tend to be more reasonable. Av. da Liberdade 204, 2nd floor. ✆ **21/311-03-50.** Metro: Avenida or Marquês de Pombal.

FOOD & WINE

Garrafeira Nacional   In the Baixa district, this wine shop, founded in 1927, has one of the best selection of wines in Portugal. The shop is staffed by 20 top professionals who will guide you to the bottle of your choice, some of which come from private cellars. You'll find ports and Madeiras along with rare whiskey, cognac, and other liquors you've never heard of. Rua de Santa Justa 18. ✆ **21/887-90-80.** www.garrafeira nacional.com. Metro: Baixa-Chiado.

Manuel Tavares Lda ★   Visiting foodies and serious gourmands call on this emporium of food and wine, one of the oldest stores in Lisbon, dating from 1860. Behind a traditional wood-framed shop front, it has a dazzling collection of Portuguese wines, liquors, and brandies. The wine comes from different regions of Portugal. The deli is well stocked with hams, cheeses, and sausages, along with dried fruits such as plums and figs. The collection of chocolates, fruit conserves, virgin olive oils, and even canned fish is mouthwatering. Rua da Betesga 1 A-B. ✆ **21/342-42-09.** www.manuel tavares.com. Metro: Rossio.

GIFTS & SOUVENIRS

Fabrico Infinito   This gallery, cafe, and design boutique in the Príncipe Real district has helped gentrify this once-sleazy area, which, in its heyday, was an aristocratic enclave. Original items for the home, along with handmade jewelry from designers in Portugal as well as Brazil, are on sale. Rua Dom Pedro V 74. ✆ **21/246-76-29.** www.fabrico infinito.com. Metro: Rato. Bus: 58.

GLOVES

Luvaria Ulisses   Without a doubt, this glove store in an Art Deco building in the Chiado is the finest such store in Lisbon—in fact, the last shop in Portugal that sells gloves, and only gloves, a tradition dating from 1925 when the store was founded. Although new styles have been introduced, the glove-making technique itself is decades old. The shop will even make gloves for you if your tastes range from the unusual or exotic. The material for the gloves comes in various offerings—satin, wool, or all types of leather (lamb, calf, game, pig, or even antelope). Whatever your choice of colors, be it sunflower yellow, turquoise, scarlet red, or spring green, it is likely to be available, even pure and simple black or brown, of course. Rua da Carmo 87. ✆ **21/342-02-95.** www.luvariaulisses.com. Metro: Rossio.

HANDICRAFTS

A Arte da Terra ★★   For that special gift or handicraft, this outlet deep in the heart of the Alfama is an idyllic hunting ground. Standing alongside the Lisbon Cathedral, the shop is housed in a building that survived the 1755 earthquake. Since the shop's creation in 1996, it has been a showcase for some of the best regional articles in the city. The owner purchases the creations of craftspeople who work in different materials such as iron, wood, stone, or sandstone, including every kind of weaving and embroidery, even hand-painted tiles or paintings. Rua Augusto Rosa 40. ✆ **21/274-59-75.** www.aartedaterra.pt. Tram: 28.

Loja dos Descobrimentos ★   In the Alfama, this handicraft shop lies in a historic building from the 16th century. Its artisans turn out some of the most beautiful hand-painted ceramics and hand-painted tiles. The designs are based on various regions throughout the country. In one part of the building is an atelier where you can see artisans painting the tiles or ceramics. The store can ship your purchases anywhere you wish, and you can even order online. Rua dos Bacalhoeiros 12A. ℂ **21/886-55-63.** www.loja-descobrimentos.com. Bus: 37.

KITSCH

A Vida Portuguesa   When it was established in 2006 by a Portuguese journalist (Catherina Portes), local residents wondered if this place was a shop or a testimonial to old-fashioned Portugal as it's remembered by anyone born during the baby boom of the 1950s. It occupies what functioned during the early 20th century as a warehouse for (very) old-fashioned cosmetics, especially rice powders and unguents that might have been in vogue before Salazar. Today, you'll wander through battered cases of retro-hip objects that you might find baffling, but which exert powerful iconic appeal to the Portuguese. What, for example, are soaps by Claus Porti, and how, exactly, should that kitschy plastic model of Saint Anthony be constructed and at what time of the year? Look for lavender waters, kitchen tools, handicrafts, artists' supplies, books, and pomades that evoke waves of memories for the Portuguese. Rua Anchieta 11. ℂ **21/346-50-73.** www.avidaportuguesa.com. Metro: Chiado.

Empório Casa Bazar   In the Príncipe real district, this is a vast emporium of flea market kitsch, and, as such, is one of the most amusing stores in Lisbon. Expect one-of-a-kind gift or household items that might have come from anywhere, certainly Iberia, but also Italy or Brazil. You might pass over those plastic Portuguese saints but latch onto some enchanting Portuguese ceramics. Rua Dom Pedro V 65. ℂ **21/096-40-93.** Metro: Rato.

MARKETS

See also the Ribeira Nova market in the "Secrets of Lisbon" box on p. 111.

Feira da Ladra   Nearly everything you can imagine is for sale at this open-air street market, which competes with the flea markets of Madrid and Paris in terms of surprising finds. Vendors peddle their wares on Tuesday and Saturday; for the finest pickings, go in the morning. The market is about a 5-minute walk from the waterfront in the Alfama district or a short walk from the Estação Santa Apolónia metro stop. It's best to start your browsing at Campo de Santa Clara and then work your way up the hilly street, lined with portable stalls and individual displays. Note that haggling is expected here.

METALS

Casa Maciel Lda   Founded in 1810 as a specialized tinker shop that created the city's best lanterns and original cake molds, this house has distinguished itself in numerous national and international contests. You can select from the in-house patterns or have the artisans create pieces from your designs; the store will also ship items. Rua da Misericórdia 63-65. ℂ **21/342-24-51.** www.casamaciel.pt. Metro: Chiado. Tram: 28. Bus: 10, 24, 29, or 30.

SHOPPING CENTERS

Centro Colombo ★★★   In the Luz district, this vast complex is the biggest shopping center on the Iberian peninsula. Its array of merchandise is stunning, a

Lisbon Shopping: From Antiques to Wine

EXPLORING LISBON

dazzling showcase of the capitalistic system, with more than 420 stores. There's everything here from an indoor amusement park to a health club to a 10-screen multiplex showing different movies. For your dining selection, you face a bewildering choice of 60 restaurants, ranging from a pizza parlor to a Chinese eatery to Burger King. Av. Lusíada. ℂ **21/711-36-36.** www.colombo.pt. Metro: Colégio Militar.

Centro Vasco da Gama   This modern shopping mall is hailed as the finest in Portugal, with 164 shops, 36 restaurants, a 10-screen movie theater, a health club, and a playground. Along with Portuguese-made products, you'll also find a lot of designer labels in clothing, including Vuitton and Hugo Boss selling at cheaper prices than you might find in other western European capitals. The shops keep hours that benefit almost all customers: They're open daily 10am to midnight. Av. Dom João II within Parque das Nações. ℂ **21/893-06-00.** www.centrovascodagama.pt. Metro: Estação Oriente.

SILVER, GOLD & FILIGREE

W. A. Sarmento ★★★   At the foot of the Santa Justa elevator, W. A. Sarmento has been in the hands of the same family for well over a century. They are the most distinguished silver- and goldsmiths in Portugal, specializing in lacy filigree jewelry, including charm bracelets. The shop has been Lisboans' favorite place to buy treasured confirmation and graduation gifts, and its clientele includes Costa do Sol aristocracy as well as movie stars and diplomats. Rua Áurea 251. ℂ **21/347-07-83** or 21/342-67-74. Metro: Chiado. Tram: 28 or 28B. Bus: 1, 21, 31, or 36.

SWEATERS

The vendors at the **Feira da Ladra** marketplace (see "Markets," above) sell a wide selection of Portuguese sweaters. **Casa Bordados da Madeira** (Rua do 1 de Dezembro 137; ℂ **21/342-14-47**) carries a fine selection of Nazaré-style fisher's sweaters.

TILES

Fábrica Viúva Lamego   Founded in 1879, this shop offers contemporary tiles—mostly reproductions of old Portuguese motifs—and pottery, including an interesting selection of bird and animal motifs. When you reach the store, you'll know you're at the right place: Its facade is decorated with colorful glazed tiles. Largo do Intendente 25. ℂ **21/885-24-08.** www.viuvalamego.com. Metro: Intendente. Tram: 28. Bus: 8.

LISBON AFTER DARK

If you have only 1 night in Lisbon, spend it at a fado club. The nostalgic sounds of fado, Portuguese "songs of sorrow," are at their best in Lisbon—the capital attracts the greatest *fadistas* (fado singers) in the world. Fado is high art in Portugal, so don't plan to carry on a private conversation during a show—it's bad form. Most of the authentic fado clubs are clustered in the Bairro Alto and in the Alfama, between St. George's Castle and the docks. You can "fado hop" between the two quarters. If you're visiting the Alfama, have the taxi driver let you off at **Largo do Chafariz,** a small plaza a block from the harbor; in the Bairro Alto, get off at **Largo de São Roque.** Most of the places we recommend lie only a short walk away.

For more information about nighttime attractions, go to the tourist office (see "Visitor Information," under "Fast Facts" in chapter 15), which maintains a list of events. Another helpful source is the **Agência de Bilhetes para Espectáculos Públicos,** in Praça dos Restauradores (ℂ **21/342-53-60**). It's open daily from 9am

FADO: THE MUSIC OF LOST love

The *saudade* (Portuguese for "longing" or "nostalgia") that infuses the country's literature is most evident in fado. The traditional songs express Portugal's sad, romantic mood. The traditional performers are women *(fadistas)*, often accompanied by a guitar and a viola.

Experiencing the nostalgic sounds of fado is essential to comprehending the Portuguese soul. Fado is Portugal's most vivid art form; no visit to the country is complete without at least 1 night spent in a local tavern listening to this traditional folk music.

A rough translation of *fado* is "fate," from the Latin *fatum* (prophecy). Fado songs usually tell of unrequited love, jealousy, or a longing for days gone by. The music, as is often said, evokes a "life commanded by the Oracle, which nothing can change."

Fado became famous in the 19th century when Maria Severa, the beautiful daughter of a Gypsy, took Lisbon by storm. She sang her way into the hearts of the people of Lisbon—especially the count of Vimioso, an outstanding bullfighter. Present-day *fadistas* wear a black-fringed shawl in her memory.

The most famous 20th-century exponent of fado was Amália Rodriguez, who was introduced to American audiences in the 1950s at the New York club La Vie en Rose. Born into a simple Lisbon family, she was discovered while walking barefoot and selling flowers on the Lisbon docks near the Alfama. For many, she is the most famous Portuguese figure since Vasco da Gama. Swathed in black, sparing of gestures and excess ornamentation, Rodriguez almost singlehandedly executed the transformation of fado into an international form of poetic expression.

to 9:30pm; go in person instead of trying to call. The agency sells tickets to most theaters and cinemas.

Also check out copies of ***What's On in Lisbon,*** available at most newsstands; *Sete,* a weekly magazine with entertainment listings; or the free monthly guides *Agenda Cultural* and *LISBOaem.* Your hotel concierge is a good bet for information, too, because one of his or her duties is reserving seats. Note that the local newspaper, *Diário de Notícias,* carries all cultural listings, but only in Portuguese.

By the standards of the United States and Canada, "the party" in Lisbon begins late. Many bars don't even open until 10 or 11pm, and very few savvy young Portuguese would set foot in a club before 1am. The Bairro Alto, with some 150 restaurants and bars, is the most happening place after dark.

The Performing Arts
CLASSICAL MUSIC
Centro Cultural de Belém ★★   This center (p. 106), is a major venue for the presentation of concerts by various international orchestras and classical recitals, even performances by top jazz artists and other visiting musicians. Some of the best dance programs in Portugal are also presented here, along with top-of-the-line theatrical productions. You can check the local newspapers upon your arrival in Lisbon to see if a featured presentation interests you. Praça do Império. ℭ **21/361-24-44.** www.ccb.pt. Tram: 15.

Museu Calouste Gulbenkian ★ From October to June, concerts, recitals, and occasionally ballet performances take place here; sometimes there are also jazz concerts. Ticket prices vary according to the performance. Av. de Berna 45. ✆ **21/782-30-00.** www.museu.gulbenkian.pt. Metro: Sebastião. Bus: 16, 56, 718, or 726.

OPERA & BALLET

Teatro Nacional de São Carlos ★★ This 18th-century theater attracts opera and ballet aficionados from all over Europe, and top companies from around the world perform here. The season begins in mid-September and extends through July. There are no special discounts. Rua Serpa Pinto 9. ✆ **21/325-30-45.** www.saocarlos.pt. Tickets 10€–100€. Box office Mon–Fri 1-7pm, Sat-Sun and holidays from 1pm to 30 min. after the show begins. Tram: 28, 58, 100, or 204 (night service). Bus: 58. Metro: Baixa-Chiado.

THEATER

Teatro Nacional D. Maria II ★ Portugal's most famous and prestigious theater dates back to the mid-19th century. The season usually begins in the autumn and lasts through spring. It presents a repertoire of both Portuguese and foreign plays, with performances strictly in Portuguese. Praça de Dom Pedro IV. ✆ **21/325-08-00** or 21/325-08-35 for reservations. www.teatro-dmaria.pt. Tickets 7€–16€, half-price for students up to 25 years old and ages 65 and older with valid ID. Metro: Rossio. Bus: 2, 9, 39, 44, 45, or 91.

The Club & Music Scene

FADO CLUBS

In the clubs listed below, it isn't necessary to have dinner; you can just have a drink. However, you often have to pay a minimum consumption charge. The music begins between 9 and 10pm, but it's better to arrive after 11pm. Many clubs stay open until 3am; others stay open until dawn.

Adega Machado ★★ This spot has been open since 1937, but has passed the test of time—it's still one of the country's favorite fado clubs. Alternating with such modern-day *fadistas* as the critically acclaimed Marina Rosa are folk dancers whirling, clapping, and singing native songs in colorful costumes. Dinner is a la carte, and the cuisine is mostly Portuguese, with a number of regional dishes. Expect to spend 25€ to 35€ for a complete meal. The dinner hour starts at 8pm, music begins at 9:15pm, and the doors don't close until 3am. It's open Tuesday through Sunday. They accept Amex, Discover, MasterCard, and Visa. Rua do Norte 91. ✆ **21/322-46-40.** www.adega machado.web.pt. Cover (including 2 drinks) 16€. Bus: 58 or 100.

A Severa ★ Although it's not quite as good as Adega Machado (see above), good food and the careful selection of *fadistas* make this a perennial favorite. Every night, top male and female singers appear, accompanied by guitar and viola music, alternating with folk dancers. In a niche, you'll spot a statue honoring the club's namesake, Maria Severa, the legendary 19th-century Gypsy *fadista*. As difficult or as unsettling as it might be to imagine, before Richard Nixon became U.S. president, he came here with his wife, Patricia, and led a congalike line between tables while warbling the refrain, "Severa . . . Severa . . . Severa." After midnight, tourists seem to recede a bit in favor of loyal habitués, who request and sometimes join in on their favorite fado number (though not usually forming Nixonian conga lines).

The kitchen turns out regional dishes based on recipes from the north of Portugal. Expect to spend at least 38€ per person for a meal with wine. An a la carte dinner will run around 18€. It's open Thursday to Tuesday noon to 3pm and 8pm to 3am, and accepts American Express, Discover, MasterCard, and Visa. Rua das Gáveas 51. © **21/346-12-04.** www.asevera.com. No cover. Bus: 20 or 24.

Café Luso In a vaulted network of 17th-century stables, Luso is one of the most famous and enduring fado clubs of the Bairro Alto. Despite a recent trend toward the touristy, it still exerts a folkloric appeal, as it has since it was transformed into a restaurant with music in the 1930s. The entertainment and regional food are presented most nights to some 160 patrons. There are three shows nightly: 8:30 to 10:30pm for the first show, 10:30pm to 12:30am for the second show, and 12:30 to 2am for the third show. Amex, Discover, MasterCard, and Visa are accepted here. Travessa da Queimada 10. © **21/342-22-81.** www.cafeluso.pt. Bus: 58 or 100.

Club de Fado In the heart of the Alfama near the cathedral, the finest guitar playing in Lisbon is heard, often as a backdrop to talented *fadista* voices. The atmosphere is traditional and rather romantic in a setting of columns, arches, and ogival ceilings. Both well-known performers and amateur artists entertain you with their singing and playing. You can order cocktails in the bar as well as a good selection of port wines, or else full meals in the restaurant, where main courses cost from 19€ to 25€. If you're not dining, the cost of the show is 7.50€. Open daily from 9pm to 2am. Rua S. João de Praça 92-94. © **21/885-27-04.** www.clube-de-fado.com. Tram: 12 or 28. Bus: 37.

Museu do Fado ★ Some of the most outstanding *fadistas*, both male and female, perform most nights at this restaurant attached to the municipal **Museu do Fado.** If you're exploring the Alfama during the day, you can drop in for a visit to the museum, which pays homage to Portugal's most distinctive musical style, fado music. The museum is entirely devoted to the world of urban song in Lisbon, tracing the origins and history of fado through photographs, sheet music, musical instruments, phonograms, collections of periodicals, costumes, trophies, and medals. The museum is open Tuesday to Sunday 10am to 6pm, charging 4€ for admission. Adjoining the museum is a restaurant serving regional food Tuesday to Sunday 7pm to 2am. Meals cost from 30€. Largo do Chafariz de Dentro 1. © **21/882-34-70.** www.museudofado.pt. Bus: 28, 735, 745, 759, or 790.

Parreirinha da Alfama Every *fadista* worth her shawl seems to have sung at this old-time cafe, just a minute's walk from the docks of the Alfama. It's fado-only here, not folk dancing, and the place has survived more or less unchanged since its establishment in the early 1950s. In the first part of the program, *fadistas* get the popular songs out of the way and then settle into their more classic favorites. You can order a good regional dinner, although many visitors opt to come here just to drink. It's open daily from 8pm to 3am; music begins at 9:30pm. The atmosphere is a lot more convivial after around 10:30pm, when local stars (who include such luminaries and divas as Lina Maria) have warmed up the crowd a bit. They accept American Express, MasterCard, and Visa. Beco do Espírito Santo 1. © **21/886-82-09.** Cover (credited toward drinks) 15€. Bus: 9, 39, or 46.

COFFEEHOUSES AND CAFES

To the Portuguese, the coffeehouse is an institution, a democratic parlor where they can drop in for their favorite libation, abandon their worries, relax, smoke, read the paper, write a letter, or chat with friends about tomorrow's football match.

The coffeehouse in Portugal, however, is now but a shade of its former self. The older and more colorful places, filled with turn-of-the-20th-century charm, are rapidly yielding to chrome and plastic.

One of the oldest surviving coffeehouses in Lisbon, **A Brasileira ★**, Rua Garrett 120 (✆ **21/346-95-41;** Metro: Rossio), is in the Chiado district. It has done virtually nothing to change the opulent but faded Art Nouveau decor that has prevailed since it became a fashionable rendezvous in 1905. Once a gathering place of Lisbon's literati, it was the favored social spot of the Portuguese poet Bocage of Setúbal, whose works are read by high school students throughout Portugal. He was involved in an incident that has since been elevated into Lisbon legend: When accosted by a bandit who asked him where he was going, he is said to have replied, "I am going to the Brasileira, but if you shoot me I am going to another world." Patrons sit at small tables on chairs made of tooled leather, amid mirrored walls and marble pilasters. A statue of the great Portuguese poet Fernando Pessoa sits on a chair amid the customers. At a table, sandwiches run 2.50€ to 3.50€, pastries are 1.25€ to 2.50€, a demitasse costs 1€ to 2€, and bottled beer goes for 1.75€ to 3€. Prices are a bit lower at the bar, but you'll probably want to linger a while—we recommend sitting down to recover from the congestion and heat. It's open daily from 8am to midnight and accepts cash only.

Although lacking A Brasileira's tradition and style, the **Pastelaria Suiça,** on the south corner of Praça de Rossio 96, in the Baixa (✆ **21/321-40-90;** www.casasuica. pt; Metro: Rossio), is a sprawling cafe-*pastelaria.* It stretches all the way back to the adjoining Praça da Figueira. This house draws more visitors than any other cafe in Lisbon. The outdoor tables fill first, especially in fair weather. In addition to serving an array of coffee and tea, the *pastelaria* is known for its tempting pastries baked on-site. The atmosphere is boisterous, and the place is generally mobbed. It's open daily from 7am to 9pm.

Another possibility is **Versailles,** Av. da República 15A (✆ **21/354-63-40;** www. pastelariaversailles.com; Metro: Saldanha), long known as the grande dame of Lisbon coffeehouses. It's also an ideal place for afternoon tea, in a faded but elegant 60-year-old setting of chandeliers, gilt mirrors, and high ceilings. As an old-fashioned and formal touch, immaculately attired waiters serve customers from silver-plated tea services. In addition to coffee and tea, the house specialty is hot chocolate. The homemade cakes and pastries are delectable. (They're baked on-site.) It's open daily from 7:30am to 10pm.

On the street level of the previously recommended Bairro Alto Hotel, the **Café Bar,** Praça Luís de Camões 8 (✆ **21/340-82-62;** www.bairroaltohotel.com; Metro:

Port Wine Tasting

Solar do Vinho do Porto (✆ **21/347-57-07;** www.ivdp.pt) is devoted exclusively to the drinking and enjoyment of port in all its glory and varieties. A quasi-governmental arm of the Port Wine Institute established the bar a few years after World War II as a low-key merchandizing tool. In a 300-year-old setting near the Glória funicular and the fado clubs of the Bairro Alto, it exudes Iberian atmosphere. The *lista de vinhos* includes more than 200 types of port wine in an amazing variety of sweet, dry, red, and white. A glass of wine costs 1€ to 25€. Open Monday to Friday 11am to midnight; Saturday 2pm to midnight. It's located at Rua de São Pedro de Alcântara 45 (Metro: Restauradores; bus: 58 or 100).

Baixa-Chiado), sprawls across three floors, with its hip minimalist decor. It is a gathering place of young Lisbon. Shared tables add to the conviviality, as DJs spin the latest hot music. If you descend to the lower level, you'll find a lounge whose vaulted ceiling once sheltered alchemists mixing up brews from an age-old pharmacy.

DANCE CLUBS & LIVE MUSIC

Alcântara Café Although this establishment draws most of its business from its sophisticated restaurant (see the Alcântara Café in "Where to Dine," in chapter 4), many club-hoppers come here only for the bar. It's in a former factory and warehouse beside the river, decorated with accessories that evoke a railway car in turn-of-the-20th-century Paris. The patrons—Americans, Portuguese, English, Germans, and Brazilians—aren't shy about striking up dialogues with attractive newcomers. Draft beer in the bar begins at 2.50€; imported whiskey sells for 6€ and up. Expect lots of deliberately provocative outrageousness, gay customers mingling with straights, and sometimes one of the highest percentages of flamboyant drag queens in Lisbon. It's open nightly from 8pm to 3am. Rua Maria Luisa Holstein 15. © **21/363-71-76.** www.alcantaracafe.com. Bus: 12 or 18.

Blues Café You'll probably like this place (as we do), even though it has very little to do with blues music and doesn't even remotely resemble a cafe. It's in a publike space on the river; an eagle's-nest balcony circles around one floor. Rather than blues, the patrons, usually in their 20s to early 30s, prefer the latest hip-hop and garage music. Beer costs 3€ to 5€ a bottle. It's open Tuesday to Thursday 8:30pm to 4am, and Friday and Saturday 8:30pm to 6am. Rua Cintura do Puerto do Lisboa 3–4. © **21/395-70-85.** www.bluescafe.pt. Cover 50€ if full; otherwise free. Tram: 15.

Cabaret Maxime ★ An old cabaret bar, a meeting place for spies in World War II, has reopened. Through its long history, it's been a brothel, a former strip club, a gay disco, and even a luxury cabaret, drawing such clients as the King of Spain. Today it's been turned into a concert venue and a first-rate bar. You can visit to enjoy the music and the exotic cocktails. Open Thursday 10pm to 2am, and Friday and Saturday from 10pm to 4am. Praça da Alegria 58. © **21/346-70-90.** Metro: Avenida.

Lux Frágil Popular, free-form, and hip, this two-story warehouse contains a labyrinth of interconnected spaces, each of which is likely to feature a radically different scene from the one in the room that's immediately adjacent. Set on the banks of the Tagus, a short walk from the Santa Apolónia railway station, it attracts and amuses counterculture hipsters, with theatrical lighting, deep sofas, cutting-edge music, and some highly unusual accessories—one of them is an enormous chandelier composed entirely of steel wire and tampons. Expect this and other forms of offbeat humor, and an ambience that might remind you of a be-in from the 1960s. The upstairs bar, where a DJ spins records, is open daily from 10pm to 6am. The more manic, street-level dance floor is open Thursday to Saturday 1am to 7am. Entrance to both areas is free before midnight; after that, a 15€ cover applies, although there might be a doorman with a velvet rope/barrier keeping out rowdies on weekends. Av. Infante Don Henrique, Armazém (Warehouse) A, Cais da Pedra a Sta. Apolónia. © **21/882-08-90.** www.luxfragil.com. Bus: 9, 39, or 46.

Musicbox Lisboa New York is not the only city that never sleeps. The night here never dies until the sun comes up. Most bars shut down at 2am. That's when the Musicbox gets started as late-night owls pour into this joint under a bridge in the Cais do Sodré sector. Fashionistas, hustlers, PR reps, and various hipsters in their 20s and

30s frequent this cavernlike setting. DJs most often rule the night but occasionally live bands are brought in to entertain. Cover ranges from 8€ to 10€. Open from midnight to 6am daily. Rua Nova de Carvalho 24. ℂ **21/347-31-88.** www.musicboxlisboa.com. Cover 8€. Metro: Cais do Sodré.

Paradise Garage   A frequently reincarnated hot spot in Lisbon for live music is set within a battered early 20th-century building in the Alcantara district. It has witnessed the rise and fall of dozens of musical trends in its role as a nightspot that every twenty-something in Lisbon seems to have visited at least once since its heyday in the 1970s, Call the box office or check one of the local newspapers to find out what's on here while you're visiting because lineups change frequently. A rock concert featuring a group from England or America might be the stars of the evening, and other times you might find a theme night. Internationally known DJs are occasionally brought in to thrill the dancers. Gay nights are also a feature, and prices and times depend on what's playing. Rua João de Oliveira Miguéns 38-48. ℂ **21/324-34-00.** www.paradisegarage.pt. Tram: 15.

Silk ★★   If we had a date for a night in Lisbon with Madonna, we'd take her to this hot spot, all black and fuchsia, with a sexy sultriness. What you see going on in its deep plush couches would bring a blush to aging party boy Jack Nicholson. The visit here would be worthy if just for the incredible vista from the floor-to-ceiling windows. You can also perch on a candlelit outdoor deck on the sixth floor. The DJ spins the tunes as chic young things sip Moët & Chandon, or whatever. The club lies on the upper two floors of Espaço Chiado with its 270-degree breathtaking view of Lisbon. Open Tuesday to Saturday 10pm to 4am. Rua da Misericórdia 14. ℂ **21/780-34-70.** www.silk-club.com.

JAZZ

Onda Jazz ★   The best jazz in Lisbon, often featuring artists from Africa, is presented here in this Alfama dive. The area is surrounded by fado bars, but the sounds coming from here are distinctly different. In addition to the wide array of jazz rhythms, the bar often features Latin and Asian jazz. The cover can vary, but it's usually around 10€. Open Tuesday, Thursday, and Sunday 8pm to 2am; Friday and Saturday 8pm to 3am. Arco de Jesus 7. ℂ 21/888-32-42. www.ondajazz.com. Tram: 28.

THE BAR SCENE

Bairru's Bodega   In a warm, inviting atmosphere this is one of the best of the wine bars in the Bairro Alto district, which comes alive at night. Against a backdrop of Portuguese music, you sit at tables made from wine barrels. There is a wide array of Portuguese wines to choose from, and you can also order by the glass, costing from 3.50€. The bartender can also introduce you to a number of exotic liqueurs such as carob or lump loquat. Unlike other bars in the district, this bodega does not serve beer. Regional cheese and local hams and sausages are also served. Open Monday to Saturday 7pm to 2am. Rua da Barroca 3. ℂ **21/346-90-60.** www.bairrusbodega.com. Metro: Chiado.

Bar Procópio ★ 🎒   A longtime favorite of journalists, politicians, and foreign actors, the once-innovative Procópio has become a tried-and-true staple among Lisbon's watering holes. Guests sit on tufted red velvet, surrounded by stained and painted glass and ornate brass hardware. Mixed drinks cost 7€ and up; beer costs 3€ and up. Procópio might easily become your favorite bar, if you can find it. It lies just off Rua de João Penha, which is off the landmark Praça das Amoreiras. Open Monday to Friday 6pm to 3am, Saturday 9pm to 3am. Alto de São Francisco 21. ℘ **21/385-28-51.** www.barprocopio.com. Closed Aug 11–Sept 8. Metro: Rato. Bus: 9.

Bora-Bora   A Polynesian bar might seem out of place in Lisbon, but the theme draws packs of locals who are tired of a constant diet of Iberian folklore. As you might expect from an urban bar with a Hawaiian theme, Bora-Bora specializes in imaginative variations on fruity, flaming, and rum-laced drinks. The couches are comfortable and inviting, angled for views of the Polynesian art that lines the walls. Beer costs 4€; mixed drinks are 6€ and up. It's open Friday and Saturday from 9pm to 3:30am. Rua da Madalena 201. ℘ **21/887-20-43.** Metro: Rossio. Tram: 12 or 28.

CINCO Lounge ★★   This is the hottest, chicest bar in all of Lisbon. Lying above the Bairro Alto section, it features an array of dazzling cocktails—some 100 in all—using only the most expensive of liquors and the freshest of fruits. Age is not a factor here, providing you're of drinking age. The waiter will exchange your drink for one you prefer, if you don't like the first choice. That is, if you order anything but The Black Amex, which costs 235€. It's a crystallized brown sugar cube dissolved in Hennessy VS Cognac and Cuvée du Centenaire Grand Marnier, spiked with Dom Perignon. The setting is elegant, with floor-to-ceiling windows, glass-topped tables, and the most flattering lighting in Lisbon. It's open daily from 5pm to 2am. Rua Ruben A. Leitão 17A. ℘ **21/342-40-33.** www.cincolounge.com. Metro: Rato.

Garrafeira Alfaia ★ ▮   This traditionally styled wine bar in the Bairro Alto is surrounded by a cultural mélange of trendy shops, restaurants, bars, and houses where *fadistas* perform. It's a good place to spend the early part of the evening before going on to dinner, attracting a mixture of locals and visitors. You can sample an impressive collection of Portuguese wines and savory tapas. Tapas include such fare as *sericaia,* an airy, eggy soufflé served with the famous sugarplums of Elvas. You can also try charcuterie from the famous "black pigs" of Portugal, or else a sheep's milk cheese coagulated with cardoon thistle. Wines range from a Chardonnay from the Alentejo region to some of the better vintages from the Upper Douro in the north. Glasses of wine cost between 3€ and 10€, with tapas priced from 6€ to 12€. Open daily 4pm to 1am. Rua do Diário de Noticias 125. ℘ **21/343-30-79.** www.garrafeiraalfaia.com. Bus: 58.

Panorama Bar   The Panorama Bar occupies the top floor of one of Portugal's tallest buildings, the 30-story Lisboa Sheraton. The view (day or night) is of the old and new cities of Lisbon, the mighty Tagus, and many of the towns on the river's far bank. The cosmopolitan decor incorporates chiseled stone and stained glass. You'll pay 8.50€ to 12€ for a whiskey and soda. Opening hours are Sunday to Wednesday noon to 2am; Thursday and Friday noon to 3am; Saturday 6pm to 3am; Sunday 6pm to 2am. In the Sheraton Lisboa Hotel & Spa, Rua Latino Coelho 1. ℘ **21/312-00-00.** www.sheratonlisboa. com. Metro: Picoas. Bus: 1, 2, 9, or 32.

Pavilhão Chines   The mother of all flea market bars, this watering hole in the Bairro Alto contains a collection of kitsch that alone is worth the trek here. Replicas of everyone from Buddha to Popeye decorate the joint, along with bronze cupids, Toby tankards, baubles and beads, and enough Victoriana to fill half the attics of London. It's a lively venue open Monday to Friday 6pm to 2am, and Saturday 9pm to 2am. Rua Dom Pedro V 89. ℘ **21/342-47-29.** Metro: Rato.

Restô do Chapitô ★ ▮   Hidden away deep in the heart of the Alfama, right below the castle, is one of the drinking (or dining) secrets of Lisbon. The weathered building that contains it has been used, during its turbulent history, as a 17th-century prison and later as a state-sponsored school for the training of circus performers. The view is one of the most panoramic in the Alfama. You can drop in for a coffee or return later, taking a candlelit table to enjoy a limited but choice menu, ranging from succulent and large steaks to a vast array of tapas, often stuffed calamari or even roasted green chili peppers, and lots more. Open Tuesday to Friday 7:30pm to 2am and Saturday and Sunday from 10am to 2am. Rua Costa do Castelo 7, São Cristóvão. ℂ **21/886-73-34.** www.chapito.org. Tram: 28.

GAY & LESBIAN BARS & CLUBS

Although this ultra-Catholic country remains one of the most closeted in western Europe, at least eight gay nightspots have sprung up in the district known as Príncipe Real. With each passing year, the gay presence in Lisbon becomes more visible. You might begin your night crawl at either of the first two establishments listed below.

Bar 106   A short walk from the also-recommended Finalmente, this is a popular bar, rendezvous point, and watering hole for gay men, most of whom arrive here after around 10pm. Expect a simple, restrained decor, a busy bar area, and enough space to allow subgroups and cliques of like-minded friends to form quickly and easily. It's open nightly from 9pm until 2am. Rua de São Marçal 106. ℂ **21/342-73-73.** www.bar106.com. Tram: 28. Bus: 100.

Finalmente Club   This is the dance club that many gay men in Lisbon end up at after an evening of drinking and talking in other bars around the Bairro Alto. There's a hardworking, hard-drinking bar area; a crowded dance floor; lots of bodies of all shapes and sizes; and a small stage upon which drag shows allow local *artistes* to strut their stuff and emulate—among others—Carmen look-alikes from Seville. A stringent security system requires that you ring a bell before an attendant will let you in. It's open daily from 1am to between 3 and 6am, depending on business. Rua da Palmeira 38. ℂ **21/347-99-23.** Cover 14€, includes 1st drink. Bus: 100.

Frágil   Don't expect a sign that indicates the location of this place: All you'll see are some blue neon lights and a vigilant doorman. Frágil devotes itself to counterculture music, gay men and women, and a scattering of heterosexuals who appreciate the cutting-edge music and permissive atmosphere. Technically, the place opens Tuesday to Saturday at 11:30pm, but don't expect a crowd until at least midnight—and a mob by around 2am. Closing is around 4am the following morning. Rua da Atalaia 126-128. ℂ **21/346-95-78.** www.fragil.com.pt. Cover 10€. Bus: 58 or 100. Metro: Chiado.

Trumps   Of the bars recommended within this nightlife section, this is the one with the most whimsical staff and the most erratic opening hours. Known to local English-speaking wits as Tramps, it's positioned near (but not in) the Bairro Alto. Several bars are scattered throughout its two levels, along with an active dance floor and lots of cruising options within its shadowy corners. Lesbians make up about a quarter of the crowd, but most of the patrons here are gay males. This place is open Friday and Saturday 11:45pm to 6am. *Our advice:* Hang out at Finalmente or Frágil, and ask one of the regular patrons there about the opening hours and ongoing viability of Trumps. Rua da Imprensa Nacional 104B. ℂ **21/397-10-59.** www.trumps.pt. Cover (credited toward drinks) 13€. Bus: 58.

ESTORIL, CASCAIS & SINTRA

L ured by Guincho (near the westernmost point in continental Europe), the Boca do Inferno (Mouth of Hell), and Lord Byron's "glorious Eden" at Sintra, many travelers spend much of their time in this region, just west of Lisbon. You could spend a day drinking in the wonders of the library at the monastery-palace of Mafra (Portugal's El Escorial), dining in the pretty pink rococo palace at Queluz, or enjoying seafood at the Atlantic beach resort of Ericeira.

However, the main draw in the area is the Costa do Sol. The string of beach resorts, including Estoril and Cascais, forms the Portuguese Riviera on the northern bank of the mouth of the Tagus. If you arrive in Lisbon when the sun is shining and the air is balmy, consider heading straight for the shore. Estoril is so close to Lisbon that darting in and out of the capital to see the sights or visit the fado clubs is easy. An inexpensive electric train leaves from the Cais do Sodré station in Lisbon frequently throughout the day and evening; its run ends in Cascais.

Although the beachfront strip of the Costa do Sol is justifiably famous, it's generally recommended that you swim in the pools (indoor or outdoor) at the resort hotels. For the most part, the waters along the coast are polluted and, therefore, not recommended for swimming. Despite this, the beaches are still great for getting a suntan.

The sun coast is sometimes known as A Costa dos Reis, the Coast of Kings, because it's a magnet for deposed royalty—exiled kings, pretenders, marquesses from Italy, princesses from Russia, and baronesses from Germany. Some live simply, as did the late Princess Elena of Romania (Magda Lupescu), a virtual recluse in an unpretentious villa. Others insist on a rigid court atmosphere, as did Umberto, who was king of Italy for 1 month in 1946 and then was forced into exile. Other nobles who settled here include Don Juan, the count of Barcelona, who lost the Spanish throne in 1969 when his son, Don Juan Carlos, was named successor by Generalissimo Franco; Joanna, the former queen of Bulgaria; and the Infanta Dona Maria Adelaide de Bragança, sister of the pretender to the Portuguese throne.

Despite the heavy concentration of royals, the Riviera is a microcosm of Portugal. Take a ride out on the train, even if you don't plan to stay here.

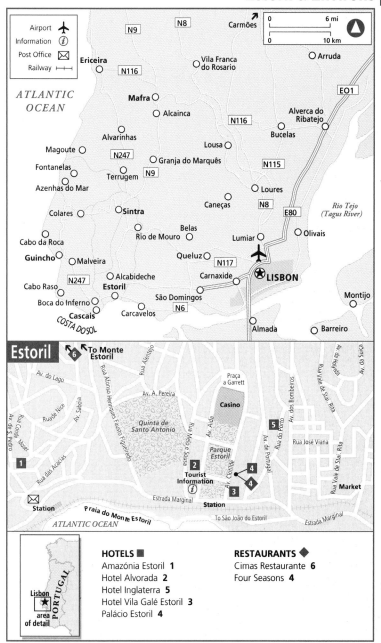

HOTELS ■
Amazónia Estoril **1**
Hotel Alvorada **2**
Hotel Inglaterra **5**
Hotel Vila Galé Estoril **3**
Palácio Estoril **4**

RESTAURANTS ◆
Cimas Restaurante **6**
Four Seasons **4**

You'll pass pastel-washed houses with red-tile roofs and facades of antique blue-and-white tiles; miles of modern apartment dwellings; rows of canna, pine, mimosa, and eucalyptus; swimming pools; and, in the background, green hills studded with villas, chalets, and new homes.

Lisbon is the aerial gateway for the Costa do Sol and Sintra. Once there, you can drive or take public transportation.

ESTORIL: PLAYGROUND OF ROYALTY ★

13km (8 miles) S of Sintra; 24km (15 miles) W of Lisbon

This chic resort with its beautiful beaches along the Portuguese Riviera has long basked in its reputation as a playground of monarchs. Fading countesses arrive at the railway station, monarchs in exile drop in at the Palácio Estoril for dinner, and the sons of deposed dictators sunbathe by the pool. Today's Estoril was the creation of Fausto Figueiredo, who built the deluxe Palácio in 1930. The casino opened in the late 1960s. During World War II, as Nazi troops advanced across Europe, many collapsed courts fled to Estoril to wait out the war in a neutral country.

Essentials

ARRIVING

BY TRAIN   Electric trains leave from the waterfront Cais do Sodré station in Lisbon. The round-trip fare is 3€, and departures are every 20 minutes for the half-hour trip. Trains operate daily 5:30am to 1:30am. For information, call ℂ **80/820-82-08;** www.cp.pt.

BY BUS   Buses from Lisbon are impractical, considering the low cost and convenience of the frequent trains. But if you're coming to Estoril from Sintra, the bus is your best bet; about a dozen buses a day make the 1-hour run. The round-trip fare is 4€.

BY CAR   From Lisbon, head west on Route 6; try to avoid driving on weekends, when there's considerable traffic in both directions. Driving time depends on traffic, which tends to be heavy almost all day and night. It's lightest Monday to Friday 10am to 4pm. Rush hours are brutal, as is the rush to the beach on Saturday and Sunday before 10am and the rush back to Lisbon on Saturday and Sunday between 4 and 6pm. It might be easier on your nerves to take the electric train and forget about driving along the coast.

VISITOR INFORMATION

Junta de Turismo da Costa do Estoril is at Avenida Aida, Edificio Arcadas Parque (ℂ **21/466-38-13;** www.estorilcoast-tourism.com), across from the train station. It's open Monday to Saturday 9am to 7pm, Sunday 10am to 6pm; summer Monday to Saturday 9am to 8pm.

Having Fun in Estoril

EXPLORING THE RESORT   Parque Estoril, in the center of town, is a well-manicured landscape. At night, when it's floodlit, you can stroll amid the subtropical vegetation. The palm trees studding the grounds have prompted many to call it "a corner of Africa." At the top of the park sits the casino, which offers gambling, international floor shows, dancing, and movies.

Across the railroad tracks is the beach, where some of the most fashionable people in Europe sun themselves on peppermint-striped canvas chairs along the Praia Estoril Tamariz. The beach is sandy, unlike the pebbly strand at Nice. Although it is a lovely stretch of sand, we don't recommend going into the water, which is almost too polluted for swimming. You can enjoy the sands and the beach scene, but for actual swimming, head to one of the many hotel pools in the area.

Tamariz draws more gay patrons than any other beach in Portugal, although the beach in general has a little bit of everything. The gay section is easy to discern; as one beach buff said, "It's easy. Just gravitate to the section with the most pumped-up bodies."

To the east is São João do Estoril, which also has a regrettably polluted beach but many handsome private villas. Most visitors go there to dine and dance.

OUTDOOR ACTIVITIES   Other than the beach, the big activity here is golf. A fixture in Estoril since 1940, **Clube de Golf do Estoril,** Avenida da República (© **21/468-01-76**), lies in the foothills of Sintra, a 3-minute drive from the casino at Estoril. The course, one of the finest in Europe, has played host to international championship matches. The club has a 9-hole course and an 18-hole course. Monday to Friday, nonmembers can play 18 holes for 55€. Saturday and Sunday are reserved for members of the club or guests of the Palácio Estoril (see below), who pay 28€ Monday to Friday and 33€ on weekends.

The most modern complex of tennis courts in town, shared by most of the city's major resorts, is the **Clube de Ténis do Estoril,** Avenida Conte de Barcelona (© **21/466-27-70;** www.clubedetenisdoestoril.com). It offers more than 20 tennis courts, including most of the newest in town, and charges between 9€ and 14€ per person per hour for play. Within a short walk of the Palácio Estoril, it's open daily from 9am until dusk.

SHOPPING   Other than the upscale hotel boutiques that sell scarves and poolside accessories, Estoril does not abound with shopping options. Most dedicated consumers head for the markets of Lisbon or for the large-scale shopping center in Cascais (see "Cascais," later in this chapter), a 10-minute drive from Estoril.

In July and August, the resort sponsors an open-air handicrafts fair, the **Feira do Artesanato,** near the casino. It's worth a visit even if you're staying in Cascais. The fair runs nightly from around 5pm until midnight. In addition to good regional specialties, the stalls sell handicrafts and art, including ceramics, from all parts of Portugal. You can also drive 6.5km (4 miles) southeast of Estoril to the town of **Carcavelos,** which has a busy market on Thursday from 7am to 5pm. You'll see local arts and crafts along with more mundane items such as food and clothing. You can also reach Carcavelos by train from Estoril; it's best to go in the morning.

Where to Stay
EXPENSIVE

Palácio Estoril ★★★   The Palácio Estoril is legendary as a retreat for exiled royalty and a center of espionage during World War II. At its 1930 debut, the Palácio received the honeymooning Japanese crown prince and his bride. Umberto, the deposed king of Italy, and Don Juan, the count of Barcelona, followed. During World

War II, when people escaped from Nazi-occupied Europe with little more than a case of jewels and the clothes on their back, the hotel accepted diamonds, rubies, and gold instead of money.

The reception rooms are Pompeian, with sienna-colored marble pillars, bold bands of orange, and handmade carpets. The intimate salons are ideal for a tête-à-tête. The large guest rooms are traditional, with fine Regency-style furnishings, walk-in closets, and luxurious bathrooms with bidets and heated towel racks. Single rooms facing the rear are the smallest but also the quietest. The hotel opens onto the side of Estoril Park, which is capped by the casino. The beach is a short walk away.

Rua Particular, 2769-504 Estoril. www.palacioestorilhotel.com. (*) **21/464-80-00.** Fax 21/464-81-59. 162 units. 320€–390€ double; from 400€ junior suite. Rates include American breakfast. AE, DC, MC, V. Free parking. **Amenities:** Restaurant; bar; babysitting; concierge; golf course nearby; outdoor pool; room service; spa. *In room:* A/C, TV, hair dryer, minibar, Wi-Fi (8€ per 24 hr.).

MODERATE

Amazónia Estoril ★★ 📠 Partially because of its emphasis on golf, this hillside hotel seems a lot like a corner of Scotland. It's located about 2km (1¼ miles) from the Clube de Golf do Estoril course. Near the bar, there's even a map of the golf course at St. Andrews, close to autographed photos of the many championship golfers who have stayed here. The gardens make this place one of the town's prime attractions.

The midsize accommodations are comfortable and attractive. The most desirable and spacious are in the main building, a former private home. All the rooms have balconies and come with stylish bathrooms. Suites are equipped with kitchenettes.

Rua Eng. Álvaro Pedro Sousa 175, 2765 Estoril. www.amazoniahoteis.com. (*) **21/468-04-24.** Fax 21/467-08-59. 32 units. 110€–196€ double; 135€–227€ suite. Rates include buffet breakfast. AE, DC, MC, V. Free parking. **Amenities:** Restaurant; 2 bars; babysitting; outdoor pool; room service. *In room:* A/C, TV, hair dryer, minibar, Wi-Fi (7.50€ per 24 hr.).

Hotel Alvorada This hotel, which opened its doors in 1969, is fully renovated but still merely functional. It provides pousada-style accommodations on a small scale. The hotel stands opposite the casino and the Parque Estoril, just a 3-minute walk from the beach. It's recommended for its well-maintained but unstylish midsize guest rooms, each of which has balconies. The top-floor solarium offers a panoramic view of the sea. Only breakfast is served.

Rua de Lisboa 3, 2765-240 Estoril. www.hotelalvorada.com. (*) **21/464-98-60.** Fax 21/468-72-50. 51 units. 90€–290€ double; 145€–330€ triple. Rates include continental breakfast. AE, DC, MC, V. Free parking. **Amenities:** Bar; babysitting; room service *In room:* A/C, TV, hair dryer, Wi-Fi (5€ per 24 hr.).

Hotel Inglaterra ★ ☺ 📠 This is a well-preserved historical gem, boasting an idyllic location on a hilltop overlooking the coast. Around the turn of the 20th century, it was constructed as a private palace, but has been cleverly repositioned as a boutique hotel. The colonial look so typical of the country's hotels is missing here—in fact, you'd think a Japanese decorator passed through here, what with all the minimalist black wooden furniture and the Asian artifacts used for decor. We like the rooms with private terraces overlooking the hills of Sintra or the bay of Cascais with all its expensive yachts the best. The hotel could serve as both a romantic retreat for couples or else a family favorite—there's even a kiddie playground.

Rua do Porto 1, 2765-271 Estoril. www.hotelinglaterra.com.pt. (*) **21/468-44-61.** Fax 21/468-21-08. 55 units. 60€–300€ double; 110€–350€ suite. AE, DC, MC, V. Free parking. **Amenities:** Restaurant; 2 bars; babysitting; bikes; children's center; concierge; exercise room; outdoor pool; room service. *In room:* A/C, TV, hair dryer, minibar, Wi-Fi (6€ per 24 hr.).

INEXPENSIVE

Hotel Vila Galé Estoril ★ Built in the late 1950s next door to the far more glamorous Palácio (see above), this hotel rises seven floors with walls of soaring glass. About half the rooms boast good-size balconies overlooking the water and the casino. Only a minute or so from the sea and the electric train station, it's in the center of Estoril's boutique district. Bedrooms feature stylish modern stained-wood furniture and a neatly kept bathroom.

Av. Marginal, Apartado 492766-901 Estoril. www.vilagale.pt. ℂ **21/464-84-00.** Fax 21/464-84-32. 126 units. 65€–156€ double. Rates include buffet breakfast. AE, DC, MC, V. Parking 7.50€. **Amenities:** Restaurant; 2 bars; babysitting; concierge; health club; Jacuzzi; golf course (nearby); outdoor pool; room service; sauna; Wi-Fi (5€ per hour, in lobby). In room: A/C, TV, hair dryer, minibar.

Nearby Places to Stay

A satellite of Estoril, Monte Estoril is less than 1km (⅔ mile) west, on the road to Cascais. Built across the slope of a hill, it opens onto a vista of Cascais Bay and the Atlantic beyond.

EXPENSIVE

Hotel Estoril Eden ★ ☺ The government-rated four-star Hotel Estoril Eden is an ideal place for families because it offers apartments. Built in 1985, the white-walled tower sits on a rocky knoll above the road paralleling the edge of the sea. The soundproof, moderately sized apartments are decently decorated with sturdy wooden furniture, comfortable armchairs, good beds with low headboards, and prints on the white walls. Each has a kitchenette, tiled bathrooms, and a balcony with a sea view.

Av. Sabóia 209, Monte Estoril, 2769-502 Estoril. www.hotelestorileden.pt. ℂ **21/466-76-00.** Fax 21/466-76-01. 162 apts. 182€–302€ apt for 2. Rates include buffet breakfast. AE, DC, MC, V. Parking 15€. **Amenities:** Restaurant; 3 bars; babysitting; exercise room; Jacuzzi; 2 pools (1 heated indoor); sauna. In room: A/C, TV, hair dryer, kitchenette, Wi-Fi (8€ per 24 hr.).

INEXPENSIVE

Saboia Estoril Hotel Just a 500m (1,640-ft.) walk from the nearest good beach, this six-floor hotel dates from the 1970s and lies next to a small garden in a tranquil residential neighborhood of mainly 19th-century private villas. Since its opening, it has been renovated on an as-needed basis. Bedrooms are midsize and tastefully, though simply, decorated with standard motel-type furnishings. The best accommodations are those with private balconies opening onto views of the sea; about half of the units fall into this category. Right next to the pool is a Jacuzzi and Turkish bath, and on-site is a small gym.

Rua Belmonte 1, Monte Estoril, 2765-398 Estoril. www.hotelsaboia.com. ℂ **21/468-02-02.** Fax 21/468-11-17. 48 units. 45€–100€ double. Rates include buffet breakfast. AE, DC, MC, V. Free parking. **Amenities:** Snack bar; babysitting; bikes; exercise room; outdoor pool. In room: A/C, TV, hair dryer, minibar, Wi-Fi (12€ per 24 hr.).

Where to Dine

EXPENSIVE

Four Seasons ★★★ INTERNATIONAL For fine food, go to the Four Seasons, whose connection with one of Portugal's most famous hotels gives it immediate cachet. But even on its own merit, it is one of the finest—and one of the most expensive—restaurants in Estoril.

The menus and the service at the Four Seasons reflect the seasons, changing four times a year. Other than the handful of intimate tables set on the upper mezzanine, the elaborately decorated tables cluster around a beautiful but purely decorative Iberian kitchen. The quiet, the candles, and the rich colors invite comparison to an elegant 19th-century Russian home. However, the discreet charm and polite manners of the well-trained staff are distinctively Portuguese.

The international cuisine is superb. For an appetizer, you might select three-cheese crepes, lobster bisque, or chilled mussel soup. To follow, try sole meunière, medallions of grouper with seaweed and salmon roe, flamed shrimp *amira*, or a *parrillada* of lobster, shrimp, mussels, and clams for two. Meat dishes include beef and veal stuffed with shrimp, medallions of venison with chestnuts, and wild boar cutlets with pineapple. The fixed-price menu includes soup or appetizer, a main course, dessert, mineral water, and coffee. Wine can be added for a supplement of 8€.

In the Palácio Estoril, Rua do Parque. ✆ **21/464-80-00.** Reservations required. Main courses 24€–48€. AE, DC, MC, V. Daily noon–3pm and 7:30–10:30pm.

MODERATE

Cimas Restaurante ★ INTERNATIONAL/PORTUGUESE In Monte Estoril, just outside the center of Estoril, this restaurant is housed in the replica of an Elizabethan cottage. Tables open onto views of the sea. You'll dine very well here on market-fresh ingredients skillfully handled by a well-trained kitchen staff. The bar that opened on this site in World War II became a haven for spies. In time, it became the unofficial headquarters of opponents of the Franco regime in Spain. Novelists, journalists, and artists flocked here. The savory sea bass with clams is a specialty. Other good dishes include salt codfish casserole; monkfish on a spit with prawns and fresh squid; and lamb kidneys in a Madeira wine sauce.

Av. Marginal, Monte Estoril. ✆ **21/468-12-54.** www.cimas.com.pt. Reservations recommended. Main courses 10€–35€. DC, MC, V. Mon–Sat 12:30–4pm and 7:30–11pm. Closed 2nd and 3rd week of Aug.

Estoril After Dark

GAMBLING An alcohol-stoked crawl through the upscale bars of such hotels as the Palácio might provide insights into the glamour of this pocket of Portugal. If you're looking for something more formal, check out the **Casino Estoril,** in the Parque Estoril, Praça José Teodoro dos Santos (✆ **21/466-77-00;** www.casino-estoril.pt). There's a cover charge of 5€ for entrance into the section with the gaming tables (roulette, French banque, *chemin de fer,* blackjack, and craps); you can gamble to your heart's content every day between 3pm and 3am. You must present a passport, driver's license, or other form of photo ID, and you must be 18 or over. A jacket is required. Entrance to the separate slot-machine room is free and requires no ID. Built in the late 1950s, the casino rises from a formally landscaped garden on a hilltop near the town center. Glass walls enclose an inner courtyard with fountains and tiled paths.

CLUBS & BARS The casino is the venue for the region's splashiest and most colorful weekend cabaret act, **Salão Preto e Prata,** in the Casino Estoril, Parque Estoril, Praça José Teodoro dos Santos (✆ **21/466-77-00;** www.casino-estoril.pt). Expect leggy, feathered, and bejeweled dancers strutting around in billowing trains and bespangled bras. Food is served in the 700-seat theater or in the 150-seat satellite restaurant. Shows are presented Saturday at 5pm and 9:30pm and again on Sunday at 5pm. Dinner, including access to the show, costs 56€ to 65€ per person. The cover charge is 21€ on both Saturday and Sunday.

CASCAIS ★★

6.5km (4 miles) W of Estoril; 61km (38 miles) W of Lisbon

In the 1930s, Cascais was a tiny fishing village that attracted artists and writers to its little cottages. But it was once known as a royal village because it enjoyed the patronage of Portugal's ruling family. When the monarchy died, the military replaced it. General António Óscar de Fragoso Carmona, president of Portugal until 1951, once occupied the 17th-century fort guarding the Portuguese Riviera.

To say Cascais is growing would be an understatement: It's exploding! Apartment houses, new hotels, and the finest restaurants along the Costa do Sol draw a never-ending stream of visitors every year.

However, the life of the simple fisher folk goes on. Auctions, called *lotas,* of the latest catch still take place on the main square. In the small harbor, rainbow-colored fishing boats share space with pleasure craft owned by an international set that flocks to Cascais from early spring until autumn.

The town's tie with the sea is old. If you speak Portuguese, chat up any of the local fishers. They'll tell you that one of their own, Afonso Sanches, discovered America in 1482. Legend has it that Columbus learned of his accidental find, stole the secret, and enjoyed the subsequent acclaim.

Essentials

ARRIVING

BY TRAIN   The round-trip fare from Lisbon's Cais do Sodré to either Estoril (the second-to-last stop) or Cascais (the end of the line) costs 4.50€. Electric trains arrive from and depart from Lisbon at intervals of every 20 minutes. Service runs daily from 5:30am to 1:30am. For information in Lisbon, in Cascais, or Estoril call ℂ **80/820-82-08.**

BY BUS   Buses from Lisbon are impractical, considering the low cost and convenience of the frequent trains. But if you're coming to Cascais from Sintra, the bus is your best bet; about a dozen buses a day make the 1-hour run. The round-trip fare is 7€.

BY CAR   From Estoril (see "Estoril," earlier in this chapter), continue west along Route 6 for another 6.5km (4 miles).

VISITOR INFORMATION

The **Cascais Tourist Office** is at Rua Visconde da Luz, 2750 Cascais (ℂ **21/486-82-04;** www.estorilcoast-tourism.com). The tourist office is open Monday to Friday 9am to 7pm, Saturday and Sunday 9am to 8pm. In summer (June to September), it's open daily 9am to 8pm.

Having Fun in Cascais

EXPLORING THE TOWN   Many visitors, both foreign and domestic, clog the roads to Cascais on summer Sundays, when bullfights are held at the **Monumental de Cascais,** a ring outside the "city" center (see "Spectator Sports," in chapter 5 for info on other bullfights in the area).

When you're not at the beach, a good place to relax is the sprawling **Parque do Marechal Carmona,** open daily from 8:30am to 7:45pm in the summer and until 5:45pm in the winter. It lies at the southern tip of the resort, near the water. Here you'll find a shallow lake, a cafe, and a small zoo. Chairs and tables are set out under shade trees if you'd like to picnic.

The most important church is the **Igreja de Nossa Senhora da Assunção (Church of Our Lady of the Assumption),** on Largo da Assunção (© 21/484-74-80), a leafy square toward the western edge of town. It's open daily from 9am to 1pm and 5 to 8pm. Admission is free, although donations for the maintenance and upkeep of the premises are accepted. Paintings by Josefa de Óbidos, a 17th-century artist, fill the nave. They're unusual because women rarely attained such artistic posts in those days. The hand-painted *azulejos* (tiles) date from 1720 and 1748. The beautiful altar dates from the end of the 16th century.

Cascais also has some minor museums, including the **Museu do Mar (Museum of the Sea),** Rua Julio Pereira de Mello (© 21/481-59-06). The museum displays fishing artifacts, including equipment and model boats. Folkloric apparel worn by residents in the 1800s is also on exhibit. Old photographs and paintings re-create the Cascais of long ago. The museum is open November to April Tuesday to Sunday 10am to 5pm, and May to October 10am to 9pm; admission is free.

Another museum is the **Museu do Conde de Castro Guimarães,** Avenida Rei Humberto II de Itália, Estrada da Boca do Inferno (© 21/481-53-04). On the grounds of the Parque do Marechal Carmona, it occupies the former 19th-century home of a family whose last surviving member died in 1927. The museum offers a rare glimpse into life in the 18th and 19th centuries, with ceramics, antiques, artwork, silver ewers, samovars, and Indo-Portuguese embroidered shawls—you name it. It's open Tuesday to Sunday 10am to 12:30pm and 2 to 5pm; admission is 2€ and free for children under 18 and seniors. Guided tours are on the hour between 10am and 5pm.

The most popular excursion outside Cascais is to **Boca do Inferno (Mouth of Hell)** ★. Thundering waves sweep in with such power that they've carved a wide hole resembling a mouth, or *boca,* into the cliffs. However, if you should arrive when the sea is calm, you'll wonder why it's called a cauldron. The Mouth of Hell can be a windswept roar if you don't stumble over too many souvenir hawkers. Take the highway toward Guincho and then turn left toward the sea.

OUTDOOR ACTIVITIES   Most visitors are content with the trio of fair beaches here, and simply lying on one of the lovely, sandy beaches is a fine way to spend the day. Fortunately, the waters of Cascais are no longer polluted as they were in the late '90s, so swimming is now also possible.

The best golf course is **Oitavos Dunes Quinta da Marinha** (© 21/486-06-00; www.quintadamarinha-oitavosgolfe.pt), 7km (4⅓ miles) west of Cascais. The course here evokes links in Scotland. Holes open onto distant views of the Atlantic and the Sintra mountain range. Designed by golf architect Arthur Hills, the course lies in the Sintra-Cascais National Park. Greens fees are 91€ in winter, rising to 155€ in summer. Hours are daily 8am to 8pm. An equestrian center with some 230 horses is on-site in addition to various indoor and outdoor riding arenas. A 30-minute ride goes for 25€; 1 hour costs 35€.

Another good golf course is **Clube de Golfe da Marinha,** Quinta da Marinha (© 21/486-01-00), which was carved out of sprawling woodlands of umbrella pines. The master himself, Robert Trent Jones, Sr., designed the 18-hole course, the showcase of an upscale residential resort complex that stretches over some 131 hectares (324 acres). Windblown dunes and sea-lashed outcroppings are part of the backdrop along its 6,120m (20,079 ft.). The 18th hole, facing a deep rocky gorge, is the most challenging. Greens fees from Monday to Sunday are 95€ or 48€ after 3:30pm.

SHOPPING As a prominent beachfront resort, Cascais offers lots of simple kiosks selling sunglasses and beachwear. The region's densest concentration of stores catering to united Europe's definition of the good life is nearby. The sprawling shopping center **Shopping Cascais,** Estrada Nacional 9, Estrada de Sintra (*©* **21/012-16-28** for information; www.cascaishopping.pt), is beside Hwy. 5A, the road between Cascais and Sintra. (Some locals refer to it as the Shopping Center of Cascais.) It contains two floors and more than 100 boutiques, with special emphasis on housewares, home furnishings and accessories, and clothing.

Tear Casa, Rua da Saudade 6 (*©* **21/484-43-36**), is our favorite emporium for hand-embroideries in all of Cascais, with a selection of sheets, tableware, and women's nightgowns. The owners also believe that a well-dressed child is a well-behaved child; as a consequence, the store carries some of the most charming children's clothes in Cascais.

If you're in the mood for more folkloric, less overtly commercial settings, you might want to ignore the megamall. Wander instead through the warren of small ceramics shops that surround Cascais's church, or walk along the town's most commercialized street, **Rua da Raita,** an all-pedestrian walkway in the town center.

The most intriguing shopping possibilities are at the markets. Head north of the center along Rua Mercado, off Avenida do 25 de Abril, on Wednesday or Saturday morning, and you'll find a fruit and vegetable market (along with a lot of other items). Another sprawling market operates at the bullring, **Praça de Touros,** on Avenida Pedro Álvares, west of the center, on the first and third Sunday of each month.

Where to Stay
VERY EXPENSIVE

Albatroz ★★★ After many decades, this monument to aristocratic glamour still reigns undisputed as the most elegant and sought-after hotel on the Costa do Sol. Today, although confronted with stiff competition from newer hotels that are almost as charming, it continues to hold its reputation as a lodging for the quietly rich. Don't expect glitziness: The property is small-scale and restrained, although in the opinion of some, a tad pretentious and even a wee bit stuffy. Its centerpiece is a pair of interconnected beach houses, one of which was originally built in 1793 for the duke of Loulé and acquired during the 19th century as a holiday home for the Count and Countess de Foz. In the 20th century, it became an inn. In 1983, a series of additions and alterations eventually engulfed the original villas, even though you can still see traces of the original architecture, especially in the foyer to the much-heralded restaurant. Today you'll find airy, open spaces, contemporary tilework, and low-slung furniture that's in keeping with its image as an upscale beach hotel. In 2000, the hotel acquired a neighboring neo-Romantic villa, which at great expense was converted into a conference center with six extremely upscale suites. Units in the building's ivy-draped main core vary in size, and all are extremely comfortable, albeit, for the most part, blandly conservative in their decor.

Rua Frederico Arouca 100, 2750-353 Cascais. www.albatrozhotels.com. *©* **21/484-73-80.** Fax 21/484-48-27. 59 units. 170€–390€ double; 300€–580€ suite. Extra bed 50€–85€. Rates include buffet breakfast. AE, DC, MC, V. Free parking. **Amenities:** Restaurant; bar; airport transfers (60€); babysitting; concierge; outdoor pool; room service. *In room:* A/C, TV, hair dryer, minibar, Wi-Fi (7€ per hour).

Grande Real Villa Itália ★★★ ☺   Except for the chic and swanky Albatroz, this is the most stunning, government-rated five-star hotel in the Greater Cascais area. Built on the site of a former Italian palace, it is a luxurious choice for a spa and beach hotel. The architects designed several balconies or terraces overlooking the sea. Tastefully furnished and spacious bedrooms are equipped to a very high standard, and the decor is inspired by shades from the sea, especially blue and gray. The suites are more exotic with warmer colors, the decorator claiming he was "inspired by the colors of a late afternoon." Many of the accommodations open onto sea-view balconies.

Rua Frei Nicolau de Oliveira 100, 2750-319 Cascais. www.realhotelsgroup.com. ✆ **21/096-60-00.** Fax 21/096-60-01. 124 units. 150€–297€ double; 800€ suite. AE, MC, V. Free parking. **Amenities:** 2 restaurants; bar; bikes; children's center; concierge; health club & spa; 2 pools (outdoor); room service. *In room:* A/C, TV, hair dryer, minibar, Wi-Fi (free).

EXPENSIVE

Estalagem Villa Albatroz ★★ 🎒   Set in the geographic heart of Cascais, a very short walk from city hall and the bandstand where midsummer civic concerts are held, this hotel was originally built in the 19th century as the beach house of the dukes of Palmela. In the late 1990s, it was acquired by the owners of the also-recommended Albatroz hotel and reconfigured as a small-scale boutique hotel. Overall, the aura is airy. Rooms are smaller than those at the Albatroz and not quite as grand as you might expect. Overall, the experience is comfortable and convenient, particularly because of the hotel's superb location and thoughtful staff.

Rua Fernandes Tomás 1, 2750-342 Cascais. www.albatrozhotels.com. ✆ **21/486-34-10.** Fax 21/484-46-80. 11 units. 177€–224€ double; 230€–285€ junior suite; 285€–385€ suite. Extra bed 60€–70€. AE, DC, MC, V. Free parking. **Amenities:** Restaurant; bar; room service; Wi-Fi (4€ per hour, in lobby). *In room:* A/C, TV, hair dryer, minibar.

Farol Design Hotel ★★ 🎒   One of the region's best government-rated five-star hotels opened in 2002 and became an instant hit with a chic crowd. Enjoying a scenic waterfront location a 10-minute walk from the center of town, this is a completely remodeled 19th-century mansion that has been handsomely converted, making it the most stylish boutique hotel along the Costa do Sol. The building rises four stories, housing rooms with mainly midsize to spacious bedrooms, and rooms with mostly monochromatic color schemes of either all-white (three of the rooms), or mostly red, mostly pink, or mostly dark gray. Furnishings are tasteful—sometimes elegant—and extra-special features such as hydromassage tubs are in each tiled bathroom. Bedrooms have parquet floors and dark-wood furnishings. You never have to leave here at night because a first-class restaurant serves international food, and two fashionable bars and a well-attended dance club entertain the young and beautiful.

Av. Rei Humberto II de Italia 7, 2750-461 Cascais. www.farol.com.pt. ✆ **21/482-34-90.** Fax 21/483-64-61. 34 units. 130€–390€ double; 250€–480€ suite. Rates include buffet breakfast. AE, DC, MC, V. Free parking. **Amenities:** Restaurant; bar; babysitting; outdoor pool; room service; sauna. *In room:* A/C, TV, hair dryer, minibar, Wi-Fi (free).

Hotel Cascais Miragem ★★ ☺   With its bedrooms opening onto the Atlantic, this is a sleek, modern, and inviting choice located between Estoril and Cascais. Its array of bedrooms are equipped with all the standard and even some luxurious features; bedrooms range from average-size to spaciously deluxe, the latter with entrance halls and marble-floored bathrooms. The bedrooms are antiallergenic with a mixture of marble and wood, and most of the accommodations also contain private terraces. The hotel does more than most to cater to families, with its children's pool, play area, kiddie menus, toys in the room, and even special excursions by prior arrangement. Its dining facilities are among the finest of any hotel along the coast, with a mixture of Portuguese dishes combined with international specialties. The staff is among the finest along the coast, and its members are helpful in arranging golf, excursions, or any number of other demands.

Av. Marginal 8554, 2754-236 Cascais. www.cascaismirage.com. ℂ **21/006-06-00.** Fax 21/006-06-01. 192 units. 150€–260€ double; 550€–650€ suite. Children 11 and under stay free. Rates include buffet breakfast. AE, DC, MC, V. Parking 12€. **Amenities:** 3 restaurants; 3 bars; babysitting; children's center; concierge; health club & spa; outdoor pool; room service. *In room:* A/C, TV, hair dryer, minibar, Wi-Fi (free).

Hotel Quinta da Marinha Resort ★★ ☺ Only a 10-minute ride west from the center of Cascais, this lavish resort sprawl appeals to those who want to settle in for a few days at a swank government-rated five-star resort. "We have everything," the manager assured us. Not quite, but there's plenty to coddle you in luxury and amuse you during your stay. Rooms are attractively and luxuriously furnished with individual balconies and double-glass windows; each comes with a roomy, tiled bathroom. Surrounded by pine woods, the resort is one of the most tranquil in the area. If you'd like to spread out close to the golf course, you can rent a villa with a kitchenette, living room with fireplace, and daily cleaning service. The food is a refined version of regional dishes and international specialties as best reflected in the Five Pines Restaurant. Golfers can enjoy lunch at the clubhouse. A seafood restaurant also opens onto the water. This is one of the few hotels in the area with a summer-only Kids Club, which brings in families.

Quinta da Marinha, 2750-715 Cascais. www.quintadamarinha.com. ℂ **21/486-01-00.** Fax 21/486-94-82. 198 units. 135€–310€ double; 240€–420€ suite. AE, DC, MC, V. Free parking. **Amenities:** 4 restaurants; 2 bars; babysitting; children's center; concierge; 18-hole golf course; health club & spa; indoor heated pool; 3 outdoor pools; room service; 6 outdoor tennis courts (lit). *In room:* A/C, TV, hair dryer, minibar, Wi-Fi (in some; 6€ per hr.).

Hotel Vila Galé Cascais ★★ In the historic quarter of Cascais, this modern hotel doesn't quite challenge the Albatroz, but it is nonetheless a first-class citadel of charm and comfort. The balconied hotel, surrounded by palaces and the Parque da Gandarinha, offers beautifully furnished bedrooms, including 70 junior suites, each with a beehive-shape balcony overlooking the sea or mountains. In terms of prestige, comfort, and desirability, this hotel is no. 2 in town. The hotel is also one of the best equipped in the area, known for its pools, bars, and restaurant.

Rua Frei Nicolau de Oliveira, Parque da Gandarinha, 2750-641 Cascais. www.vilagale.pt. ℂ **21/482-60-00.** Fax 21/483-73-19. 233 units. 75€–218€ double; 98€–287€ suite. AE, DC, MC, V. Free parking. **Amenities:** Restaurant; 2 bars; babysitting; children's center; 2 outdoor pools; room service; sauna. *In room:* A/C, TV, hair dryer, minibar, Wi-Fi (15€ per 24 hr.).

MODERATE

Casal Antigo ★ 🏠 To escape the hordes along the Costa do Sol, more and more visitors are discovering this restored old villa lying in the Sintra-Cascais natural park, a 10-minute drive from the center of Cascais and a 25-minute taxi ride from the Lisbon airport. This is a modernized, tastefully furnished, and well-run B&B that has already gained a devoted list of habitués. Much of the original structure has been preserved, although modern amenities such as up-to-date plumbing have been added to this family-run establishment, one of the most tranquil oases in the resort area.

Families can check into a suite around the swimming pool. Bedrooms are midsize and comfortably furnished.

Rua do Cabo 467, Malveira de Serra 2750-518 Cascais. www.casalantigo.com. ✆/fax **21/485-20-24.** 8 units. 85€–95€ double; 100€–180€ family suite. Rates include buffet breakfast. MC, V. Free parking. **Amenities:** Outdoor pool; room service; Wi-Fi (free, in lobby). *In room:* A/C, TV/DVD.

Hotel Baía   One of the most appealing things about this well-managed, government-rated three-star hotel is its location directly above the town's fishing port, adjacent to the town hall and within a short walk of five-star hotels whose accommodations cost a whole lot more. Originally built in the 1960s, it was extensively renovated, enlarged, and modernized. Today its five floors contain contemporary furnishings and a simple decor.

Av. Marginal, 2754-509 Cascais. www.hotelbaia.com. ✆ **21/483-10-33.** Fax 21/483-10-95. 113 units. 70€–144€ double. Rates include buffet breakfast. AE, DC, MC, V. Parking 10€. **Amenities:** 2 restaurants; bar; bikes; indoor heated pool; Wi-Fi (free, in lobby). *In room:* A/C, TV.

Pestana Cascais ★★   On the road to Guincho (see below) stands one of the most modern and best-equipped hotels in Cascais, located only .8km (half a mile) from the center of the resort. It caters to activity-oriented families and the staff can arrange a host of activities, including golf nearby, and even horseback riding in the hills or along the beach. Bedrooms are spacious and attractively furnished with contemporary, comfortable pieces. Most of the accommodations have a balcony facing the sea, along with a small living room, plus a kitchenette—ideal for a longer stay. A generous breakfast is also offered, and if you book early, the staff might quote you a special discounted rate.

Av. Manuel Júlio Carvalho e Costa 115, 2754-518 Cascais. www.pestana.com. ✆ **21/482-59-00.** Fax 21/482-59-77. 149 units. 75€–202€. AE, DC, MC, V. Rates include buffet breakfast. Free parking. **Amenities:** Restaurant; bar; children's center; concierge; golf nearby; health club & spa; outdoor pool; room service; 2 tennis courts (lit); watersports equipment/rentals. *In room:* A/C, TV, hair dryer, minibar, Wi-Fi (5€ per 24 hr.).

INEXPENSIVE

Albergaria Valbom   Built in 1973, this hotel offers an indistinct white-concrete facade with recessed balconies. It is battered but acceptable, and the staff is helpful and polite. Conservatively decorated guest rooms surround the sun-splashed TV lounge. Some of the rooms have TVs. The quieter accommodations look out over the back. The Valbom lies on a drab commercial-residential street close to the center of Cascais, near the rail station.

Av. Valbom 14, 2750-508 Cascais. www.albergariavalbom.com. ✆ **21/486-58-01.** Fax 21/486-58-05. 40 units. 50€–70€ double. Rates include buffet breakfast. AE, DC, MC, V. Parking 7.50€. **Amenities:** Babysitting; bikes. *In room:* A/C, Wi-Fi (7.50€ per 24 hr.).

Casa da Pergola ★★ ✦   Built in the 18th century, this elegant villa behind a garden offers one of the most tranquil interiors in Cascais. In the center of town, it stands in a neighborhood filled with restaurants and shops. The manager/owner is Patricia Gonçalves. It was her childhood home, and today she maintains it as if it were still her private domain. Her genteel staff proudly displays a collection of antique furniture and blue-and-white tiles that surround the elegant ground-floor parlor and second-floor sitting room. All of the small accommodations are well furnished, with well-maintained bathrooms. Reserve in advance. Although it's technically closed in winter, the hotel will open during that time for any party that reserves five or more rooms.

Av. Valbom 13, 2750-508 Cascais. www.casadapergola-cascais-lisbon.com. ℂ **21/484-00-40.** Fax 21/483-47-91. 10 units. 88€–150€ double. Rates include buffet breakfast. No credit cards. Parking (in nearby lot) 8€. Closed Dec 16–Feb 14. *In room:* A/C (in some), hair dryer.

Residencial Solar Dom Carlos ⚓ If you're saving money and your expectations aren't too high, this little back-street inn is most inviting. Once the mansion of a local aristocrat, it dates from the 1500s. An original chapel from the nobleman's home remains intact. The place is immaculately kept and makes heavy use of tiled floors. The comfortably furnished rooms are often large and have good beds but not a lot of other luxuries. The inn also has a private garden.

Rua Latina Coelho, 2750-408 Cascais. www.solardomcarlos.com. ℂ **21/482-81-15.** Fax 21/486-51-55. 18 units. 48€–84€ double. Rates include buffet breakfast. AE, DC, MC, V. Free parking. **Amenities:** Babysitting; bikes; Wi-Fi (free, in lobby). *In room:* TV, minibar (in some).

Where to Dine

After Lisbon, sprawling Cascais offers the second-highest concentration of quality restaurants in Portugal. Even if you're based in the capital, consider a trip to Cascais for seafood.

EXPENSIVE

Baluarte ★★ PORTUGUESE/SEAFOOD This restaurant is one of the most sought after in town by some of the coast's most discerning palates—it attracts mainly foreign vacationers who often come here to show off their chic resort apparel at night. The decor is sleek and modern, with comfortable, upholstered chairs set at tables with crisp white linens and crystal. Some of the dishes, especially those of the sea, fairly explode with sublime flavors. The house specialty is *bacalhau* or dried cod à Baluarte, an elegant interpretation of this rather peasant dish. We also revel in the chef's medallions of grouper with fresh shrimp.

Av. D. Carlos 1-6. ℂ **21/486-51-57.** www.restbaluarte.com. Reservations required. Main courses 16€– 38€. AE, DC, MC, V. Tues–Sun 12:30–3pm and 7–10:30pm.

Restaurant Albatroz ★★★ INTERNATIONAL/PORTUGUESE One of the finest places to dine along the Costa do Sol, this elegantly decorated restaurant is part of the most famous hotel on the coast (see "Where to Stay," above). From its windows, you'll have a sweeping view of one of the Costa do Sol's most popular beaches. Its summer-style decor is inviting year-round. The room is not grand or stuffy, but the service is rather formal. Diners' attire is probably best described as "neat casual."

Begin with an aperitif on the covered terrace. Afterward, you'll be ushered into a glistening dining room that serves some of the finest Portuguese and international cuisine in Cascais. Your options might include poached salmon, partridge stew, chateaubriand, or a savory version of stuffed sole with shellfish. Daily fresh fish specials are served; one especially succulent offering is monkfish with sea clams. For dessert, choices range from crêpes suzette to iced soufflé. There's a wide selection of Portuguese and international wines, too.

In the Albatroz, Rua Frederico Arouca 100. ℂ **21/484-73-80.** Reservations required. Main courses 25€–46€. AE, DC, MC, V. Daily 12:30–3pm and 7:30–10:30pm.

Restaurante Luzmar PORTUGUESE There is no more centrally located restaurant than this one, as it lies on the main street of town close to the beach. Decorated in a typical tavern style, it is air-conditioned inside but has outdoor dining on its terrace. The chefs are known for their wide variety of freshly caught fish, shellfish, and such typically Portuguese meat dishes as lamb chops with garlic or grilled *entrecôte* (steak). Shellfish rice is another favorite, as is a buffet of grilled fish. Watch those shellfish dishes: The price adds up quickly, and is based on the market price of the day. Start, perhaps, with stuffed spider crabs or melon with smoked ham. For dessert, the hazelnut mousse or chocolate cake is a guilty pleasure.

Alameda dos Combatentes da Grande Guerra 104. ☎ **21/484-57-04.** www.luzmar.dcsa.pt. Reservations recommended. Main courses 16€–38€. AE, DC, MC, V. Tues–Sun 12:30–4:30pm and 7pm–midnight.

Restaurante Visconde da Luz ★ PORTUGUESE/SEAFOOD This well-known restaurant sits in a low-slung bungalow at the edge of a park in the center of Cascais. The view encompasses rows of lime trees and towering sycamores where flocks of birds congregate at dusk (be warned if you're walking underneath). The decor is modernized Art Nouveau. The uniformed staff is polite and eager. The Portuguese food is well prepared with fresh ingredients. A meal might include fried sole, shellfish, pork with clams, seafood curry, or clams in garlic sauce, finished off with almond cake. Many seafood choices are sold by the kilogram (2.2 lb.), a generous portion that can easily feed two.

In the Jardim Visconde da Luz. ☎ **21/484-74-10.** www.viscondedaluz.dcsa.pt. Reservations required. Main courses 16€–32€. AE, DC, MC, V. Tues–Sun 12:30–4:30pm and 7pm–midnight.

MODERATE
Beira Mar Restaurante ★★ PORTUGUESE Cozy and crowded, with a terrace that spills onto a traffic-free plaza in front, this is the best restaurant in the center of Cascais. Established in the 1950s, with present management in place since 1973, it evokes a relatively simple seafront tavern, except that the food and service are a lot better than that cliché might imply. Within sight of a well-scrubbed kitchen, you'll enjoy such menu items as a savory *sopa de marisco* (shellfish soup), filet of whitefish with shellfish rice, baked sea bass in a salt crust, or whitefish crowned with a banana. Grilled sole and several kinds of shellfish round out the menu.

Rua das Flores 6. ☎ **021/482-73-80.** www.beiramarcascais.com. Reservations recommended. Main courses 15€–35€. AE, DC, MC, V. Wed–Mon noon–4pm and 7pm–midnight.

Eduardo's BELGIAN/PORTUGUESE/THAI Rustically decorated with regional artifacts, this provincial restaurant occupies the street level of a postwar apartment building in the center of Cascais. It's named after its Belgian-born owner, Edouard de Beukelaer, who turns out savory Portuguese and Belgian meals. The well-prepared food might include filet steaks, braised filet of turbot, crayfish in butter sauce with capers, and veal liver. Savory Thai dishes feature prawns tossed with coconut milk and red curry or fried sea bass topped with a sweet and sour sauce.

Largo das Grutas 3. ☎ **21/483-19-01.** Reservations recommended. Main courses 9.50€–22€. AE, DC, MC, V. Mon–Sat noon–3pm and 7–11pm.

Reijos ★ 🍴 INTERNATIONAL/PORTUGUESE This place is likely to be crowded, so in high season you'll have to wait for a table or abandon all hope—this intimate, informal bistro is that good. The menu combines fine American and Portuguese foods with pleasing results. Justifiably popular items include grilled lobster with butter sauce, shrimp curry, and filet mignon. Two dishes from Macau are prepared at your table: beef with garden peppers, and shrimp with cucumbers. Fresh seafood includes sole, sea bass, grouper, fresh salmon, and *bacalhau a Reijos* (oven-baked dry codfish with cheese sauce). Unlike many European restaurants, Reijos serves fresh vegetables with its main dishes at no extra cost. The service is excellent.

Rua Frederico Arouca 35. ✆ **21/483-03-11.** Reservations required for dinner. Main courses 18€-35€. AE, DC, MC, V. Mon-Sat 12:30-3:30pm and 7-11pm. Closed Dec 15-30.

INEXPENSIVE

B&B Restaurante 🍴 PORTUGUESE   No, the B&B in the name doesn't stand for bed-and-breakfast—rather for *bom* and *baratoa,* meaning good and cheap in Portuguese. The little eatery lives up to its namesake. One reader wrote that she would gladly have paid double for the meal she consumed here. The restaurant is run by a expat Frenchman who arrived in town some 30 years ago. The octopus usually wins a rave from most clients; it's slowly cooked in the oven for about 2 hours before it's lightly grilled in olive oil and fresh herbs. The catch of the day can also be served grilled and golden brown. The cook is superb at turning out shrimp as well. Many diners end their meal with a glass of port.

Rua do Poço Novo. ✆ **21/482-06-86.** Reservations recommended. Main courses 9€-16€. No credit cards. Mon-Sat noon-2:30pm and 6:30-9:45pm.

Dom Manolo 🍴 PORTUGUESE   In the center of Cascais—in fact, on its main street—this Spanish-operated restaurant and grill looks like an Iberian tavern. The kitchen dishes out reasonably priced, tasty, uncomplicated regional fare. It attracts more local residents than fancy foreign visitors. The perfectly cooked spit-roasted chicken, with french fries or a salad, is a favorite. Other good choices are the savory grilled sardines, any shrimp dish, and most definitely the fresh catch of the day. For dessert, there's velvety flan.

Av. Marginal 11. ✆ **21/483-11-26.** Main courses 10€-18€. No credit cards. Daily 10am-11:30pm. Closed Jan.

John Bull/Restaurant & Bar AMERICAN/ENGLISH/PORTUGUESE   This centrally located pub and restaurant shows its English roots in both the black-and-white timbered Elizabethan facade and the John Bull Pub. The street-level room has dark wooden paneling, oak beams, a fireplace, rough-hewn stools and tables, and pewter pots. Pints of hand-pumped ales and lagers are popular with those who want only to drink and talk. Hungry customers head upstairs to the Britannia Restaurant, where the menu features English, American, and Portuguese dishes. Popular items include cottage pie, Southern fried chicken, T-bone steaks, and local seafood. The food is solid and reliable—nothing more.

Largo Luís de Camões 4. ✆ **21/483-33-19.** Main courses 8€-23€. AE, DC, MC, V. Daily 9am-3:30pm and 7:30-11:30pm (bar open until 2am).

La Brasserie de L'Entrecôte 🍴 FRENCH   At first glance, this restaurant resembles the kind of turn-of-the-20th-century brasserie you'd find in central France, with mahogany paneling, polished brass, and apron-clad staff members. A glance at the menu, however, quickly reveals that this is a French brasserie with a twist: The only available choice is *entrecôte* with french fries, accompanied with a salad and your choice of sauces. But despite the limited menu, the place is crowded, especially in high season. You can order, for a supplement, any of five kinds of dessert that include tarts, sorbets (lime or mango), and fruit salads, as well as wines from a savvy list of mostly Portuguese vintages. Overall, if you don't mind the limited menu, the place is one of the best bets in Cascais for the presentation of satisfyingly generous meals at rock-bottom prices in a good-looking setting.

Marina de Cascais, Loja 43. ✆ **21/481-81-96.** www.brasserieentrecote.pt. Reservations recommended for dinner on weekends. Main courses 18€-25€. AE, DC, MC, V. Daily 12:30-3:30pm and 7:30-11:30pm.

Vin Rouge ★ CONTINENTAL/FUSION Stylish, even debonair, this sophis-ticated restaurant pairs good value with excellent cuisine. It operates from within a minimalist-looking dining room outfitted in tones inspired by the magenta and ruby tones of red wine. Additional seating spills onto an open veranda with one of Cascais's best views of the bay. It's set inside the sea-fronting Estalagem Villa Albatroz, about 500 yards from the legendary Albatroz hotel. Menu items vary with the season, but invariably include a starting platter of foie gras, grilled scallops with a coulis of mango, and salad greens; deboned skate poached in shellfish consommé and served with baby gnocchi and summer vegetables; and rack of lamb with rosemary and a creamy garlic sauce.

Rua Fernandes Tomas 1, Villa Cascais (in the Estalagem Villa Albatroz). ℗ **021/468-44-39.** www.restaurantevinrouge.blogspot.com. Reservations recommended. Main courses 10€–20€. MC, V. Tues-Sun 12:30–3pm and Tues-Sat 7:30–10:30pm.

Cascais After Dark

Baluarte Bar Spacious, streamlined, and airy, this is the bar that many employees of local hotels and restaurants drop into when their work day is finished. It evokes the kind of hip, youth-oriented place that you might expect within the Bairro Alto of Lisbon, except that it occupies the street level of a condominium complex directly across the street from the town's most central beach, the Praia do Peixe. Although it's associated with a restaurant directly above it, most clients come here just for a drink and a chat with their friends, and never actually climb the stairs for a meal. It's open daily from 4pm to 4am. Av. Don Carlos I, no. 6 (Marginal). ℗ **21/486-51-57.** www.restbaluarte.com.

O'Neill's Irish Pub Set within a few steps of Cascais's town hall, this is a genuine Irish pub with a rowdy permissiveness. Amid dark paneling and etched mirrors, you'll hear live Irish music (Wed–Sat beginning at 11pm) and can order snack items that include chili and full Irish breakfasts. It's open daily from noon to 2am. Rua Afonso Sanches 8. ℗ **21/486-82-30.**

GUINCHO ★

6.5km (4 miles) N of Cascais; 9.5km (6 miles) N of Estoril

The word *guincho* is best translated as "caterwaul," the cry that swallows make while darting along the air currents over the wild sea. The swallows stay at Guincho year-round. Sometimes at night, the sea, driven into a frenzy, howls like a wailing ban-shee—and that, too, is *guincho.*

The town lies near the westernmost point on the European continent, known to the Portuguese as **Cabo da Roca ★**. The beaches are spacious and sandy, the sun-shine is incandescent, and the nearby promontories, jutting into white-tipped Atlantic waves, are spectacular. Wooded hills back the windswept dunes; and to the east, the Serra de Sintra is silhouetted on the distant horizon.

Essentials

ARRIVING

BY BUS From the train station at Cascais, buses leave for the Praia do Guincho every hour. The trip takes 20 minutes.

BY CAR From Cascais, continue west along Route 247.

VISITOR INFORMATION

The nearest tourist office is in Cascais (p. 149).

Treacherous Beaches & Seafood Feasts

Praia do Guincho draws large beach crowds. The undertow is treacherous, so swim at your own risk. Keep in mind the advice of Jennings Parrott, writing in the *International Herald Tribune:* "If you are caught up by the current, don't fight it. Don't panic. The wind forces it to circle, so you will be brought back to shore." A local fisherman, however, advises that you take a box lunch along. According to him, "Sometimes it takes several days to make the circle."

Despite the danger, Praia do Guincho is popular with surfers and windsurfers. There is no place to rent sailboards, but windsurfers show up here from other parts of Europe, bringing their own sailboards and taking their lives into their own hands.

One of the primary reasons for coming to Guincho is to sample its seafood restaurants (see "Where to Dine," below). You can try the crayfish-size box-jaw lobsters known as *bruxas,* which in Portuguese means "sorcerer," "wizard," "witch doctor," and even "nocturnal moth." To eat like the Portuguese, you must also sample the barnacles, called *percebes.* (Many foreign visitors fail to comprehend their popularity.) The fresh lobsters and crabs are cultivated in nearby shellfish beds, which are fascinating sights in themselves.

Where to Stay

EXPENSIVE

Fortaleza do Guincho ★★★   This Relais & Châteaux hotel is one of the grandest and most prestigious hotels in the region. It originated in the 17th century within a few hundred feet of the westernmost point in Europe, when an army of stonecutters built one of the most forbidding fortresses along the coast. The twin towers that flank the vaguely Moorish facade still stand sentinel over a sun-bleached terrain of sand and rock.

The public rooms contain all the antique trappings of an aristocratic private home. In cold weather, a fire might blaze in a granite-framed fireplace, illuminating the thick carpets and the century-old furniture. Each small but luxuriously furnished guest room is behind a thick pine door heavily banded with iron under a vaulted stone ceiling. Most rooms overlook the savagely beautiful coastline. Some beds are set in alcoves. There are also three small but elegant suites, some with their own fireplaces.

Estrada do Guincho, 2750-642 Cascais. www.guinchotel.pt. ℂ **21/487-04-91.** Fax 21/487-04-31. 27 units. 130€–345€ double; 230€–415€ suite. Rates include buffet breakfast. AE, DC, MC, V. Free parking. **Amenities:** Restaurant; bar; babysitting; bikes; room service. *In room:* A/C, TV, hair dryer, minibar, Wi-Fi (free).

MODERATE

Senhora da Guia ★★ 🎁   After returning to their native Portugal following a sojourn in Brazil, the Ornelas family set their sights on restoring this former country villa of the Sagres brewery family to its former glory. Because of their efforts, it's now one of the loveliest hotels in the region. The 1970 house has thick walls, high ceilings, and elaborately crafted moldings that give the impression of a much older building. The elegant midsize guest rooms and suites contain reproductions of 18th-century Portuguese antiques, thick carpets, louvered shutters, and spacious modern bathrooms. The villa sits on a bluff above the sea, and the views are panoramic.

Estrada do Guincho, 2750-642 Cascais. www.senhoradaguia.com. ☎ **21/486-92-39.** Fax 21/486-92-27. 41 units. 110€–245€ double; 280€–550€ suite. Rates include buffet breakfast. AE, DC, MC, V. Free parking. **Amenities:** Restaurant; bar; airport transfers (60€); babysitting; bikes; exercise room; Jacuzzi; outdoor saltwater pool; room service; sauna. *In room:* A/C, TV, hair dryer, minibar, Wi-Fi (17€ per 24 hr.).

Where to Dine
VERY EXPENSIVE
Restaurant Fortaleza do Guincho ★★ CONTINENTAL/FRENCH   No other restaurant along the coast between Cascais and Guincho can compete with the sheer drama and majesty of this one. Set directly atop jagged rocks a few feet from the surf, it's part of what was once a military outpost for the Portuguese monarchs, built on this isolated site in the 17th century. In 2001, the restaurant was designated as a Relais & Châteaux establishment, thanks partly to its devoted allegiance to the tenets of modern French cuisine. A disciple (Vincent Farges) of one of eastern France's most celebrated chefs (Antoine Westermann, owner of Buerehiesel, in Alsace) was installed as the hardworking director of the kitchens. Since then, the site has been acknowledged as the most gastronomically sophisticated in the region, with a world-class cuisine and impeccable service. Menu items change with the seasons and the inspiration of the chef but are likely to include shellfish soup with basil and saffron sauce, roasted monkfish in a red-wine sauce with a comfit of garlic and onions, and shoulder of lamb in an herb-and-salt crust with thyme-flavored potatoes.

In the Fortaleza do Guincho hotel, Praia do Guincho. ☎ **21/487-04-91.** Reservations recommended. Main courses 30€–68€. AE, DC, MC, V. Daily 12:30–3pm and 7–10:30pm.

MODERATE
Monte Mar 🎁 PORTUGUESE/SEAFOOD   One of the most appealing restaurants in the region around Cascais occupies a low-slung seafront pavilion set above jagged rocks and a savagely beautiful landscape about 5km (3 miles) west of Cascais, beside the highway leading to Guincho. It contains two sun-flooded, contemporary-looking dining rooms separated by a busy, open kitchen. The entire structure is ringed with wide balconies. This has been a much-respected staple in Cascais for nearly a decade, thanks to an attentive staff and a policy of buying very fresh fish at least once (and usually twice) a day. Don't be fooled by what looks like a drainage ditch for storm water between the restaurant and the nearby sea. Beneath it are massive holding tanks that are likely to have contained some of the specialties that later appear at your table. All the seafood is beautifully prepared and served. But if you're unsure of what to order, consider sea bass or golden bream baked in a salt crust (usually prepared for two diners at a time). Or, opt for the time-tested dish on which this place has built its reputation: deep-fried filets of hake served with tartar sauce and new potatoes or rice. Buttery and firm-fleshed, it's one of the most delicious—and artfully simple—dishes in the region.

Oitavos, Estrada do Guincho. ☎ 21/486-92-70. www.montemar.pt. Reservations recommended. Main courses 15€–55€. AE, DISC, MC, V. Tues–Sat noon–4pm and 7–11pm.

Porto de Santa Maria ★★★ PORTUGUESE/SEAFOOD   If you drive to this isolated windswept bluff, 8km (5 miles) west of Cascais, you won't be alone. This restaurant serves some of the best seafood in the area, making it quite popular—many folks even ride out from Lisbon to dine here. The low-lying seafront building sports a trussed wooden ceiling and large windows that take in views of the occasionally treacherous surf. The polite staff serves every conceivable form of succulent shellfish, priced by the gram, as well as such house specialties as grilled sole. *Arroz de mariscos* (shellfish rice) is the most popular specialty—and justifiably so. Try the rondelles of pungent sheep's milk cheese that await you on the table.

Estrada do Guincho. ✆ **21/487-10-36** or 21/487-02-40. www.portosantamaria.com. Reservations recommended. Regular main courses 12€–33€. AE, DC, MC, V. Tues–Sun 12:30–3:30pm and 7:30-10:30pm.

Restaurante Furnas do Guincho ★ PORTUGUESE/SEAFOOD Leaving Cascais, heading toward Guincho, you'll find one of the better fish and seafood restaurants along the coast. It's a favorite of both visitors and expat residents. Codfish is prepared in a number of ways, and monkfish and freshly caught hake appear regularly on the menu. Most in-the-know diners seem to prefer one of the shellfish dishes, as the fishing areas nearby produce some of the best catches along the Costa do Sol. *Arroz de mariscos* is a specialty. It's like a Portuguese version of paella. Service is efficient and many of the recipes are time-tested—not a lot of experimentation here.

Estrada do Guincho (via Av. 25 de Abril). ✆ **21/486-92-43.** www.furnasdoguincho.pt. Reservations recommended. Main courses 15€–28€. AE, MC, V. Daily noon-4pm and 7:30-11pm.

QUELUZ

15km (9⅓ miles) NW of Lisbon

Queluz, only 20 minutes from Lisbon, makes a great excursion from the capital or en route to Sintra. The Queluz Palace (see "Exploring the Palace," below), in its pink rococo glory, offers storybook Portuguese charm.

Essentials

ARRIVING

BY TRAIN From the Estação do Rossio in Lisbon, take the Sintra line to Queluz. Departures during the day are every 15 minutes. The trip takes 30 minutes. There are two train stations in town. Get off at Queluz-Massamá, as it is closer to the palace. A one-way ticket costs 1.50€. Call ✆ **80/820-82-08** for schedules. At Queluz, turn left and follow the signs for less than 1km (⅔ mile) to the palace. Or else take bus no. 101 or 103, both of which run in front of the palace.

BY CAR From Lisbon, head west along the express highway (A1), which becomes Route 249. Turn off at the exit for Queluz. It usually takes 20 minutes.

VISITOR INFORMATION

You can ask for information at the tourist office in Sintra (see below).

Where to Stay

Pousada D. Maria I ★★★ Uniquely located on the grounds of a palace, this is one of the gems of Portugal's network of pousadas. This building's function during the 17th century was to house the staff that maintained the Palace of Queluz, which rises in stately majesty across the road. The pousada is graced with an ornate clock tower that evokes an oversize ornament in the garden of a stately English home. In addition to the pousada's comfortable midsize guest rooms and well-managed dining room, the premises contain touches of complicated Manueline stonework. The 17th-century theater holds occasional concerts. The high-ceilinged rooms are severely dignified and contain fine beds and neatly kept bathrooms.

Largo do Palácio, 2745-191 Queluz. www.pousadas.pt. ✆ **800/223-1356** for reservations in the U.S., or 21/435-61-58. Fax 21/435-61-89. 26 units. 94€–215€ double; 127€–230€ suite. Rates include buffet

EXPLORING THE palace

Palácio Nacional de Queluz ★★, Largo do Palácio, 2745-191 Queluz (© **21/434-38-60;** www.pnqueluz.imc-ip.pt), on the highway from Lisbon to Sintra, shimmers in the sunlight. It's a brilliant example of the rococo in Portugal. Pedro III ordered its construction in 1747, and the work dragged on until 1787. The architect Mateus Vicente de Oliveira was later joined by the French decorator-designer Jean-Baptiste Robillon, who was largely responsible for planning the garden and lakeside setting.

Pedro III had adapted an old hunting pavilion that once belonged to the Marquis Castelo Rodrigo but later came into the possession of the Portuguese royal family. Pedro III liked it so much that he decided to make it his summer residence. What you'll see today is not what the palace was like in the 18th century; during the French invasions, almost all of its belongings were transported to Brazil with the royal family. A 1934 fire destroyed a great deal of Queluz, but tasteful and sensitive reconstruction restored the lighthearted aura of the 18th century.

Blossoming mauve petunias and red geraniums highlight the topiary effects, with closely trimmed vines and sculptured box hedges. Fountain pools on which lilies float are lined with blue tiles and reflect the muted facade, the statuary, and the finely cut balustrades.

Inside you can wander through the queen's dressing room, lined with painted panels depicting a children's romp; the Don Quixote Chamber (Dom Pedro was born here and returned from Brazil to die in the same bed); the Music Room, complete with a French *grande pianoforte* and an 18th-century English harpsichord; and the mirrored throne room adorned with crystal chandeliers. The Portuguese still hold state banquets here.

Festooning the palace are all the eclectic props of the rococo era. You'll see the inevitable chinoiserie panels from Macau, Florentine marbles from quarries once worked on by Michelangelo, Iberian and Flemish tapestries, Empire antiques, Delft indigo-blue ceramics, 18th-century Hepplewhite armchairs, Austrian porcelains, Rabat carpets, Portuguese Chippendale furnishings, and Brazilian jacaranda wood pieces—all of exquisite quality. When they visited Portugal, Presidents Eisenhower, Carter, and Reagan stayed in the 30-chambered Pavilion of Dona Maria I, as did Elizabeth II and the prince and princess of Wales. These fabled chambers are said to have reverberated with the rantings of the grief-stricken monarch Maria I, who reputedly had to be strapped to her bed at times. Before becoming mentally ill, she was an intelligent, brave woman who did a great job as ruler of her country in a troubled time.

The palace is open Wednesday to Monday 9am to 5pm. It's closed on holidays. Admission is 7€, free for children under 14.

breakfast. AE, DC, MC, V. Free parking. From Sintra, take Hwy. IC-19 and follow signs to Queluz. **Amenities:** Restaurant; bar; exercise room; room service. *In room:* A/C, TV, hair dryer, minibar, Wi-Fi (in some; 12€ per day).

Where to Dine

Cozinha Velha (The Old Kitchen) ★★★ INTERNATIONAL/PORTUGUESE

If you have time for only two or three meals in the Lisbon area, take one at the Cozinha Velha. Once it was the kitchen of the palace, built in the grand style; it has since been converted into a colorful dining room favored by those seeking a gourmet dinner in a romantic setting.

The dining room is like a small chapel, with high stone arches, a free-standing fireplace, and marble columns. Along one side is a 6m (20-ft.) marble table laden with baskets of fruit and vases of flowers. You sit on ladder-back chairs surrounded by shiny copper, oil paintings, and torchieres. The innovative handling of regional ingredients pleases most diners, and the cooking uses spices, herbs, and textures well. We recommend the hors d'oeuvres for two, followed by a main course such as black grouper medallions with prawn béchamel, poached sole Cozinha Velha, fried goat with mashed turnip sprouts, or pepper steak with spinach mousse. For dessert, try the crepes Cozinha Velha with champagne sorbet.

In the Pousada D. Maria, Largo do Palácio. ✆ **21/435-02-32.** Reservations recommended. Main courses 18€–26€. AE, DC, MC, V. Daily 12:30–3pm and 7:30–10pm.

SINTRA: BYRON'S "GLORIOUS EDEN" ★★★

29km (18 miles) NW of Lisbon

Writers have sung Sintra's praises ever since Portugal's national poet, Luís Vaz de Camões, proclaimed its glory in *Os Lusíadas* (The Lusiads). Lord Byron called it "glorious Eden" when he and John Cam Hobhouse included Sintra in their 1809 grand tour. English romantics thrilled to its description in Byron's autobiographical *Childe Harold's Pilgrimage.*

Picture a town on a hillside, with decaying birthday-cake villas covered with tiles coming loose in the damp mist. Luxuriant vegetation covers the town: camellias for melancholic romantics, ferns behind which lizards dart, pink and purple bougainvillea over garden trelliswork, red geraniums on wrought-iron balconies, eucalyptus branches fluttering in the wind, lemon groves, and honey-sweet mimosa scenting the air. But take heed—some who visit Sintra fall under its spell and stay forever.

Sintra is one of the oldest towns in the country. When the crusaders captured it in 1147, they fought bitterly against the Moors firmly entrenched in their hilltop castle, the ruins of which remain today.

Essentials

ARRIVING

BY TRAIN   Sintra is a 45-minute ride from the Estação do Rossio at the Rossio in Lisbon. A train leaves every 10 to 20 minutes. The round-trip fare is 3.80€. For information, call ✆ **80/820-82-08.**

BY BUS   The bus from Lisbon is not recommended because service is too slow. Visitors staying on the Costa do Sol can make bus connections at Cascais or Estoril. The Sintra depot is on Avenida Dr. Miguel Bombarda, across from the main train station. Departures from in front of the Estoril rail station are every 45 minutes during the day. A one-way ticket costs 4€, and the trip takes 40 minutes. Eleven buses a day run between Sintra and Cascais. The journey takes 1 hour, and the round-trip fare is 4€. Once you're in Sintra, you can take bus no. 434, which traverses the tourist loop year-round, costing 4.50€ one-way. Departures are every half-hour during weekdays, more frequently as demand dictates on Saturday and Sunday. From the train station in the heart of Sintra, the bus goes up to Castelo dos Mouros and on to Pena Palace. A schedule is posted at the tourist information booth in the train station.

BY CAR   From Lisbon, head west along A1, which becomes Route 249 on its eastern approach to Sintra.

VISITOR INFORMATION
The tourist office, **Sintra Câmara Municipal,** is at Praça da República 23 (© **21/ 923-11-57;** www.cm-sintra.pt). It's open daily 9am to 7pm from October to May, and daily 9am to 8pm from June to September.

SPECIAL EVENTS
From later May to early July, the **Sintra Festival** (© **21/910-71-17;** www.festival desintra.pt) attracts many music lovers. The program consists entirely of a piano repertoire from the romantic period, with the best interpreters from today's international music scene. The concerts, about eight in all, usually take place in the region's churches, palaces (Palácio da Vila, Palácio da Pena, and Palácio de Queluz), parks, and country estates. Each concert costs 15€ to 30€, depending on the event. The tourist office (see "Visitor Information," above) will furnish details.

Exploring Sintra
PALACES, CASTLES & CONVENTS
You can take an organized tour of Sintra out of Lisbon (or book one within Sintra itself), but this approach allows no time for personal discovery, a must in Sintra.

Horse-drawn carriages are available for rent between the town and Serra de Sintra. The 45-minute tour costs 30€ to 50€ for up to five passengers. It's well worth the price for a most agreeable trip under the shady trees. The carriages start from and return to the large square in front of the National Palace of Sintra.

If you arrive in Sintra by train, you'll have to either take a taxi to the sights or trek up the long, lush hill to the national palace—a very long walk.

Castelo dos Mouros ★   The Castle of the Moors was built sometime between the 8th and 9th centuries in a position 412m (1,352 ft.) above sea level. In 1147, Scandinavian crusaders besieged and captured it from its Moorish occupants. Ferdinand of Saxe-Coburg-Gotha, the royal consort responsible for Pena palace (see below), attempted to restore the castle in the 19th century. He was relatively unsuccessful. From the parking area, a guide will send you in the right direction. From the royal tower, the view of Sintra, its palace and castle, and the Atlantic coast is stunning.

Calçada dos Clérigos. © **21/923-73-00.** www.parquesdesintra.pt. Admission 5€ adults, 4€ seniors and children 6–17, free for children under 6. Oct 16–Mar Tues–Sun 10am–6pm; Apr–Oct 15 Tues–Sun 10am–6:30pm. From Pena palace (10-min. walk), follow signs to the castelo.

Crime Watch
Warning: Don't leave valuables in unguarded cars in Sintra, and beware of pickpockets and purse-snatchers. Not only does the town attract virtually every tourist in Portugal, but it also attracts those who prey on them. While violence is not generally a problem, theft is.

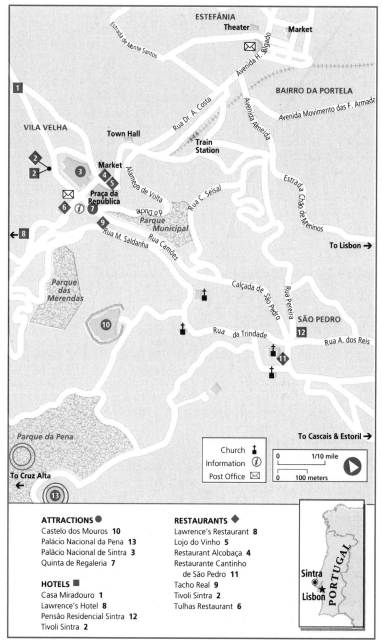

ATTRACTIONS ●
Castelo dos Mouros **10**
Palácio Nacional da Pena **13**
Palácio Nacional de Sintra **3**
Quinta de Regaleria **7**

HOTELS ■
Casa Miradouro **1**
Lawrence's Hotel **8**
Pensâo Residencial Sintra **12**
Tivoli Sintra **2**

RESTAURANTS ◆
Lawrence's Restaurant **8**
Lojo do Vinho **5**
Restaurant Alcobaça **4**
Restaurante Cantinho
  de São Pedro **11**
Tacho Real **9**
Tivoli Sintra **2**
Tulhas Restaurant **6**

165

Convento de Santa Cruz dos Capuchos ★ In 1560, Dom Álvaro de Castro ordered that this unusually structured convent be built for the Capuchins. The construction used cork so extensively that the building is sometimes known as the cork monastery.

The convent is in a secluded area 7.3km (4½ miles) from Sintra. You walk up a moss-covered path and ring the bell, and a guide will come to show you around the miniature cells. Today the convent seems forlorn and forgotten. Even when it was in use, it probably wasn't noted for its liveliness. The Capuchins who lived here, perhaps eight in all, had a penchant for the most painstakingly detailed work. For example, they lined the monastery walls with cork-bark tiles and seashells. They also carved a chapel out of rock, using cork for insulation. Outside there's an altar fresco in honor of St. Francis of Assisi. In 1834, the monks suddenly abandoned the convent, most likely to escape the crowded, primitive conditions in which the harsh environment forced them to live.

There's no bus service; if you're not driving, take a taxi from Sintra's main square.

Estrada de Pena. ℭ **21/923-73-00.** www.parquesdesintra.pt. Admission 5€. Oct 16–Mar Tues–Sun 10am–6pm; Apr–Oct 15 Tues–Sun 10am–6:30pm.

Palácio Nacional da Pena ★★ Pena perches above Sintra on a plateau about 450m (1,476 ft.) above sea level. Part of the fun of visiting the castle is the ride up the verdant, winding road through the Parque das Merendas.

The inspiration behind this castle in the sky was Ferdinand of Saxe-Coburg-Gotha, the husband of Maria II. Ferdinand called on a fellow German, Baron Eschwege, to help him build his fantasy. You can see a sculpture of the baron if you look out from the Pena toward a huge rock across the way. The palace's last royal occupant was Queen Amélia. One morning in 1910, she clearly saw that the monarchy in Portugal was ending. Having lost her husband and her soldier-son to an assassin 2 years before, she was determined not to lose her second son, Manuel II. Gathering her most precious possessions, she fled to Mafra, where her son waited. She did not see the Pena palace again until 1945, when she returned to Portugal under much more favorable conditions. Pena has remained much as Amélia left it, making it a rare record of European royal life in the halcyon days preceding World War I.

In the early 16th century, Manuel the Fortunate ordered a monastery for the Jerónimos monks built on these lofty grounds, and you can visit the preserved cloister and small oval chapel today.

Pena Park was designed and planted for more than 4 years, beginning in 1846. Ferdinand was the force behind the landscaping. He built one of the most spectacular parks in Portugal, known for the scope of its shrub and tree life. Admission to the park is included in the price of a ticket for entrance to the palace. A little carriage service inside the gate of the palace will take you up the steep hill to the palace for 2€ each way.

Estrada de Pena. ℭ **21/910-53-40.** www.parquesdesintra.pt. Admission 9€, 7€ children 6–17, 9€ seniors, free for children 5 and under. Oct 16–Mar Tues–Sun 10am–6pm; Apr–Oct 15 Tues–Sun 10am–6:30pm.

Palácio Nacional de Sintra ★★★ A royal palace until 1910, the Sintra National Palace was last inhabited by Queen Maria Pia, the Italian grandmother of Manuel II, the last king of Portugal. Much of the palace was constructed in the days of the first Manuel, the Fortunate. Long before the arrival of the crusaders under Afonso Henríques, this was a summer palace of Moorish sultans. The original palace was torn down in 1863, and Moorish-style architecture was incorporated into latter-day versions.

The structure is now a conglomeration of styles, with Gothic and Manueline predominant. The glazed earthenware tiles lining many of the chambers are among the most beautiful in Portugal, but some of the chambers stand out for other reasons. The Swan Room was a favorite of João I, one of the founding kings of Portugal, father of Henry the Navigator and husband of Philippa of Lancaster. The Room of the Sirens or Mermaids is one of the most elegant in the palace. The Heraldic or Stag Room holds coats of arms of aristocratic Portuguese families, and hunting scenes. Tile-fronted stoves are in the Old Kitchen, where feasts were held in bygone days.

The palace is also rich in paintings and Iberian and Flemish tapestries, but perhaps it's simply worth a visit for its good views: In most of the rooms, wide windows look out onto attractive views of the Sintra mountain range.

As you approach the palace, you can buy a ticket at the kiosk on your left. The palace opens onto the central town square. Outside, two conical chimney towers form the most distinctive landmark on the Sintra skyline. The walk from the train station at Sintra to the national palace takes about 10 minutes. After leaving the station, take a left and follow the road.

Largo da Rainha Dona Amélia. © **21/910-68-40.** http://pnsintra.imc-ip.pt. Admission 7€ adults, 5€ ages 15–25, free for children under 14; free admission on Sun and some holidays. Thurs-Tues 9:30am–5:30pm.

Quinta da Regaleria Classified as a World Heritage Site by UNESCO, this *quinta* (manor house) in the old quarter was built at the turn of the 20th century. It incorporates architectural elements of the Gothic, Manueline, and Renaissance styles. You can take a tour of the property, which is filled with antiques and artifacts. The building's turrets afford panoramic views of the countryside. After touring the house, visitors can stroll through the surrounding park.

Rua Visconde de Monserrate. © **21/910-66-50.** www.regaleira.pt. Admission with tour guide 11€ adults, 6€ children 8-14, 3.50€ for children under 8; without tour guide 6€ adults. Daily 10:30am–5:30pm.

SHOPPING

Folkloric, history-rich Sintra has been a repository of salable Portuguese charm since the dawn of modern tourism. As you wander through its cobblestone streets and alleyways, you'll find many intriguing outlets for handmade folk art from the region and the rest of Portugal.

The best shops include **A Esquina,** Praça da República 20 (© **21/923-34-27**). It carries many hand-painted ceramics, some of which are reproductions of designs that originated between the 15th and 18th centuries. **Almorávida,** Rua Visconde de Monserrate 12–14 (© **21/924-05-39**), in front of Sintra Palace, sells Arraiolos carpets, lace, and intricately hammered copperware. A worthy antiques shop close to the town center is **Henrique Teixeira,** Rua Consigliéri Pedroso 2 (© **21/923-10-43**). It carries sometimes dauntingly expensive furniture and accessories, including an exceptional collection of antique brass and bronze hardware.

Casa Branca, Rua Consigliéri Pedroso 12 (© **21/923-05-28;** www.casabranca. gruposilvacarvalho.com), is *the* shop for linens. Recent clients have included former U.S. secretary of state Madeleine Albright, who binge-shopped here for what we were told was more than 30,000€ worth of bed- and tableware. Inventories include embroideries from Madeira, the Azores, and the north of Portugal. Nightdresses and negligees, some of them with rich embroideries on silk or cotton, are particularly beautiful, often with provocatively flimsy décolletage.

Violeta, Rua das Padarias 19 (☎ **21/923-40-95**), stocks hand-embroidered linen tablecloths, towels, sheets, and bedspreads.

Where to Stay

VERY EXPENSIVE

Tivoli Palácio de Seteais ★★★   This is one of the most luxurious palaces to stay in all of Portugal and advance reservations are a must. Lord Byron worked on *Childe Harold's Pilgrimage* in the front garden of this palace, which later became a hotel. Seteais looks older than it is—a Dutch Gildemeester built it in the late 18th century. The fifth marquês de Marialva, who sponsored many receptions and galas for the aristocrats of his day, later took over and restored the palace.

The hotel lies at the end of a long driveway. An arched entryway dominates the formal stone architecture. The palace is on the crest of a hill; most of its drawing rooms, galleries, and chambers overlook the formal terraces, flower garden, and vista toward the sea. A long hall and a staircase with white-and-gilt balustrades and columns lead to the lower-level dining room, drinking lounge, and garden terraces. The library and adjoining music room are furnished with period pieces. The main drawing room contains antiques and a fine mural extending around the cove and onto the ceiling. The beautiful and spacious guest rooms are furnished with antiques or tasteful reproductions. There are also some less desirable and smaller rooms that are quite reasonable in price.

Rua Barbosa do Bocage 8, Seteais, 2710-517 Sintra. www.tivolihotels.com. ☎ **21/923-32-00.** Fax 21/923-42-77. 30 units. 160€–680€ double. Rates include buffet breakfast. AE, DC, MC, V. Free parking. **Amenities:** Restaurant; bar; babysitting; bikes; outdoor freshwater pool; room service; outdoor tennis court (lit); Wi-Fi (free, in lobby). *In room:* TV, hair dryer, minibar.

EXPENSIVE

Penha Longa Hotel & Golf Resort ★★★ ☺   This is the grandest resort in the Sintra area, especially for golfers, as it offers two world-class courses designed by Robert Trent Jones, Jr. Its recreational facilities beat all other resorts in the area—no competition at all. Long before it became a grand hotel, the site was a retreat of royalty since the 14th century, and it still has a landmark monastery on the grounds. The present building is a graceful palazzo-style structure set among the rolling hills, clear lakes, and lush gardens of the southern tier of the Sintra mountains.

The guest rooms are luxuriously furnished with private balconies opening onto panoramic views and large marble bathrooms. Amenities run the gamut from Bulgari bath products and plush bathrobes to espresso coffee machines. The most elite services are found on the Club Level on the top floor. Five gourmet restaurants and the best spa in the area are just part of its many attractions.

Estrada da Lagoa Azul-Malveira, 2714-511 Sintra. www.penhalonga.com. ☎ **21/924-90-11.** Fax 21/924-90-11. 194 units. 150€–245€ double; 300€–1,500€ suite. AE, DC, MC, V. Free parking. **Amenities:** 5 restaurants; 4 bars; babysitting; children's center; concierge; exercise room; 2 golf courses; 2 freshwater pools (indoor and outdoor); room service; spa; 4 outdoor tennis courts (lit); Wi-Fi (20€ per hour). *In room:* A/C, TV, CD player, hair dryer, minibar.

Pestana Sintra Golf ★★ ☺   Those who want the best of both worlds—the glories of Sintra and the beaches of Cascais—might want to lodge at one of the best-equipped hotels in the area, featuring a wide array of sports, both land and sea. The hotel also lies close to some of the best golf courses in the area and is one of the most

modern and efficient in the area, with spacious bedrooms, tasteful furnishings, and grand comfort. The bedrooms seem to have more extras than most we have inspected, everything from a working desk to a shaving mirror. One aspect we especially like are the furnished balconies opening onto views of the pool. The location is 8km (5 miles) southeast of the center of Sintra reached along N9.

Rua Mato da Mina 1, Quinta da Beloura, 2710-692 Sintra. www.pestana.com. 🄲 **21/042-43-00.** Fax 21/042-43-98. 137 units. 100€–288€. Rates include breakfast. AE, DC, MC, V. Free parking. **Amenities:** Restaurant; bar; children's center; concierge; 18-hole golf course nearby; health club & spa; outdoor pool; 2 tennis courts (lit); room service; watersports equipment/rentals. *In room:* A/C, TV, hair dryer, Internet (15€ per hour).

MODERATE

Lawrence's Hotel ★★ 👔   Lawrence's Hotel boasts a pedigree that's older than that of any other hotel in Iberia. It originated in the 1760s, when an eccentric but formidable English innkeeper (Jane Lawrence) established the hotel. Its fortunes were assured in 1809, when Lord Byron stayed here for a 12-day visit and publicized the virtues of Sintra and the hotel in his writings. After millions of dollars of expenditures, the hotel is now one of the most desirable inns in Portugal. It occupies a low-slung yellow building a short walk uphill from the center of town, on the road that leads to the Pena Palace. Because of the sloping terrain on which it sits, you enter from the street onto the third floor of a six-story building with a tasteful, completely unglitzy decor and the most recent in electronics and security devices. Bedrooms are airily furnished with tasteful replicas of 19th-century furniture, in a spirit of thrift that emulates that of a discreetly upscale private home. Some units have private terraces.

Rua Consiglièri Pedroso 38-40, 2710-550 Sintra. www.lawrenceshotel.com. 🄲 **21/910-55-00.** Fax 21/910-55-05. 16 units. 100€–174€ double; 190€–264€ suite. Rates include buffet breakfast. AE, DC, MC, V. **Amenities:** Restaurant; bar; babysitting; Wi-Fi (free, in lobby). *In room:* A/C, TV, hair dryer.

Quinta das Sequóias ★★ 👔   Standing on 16 hectares (40 acres) of wooded grounds, this beautiful 19th-century manor house lies less than 1km (⅔ mile) below the Tivoli Palácio de Seteais (see above). The manor house was originally built as a rural annex of a much larger palace (the Palácio do Relógio) in Sintra's center. The generally spacious rooms have high ceilings and formal 19th-century furniture. On the premises is a verdant English-style garden. Within a 16km (10-mile) walk from the main house are an archaeological dig, where Roman coins and artifacts from the Bronze Age have been unearthed, and bubbling springs whose pure waters were noted by historians during the 15th century.

Abdo. 1004, 2710-801 Sintra. www.quintadasequoias.com. 🄲 **21/923-03-42.** Fax 21/910-60-65. 5 units. 145€–170€ double. Rates include buffet breakfast. AE, DC, MC, V. Closed Oct 31–Mar 31. From Sintra, take the road signposted for Montserrat and then fork left at signpost for hotel. **Amenities:** Bar; outdoor pool; room service; sauna. *In room:* A/C, hair dryer.

Quinta de São Thiago ★   Quinta de São Thiago is smaller and more intimate than Tivoli Palace, and certainly not as grand as Lawrence's Hotel, but like those two hotels, it too was visited by Byron years ago. In many ways, it also offers a more authentic experience of what a *quinta* (manor house) looked like in another century. Reached on a rough road, it edges up the side of a mountain in a woodland setting. Its origins as a *quinta* go back to the 1500s, but it's now refurbished and decked out with antiques. The midsize guest rooms are comfortably furnished and attractively decorated, with tidy bathrooms equipped with modern plumbing. Many of the units open onto views of the valley of Colares and the water beyond. The pool offers views of Monserrate and the Atlantic coastline.

In the finest British tradition, tea is offered in the parlor, which was transformed from the original kitchen. Dances are held in summer in the music room, as well as summertime buffets.

Estrada de Monserrate, 2710-610 Sintra. ℂ **21/923-29-23.** Fax 21/923-43-29. 9 units. 80€–115€ double; 130€–145€ suite. Rates include buffet breakfast. MC, V. Free parking. **Amenities:** Bar; outdoor pool; outdoor tennis court.

Tivoli Sintra ★★ Opened in 1981, this modern and airy property is the finest hotel in the center of Sintra and a favorite with groups. It lies only a few doors from the National Palace and offers an abundance of modern conveniences, including a garage. The spacious guest rooms are comfortably furnished, with large beds and big easy chairs. The balconies and the public rooms look out onto a wooded hill with views of Sintra's *quintas*. The sight, according to one reader, "could have inspired mad Ludwig of Bavaria or at least Walt Disney." The hotel has a restaurant with panoramic views of Monserrate.

Praça da República, 2710-616 Sintra. www.tivolihotels.com. ℂ **21/923-72-00.** Fax 21/923-72-45. 77 units. 97€–180€ double; 137€–250€ suite. Rates include buffet breakfast. AE, DC, MC, V. **Amenities:** Restaurant; bar; babysitting; concierge; exercise room; room service; Wi-Fi (free, in lobby). *In room:* A/C, TV, hair dryer, minibar.

INEXPENSIVE

Casa Miradouro ★★ 🏠 At the edge of Sintra, this candy-striped house is a snug, cozy retreat. From its 1894 construction until 1987, it belonged to several generations of a family that included important figures in the Portuguese army. It's now a well-managed, attractively indulgent B&B. About .5km (⅓ mile) north of Sintra, it boasts a small garden, very few amenities other than the owner's genteel goodwill, and a facade that art historians have defined as Iberian chalet-style. The excellently maintained rooms are most inviting, with provincial carpets, tile floors, and wrought-iron bedsteads. Views from upper-floor rooms include the Pena Palace and, on clear days, the faraway Atlantic.

Rua Sotto Mayor 55, 2710-801 Sintra. www.casa-miradouro.com. ℂ **21/910-71-00.** Fax 21/924-18-36. 6 units. 95€–135€ double. Rates include buffet breakfast. AE, MC, V. Closed Jan 8–Feb 24. From the Tivoli Sintra (see above), take Rua Sotto Mayor for .4km (¼ mile). **Amenities:** Bar; babysitting; Wi-Fi (free, in lobby). *In room:* No phone.

Hotel Arribas This hotel is an affordable selection with quite decent accommodations that range from midsize to spacious. One of its biggest assets is its location over the Atlantic-washed cliffs at the top of Praia Grande—it's one of the best beaches in the surroundings of Lisbon. If you don't want to walk to the beach, you can always use the hotel's saltwater swimming pools. The panoramic restaurant serves good cuisine, featuring traditional Portuguese specialties as well as international dishes.

Praia Grande, Av. Alfredo Coelho, 2706-329 Colares. www.hotelarribas.com. ℂ **21/928-90-50.** Fax 21/929-24-20. 58 units. 60€–132€ double; 76€–176€ triple. AE, DC, MC, V. **Amenities:** Restaurant; 2 bars; outdoor saltwater pool; room service. *In room:* A/C, TV, hair dryer, minibar.

Pensão Nova Sintra Rising like a private villa, this restored pension from 1875 stands in the satellite of Sintra known as Estefânia, right on the outskirts of town. When the little inn was restored and opened to receive guests, the 19th-century architectural features were maintained. The atmosphere is heavily laced with tradition, from the choice of furniture to the welcome. Umbrella-shaded tables and chairs are placed outside in fair weather.

Largo Afonso de Albuquerque 25, Estefânia, 2710-519 Sintra. www.novasintra.com. © **21/923-02-20.** Fax 21/910-70-33. 9 units. 65€–85€ double. AE, DC, MC, V. **Amenities:** Restaurant; bar; babysitting. *In room:* Ceiling fan, hair dryer, Wi-Fi (free).

Pensão Residencial Sintra   In São Pedro, a verdant suburb of Sintra, this 1850s stone house was commissioned by its former occupant, Viscount Tojal. Shortly after World War II, the German-born parents of the present owner, Susana Rosner Fragoso, bought the house and transformed it into a dignified *pensão* (boarding-house). Surrounded by a spacious garden with venerable trees, the pastel-colored midsize rooms contain simple but comfortable furniture.

Travessa dos Avelares 12, 2710-506 Sintra. ©/fax **21/923-07-38.** 15 units. 60€–110€ double. Rates include buffet breakfast. MC, V. From Sintra, take a bus marked São Pedro or Mira-Sintra. **Amenities:** Bar; outdoor pool; room service. *In room:* TV.

Where to Dine
MODERATE

Lawrence's Restaurant ★ INTERNATIONAL   The owners of this restaurant describe it as the main focus of the hotel that houses it, occupying more of their attention than the hotel itself. Outfitted in a tasteful interpretation of a late-19th-century decor, it has welcomed diners that have included presidents, statesmen, diplomats, and actors—all of whom seem to appreciate the superb cuisine and grace-ful service. The menu changes frequently, but it's likely to include a sophisticated version of fish soup; black tagliolini with grilled octopus, squid ink, and fresh sweet basil; house-style codfish; and grilled filet of sea bass with a comfit of leeks. Meat items include a roasted spit that contains both venison and white veal, and a roasted magret of duck served with Rösti potatoes and wild berry sauce.

In Lawrence's Hotel, Rua Consigliéri Pedroso 38-40. © **21/910-55-00.** Reservations recommended. Main courses 15€–28€. AE, DC, MC, V. Daily 12:30-3pm and 7:30-10pm.

Restaurante Cantinho de São Pedro ★ FRENCH/PORTUGUESE   Less than 2km (1¼ mile) southeast of Sintra, in São Pedro de Sintra, this is one of the hillside village's finest dining choices. It's right off the main square, Praça Dom Fernando II, where the *Feira da Sintra* (Sintra Fair) is staged every second and fourth Sunday of the month. Dating from the time of the Christian Reconquest, the fair is one of the oldest in the country. Look for the *pratos do dia* (daily specials), or save your appetite for the tasty specialties. They include velvety crepes stuffed with fresh lob-ster, and meltingly tender beefsteak in green-pepper sauce. Try salmon and shrimp au gratin or pork with clams in the style of the province of Alentejo.

Praça Dom Fernando II 18 (at Lojas do Picadeiro). © **21/923-02-67.** www.cantinhosaopedro.com. Reservations recommended. Main courses 12€–20€; 17€ tourist menu. AE, DC, MC, V. Daily noon–3pm and 7:30-10pm.

Tacho Real ★★ FRENCH/PORTUGUESE   Lisboans come in from the city to enjoy the well-prepared meals at this chic, elegant, and stylish restaurant. It's set at the top of a steep flight of cobble-covered steps and ramps that lead uphill, after a huff-and-puff short walk from the Praça da República below. The kitchen deftly handles fish and meat dishes, and some succulent poultry dishes also appear on the menu. Two popular house specialties are fish filet with shrimp sauce and rice, and filet steak with cream sauce and mushrooms. We always like the bubbling fish stew. The fixed-price menu is a bargain that includes soup, a main course, dessert, coffee, and half a bottle of wine. Service is efficient and polite (waiters speak English).

Rua da Ferraria 4. *©* **21/923-52-77.** Reservations recommended. Main courses 12€–30€. AE, DC, MC, V. Thurs-Tues noon-3pm and 7:30-10:30pm.

Tivoli Sintra ★ INTERNATIONAL/PORTUGUESE   Because this restaurant is within the concrete-and-glass walls of the town center's most desirable hotel, many visitors might overlook the Tivoli Sintra as a dining spot. That would be a shame—it serves some of the finest food in town. Staffed by a battalion of uniformed waiters, the room has a shimmering metallic ceiling, dark paneling, and floor-to-ceiling windows on one side. The daily menu is likely to include such carefully crafted dishes as tournedos Rossini, fish soup, and filet of turbot with mushrooms and garlic.

Praça da República. *©* **21/923-72-00.** Reservations recommended. Main courses 15€–29€. AE, DC, MC, V. Daily 12:30-3pm and 7:30-10pm.

INEXPENSIVE

Lojo do Vinho CAFE/WINE BAR   Set directly on the town's main square, this establishment combines aspects of both a restaurant and a wine shop. No one will mind if you browse the inventory of wine and port from throughout the country. But if you're hungry, you can sit at any of several low-slung tables and enjoy wine by the glass with some simple snacks. These might include a selection of Portuguese cheese, sausages, olives, or smoked ham. Additional bottles are on display in the slightly claustrophobic setting. Overall, a visit here is a fine way to acquaint yourself with ethnic Portuguese wines in a setting that evokes a medieval wine cellar.

Praça da República 3. *©* **21/924-44-10.** Snacks, platters, and sandwiches 8€–21€. AE, DC, MC, V. Daily 9am-10:30pm.

Restaurant Alcobaça PORTUGUESE   Popular with English visitors, this shop-size restaurant occupies two floors of a centrally located building on a steep, narrow pedestrian street. You can get one of the cheapest meals in town here. The Alcobaça serves typical Portuguese cuisine, including flavorful monkfish rice, tasty roast sardines, *caldo verde* (a soup with ham hock, greens, and potatoes), hake filet with rice, octopus, Alcobaça chicken, and succulent pork with clams. It's the kind of robust food beloved by locals.

Rua das Padarias 7, 9, and 11. *©* **21/923-16-51.** Reservations not necessary. Main courses 8€–35€. No credit cards. Daily 11am-11pm.

Tulhas Restaurant PORTUGUESE   This restaurant, decorated with tiles and wood, is between the tourism office and San Martin Church. Specialties of the house are codfish in cream sauce with potatoes, roasted lamb or duck with rice, steak au poivre (pepper steak with pepper sauce), and veal Madeira. You'll find better food elsewhere, but the quality of the meat and fish is good, and the chefs present platters with perfectly balanced flavors.

Gil Vicente 4. *©* **21/923-23-78.** Main courses 8€–22€. AE, DC, MC, V. Thurs-Tues noon-3:30pm and 7:30-10pm.

Sintra After Dark

Sintra is not a party town; the most intriguing soirees are private. A worthy bar in the center of town, where you might meet people from any country in Europe, is **Adega das Caves,** Praça da República 2–10 (*©* **21/923-08-48**). The establishment is a restaurant that does a busy lunch trade. After dark, it mellows into a likable bar and bodega, specializing in beer and Portuguese wine. It's open every day until around 2am. A nearby competitor is the **Taverna dos Trovadores,** Largo D. Fernando II, São Pedro (© **21/923-35-48;** www.taverna-trovadores.com), which lies in the center of the tiny hamlet of São Pedro, less than 2km (1¼ miles) south from the center of Sintra. Popular and convivial, it incorporates aspects of an old-fashioned *tasca* (tavern) with a modern singles bar and it features recorded and (on rare occasions) live music, a long drink list, and a cross section of residents from throughout the region.

ERICEIRA ★

21km (13 miles) NW of Sintra; 50km (31 miles) NW of Lisbon

This fishing port is nestled on the Atlantic shore. Whitewashed houses accented with pastel-painted corners and window frames line its narrow streets. To the east rise the mountains of Sintra.

The sea gives life to Ericeira, as it has for some 700 years. Fishermen still pluck their food from it. The beach lures streams of visitors every summer, giving a much-needed boost to the local economy. Along the coast, cliffside nurseries called *serrações* breed lobsters. Lobster is the house specialty at every restaurant in Ericeira.

In 1584, Mateus Álvares arrived in Ericeira from the Azores, claiming to be King Sebastião, who had reportedly been killed on the battlefields of North Africa. Álvares and about two dozen of his chief supporters were executed after their defeat by the soldiers of Philip II of Spain, but today he is regarded as the king of Ericeira. In October 1910, the fleeing Manuel II and his mother, Amélia, set sail from the Ericeira harbor to a life of exile in England.

The crescent-shape, sandy **Praia do Sol,** the favorite beach of Portuguese and foreign visitors, attracts many travelers here. There are three other good beaches: **Ribeira Beach, North Beach,** and **St. Sebastian Beach.** All are suitable for swimming, unlike the beaches at Estoril and Cascais.

Essentials

ARRIVING

There is no direct rail service to Ericeira.

BY BUS   **Mafrense buses** (www.mafrense.pt) from both Sintra and Lisbon serve Ericeira. One bus per hour leaves Lisbon's Campo Grande Station for the 1¼-hour trip. A one-way ticket costs 6.50€. From Sintra, there's one bus per hour. The trip takes 1 hour and costs 3.80€ one-way.

BY CAR   From Sintra (p. 163), continue northwest along Route 247.

VISITOR INFORMATION

The **Ericeira Tourist Office** is at Rua Mendes Leal (© **26/186-31-22;** www. ericeira.net). It's open daily 9:30am to 7pm, and Saturday 9:30am to 10pm.

Exploring the Town

A NEARBY ATTRACTION

Palácio Nacional de Mafra ★★   This palace is a work of extraordinary discipline, grandeur, and majesty. At the peak of its 13-year construction, it reputedly employed 50,000; a small town was built just to house the workers. Its master model was El Escorial, the Daedalian maze constructed by Philip II outside Madrid. Mafra's might not be as impressive or as labyrinthine, but the diversity of its contents is amazing. Its 880 rooms housed 300 friars who could look through 4,500 doorways and windows.

The summer residence of kings, Mafra, 40km (25 miles) northwest of Lisbon, was home to the banished queen Carlota Joaquina. In addition to having a love of painting, Carlos I, the Bragança king assassinated at Praça do Comércio in 1908, was an avid hunter. In one room he had chandeliers made out of antlers and upholstery of animal skins. His son, who ruled for 2 years as Manuel II, spent his last night on Portuguese soil at Mafra before fleeing to England with his mother, Amélia.

Two towers hold more than 110 chimes, made in Antwerp, Belgium, that can be heard for up to 24km (15 miles) when they're played at Sunday recital. The towers flank a basilica, capped by a dome that has been compared to that of St. Paul's in London. The church contains an assortment of chapels, 11 in all, expertly crafted with detailed jasper reredos, bas-reliefs, and marble statues from Italy. The monastery holds the pride of Mafra, a 40,000-volume library with tomes hundreds of years old—many gold-leafed. Viewed by some more favorably than the world-famous library at Coimbra, the room is a study in gilded light. The collection of elaborately decorated vestments in the Museum of Religious Art here is outstanding.

2640 Mafra. 🕐 **26/181-75-50.** www.cm-mafra.pt/turismo/palacio.asp. Admission 6€ adults, 3€ seniors (65 and over) and students 15-18, free for children under 15. Wed–Mon 10am–5:30pm. Bus: Mafrense bus from Lisbon.

Where to Stay

Hotel Pedro o Pescador   This is a relatively modest inn that attracts a devoted clientele from Lisbon. Though relatively lean on amenities, the immaculate rooms are comfortably furnished, each with a private shower-only bathroom, and the owners are friendly. Call ahead to see if the restaurant, once a well-known destination, will be open when you visit.

Rua Dr. Eduardo Burnay 22, 2655-370 Ericeira. www.hotelpedropescador.com. 🕐 **26/186-40-32.** Fax 26/186-23-21. 25 units. 40€–70€ double. Rates include buffet breakfast. AE, DC, MC, V. **Amenities:** Bar; room service. *In room:* TV.

Hotel Vila Galé Ericeira ★★   Overlooking the beaches and the waters of the Atlantic, the government-rated four-star Hotel Vila Galé Ericeira is the westernmost hotel in Europe, and brings a bit of luxury to the center of town. An older structure was completely renovated and made both stylish and up-to-date in this reincarnation, everything resting under a glistening green tiled roof. The typical Portuguese glazed tiles have been used effectively throughout the building, both to adorn the walls and to cover the floors. Bedrooms are midsize to spacious and are tastefully and comfortably furnished. The magnet in summer is the alfresco bar extending like the prow of a ship toward the sea.

Largo dos Navegantes, 2655-320 Ericeira. www.vilagale.pt. 🕐 **26/186-99-00.** Fax 26/186-99-50. 202 units. 80€–169€ double. AE, DC, MC, V. Free parking. **Amenities:** Restaurant; bar; babysitting; bikes; children's center; exercise room; 3 outdoor pools; room service; spa; Wi-Fi (5€ per hour, in lobby). *In room:* A/C, TV, hair dryer, minibar.

Vilazul Hotel ★ 🍴   If you prefer a small hotel with affordable rooms that also serves a regional cuisine, mostly seafood, consider this long-enduring favorite. Rooms are simply furnished but comfortable, and some have small private balconies. On the third floor of the hotel is a pleasant TV lounge with a view over the south side of Ericeira.

Calçada da Baleia 10, 2655-238 Ericeira. www.hotelvilazul.com.℗ **26/186-00-00.** Fax 26/186-29-27. 21 units. 44€–90€ double. Rates include buffet breakfast. AE, DC, MC. V. **Amenities:** Restaurant; 2 bars; bikes; Wi-Fi (free, in lobby). *In room:* A/C, TV.

Where to Dine

O Barco PORTUGUESE   This is the port's best independent restaurant outside its hotels. The kitchen takes full advantage of the ocean's riches but also brings in fresh meat and poultry supplies from neighboring farms. You'll be courteously welcomed into an unpretentious dining room. As you sit back enjoying an aperitif, you can study the specialties of the day offered on the limited but choice menu. Codfish invariably appears, perhaps with creamy potatoes and fresh vegetables. One of the best main courses is a platter of savory shrimp in a tangy garlic sauce; grilled beef is the favorite meat course. Desserts are often worthy, especially in summer when made with fresh fruit from nearby orchards.

Rua Capitão João Lopes.℗ **26/186-28-57.** Reservations not necessary. Main courses 12€–25€. AE, DC, MC, V. Fri–Wed noon–3pm and 7–10pm. Closed Nov 20–27.

O Poço INTERNATIONAL/PORTUGUESE   The Vilazul Hotel (see above) is also the site of one of Ericeira's best restaurants. The decor is rather formal, vaguely English country house in motif. With the sea at their doorstep, the chefs turn to the ocean for their specialties. Their best dish is Pescado a la Sal. The cooks bake a fish in salt to seal its natural juices. When the salt is peeled away, the fish is both pleasantly aromatic and juicy. You can also order the catch of the day, grilled as you like it. Meat and poultry dishes, especially a tasty chicken *cordon bleu* served with potatoes and a mixed salad, are well prepared. Vegetables—often from the nearby countryside—are fresh and not overcooked, and the pastries are made fresh daily.

Calçada de Baleia 10.℗ **26/186-00-00.** Reservations not necessary. Main courses 9€–21€. AE, DC, MC, V. Apr–Sept daily noon–3pm and 9–11pm; Oct–Mar daily noon–3pm and 9–11pm.

SOUTH OF THE TAGUS

Historically cut off from Lisbon, the narrow isthmus south of the Tagus is wild and rugged as well as lush. In different places, this strip of land plummets toward the sea, stretches along miles of sandy beaches, and rolls through groves heavy with the odors of ripening oranges. With craggy cliffs and coves in the background, the crystalline Atlantic is ideal for swimming, skin-diving, or fishing for tuna, swordfish, and bass.

The area has enjoyed an upsurge of interest since the construction of the Ponte do 25 de Abril, a long suspension bridge that makes it possible to cross the Tagus in minutes—though traditionalists prefer taking the ferry from Praça do Comércio in Lisbon and docking in Cacilhas. Whichever way of crossing you prefer, once you get to Lisbon's left bank, good roads will help you head rapidly through pine groves to the apex of the triangle known as The Land of the Three Castles: Sesimbra, Setúbal, and Palmela.

The land south of the Tagus River retains vivid reminders of its past, reflected in its Moorish architecture, Roman ruins and roads, Phoenician imprints, and Spanish fortresses. The region's proximity to Lisbon (Setúbal is only 40km/25 miles southeast of the capital) makes it perfect for a 1-day excursion. Though train travel is very limited, the area has an extensive network of ferry connections as well as bus services from Lisbon. You'll find driving to be the ideal way to explore the district at your leisure. Otherwise, you can take a bus from Lisbon to the beaches at Caparica in about 45 minutes.

If you take a ferry from Lisbon's Praça do Comércio to Cacilhas, you can catch a bus there for the beaches of Caparica. If you're visiting the peninsula by bus, use Setúbal as your hub; from there you can take local buses to Palmela and Sesimbra.

In summer, a narrow-gauge railway runs for 8km (5 miles) along the Costa da Caparica, making 20 stops at beaches along the way. If you go by rail to the peninsula, service is from Lisbon to Setúbal. From there, you must rely on buses to visit the fishing villages along the southern coast.

AZEITÃO

15km (9½ miles) NW of Setúbal; 25km (16 miles) SE of Lisbon

This sleepy village lies in the heart of *quinta* country. In its most meager manifestation, a *quinta* is a simple farmhouse surrounded by land. At its best, it's a mansion of great architectural style filled with art. Azeitão

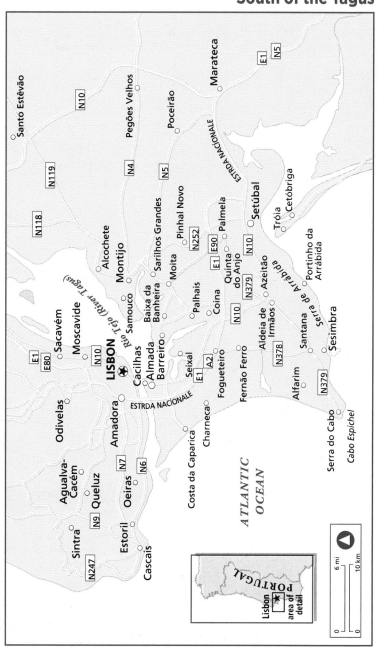

boasts some of the finest *quintas* in the country. The village makes a good base for trekkers, especially those who want to scale the limestone Serra de Arrábida. For others, long walks through scented pinewoods or silvery olive groves will suffice. To cap off your day, try some Azeitão cheese and a bottle of local muscatel wine.

Azeitão is also home to one of the region's biggest ceramics factories: **São Simão Arte** (© **21/218-31-35**). The factory outlet sells its products at prices that are somewhat less than in equivalent retail shops.

Essentials

ARRIVING

Because the village is not served by public transportation, you'll need a car. After crossing one of the bridges across the Tagus, continue south along the old road to Setúbal (N10) until you see the turnoff for the village of Azeitão.

Visiting a Quinta

Quinta da Bacalhôa ★   Manuel I reputedly introduced the concept of *quintas* in the early 16th century when he built the Quinta da Bacalhôa, about 10 km (6¼ miles) from the center of Setubal. Eventually, the 16th-century mansion associated with this *quinta* fell into disrepair and vandals carted off many of its decorations, specifically the antique tiles. An American woman, Orlena Scoville, bought the mansion in 1936 and worked for years to restore it to its original condition. Some architectural critics have suggested that it's the first example of the Renaissance in Portugal.

Bacalhôa is a private villa, and with the exception of a small reception area, the bulk of the premises cannot be visited, but the Italian/Portuguese Renaissance gardens, originally installed by Alfonso de Albuquerque, a former viceroy of India who imported his gardening aesthetic after months of travel in Italy, are open to the public on request when you arrive. Expect lots of sheared topiary and rigorously clipped boxwood hedges in serpentine patterns. The *quinta's* farmland, part of which is visible beyond the walls of the garden, is devoted to vineyards owned by **J. M. da Fonseca,** International-Vinhos, Ltda., makers of Lancers wine.

Fonseca's corporate headquarters, and processing plants, as well as the 19th-century house that originally functioned as the Fonseca's family home are 2km (1¼ miles) away, close to the center of the village of Azeitão. There's an on-site museum, whose exhibits consist mainly of unimportant antique paintings, plus a scattering of battered artifacts related to the history of winemaking. The century-old Fonseca wineries have made their product from grapes grown on the slopes of the Arrábida Mountains since the early 19th century. The top product is a muscatel called Setúbal, rarely sent abroad but well regarded by wine connoisseurs.

Gardens: Vila Fresca de Azeitão. © **21/218-00-11.** Admission 8€ adults, free for children under 13. Tues–Sat 1–5pm. Winemaking museum: Estrada Nacional 10, Vila Nogueira de Azeitão, 2925-901 Azeitão. © **21/219-80-60.** www.bacalhoa.com. Admission 4€ adults, free for children under 13. Mon–Fri 9am–5pm.

Where to Stay & Dine

Quinta das Torres ★ 🏠   A 16th-century baronial mansion of deteriorating elegance, Quinta das Torres is still intact for those who want to step back in time. Each guest room is unique; they range from smaller chambers to a ballroom-size suite dominated by princess-style brass beds. Some units have high shuttered windows, time-mellowed tile floors, antique furnishings, and niches with saints or Madonnas. The bungalows, which sleep four and have kitchenettes, ensure privacy.

The dining room (also open to those who aren't guests) has a tall stone fireplace where log fires burn on chilly evenings, plus elaborate scenic tiles depicting *The Rape of the Sabine Women* and *The Siege of Troy.* The chef specializes in regional cuisine, which is rich in sauces and strong in flavors. *Bacalhau* (dried codfish) is cooked to a golden-brown perfection, and tender cutlets of acorn-fed pork meat are sautéed and served with the fresh vegetable of the season. The roasted pheasant is a must-try when it appears on the menu.

Estrada Nacional 10, Azeitão 2925-601. ℂ **21/218-00-01.** Fax 21/219-06-07. 10 units, 2 bungalows. 75€–110€ double; 105€–175€ bungalow. Rates include buffet breakfast. AE, DC, MC, V. **Amenities:** Restaurant; bar; outdoor pool; room service. *In room:* TV, kitchenette (in bungalow), hair dryer.

SESIMBRA

26km (16 miles) SW of Setúbal; 43km (27 miles) S of Lisbon

Among the Portuguese, Sesimbra used to be a closely guarded secret. It was justifiably considered one of the most unspoiled fishing villages in the country. Today signs of rapid growth are apparent. However, fishermen still go about the time-honored task of plucking their livelihood from the Atlantic. When the fleet comes in, the day's catch is auctioned at the harbor (Porto Abrigo). Sesimbra is also a popular sportfishing center.

Essentials

ARRIVING

BY TRAIN   From Lisbon, the bus is a better choice. Rail passengers go to Setúbal by train and then have to double back on a bus to get to Sesimbra.

BY BUS   Buses to Sesimbra leave regularly from Lisbon's Praça de Espanha (Metro: Palhavã) and from Cacilhas, across the Tagus from the center of Lisbon. The 1-hour trip costs 6€. For information and schedules, call **Transportes Sul do Tejo** (ℂ **21/112-62-00;** www.tsuldotejo.pt).

BY CAR   From Lisbon, cross the Ponte do 25 de Abril bridge and continue southwest on the expressway to Setúbal. At the junction of N378, head directly south into Sesimbra.

BY FERRY   Take the ferry to Cacilhas from the Praça do Comércio wharf in Lisbon (Metro: Rossio). Then take a bus from Cacilhas.

VISITOR INFORMATION

The **tourist office** is on Largo da Marinha 26–27 (ℂ **21/228-85-40;** www.visit. sesimbra.pt). June to September, hours are daily 9:30am to 8pm; October to May, it's open daily 9am to 12:30pm and 2 to 5:30pm.

SPECIAL EVENTS

Sesimbra has many fairs and festivals during which the town attracts a lot of visitors, making accommodations hard to come by unless reservations are made well in advance. Each year, in February or early March (dates vary), Sesimbra stages **Cegadas,** which are a series of street theater presentations. Unless you speak Portuguese, it's more interesting for the casual visitor to attend the **Festa dos Pescadores** (or festival of the fishermen) celebrated every year on May 4. This is the most exciting, biggest, and best festival, but hotels are impossibly crowded in early May because of it. From June 23 to June 30, Sesimbra stages the annual **Festival of the Popular**

Saints, which is an exciting event—even for non-Catholics. The town is gaily decorated with paper flowers, parades are staged, and live music drifts through the streets.

Exploring Sesimbra

EXPLORING THE AREA The most intriguing sight in Sesimbra is the picturesque (and often photographed) **harbor ★**, which lies against the foot of a cliff, away from the city center.

Farther down the beach, beyond the boat-clogged harbor, is the 17th-century **Fortress of St. Teodósio.** It was built to fortify the region against pirates. The site is not open to the public and must be viewed from outside. However, even though the fortress can't be visited, this is the town's most scenic walk, taking you along the old port, with dramatic views of the sea on one side and colorful cliffs on the other.

A walk along the ruined battlements of the five-towered **Castle of Sesimbra** reduces the village to a miniature. The castle encloses a 12th-century church, the oldest in Sesimbra. The site is open daily from 7am to 7pm. Admission is free.

From Sesimbra, you can head west to the headland of **Cabo Espichel,** with views of arcaded pilgrim hospices dating from the 1700s. The baroque interior (gilded wood and sculpture) of a pilgrimage church, the **Santuário de Nossa Senhora do Cabo,** can be inspected daily between 9:30am to 1pm and 3 to 6pm. Admission is free. Later, walk to the edge of the cliffs behind the church for a panoramic view of the sea. At the southern end of the Arrábida Mountain chain, this pilgrimage site has been popular since the 13th century. Modern sculpture now stands in the forlorn setting. There's no guardrail, and it's a sheer drop of more than 100m (328 ft.) to the ocean waters, so be very careful. From Sesimbra, six buses a day make the 30-minute journey to this southwestern cape.

OUTDOOR ACTIVITIES Sesimbra's popularity stems from its position on a long, lovely sandy **beach.** The beach is overpopulated in summer, but the unpolluted water is ideal for swimming.

Sesimbra is also a center for **fishing.** The locals are famous for their swordfish catches, and many will take visitors out in their boats for a negotiated fee. Inquire at the tourist office (see "Visitor Information," above) about making arrangements.

SHOPPING **Avenida da Liberdade,** in the heart of town, is lined with all kinds of souvenir shops. The ceramics outlet at Azeitão (see above) is just 15km (9⅓ miles) from the center of town, along the road to Setúbal.

Where to Stay

EXPENSIVE

Sesimbra Hotel & Spa ★★ ☺ This government-rated four-star hotel now offers the most extensive facilities and the most luxe living in the area of Sesimbra. Set against the backdrop of the Arrábida Natural Reserve, the hotel opens right on the water, with 100% of its bedrooms fronting a sea view best enjoyed from one of the private balconies. All the accommodations are well equipped and comfortably and tastefully furnished, and you can live here at various levels, including in one of the elegant suites or a deluxe penthouse apartment. However, the regular doubles are midsize to spacious and are adequate in every way. A family favorite, complete with a kids club, the hotel is also a choice for honeymooners who prefer one of the more private suites. The modern spa with a gym is the best equipped south of the Tagus. The on-site dining facilities are also the finest in the area, especially with regard to

THE BEST BEACHES: WHERE THE locals SUN

The beaches along the Costa da Caparica, on the left bank of the Tagus, across from the center of Lisbon, are not as polluted as those along the more fashionable Costa do Sol (Estoril and Cascais). Surprisingly, foreigners still flock to the Costa do Sol, leaving much of the Costa da Caparica to locals.

The *costa*, on the west side of the Setúbal peninsula, stretches for some 9km (5⅗ miles) and abounds with sandy beaches and coves. Rocky outcroppings and clear, placid lagoons characterize these beaches. The farther you go from the little resort of Caparica, the better and more beautiful the beaches become.

A narrow-gauge railway serves the coast, making 20 stops over 8km (5 miles). Each white-sand beach along the way has a different allure. In general, families of all age groups are attracted to the beaches along the first eight stops. Beginning at stop 9, gay visitors become more prominent. As you travel the greater length of Costa da Caparica, the beaches become less crowded, and in the final southern stretches, nudists are often seen.

To reach the beach strip by public transport, you can take a ferry from Lisbon to Cacilhas, on the other side of Tagus. They leave every 15 minutes from Praça do Comércio's Terminal Fluvial (Metro: Rossio). You then board a bus marked CAPARICA at the station next door to the ferry terminal. The trip to the beaches takes about 45 minutes. The narrow-gauge train runs from June to September, and the bus from Cacilhas stops at the rail terminus, where you can connect with the little train.

The Setúbal peninsula has many other wonderful beaches. There are sandy beaches at Sesimbra (see above), but they are likely to be overcrowded from June to August.

The most alluring beach strip is across the mouth of the Sado, at Tróia (p. 188), a major resort with some utterly charmless apartment complexes. Ferries leave from Setúbal harbor every 45 minutes throughout the day. Trip time is 15 minutes. The ocean side of the promontory at Tróia is less filled with beach buffs and is less polluted.

fresh fish. The catch of the day is unloaded by local fishermen on the same day you consume it, and is later elegantly served in the Aquarium Restaurant. Guests also have vegetarian and low-cal options on hand at the Mosaico Restaurant & Bar.

Praça da Califórnia, 2970-773 Sesimbra. www.sesimbrahotelspa.com. ✆ **21/330-05-41.** Fax 21/223-48-65. 100 units. 75€–200€ double; 135€–400€ suite. AE, MC, V. Free parking. **Amenities:** 2 restaurants; 2 bars; children's center; exercise room; 2 freshwater pools (1 heated indoor); room service; spa. *In room:* A/C, TV, minibar.

MODERATE

Hotel do Mar ★★   One of the most unusual self-contained beach-resort hotels south of the Tagus, Hotel do Mar spreads from a high cliff to the water below. The main lobby houses a glassed-in tropical bird aviary, and the passageways are like art galleries, with contemporary paintings and ceramic plaques and sculpture. All the airy guest rooms have private terraces, with views of the ocean and gardens sweeping down the hillside. Suites vary widely in size, facilities, and price. Less-expensive suites are comfortable standard accommodations; the more expensive deluxe unit features a pool and Jacuzzi. Breakfast is served on a flower-filled terrace, and the wood-paneled restaurant overlooks the sea.

Rua General Humberto Delgado 10, 2970-628 Sesimbra. www.hoteldomar.pt. ℂ **21/228-83-00.** Fax 21/223-38-88. 168 units. 72€–210€ double; 245€–310€ junior suite; 515€–600€ suite. Rates include buffet breakfast. AE, DC, MC, V. Free parking. **Amenities:** Restaurant; bar; Jacuzzi; 2 pools (1 heated indoor); room service; sauna; 2 outdoor tennis courts; Wi-Fi (5€ per hour, in lobby). *In room:* A/C, TV, hair dryer.

SANA Sesimbra Hotel ★ A modern balconied hotel, this is the second-best choice in this resort town. Completely modernized and up-to-date, it offers comfortably and tastefully furnished bedrooms. A government-rated four-star hotel, SANA Sesimbra also offers many rooms with views. In terms of facilities, it's one of the better-equipped hotels in the area, especially with its pool, exercise room, and sauna. The restaurant's food is good, especially the fresh fish brought in by the local fishermen.

Av. 25 de Abril, 2970-628 Sesimbra. www.sanasesimbrahotel.com. ℂ **21/228-90-00.** Fax 21/228-90-01. 100 units. 129€–160€ double. Rates include buffet breakfast. AE, DC, MC. Parking 6€. **Amenities:** Restaurant; bar; babysitting; concierge; exercise room; Jacuzzi; outdoor pool; room service; sauna; Wi-Fi (10€ per 24 hr.). *In room:* A/C, TV, hair dryer, minibar.

Where to Dine

Restaurante Ribamar ★ INTERNATIONAL/PORTUGUESE This restaurant serves the best Portuguese cooking in the area, tucked away in a building a short stroll from the beach, with a view of the bay from most of the indoor and outdoor seating. It specializes in seafood fresh from local waters. The standout menu choice is the platter of mixed fish and shellfish for two, flavored with herbs, steamed in wine, and served cold with fresh lemon, if you wish. Swordfish caught in local waters is another favorite. The reasonable fixed-price menu includes soup, a main course, dessert, wine, and coffee.

Av. dos Náufragos 29. ℂ **21/223-48-53.** www.ribamar.com.pt. Reservations recommended. Main courses 18€–26€. MC, V. Daily noon–11pm.

PORTINHO DA ARRÁBIDA

13km (8 miles) SW of Setúbal; 37km (23 miles) SE of Lisbon

The fishing village of Portinho da Arrábida, a favorite with vacationing Lisbon families, is at the foot of the **Serra da Arrábida** ★. If you drive here in July and August, watch out. There's virtually no parking, and the road should be one-way but isn't—you can wait for hours to get back up the hill. In addition, the walk down and back could qualify you for the Olympics. Try to park on a wider road above the port, and then negotiate the hordes of summer visitors on foot.

There's really no place to stay in Portinho. Your best bet is to return to Sesimbra or to drive on to Setúbal for the night.

Essentials
ARRIVING
BY BUS There is no bus service between Sesimbra and Portinho da Arrábida.

BY CAR From Sesimbra, continue along N379 toward Setúbal, forking right at the turnoff for Portinho da Arrábida. But first, see the warning about parking, above. Portinho makes a good lunch stop for motorists exploring the foothills of the Serra da Arrábida.

EXPLORING THE mountains

The limestone, whale-backed Serra da Arrábida stretches for about 36km (22 miles), beginning at Palmela and rolling to a dramatic end at Cabo Espichel on the Atlantic. The Portuguese government has wisely set aside 10,800 hectares (26,687 acres) as a sanctuary between Sesimbra and Setúbal to protect the area from developers and to safeguard the local scenery and architecture.

At times, the cliffs and bluffs are so high that it seems you have to peer through clouds to see the purple waters of the Atlantic below. More than 1,000 species of plant life have been recorded, including holm oaks, sweet bay, pines, laurel, juniper, cypress, araucaria, magnolia, lavender, myrtle, and pimpernels.

Our favorite time to visit is in late March or the beginning of April (around Easter), when wildflowers—everything from coral-pink peonies to Spanish bluebells—cover the mountains.

Numerous sandy coves lie at the foot of the Serra da Arrábida's limestone cliffs. One of the finest beaches is **Praia de Galapos.** Another popular beach is **Praia de Figueirinha,** between Portinho da Arrábida and Setúbal, known for sport fishing, windsurfing, and sailing. The *serra* (mountain ridge) abounds with caves and grottoes. The best known is **Lapa de Santa Margarida,** of which Hans Christian Andersen wrote, "It is a veritable church hewn out of the living rock, with a fantastic vault, organ pipes, columns, and altars."

VISITOR INFORMATION

The nearest tourist offices are at Setúbal (© 26/553-91-20) or Sesimbra (© 21/228-85-40), but they offer little help to visitors to Portinho.

SETÚBAL ★

40km (25 miles) SE of Lisbon

On the right bank of the Sado River lies one of Portugal's largest and oldest cities, said to have been founded by Noah's grandson. Motorists often include it on their itineraries because of the exceptional inn, the **Pousada de Setúbal, São Filipe,** in a late-16th-century fort overlooking the sea (see "Where to Stay," below).

Setúbal, the center of Portugal's sardine industry, is known for the local production of the most exquisite muscatel wine in the world. Orange groves, orchards, vineyards, and outstanding beaches such as the popular Praia da Figueirinha all lie near Setúbal. The white pyramidal mounds dotting the landscape are deposits of sea salt drying in the sun, another major commercial asset of this seaside community.

Many artists and writers have come from Setúbal, most notably the 18th-century Portuguese poet Manuel Maria Barbosa du Bocage, forerunner of the Romantics. A monument honors him at Praça do Bocage.

Essentials

ARRIVING

BY TRAIN   The trip from Lisbon takes 1½ hours, and a one-way ticket costs 9€. For more information and schedules, call © 80/820-82-08.

BY BUS   Buses from Lisbon arrive every hour or two, depending on the time of day. The trip takes an hour, and a one-way ticket costs 6.50€. For more information and schedules, call ℂ**70/722-33-44** (www.rede-expressos.pt).

BY CAR   After crossing one of the Tagus bridges from Lisbon, follow the signs to Setúbal along the express highway, A2, until you see the turnoff for Setúbal. The old road (N10) to Setúbal is much slower.

VISITOR INFORMATION

The **Setúbal Tourist Office** is at Travessa Frei Gaspar 10 (ℂ **26/553-91-20;** www.turismolisboavaledotejo.pt). The office is open June to September Monday to Saturday 9:30am to 7pm and Sunday 9:30am to 12:30pm. From October to May, hours are Monday to Saturday 9:30am to 6pm.

Exploring Setúbal

Convento de Jesús ★
This church is a late-15th-century example of the Manueline style of architecture. Of particular interest are the main chapel, the ornate decorations on the principal doorway, and the Arrábida marble columns. Hans Christian Andersen called the monument "one of the most beautiful small churches that I have ever seen." The church has been extensively restored; the latest wholesale renovation took place in 1969 and 1970.

Praça Miguel Bombarda (off Av. do 22 de Dezembro). ℂ **26/553-78-90** or 26/552-41-50. Suggested donation 1€. Tues–Sat 9am–1pm and 1:30–5:30pm. Bus: 1, 4, 7, 10, or 12.

Museu da Setúbal
Adjoining the Igreja de Jesús, this unpretentious town museum houses some early-16th-century Portuguese paintings, as well as Spanish and Flemish works and contemporary art. The museum is also rich in antique *azulejos* (hand-painted tiles) and has a large antique coin collection, plus artifacts from archaeological digs in the area. Don't miss the collection of ecclesiastical gold and silver, especially a Gothic processional cross in crystal and gilt from the 15th century. If you have an hour or so, this museum is well worth a visit.

Rua Balneário Paula Borba. ℂ **26/553-78-90.** Admission 1.50€. Tues–Sat 9am–noon and 1:30–5:30pm. Bus: 1, 4, 7, 10, or 12.

OUTDOOR ACTIVITIES
The playground of Setúbal is the Peninsula of Tróia (see below), site of some excellent white-sand beaches. Parts of the lonely, rocky stretches of land between Lisbon and Setúbal have undergone massive upgrades, making way for some of Europe's best golf courses to emerge.

Portugal's most acclaimed golf course is the **Aroeira Clube de Golf ★★**, Herdade de Aroeira, Fonte da Telha, 2825 Monte de Caparica, Aroeira (ℂ **21/297-91-00;** www.aroeira.com). Designed as a 364-hectare (899-acre) "golf estate" in the early 1970s by the English architect Frank Pennink, it's a par-72, 6,040m (19,816-ft.) course. International golf magazines have hailed the layout as one of the finest in Europe. Low, rocky cliffs and a network of lakes separate the long, lush fairways and copses of pine trees from the surging Atlantic. Advance reservations are essential. Greens fees for 18 holes run 52€ to 82€, depending on the time and day. Golf clubs can be rented for 40€, and an electric cart costs 18€ for 18 holes. To reach the club from Lisbon (a 25km/16-mile ride, which takes about 35 min.), take one of the bridges over the Tagus. Drive south for 32km (20 miles), and exit the highway at Costa da Caparica. From Setúbal (a 40km/25-mile ride, which takes about 1 hr.), take Hwy. N10 northwest to Lisbon and exit at Fogueteiro.

If the Aroeira course is booked, you can schedule a round at another course in the region. **Quinta do Perú Golf & Country Club,** Alameda da Serra 2, is near the hamlet of Negreiros (© **21/213-43-20;** www.golfquintadoperu.com). From Setúbal, take Estrada Nacional 10 for about 19km (12 miles), following signs to Lisbon. Reservations are required. Another, less prestigious, option is the **Golfe do Montado,** in the hamlet of Montado (© 26/570-8150; www.montadoresort.com). From Setúbal, drive 10km (6¼ miles) south along the Estrada Nacional, following signs to Alentejo and Algarve. Greens fees are comparable to those at the Aroeira, but professionals don't consider either of those newcomers as exciting.

SHOPPING Setúbal offers enough outlets for local handicrafts to keep any devoted shopper busy for at least a full afternoon.

Fortuna (© **21/287-10-68**), a ceramics factory and technical school, dominates the hamlet of **Quinta do Anjo,** 6.5km (4 miles) northeast of Setúbal. To reach it, follow signs to Palmela. **São Simão Arte** (© **21/218-31-35**), a leading competitor, manufactures ceramics that are glazed and painted fancifully with renditions of flowers, vines, and woodland animals, some of them mythical. The store is the focal point of the hamlet of **Azeitão,** 15km (9⅓ miles) northwest of Setúbal. Both offer factory tours and ample shopping opportunities.

Where to Stay
EXPENSIVE
Estalagem Do Sado ★★ It lacks the history and ambience of the Pousada de Setúbal, São Filipe (see below), but this hotel has superior amenities and facilities. Its older four-story section, containing a series of nine junior suites, is housed in a pink-painted structure with sections built in 1963 and 1993. Other more modern rooms were added in a new wing. All of the accommodations open onto a small balcony overlooking cityscapes. Some of the bedrooms are in a very contemporary style, whereas others are more classical. If you want smaller rooms that ooze atmosphere, check into the older section; if you seek spacious and modern, then head for the newer wing.

Rua Irene Lisboa 1 and 3, 2900-028 Setúbal. www.estalagemdosado.com. © **26/554-28-00.** Fax 26/554-28-28. 66 units. 110€–175€ double; 140€–300€ suite. Rates include buffet breakfast. AE, DC, MC, V. Free parking. **Amenities:** Restaurant; bar; babysitting; bikes; room service; Wi-Fi (free, in lobby). *In room:* A/C, TV, hair dryer, minibar.

Pousada de Setúbal, São Filipe ★★ This fortress-castle, built by Philip I (Philip II of Spain) on a hilltop overlooking the town and the harbor, dates from the 17th century. It's the work of Italian architect Philipe Terzi. The road leading to the pousada winds up a mountain and passes through a stone arch and past towers to the belvedere. The walls of the chapel and the public rooms contain tile dados depicting scenes from the life of São Filipe and the life of the Virgin Mary. They're dated 1736 and signed by Policarpo de Oliveira Bernardes.

Guest rooms that once housed soldiers and the governor have been tastefully furnished with antiques and reproductions of 16th- and 17th-century pieces. Guns and ammunition have given way to soft beds and ornate Portuguese-crafted headboards. The hotel is flooded with what seems like miles of plant-filled corridors.

If you're not driving, take a taxi from Setúbal—the walk is too long for most people.

Castelo de São Filipe, 2900-300 Setúbal. www.pousadas.pt. © **26/555-00-70.** Fax 26/553-92-40. 16 units. 145€–240€ double; 190€–270€ suite. Rates include buffet breakfast. AE, DC, MC, V. Free parking.

Amenities: Restaurant; bar; bikes; room service; watersports equipment/rentals. *In room:* A/C, TV, hair dryer, minibar, Wi-Fi (in some; 12€ per day).

MODERATE

Luna Esperança Centro Hotel   This hotel is suitably functional and has been brought up-to-date with a series of renovations. In the center of Setúbal, it offers a view of the Sado River from many of its rooms. Suitable for both the business traveler and the vacationer, it features midsize bedrooms that are simply but comfortably furnished and well maintained. There is no restaurant, but the lobby bar is a popular gathering place.

Av. Luisa Todi 220, 2900-452 Setúbal. www.lunahoteis.com. (©) **26/552-17-80.** Fax 26/552-17-89. 80 units. 64€ double; 119€ suite. MC, V. **Amenities:** Lobby bar; room service. *In room:* A/C, TV, hair dryer, minibar, Wi-Fi (free).

INEXPENSIVE

Setúbalense Residencial   About a minute's walk north of Setúbal's central plaza, Largo da Misericórdia, this is a family-run hotel that opened in the early 1990s. The carefully restored three-story building was erected 200 years ago as a substantial private home. The midsize rooms have high ceilings and streamlined modern furniture, including neatly kept bathrooms with tub/shower combos.

Rua Major Afonso Pala 17, 2900-127 Setúbal. www.setubalense.com. (©) **26/552-57-90.** Fax 26/552-57-89. 24 units. 50€–60€ double. Rates include buffet breakfast. AE, DC, MC, V. **Amenities:** Bar; room service. *In room:* TV, fan, hair dryer.

Where to Dine

INEXPENSIVE

El Toro PORTUGUESE/SPANISH   Established in the commercial core of Setúbal in the late 1990s, with a dining room outfitted in tones of salmon and white, this is one of the most consistently popular restaurants in town, packed every day with office workers at lunchtime and gaggles of family and friends in the evening. Much about it will remind you of a *tasca* in Andalusia, in neighboring Spain, thanks to bullfighting memorabilia, and a well-accessorized roster of tapas (served at table or at a bar near the front). Expect platters brimming with roasted meats, well-prepared fish, and the kind of succulent tidbits such as stuffed mushrooms or slices of Serrano ham that go well with *fino Porto* or *Xeres*.

Rua António José Baptista 111. (©) **26/552-49-95.** Reservations recommended for dinner. Main courses 13€–27€. AE, DC, MC, V. Daily 12:30–3pm and 7:30–11pm. Closed Wed and Sat Aug 1–14 and daily Aug 15–30.

Estalagem do Sado Restaurant ★ CONTINENTAL/PORTUGUESE   This is the showcase restaurant of Setúbal's best hotel, a previously recommended much-renovated 19th-century palace. The restaurant lies within a 5-minute drive from the city's core, on the building's uppermost (eighth) floor, and is directly accessible via a dramatically angular elevator whose shaft rises as a distinctly separate structure from the building's historic core. At the summit, wide-angled views extend outward in all directions, sweeping out over the surrounding coastline and the estuary of the Sado River. Many guests opt for selections from the menu's "daily fish market," which allows anything from the catch of the day to be grilled and served with whatever sauce and trimmings you specify. Other choices include codfish stuffed with local cheese; monkfish with coriander sauce; fried lamb chops with potatoes and tomatoes; and grilled filet steak with béarnaise.

Irene Lisboa 1-3. (C) **26/554-28-00.** Reservations recommended. Main courses 11€–22€. AE, DC, MC, V.
Mon–Sat 12:30–3pm and 7:30–10:30pm.

Setúbal After Dark

The densest concentration of nightlife options lies near the western terminus of
Avenida Luisa Todi, the road leading west to a string of beaches. Another rich concentration of nightlife options is in the seafront village of **Albarquel,** less than 2km
(about 1¼ miles) west of Setúbal. Try the late-night eatery **Restaurant All-Barquel,**
Praia de Albarquel ((C) **26/522-19-46**), which caters to night owls of all ages.

PENINSULA DE TRÓIA

20 min. from Setúbal by ferry

Tróia is a long, sandy peninsula across the River Sado estuary that is accessible by
ferry from Setúbal. It is graced with many good sandy beaches and crystal-clear
waters, which makes it a choice vacation spot for families who flock here in summer.
Its appeal had begun to wane around the turn of the millennium but now it's making
a comeback, especially with the opening of the Tróia Design Hotel (see below).

Essentials

ARRIVING

BY FERRY   From Setúbal, **Atlantic Ferries,** Doca do Comércio ((C) **26/523-51-
01**), operates both car and passenger ferries to the peninsula every half-hour to the
hour 24 hours a day. From the port of Setúbal, the cost is 2.50€ per person on the
passenger ferry or 11€ per person in a car headed to Tróia.

BY CAR   Because Tróia is a peninsula, it's possible to drive there along Route
N251 to reach it, but the road is circuitous and not a very good one. The car ferry is
better.

VISITOR INFORMATION

There is no tourist office but you can call **Tróia Resort,** Tróia-Carvalhal at
(C) **26/510-55-00** during the day or look for information at **www.troiaresort.net**.

Exploring the Area

Cetóbriga, on the peninsula, contains ruins of a thriving Roman port. Excavations
began in the mid–19th century. The city, dating from the 3rd and 4th centuries, was
destroyed by the ocean, but traces of villas, bathing pools, a fresco-decorated temple,
and a place for salt preservation of fish have been unearthed. Cetóbriga's ruins are
about 2.5km (1½ miles) from the site of the present tourist development of Tróia but
are worth seeing only if you have time. Otherwise, the simple foundations of long-
gone buildings are too minor to merit a special visit.

One of the attractions of the island is the **Tróia Golf Course** designed by Robert
Trent Jones at Complexo Turistico de Tróia, Carvalhal ((C) **26/549-41-12;** www.
troiagolf.com). This is an 18-hole, 6,374m (20,912-ft.), par-72 course that features a
pro shop, restaurant, and bar. This course lies close to the sea and has a lot of
obstacles in its setting of maritime pines, tropical flora, and plenty of sand. Beginning
players often find it too difficult; even to more experienced golfers, it's a big challenge.
The cost is 73€ on Saturday and Sunday, lowered to 61€ weekdays. A handicap certificate is required.

Where to Stay & Dine

You can rent an apartment on the island if you'd like a seaside holiday. Further information is available from **Sonae Turismo SGPS, S.A.,** Rua do Viriato 13, 1060 Lisboa (© **21/011-91-00;** www.sonaeturismo.com).

Tróia Design Hotel ★★ ☺   This is the most luxurious resort in this area of Portugal. The creation of a number of the country's leading designers and architects, this government-rated, five-star hotel overlooks the marina, which you can see from the balcony of your room. A special feature is the two rooftop pools, one for the kids, another an infinity pool, overlooking the Serra da Arrábida range in the background.

It's a family favorite because accommodations can be rented as one-, two-, or three-bedroom apartment units, with their own private Jacuzzi. Bedrooms are spacious and well furnished, and the hotel opens right onto a good beach.

The complex rises 14 floors, its undulating facade studded with balconies. A sleek contemporary design, the structure consists of glass, concrete, and chrome crossed with wood and lacquer. The on-site spa is the best in this part of Portugal, with four distinct areas of treatment. More than 70 different treatments are performed by qualified therapists. A children's center keeps kids occupied between 3 and 12 years old. The Salinas Brasserie is a stylish place for seafood and other dishes, and the B&G is more sophisticated with a more refined cuisine.

Marina de Tróia-Carvalhal, 7570-789 Grândola. www.troiadesignhotel.com. © **26/549-80-00.** 205 units. 199€-219€ double; 259€-438€ suite. AE, DC, MC, V. **Amenities:** 2 restaurants; bar; bikes; children's programs; concierge; exercise room; golf course; room service; spa. *In room:* A/C, TV, fridge (in some), hair dryer, kitchen (in some), minibar, Wi-Fi (free).

PALMELA

8km (5 miles) N of Setúbal; 32km (20 miles) SE of Lisbon

The village of Palmela lies in the heart of wine country, the foothills of the Arrábida Mountains. It's famous for its fortress, which offers one of the best views in Portugal from an elevation of 366m (1,201 ft.). From this vantage point, you can see over sienna-hued valleys and vineyards flush with grapes to the capital in the north and to the estuary of the Sado to the south.

Essentials

ARRIVING

There is no bus or train service to Palmela.

BY CAR   From Lisbon, cross the Ponte do 25 de Abril bridge and head south along E1. Exit at the cutoff marked Palmela. From Setúbal, continue north along A2 to the same exit.

VISITOR INFORMATION

The local tourist office (© **21/233-21-22**) is at the Posada de Palmela, Castelo de Palmela (see below). The office is open in summer Monday to Friday 9:30am to 8:30pm; in winter, hours are Monday to Saturday 9am to 1pm and 2 to 5:30pm.

Where to Stay & Dine

EXPENSIVE

Pousada de Palmela, Castelo de Palmela ★★★   This is one of the last remaining segments of the town's 12th-century castle. It was built as a monastery

Exploring Palmela's Castle

Palmela is famous as the site of a 12th-century fortress built by Afonso Henríques, the first king of Portugal, who drove out the Moors and secured control of the fertile lands south of the Tagus. Into the medieval walls of this fortress the Portuguese government built the **Pousada de Palmela,** in the Castelo de Palmela (see description, below). Today, part of the castle/fortress's complex incorporates the pousada, with the remainder open for visits, without charge, to anyone who drops in. On the premises, what was originally built in the 15th century as a church (Igreja de Santiago) is now a museum dedicated to a changing array of temporary exhibitions related to the art, folklore, and history of the region. It's open without charge Tuesday to Sunday from 10am to noon and from 2 to 6pm. For more information about the fortress, the church and its temporary exhibitions, or the dining and accommodations within the castle, contact the pousada (see below).

within the castle walls in 1482, on orders of João I and dedicated to St. James. Its use as a pousada kept it from falling into ruin, and the skillful, unobtrusive conversion preserved the classic look and feel of a cloister. On the crest of a hill, the pousada is traditional in design; a huge square building opens onto a large courtyard, and the lower-level arches have been glassed in and furnished with lounge chairs.

Most of the guest rooms have been opened up, enlarged, and brought glamorously up-to-date. They're furnished in Portuguese style with hand-carved pieces and fine fabrics, and most of the rooms open onto nice views. Near the dining room is a comfortable drawing room with a noteworthy washbasin that the monks once used for their ablutions.

2950-997 Palmela. www.pousadas.pt. ② **21/235-12-26.** Fax 21/233-04-40. 28 units. 94€–230€ double; from 127€ suite. Rates include buffet breakfast. AE, DC, MC, V. Free parking. **Amenities:** Restaurant; bar; babysitting; bikes; room service. In room: A/C, TV, hair dryer, minibar, Wi-Fi (in some; 12€ per day).

INEXPENSIVE

Quinta do Patrício ★ 🏠 The oldest part of this charming, family-run bed-and-breakfast hotel is its stone-sided windmill. Built in 1798, it's now the establishment's most comfortable place to stay. Other rooms are in the main house, a short walk away through a nice garden. Don't expect a conventional, international feel: Life here is slow, revolving around the pleasant garden and tastefully decorated public areas. The simple guest rooms are small, comfortable, and well maintained, with neatly kept bathrooms. Breakfast is the only meal served. The *quinta* lies about .4km (¼ mile) west of the center of town.

Estrada do Castelo de São Felipe, 2900-300 Setúbal. www.quintadopatricio.com. ② **26/555-04-75.** 3 units. 95€–1120€ double. Rates include buffet breakfast. No credit cards. **Amenities:** Outdoor pool. In room: No phone.

ESTREMADURA

E stremadura is a land of contrasts. The Atlantic crashes upon the southern coast, but farther up in the snug cover of São Martinho do Porto, the ocean can hardly muster a ripple. Although two mountain ranges loom to the east of the flat western seascapes, the sea's presence permeates the entire region. Even in the many examples of Manueline architecture, especially at Batalha, the tie with the sea remains unbroken. Its nautical designs—ropes, cables, armillary spheres, and seascape effects—reflect Portugal's essential connection to the sea.

8

Estremadura contains lovely towns as old as Portuguese nationhood whose beauty has not been diminished by time. Despite the name (which means "extremities"), the region is neither extremely harsh nor especially remote. Rather, it is in many ways the spiritual heart of Portugal. Its isolation derives more from the slow, erratic, and sometimes undependable public transportation, which makes the region best suited to a driving tour.

ÓBIDOS ★★

93km (58 miles) N of Lisbon; 7km (4⅓ miles) S of Caldas da Rainha

The poet king Dinis and his saintly wife, Isabella of Aragón, once passed by the walls of this medieval village and noted its beauty. The queen likened the village to a jewel-studded crown. Eager to please, Dinis made her a present of the village. He established a tradition: Instead of precious stones, Portuguese royal bridegrooms presented Óbidos to their brides.

Entered through a tile-coated gatehouse, the town is definitely a trip back in time. The **medieval city ★★** rises on a sugar-loaf hill above a valley of vineyards. Its golden towers, crenellated battlements, and ramparts (which afford views of the tranquil Valley of the Ria Arnóia, vineyards, tiny cottages, and cultivated fields) contrast with gleaming white houses and the rolling countryside, where windmills clack in the breeze.

Essentials

ARRIVING

BY TRAIN From the Estação do Rossio station in Lisbon (Metro: Rossio), commuter trains run to Cacém, where you can change trains for Óbidos. About 11 trains a day make the approximately 2-hour run; the one-way fare is 8.50€. For information and schedules, call ✆ **80/820-82-08.**

BY BUS You can take a connecting bus from Lisbon, but the train is easier. Buses leave from Avenida Casal Ribeiro in Lisbon for the 75-minute trip to Caldas da Rainha, where you transfer to another bus to Óbidos.

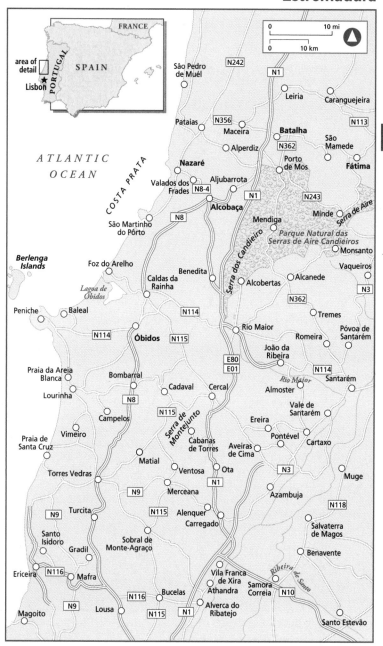

The one-way fare is 8€. About six buses a day make the 20-minute trip from Caldas da Rainha to Óbidos. For information, call ✆ 26/283-10-67 in Caldas da Rainha.

BY CAR   From Lisbon, N8 runs north to Óbidos via Torres Vedras. This trip takes about an hour. You can also take Hwy. A8.

VISITOR INFORMATION

You'll find the **Óbidos Tourist Office** on Porta da Vila (✆ 26/295-92-31; www. rt-oeste.pt). It's open May to September daily from 9:30am to 7:30pm, and October to April daily from 9:30am to 6pm.

Exploring the Town

In the Renaissance church **Igreja de Santa Maria,** blue-and-white *azulejos* (tiles) line its **interior ★**. Look for the Renaissance **tomb ★** and the paintings of Josefa of Óbidos, a 17th-century artist. The church lies to the right of the post office in the central square. It's open daily 9:30am to 12:30pm and 4:30 to 7pm April to September, and 9:30am to 12:30pm and 2:30 to 6pm October to March. Admission is free. For information, call ✆ 26/295-96-33.

The other major attraction in Óbidos is the castelo (part of which is now a tourist inn; see "Where to Stay," below). The castle suffered severe damage in the 1755 earthquake but was restored. It's one of Portugal's greatest medieval castles, with a host of Manueline architectural elements. In 1148, Dom Afonso Henríques and his troops, disguised, incredibly, as cherry trees, captured the castle from the Moors. The Moors were driven from the land, and Henríques went on to become the founding father of Portugal; he was proclaimed its first king.

The main entrance to Óbidos is a much-photographed gate, the narrow, zigzag **Porta da Vila.** Be sure to watch your car mirrors as you pass through it.

Outdoor Activities

Ideal for general sunning and swimming is the beach at Lagoa de Óbidos, northwest of Óbidos and west of Caldas da Rainha. You can rent windsurfing boards and rigs on the beach here; surfers generally prefer the beach at Peniche, southwest of Lagoa de Óbidos, because the waves are better there.

One of the best golf courses in the region, the **Golf do Vimeiro,** is allied with the **Hotel Golf Mar,** at Torres Vedras (✆ 26/198-08-00; www.golfvimeiro.com), which towers over the cliff. The course has 9 holes, all relatively narrow and well defined by trees and shrubs; the river is an ever-present hazard. The first-class hotel, the best sports complex in the area, also offers tennis, three swimming pools (one heated), horseback riding, fishing, great views, access to several beaches, and a recommended restaurant, all for a reasonable price. Doubles are 45€ to 115€. The thermal spa of Vimeiro, with its curative waters, is close by. The course is 34km (21 miles) south of Óbidos, and greens fees are 25€ for 9 holes.

Shopping

Save some time for browsing through the **shops** and searching out thick woven fabrics, regional rugs (both hand- and machine-made), raffia and handmade bags, and local lace.

Óbidos is one of the most folkloric towns in Portugal; dozens of boutiques line the town's main street, **Rua Direita ★**. These stores are loaded with ceramics, embroideries, wine, and woodcarvings. Individual outlets of note include the **Oficina do**

Barro, Praça de Santa Maria (📞 **26/295-92-31**), which is associated with the town's tourist office. It maintains a studio (open to visitors) that produces delicate ceramics—usually glazed in white—that resemble the texture of a woven basket. **Loja dos Arcos,** Rua Direita (📞 **26/295-98-33**), sells wine, leather, and ceramics that are usually a bit more interesting than the wares at equivalent shops nearby.

Where to Stay
EXPENSIVE
Pousada de Óbidos, Castelo de Óbidos ★★   This Manueline-trimmed stone palace is one of the most heavily booked in the country, so you should reserve rooms as far in advance as possible. Rooms vary in size, but most of them are quite comfortable and well furnished with reproduction furniture inspired by the 16th and 17th centuries. Deep-set windows have tiny ledges where you can look out onto views of the countryside. Homemade quilts or fabrics cover the beds, and the bathrooms, a bit small, are covered with hand-painted *azulejos* (tiles). The cuisine and service are the finest in Óbidos.

Paço Real (Abdo. 18), 2510-999 Óbidos. www.pousadas.pt. 📞 **26/295-50-80.** Fax 26/295-91-48. 9 units. 136€–250€ double; from 184€–360€ suite. Rates include buffet breakfast. AE, DC, MC, V. **Amenities:** Restaurant; bar; bikes; Wi-Fi (free, in lobby). *In room:* A/C, TV, hair dryer, minibar.

Praia D'El Rey Marriott Golf & Beach Resort ★★★ ☺   You'll find the most luxurious hotel in the area lying 16km (10 miles) west of Óbidos. This government-rated five-star hotel opens onto a splendid sandy beach stretching for 4km (2½ miles). The resort hotel itself, with its 18-hole championship golf course, stands on 243 hectares (600 acres) of oceanfront property. Even in rainy weather, you can swim in the indoor pool, where columns evoke a Roman bath. The bedrooms, roomy and light, are the most luxurious in the area, containing all those extras that make for a good stay, including bottled water, bathrobes, and individual climate control. The rooms feature private terraces or balconies opening onto ocean views. Restaurant facilities range from a pool grill to alfresco dining on a terrace overlooking the ocean.

Av. D. Inês de Castro, 2510-451 Vale de Janelas, Amoreira. www.marriott.com/lisdr. 📞 **26/290-51-00.** Fax 26/290-51-01. 179 units. 135€–550€ double; 328€–1,100€ suite. AE, DC, MC, V. **Amenities:** 3 restaurants; 4 bars; babysitting; bikes; children's center; concierge; 18-hole golf course; health club & spa; 2 freshwater pools (1 heated indoor); 7 outdoor tennis courts (lit); extensive watersports equipment/rentals. *In room:* A/C, TV/DVD, hair dryer, minibar, Wi-Fi (free).

MODERATE
Casa das Senhoras Rainhas   Although it hardly ranks up there with the Pousada de Óbidos, this substantial but small inn is installed in a tiled roofed villa that was constructed to blend harmoniously with the antique architecture of Óbidos. The tastefully modern rooms are attractively furnished and comfortable. On-site is the Restaurant Cozinha das Rainhas, which you can patronize even if you're not a guest of the hotel; however, you should call ahead for reservations.

Rua Padre Nunes Tavares 6, 2510-070 Óbidos. www.senhorasrainhas.com. 📞 **26/295-53-60.** Fax 26/295-53-69. 10 units. 149€–179€ double; 181€–204€ suite. AE, MC, V. **Amenities:** Restaurant; bar; babysitting; bikes; Wi-Fi (free, in lobby). *In room:* A/C, TV, hair dryer.

Casa de S. Thiago ★ 🔥   You get comfort and tranquillity in an intimate atmosphere in this manorial guesthouse situated inside the walls near the castle. Walls are covered with authentic Portuguese *azulejos,* and all the bedrooms are midsize, each

THE beaches OF ESTREMADURA

Take your pick from the ribbonlike string of beaches that stretches almost continuously along the coast of Estremadura. Some 240km (149 miles) of sand extend all the way to its northern edge, just south of the beach resort of **Figueira da Foz.**

Many of Estremadura's beaches are uncrowded and filled with powdery sand bordering crystal-clear waters. Others, especially those near industrial wastelands, are much less desirable and might be polluted. Look for beaches flying a blue banner, which indicates that the European Union has granted its seal of approval to the beach's hygiene and safety.

One of our favorites is the seaside village of **São Martinho do Porto,** 116km (72 miles) north of Lisbon and a short run south of overcrowded Nazaré. This resort nestles between pine-covered foothills and the ocean, and its waters are calm and clear. Another good beach, north of Nazaré, is at **São Pedro de Moel,** 135km (84 miles) north of Lisbon. It has a 63-room resort hotel, **Hotel Mar e Sol,** Av. da Liberdade 1 (🕾 24/459-00-00; www.hotelmaresol.com), where you can take a room or a meal. Rooms range from 70€ to 95€ for a double, including breakfast. The chefs here serve an excellent regional cuisine for lunch and dinner, focused mainly on locally caught fish. Main courses cost 8€ to 20€.

Another place worth seeking out is the town of **Peniche,** 92km (57 miles) north of Lisbon. This fishing port stands high on a peninsula, with wide, sandy beaches at the foot of rocky cliffs. Peniche doesn't always have the cleanest water (compared to other uncrowded, remote places), but it is nevertheless a family favorite. When you tire of the beach, you can explore **Cabo Carvoeiro** on the peninsula, about 4.8km (3 miles) east of Peniche. It offers panoramic views of the surf smashing against the rock formations hundreds of feet below the road. Or, you can go to the large water-park complex, **Sportágua,** Avenida Monsenhor Bastos (🕾 26/278-91-25; www.sportagua. com), which has water slides and swimming pools for adults and separate ones for children, plus snack bars and dining places. Admission is 12€ for adults, 10€ for children 6 to 10, and free for children under 5. Hours are daily 10am to 7pm from mid-July to mid-September.

Many of the area's most popular beaches, those with the most facilities, are frequented for their sands, not for swimming. (They might not have blue flags, depending on conditions, when you visit.) These include **Milfontes, Foz do Arelho,** and **Nazaré.** Other less frequented but good beaches are at **Pedrógão, Baleal, Consolação, Porto Covo, Porto Dinheiro,** and **Santa Cruz.** All are signposted from the highway.

with a fireplace and tiled private bathroom. You find personalized hospitality here that makes you feel as if you're staying in a private home.

Largo de S. Tiago do Castelo, 2510 Óbidos. www.casas-sthiago.com. 🕾/fax **26/295-95-87.** 8 units. 90€–110€ double. Rates include buffet breakfast. AE, DC, MC, V. *In room:* TV.

Casa d'Óbidos ★★ 🛏 The most atmospheric accommodations in the area lie right outside Óbidos in a carefully restored manor house dating from the 19th century. Standing in the midst of well-landscaped gardens, the house is furnished with antiques and tiles made by local artisans. Both the public and private rooms are beautifully decorated. Rooms are available both in the main house and in a cottage, also handsomely restored, on the grounds. The breakfast is the finest in the area, including five types of bread, along with fluffy scrambled eggs, freshly squeezed juice, and fruits such as kiwi.

Quinta de S. José, 2510-135 Óbidos. 9 units. www.casadobidos.com. ✆ **26/295-09-24.** Fax 26/295-99-70. 90€–140€ double. Extra bed 23€. MC, V. **Amenities:** Outdoor pool; outdoor tennis court. *In room:* Fans, TV.

Estalagem do Convento ★ These are the second-finest accommodations in Óbidos. The inn, installed in a former nunnery, is handsomely decorated in a rustic Iberian style. Bedrooms are small but well furnished, mainly with reproductions of furnishings from the 17th and 18th centuries. Housekeeping is top-notch here, and the little tiled bathrooms are immaculately clean.

Rua Dom João de Ornelas, 2510 Óbidos. www.estalagemdoconvento.com. ✆ **26/295-92-16.** Fax 26/295-91-59. 31 units. 76€–106€ double; 89€–150€ suite. Rates include buffet breakfast. AE, MC, V. **Amenities:** Restaurant; bar; room service; Wi-Fi (free, in lobby). *In room:* TV, hair dryer, minibar.

Hotel Real d'Óbidos ★ Other than the Pousada de Óbidos, this is the ranking inn of town. The present owners took over a property that dated from the 14th century and rebuilt it according to the original architectural plan, although installing modern bathrooms and other conveniences. The bedrooms are beautifully furnished and well maintained, each with a state-of-the-art tiled bathroom. All of the guest rooms are about the same size, each one individually designed to reflect an element of the region's diverse history. Guests have a choice of double beds or twins.

Rua D. João de Ornelas, 2510-074 Óbidos. www.hotelrealdobidos.com. ✆ **26/295-50-90.** Fax 26/295-50-99. 15 units. 135€–195€ double; 150€–230€ suite. Rates include buffet breakfast. AE, MC, V. **Amenities:** Restaurant; bar; babysitting; outdoor pool; room service; Wi-Fi (5€ per hour). *In room:* A/C, TV/DVD, CD player, hair dryer, minibar.

INEXPENSIVE

Albergaria Josefa d'Óbidos Hotel ★ 🛏 This flower-bedecked inn lies outside the old town's fortifications. The inn lies on a hillside that overlooks the main gate into Óbidos. The guest rooms range from small to midsize and are furnished with 18th-century reproductions of regional furniture. Each unit comes with a tiny, neatly kept bathroom covered with hand-painted tiles. The restaurant, in the classic style of an old-fashioned Portuguese tavern, serves excellent regional and international cuisine with an emphasis on fish. Main courses cost 10€ to 24€, and the restaurant is open for lunch and dinner.

Rua Dom João de Ornelas, 2510 Óbidos. www.josefadobidos.com. ✆ **26/295-92-28.** Fax 26/295-95-33. 34 units. 60€–80€ double; 110€–115€ suite. Rates include buffet breakfast. AE, DC, MC. Free parking. **Amenities:** Restaurant; 2 bars; room service; Wi-Fi (free, in lobby). *In room:* A/C, TV, hair dryer, minibar (in some).

Albergaria Rainha Santa Isabel ⚑ On a narrow cobblestone street running through the center of town, this building, once a private home, is many centuries old. Blue, white, and yellow tiles cover the high-ceilinged lobby. The comfortable bar area is filled with leather sofas and Victorian-style chairs. An elevator runs to the simply furnished but immaculate guest rooms. Most guests deposit their luggage at the reception desk before parking for free on the square in front of the village church nearby.

Rua Direita, 2510 Óbidos. www.obidoshotel.com. ✆ **26/295-93-23.** Fax 26/295-91-15. 20 units. 79€–90€ double. Rates include buffet breakfast. AE, DC, MC, V. **Amenities:** Bar; room service. *In room:* A/C, TV, minibar.

A SIDE TRIP TO caldas da rainha

The rheumatic sister-queen of Manuel the Fortunate, Leonor, discovered the therapeutic value of the springs here on a trip to Óbidos. The town has been a spa ever since.

Leonor returned to Caldas da Rainha again and again, and she constructed a hospital and an adjoining church. The chapel, **Nossa Senhora do Pópulo,** was built in the early 16th century in the Manueline style, then at its apex. The spa, which was particularly popular in the 19th century, lies some 95km (59 miles) north of Lisbon. People usually visit it after stopping at Óbidos, 6.5km (4 miles) away. It's worth the 30 minutes or so needed to explore the interior of the church: The walls are entirely covered in beautiful hand-painted *azulejos.* The outstanding artistic treasure of the church is a **triptych ★** of the Crucifixion, which lies above the triumphal arch of the church.

Caldas da Rainha is also noted for its ceramics. Many roadside stands charge far lower prices than you'd pay in Lisbon. The best selections are in the showrooms of factories, notably **Secla,** Rua São João de Deus (✆ **26/284-21-51;** www.secla.pt).

Where to Dine
MODERATE

Most visitors to Óbidos like to dine at Pousada de Óbidos, Castelo de Óbidos (see "Where to Stay," above). However, you get far better value, less formality, and more local color at one of the typical little restaurants inside or outside the city's walls.

Café/Restaurante 1 de Dezembro PORTUGUESE   This snack bar and restaurant is known for its reliable *pratos do día* (plates of the day), made with market-fresh ingredients. The two most popular specialties are a typical Portuguese *cocido,* which is a thick meat and vegetable stew, or else *caldeirada,* a seafood stew. You can drop in for something quick to eat at just about any time. The format is friendly, simple, and convenient.

Largo São Pedro 3. ✆ **26/295-92-98.** Main courses 10€–20€. MC, V. Mon–Sat 8am–midnight.

Restaurante Alcaide ★ 🍴 REGIONAL PORTUGUESE   A local favorite inside the city walls, this spot is known for its tasty regional dishes and good, inexpensive wines. Appetizers that might tempt here include a delicious Iberian smoked ham. From there, you can go on to such excellent fish dishes as grouper filet gratin or one of the meat specialties, such as escalopes of veal in a tangy Madeira sauce. The chef also prepares a tender and well-flavored Portuguese beefsteak and small pork tournedos with *fines herbes,* another specialty.

Rua Direita 60. ✆ **26/295-92-20.** www.restaurantealcaide.com. Reservations recommended. Main courses 10€–40€. AE, DC, MC, V. Thurs–Tues 12:30–3pm and 7:30–10pm. Closed last 2 weeks in Nov and last 2 weeks in Mar.

ALCOBAÇA ★★

108km (67 miles) N of Lisbon; 16km (10 miles) NE of Caldas da Rainha

The main attraction in Alcobaça is its stately monastery. But the shopping is worthy, too—the nearby market is said to sell the best fruit in Portugal. (The peaches, grown in surrounding orchards originally planted by the Cistercian monks, are especially succulent.) Many market stalls also sell the blue-and-white pottery typical of Alcobaça.

Essentials

ARRIVING

BY TRAIN   There is no direct train service from Lisbon and connections are awkward. Your best bet is to take the bus.

OFF THE BEATEN PATH: NATURE IN THE raw

The area around Alcobaça contains two of the least discovered but most dramatic havens for nature in Portugal: a national park and an offshore island that's ideal for scuba diving.

Parque Natural das Serras de Aire e Candeeiros straddles the border between Estremadura and Ribatejo, almost halfway between Lisbon and Coimbra. Encompassing more than 30,000 hectares (74,132 acres) of moors and scrubland, the rocky landscape is sparsely settled. A center for hikers is the small hamlet of **Minde,** where women weave patchwork rugs that are well known in the region. Take along plenty of supplies (water, lunch, sunscreen, and so on) for a day's hike in the wilderness.

In this rocky landscape, farmers barely eke out a living. They gather local stones to build their shelters, and they get energy from windmills. If you'd rather drive than hike through the area, take N362, which runs for some 45km (28 miles) from Batalha in the north to Santarém in the south.

The other great area of natural beauty is **Berlenga Island ★★★**. A granite rock in the Atlantic, Berlenga is an island hideaway and nature preserve. Eleven kilometers (6¾ miles) out in the ocean west of Peniche, a medieval fortress once stood guard over the Portuguese coastline from this island. Berlenga is the largest island in a little archipelago made up of three groups of

rocky rises known as the Farilhões, the Estrelas, and the Forcadas.

The medieval fortress on Berlenga, **Forte de São João Batista,** was destroyed in 1666 when 28 Portuguese tried to withstand a force of 1,500 Spaniards who bombarded it from 15 ships. Rebuilt toward the end of the 17th century, it now houses a hostel. You can take a stairway from the fortress to the lighthouse, stopping along the way to look over the panorama of the archipelago. A cobblestone walk from the top of the lighthouse site takes you down to a little bay with fishermen's cottages along a beach.

The **Furado Grande** is a long marine tunnel that leads to a creek walled in by the granite cliffs. Under the fortress is a cave the locals call the **blue grotto,** but its pool is really closer to emerald green. The clear waters of the grotto and the island itself make Berlenga a mecca for snorkelers and scuba divers. Local waters contain an array of fish, including bream, red mullet, and sea bass. To reach the island, head first for Peniche, 92km (57 miles) north of Lisbon. A ferry makes two trips a day to the island in July and August; the first leaves at 9:30am. A same-day round-trip ticket costs 20€. From September to June, one ferry a day leaves at 10am and returns at 6pm. *A word of caution:* This boat ride is rough: If you're prone to getting seasick, take the proper precautions.

FOLKLORE—ROOSTERS RISING FROM THE DEAD

Portugal's Atlantic melancholy, its majestic vistas, and its history's drama and occasional madness have all contributed to a rich body of legend, lore, and folklore. Some of these tales and myths were promoted as ideology that unified the country against the menace of neighboring Spain. Other tales were borrowed from Christian, Moorish, and—in some cases—Celtic mythology that permeated the land in prehistoric times. Even St. Martin of Dume—the Hungarian-trained 5th-century saint, credited with converting the Portuguese to Christianity—railed against the Portuguese tendency to rely on charms, divination, good-luck symbols, and invocations of the dead.

The religious and pagan themes run deep. Churches throughout the country are adorned with unusual votive offerings, often made of wax, which hang on strings near the altar or near the votive candles. Intended to promote divine healing for ailments, they are shaped like heads, hands, breasts, babies, pigs, or oxen. They might include yellowing wedding dresses or hair braids and are sometimes the more bizarre (yet touching) sights in a rural chapel. Votives are offered to any of a number of saints in thanks for blessings prayed for and received. If votives are not offered to the saint, it is sometimes believed the saint will take revenge. Today, the church is more critical of these gifts, but as late as the 1960s, the gift-giving rituals were tolerated and encouraged in many parts of the country.

The phases of the moon are said to be important to the health of vegetables, crops, and babies. The most vigorous of any of these will be sown or conceived, it is believed, during the waxing of the moon. Certain fountains are claimed to contain healing powers and to conceal the entrances to underground chambers where Enchanted Mooresses are said to be hiding, guarding great treasures. A mother should not breastfeed her infant and eat simultaneously lest the baby grow up to be greedy. And an hours-old infant should not be taken outdoors immediately for fear of inciting the evil eye; rather, it should be placed on a bed near a pair of his or her father's outstretched trousers, the symbol of which will frighten away witches.

A respect for death and bereavement is pervasive. Black is probably the most popular color for clothes in Portugal today, as it is the traditional color for anyone in mourning. Though followed less strictly today than 30 years ago, widows are expected to remain in black for around 7 years after the death of their husbands, and many choose to continue to wear it the rest of their lives. Mourning the loss of a parent is expected to last around 2 or 3 years. Oddly, the loss of a child is not associated with any formal period of mourning.

The land is rife with many different legends as well, some popularized as unifying tales for the Portuguese. Among them is the Rooster of Barcelos, who—although cooked and about to be served as the main course in a magistrate's

BY BUS   From Lisbon four *expressos* depart each day for Alcobaça, the trip taking 2 hours and costing 9€ one-way. Buses are run by **Rede Expressos** (© 70/722-33-44; www.rede-expressos.pt).

BY CAR   From Caldas da Rainha, continue northeast along N8 for 16km (10 miles).

AND A necrophiliac queen

dinner—crowed ecstatically to prove the innocence of a pilgrim wrongfully accused of theft. Equally touching is the Legend of the Almond Blossoms, which dates from the 10th century's Moorish occupation of the Algarve. A Viking maiden, captured as a child during battle, fell in love with the son of the local Caliph and married him. Despite their joy, only the sight of a field of almond trees, reminiscent of the snow of her native Norway, could keep her happy and healthy in her adopted Moorish home. In gratitude, the Caliph ordered the planting of thousands of almond trees. Today, residents of the Algarve recall this myth every February when the almond trees bloom.

Another legend involves Dom Fuas Ropinho, one of Portugal's founders and the subject of several poems by Camões. The devil, vengeful at the rare instance of facing a virtuous and incorruptible man, disguised himself as a stag during a hunt and led Dom Fuas to the edge of a steep rocky cliff. Only the image of the Virgin (which appeared suddenly in a blaze of light) caused the hunter to stop, only moments before he'd have been thrown by his horse over the rocks to his death. In 1182, Dom Fuas built near the cliffs a chapel to Our Lady of Nazaré. Rebuilt in the 1500s, it was visited by Vasco da Gama, who prayed there in thanks after discovering the sea route to India in 1498.

Finally, there is the Miracle of the Roses: The Aragonese Princess Isabella spent the bulk of her personal fortune to help the penniless nuns of Santa Clara. Her kind but thrifty husband, Dinis, was about to punish her severely for donating her final funds to the order but was stopped when the loaves of bread Isabella was carrying were miraculously transformed into roses. Since it was January, when roses were out of season, the king fell on his knees in thanks; to everyone's delight, Dinis massively increased her annual income so she could continue to make charitable gifts as she saw fit. Today, the sainted queen is the patron saint of Coimbra, with biannual torchlight processions held in her honor.

Other legends reflect the madness of some of the country's rulers and are in some cases historically true. In the 1300s, Prince Dom Pedro fell in love with one of his wife's ladies-in-waiting, a Spanish-born girl named Inês de Castro. Soon Inês was banished from the country. When Pedro's wife died, Inês returned to live openly with him. Fearing that Inês was fomenting a plot against the monarchy, a group of nobles (including Afonso IV, Pedro's father) arranged to have her killed. Pedro, upon finding her body, became insane. When he ascended the throne 2 years later, he had the hearts of Inês's murderers torn from their bodies, ordered that she be exhumed and dressed in royal clothes, and arranged for her coronation as queen of Portugal in the monastery of Alcobaca (see above). Part of the ceremony involved the obligatory kissing of the skeletal royal hand by all the nobles present. Today, the tomb of Inês that Pedro commissioned for Alcobaca is considered one of the most beautiful in Portugal.

8

ESTREMADURA | Alcobaça

VISITOR INFORMATION

The **Alcobaça Tourist Office** is on Praça do 25 de Abril (© **26/258-23-77;** www. cm-alcobaca.pt). It's open May to July and September daily 10am to 1pm and 3 to 7pm; August daily 10am to 7pm; October to April daily 10am to 1pm and 2 to 6pm.

Exploring the Town

VISITING THE MONASTERY   In the Middle Ages, the Cistercian **Mosteiro de Santa Maria (St. Mary Monastery)** ★★ was one of the richest and most prestigious in Europe. Begun in 1178, it was founded to honor a vow made by Portugal's first king, Afonso Henríques, before he faced the Moors at Santarém. Alcobaça, at the confluence of the Alcoa and Baça rivers, was built to show his spiritual indebtedness to St. Bernard of Clairvaux, who inspired (some say goaded) many Crusaders into battle against the infidels.

Today, in spite of its baroque facade and latter-day overlay, the monastery is a monument to simplicity and majesty. Above the 98m-long (322-ft.) nave, quadripartite vaulting is supported on transverse arches. These rest on towering pillars and columns. The aisles, too, have stunning vertical lines and are practically as tall as the nave itself.

The transept shelters the **Gothic tombs** ★★ of two star-crossed lovers, the Romeo and Juliet of Portuguese history. Though damaged, their sarcophagi are the greatest pieces of sculpture from 14th-century Portugal. The artist is unknown.

The Cloisters of Silence, with their delicate arches, were favored by Dinis, the poet-king. He sparked a thriving literary colony at the monastery, where the monks were busily engaged in translating ecclesiastical writings. Aside from the tombs and cloisters, the curiosity is the kitchen, through which a branch of the Alcoa River was routed. As in most Cistercian monasteries, the flowing brook was instrumental for sanitation purposes. Chroniclers have suggested that the friars fished for their dinner in the brook and later washed their dishes in it.

In the 18th-century Salon of Kings are niches with sculptures of some Portuguese rulers. The empty niches, left waiting for the rulers who were never sculptured, lend a melancholic air. The tiles in the room depict, in part, Afonso Henríques's triumph over the Moors.

The monastery (© **26/250-51-20**; www.mosteiroalcobaca.pt) is located on Praça do 25 de Abril and is open daily April to September from 9am to 7pm and October to March from 9am to 5pm. Admission costs 6€.

SHOPPING   You'll find a dozen or so handicraft and ceramics shops lining the square in front of the monastery. One of the best outlets is **Casa Artisate Egarafeira,** Praça do 25 de Abril 51–52 (© **26/259-01-20**), which sells antiques, ceramics, and regional wine, among other offerings.

Where to Stay

MODERATE

Challet da Fonte Nova ★ 📷   A majestic iron gate dating from the 19th century guards the entrance to this traditional chaletlike structure—the best accommodations in town. Once a private mansion, this is now a charming, graceful inn, consisting of three floors plus a basement that has been turned into a saloon with a pool table and bar. Bedrooms vary in size and dimensions, but all are comfortable, excellently maintained, and have midsize private bathrooms.

Rua da Fonte Nova, 2461-601 Alcobaça. www.challetfontenova.pt. © **26/259-83-00.** Fax 26/259-84-30. 10 units. 125€ double; 145€ junior suite. Rates include buffet breakfast. AE, MC, V. Free parking. **Amenities:** Bar. *In room:* A/C, TV, hair dryer, Wi-Fi (free).

Hotel D. Inês de Castro   One of the town's leading inns, this small hotel is strictly functional and of recent construction. It is, nonetheless, comfortable and convenient for an overnight stopover. Bedrooms are midsize and tastefully furnished, with immaculately maintained tiled bathrooms. Rated three stars by the government, the hotel serves a generous breakfast.

Rua Costa Veiga 44–48, 2460-028 Alcobaça. www.hotel-inesdecastro.com. (C) **26/258-23-55.** Fax 26/258-12-58. 37 units. 50€–100€. MC, V. Free parking. *In room:* A/C, TV.

INEXPENSIVE

Hotel Santa Maria ★   The most attractive modern hotel in town is ideally located in a quiet but central part of the historic city, on a sloping street just above the plaza in front of the monastery. Guest rooms are small and a bit cramped but filled with polished paneling cut into geometrical shapes. They contain comfortable contemporary chairs, and some have views and balconies over the monastery and square. If parking is a problem, the hotel will open its garage for free.

Rua Francisco Zagalo 20–22, 2460-041 Alcobaça. www.hotelsantamaria.com.pt. (C) **26/259-01-60.** Fax 26/259-01-61. 76 units. 45€–69€ double; 80€ suite. Rates include buffet breakfast. AE, MC, V. **Amenities:** Bar; room service. *In room:* A/C, TV, hair dryer.

Where to Dine

Trindade PORTUGUESE   The most popular restaurant in town opens onto a side of the monastery fronting a tree-shaded square. Trindade has both full restaurant service and a snack bar. Your meal here is likely to include shellfish soup, roast rabbit, or the fresh fish of the day. Tender roast chicken is also available. The food is hearty and full of flavor, but the place is often overrun with international religious pilgrims and is a popular hangout for locals.

Praça do Dom Afonso Henríques 22. (C) **26/258-23-97.** Main courses 9€–22€. AE, MC, V. Daily 9:30am–11pm (bar open until 2am). Closed 2 weeks in Oct or Nov.

NAZARÉ ★★

132km (82 miles) N of Lisbon; 13km (8 miles) NW of Alcobaça

The inhabitants of Portugal's most famous fishing village live in a unique, tradition-bound world that tourists threaten to overthrow. Many residents have never left their village, except perhaps to make the pilgrimage to nearby Fátima. The people remain insular, even as their village blossoms into a big summer resort.

Nazaré is probably best experienced in the off season; chances are that you won't really get to see it in summer. You'll be too busy looking for a parking place (good luck) or elbowing your way onto the beach. The crowds who come to visit the "most picturesque fishing village in Portugal," coupled with widespread high-rise construction, have made people wonder what happened to the fishing village. Amazingly, it's still here—you just have to look for it.

Essentials

ARRIVING

BY TRAIN   Valado dos Frades is the closest main train station to Nazaré, but there is no direct train service from Lisbon to Valado dos Frades. From Lisbon take the train to Cacém; in Cacém take another train to Caldas da Rainha. In Caldas da Rainha take the train to Valado dos Frades. The trip takes 3½ hours and costs 11€.

BY BUS   About a dozen buses a day make the short run between Nazaré and Valado dos Frades. A one-way ticket costs 1.50€. Eight express buses per day arrive from Lisbon. The trip takes 2 hours (1 hr. less than the train) and costs 10€ one-way. For information, call ✆ **96/744-98-68.**

BY CAR   From Alcobaça (see above), continue northwest along N8-5 for about 13km (8 miles). From Lisbon, take Hwy. A-8.

VISITOR INFORMATION

The **Nazaré Tourist Office** is on Avenida Manuel Remígio (✆ **26/256-19-44**). It's open daily, but hours vary depending on the time of year, so you should call ahead.

Exploring the Village

PEOPLE-WATCHING   Don't expect stunning architecture or historic sights—the big attractions in Nazaré are the people and their fabled boats. The villagers' clothes are patchwork quilts of sun-faded colors. The rugged men don rough woolen shirts and trousers, patched in kaleidoscopic rainbow hues resembling tartan, as well as long woolen stocking caps, in the dangling ends of which they keep their prized possessions—a favorite pipe or a crucifix. The women walk about mostly barefoot wearing embroidered, handmade blouses and pleated skirts of patched tartan woolens.

The fishing boats here are Phoenician in design: slender, elongated, and boldly colored. Painted on the high, knifelike prows, you'll often see crudely shaped eyes—eyes supposedly imbued with the magical power to search the deep for fish and to avert storms. Even so, the boats sport lanterns for the dangerous job of fishing after dark. During the gusty days of winter or at high tide, the boats are hauled into a modern harbor about 10 minutes from the city's center. If you want to look at a boat, one of the locals will lead you—for a price.

Nazaré consists of two sections: the fishing quarter and the **Sítio ★**, the almost exclusively residential upper town. Near the beach you'll find handicraft shops, markets, restaurants, hotels, and boardinghouses. The main square opens directly onto the sea, and narrow streets lead to the smaller squares, evoking a medina in a Moorish village. At the farthest point from the cliff and square are the vegetable and fish markets, where auctions are held.

Jutting out over the sea, the promontory of the Sítio is a sheer drop to the ocean and the beach below. It's accessible by either a funicular or a steep cobblestone pathway. The Virgin Mary supposedly appeared here in 1182: A young horseback-riding nobleman, Dom Fuas Roupinho, was pursuing a wild deer near the precipice, which was shrouded in mist. The fog lifted suddenly to reveal the Virgin and the chasm below. In honor of this miracle, the nobleman built the **Chapel of Memory.** Today, near the spot, you can go inside the 18th-century structure honoring the event. The tiny chapel is known for its *azulejos,* or hand-painted tiles, that cover its facade, roof, and interior. Many of the tiles depict the legend of Dom Fuas Roupinho. A staircase leads down into a small crypt, and here, in a recess, is what is said to be the hoof-print left by Roupinho's horse as it came to a screeching halt at the edge of the cliff, saving its rider's life. The **panoramic view ★★** of Nazaré and the Atlantic coast is one of the great seascapes in Estremadura.

SHOPPING   Few other towns in Portugal have so many shops—but so few that aren't disappointing. Perhaps it's the sheer volume of merchandise in the crammed boutiques, all featuring much-the-same wares. The residents of tourist-conscious Nazaré long ago lost their enthusiasm for their ubiquitous, rough-textured fisher's sweaters, which seem to spill over shelves of virtually every boutique in town. The robust *varinas* (fishwives) of Nazaré have given up knitting in favor of more modern commercial pursuits, such as running snack bars, souvenir shops, and postcard kiosks. Most of the knitwear you'll see here is imported from less prosperous communities in Portugal's far north.

Where to Stay

Although Nazaré is one of the most popular destinations in Portugal, for some reason it has never had a first-rate hotel.

MODERATE

Hotel Miramar ★ This modern, well-run hotel is as good as it gets in Nazaré. Lying a short walk from Praia de Nazaré (the beach), the Hotel Miramar is as close as Nazaré comes to having a resort hotel, with a swimming pool and a health club. Bedrooms are well furnished with functional, modern pieces, along with tiled bathrooms, each immaculately kept. The on-site restaurant is first class, specializing in the catch of the day, along with shellfish. The government rates this one four stars.

Rua Abel da Silva 36, 2450-060 Nazaré. www.hotelmiramar.pt. 26/255-00-00. Fax 26/255-00-01. 40 units. 70€–180€ double. AE, MC, V. Free parking. **Amenities:** Restaurant; bar; babysitting; exercise room; Internet (free, in lobby); Jacuzzi; outdoor pool; room service; sauna. *In room:* A/C, TV, hair dryer.

Hotel Praia The Praia (literally, "Beach") is the second-best hotel in town after the Miramar (see above). The six-floor hotel is decorated in a modern but uninspired style. It's about a 3-minute walk from the sandy beach where the fishing boats and bathing cabins lie. The midsize rooms are reasonably comfortable and well maintained.

Av. Vieira Guimarães 39, 2450-159 Nazaré. www.hotelpraia.com. 26/256-14-23. Fax 26/256-14-36. 40 units. 75€–130€ double; 95€–190€ junior suite. Rates include buffet breakfast. AE, DC, MC, V. Parking 10€. **Amenities:** Restaurant; bar; concierge; exercise room; 2 pools (1 indoor); room service; sauna; Wi-Fi (free, in lobby). *In room:* A/C, TV, hair dryer, kitchenette (in some), minibar.

Mar Bravo Considerably improved in recent years, this place is now a government-rated four-star inn. The small guest rooms are comfortably furnished, and modern facilities such as private bathrooms have been added. The location on the main square in front of the beach is ideal only if you like lots of tourists.

Praça Sousa Oliveira 70–71, 2450-159 Nazaré. www.marbravo.com. 26/256-91-60. Fax 26/256-91-69. 16 units. 90€–155€ double. Rates include buffet breakfast. AE, DC, MC, V. Free parking nearby. **Amenities:** 2 restaurants; bar; concierge; room service. *In room:* A/C, TV, Wi-Fi (7€ per 24 hr.).

INEXPENSIVE

Hotel Da Nazaré Hotel da Nazaré occupies third place in our ranking of Nazaré's hotels, after the Miramar and Praia (see above). This hotel doesn't please everybody, yet many patrons count themselves lucky if they can get a room because it books up so quickly, especially in July and August. The hotel is on a busy and noisy street set back from the water, about a 3-minute walk from the promenade. It opens onto a tiny plaza, and many of the front guest rooms have private balconies. The small, simply furnished rooms have good beds and well-kept bathrooms. A rooftop sun terrace has views of Nazaré and the cliff-top Sítio.

The best features of this hotel are its fourth- and fifth-floor restaurant and bar. The dining room opens onto windowed walls peering out over the village housetops, the rugged cliffs, and the harbor.

Largo Afonso Zuquete, 2450-065 Nazaré. www.hoteldanazare.com. 26/256-90-30. Fax 26/256-90-38. 52 units. 40€–90€ double; 95€–115€ suite. Rates include buffet breakfast. AE, DC, MC, V. Free parking. **Amenities:** Restaurant; bar; room service. *In room:* A/C, TV, hair dryer, minibar.

Hotel Maré   Although several notches down from the recommendations above, this small hotel is a budget favorite, lying in the center just a short walk inland from the ocean. Completely modern and up-to-date, it is efficiently run and offers midsize bedrooms with modern furnishings and tiled bathrooms. Families with young children are welcomed. On-site is a restaurant specializing in regional favorites, especially the catch of the day.

Rua Mouzinho de Albuquerque 8, 2450-901 Nazaré. www.hotelmare.pt. (C) **26/255-01-80.** Fax 26/255-01-81. 36 units. 70€–125€ double. AE, MC, V. Free parking nearby. *In room:* A/C, TV, Wi-Fi (free).

Pensão Restaurante Ribamar ★   This genuine restaurant-inn is right on the water, and most of its small guest rooms open onto balconies. A twisting stairway in the rear leads to the old-style rooms. Each immaculate room is individually decorated and comfortable, equipped with a well-kept bathroom.

Rua Gomes Freire 9, 2450-222 Nazaré. www.ribamar.pa-net.pt. (C) **26/255-11-58.** Fax 26/256-22-24. 25 units. 50€–80€ double; 70€–95€ suite. Rates include continental breakfast. MC, V. Parking 5€–10€. **Amenities:** Restaurant; bar. *In room:* TV.

Where to Dine

Mar Bravo PORTUGUESE   One of the busiest of the dozens of overpriced restaurants in this bustling village is Mar Bravo, on the corner of the square overlooking the ocean. A complete and consistently pleasing meal consists of soup followed by a fish or meat dish and bread. An English-language menu lists a la carte specialties such as classic bass caprice, fish stew Nazarena, lobster stew, and grilled pork. Dessert might be a soufflé, fruit salad, or pudding. Upstairs is a second dining room, with an ocean view.

Praça Sousa Oliveira 71. (C) **26/256-91-60.** www.marbravo.com. Reservations recommended. Regular main courses 14€–48€. AE, DC, MC, V. Daily 11am–midnight.

Os Antónios SEAFOOD/PORTUGUESE   If you don't like the fish harvested daily in this famous little seaport, you may have come to the wrong place. But you'll find some meat dishes as well, including roast kid on the barbecue, tender lamb from the hinterlands, and "steak on the stone," a specialty. Begin perhaps with the fish soup of the day or a shrimp cocktail. You can even order a plate of pig ears, but you might settle instead for the fresh octopus salad. A savory platter of seafood rice is served for two people, and tiger prawns emerge from the grill as a succulent treat. Desserts are superb, especially the mango mousse, the orange pie, and the wine-soaked fresh pears.

Largo Vasco da Gama. (C) **23/294-95-15.** www.osantonios.com. Main courses 14€–28€. AE, MC, V. Daily noon–2:30 and Mon–Sat 7–10pm.

BATALHA

118km (73 miles) N of Lisbon

Batalha merits a visit for only one reason: to see the monastery. Most visitors choose to stay in Fátima or Nazaré, which have more hotels and restaurants, but we've included the best options for sleeping and eating in town below, in case you decide to linger.

Essentials

ARRIVING

BY BUS   From Nazaré (see above), seven buses a day make the 1-hour trip to Batalha, with a change at Alcobaça; one-way tickets cost 4.50€. From Lisbon, six *expresso* buses operate daily; the trip lasts 2 hours and costs 11€ one-way.

BY CAR From Alcobaça (see earlier), continue northeast along N8 for about 20 minutes.

VISITOR INFORMATION

The **Batalha Tourist Office** is on Praça Mouzinho de Albuquerque (© **24/476-51-80**). If you're traveling by bus, the tourist office keeps detailed schedules of the best connections to surrounding towns. It's open daily from 10am to 1pm and 3 to 7pm. In August, it's open daily 10am to 7pm.

Visiting the Monastery

Mosteiro de Santa Maria da Vitória ★★★ In 1385, João I vowed on the plains of Aljubarrota that if his underequipped and outnumbered army defeated the invading Castilians, he would commemorate his spiritual indebtedness to the Virgin Mary. The result is the magnificent Monastery of the Virgin Mary, designed in splendid Gothic and Manueline style.

The **western porch ★**, ornamented by a tangled mass of Gothic sculpture of saints and other figures, sits beneath stained-glass windows of blue, mauve, and amber. The windows are exceptionally beautiful and are best enjoyed on a sunny day. Because the windows were damaged over the centuries, various artisans have replaced them in their original 16th-century Manueline detail.

In the **Founder's Chapel ★**, João I and his English queen, Philippa of Lancaster (daughter of John of Gaunt), lie in peaceful repose, their hands entwined on their stone effigies beneath an exquisite octagonal lantern. Prince Henry the Navigator's tomb is near that of his parents. His fame eclipsed theirs even though he never sat on the throne. The **Royal Cloisters ★★★** reveal the beginnings of the nautically oriented Manueline architecture.

The magnum opus of the monastery is the **Chapter House ★★**, a square chamber whose **vaulting ★★★** is an unparalleled example of the Gothic style, bare of supporting pillars.

Sentinels and the glow of an eternal flame guard the two tombs of Portugal's Unknown Soldiers from World War I. In one part of the quadrangle is the Unknown Soldiers Museum, which houses gifts to the fallen warriors from the people of Portugal and other countries. Beyond the crypt are the remains of the old wine cellars. You can visit the crypts daily from 9am to 5pm, but you might not want to unless you're a crypt aficionado. These consist of a series of dank and gloomy ancient tombs, but no notable treasures.

Stunning filigree designs ornament the coral-stone entrance to the seven unfinished **chapels ★★**. The *capelas,* under a "sky ceiling," are part of one of the finest examples of the Manueline style, a true stone extravaganza. Construction was abandoned so workers for Manuel I could help build his monastery at Belém.

Praça Mouzinho de Albuquerque. © **24/476-54-97.** Admission 5€, free for children under 14. Oct–Mar daily 9am–5pm; Apr–Sept daily 9am–6pm.

Where to Stay & Dine

MODERATE

Hotel Mestre Afonso Domingues This pousada fills a big accommodations gap in this part of the country. It stands right across the square from the monastery. Guests can relax in well-kept modern comfort, if not great style. The good-size rooms are well furnished, with comfortable beds. The staff is helpful and friendly. And the restaurant here serves the finest cuisine in town to nonguests as well as guests, although that's no great compliment because Batalha is hardly a gourmet citadel.

Largo do Mestre Afonso Domingues 6, 2440-102 Batalha. www.hotel.mestreafonsodomingues.pt. *☎* **24/476-52-60.** Fax 24/476-52-47. 21 units. 90€–100€ double; 140€–160€ suite. Rates include buffet breakfast. AE, DC, MC, V. **Amenities:** Restaurant; bar; bikes; room service; Wi-Fi (free, in lobby). *In room:* A/C, TV, hair dryer, minibar.

Hotel Villa Batalha ★★   At long last Batalha has a first-rate hotel built in the center of town, within view of the monastery. The government-rated four-star hotel, by far the most superior in town, has brought a high level of comfort and conveniences to the town that heretofore had mainly some inns. The interior space is flooded with natural light, and most bedrooms open onto private balconies overlooking the monastery. The hotel is imbued with a warm atmosphere and filled with tasteful furnishings in both the bedrooms and public areas.

The decorators weren't afraid of color, imbuing the hotel with creamy chocolate browns and sienna reds. The on-site restaurant, Adega dos Frades, specializes in regional dishes, and does so exceedingly well. The hotel offers one of the best spas in the region, complete with steam room, sauna, Jacuzzi, and indoor pool.

Rua Dom Duarte I, 248 2440-415 Batalha. www.hotelvillabatalha.com. *☎* **24/424-04-00.** 93 units. 105€–120€ double; from 175€ suite. AE, MC, V. **Amenities:** Restaurant; bar; bikes; concierge; golf course; indoor pool; room service; spa; outdoor tennis court (lit). *In room:* A/C, TV, hair dryer, minibar, Wi-Fi (free).

INEXPENSIVE

Hotel Casa do Outeiro *⚑*   If you get the right room here, you'll wake up in the morning to look upon a view of the monastery itself from your own private terrace. This is a homelike and most welcoming little pension (boardinghouse). It is completely modern with individually designed, midsize bedrooms that are both tasteful and comfortable, with small private bathrooms. Breakfast is served by the pool.

Largo Carvalho do Outeiro 4, 2440-128 Batalha. www.casadoouteiro.com. *☎* **24/476-58-06.** Fax 24/476-88-92. 15 units. 51€–90€. AE, DC, MC, V. **Amenities:** Children's center; exercise room; outdoor pool. *In room:* A/C, hair dryer, minibar, Wi-Fi (free; in some).

Motel S. Jorge ☺   Catering to motorists and families in general, this is a well-laid-out motel complex with a choice of regular rooms or bungalows on the grounds. Families most often go for the bungalows, which are equipped for guests to do their own cooking. The small-to-midsize bedrooms are furnished in a standard motel fashion—nothing special here—but they are well maintained and comfortable. The motel has the best recreational facilities of any accommodations in the area, including a diamond-shaped outdoor pool with a special section reserved for kids. Scattered about the lawns are umbrellas and chairs. On-site is a basic restaurant decorated with local artifacts and serving affordable regional cuisine.

Estrada Nacional 1, Casal da Amieira, 2440-011 Batalha. www.motelsjorge.com. *☎* **24/476-97-10.** Fax 24/476-97-11. 67 units. 45€–65€ double; bungalows 75€–110€. AE, DC, MC, V. **Amenities:** Restaurant; bar; outdoor pool; outdoor tennis court (lit). *In room:* A/C, TV.

FÁTIMA

142km (88 miles) N of Lisbon; 58km (36 miles) E of Nazaré

Fátima is a world-famous pilgrimage site because of reported sightings of the Virgin Mary in the early 20th century. The terrain around the village is wild, almost primitive,

THE ROLE OF THE church IN PORTUGAL

From its medieval origins, Portugal has been intricately bound in an allegiance to the Church. (The existence of the country itself in the early days of Afonso Henriques probably stemmed from a religion-based hatred of the Moors.) Although they were devout, the Portuguese monarchs never seemed as rabidly fanatical in their faith as their neighbors in Spain. Likewise, although Portugal endured an Inquisition, its purges never ran as deep or were quite as bloody as those of the Spaniards.

Today, although observant of Roman Catholic doctrine and reasonably devout, the country seems more interested in the melancholy passion of the fado and the fanfare of football (soccer) than in the passions of religion. Since the Industrial Revolution and the social unrest that accompanied it, Portugal has maintained an uncomfortable duality between its allegiance to the Roman Catholic Church and a general dislike for clerical directives coming from beyond their village or town. Nonetheless, applications to God tend to increase during times of trouble. According to an ancient Portuguese proverb, "When food is on the table, the Saints are left in peace."

Despite the influences of socialist politics and a general disillusionment, the Church continues to inspire great loyalty, especially in rural areas and probably more among women than among men. In some villages, especially in the more devout northern sections, at least half of an entire village might be found in church on Sunday.

In rural areas, religion is closely associated with protection of fields, family, households, and domestic animals and used as a kind of appeasement against the many ills that might potentially cause damage. Significantly, some of the most sought after rustic antiques in Portugal are traditional 19th-century ox yokes, lavishly carved from timbers into ornate depictions of Christian imagery, complete with crosses and symbols of fertility to bless and protect the oxen plowing the fields.

Today, despite tendencies within Portugal to both respect and condemn the Church, more than 85% of the people still professes to be Roman Catholic. In 1940, a concordar was signed with the Holy See in Rome, an act that defined the relationship between the Portuguese state and the Catholic Church. The mainland of Portugal today comprises three metropolitan archdioceses under archbishops in Lisbon, Braga, and Évora. There are 20 dioceses. Throughout the country, there is freedom of worship, both public and private.

Despite the decay of allegiance to the church and the unending diversions of football and politics, a still popular pastime in Portugal involves going on pilgrimages, usually to one or another of the many holy shrines scattered throughout the country. Foremost among them is the shrine of Fátima (see below).

with an aura of barren desolation hanging over the countryside. However, when religious pilgrims flock to the town twice a year, its desolation quickly turns to fervent drama.

Essentials

ARRIVING

BY TRAIN   Ten trains run daily from Lisbon to Caxarias, 10km (6¼ miles) outside Fátima. A ticket costs 12€, and the trip takes 1 hour and 10 minutes. For information and schedules, call ☎ **80/820-82-08.** Buses await passengers at Caxarias and run into Fátima. The fare is 4€, and buses between Caxarias and Fátima operate at the rate of seven per day, with a one-way ticket costing 4€.

BY BUS   On bus schedules, Fátima is often listed as Cova da Iria, which leads to a lot of confusion. Cova da Iria is less than 1km (⅔ mile) from Fátima and is the focus of pilgrimages and the site of the alleged religious miracles. About three buses a day connect Fátima with Batalha. The trip takes 40 minutes and costs 4€ one-way. Fifteen buses a day arrive from Lisbon. The 1½-hour trip costs 8.50€ one-way. For information and schedules, call ☎ **24/953-16-11.**

BY CAR   From Batalha (see above), continue east along Route 356 for 15km (9¼ miles).

VISITOR INFORMATION

The **tourist office** is on Avenida Dom José Alves Correia da Silva (☎ **24/953-11-39;** www.rt-leiriafatima.pt) and is open daily from 10am to 1pm and 3 to 7pm. In August, it's open daily 10am to 9pm.

Exploring the Town

A PILGRIMAGE TO FÁTIMA   On May 13 and October 13, pilgrims overrun the town, causing the roads leading to Fátima to be choked with pilgrims in donkey carts, on bicycles, or in cars. Many also approach on foot; some even "walk" on their knees in penance. Once in Fátima, they camp out until day breaks. In the central square, which is larger than St. Peter's in Rome, a statue of the Madonna passes through the crowd between about 10am and 12:30pm. When it does, some 75,000 handkerchiefs flutter in the breeze.

Then as many as are able crowd in to visit a small slanted-roof shed known as the **Chapel of the Apparitions.** Inside stands a single white column marking the spot where a small holm oak once grew. An image of the Virgin Mary reputedly appeared over this oak on May 13, 1917, when she is said to have spoken to three shepherd children. That oak long ago disappeared, torn to pieces by souvenir collectors. The original chapel constructed here was dynamited on the night of March 6, 1922, by skeptics who suspected the church of staging the so-called miracle.

While World War I dragged on, three devout children—Lúcia de Jesús and her cousins, Jacinta and Francisco Marto—claimed that they saw the first appearance of "a lady" on the tableland of Cova da Iria. Her coming had been foreshadowed in 1916 by what they would later cite as "an angel of peace," who is said to have appeared before them.

Attempts were made to suppress their story, but it spread quickly. During the July appearance, the lady was reported to have revealed three secrets to them, one of which prefigured the coming of World War II; another was connected with Russia's "rejection of God." The final secret, a "sealed message" recorded by Lúcia, was opened by church officials in 1960, but the contents of that message were only recently published. According to the Vatican, it predicted that Pope John Paul II would be shot. Acting on orders from the Portuguese government, the mayor of a nearby town threw the children into jail and threatened them with torture, even death in burning oil. Still, they would not be intimidated and stuck to their story. The lady reportedly made six appearances between May and the final one on October 13,

ESTREMADURA | Fátima

1917, when the children were joined by an estimated 70,000 people who witnessed the famous Miracle of the Sun. The day had begun with pouring rain and driving winds. Observers from all over the world testified that at noon "the sky opened up" and the sun seemed to spin out of its axis and hurtle toward the earth. Many at the site feared the Last Judgment was upon them. Others later reported that they thought the scorching sun was crashing into the earth and would consume it in flames. Many agreed that a major miracle of modern times had occurred. Only the children reported seeing Our Lady, however.

Both Francisco and Jacinta died in the influenza epidemic that swept Europe after World War I. Lúcia became a Carmelite nun in a convent in the university city of Coimbra. She returned to Fátima in 1967 to mark the 50th anniversary of the apparition, and the pope flew in from Rome.

A cold, pristine white basilica in the neoclassical style was erected at one end of the wide square. If you want to go inside, you might be stopped by a guard if you're not suitably dressed. Women are asked not to enter wearing slacks or "other masculine attire." Men wearing shorts are also excluded.

SHOPPING   Many of the souvenirs you'll find in Fátima are religious in nature. If you're interested in an evenhanded mixture of religious and secular objects, head for the town's biggest gift shop, **Centro Comercial Fátima (Fátima Shopping Center),** Estrada de Leiria (✆ **24/953-23-75;** www.fatimashoppingcenter.com). The staggering inventory is piled to the ceiling. If you're looking for devotional statues or a less controversial example of regional porcelain, you'll find it here, 450m (1,476 ft.) from the town's main religious sanctuary. Another well-stocked gift shop is in the **Pax Hotel,** Rua Francisco Marto (✆ **24/953-94-00;** www.hotelpax.com).

Where to Stay

On major pilgrimage days, it's just about impossible to secure a room unless you've reserved months in advance.

MODERATE

Casa Alta Royal Lodge ★★★   The pilgrimage center of Fátima attracts millions of visitors annually but has never had an atmospheric or romantic place to stay until the opening of this elegant retreat with only three bedrooms. In the village of Ourém, it lies only a 12-minute drive from the center of Fátima. This former royal lodge offers the grandest accommodations in the area, with beautifully furnished bedrooms filled with antiques, embroidered sheets, and even robes and slippers. A full English-style breakfast is included in the rates, and candlelit dinners with sterling silver table service are just part of the allure of this charmer.

2490-481 Ourém. www.casaaltaroyallodge.com. ✆ **24/954-35-15.** Fax 24/954-35-30. 3 units. 150€–230€ double. Rates include an English breakfast. MC, V. **Amenities:** Restaurant; outdoor pool; room service. *In room:* A/C, TV, hair dryer.

INEXPENSIVE

Dom Gonçalo & Spa   This modern hotel sits in a large garden at the entrance to town, only 365m (1,198 ft.) from the Sanctuary of Our Lady of Fátima. The small to midsize guest rooms are among the town's finest, although Hotel Fátima probably has the edge. All are comfortably and attractively furnished, with firm beds and a functional decor. The bathrooms are small but well maintained.

Rua Jacinta Marto 100, 2495-450 Fátima. www.hoteldg.com. 📞 **24/953-93-30.** Fax 24/953-93-35. 42 units. 72€–90€ double; 116€–135€ suite. Rates include buffet breakfast. AE, DC, MC, V. **Amenities:** Restaurant; bar; babysitting; bikes; children's center; exercise room; indoor heated pool; room service; spa; Wi-Fi (free, in lobby). *In room:* A/C, TV, hair dryer, minibar.

Hotel Fátima ★ Hotel Fátima is the leading hotel in a town full of fairly standard but decent hotels (which are clean, comfortable, and decently run, but not luxurious or architecturally distinguished in any way). Many of the midsize rooms here overlook the sanctuary. The best rooms are in the newer 45-room addition. This is the only hotel in town that can be rated as first class.

Rua João Paulo II, 2495-308 Fátima. www.hotelfatima.com. 📞 **24/953-33-51.** Fax 24/953-26-91. 126 units. 70€–110€ double; 100€–155€ suite. Rates include buffet breakfast. AE, DC, MC, V. Parking 6.50€. **Amenities:** Restaurant; bar; room service; Wi-Fi (5€ per hour, in lobby). *In room:* A/C, TV, minibar.

Hotel Santa Maria This comfortable modern hotel is on a quiet side street just a few steps east of the park surrounding the sanctuary. Each modern room, attended by a well-trained staff, contains a balcony and a well-maintained bathroom. The small accommodations are plain but entirely acceptable.

Rua de Santo António, 2495-430 Fátima. www.hotelstmaria.com. 📞 **24/953-01-10.** Fax 24/953-01-19. 120 units. 78€–120€ double; 130€–190€ suite. Rates include continental breakfast. AE, MC, V. Free parking. **Amenities:** Restaurant; bar; concierge; room service; Wi-Fi (free, in lobby). *In room:* A/C, TV, hair dryer, minibar.

Hotel São José On one of the busiest streets in Fátima, within walking distance of the sanctuary, this modern balconied hotel is large and urban. It has a uniformed staff, a marble-floor lobby, and comfortable midsize rooms. This hotel seems to have a bit more style than some of its more spartan competitors.

Av. Dom José Alves Correia da Silva, 2495-402 Fátima. www.hotelsaojose.com. 📞 **24/953-01-20.** Fax 24/953-01-29. 76 units. 65€–85€ double; 100€–125€ suite. Rates include buffet breakfast. AE, MC, V. **Amenities:** Restaurant; 2 bars; exercise room; room service; sauna. *In room:* A/C, TV, hair dryer, Wi-Fi (free).

Where to Dine

Grelha GRILL/PORTUGUESE   If you don't want to eat at a hotel, try Grelha, one of the best of a meager selection. It's 275m (902 ft.) from the sanctuary at Fátima. Grelha offers regional specialties but is known for its grills, especially steaks and fish. Grilled codfish is an especially good choice. In the cooler months, the fireplace is an attraction, and the bar is busy year-round.

Rua Jacinta Marto 78. 📞 **24/953-16-33.** Main courses 9€–25€. AE, DC, MC, V. Fri–Wed noon–3pm and 7–10:30pm. Closed 2 weeks in Nov.

Tia Alice ★ PORTUGUESE   This simple, rustic restaurant offers copious portions of food inspired by the rural traditions of Estremadura. It's the finest dining choice in the area, though that's not saying a lot. Specialties include broad-bean soups, roast lamb with rosemary and garlic, fried hake with green sauce, chicken, Portuguese sausages, and grilled lamb or pork chops.

Rua do Adro. 📞 **24/953-17-37.** Reservations required. Main courses 15€–26€. AE, MC, V. Tues–Sat noon–3pm and 7:30–10pm; Sun noon–6pm. Closed July.

Fátima After Dark

As you might expect of a destination for religious pilgrimages, Fátima is early to rise (in many cases, for morning Mass) and early to bed. Cafes in town tend to be locked tight after around 10pm, so religion-weary residents who want to escape drive 4km (2½ miles) south of town along Estrada de Minde to the village of Boleiros. Here you'll find **Bar Truão** (© **24/952-15-42;** www.truao.com), a music bar that is much more attuned to human frailties than the ecclesiastical monuments in the core. It's open Friday and Saturday nights from 11pm to 2am.

THE ALGARVE

I n the ancient Moorish town of Xelb (today called Silves), a handsome and sensitive vizier once lived. During one of his sojourns into northern lands, he fell in love with a beautiful Nordic princess. After they married, he brought her back to the Algarve. Soon the young princess began to pine for the snow-covered hills and valleys of her native land. The vizier decreed that thousands of almond trees would be planted throughout his realm. Since that day, pale-white almond blossoms have blanketed the Algarve in late January and early February. The young princess lived happily ever after in her vizier's sun-drenched kingdom, with its sweet-smelling artificial winters—or so the story goes.

The maritime province of the Algarve, often called the Garden of Portugal, is the southwesternmost part of Europe. Its coastline stretches 160km (99 miles) from Henry the Navigator's Cape St. Vincent to the border town of Vila Real de Santo António, fronting once-hostile Spain. The varied coastline contains sluggish estuaries, sheltered lagoons, low-lying areas where clucking marsh hens nest, long sandy spits, and promontories jutting out into the white-capped aquamarine foam.

Called Al-Gharb by the Moors, the land south of the *serras* (mountains) of Monchique and Caldeirão remains a spectacular anomaly that seems more like a transplanted section of the North African coastline than a piece of Europe. The temperature averages around 60°F (16°C) in winter and 74°F (23°C) in summer. The countryside abounds in vegetation: almonds, lemons, oranges, carobs, pomegranates, and figs.

Even though most of the towns and villages of the Algarve are more than 240km (149 miles) from Lisbon, the great 1755 earthquake shook this area. Entire communities were wiped out; however, many Moorish and even Roman ruins remain. In the fret-cut chimneys, mosquelike cupolas, and cubist houses, a distinct Oriental flavor prevails. Phoenicians, Greeks, Romans, Visigoths, Moors, and Christians all touched this land.

Much of the historic flavor, however, is gone forever, swallowed by a sea of dreary high-rise apartment blocks surrounding most towns. Years ago, Portuguese officials, looking in horror at what happened to Spain's Costa del Sol, promised more limited and controlled development so that they wouldn't make "Spain's mistake." That promise, in our opinion, has not been kept.

Algarvian beaches are some of the best in Portugal. Their quality has led to the tourist boom across the southern coastline, making it a formidable rival of Lisbon's Costa do Sol and Spain's Costa del Sol. There are literally hundreds of beaches, many with public showers and watersports

9

THE ALGARVE | Introduction

Rio Guadiana

Vila Real de Santo António

Monte Gordo

Castro Marim

IP1

Golfo de Cádiz

N122

N124

Rio de Foupana

Rio de Odeleite

Tavira

Ribeira de Carreiras

Rio Vascão

N397

Ilha de Armona

N267

Barronca Velho

Ribeira de Alportel

São Brás de Alportel

Olhão

Cabo de Santa Maria

N2

Estói

Faro

Loulé

Almancil

N125

Serra do Caldeirão

Quarteira

Ilha da Barreta

N124

Vilamoura

IP1

Ferreiras

Albufeira

IP2

São Bartolomeu de Messines

Armação de Pêra

ATLANTIC OCEAN

E01

IP1

Lagoa

IP1

São Marcos da Serra

Silves

Carvoeiro

N266

Portimão

Praia da Rocha

Caldas de Monchique

Odemira

Rio Mira

Serra do Espinhaço de Cão

Lagos

Odeceixe

IC4

Aljezur

IC4

N125

Sagres

Ponta de Sagres

Carrapateira

N268

Vila do Bispo

Cabo de São Vicente

PORTUGAL

Lisbon

area of detail

6 mi

10 km

213

equipment available for rent. Not all beaches are suitable for swimming because some have sloping seabeds or swift currents—heed local warnings.

Since around 1965, vast stretches of coastal terrain have been bulldozed, landscaped, irrigated, and reconfigured into golf courses. Many are associated with real-estate developments or major resorts, such as the 800-hectare (1,977-acre) Quinta do Lago, where retirement villas nestle amid vegetation at the edges of the fairways. Most are open to qualified golfers who inquire in advance.

Many former fishing villages—now summer resorts—dot the Algarvian coast: Carvoeiro, Albufeira, Olhão, Portimão. The sea is the source of life, as it always has been. The village marketplaces sell esparto mats, copper, pottery, and almond and fig sweets, sometimes shaped like birds and fish. Through the narrow streets comes the fast sound of little accordions pumping out the rhythmical *corridinho*.

SAGRES: "THE END OF THE WORLD" ★

280km (174 miles) S of Lisbon; 34km (21 miles) W of Lagos; 114km (71 miles) W of Faro

At the extreme southwestern corner of Europe—once called *o fim do mundo* (the end of the world)—Sagres is a rocky escarpment jutting into the Atlantic Ocean. From here, Henry the Navigator, the Infante of Sagres, launched Portugal and the rest of Europe on the seas of exploration. Here he established his school of navigation, where Magellan, Diaz, Cabral, and Vasco da Gama apprenticed. A virtual ascetic, Henry brought together the best navigators, cartographers, geographers, scholars, sailors, and builders; infused them with his rigorous devotion; and methodically set Portuguese caravels upon the Sea of Darkness.

Essentials

ARRIVING

BY FERRY & TRAIN   From Lisbon, take an Algarve-bound train to the junction at Tunes, where a change of trains will take you south all the way to Lagos. The rest of the distance is by bus (see below). For information and schedules, call ✆ **80/820-82-08** (www.cp.pt). From Lagos, buses go to Sagres.

BY BUS   Ten EVA buses (✆ **28/989-97-60;** www.eva-bus.com) in Lagos run hourly from Lagos to Sagres each day. The trip time is 1 hour, and a one-way ticket costs 3.60€.

BY CAR   From Lagos, drive west on Route 125 to Vila do Bispo, and then head south along Route 268 to Sagres.

Exploring Sagres

Both the cape and Sagres offer a view of the sunset. In the ancient world, the cape was the last explored point, although in time the Phoenicians pushed beyond it. Many mariners thought that when the sun sank beyond the cape, it plunged over the edge of the world.

Today, at the reconstructed site of Henry's windswept fortress on Europe's Land's End (named after the narrowing westernmost tip of Cornwall, England), you can see a huge stone compass dial. Henry supposedly used the Venta de Rosa in his naval studies at Sagres. Housed in the **Fortaleza de Sagres,** Ponta de Sagres, is a small museum of minor interest that documents some of the area's history. It's open May to September daily 9:30am to 8pm, October to April 9:30am to 5:30pm. Admission is 3€ for adults, 1.50€ for ages 15 to 25, and free for children 14 and under. At a simple chapel, restored in 1960, sailors are said to have prayed for help before setting out into uncharted waters. The chapel is closed to the public.

About 5km (3 miles) away is the promontory of **Cabo de São Vicente ★★**. It got its name because, according to legend, the body of St. Vincent arrived mysteriously here on a boat guided by ravens. (Others claim that the body of the patron saint, murdered at Valencia, Spain, washed up on Lisbon's shore.) A lighthouse, the second most powerful in Europe, beams illumination 100km (62 miles) across the ocean. To reach the cape, you can take a bus Monday through Friday only leaving from Rua Comandante Matoso near the tourist office. Trip time is 10 minutes, and departures are at 11:15am and 2:25pm, a one-way ticket costs 2€.

Outdoor Activities

BEACHES   Many beaches fringe the peninsula; some attract nude bathers. Mareta, at the bottom of the road leading from the center of town toward the water, is the best and most popular. East of town is Tonel, also a good sandy beach. The beaches west of town, Praia da Baleeira and Praia do Martinhal, are better for windsurfing than for swimming.

FISHING   Fishing is worthwhile (and legal) between October and January, although you should be warned in advance that quantities of fish seem to have diminished in recent years. You can walk down to almost any beach and hire a local fisherman to take you out for a half-day, and just about every large-scale hotel along the Algarve will arrange a fishing trip for you. Most fishing excursions are configured as half-day events, priced, with equipment included, at around 40€ per adult per half-day excursion.

Where to Stay

MODERATE

Memmo Baleeira Hotel   Named after the whaleboats (*baleeira*) whose mariners sailed to distant ports of the Atlantic, Memmo Baleeira Hotel occupies a tastefully simple, angular, and minimalist complex that's perched on a low cliff above the jagged and rocky coastline of Sagres, above the fishing port, 50m (164 ft.) from a pleasant beach. The largest hotel on Sagres, and perhaps the most self-consciously "artful" in the calculated simplicity of its sun-flooded, mostly white interiors, it offers guest rooms with balconies and views over the open sea, the harbor, the gardens, or, at the cheapest level, a parking lot. The number of its rooms has nearly doubled in recent years; the older ones are quite small.

Sítio da Baleeira, Sagres, 8650 Vila do Bispo. www.memmohotels.com. © **28/262-42-12.** Fax 28/262-44-25. 144 units. 95€–190€ double; 171€–225€ suite. Rates include buffet breakfast. AE, DC, MC, V. Free parking. **Amenities:** Restaurant; bar; babysitting; bikes; children's center; exercise room; 2 freshwater pools (1 heated indoor); room service; spa; outdoor tennis court (lit); limited watersports equipment/rentals; Wi-Fi (free, in lobby). *In room:* A/C, TV, DVD player (in some), kitchenette (in some); minibar.

Pousada do Infante ★★   Pousada do Infante, the best address in Sagres, seems like a monastery built by ascetic monks who wanted to commune with nature. You'll be charmed by the rugged beauty of the rocky cliffs, the pounding surf, and the sense of the ocean's infinity. Built in 1960, the glistening white government-owned tourist inn spreads along the edge of a cliff that projects rather daringly over the sea. It boasts a long colonnade of arches with an extended stone terrace set with garden furniture, plus a second floor of accommodations with private balconies. Each midsize guest room is furnished with traditional pieces. Room nos. 1 to 12 are the most desirable.

The public rooms are generously proportioned, gleaming with marble and decorated with fine tapestries depicting the exploits of Henry the Navigator. Large velvet couches flank the fireplace.

Ponta da Atalaia, 8650-385 Sagres. www.pousadas.pt. ✆ **28/262-02-40.** Fax 28/262-42-25. 39 units. 92€–240€ double; 115€–300€ suite. Rates include buffet breakfast. AE, DC, MC, V. Free parking. **Amenities:** Restaurant; bar; babysitting; outdoor freshwater pool; room service; outdoor tennis court (lit). *In room:* A/C, TV, hair dryer, minibar, Wi-Fi (in some; 12€ per 24 hr.).

Romantik Villa Vivenda Felicidade ★★ 🎁 As popular resorts along the Algarve become overcrowded in summer, more discerning visitors are finding hideaways in remote villages. Such a village is Salema, between Sagres and Lagos, where you'll find this lush villa lying along Route 125. In a landscaped setting, it features a swimming pool and a garden overlooking the ocean. Bedrooms are done in regional styling, with well-crafted furniture often placed against stone walls. Bathrooms are sleek and modern. There's no Internet access, but there is an Internet cafe in the little village of Salema.

Salema M5, 8650-191 Budens. www.romantikvilla.com. ✆ **28/269-56-70.** 4 units. 80€–90€ double; 100€–120€ suite. No credit cards. Free parking. **Amenities:** Outdoor pool. *In room:* A/C, TV, hair dryer.

Where to Dine

Restaurante O Telheiro do Infante ★ SEAFOOD This two-floor restaurant is the best place for dining in the area, especially if you like your food fresh from the sea. There may be a bit of a wait, as all the dishes are prepared to order to maintain freshness. Originally, the location was a small farm, which grew and changed into its present role as tourism to the area increased. Raw ingredients are prepared with succulent simplicity. We always like to begin with the fresh oysters or the shrimp cocktail. Our favorite salad is the one made with fresh asparagus. Your best seafood selection is always the *peixe do dia*, or fresh catch of the day. It can be grilled to your specifications, or the fish can also be sautéed and served in a butter sauce with fresh vegetables. An array of pork and beef dishes from the Portuguese plains north of here should satisfy any meat eater. (The pork is very sweet because the pigs are often fed a diet of acorns.) Some tables are placed outside so you can enjoy the view of the ocean.

Praia da Mareta. ✆ **28/262-41-79.** www.telheirodoinfante.com. Reservations recommended in summer. Main courses 13€–28€. AE, DC, MC, V. Wed–Mon 10am–10pm.

Restaurante Vila Velha ★★ INTERNATIONAL In a rustic setting in a villa, this first-class restaurant with its covered terrace in summer is elegant. It's air-conditioned in summer, but in winter a cozy fire awaits you. Pleasure will explode on your palate as you sample such great dishes as stuffed quail in wine sauce; prawn curry; small pork filets with mango sauce; hake filets with scallops and hollandaise sauce; or tagliatelle with prawns and monkfish. Desserts are sumptuous, especially the homemade walnut ice cream with flambé bananas and a chocolate sauce. Prepare yourself for one of your finest gastronomic evenings on the Algarve if you eat here.

Rua Patrão António Faustino. ✆ **28/262-47-88.** www.vilavelha-sagres.com. Reservations required. Main courses 28€–38€. MC, V. Tues–Sun 6:30–10pm (until 10:30pm July 15–Sept 15).

Sagres After Dark

The best of the many nightspots in the town's historic core include the **Bar Dromedário,** Rua Comandante Matos (⌀ **28/262-42-19;** www.dromedariosagres.com), and the **A Rosa dos Ventos (Pink Wind) Bar,** Praça da República (⌀ **28/262-44-80;** www.rosadosventos.info). Folks from all over Europe talk, relax, and drink beer, wine, or sangria.

LAGOS ★

34km (21 miles) E of Sagres; 69km (43 miles) W of Faro; 264km (164 miles) S of Lisbon; 13km (8 miles) W of Portimão

Lagos, known to the Lusitanians and Romans as Lacobriga and to the Moors as Zawaia, became a shipyard of caravels during the time of Henry the Navigator. Edged by the Costa do Ouro (Golden Coast), the Bay of Sagres was at one point in its epic history big enough to allow 407 warships to maneuver with ease.

An ancient port city (one historian traced its origins to the Carthaginians, 3 centuries before the birth of Christ), Lagos was well known by the sailors of Admiral Nelson's fleet. From Liverpool to Manchester to Plymouth, the sailors spoke wistfully of the beautiful green-eyed, olive-skinned women of the Algarve. Eagerly they sailed into port, looking forward to carousing and drinking.

Actually, not that much has changed since Nelson's day. Few go to Lagos wanting to know its history; rather, the mission is to drink deeply of the pleasures of table and beach. In winter, the almond blossoms match the whitecaps on the water, and the weather is often warm enough for sunbathing. In town, a flea market sprawls through the narrow streets.

Less than 2km (1¼ miles) down the coast, the hustle and bustle of market day is forgotten as the rocky headland of the **Ponta da Piedade (Point of Piety) ★★** appears. This spot is the most beautiful on the entire coast. Amid the colorful cliffs and secret grottoes carved by the waves are the most flamboyant examples of Manueline architecture.

Much of Lagos was razed in the 1755 earthquake, and it lost its position as the capital of the Algarve. Today only the ruins of its fortifications remain. However, traces of the old linger on the back streets.

Essentials

ARRIVING

BY FERRY & TRAIN From Lisbon, take an Algarve-bound train to the junction at Tunes, where a change of trains will take you south all the way to Lagos. Five trains a day arrive from Lisbon. The trip takes 5½ hours and costs at least 22€ one-way. For more information and schedules, call ⌀ **80/820-82-08.**

BY BUS Six buses a day make the run between Lisbon and Lagos. The trip takes 4 hours and costs 19€ each way. Call ⌀ **28/989-97-60** for schedules.

BY CAR If you're coming from Lisbon, after leaving Sines, take Route 120 southeast toward Lagos and follow the signs into the city. From Sagres, take N268 northeast to the junction with N125, which will lead you east to Lagos.

VISITOR INFORMATION

The **Lagos Tourist Office,** Praça Gil Eanes, Lagos (**© 28/276-30-31;** www.visit algarve.pt), is open daily 9:30am to 1pm and 2 to 5:30pm.

Exploring the Town

Antigo Mercado de Escravos The Old Customs House stands as a painful reminder of the Age of Exploration. The arcaded slave market, the only one of its kind in Europe, looks peaceful today, but under its four Romanesque arches, captives were once sold to the highest bidders. The house opens onto the tranquil main square dominated by a statue of Henry the Navigator.

Praça do Infante Dom Henríques. Free admission. Daily 24 hr.

Igreja de Santo António ★ The 18th-century Church of St. Anthony sits just off the waterfront. The altar is decorated with some of Portugal's most notable baroque **gilt carvings ★**, created with gold imported from Brazil. Begun in the 17th century, they were damaged in the earthquake but subsequently restored. What you see today represents the work of many artisans—each, at times, apparently pursuing a different theme.

Rua General Alberto Carlos Silveira. © **28/276-23-01.** Admission 2€ adults, 1€ students and seniors 65 and older, free for children under 12. Tues–Sun 9:30am–12:30pm and 2–5pm.

Museu Municipal Dr. José Formosinho The Municipal Museum contains replicas of the fret-cut chimneys of the Algarve, three-dimensional cork carvings, 16th-century vestments, ceramics, 17th-century embroidery, ecclesiastical sculpture, a painting gallery, weapons, minerals, and a numismatic collection. There's also a believe-it-or-not section displaying, among other things, an eight-legged calf. In the archaeological wing are Neolithic artifacts, Roman mosaics found at Boca do Rio near Budens, fragments of statuary and columns, and other remains of antiquity from excavations along the Algarve.

Rua General Alberto Carlos Silveira. © **28/276-23-01.** Admission 3.50€ adults; 2.50€ children 12–14. Tues–Sun 9:30am–12:30pm and 2–5pm. Closed holidays.

Outdoor Activities

BEACHES Some of the best beaches—including Praia de Dona Ana, the most appealing—are near Lagos, south of the city. Follow signs to the Hotel Golfinho. If you go all the way to the southernmost point, Ponta da Piedade, you'll pass some pretty cove beaches set against a backdrop of rock formations. Steps are sometimes carved into the cliffs to make for easier access. Although it's crowded in summer, another good white-sand beach is at the 2.5km-long (1½-mile) Meia Praia (Half Beach), across the river from the center of town.

DIVING One of the Algarve's most highly recommended outlets for scuba diving is **Blue Ocean Divers,** Estrada de Porto de Mós (Motel Ancora; **© 96/466-56-67;** www.blue-ocean-divers.de), one of the region's few fully licensed and insured scuba outfits. It pays special attention to safety, and its staff focuses on the coastline between Lagos and Sagres, site of numerous underwater caves and (mostly) 20th-century shipwrecks at depths of between 12m (39 ft.) and 35m (115 ft.) beneath the high-tide level. One dive with full equipment costs 50€; a PADI scuba course of 3 days and two dives costs 250€.

GOLF **Palmares Golf,** Meia Praia, 8600 Lagos (℃ **28/279-05-00;** www.palmares
golf.com), is not a particularly prestigious or championship-level course—it's "medium"
in both difficulty and desirability. Frank Pennink designed it in 1975 on land with many
differences in altitude. Some fairways require driving a ball across railroad tracks, over
small ravines, or around palm groves. Its landscaping suggests North Africa, partly
because of its hundreds of palms and almond trees. The view from the 17th green is
exceptionally dramatic. Par is 71. Greens fees are 63€ to 95€, depending on the season.
The course lies on the eastern outskirts of Lagos, less than 1km (⅔ mile) from the
center. To reach it from the heart of town, follow signs toward Meia Praia.

Another course is **Parque da Floresta,** Budens, Vale do Poço, 8650 Vila do Bispo
(℃ **28/269-00-54;** www.parquedafloresta.com). One of the few important Algarvian
courses west of Lagos, it's just inland from the fishing hamlet of Salema. Designed by
the Spanish architect Pepe Gancedo and built as the centerpiece of a complex of
holiday villas completed in 1987, the par-72 course offers sweeping views; we find it
to be more scenic and more challenging than the Palmares course. Some shots must
be driven over vineyards, and others over ravines, creeks, and gardens. Critics of the
course have cited its rough grading and rocky terrain. Some of these drawbacks are
offset by a clubhouse with a sweeping view over the Portuguese coast. Greens fees
are 25€ to 50€ for 9 holes, and 40€ to 95€ for 18. To reach the course from the center of Lagos, drive about 15km (9⅓ miles) west, following road signs toward Sagres
and Parque da Floresta.

Go to **www.algarvegolf.net** for more information on courses in the Algarve
region.

Shopping

At **Terracota,** Praça Luís de Camões (℃ **28/276-33-74**), you'll find pottery from
Spain, art objects from Portugal, and inlaid wood and artfully ornate brass and copper
from Morocco, Tunisia, Egypt, and Greece.

Where to Stay

EXPENSIVE

Romantik Hotel Vivenda Miranda ★★★ 🎁 A real discovery, this small,
Moorish-style hotel towers on a cliff overlooking the coast, 2.8km (1¾ miles) south
of Lagos near the beach of Praia do Porto de Mós. Surrounded by exotic gardens and
terraces, the inn opens onto the most panoramic views of any hotel in the area. Midsize to spacious bedrooms are stylish and exceedingly comfortable, with first-class
tiled bathrooms. This is the kind of hotel that would be ideal for a honeymoon or
romantic getaway. The cuisine in its restaurant is so good that you might want to
indulge in a gourmet dinner featuring organic produce, along with an excellent selection of regional wines.

Porto de Mós, 8600-282 Lagos. www.vivendamiranda.com. ℃ **28/276-32-22.** Fax 28/276-03-42. 28
units. 130€–240€ double; 140€–450€ suite. Rates include buffet breakfast. AE, MC, V. Free parking.
Amenities: Restaurant; bar; babysitting; bikes; outdoor freshwater pool; room service; spa; Wi-Fi (free,
in lobby). *In room:* TV, hair dryer, minibar.

Tivoli Lagos ★ A 20th-century castle of Moorish and Portuguese design, Tivoli
Lagos lies within its own ramparts and moats—okay, a swimming pool and a paddling
pool. It's at the eastern side of the old town, far removed from the beach. This first-class

hotel spreads over 1.2 hilltop hectares (3 acres) overlooking Lagos; no matter which room you're assigned, you'll have a view, even if it's of a sun-trap courtyard with semi-tropical greenery. The main room has a hacienda atmosphere, with white-plaster walls enlivened by sunny colors.

Some of the midsize guest rooms have ground-level patios, but most are on the upper six floors and have a 1960s feel. A 31-room wing, complete with pool and health club, was added in 1989. The hotel owns the Duna Beach Club, on Meia Praia beach, which has a saltwater pool, a restaurant, and three tennis courts; guests have free membership during their stay. A private motorcoach makes regular trips to the beach club, 5 minutes from the hotel.

Rua António Crisógono dos Santos, 8600-678 Lagos. www.tivolihotels.com. © **28/279-00-79.** Fax 28/279-03-45. 324 units. 50€–151€ double; 100€–306€ suite. Rates include buffet breakfast. AE, DC, MC, V. Parking 3€. **Amenities:** 2 restaurants; 2 bars; babysitting; bikes; children's center; health club & spa; 3 freshwater pools (1 heated indoor); room service; 3 outdoor tennis courts (lit); Wi-Fi (free, in lobby). *In room:* A/C, TV, hair dryer, minibar.

MODERATE

Albergaria R Marina Rio   This government-rated four-star hotel is in the center of town opposite the Lagos marina. Its small to midsize guest rooms are nicely decorated, and many open onto views of the sea. On the top floor is a sun terrace with pool overlooking the Bay of Lagos. In summer, a courtesy bus takes guests to the beaches and golfers to the course at Palmares. The biggest problem with staying here is that tour agents from Germany often book all the rooms en masse.

Av. dos Descobrimentos (Abdo. 388), 8600-645 Lagos. www.marinario.com. © **28/276-98-59.** Fax 28/276-99-60. 36 units. 58€–120€ double. Rates include buffet breakfast. AE, MC, V. Parking 10€. **Amenities:** Bar; babysitting; outdoor freshwater pool. *In room:* A/C, TV, hair dryer, Wi-Fi (free).

INEXPENSIVE

Casa da Moura ★ ⚑   The "House of Moors" was built originally in 1892 for a rich Lagos family. It has been brought completely up-to-date with a pool and a rooftop terrace overlooking the Atlantic Ocean. Lying inside the ramparts, a 5-minute walk from the center, the Casa imported much of its raw materials from Morocco. The manor house is filled with wood-lined ceilings, stone and wooden floors, and wide corridors. For rent are two attractively furnished studios and six apartments. All accommodations have a different decoration and color scheme. Breakfast is served on an open air terrace.

Rua Cardeal Neto 10, 8600-645. www.casadamoura.com. © **28/277-07-30.** Fax 28/278-05-89. 8 units. 49€–149€. AE, MC, V. Free parking. **Amenities:** Outdoor pool. *In room:* A/C, TV, hair dryer, kitchenette, Wi-Fi (free).

Where to Dine

MODERATE

Restaurante D. Sebastião ★ REGIONAL PORTUGUESE   This rustically decorated tavern on the main pedestrian street is one of the finest dining choices in Lagos. Portuguese-owned and -operated, it offers a varied menu of local specialties. Options include lip-smacking pork chops with figs, succulent shellfish dishes like clams and shrimp cooked with savory spices, and grills. Live lobsters are kept on the premises. One of the best selections of Portuguese vintage wines in town accompanies the filling, tasty meals. In summer, outdoor dining is available.

Rua do 25 de Abril 20-22. © **28/278-04-80.** www.restaurantedonsebastiao.com. Reservations recommended. Main courses 9€–25€. AE, MC, V. Daily noon–10pm. Closed Dec 24–26 and Dec 31–Jan 2.

Rouxinol ★ PORTUGUESE   Motorists can seek out this restaurant lying 42km (26 miles) from Lagos near the little town of Monchique. Discerning palates know they'll be served some of the best regional cuisine in the area. The first-class restaurant is installed in an old hunting lodge that has been restored by its owner/chef Stefhan. The chef has operated restaurants in West Africa, Morocco, the Canary Islands, and the Caribbean, and has brought the flavors of those exotic destinations with him to his Rouxinol (nightingale, in English). Food is served on an open-air terrace on balmy summer nights. Most guests order the freshly caught fish of the day, although the shellfish stew is the chef's signature dish. We can't wait to sample once again the grilled lamb from the Alentejo, followed by a warm raspberry pie with ice cream.

Estrada de Monchique. ✆ **28/291-39-75.** Reservations required. Main courses 8€–23€. AE, MC, V. Tues–Sun noon–9:30pm (until 10pm in summer). Closed Dec–Jan.

Lagos After Dark

You'll find hints of big-city life in Lagos and a devoted cadre of night owls. On Rua Cândido dos Reis, are lots of hot spots including **Inside Out Bar,** Rua Cândido dos Reis 119 (no phone), with a fun staff and the largest *carte* of drinks in town. It usually stays open until 4am. Equally popular is the **Red Eye,** Rua Cândido dos Reis 63 (no phone), attracting a lot of Londoners and Aussies as well, who pile in here for the inexpensive drinks and the rock music. It's said to be the best place to find a partner (of either sex) for the night. It stays open until 2am.

PORTIMÃO

18km (11 miles) E of Lagos; 61km (38 miles) W of Faro; 290km (180 miles) SE of Lisbon

Portimão is perfect if you want to stay in a bustling fishing port rather than a hotel perched right on the beach. Since the 1930s, **Praia da Rocha ★★**, 3km (1¾ miles) away, has snared sun-loving traffic. Today it's challenged by Praia dos Três Irmãos, but tourists still flock to Portimão in the summer.

The aroma of the noble Portuguese sardine permeates every street. Portimão is the leading fish-canning center in the Algarve. For a change of pace, this town, on an arm of the Arcade River, makes a good stopover for its fine dining. Stroll through its gardens and its shops (especially noted for their pottery), drink wine in the cafes, and roam down to the quays to see sardines roasting on braziers. The routine activity of the Algarvians is what gives the town its charm.

Essentials

ARRIVING

BY TRAIN   From Lagos (p. 217), trains on the Algarve Line run frequently throughout the day to Portimão. The trip takes 15 minutes and costs 1.50€. For information and schedules, phone ✆ **80/820-82-08.**

BY BUS   An express bus from Lisbon makes the 3½-hour trip and costs 19€. A bus runs from the beach at Portimão, 3km (1¾ miles) away. For **information** and schedules, call ✆ **28/989-97-60** or consult **www.eva-bus.com**.

BY CAR   The main highway across the southern coast, Route 125, makes a wide arch north on its eastern run to Portimão.

VISITOR INFORMATION

At Praia da Rocha, the **tourist office** (② **28/247-07-32;** www.visitalgarve.pt) is on Avenida Zeca Alfonso and is open daily 9:30am to 1pm and 2 to 5:30pm (closes in summer at 7pm).

Exploring the Town

Although it lacks great monuments and museums, Portimão is worth exploring. Just wander through its colorful streets, stopping at any sight that interests you. The once-colorful fishing boats used to unload their catch here at the port but have moved to a terminal across the river. High-rise buildings ring the area, but the core of the old town is still intact.

Try to be in Portimão for lunch. Of course, you can dine at a restaurant, but it's even more fun to walk down to the harborside, where you can find a table at one of the low-cost eateries. The specialty is chargrilled sardines, which taste like nothing you get from a can. They make an inexpensive meal accompanied by chewy, freshly baked bread; a salad; and a carafe of regional wine. If you're in town in August, stay for the **Sardine Festival** (dates vary), where the glory that is the Portuguese sardine is honored, lauded, and, finally, devoured.

If you'd like to go sightseeing, you can visit **Ferragudo,** a satellite of Portimão, 5km (3 miles) east and accessible by bridge. The beach area here is being developed rapidly but remains largely unspoiled. The sandy beach lies to the south, and kiosks rent sailboards and sell seafood from a number of waterside restaurants. In the center you can see the ruins of the **Castelo de São João,** which was constructed to defend Portimão from English, Spanish, and Dutch raids. There's no need to return to Portimão for lunch.

At Praia da Rocha, 3km (1¾ miles) south of Portimão, you can explore the ruins of the 16th-century **Fortaleza de Santa Catarina,** Avenida Tomás Cabreira, which was constructed for defensive purposes.

Outdoor Activities

BEACHES Even those staying in Portimão head for the beach first thing in the morning. The favorite is **Praia da Rocha,** a creamy yellow strand that has long been the most popular seaside resort on the Algarve. English voyagers discovered the beauty of its rock formations around 1935. At the outbreak of World War II, there were only two small hotels and a few villas on the Red Coast, most built by wealthy Portuguese. Nowadays, Praia da Rocha is booming. At the end of the mussel-encrusted cliff, where the Arcade flows into the sea, lie the ruins of the Fortress of Santa Catarina. The location offers views of Portimão's satellite, Ferragudo, and of the bay.

Although **Praia dos Três Irmãos** is more expensive, you might want to visit its beach, 5km (3 miles) southwest of Portimão. From Portimão's center, you can take a public bus; they run frequently throughout the day. The bus is marked PRAIA DOS TRÊS IRMÃOS. Departures are from the main bus terminal in Portimão, at Largo do Duque (② **28/989-97-60**).

Praia dos Três Irmãos has 15km (9⅓ miles) of burnished golden sand, interrupted only by an occasional crag riddled with arched passageways. This beach has been discovered by skin divers who explore its undersea grottoes and caves.

Nearby is the whitewashed fishing village of Alvor, where Portuguese and Moorish arts and traditions have mingled since the Arab occupation ended. Alvor was a favorite

Portimão

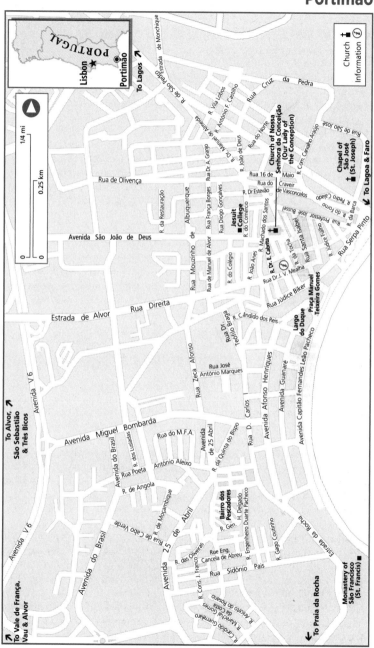

Church ✚
Information ⓘ

PORTUGAL
Lisbon ★
Portimão ⦿
To Lagos →

1/4 mi
0.25 km

Estrada de Monchique
R. de São Pedro
Rua Vila Lobos
Rua R. Antonio F. Castilho
Dr. Manuel de Almeida
Rua Cruz da Pedra
Rua do Norte
R. João de Deus
Church of Nossa Senhora da Conceição (Our Lady of the Conception)
Rua de São José
R. Com. Carvalho Araújo
Chapel of São José (St. Joseph)
→ To Lagoa & Faro

Rua de Olivença
R. da Restauração
Albuquerque
Rua Franca Borges
Rua Dr. A. Granjo
Rua Diogo Gonçalves
Rua 16 de Maio
Rua do Craveir de Vasconcelos
R. Dr.Estêvão
Rua Professor José Bussel
R. do Forno
R. Pedro C. Calado
R. da Boca

Avenida São João de Deus
Rua Mouzinho de Albuquerque
Rua de Manuel de Alvor
R. do Colégio
Jesuit College
R. do Comércio
R. Machado dos Santos
R. João Aires
R. da Rocha
R. Dr. E. Cabrita
Rua Santa Isabel
Rua Dr.J. V. Mealha
Rua Júdice Fialho
Rua Serpa Pinto

Estrada de Alvor
Rua Direita
Rua Dr. Teófilo Braga
R. Cândido dos Reis
Rua Júdice Biker
Praça Manuel Teixeira Gomes
Largo do Duque
Avenida Capitão Fernandes Leão Pacheco

↖ To Alvor, São Sebastião & Três Bicos
Avenida V 6

Rua Zeca Afonso
Rua José António Marques

Avenida Miguel Bombarda
Avenida do Brasil
Rua dos Lusíadas
Rua Poeta António Aleixo
Rua do M.F.A.
Rua da Quinta do Bispo
Avenida de 25 Abril
Rua D. Carlos
Avenida Afonso Henriques
Avenida Guanaré

↖ To Vale de França, Vau & Alvor
Avenida V 6
Avenida do Brasil
R. de Angola
Avenida 2,5 de Abril
Rua de Moçambique
Av. de Cabo Verde
R. das Oliveiras
Cancela de Abreu
Rue Eng.
Rua Sidónio Pais
R. Gen. H. Delgado
Bairro dos Pescadores
R. Engenheiro Duarte Pacheco
R. Gago Coutinho
Estrada da Rocha

R. Cândido Guerreiro
R. Marechal Gomes da Costa
R. Aníbal do Aposno
R. Cons. J. Franco
Monastery of São Francisco (St. Francis) ■

↓ To Praia da Rocha

9

THE ALGARVE | Portimão

coastal haunt of João II, and now summer hordes descend on the long strip of sandy beach. It's not the best in the area, but at least you'll have plenty of space. Alvor is accessible by public bus from Portimão's center.

GOLF Penina (© 28/242-02-00; www.lemeridienpenina.com) is 5km (3 miles) west of the center of Portimão, farther west than many of the other great golf courses. Completed in 1966, it was one of the first courses in the Algarve and the universally acknowledged masterpiece of the British designer Sir Henry Cotton. It replaced a network of marshy rice paddies on level terrain that critics said was unsuited for anything except wetlands. The solution involved planting groves of eucalyptus (350,000 trees in all), which grew quickly in the muddy soil. Eventually they dried it out enough for the designer to bulldoze dozens of water traps and a labyrinth of fairways and greens. The course wraps around a luxury hotel (Le Méridien Penina Golf & Resort). You can play the main championship course (18 holes, par 73), and two 9-hole satellite courses, Academy and Resort. Greens fees for the 18-hole course are 50€ to 120€; for either of the 9-hole courses, they're 33€ to 65€. To reach it from the center of Portimão, follow signs to Lagos, turning off at the signpost for Le Méridien Penina Golf & Resort.

Amid tawny-colored rocks and arid hillocks, **Vale de Pinta** (© 28/234-09-00; www.pestanagolf.com), Praia do Carvoeiro, sends players through groves of twisted olive, almond, carob, and fig trees. Views from the fairways, designed in 1992 by Californian Ronald Fream, sweep over the low masses of the Monchique mountains, close to the beach resort of Carvoeiro. Experts say it offers some of the most varied challenges in Portuguese golf. Clusters of "voracious" bunkers, barrier walls of beige-colored rocks assembled without mortar, and abrupt changes in elevation complicate the course. Par is 71. Greens fees are 60€ to 90€. From Portimão, drive 14km (8⅔ miles) east on N125, following signs to Lagoa and Vale de Pinta/Pestana Golf.

Visit **www.algarvegolf.net** for more information on courses in the Algarve region.

Shopping

The fishers unload their boats by tossing up wicker baskets full of freshly caught fish Monday through Saturday between 9:30 and 10:30am. Fish, fruit, and vegetable markets are held every morning (except Sun) until 2pm in the market building and open square. On the first Monday of every month, a gigantic daylong regional market sells local artifacts, pottery, wicker, and even snake oil. Boutiques offering the Algarve's best selection of sweaters, porcelain, and pottery abound.

You'll find modern, Pan-European commercialism in this once-sleepy fishing village—most noticeably on such busy shopping streets as **Rua Comerciale** and **Rua Vasco da Gama.** Goods include hand-knit sweaters, hand-painted porcelains, and tons of pottery from factories and individual artisans throughout Portugal. Some of the best of it is available from two connected stores, **Aquarius I** and **II** (Rua Vasco da Gama 42 and 46; © 28/242-66-73). Look for knitwear, ceramics, pottery, leatherwear, and woodcarvings.

Where to Stay

Hotels are limited in the center of Portimão, but Praia da Rocha has one of the largest concentrations on the Algarve. Praia dos Três Irmãos, though less developed, is the challenger to Praia da Rocha. In summer, don't even consider arriving at one of these beachfront establishments without a reservation.

CENTRAL PORTIMÃO
Inexpensive
Albergaria Miradouro Albergaria Miradouro benefits from a central location on a quiet square opposite an ornate Manueline church. Its modern facade is banded with concrete balconies. A few of the no-frills guest rooms, which are rather small, have terraces. Furnishings are meager, but the beds are reasonably comfortable. All units have well-maintained bathrooms equipped with tub/shower combinations and decent plumbing. Here you're likely to meet an array of European backpackers eager to converse and share travelers' tales. Motorists can usually find a parking space in the square just opposite the hotel.

Rua Machado Santos 13, 8500-581 Portimão. ✆/fax **28/242-30-11.** 25 units. 40€–70€ double. Rates include buffet breakfast. No credit cards. *In room:* TV.

Hotel Globo ★ Despite its location in the heart of the old town, the Globo is contemporary. A first-class hotel, it's recommended for its good design. Snug modern balconies overlook the tile rooftops crusted with moss. In 1967, the owner and manager imported an architect to turn his inn into a top-notch hotel. Each midsize guest room exhibits good taste in layout and furnishings: matching ebony panels on the wardrobes, built-in headboards, and marble desks. Each unit also has a well-maintained bathroom with a tub/shower combination.

On the ground floor is an uncluttered, attractive lounge with an adjoining bar. Crowning the top floor is a dining room, open for breakfast only. Its four glass walls permit unblocked views of the harbor, ocean, or mountains.

Rua do 5 de Outubro 26, 8500-581 Portimão. www.hoteisalgarvesol.pt. ✆ **28/240-50-30.** Fax 28/248-31-42. 71 units. 43€–105€ double; 70€–142€ junior suite. Rates include buffet breakfast. AE, DC, MC, V. **Amenities:** Restaurant; bar; bikes; exercise room; room service; sauna; Wi-Fi (5€ per hour, in lobby). *In room:* A/C, TV, hair dryer.

PRAIA DA ROCHA
Expensive
Hotel Algarve Casino ★★★ The leading hotel in this area is strictly for those who love glitter and glamour and don't object to the prices. With a vast staff at your beck and call, you'll be well provided for in this elongated block of rooms poised securely on the top ledge of a cliff. The midsize to spacious guest rooms have white walls, colored ceilings, intricate tile floors, mirrored entryways, indirect lighting, balconies with garden furniture, and bathrooms with separate tub/shower combinations. Many are vaguely Moorish in design, and many have terraces opening onto the sea. The Yachting, Oriental, Presidential, and Miradouro suites are decorative tours de force.

Av. Tomás Cabreira, Praia da Rocha, 8500-802 Portimão. www.solverde.pt. ✆ **28/240-20-00.** Fax 28/240-20-99. 208 units. 78€–248€ double; 121€–452€ suite. Rates include buffet breakfast. AE, DC, MC, V. Parking 12€. **Amenities:** 2 restaurants; 2 bars; babysitting; children's center; exercise room; Jacuzzi; 2 seawater pools (1 heated indoor); room service; sauna; 2 outdoor tennis courts (lit); limited watersports equipment/rentals. *In room:* A/C, TV, hair dryer, minibar, free Wi-Fi (in some).

Moderate
Hotel Júpiter Hotel Júpiter occupies the most prominent street corner in this bustling summer resort. Boutiques fill the wraparound arcade, and guests relax, sometimes with drinks, on comfortable couches in the lobby. The midsize guest rooms are comfortably modern but uninspired. They have balconies with views of the

river or the sea. The hotel is just across from a wide beach. The Blexus dance club provides late-night diversion.

Av. Tomás Cabreira, Praia da Rocha, 8500-802 Portimão. www.hoteljupiter.com. ℭ **28/247-04-70.** Fax 28/241-53-19. 180 units. 40€–160€ double; 80€–195€ junior suite. Rates include buffet breakfast. AE, DC, MC, V. **Amenities:** Restaurant; bar; babysitting; exercise room; outdoor freshwater heated pool; room service; spa; Wi-Fi (5€ per hour, in lobby). *In room:* A/C, TV, hair dryer, minibar.

Inexpensive

Residencial Sol ⚑ Partly because of its location near the noisy main street, the painted concrete facade of this establishment appears somewhat bleak. In this case, however, appearances are deceiving. The small to midsize guest rooms offer some of the tidiest, least pretentious, most attractive accommodations in town. Each unit is designed for two and contains a neatly kept bathroom. The accommodations in back are quieter, but the front units (some with terrace) look across the traffic toward a bougainvillea-filled park.

Av. Tomás Cabreira 10, Praia da Rocha, 8500-802 Portimão. ℭ **28/242-40-71.** Fax 28/241-99-44. 30 units. 50€–65€ double. Rates include continental breakfast. AE, DC, MC, V. Closed Nov–Mar. *In room:* No phone.

PRAIA DOS TRÊS IRMÃOS
Expensive

Le Méridien Penina Golf & Resort ★★★ Located between Portimão and Lagos, this property was the first deluxe hotel to be built on the Algarve. Nowadays it has serious competition from the other luxury hotels, but fans of golf (see "Outdoor Activities," above) remain loyal to the Penina. It's a big sporting mecca and stands next to the Algarve's major casino. Besides the golf courses, the hotel has a private beach with its own snack bar and changing cabins, reached by a shuttle bus.

Most of the guest rooms contain picture windows and honeycomb balconies with views of the course and pool, or vistas of the Monchique hills. The standard rooms are furnished pleasantly, combining traditional pieces with Portuguese provincial spool beds. All rooms are spacious, with well-stocked bathrooms and good-size beds. The so-called attic rooms have the most charm, with French doors opening onto terraces. On the fourth floor are some duplexes, often preferred by families.

Estrada Nacional 125, 8501-952 Portimão. www.starwoodhotels.com. ℭ **800/225-5843** in the U.S., or 28/242-02-00. Fax 28/242-03-00. 196 units. 116€–290€ double; 267€–509€ junior suite. Rates include buffet breakfast. AE, DC, MC, V. Free parking. **Amenities:** 5 restaurants; 3 bars; babysitting; bikes; children's programs; 3 golf courses; outdoor freshwater pool; room service; sauna; 6 outdoor tennis courts (lit); extensive watersports equipment/rentals; Wi-Fi (5€ per hour, in lobby). *In room:* A/C, TV, hair dryer, minibar.

Pestana Alvor Praia ★★★ This citadel of hedonism, built in 1968 and constantly renewed, has more *joie de vivre* than any other hotel on the Algarve. Its location, good-size guest rooms, decor, service, and food are ideal. "You'll feel as if you're loved the moment you walk in the door," one guest of the hotel told us. Poised regally on a landscaped crest, many of the guest and public rooms face the ocean, the gardens, and the free-form Olympic-size pool. Gentle walks and an elevator lead down the palisade to the sandy beach and the rugged rocks that rise out of the water.

Accommodations vary from a cowhide-decorated room evoking Arizona's Valley of the Sun to typical Portuguese-style rooms with rustic furnishings. Most contain oversize beds, plenty of storage space, long desk-and-chest combinations, and well-designed bathrooms. All rooms have balconies and most have sea views.

Praia dos Três Irmãos, Alvor, 8501-904 Portimão. www.pestana.com. © **28/240-09-00.** Fax 28/240-09-75. 195 units. 82€–300€ double; 140€–460€ suite. Rates include buffet breakfast. AE, DC, MC, V. Free parking. **Amenities:** 2 restaurants; 2 bars; babysitting; bikes; health club; 3 saltwater pools (1 heated indoor); room service; sauna; 7 outdoor tennis courts (lit); Wi-Fi (18€ per 24 hr., in lobby). *In room:* A/C, TV, hair dryer, minibar.

Pestana Delfim ★★ The developers of this all-inclusive haven chose their site wisely; it's near the beach Três Irmãos, on a scrub-covered hillside which offers a sweeping view of the coastline and its dozens of high-rises. With a central tower and identical wings splayed like a boomerang in flight, the hotel, a well-designed landmark originally built in 1982 and frequently renovated since then, is one of the region's most dramatic modern buildings. In spite of the proximity of the beach, many guests prefer the parasol-ringed pool, which encloses a swim-up bar. Each well-furnished, midsize guest room has a private terrace.

Praia dos Três Irmãos, 8501-904 Alvor. www.pestana.com. © **28/240-08-00.** Fax 28/240-08-99. 312 units. 166€–312€ double; 213€–356€ suite. Rates include all meals and drinks. AE, DC, MC, V. **Amenities:** Restaurant; 3 bars; babysitting; exercise room; Jacuzzi; 2 saltwater pools (1 heated indoor); room service; sauna. *In room:* A/C, TV, hair dryer, minibar (in some).

Where to Dine

If you're sightseeing in Portimão, you might want to seek out a restaurant here; otherwise, most people dine along the beaches, especially those at Praia da Rocha and Praia dos Três Irmãos. All the major hotels have at least one deluxe or first-class restaurant. There's a wide selection catering to a range of budgets.

PRAIA DA ROCHA

Bamboo Garden ★ ❚❚ CHINESE Bamboo Garden, which has a classic Asian decor, serves some of the best Chinese food on the coast. The large menu includes everything from squid chop suey to prawns with hot sauce. After deciding on a soup or an appetizer (try the spring roll), guests can select from various categories, including chicken, beef, squid, and prawns. You might, for example, try fried duck with soybean sauce or chicken with almonds from the Algarve. Peking duck is the chef's specialty. This air-conditioned spot is a safe haven for reliable food when you've overdosed on Portuguese codfish.

Edifício Lamego, Loja 1, Av. Tomás Cabreira. © **28/248-30-83.** Reservations recommended. Main courses 10€–18€. DC, MC, V. Daily 12:30–3pm and 6–11:30pm.

Restaurante Titanic ★★★ INTERNATIONAL Replete with gilt and crystal, the 100-seat air-conditioned Titanic is the most elegant restaurant in town. Its open kitchen serves the best food in Praia da Rocha, including shellfish and flambé dishes. Despite the name, it's not on—or in, thank goodness—the water, but in a modern residential complex. You can dine very well here on such appealing dishes as the fish of the day, pork filet with mushrooms, prawns *a la plancha* (grilled on a plank of wood), Chinese fondue, or excellent sole Algarve. Service is among the best in town.

In the Edifício Colúmbia, Rua Eng. Francisco Bivar. © **28/242-23-71.** www.titanic.com.pt. Reservations recommended, especially in summer. Main courses 12€–32€. AE, DC, MC, V. Daily 7pm–midnight. Closed Nov 27–Dec 27.

Safari ★ ❚❚AFRICAN/PORTUGUESE Safari is a Portuguese-run restaurant with a "taste of Africa" in its cuisine; the former Portuguese colony of Angola inspired many of its savory specialties. The name also suggests a faux-African tourist trap, but this

MONCHIQUE: ESCAPE TO THE COOL mountains

The Monchique range of hills is the Algarve at its coolest and highest. The rocky peak of the range, some 900m (2,953 ft.) high, looks down on forested slopes and green valleys, burgeoning with orange groves, Indian corn, heather, mimosa, rosemary, oleander bushes, and cork-oak, chestnut, pine, and eucalyptus trees. Icy water springs from the volcanic rock that makes up the range, flowing down to the foothills.

The largest town in the borough, also named Monchique, lies on the east side of Mount Fóia, 26km (16 miles) north of Portimão. The town was once engaged in the manufacture of wooden casks and barrels and the making of oakum and rough cloth. The Manueline-style parish church, with its interesting radiated door facing, dates from the 16th century. Colorful decorated tiles and carved woodwork grace the interior, along with a statue of Our Lady of the Immaculate Conception, an 18th-century work attributed to Machado de Castro. The convent of Nossa Senhora do Desterro is in ruins, but you can look at the curious tiled fountain and the impressive old magnolia tree on its grounds.

Caldas de Monchique was discovered in Roman days and turned into a spa.

The waters, from springs in volcanic rock, are still considered good treatment for respiratory disorders, accompanied as they are by the clear air of the highlands.

Nearly 13km (8 miles) from the town of Monchique, Alferce, nestled among trees and mountains, has traces of an ancient fortification. There's also an important handicraft center here. In the opposite direction, about 13km (8 miles) west of Monchique, is Fóia, the highest point in the Algarve. From here you have splendid views of the hills and the sea.

A small inn in the town of Monchique, the **Estalagem Abrigo da Montanha,** 8550-257 Monchique (℡ **28/291-21-31;** fax 28/291-36-60; www.abrigodamontanha.com), is in a botanical garden. With all the blooming camellias, rhododendrons, mimosa, banana palms, and arbutus, plus the tinkling waterfalls, you'd never believe the hot Algarve coast was in the same province. The inn has 11 doubles and three suites. Rates are 60€ to 85€ for a double or 80€ to 105€ for a suite, including breakfast. On chilly evenings, guests gather before a fireplace in the lounge.

place isn't. Safari offers good value and is known for its commendable fresh fish and seafood. Many guests in neighboring hotels escape their board requirements just to sample the good home-cooked meals. On summer weekends you might hear live Brazilian or African music. The fare includes steak, curries, and shrimp, and such dishes as swordfish steak in pepper sauce, charcoal-grilled fresh fish, and *bacalhau a Safari* (fried codfish with olive oil, garlic, and peppers, served with homemade potato chips). It's customary to begin with a bowl of savory fish soup. The building stands on a cliff overlooking the beach and has a glass-enclosed terrace.

Rua António Feu. ℡ **28/242-35-40.** Reservations recommended. Main courses 9€–21€. AE, DC, MC, V. Daily noon–midnight. Closed Dec.

PRAIA DOS TRÊS IRMÃOS

Restaurante Búzio ★ INTERNATIONAL   Restaurante Búzio stands at the end of a road encircling a resort development dotted with private condos and exotic shrubbery. In summer, so many cars line the narrow road that you'll probably need to park near the resort's entrance and then walk downhill to the restaurant. Dinner is served in a room whose blue curtains reflect the shimmering ocean at the bottom of the cliffs. Your meal might include excellent fish soup, refreshing gazpacho, or *carré de borrego Serra de Estrela* (gratinée of roast rack of lamb with garlic, butter, and mustard). Other good choices are Italian pasta dishes, boiled or grilled fish of the day, flavorful pepper steak, and lamb kabobs with saffron-flavored rice. The restaurant maintains an extensive wine cellar.

Aldeamento da Prainha, Praia dos Três Irmãos. *C* **28/245-87-72.** www.restaurantebuzio.com. Reservations recommended. Main courses 10€–30€; fixed-price menus at 30€–54€. AE, DC, MC, V. Daily 7–10:30pm. Closed Dec 15–Jan 7.

Portimão After Dark

The town center has about a dozen *tascas* (taverns) and bodegas, but you might be happier with the glossier after-dark venues in internationally minded Praia da Rocha. Many bars and pubs, as well as the resort's casino (see below), line Avenida Tomás Cabreira. Depending on your mood, you might enjoy popping in and out of several of them—a ritual akin to a London pub-crawl. The most active and intriguing hangouts include **Farmer's Bar,** Rua Engenheiro José Bívar Edifício Serra Mar-lj 10 (*C* **28/242-57-20**), which serves wine, beer, and cocktails. It's open daily from 10am to 4am. Danceaholics and devoted night owls appreciate the shenanigans at **Disco Pé de Vento,** Avenida Tomás Cabreira (no phone). It gets going after midnight every night in high season and remains open until the last person staggers off the next morning. The cover charge is 10€.

Casino Praia da Rocha ★ is on the glittering premises of the five-star Hotel Algarve Casino, Avenida Tomás Cabreira (*C* **28/240-20-00**). Its gaming tables and slot machines open every night at 4pm and shut down at 3am, or later if business warrants. Its entertainment highlight is the cabaret show, featuring lots of dancers in spangles and feathers, magicians, and a master of ceremonies telling not-very-subtle jokes. Dinner, served beginning at 8:30pm, precedes the show and costs 45€. If you skip dinner, the entrance fee of 14€ includes the first drink. Showtime is 11pm. Also look for other forms of entertainment, such as live concerts or fado.

SILVES ★

6.5km (4 miles) N of Lagoa; 11km (6¾ miles) NE of Carvoeiro

When you pass through its Moorish-inspired entrance, you'll quickly realize that Silves is unlike other towns and villages of the Algarve. It lives in the past, recalling its heyday when it was known as Xelb. It was the seat of Muslim culture in the south before it fell to the Crusaders. Christian warriors and earthquakes have been rough on Silves.

The Castle of Silves, crowning the hilltop, has held on, although it has seen better days. Once the blood of the Muslims, staging their last stand in Silves, "flowed like red wine," as one Portuguese historian wrote. The cries and screams of women and children resounded over the walls. Nowadays the only sound you're likely to hear is the loud rock music coming from the gatekeeper's house. Silves is most often visited on a day trip from one of the beach towns to the south.

Essentials

ARRIVING

BY TRAIN   Trains from Faro serve the Silves train station, 1.8km (1 mile) from the center of the town. For information, call ℂ **80/820-82-08.**

BY CAR   Coming east or west along Route 125, the main road traversing the Algarve, you arrive at the town of Lagoa (not to be confused with Lagos). From there, head north to Silves along Route 124.

VISITOR INFORMATION

The **tourist office** (ℂ **28/244-22-55;** www.visitalgarve.pt) is located on Rua 25 de Abril and is open Monday to Friday 9:30am to 12:30pm and 2 to 5pm.

Exploring the Town

The red-sandstone **Castelo dos Mouros** ★ (ℂ **28/244-56-24**) might date from the 9th century. From its ramparts you can look out on the saffron-colored, mossy tile roofs of the village houses down the narrow cobblestone streets where roosters strut and scrappy dogs sleep peacefully in doorways. Inside the walls, the government has planted a flower garden with golden chrysanthemums and scarlet poinsettias. In the fortress, water rushes through a huge cistern and a deep well made of sandstone. Below are dungeon chambers and labyrinthine tunnels where the last of the Moors hid out before the Crusaders found them and sent them to their deaths. The site is open daily from 9am to 5pm (until 7pm in summer). Admission is 3.50€ and free for children 11 and under.

The 13th-century former **Cathedral of Silves** ★ (ℂ **28/244-08-00**), on Rua de Sé, was built in the Gothic style. It is one of the most outstanding religious monuments in the Algarve. The aisles and nave are beautiful in their simplicity. The flamboyant Gothic style of both the chancel and the transept dates from a later period. The Christian architects who originally constructed the cathedral might have torn down an old mosque to do so. Many of the tombs here are believed to be the graves of Crusaders who took the town in 1244. It's open daily from 8:30am to 1pm and 2:30 to 5:30pm, and until 6pm from June to September. Admission is free, but donations are welcome.

The best artifacts found in the area are on display at the **Museu Arqueologia,** Rua das Portas de Loulé (ℂ **28/244-48-32**), a short walk from the Sé. The museum's major sight is an ancient Arab water cistern preserved as part of a 9m-deep (30-ft.) well. Admission is 2.50€. It's open Monday to Saturday 9am to 6pm.

Outside the main part of town, on the road to Enxerim, near an orange grove, a lonely open-air pavilion shelters a 15th-century stone lacework cross. This ecclesiastical artwork, **Cruz de Portugal,** is two-faced, depicting a *pietà* (the face of Christ is destroyed) on one side and the Crucifixion on the other. It has been declared a national monument of incalculable value. A guide isn't really necessary, but if you'd like, one of the local boys will serve as your guide for a modest fee.

Where to Stay

Colina dos Mouros Hotel ★ 🏨   On the outskirts of town, this modern inn at last provides a decent place to stay in the historic town of Silves. Only a short walk from the historic core, the well-managed and well-furnished hotel offers midsize to spacious bedrooms that are comfortably and immaculately kept. You approach the hotel across a Roman bridge spanning the River Arade. Enveloped by gardens, the hotel is completely modern and up-to-date. The building opens onto views of the rooftops of Silves and its major monuments. Beaches are a short drive from the inn.

Pocinho Santo, 8300-999 Silves. www.colinahotels.com. ✆ **28/244-04-20.** Fax 28/244-04-26. 57 units. 37€–72€ double. AE, MC, V. Free parking. **Amenities:** Restaurant; 2 bars; bikes; outdoor freshwater pool. *In room:* A/C, TV, hair dryer.

Where to Dine

Rui I PORTUGUESE   This regional restaurant, decorated with whitewashed walls and Algarvian handicrafts, draws more locals than visitors. The cooking is competent and hearty, the way the townspeople like it. Many dishes such as roast lamb are remembered fondly from the diners' childhoods. Most patrons are attracted to the fish, which is delivered fresh every morning from the coast down below. Our favorite dish here is the herb-flavored kettle of shellfish rice, the local version of paella. In the autumn the chef prepares savory game dishes, especially partridge, wild boar, and Algarvian rabbit.

Rua Comendador Vilarim 27. ✆ **28/244-26-82.** Main courses 9€–26€. AE, MC, V. Wed–Mon noon–3:30pm and 6:30–10:30pm.

ALBUFEIRA ★

37km (23 miles) W of Faro; 325km (202 miles) SE of Lisbon

This cliffside town, formerly a fishing village, is the St. Tropez of the Algarve. The lazy life, sunshine, and beaches make it a haven for young people and artists, although the old-timers still regard the invasion that began in the late 1960s with some ambivalence. That development turned Albufeira into the largest resort in the region. Some residents open the doors of their cottages to those seeking a place to stay. Travelers with less money often sleep in tents.

Essentials

ARRIVING

BY TRAIN   Trains run between Albufeira and Faro (see "Faro," later), which has good connections to Lisbon. For schedule information, call ✆ **80/820-82-08.** The train station lies 6.5km (4 miles) from the town's center. Buses from the station to the resort run every 30 minutes; the fare is 3.50€ one-way.

BY BUS   Buses run between Albufeira and Faro every hour. Trip time is 1 hour, and a one-way ticket costs 4.50€. Twenty-three buses per day make the 1-hour trip from Portimão to Albufeira. It costs 4.30€ one-way. For information and schedules, call ✆ **28/989-97-60.**

BY CAR   From east or west, take the main coastal route, N125. Albufeira also lies near the point where the express highway from the north, N264, feeds into the Algarve. The town is well signposted in all directions. Take Route 595 to reach Albufeira and the water.

VISITOR INFORMATION

The **Tourist Information Office** is at Rua do 5 de Outubro (✆ **28/958-52-79;** www.visitalgarve.com). From July to September, hours are daily from 9:30am to 7pm; October to June, they're from 10am to 5:30pm.

Exploring the Town

With steep streets and villas staggered up and down the hillside, Albufeira resembles a North African seaside community. The big, bustling resort town rises above a sickle-shape beach that shines in the bright sunlight. A rocky, grottoed bluff separates the strip used by sunbathers from the working beach, where brightly painted fishing boats are drawn up on the sand. Access to the beach is through a tunneled rock passageway.

After walking Albufeira's often hot but intriguing streets, you can escape and cool off at **Zoomarine,** N125, Guia (© **28/956-03-00;** www.zoomarine.pt), 6.5km (4 miles) northwest. It's a popular water park, with rides, swimming pools, gardens, and even sea lion and dolphin shows. Opening hours are March 1 to June 19 and September 3 to October 31 Tuesday to Sunday 10am to 6pm, June 20 to September 2 Tuesday to Sunday 10am to 7:30pm. Admission is 25€ for adults and 16€ for children 10 and under.

Outdoor Activities

BEACHES   Some of the best beaches—but also the most crowded—are near Albufeira. They include Falésia, Olhos d'Água, and Praia da Oura. Albufeira, originally discovered by the British, is now the busiest resort on the Algarve. To avoid the crowds on Albufeira's main beaches, head west for 4km (2½ miles) on a local road to São Rafael and Praia da Galé. You might also go east to the beach at Olhos d'Água.

GOLF   Many pros consider the extremely well-maintained **Pine Cliffs** course, Praia da Falésia 644, 8200 Albufeira (© **28/950-01-00;** www.pinecliffs.com), relaxing but not boring. It has only 9 holes scattered over a relatively compact area. Opened in 1990, its fairways meander beside copper-colored cliffs that drop 75m (246 ft.) down to a sandy beach. Par is 33. The green fees are 39€ to 49€ for Sheraton Algarve Hotel guests and 45€ to 59€ for nonguests. The course lies 6.5km (4 miles) west of Vilamoura and less than 5km (3 miles) east of Albufeira. To reach it from Albufeira, follow signs to the hamlet of Olhos d'Água, where more signs direct you to the Sheraton Algarve Hotel and Pine Cliffs.

Visit **www.algarvegolf.net** for more information on courses in the Algarve region.

Shopping

One of the busiest resorts along the Algarve, Albufeira maintains an almost alarming roster of seafront kiosks, many selling fun-in-the-sun products of dubious (or, at best, transient) value. The main shopping areas are along Rua do 5 de Outubro and Praça Duarte de Pacheco. An even denser collection of merchandise is on display in the town's largest shopping plaza, **Modelo Shopping Center,** Rua do Município, about .5km (⅓ mile) north of the town center. Most of the independently operated shops inside are open daily from 10am to 10pm. Although Albufeira produces limited amounts of ceramics, you'll find a wide selection of pottery and glazed terra cotta from throughout Portugal at the **Infante Dom Henrique House,** Rua Cândido do Reis 30 (© **28/951-32-67**). Also look for woven baskets and woodcarvings.

Where to Stay

Though Albufeira has many accommodations, many establishments charge rates more suited to the middle-of-the-road traveler than to the young people who favor the place. Below are some of the best options for all price ranges.

THE ALGARVE | Albufeira

EXPENSIVE

Club Med da Balaïa ★ On 16 hectares (40 acres) of sun-drenched scrubland about 6.5km (4 miles) east of Albufeira, this all-inclusive high-rise resort is one of the most stable in the Club Med empire. Favored by vacationers from northern Europe, it encompasses a shoreline of rugged rock formations indented with a private beach and a series of coves for surf swimming. The small accommodations have twin beds, two safes, and piped-in music. They're decorated in understated, uncluttered style, with private balconies or terraces. Many vacationers here appreciate the nearby golf course; others opt to participate in semiorganized sports. Meals are usually consumed at communal tables; there are many lunchtime buffets and copious amounts of local wine.

Praia Maria Luisa, 8200-854 Albufeira. www.clubmed.com. ℂ **800/CLUB-MED** (258-2633) in the U.S., or 28/951-05-00. Fax 28/958-71-79. 372 units. 275€–570€ double. Rates include full board and use of most sports facilities. Children 4-12 20% discount in parent's room. AE, DC, MC, V. Free parking. Closed mid-Oct to mid-Apr. **Amenities:** 3 restaurants; 3 bars; children's center; exercise room; 9-hole golf course; outdoor freshwater pool; room service; spa; 7 outdoor tennis courts (lit). *In room:* A/C, TV, hair dryer, minibar.

Real Bellavista ★★ ☺ The finest hotel within the town center, Real Bellavista is a luxurious government-rated four-star hotel that has the aura of a city hotel but the facilities of a holiday resort. A favorite with European families, it can also be an adult retreat, lying 1.5km (1 mile) from the beach to which a courtesy hotel bus runs frequently. Bedrooms come in a wide range, including "classic" accommodations with twin beds, balconies, and a tiled bathroom. More expensive are the premium rooms which are more spacious. Even roomier and better equipped are the junior and executive suites, the latter with a separate living room. The spa and health club is one of the finest in the area; a team of hydrotherapists, beauticians, masseurs, and fitness trainers await you. Guests with children can patronize at Mini Club at the hotel's sister, Grande Real Santa Eulália. The hotel restaurant, Cozinha do Real, is known for its lavish buffets, but also serves a la carte meals and caters to special diets.

Av. do Estádio, 8200-127 Albufeira. www.realbellavistahotel.com. ℂ **28/954-00-60.** 190 units. 100€–215€; from 250€ suite. AE, MC, V. **Amenities:** Restaurant; bar; babysitting; concierge; exercise room; 2 pools (indoor and outdoor); room service; spa. *In room:* A/C, TV, hair dryer, minibar, Wi-Fi (free).

MODERATE

Hotel Montechoro ★ The leading choice in Montechoro, just more than 3km (1¾ miles) northeast of the center of Albufeira, looks like a hotel you might encounter in North Africa. It's a fully equipped, self-contained, government-rated four-star resort complex, with such ample facilities that you might get lost—which is just as well because the one thing it lacks is a beach. The spacious rooms afford views of the countryside and are generally done in modern style, with excellent beds and tidily kept bathrooms.

Rua Alexandre O'Neill (Abdo. 928), 8201-912 Albufeira. www.hotelmontechoro.pt. ℂ **28/959-71-50.** Fax 28/958-99-47. 362 units. 57€–162€ double; 77€–189€ suite. Rates include buffet breakfast. AE, DC, MC, V. Free parking. **Amenities:** 2 restaurants; 2 bars; babysitting; bikes; exercise room; 2 freshwater pools (1 heated indoor); room service; sauna; 8 outdoor tennis courts (lit). *In room:* A/C, TV, hair dryer, Wi-Fi (20€ per 24 hr.).

Hotel Vila Galé Cerro Alagoa ★★ ☺ A sort of South Seas ambience predominates at this fine resort. Most guests hail from northern Europe, and they find this a relaxing environment in which to soak up the sun. A large, sprawling property, it lies near the sandy beach of Albufeira and is also within an easy commute of several other Algarvian beaches, both east and west. Each room has a balcony; comfortable, durable furnishings; and tiled bathrooms. You can also dine in style here; the chefs are fond of presenting theme evenings, and the restaurants offer a great variety of cuisines. Nonguests often drop in here to patronize the Dog & Duck Pub, a British-style bar featuring live music and karaoke.

Rua do Município, 8200-916 Albufeira. www.vilagale.pt. ✆ **28/958-31-00.** Fax 28/958-31-99. 310 units. 65€–214€ double; 85€–130€ junior suite. Rates include buffet breakfast. AE, DC, MC, V. Parking 8€. **Amenities:** Restaurant; 2 bars; bikes; children's center; exercise room; Jacuzzi; 2 freshwater pools (1 heated indoor); room service; sauna. *In room:* A/C, TV, minibar, Wi-Fi (5€ per hour).

INEXPENSIVE

Albufeira Jardim   This establishment is especially popular with northern Europeans, Spaniards, and North Americans who want to linger a while before resuming their tours of the Algarve. On a hill high above Albufeira, it opened in the 1970s as Jardim I. In the late 1980s, it gained another section, Jardim II, a 5-minute walk away. The older section is larger and has gardens that are a bit more mature. The attractively furnished, good-size units are in four- and five-story buildings. Each apartment has a kitchenette and a balcony with a view of the faraway ocean and the town. Guests usually prepare breakfast (which is not included in the rates) in their rooms. A minibus makes frequent runs from the apartments to the beach, a 10-minute drive away.

Cerro da Piedade, 8200-916 Albufeira. www.albufeira-jardim.com. ✆ **28/957-00-70.** Fax 28/957-00-71. 243 apts. 32€–85€ 1-bedroom apt; 40€–115€ 2-bedroom apt. AE, DC, MC, V. Free parking. **Amenities:** 2 restaurants; 2 coffee shops; 2 bars; babysitting; 3 outdoor freshwater pools (1 heated in winter); 3 outdoor tennis courts (2 are lit). *In room:* Kitchenette.

Auramar Beach Resort   One of the resort's largest hotels sits about 1.5km (1 mile) east of the center, in large gardens on a low cliff overlooking a sandy beach. Built in 1974, it resembles a series of fortresses facing the ocean. The complex consists of a quartet of three-, four-, and five-story buildings separated by wide stretches of greenery. Because of last-minute discounts, this hotel can be very inexpensive during off season, when special promotions sometimes bring doubles, with breakfast, to rates about 60% of what we've quoted below. But regrettably, because its rooms are sold as blocks to European tour operators during midsummer, it's often completely sold out during July and August. Check the website for last-minute specials, as this hotel offers them unexpectedly.

Praia dos Aveiros, Areias de São Albufeira, 8200-777 Albufeira. www.booking.com/Auramar BeachResort. ✆ **28/959-91-00.** Fax 28/959-91-95. 287 units. 58€–105€ double. Extra bed 27€–32€. Rates include buffet breakfast. AE, DC, MC, V. Free parking. **Amenities:** Restaurant; bar; bikes; children's center; exercise room; 2 freshwater pools (1 heated indoor); sauna; 2 outdoor tennis courts (lit); Wi-Fi (9€ per hour, in lobby). *In room:* A/C, TV.

Estalagem do Cerro Hotel & Spa ★ 🛏   Built in 1964, this hotel captures Algarvian charm without neglecting modern amenities. This Inn of the Craggy Hill is at the top of a hill overlooking Albufeira's bay, about a 10-minute walk from the beach. A similar Moorish style unites an older, regional-style building and a more modern structure. The tastefully furnished midsize guest rooms have verandas overlooking the sea, pool, or garden. Ten units are large enough for families.

Rua Samora Barros, Cerro da Piedade, 8200-320 Albufeira. www.docerro.com. ✆ **28/959-80-84.** Fax 28/959-80-01. 92 units. 70€–110€ double. Rates include buffet breakfast. AE, DC, MC, V. Limited free parking on street. **Amenities:** 2 restaurants; 2 bars; babysitting; bikes; children's center; exercise room; Jacuzzi; 2 freshwater pools (1 heated indoor); room service; sauna; Wi-Fi (free, in lobby). *In room:* A/C, TV, hair dryer, minibar.

Hotel Sol e Mar This government-rated four-star hotel occupies a prime location in the heart of Albufeira above the beach. It dates from 1969 and was enlarged in 1975. The two-story entrance on the upper palisade can be deceiving—when you walk across the spacious sun-filled lounges to the picture windows and look down, you'll see a six-story drop. Hugging the cliff are midsize guest rooms and a wide stone terrace with garden furniture and parasols. On a lower level is a sandy beach. The guests are a Continental crowd with a sprinkling of Americans. All units have private balconies, good bathrooms, wooden headboards, locally painted seascapes, slim-line armchairs, and plenty of wardrobe space.

Rua Bernardino de Sousa, 8200-071 Albufeira. www.grupofbarata.com. ✆ **28/958-00-80.** Fax 28/958-70-36. 74 units. 65€–125€ double. Rates include buffet breakfast. AE, DC, MC, V. No parking available. **Amenities:** 2 restaurants; bar; indoor freshwater heated pool; room service; Wi-Fi (5€ per hour, in lobby). *In room:* A/C, TV, hair dryer, minibar.

Rocamar Beach Hotel You might think that this cubistic hotel looks like an updated version of a Moorish castle, a well-ordered assemblage of building blocks, or the partially excavated side of a stone quarry. Built in 1974, it was enlarged in 1991 and completely restored in 2007. It rises six stories above the tawny cliffs that slope down to one of the most inviting beaches on the Algarve. Many of its windows and all of its balconies benefit from the view (ask for a sea-view room). The hotel is a 5-minute walk from the town's attractions. Rooms are tastefully furnished and sun-washed, most comfortable, with spotless bathrooms.

Largo Jacinto d'Ayet 7, 8200-071 Albufeira. www.rocamarbeachhotel.com. ✆ **28/954-02-80.** Fax 28/954-02-81. 91 units. 50€–131€ double. Rates include buffet breakfast. AE, DC, MC, V. Limited free parking on street. **Amenities:** Restaurant; bar; room service; spa. *In room:* A/C, TV, Wi-Fi (free).

Where to Stay Nearby

AT SESMARIAS

São Rafael Suite Hotel ★★ ☺ Lying 4km (2½ miles) west of the center of Albufeira, this is one of the best resort hotels in the area—modern, tranquil, and most functional. The all-suite hotel offers spacious and comfortable accommodations, suitable for a couple who like a lot of room or else a family. The government rates it five stars because of its many facilities, including indoor and outdoor pools, one just for children. In summer the staff offers a Kids Club. The beachside hotel enjoys a garden setting, and its Relax Centre is well equipped with a Jacuzzi, sauna, Turkish bath, an indoor heated pool, and massage and treatment rooms. The staff will also arrange many outdoor activities, including diving, snorkeling, sailing, windsurfing, water-skiing and canoeing. The hotel operates both a buffet restaurant and a more gourmet a la carte dining room, and in season features lunch around the pool.

Sesmarias, 8200-613 Albufeira. www.cshotelsandresorts.com. ✆ **28/954-03-30.** Fax 28/954-03-14. 101 units. 175€–225€ suite. AE, DC, MC, V. **Amenities:** 3 restaurants; babysitting; bar; children's club; concierge; exercise room; 3 pools (1 indoor); room service. *In room:* A/C, TV/DVD, hair dryer, minibar, Wi-Fi (free).

PRAIA DE SANTA EULÁLIA

Grande Real Santa Eulália Resort & Hotel Spa ★★★ ☺ One of the most luxurious hotel resorts in the area opens onto a good sandy beach, 4km (2½ miles) from the center of Albufeira. This posh resort offers a choice of standard double rooms and luxurious apartment suites. Some of the suites are ideal for singles or couples, though larger families can rent two- or three-bedroom suites as well. Windows in these accommodations open either onto the Atlantic or else a well-landscaped garden. Bedrooms are spacious and beautifully furnished, each with a tiled modern bathroom. The most luxurious units contain kitchenettes and a heated Jacuzzi on their private terraces.

The main restaurant, Real, serves buffet-style meals from breakfast to dinner, but we prefer Le Club with its superb Italian cuisine, plus international specialties. The spa, with its range of treatments using seawater, is one of the best along the coast, with a team of hydrotherapists, beauticians, masseurs, and fitness trainers. The hotel is also one of the best on the Algarve for families with children, with a kiddie center with trained professionals, plus many facilities such as small pools just for the kids.

Praia de Santa Eulália, 8200-916 Albufeira. www.granderealsantaeulaliahotel.com. ✆ **28/959-80-00.** Fax 28/959-80-01. 158 units. 83€–295€ double; 132€–437€ suite. Rates include buffet breakfast. AE, DC, MC, V. Parking 10€. **Amenities:** 4 restaurants; 8 bars; babysitting; children's center; 4 freshwater pools (1 heated indoors); room service; spa; 2 outdoor tennis courts (lit); Wi-Fi (free, in lobby). *In room:* A/C, TV, hair dryer, kitchens (in some), minibar.

PRAIA DA FALÉSIA

Sheraton Algarve Hotel ★★★ Opened in 1992 about 8km (5 miles) east of Albufeira, this government-rated five-star hotel is laid out like an Algarve village, with no building rising higher than three floors. The property was designed to blend tastefully into its oceanfront location and its wings ramble through a subtropical garden dotted with copses of the site's original pine trees. Conceived as a complete resort incorporating a 9-hole golf course, the hotel caters to an international clientele. Accommodations range from midsize to spacious and open onto land, garden, or sea views. Each is traditionally furnished with luxurious pieces, including quality beds and state-of-the-art plumbing.

Praia da Falésia (P.O. Box 644), 8200-909 Albufeira. www.pinecliffs.com/en/resort_hotel.php. ✆ **800/325-3535** in the U.S., or 28/950-01-00. Fax 28/950-19-50. 215 units. 111€–490€ double; 185€–615€ suite. Rates include buffet breakfast. AE, DC, MC, V. Free parking. **Amenities:** 9 restaurants; 5 bars; babysitting; bikes; children's center; concierge; golf course; health club & spa; 5 outdoor freshwater pools (1 heated); room service; 5 outdoor tennis courts (lit); extensive watersports equipment/rentals. *In room:* A/C, TV, hair dryer, minibar.

PRAIA DA GALÉ

Vila Galé Praia ★★ Like the even more glamorous hotel below, this is another winner positioned about 15km (9⅓ miles) west of Albufeira, an easy commute. In a room here, you're just 2 minutes from a good beach. A government-rated four-star hotel, this resort is small enough to be called a "boutique." It is mainly for romantic couples, as the rooms are a bit small, not suitable for an extra bed. Most of the accommodations open onto balconies and are furnished with such amenities as bathrobes, ceiling fans, and blackout draperies. A Portuguese and international menu is served in the main restaurant or less formally in the bar lounge. The hotel emphasizes its spa and health facilities, with its mega-sized Jacuzzi and sauna, steam baths, special treatments, and massages; trainers even give yoga lessons. Courtesy buses take visitors into the center of Albufeira.

Praia da Galé, 8201-917 Albufeira. www.vilagale.com. ℰ **28/959-01-90.** 40 units. 88€–220€. AE, DC, MC, V. **Amenities:** Restaurant; bar; exercise room; 2 pools (outdoor); room service; spa. *In room:* A/C, TV/DVD, CD player, hair dryer, minibar, Wi-Fi (free).

Vila Joya ★★★ The most luxurious and intimate inn in the Algarve, the Vila Joya is especially favored by Germans (ex-Chancellor Willy Brandt came here just before his death). The establishment lies 15km (9⅓ miles) west of Albufeira in a residential neighborhood dotted with other dwellings, but within the confines of its large gardens, visitors can easily imagine themselves in the open countryside. A footpath leads down to the beach. All of the beautiful accommodations have a view of the sea and a private bathroom (some of which are tiled in traditional *azulejos*).

Praia da Galé (Abdo. Postal 120), 8200-917 Albufeira. www.vilajoya.com. ℰ **28/959-17-95.** Fax 28/959-12-01. 20 units. 385€–860€ double; from 815€ suite. Rates include half-board. AE, DC, MC, V. Free parking. **Amenities:** Restaurant; bar; airport transfers (235€); babysitting; bikes; exercise room; golf course; Jacuzzi; outdoor heated pool; room service; sauna; spa; outdoor tennis court (lit). *In room:* A/C, TV/DVD, hair dryer, minibar, Wi-Fi (free).

Where to Dine

EXPENSIVE

O Cabaz da Praia (The Beach Basket) FRENCH/PORTUGUESE The Beach Basket, near the Hotel Sol e Mar (see above), sits on a colorful little square near the Church of São Sebastião. In a former fishermen's cottage, the restaurant boasts a large, sheltered terrace with a view over the main Albufeira beach. The food's good, too. Main courses, including such justifiable favorites as cassoulet of seafood, *salade océane,* monkfish with mango sauce, and beef filet with garlic and white-wine sauce, are served with a selection of fresh vegetables.

Praça Miguel Bombarda 7. ℰ **28/951-21-37.** Reservations recommended. Main courses 22€–28€. AE, MC, V. Fri–Wed noon–3pm and 7:30–11pm.

MODERATE

A Casa do Avo ★ PORTUGUESE In the Vale de Parra, a scenic valley, this restaurant is 6km (3¾ miles) west of Albufeira and makes a good dining choice for motorists who like to escape the summer bustle of Albufeira itself. Traditional in style, the restaurant specializes in regional dishes from the Algarve, taking special care with the catch of the day. If you don't like fish, you'll find an array of meats from the Monchique, and can order some of the delightful regional wines, followed by a selection of Portuguese desserts made fresh daily. A traditional menu, called "The Grandfather's Menu," is a three-course meal at a very reasonable price. It includes a buffet of 30 hors d'oeuvres, both hot and cold, followed by the chef's special (an option of two main courses) and then a dessert or fresh fruit. There is an a la carte menu as well, but the buffet is the one for great value.

Sitio de Vale de Parra, outside Guia. ℰ **28/951-32-82.** www.restaurante-acasadoavo.com. Reservations recommended. Fixed-price menu 18€; main courses 14€–28€. AE, MC, V. May–Sept daily 12:30–3pm and 6:30–10pm; Oct–Apr Wed–Sun 12:30–3pm and Tues–Sun 6:30–10pm.

Café Doris GERMAN/PORTUGUESE This German-operated rotisserie-creperie-restaurant turns out well-prepared crepes, home-baked cakes, and ice cream in many flavors, as well as heartier fare. Rich-tasting goulash-meat soup is always offered as an appetizer, as is savory goat stew. You might move on to roast pork with onion sauce, monkfish with rice curry, or a good steak with cream sauce, herbs, lyonnaise potatoes, and a salad. Doris has an unusual selection of hot drinks, including coffee Algarve (with Medronho). The cafe has an intimate vibe, with wooden tables and chairs and regional art adorning its white walls.

Av. Dr. Francisco Sá Carneiro, Areias de São João. ✆ **28/951-24-55.** Reservations required in summer. Main courses 8€–16€. MC, V. Daily 9am–1am. Closed Nov–Feb.

Fernando 🐟 PORTUGUESE   Fernando, with its large terrace and pleasant dining room, serves tempting, economical fare. We always go here for the fish of the day. You can count on good soup, usually fish-based. If you're tired of fish, the chef will fix you a simple steak or a Portuguese specialty such as clams with pork. Several varieties of tempting kabobs are also available. Desserts aren't anything special.

Rua Bernardino de Sousa. ✆ **28/951-21-16.** Main courses 14€–18€. AE, DC, MC, V. Daily noon–midnight.

La Cigale FRENCH/PORTUGUESE   Right on the beach, 7.3km (4½ miles) from Albufeira, La Cigale has a terrace that makes it a romantic choice at night. Its atmosphere reflects the mood of the sunny southern coast of Europe—and, fortunately, the food matches the atmosphere. The wine list is fairly distinguished, in keeping with the impressive menu. The amiable management works efficiently. Specialties include clams a la Cigale, shellfish rice, steak with pepper sauce, sea bass, and a daily selection of fresh-caught fish.

Praia de Olhos d'Água. ✆ **28/950-16-37.** www.restaurantelacigale.net. Reservations required. Main courses 15€–32€. AE, MC, V. Daily noon–5:30pm and 7–11pm. Closed Dec 1–26 and Jan 5–31.

O Marinheiro ★ ☺ PORTUGUESE/INTERNATIONAL   Ever since Monika and Joaquim Coelho came here around the turn of the millennium, they have been known for serving the best market-fresh cuisine in the area. All their dishes, whenever possible, use the freshest of seasonal ingredients. There's also a children's selection on the menu, since this dining room is a family favorite. Many diners begin their evening hanging at the well-stocked bar, sampling a glass or two of regional wine. In summer guests retreat to the shady garden terrace. There is also an air-conditioned winter garden, plus a playground for kids.

Freshly caught fish is the prize of the menu—called "fruits of the sea" here. A number of vegetarian dishes are always offered, but the specialties are two kinds of salmon—one with a dill-laced lemon mayonnaise and another served with horseradish sauce and capers. The choice meat dish is filet of beef carpaccio—thin slices of filet of beef with pink peppercorns, virgin olive oil, and Parmesan cheese. A tantalizing selection of desserts is also available, including blackberry sorbet or a combination white and brown chocolate mousse.

Estrada da Praia da Coelha, Sesmarias. ✆ **28/959-23-50.** www.o-marinheiro.com. Reservations required. 18€–36€. MC, V. Mar–Nov daily 6:30pm–midnight.

Restaurante A Ruína ★ PORTUGUESE   This restaurant sits opposite the fish market, overlooking the main beach. From the arcaded dining room, with its long candlelit wooden tables, you can watch the fishers mending their nets. Another cave-like room has more tables and a bar. The decor is unpretentious, and the reasonably priced seafood is fresh. A bowl of flavorful soup will get you going; then it's on to one of the fish specialties, such as grilled fresh tuna. The fish stew, *caldeirada,* is the chef's specialty and our favorite dish. Typical desserts are custard and mousse.

Cais Herculano, Albufeira. ✆ **28/951-20-94.** www.restaurante-ruina.com. Reservations recommended. Main courses 15€–30€. AE, DC, MC, V. Daily 12:30–3pm and 7–11pm.

Albufeira After Dark

You can have a lot of fun in this hard-drinking, fun-in-the-sun town, discovering your own favorite tucked-away bar. To get rolling, you might begin at the **Falan Bar,** Rua São Gonçalo de Lagos (no phone), or the nearby **Fastnet Bar,** Rua Cândido dos Reis 10 (© **28/958-91-16**), where no one will object if you jump to your feet and begin to dance. A few storefronts away is the **Classic Bar,** Rua Cândido dos Reis 8 (© **28/951-20-75**), a folksy, comfortably battered place that's almost completely devoid of pretension. The bars are usually open until 3 or 4am, depending on business.

QUARTEIRA

23km (14 miles) W of Faro; 307km (191 miles) SE of Lisbon

This once-sleepy fishing village between Albufeira and Faro used to be known only to a handful of artists who amused the local fisher folk. Now, with the invasion of outsiders, the traditional way of life has been upset. A sea of high-rise buildings has swallowed Quarteira, and the place is now a bustling, overgrown resort. The big attraction is one of the Algarve's longest beaches. In summer it's filled with vacationing Portuguese and other Europeans who supply a much-needed boost to the local economy.

Golfers who don't want to pay the high rates at Vale do Lobo or Vilamoura (both of which have 18-hole courses) can stay inexpensively in Quarteira (see "Where to Stay," below). The courses are only a 10-minute drive away, and Quarteira lies about 11km (6¼ miles) from the Faro airport.

The largest concentration of quality hotels and restaurants is not in Quarteira or even Praia de Quarteira, but in the satellite of Vilamoura, west of Quarteira. Buses run between Quarteira and Vilamoura frequently throughout the day. Tourist information is available in Quarteira (see below).

At a central point on the Algarve coast, only 18km (11 miles) west of Faro airport, Vilamoura is an expansive land-development project, the largest private tourist "urbanization" in Europe. Although the remains of a Roman villa were discovered when builders were working on the local marina, the history of Vilamoura is yet to be written. Plans call for a city larger than Faro and an interior lake linked with the bay and ocean by two canals. There's already a marina that can hold 1,000 pleasure boats. Vilamoura is now filled with "holiday villages" and apartment complexes.

Essentials
ARRIVING

BY BUS If you're dependent on public transportation, take a plane, bus, or train from Lisbon to Faro (see "Faro," later), and then catch one of the buses that runs frequently between Faro and Quarteira. Contact EVA (© **28/989-97-60;** www.eva-bus.com) for schedules and information.

BY CAR From Albufeira, head east along Route 125; from Faro, go west on Route 125. Signposts point to the little secondary road that runs south to Quarteira, which is the center for exploring the more extensive tourist developments along Praia de Quarteira and Vilamoura.

VISITOR INFORMATION
The **tourist information office** is at Avenida Infante Sagres, Praça do Mar (© **28/938-92-09;** www.visitalgarve.pt). It's open October to May Tuesday to Thursday

from 9:30am to 5:30pm, and Friday and Monday 9:30am to 1pm and 2 to 5:30pm. June to September, it's open Tuesday to Thursday 9:30am to 7pm, and Friday to Monday 9:30am to 1pm and 2 to 5:30pm.

Having Fun in Quarteira

OUTDOOR ACTIVITIES

Sports are a main attraction here. There are 18-hole golf courses, watersports, tennis courts, a riding center, and yachting. Shops and other tourist facilities, including restaurants and bars, also provide pleasant diversions.

BOATING Marinas have been tucked into virtually every navigable cove along the Algarve, and most contain a handful of sailboats or motorboats that can be rented, with or without a skipper, to qualified sailors. *Note:* Before you can rent, you must present accreditation or some certificate from a yacht club proving your seaworthiness.

Algariate operates a boat-charter business from the 100-berth Marina de Vilamoura, 8125 Quarteira (*©* **28/938-99-33**). Algariate was established in 1993 and is one of the largest yacht and motorboat charterers in the Algarve. Boats up to 14m (46 ft.) in length are available. Without a crew, they rent from 2,000€ per week, depending on size and season. Clients often use Vilamoura as a point of origin for visits to Madeira, North Africa, or the southern coast of Spain. If you prefer to have someone else worry about navigation, you can sail on the *Condor de Vilamoura* (*©* **28/931-40-70**), which departs from the Vilamoura Marina at least once a day, depending on business, for 3-hour cruises toward Albufeira. The cost is 35€ per person. A full-day cruise lasting about 7 hours costs from 55€, with lunch included.

GOLF **Vila Sol,** Alto do Semino, Vilamoura, 8125 Quarteira (*©* **28/930-05-05;** www.vilasol.pt), has the best fairways and the boldest and most inventive contours of any golf course in the Algarve. Designed by the English architect Donald Steel, it opened in 1991 as part of a 147-hectare (363-acre) residential estate. Steele took great care in allowing the terrain's natural contours to determine the layout of the fairways and the impeccable greens. Although it hasn't been around long, Vila Sol has twice played host to the Portuguese Open. Golfers especially praise the configuration of holes 6, 8, and 14, which incorporate ponds, creek beds, and pine groves in nerve-racking order. Par is 72. Greens fees are 95€. From Quarteira, drive east for about 5km (3 miles), following signs to Estrada Nacional 125, and turn off where signs point to Vila Sol.

Vilamoura has three famous courses, each with its own clubhouse, managed and owned by the same investors. They're 4km (2½ miles) east of Quarteira and are carefully signposted from the center of town. Discounts on greens fees are offered to the guests of five nearby hotels according to a complicated, frequently changing system of hierarchies and commercial agreements.

The most famous and most sought-after of Vilamoura's trio of golf courses is the **Oceanico Old Course,** 8125 Vilamoura, sometimes referred to as Vilamoura I (*©* **28/931-03-41** for information). Noted English architect Frank Pennink laid out the course in 1969, long before American tastes in golf influenced Portugal. In design, texture, and conception, it's the most English of southern Portugal's golf courses, and it's invariably cited for its beauty, its lushness, and the maturity of its trees and shrubbery. Although some holes are almost annoyingly difficult (four of them are par 5), the course is among the most consistently crowded on the Algarve. Par is 73. Greens fees are 120€.

Adjacent to the Old Course are a pair of newer, less popular par-72 courses that nonetheless provide challenging golf for those who prefer different terrain. The first is the **Pinhal Golf Course,** 8125 Vilamoura, also known as Vilamoura II (✆ **28/931-03-90**), which opened in the early 1970s. It's noted for the challenging placement of its many copses of pine trees. Greens fees run 52€ to 100€, depending on the season and the time of day. Nearby is the most modern course, the **Laguna Golf Course,** 8125 Vilamoura, or Vilamoura III (✆ **28/931-01-80**). Known for its labyrinth of water traps and lakes, it opened in the late 1980s. Greens fees are 75€. Tee times during the midday heat are less expensive than those in the early morning.

Visit **www.algarvegolf.net** for more information on courses in the Algarve region.

TENNIS The English influence in southern Portugal is so strong that no self-respecting resort would be built without at least one tennis court. The **Vilamoura Ténis Center,** 8125 Vilamoura (✆ **28/932-41-23;** www.premier-sports.org), has 12. They're open to suitably dressed players for 19€ per hour. Hours are daily from 9:30am to 8pm. Tennis racquets and balls rent for 5€, and four tennis balls can be purchased for 5€.

Where to Stay

Vilamoura is a better place to use as a base than Praia de Quarteira, whose less attractive accommodations are often filled with tour groups.

PRAIA DE QUARTEIRA

Atismar Hotel High-rise apartment blocks line the street the Atismar calls home so completely that it resembles Manhattan. Fortunately, many of the Hotel Atismar's balconied, tastefully decorated rooms look away from the street and out over the beach, 50m (164 ft.) away. Though small, rooms are comfortable, with well-maintained bathrooms. A fence separates the tiny outdoor pool from the sidewalk; many guests prefer to swim at the beach.

Av. Francisco Sá Carneiro, 8125-145 Quarteira. ✆ **28/938-97-71.** Fax 28/938-97-74. 97 units. 60€–110€ double. Rates include buffet breakfast. AE, DC, MC, V. Free parking. Closed Nov–Apr. **Amenities:** Restaurant; bar; babysitting; bikes; outdoor freshwater pool; room service; Wi-Fi (free, in lobby). *In room:* A/C, TV.

Hotel Dom José Hotel Dom José is sometimes completely booked, often by vacationers from Britain who consider its amenities considerably better than its three-star status dictates. At its tallest point, the hotel has eight balconied stories; the outlying wings are shorter. The double rooms are small and plain but comfortably furnished. A low wall separates the pool from the town's portside promenade. The public rooms fill every evening as guests enjoy drinks, live music, and the air-conditioned sea view. In another corner of the ground floor, a lattice-covered room contains a wide-screen TV.

Av. Infante do Sagres 141-143, 8125-157 Quarteira. www.hoteldomjose.com. ✆ **28/931-02-10.** Fax 28/930-27-55. 154 units. 60€–173€ double. Rates include buffet breakfast. AE, DC, MC, V. **Amenities:** Restaurant; 2 bars; babysitting; outdoor freshwater pool; Wi-Fi (5€ per hour, in lobby). *In room:* A/C, TV, hair dryer.

Hotel Zodiaco ☺ This modern resortlike hotel, located only 400m (1,312 ft.) from Forte Novo Beach, is an economical choice. Its bedrooms, though lackluster, are well maintained and comfortable. Most of them are midsize, with tiled bathrooms.

For those who want to lodge in the center of Quarteira itself, the Zodiaco ranks just under the Atismar. Its kindergarten makes it popular with families.

Fonte Santa, 8125-298 Quarteira. www.hotel-zodiaco.com. © **28/938-14-20.** Fax 28/938-14-25. 60 units. 37€–100€ double. Rates include buffet breakfast. AE, DC, MC, V. Free parking. **Amenities:** Restaurant; bar; babysitting; outdoor freshwater pool; room service; outdoor tennis court (lit); Wi-Fi (free, in lobby). *In room:* A/C, TV.

VILAMOURA
Expensive
Hilton Vilamoura As Cascatas Golf Resort & Spa ★★★ ☺   In 2009, *Business Destination Magazine* awarded this pocket of posh the "Best Luxury Hotel in Portugal." It is expected to keep that position, or at least remain at the top, for many years to come. With its enormous pools with cascading waterways and pavilions, this is a bit of a fantasyland. Stylish bars and gourmet restaurants add to its allure. The luxurious bedrooms are among the best along the Algarve, opening onto balconies with views of the ocean. The marble-clad bathrooms are also opulent. Of all the major resorts along the coast, this one has more to offer children than all others, ranging from an on-site day camp to a child care center with special kiddie menus.

Rua da Torre D'Água Lote 4, 8125-615 Vilamoura. www.hilton.com. © **28/930-40-00.** Fax 28/930-40-05. 135 units. 120€–405€ double; 260€–635€ suite. AE, DC, MC, V. Free parking. **Amenities:** 3 restaurants; 3 bars; babysitting; bikes; children's center; concierge; 18-hole golf course; health club & spa; 6 freshwater pools (1 heated indoor); room service; outdoor tennis court (lit). *In room:* A/C, TV/DVD, CD player, hair dryer, minibar, Wi-Fi (22€ per day).

Tivoli Marina Vilamoura ★★★   The government-rated five-star Tivoli Marina is one of the finest deluxe hotels on the Algarve, standing in the midst of 30,000 sq. m (322,917 sq. ft.) of landscaped gardens with direct access to a splendid private beach. The hotel is popular with well-heeled Portuguese and international visitors. During the slower winter months, it accommodates conventions. The massive, rectangular hotel also sits next to the Vilamoura marina. Each well-furnished guest room has a view of the marina or the ocean, but views from floors eight and nine are the most panoramic. The high-ceilinged interior, with a huge lounge with space for 500, is decorated in traditional and modern designs, although the lobby is brassy and garish.

Marina de Vilamoura, 8125-901 Quarteira. www.tivolihotels.com. © **28/930-33-03.** Fax 28/930-33-45. 383 units. 106€–540€ double; 351€–1,100€ junior suite; 555€–1,210€ executive suite. Rates include buffet breakfast. AE, DC, MC, V. Free parking. **Amenities:** 2 restaurants; 4 bars; babysitting; bikes; children's center; concierge; exercise room; 3 pools (1 heated indoor); room service; spa; 2 outdoor tennis courts (lit); Wi-Fi (5€ per hour, in lobby). *In room:* A/C, TV, hair dryer, minibar.

Moderate
Dom Pedro Golf ★★   This 10-story hotel offers first-class comfort in the tourist whirl of Vilamoura. It's close to the casino and a short walk from the sands. The public rooms are sleekly styled. The midsize guest rooms are pleasantly furnished and carpeted, with private terraces, but the overall effect is uninspired. The hotel is a favorite with touring groups from England and Scandinavia. The house band provides nightly entertainment, and there's a casino in front of the hotel. Deep-sea fishing and horseback riding can be arranged, and guests receive a 15% to 20% discount on greens fees at various area golf courses.

Rua Atlântico, Vilamoura 8125-478 Quarteira. www.dompedro.com. © **28/930-07-80.** Fax 28/930-07-01. 266 units. 63€–240€ double. Rates include buffet breakfast. AE, DC, MC, V. Free parking. **Amenities:** 2 restaurants; 2 bars; airport transfers (40€); babysitting; children's center; concierge; 3 freshwater pools (1 heated indoor); room service; spa; 3 outdoor tennis courts (lit); Wi-Fi (6€ per hour, in lobby). *In room:* A/C, TV, hair dryer, minibar.

Where to Dine

VILAMOURA

Peppers Steakhouse ★ INTERNATIONAL/PORTUGUESE   The most exclusive and expensive dining spot in the Tivoli Marina Vilamoura (reviewed separately, above) is this steakhouse, on the main floor. A grand piano on a dais separates the restaurant from the chic Canela Bar. Live music filters into both areas. The stylish bar offers a large variety of drinks daily from 10:30am to 1am. Overlooking the marina under high ceilings, the steakhouse is sophisticated but not fussy. You might begin with assorted smoked fish and follow with a seafood specialty, such as divinely smooth lobster cassoulet, turbot in seafood sauce, sea bass flambé with fennel, stuffed trout, or excellent filet of sole. Meat dishes use only the finest cuts—rack of lamb, T-bone steak, and tournedos stuffed with shrimp and scallops and served with béarnaise.

In the Tivoli Marina Vilamoura. ✆ **28/930-33-03.** Reservations recommended. Main courses 23€–30€. AE, DC, MC, V. Daily 7:30–11pm.

Willie's Restaurant ★★★ INTERNATIONAL   Wilhelm Wurger is "Willie," and he's one of the grand chefs along the entire Algarve, winning a coveted Michelin star. His cuisine is served in an opulent setting with fine crystal and silver, enhanced with fresh flowers. The setting is in an upscale residential area close to the Pinhal Golf Course. Willie likes to share his love of good food with you, offering you such sublime dishes as a homemade seafood ravioli in a vermouth cream sauce followed by such mains as saddle of monkfish in a mustard cream sauce with potato mousse. He selects only the choicest cuts of beef which can be roasted or grilled to your taste. The wine *carte* is also the finest in the area, as is the efficient, polite staff.

Rua do Brasil. ✆ **28/938-08-49.** Reservations required. Main courses 25€–32€. AE, DC, MC, V. Daily 7–10pm. Closed Jan 10–Feb 4.

Quarteira After Dark

Much of the tourist expansion in this region has occurred outside the immediate confines of Quarteira, so you're likely to find only a handful of sleepy bodegas and *tascas* (taverns) inside the city limits. Most cater to locals and serve beer and wine.

Glossier diversions are the norm in the massive marina and tourist developments of nearby Vilamoura. Foremost among these is the **Casino Vilamoura** ★, Vilamoura, 8125 Quarteira (✆ **28/931-00-00;** www.solverde.pt), one of the finest nightspots in the Algarve. Its most appealing feature is a gambling salon that offers roulette, blackjack, French banque, and baccarat. It's open every day from 3pm to 3am. To enter, you must present a passport or photo ID and pay 10€. A separate, less glamorous slot-machine salon at the casino, open daily from 4pm to 4am, doesn't charge admission.

The casino's 600-seat supper club serves meals nightly starting at 8:30pm; one of the Algarve's splashiest floor shows and cabaret revues begins at 10:30pm. A fixed-price meal costs 40€, including the show. You must make a reservation at the supper club. The show alone costs 14€, which includes one drink. Physically part of the casino, but with a separate entrance and separate staff, is Vilamoura's most action-oriented dance club, **Black Jack** (✆ **28/938-91-47**). Every clubber in the region comes to dance here. It's open Thursday, Friday, and Saturday 11pm to 6am. The cover charge is 30€ and includes the first drink. The casino and its facilities are open every night except December 24 and 25.

ALMANCIL

13km (8 miles) W of Faro; 306km (190 miles) SE of Lisbon

Almancil is a small market town of little tourist interest, but it's a center for two of the most exclusive tourist developments along the Algarve. **Vale do Lobo** lies 6.5km (4 miles) southeast of Almancil, and **Quinta do Lago** is less than 10km (6¼ miles) southeast of town.

The name *Vale do Lobo* (Valley of the Wolf) suggests a forlorn spot, but in reality the vale is the site of a golf course designed by Henry Cotton, the British champion. It's west of Faro, about a 20-minute drive from the Faro airport. Some holes are by the sea, which results in many an anxious moment as shots hook out over the water. The property includes a 9-hole course, a 9-hole par-3 course, a putting green, and a driving range. The tennis center is among the best in Europe.

Quinta do Lago, one of the most elegant "tourist estates" on the Algarve, also has superb facilities. The pine-covered beachfront property has been a favored retreat of movie stars and European presidents. The resort's 27 superb holes of golf are also a potent lure. This is true luxury—at quite a price.

Essentials

ARRIVING

BY TRAIN   Faro, the gateway to the eastern Algarve, makes the best transportation hub for Almancil and its resorts. Go to Faro by train (see "Faro" on p. 248) and then take a bus the rest of the way.

BY BUS   Almancil is a major stop for buses to the western Algarve; about 17 a day run from Faro to Albufeira. Travel time is about 50 minutes. Whereas a taxi will cost around 40€ for up to four passengers, bus transit costs only around 5.50€ per person, with a stop at Almancil. For more information, call ☎ **28/989-97-60.**

BY CAR   From Faro, head west along Route 125; from Albufeira or Portimão, continue east along Route 125.

VISITOR INFORMATION

Almancil's tourist office is at Av. 25 Abril 9 (☎ **28/939-26-59**). The opening hours are Monday to Friday 9am to 12:30pm and 2 to 3:30pm.

Outdoor Activities

GOLF   One of the most deceptive golf courses on the Algarve, **Pinheiros Altos,** Quinta do Lago, 8135 Almancil (☎ **28/935-99-00;** www.pinheirosaltos.com), has contours that even professionals say are far more difficult than they appear at first glance. American architect Ronald Fream designed the 100 hectares (247 acres), which abut the wetland refuge of the Rio Formosa National Park. Umbrella pines and dozens of small lakes dot the course. Par is 72. Greens fees are 45€ to 60€ for 9 holes and 90€ to 120€ for 18 holes. Pinheiros Altos lies about 5km (3 miles) south of Almancil. From Almancil, follow the signs to Quinta do Lago and Pinheiros Altos.

The namesake course of the massive development, **Quinta do Lago,** Quinta do Lago, 8135 Almancil (☎ **28/939-07-00;** www.quintadolagogolf.com), consists of two 18-hole golf courses, Quinta do Lago and Rio Formosa. Together they cover more than 240 hectares (593 acres) of sandy terrain that abuts the Rio Formosa Wildlife Sanctuary. Very few long drives here are over open water; instead, the fairways undulate through cork forests and groves of pine trees, sometimes with abrupt changes in elevation. Greens fees are 139€ to 178€ depending on the season. The courses are 6km (3¾ miles) south of Almancil. From Almancil, follow signs to Quinta do Lago.

Of the four golf courses at the massive Quinta do Lago development, the par-72 **San Lorenzo (São Lourenço)** course, Quinta do Lago, Almancil, 8100 Loulé (© **28/939-65-22;** www.sanlorenzogolfcourse.com), is the most interesting and challenging. San Lorenzo opened in 1988 at the edge of the grassy wetlands of the Rio Formosa Nature Reserve. American golf designers William (Rocky) Roquemore and Joe Lee created it. The most panoramic hole is the 6th; the most frustrating is the 8th. Many long drives, especially those aimed at the 17th and 18th holes, soar over a saltwater lagoon. Greens fees are 85€ for 9 holes and 165€ for 18 holes. From Almancil, drive 8km (5 miles) south, following signs to Quinta do Lago.

The **Vale do Lobo** course, Vale do Lobo, 8135 Almancil (© **28/935-34-65;** www.valedolobo.com), technically isn't part of the Quinta do Lago complex. Because it was established in 1968, before any of its nearby competitors, it played an important role in launching southern Portugal's image as a golfer's mecca. Designed by the late British golfer Henry Cotton, it contains four distinct 9-hole segments. All four include runs that stretch over rocks and arid hills, often within view of olive and almond groves, the Atlantic, and the high-rise hotels of nearby Vilamoura and Quarteira. Some long shots require driving golf balls over two ravines, where variable winds and bunkers that have been called "ravenous" make things particularly difficult. Greens fees, depending on the day of the week and other factors, range from 83€ to 155€ for 18 holes. From Almancil, drive 4km (2½ miles) south of town, following signs to Vale do Lobo.

Visit **www.algarvegolf.net** for more information on courses in the Algarve region.

Where to Stay

VALE DO LOBO

Dona Filipa Hotel ★★★ ☺ This deluxe golf hotel is a citadel of ostentatious living. The grounds are impressive, embracing 180 hectares (445 acres) of rugged coastline with steep cliffs, inlets, and sandy bays. The hotel's exterior is comparatively uninspired, but the interior features such lavish touches as green silk banquettes, gold-painted palms holding up the ceiling, marble fireplaces, Portuguese ceramic lamps, and old prints over baroque-style love seats. The midsize to spacious guest rooms are handsomely decorated with antiques, rustic accessories, and handmade rugs. Most have balconies and twin beds.

Vale do Lobo, 8135-901 Almancil. www.donafilipahotel.com. © **28/935-72-23.** Fax 28/935-72-01. 154 units. 189€–290€ double; 315€–510€ junior suite; 450€–665€ deluxe suite. Rates include buffet breakfast. AE, MC, V. Free parking. **Amenities:** 2 restaurants; bar; babysitting; bikes; children's center; concierge; outdoor heated pool; room service; spa; 3 outdoor tennis courts (lit); Wi-Fi (3€ per hour, in lobby). *In room:* A/C, TV, hair dryer, minibar.

QUINTA DO LAGO

Hotel Quinta do Lago ★★★ A pocket of the high life since 1986, Hotel Quinta do Lago is a sprawling 800-hectare (1,977-acre) estate that contains some private plots beside the Ria Formosa estuary. Its riding center and 27-hole golf course are among the best in Europe. The estate's contemporary Mediterranean-style buildings rise three to six floors. The luxurious guest rooms overlook a saltwater lake and feature modern comforts. Decorated with thick carpeting, pastel fabrics, contemporary art, and light-wood furniture, the rooms are generally spacious, with tile or marble bathrooms and balconies that open onto views of the estuary.

Quinta do Lago, 8135-024 Almancil. www.quintadolagohotel.com. © **800/223-6800** in the U.S., or 28/935-03-50. Fax 28/939-63-93. 141 units. 213€–569€ double; 569€–2,650€ suite. Rates include buffet breakfast. AE, DC, MC, V. Free parking. **Amenities:** 2 restaurants; bar; babysitting; bikes; children's center; exercise room; 2 freshwater heated pools (1 indoor); room service; spa; 2 outdoor tennis courts (lit). *In room:* A/C, TV, hair dryer, minibar, Wi-Fi (7€ per 24 hr.).

Where to Dine

Casa do Campo ★ PORTUGUESE/SEAFOOD   This old Algarvian house filled with cozy charm is 8.5km (5¼ miles) south of Almancil. Serving a superb cuisine, it accurately bills itself as a restaurant for all seasons. Diners enjoy a blazing fireplace in winter or alfresco dining under an old fig tree in summer. The food is prepared by first-class chefs who turn out such dishes as the fresh catch of the day which is grilled to perfection. The house is also known for its pepper steak flambé (prepared at your table) and its cuts of filet mignon. Other temptations on the menu include fresh Atlantic sole on the grill or an Algarvian *cataplana* of fresh fish and clams in a savory kettle. Desserts such as mango au gratin with an orange sabayon are scrumptious.

Quinta do Lago. © **28/939-91-09.** Reservations required. Main courses 22€–27€. AE, MC, V. June-Sept Mon-Sat 7:30–10:30pm; off-season Mon-Sat 7–10pm.

Casa Velha ★★★ FRENCH   Set on a hillside behind the massive Quinta do Lago resort, the excellent Casa Velha overlooks the resort's lake from the premises of a century-old farmhouse that has functioned as a restaurant since the early 1960s. The cuisine is mainly French, with a scattering of Portuguese and international dishes. Start with foie gras or marinated lobster salad. Specialties include a salad of chicken livers and gizzards with leeks and vinaigrette, and lobster salad flavored with an infusion of vanilla. Other good choices are carefully flavored preparations of sea bass, filet of sole, and breast of duck with 12 spices.

Quinta do Lago. © **28/939-49-83.** www.restaurante-casavelha.com. Reservations recommended. Main courses 18€–36€; fixed-price menus at 49€–119€. AE, MC, V. Mon-Sat 7–10:30pm.

Fuzios ★ ITALIAN/SEAFOOD   Tasty dishes and market-fresh ingredients are a mark of this cozy restaurant, decorated in a tavern style and only minutes from the resort complexes of Vale de Lobo and Quinta do Lago. The decor is warm and inviting, as is the welcome. Art by a local artist decorates the walls, and in summer you can dine outside on the terrace. In winter, log-burning fires warm the night. Both fresh local products and imported Italian ingredients go into the dishes. The chef is known for his prawns *piri-piri* (very hot), and his herb-crusted rack of lamb, sautéed scallops, beef Marsala, and very succulent pastas. The lemon cheesecake would please even the pickiest palette.

Rua do Comércio 286, Estrada de Quarteira. © **28/939-90-19.** Reservations required. Main courses 15€–30€. AE, MC, V. Thurs-Tues 6:30–11pm. Closed Nov 15–Dec.

Mr. Freddie's INTERNATIONAL   On the Almancil to Vale do Lobo highway, this restaurant with its terrace and beautifully set tables is increasingly known for its excellent cuisine and refined service. The market-fresh specialties keep satisfied diners coming back for more. Whether you opt for the roast duck or the pepper steak (or our recommendation, the fresh fish), all your platters will be accompanied by the season's freshest and best vegetables. You should start your meal with a selection of cold starters—none is better than the smoked swordfish with horseradish sauce—or one of the hot starters, such as sautéed clams delicately flavored with coriander and seasoned with fresh lemon and olive oil. We really like the filet of pork with apple slices and honey, and the roast rack of lamb in a rosemary and mustard sauce.

Escanxinas—Estrada de Vale do Lobo. ✆ **28/939-36-51.** www.mrfreddies.net. Reservations recommended. Main courses 14€–39€. AE, DC, MC, V. Mon–Sat 7–10:30pm. Closed Dec 25–Jan 1.

Pequeno Mundo ★ FRENCH In Almancil itself, this is the most tranquil and elegant—and, in fact, the best overall—choice for dining. It's a delightful house with a lovely courtyard that is romantic on a summer night. Reached by following a signposted, rough dirt track, Pequeno Mundo was converted from an old farmhouse. The finely tuned cuisine makes the trip worthwhile. The chef's specialty is chateaubriand, and it's the best we've had on the coast, served with a perfectly made béarnaise sauce and accompanied by sautéed potatoes. Alternately, you can also order a tender filet steak in a green-pepper sauce or a filet of lamb with fresh vegetables. The fish stew is the best in the area, and the fresh fish of the day can be prepared "as you like it."

Pereiras-Oeste. ✆ **28/939-98-66.** www.restaurantepequenomundo.com. Reservations required. Main courses 16€–35€. AE, MC, V. Mon–Sat 7–10:30pm. Closed Dec 1–Jan 31.

Restaurante Amadeus ★★★ INTERNATIONAL One of the very few restaurants in Portugal to be granted a coveted Michelin star, Amadeus is known for its innovative cuisine and outstanding cellar. As you might expect, the menu strikes rich, full chords and seemingly avoids all pitfalls. If the weather's fine (and it usually is), you can dine outside, enjoying the seductive cuisine in a modern setting. You are likely to have one of your finest Algarvian dining experiences here as you sample such sublime dishes as ravioli with wild broccoli, wild white sea bass with stewed fennel, filet of John Dory flavored with Spanish manzanilla olives, or a paprika risotto with wild octopus. The desserts are among the finest along the coast; you might opt for an orange crème brûlée with a carob tree tartlet or else prickly pears with a white chocolate sorbet.

Escanxinas, Estrada Almancil-Quarteira. ✆ **28/939-91-34.** www.amadeus.hm. Reservations required. Fixed-price menus 69€, 79€, and 98€. AE, DC, MC, V. Wed–Mon 6:30–11pm.

Restaurante Henrique Leis ★★★ FRENCH/INTERNATIONAL In Vale Formoso, 3km (1¾ miles) from Almancil, is one of the region's most outstanding restaurants, fully the equal of São Gabriel (see below). The restaurant takes its name from chef Henrique Leis, who is a whiz in the kitchen, turning out one sumptuous platter after another and winning a devoted following with his top-class dining and elegant, tranquil surroundings. The cuisine is vivid and modern, including such appetizers as a fresh goose foie gras prepared two different ways, or scallop and langoustine supreme with a boletus sabayon. The quail salad with foie gras and truffles from the Périgord region adds divine taste and a touch of class. Signature main courses include breast of Barbary duck with caramelized apples and passion fruit, and a piccata of veal tenderloin with a light sabayon of two mustards and honey. Fish depends on the catch of the day and is always very fresh.

Vale Formosa. ✆ **28/939-34-38.** www.henriqueleis.com. Reservations required. Main courses 28€–42€; 6-course menu 76€. AE, MC, V. Mon–Sat 7–10pm. Closed Nov 15–Dec 25.

São Gabriel ★★★ CONTINENTAL/SWISS A classic, elegant restaurant, this deluxe choice lies directly southeast of the center of Almancil. Gourmets drive for miles around to sample the food and wine in the refined dining room, which also features a summer terrace. The actual dishes served depend on the time of the year and the mood of the chef. You might encounter lamb perfectly roasted in an old oven, tender duck flavored with port wine, or roasted veal cutlets with Swiss-style hash browns. The cuisine is remarkably well crafted, though not daringly original. You are, however, assured of the freshest of ingredients and a changing array of tempting desserts.

Estrada Vale do Lobo. 🕾 **28/939-45-21.** www.sao-gabriel.com. Reservations required. Main courses 21€–33€; tasting menu 65€. AE, MC, V. Wed–Sat 7–10:30pm, Sun noon–2:30pm and 7–10:30pm. Closed Nov–Mar 2.

FARO ★

258km (160 miles) SE of Setúbal; 309km (192 miles) SE of Lisbon

Once loved by the Romans and later by the Moors, Faro is the provincial capital of the Algarve. In this bustling little city of some 30,000 permanent residents, you can sit at a cafe, sample the wine, and watch yesterday and today collide as old men leading donkeys brush past German backpackers in shorts. Faro is a hodgepodge of life and activity: It has been rumbled, sacked, and "quaked" by everybody from Mother Nature to the Earl of Essex (Elizabeth I's favorite).

Since Afonso III drove out the Moors for the last time in 1266, Faro has been Portuguese. On its outskirts, an international airport brings in thousands of visitors every summer. The airport has done more than anything else to increase tourism not only to Faro, but also to the entire Algarve.

Many visitors use Faro only as an arrival point, rushing through en route to a beach resort. Those who stick around will enjoy the local charm and color, exemplified by the tranquil fishing harbor. A great deal of antique charm is gone, thanks to the Earl of Essex, who sacked the town in 1596, and the 1755 earthquake. Remnants of medieval walls and some historic buildings stand in the Cidade Velha, or Old Town, which can be entered through the Arco da Vila, a gate from the 18th century.

Essentials

ARRIVING

BY PLANE Jet service makes it possible to reach Faro from Lisbon in 30 minutes. For flight information, call the **Faro airport** (🕾 28/980-08-00). To get from the airport to the rail station, take one of the **EVA Buses** (🕾 28/989-97-60; www.eva-bus.com). EVA runs 20 buses per day from the airport to the railway station, from 7:10am to 9:15pm, costing 1.70€.

BY TRAIN Trains arrive from Lisbon five times a day. The trip takes 4¾ hours and costs 20€. The train station is at Largo da Estação (🕾 80/820-82-08). This is the most strategic railway junction in the south of Portugal, thanks to its position astride lines that connect it to the north-south lines leading from Lisbon.

BY BUS There are five buses per day from Lisbon to Faro. The journey takes 3½ hours. The bus station is on Av. da República 5 (🕾 28/989-97-60; www.eva-bus.com); a one-way ticket costs 19€.

BY CAR From the west, Route 125 runs into Faro and beyond. From the Spanish border, pick up N125 west.

VISITOR INFORMATION

The **tourist office** is at Rua da Misericórdia 8–11 (℃ **28/980-36-04**) or at the airport (℃ **28/981-85-82**). It's open daily 9:30am to 5:30pm September to May, and 9:30am to 7pm June to August.

Exploring the Town

The most bizarre attraction in Faro is the **Capela dos Ossos (Chapel of Bones).** Enter through a courtyard from the rear of the **Igreja de Nossa Senhora do Monte do Carmo do Faro,** Largo do Carmo (℃ **28/982-44-90**). Erected in the 19th century, the chapel is completely lined with human skulls (an estimated 1,245) and bones. It's open daily 10am to 2pm and 3 to 5:30pm. Entrance is free to the church and 1€ to the chapel.

The church, built in 1713, contains a gilded baroque altar. Its facade is also baroque, with a bell tower rising from each side. Topping the belfries are gilded, mosquelike cupolas connected by a balustraded railing. The upper-level windows are latticed and framed with gold; statues stand in niches on either side of the main portal.

Other religious monuments include the old **Sé** (cathedral), on Largo da Sé (℃ **28/989-83-00**). Built in the Gothic and Renaissance styles, it stands on a site originally occupied by a mosque. Although the cathedral has a Gothic tower, it's better known for its tiles, which date from the 17th and 18th centuries. The highlight is the Capela do Rosário, on the right. It contains the oldest and most beautiful tiles, along with sculptures of two Nubians bearing lamps and a red chinoiserie organ. Admission is free. The beautiful cloisters are the most idyllic spot in Faro. The cathedral is open daily from 10am to 5:30pm. Admission is 2€.

Igreja de São Francisco, Largo de São Francisco (℃ **28/987-08-70**), is the other church of note. Its facade doesn't even begin to hint at the baroque richness inside. Panels of glazed earthenware tiles in milk-white and Dutch blue depict the life of the patron saint, St. Francis. One chapel is richly gilded. Hours are Monday through Friday from 8 to 9:30am and 5:30 to 7pm (but in the sleepy Algarve, you might sometimes find it closed).

If it's a rainy day, two minor museums might hold some interest. The municipal museum, or **Museu Municipal de Faro,** Largo Dom, Afonso III 14 (℃ **28/989-74-19**), is in a former 16th-century convent, the Convento de Nossa Senhora da Assunção. Even if you aren't particularly interested in the exhibits, the two-story cloister is worth a visit. Many artifacts dating from the Roman settlement of the area are on display. Some of the Roman statues are from excavations at Milreu. The museum is open Monday to Saturday 10am to 6pm. Admission is 2€ for adults, 1€ for those 13 to 26 years old, and free to those 12 and under.

The dockside **Museu Marítimo,** Rua Comunidade Lusíada (℃ **28/989-49-90**), displays models of local fishing craft and of the boats that carried Vasco da Gama and his men to India in 1497. There are replicas of a boat the Portuguese used to sail up the Congo River in 1492 and of a vessel that bested the entire Turkish navy in 1717. It's open Monday to Friday 9am to noon and 2:30 to 4:30pm. Admission is 2€.

OUTDOOR ACTIVITIES   Most visitors don't come to Faro to look at churches or museums, regardless of how interesting they are. Bus no. 16, leaving from the terminal, runs to Praia de Faro; the one-way fare is 1€. A bridge also connects the mainland and the beach, about 6km (3¾ miles) from the town center. At the shore, you can water-ski, fish, or just rent a deck chair and umbrella and lounge in the sun.

SHOPPING   Most of the shopping outlets in Faro are on Rua Santo António or its neighbor, Rua Francisco Gomes, in the heart of town. Check out **Carminho,** Rua Santo António 29 (✆ **28/982-65-22**), a well-recommended outlet for handicrafts and, to a lesser extent, traditional clothing. If you're interested in wandering like a local resident amid stands and booths piled high with the produce of southern Portugal, consider a trek through the **Mercado de Faro,** Largo do Mercado, in the town center. It's open daily from 6:30am to 1:30pm.

Where to Stay

Eva Hotel ★   Eva dominates the harbor like a fortress. It's a modern, eight-story hotel that occupies an entire side of the yacht-clogged harbor. Most of the midsize, albeit austere guest rooms offer direct sea views. The better rooms have large balconies and open onto the water. Eva's best features are its penthouse restaurant and rooftop pool, supported on 16 posts, with sun terraces and a bar.

Av. da República 1, 8000-078 Faro. www.tdhotels.pt. ✆ **28/900-10-00.** Fax 28/900-10-02. 134 units. 106€-165€ double; 141€-225€ suite. Rates include buffet breakfast. AE, DC, MC, V. Limited free parking available on street. **Amenities:** 2 restaurants; 3 bars; babysitting; concierge; exercise room; outdoor freshwater pool; room service; spa. *In room:* A/C, TV, hair dryer, minibar, Wi-Fi (4€ per hour).

Hotel Residencial S. Algarve ★ 🍴   Faro's best hotel deal opened in 1999, but in 2006 it added a modern annex that greatly increased its room count. The inn was created from an 1880s private dwelling that once belonged to a rich seafarer. When the present owner took over the premises, the building had deteriorated to the point that it had to be demolished. The reconstruction, however, honored the original architectural style. Some of the original hand-painted tiles have been preserved in glass cabinets in the foyer. Only a short walk from the historic core of Faro, the inn is most inviting. All the midsize to spacious bedrooms are well furnished and comfortable, with up-to-date amenities and bathrooms that rival those of many a first-class hotel.

Rua Infante Dom Henrique 62, 8000-363 Faro. www.residencialalgarve.com. ✆ **28/989-57-00.** Fax 28/989-57-03. 40 units. 45€-80€ double; 60€-95€ triple. Rates include continental breakfast. AE, DC, MC, V. Parking 5€. **Amenities:** Bar; babysitting; Wi-Fi (free, in lobby). *In room:* A/C, TV, hair dryer, minibar.

Hotel Santa Maria   This government-rated three-star hotel in the center of Faro has emerged as the best in town after a recent remodeling. The five-floor corner hotel is somewhat of a conventional commercial traveler's stopover, but could come in handy if you're in Faro waiting for a flight the following day. Bedrooms are adequately furnished and well maintained and are spread over five floors. The staff is efficient and will guide you through the intricacies of Faro.

Rua de Portugal 17, 8000-281 Faro. www.jcr-group.com. ✆ **28/989-80-80.** Fax 28/989-80-89. 60 units. 54€-122€ double; 84€-147€ suite. AE, MC, V. Parking 10€. **Amenities:** Bar; bikes; room service. *In room:* A/C, TV, hair dryer, Wi-Fi (free).

Where to Dine

Adega Nortenha 🍴 PORTUGUESE   It's hardly a deluxe choice, but if you gravitate to simple yet well-prepared regional food, this little restaurant does the job. It's also one of the best value spots in town, which is probably why locals swear by it. Fresh tuna steak is a delicious choice, as is the roast lamb, which is herb-flavored and perfumed with garlic. The service is friendly and efficient, and the restaurant is done up in typical Algarvian style—there's even a balcony that's great for people-watching on the street below.

Praça Ferreira de Almeida 25. (*C*) **28/982-27-09.** Main courses 7€–€. AE, DC, MC, V. Daily noon–3pm and 7–10:30pm.

Dois Irmãos PORTUGUESE   This popular bistro, founded in 1925, offers a no-nonsense atmosphere and has many devotees. The menu is as modest as the establishment and its prices, but you get a good choice of fresh grilled fish and shellfish dishes. Ignore the paper napkins and concentrate on the fine kettle of fish before you. Clams in savory sauce are a justifiable favorite, and sole is regularly featured—but, of course, everything depends on the catch of the day. Service is slow but amiable.

Largo do Terreiro do Bispo 20. (*C*) **28/982-33-37.** Reservations recommended. Main courses 12€–26€. AE, DC, MC, V. Daily noon–4pm and 6–11pm.

Faro After Dark

What Bourbon Street is to New Orleans, **Rua do Prior** is to Faro. In the heart of town, adjacent to the Faro Hotel, it's chockablock with dozens of night cafes, pubs (English and otherwise), and dance clubs that rock from around 10:30pm until dawn. Head to this street anytime after noon for insights into the hard-drinking, hard-driving nature of this hot southern town. Our favorite watering hole along this street is **CheSsenta Bar,** Rua do Prior 34 ((*C*) **91/874-58-37**), where the crowd is in their 20s and 30s, and downs one beer after another at 1.50€ a mug. It's open daily 9pm to 4am. Karaoke on Wednesday and Friday often rules the night at **O Conselheiro,** in the center of Rua Conselheiro Bívar (no phone). The best recorded music in town is played here by a DJ, and sometimes the bar converts to a dance floor. It too is open daily 10pm to 4am, and charges the same for beer.

Easy Excursions from Faro

Some of the most interesting towns in the Algarve surround the capital. Exploring any one takes a half-day.

LOULÉ   This market town 15km (9⅓ miles) north of Faro lies in the heart of the Algarve's chimney district. If you think chimneys can't excite you, you haven't seen the ones here. The fret-cut plaster towers rise from many of the cottages and houses (and even the occasional doghouse).

Bus service is good during the day; about 40 buses arrive from various parts of the Algarve, mainly Faro. Five trains per day arrive from Faro at the Loulé rail station, about 5km (3 miles) from the center of town. There are bus connections to the center of town from the station, or you can take a taxi.

The **Loulé Tourist Information Office** is on Avenida 25 de Abril ((*C*) **28/946-39-00**). It's open October to May Monday to Friday 9:30am to 5:30pm, and Saturday 9:30am to 3:30pm; and June to September Monday to Friday 9:30am to 7pm, and Saturday 9:30am to 3:30pm.

Loulé and the villages around it are known for their handicrafts. They produce work in palm fronds and esparto, such as handbags, baskets, mats, and hats. Loulé artisans also make copper articles, bright harnesses, delicate wrought-iron pieces, clogs, cloth shoes and slippers, tinware, and pottery. Products are displayed in workshops at the foot of the walls of an old fortress and in other showrooms, particularly those along Rua do 9 de Abril.

In Loulé, you might want to visit the Gothic-style **Igreja de São Clemente, Matriz de Loulé,** or parish church, Largo do Matriz 19 (✆ **28/941-51-67**). It was given to the town in the late 13th century. It's open Monday to Friday 9 to 11am, Saturday 9am to 7pm. Admission is free though donations are welcome.

The remains of the **Moorish castelo** are at Largo Dom Pedro I (no phone). The ruins house a historical museum and are open Monday to Friday 9am to 5:30pm, and Saturday 10am to 2pm. Admission is 2€.

For meals, try the Portuguese cuisine at **O Avenida,** Av. José da Costa Mealha 13 (✆ **28/946-21-06**), on the main street close to the traffic circle. It's one of the finest restaurants in the Algarve. The specialty is shellfish cooked *cataplana*-style. You can also order beefsteak à Avenida or sole meunière. The restaurant is open Monday through Saturday from noon to 3:30pm and 7 to 10pm; it's closed for most of November. Meal prices start at 7€ to 15€. Occasional live entertainment is featured. O Avenida accepts most major credit cards.

SÃO BRÁS DE ALPORTEL Traveling north from Faro, you'll pass through groves of figs, almonds, and oranges, and through pine woods where resin collects in wooden cups on the tree trunks. After 20km (12 miles) you'll come upon isolated São Brás de Alportel, one of the most charming and least-known spots on the Algarve. Far from the crowded beaches, this town attracts those in search of pure air, peace, and quiet. It's a bucolic setting filled with flowers pushing through nutmeg-colored soil. Northeast of Loulé, the whitewashed, tile-roofed town livens up only on market days. Like its neighbor, Faro, it's noted for its perforated plaster chimneys. The area at the foot of the Serra do Caldeirão has been described as one vast garden.

OLHÃO This is the Algarve's famous cubist town, long beloved by painters. In its heart, white blocks stacked one upon the other, with flat red-tile roofs and exterior stairways on the stark walls, evoke the casbahs of North Africa. The cubist buildings are found only at the core. The rest of Olhão has almost disappeared under the onslaught of modern commercialism.

While you're here, try to attend the fish market near the waterfront when a *lota*, or auction, is underway. Olhão is also known for its "bullfights of the sea," in which fishers wrestle with struggling tuna trapped in nets en route to the smelly warehouses along the harbor.

If you're here at lunchtime, go to one of the inexpensive markets along the waterfront. At **Casa de Pasto O Bote,** Av. do 5 de Outubro 122 (✆ **28/972-11-83**), you can select your food from trays of fresh fish. Your choice is then grilled to your specifications. Meal prices start at 10€. It's open Monday to Saturday noon to 3pm and 7 to 10pm.

For the best view, climb **Cabeça Hill,** with grottoes punctured by stalagmites and stalactites, or St. Michael's Mount, offering a panorama of the casbahlike Baretta. Finally, to reach one of the most idyllic beaches on the Algarve, take a 10-minute motorboat ride to the Ilha da Armona, a nautical mile away. Ferries run hourly in summer; the round-trip fare is 5.50€. Olhão is 8km (5 miles) east of Faro.

TAVIRA A gem 31km (19 miles) east of Faro, Tavira is approached through green fields studded with almond and carob trees. Sometimes called the Venice of the Algarve, Tavira lies on the banks of the Ségua and Gilão rivers, which meet under a seven-arched Roman bridge. In the town square, palms and pepper trees rustle under the cool arches of the arcade. In spite of modern encroachments, Tavira is festive looking. Floridly decorated chimneys top many of the houses, some of which are graced with emerald-green tiles and wrought-iron balconies capped by finials. Fretwork adorns many doorways. The liveliest action centers are the fruit and vegetable market on the river esplanade.

The **Tavira Tourist Office** is on Rua da Galeria 9 (℡ **28/132-25-11**). Tavira has frequent bus connections with Faro throughout the day. It's open June to September daily 9:30am to 7pm; and October to May Monday to Friday 9:30am to 1pm and 2 to 5:30pm.

Climb the stepped street off Rua da Liberdade, and you can explore the battlemented walls of a castle once known to the Moors. From here you'll have the best view of the town's church spires; across the river delta, you can see the ocean. The castle is open daily from 9am to 5pm. Admission is free.

A tuna-fishing center, Tavira is cut off from the sea by an elongated spit of sand. The **Ilha de Tavira** begins west of Cacela and runs all the way past the fishing village of Fuzeta. On this sandbar, accessible by motorboat, are two beaches: the Praia de Tavira and the Praia de Fuzeta. Some people prefer the beach at the tiny village of Santa Luzia, about 3km (1¾ miles) from the heart of town.

If you're here for lunch, try the **Restaurante Imperial,** Rua José Pires Padinha 22 (℡ **28/132-23-06**). A small, air-conditioned place off the main square, it serves regional food, including shellfish, shellfish rice, garlic-flavored pork, roast chicken, fresh tuna, and other Portuguese dishes, accompanied by vegetables and good local wines. A favorite meal is pork and clams with french fries, topped off with a rich egg-and-almond dessert. Meals cost 8€ to 22€ or more, including wine. Food is served daily from noon to 3:30pm and 7 to 11pm. American Express, MasterCard, and Visa are accepted.

If you'd like to stay a while, consider checking into **Pousada de Tavira, Convento da Graça ★★**, Rua D. Paio Peres Correia, 8800-407 Tavira (℡ **28/132-90-40;** fax 28/138-17-41; www.pousadas.pt), a 36-room hotel charging 130€ to 300€ for a double, 176€ to 438€ for a suite. Beginning in 1569, cloistered Augustinian nuns lived in the convent founded on this site. Today this historic building with its Renaissance cloister and baroque central staircase has been turned into one of the most colorful hotels in the Algarve. All the modern equipment has been installed, but much remains from its convent heyday. The bedrooms are the finest in the area, many with small balconies and one with a mezzanine. The accommodations are stylishly furnished and exceedingly comfortable. The suites are superb, one with a private garden. Archaeological traces of Islamic origin were discovered during the restoration. Some of these features are partially visible from the bar. The pousada has a good restaurant, a lively bar, and 2 outdoor pools.

American Express, Diners Club, MasterCard, and Visa are accepted.

ESTÓI A little village some 8km (5 miles) northeast of Faro, Estói is still mainly unspoiled by tourists. Buses run to the area from Faro. Visitors are objects of some curiosity, stared at by old women sheltered behind the curtains of their little houses and followed by begging children. Sometimes you see women washing their clothing in a public trough. Garden walls are decaying here, and the cottages are worn by time and the weather.

The principal sight in Estói is the **Palácio do Visconde de Estói.** The villa, with its salmon-pink baroque facade, has been described as a cross between Versailles and the water gardens of the Villa d'Este near Rome. It was built in the late 18th century for Francisco José de Moura Coutinho; José Francisco da Silva rescued it from near ruin between 1893 and 1909. A palm-lined walk leads to terraced gardens with orange trees along the balusters.

The villa is not open to the public, but the grounds can be visited Tuesday to Saturday from 10am to 5pm. To enter, ring a bell at the iron gates outside the palm-lined walk, and a caretaker will guide you to the gardens. There's no entrance fee, but tip the caretaker.

Monte do Casal ★★, Cerro de Lobo-Estói, 8005-436 Faro (✆ **28/999-01-40;** www.montedocasal.pt), is a country house from the 18th century that is one of the most sedate and charming places to stay in the region. Totally renovated, the British-owned inn lies on 3 hectares (7½ acres) of grounds planted with olive, fruit, and almond trees along with bougainvillea climbing white walls. The well-manicured garden contains a swimming pool. The spacious and comfortably furnished bedrooms, with tub/shower combinations, have terraces with panoramic views of the countryside. This inn represents gracious Algarvian living at its best. In the regional-style dining room, an excellent French cuisine is served nightly in a setting that was originally part of an old farmhouse. Guests meet and mingle in the spacious drawing room with luxurious furnishings, a bookcase, oil paintings, and a fireplace. Doubles cost 105€ to 255€; suites cost 170€ to 300€. It's closed January 4 to February 12.

If you'd like to spend the night in this historic town, you can check into the **Pousada do Palacio de Estói,** Rua São José, 8005-465 Estói (✆ **28/999-01-50;** www.pousadas.pt), installed in a 19th-century palace, formerly the home of the Viscounts of Estói. The palace was lived in by his descendants until they sold it to Faro in 1987. Today, it has been turned into one of the charming pousadas of Portugal, with tea pavilions and a little Versailles-style garden. The entire aristocratic complex consists of 4 hectares (10 acres), including the old stables. A modern wing of first-class bedrooms has been installed, each room air-conditioned and beautifully and comfortably furnished in modern styling. Luxurious touches include an outdoor swimming pool and spa. Architecturally, many of the neo-baroque and neo-rococo features have been maintained, and the interior contains plaster ceilings, the finest in the Algarve. You can wander at leisure through the statue-studded gardens, which can also be enjoyed from a balcony from your bedroom. The 60-room inn charges from 200€ to 300€ in a double, 270€ to 405€ in a suite. Amenities include a restaurant, bar, and free Wi-Fi in the public areas.

VILA REAL DE SANTO ANTÓNIO

314km (195 miles) SE of Lisbon; 85km (53 miles) E of Faro; 50km (31 miles) W of Huelva, Spain

Twenty years after the Marquês de Pombal rebuilt Lisbon, which had been destroyed in the great 1755 earthquake, he sent architects and builders to Vila Real de Santo António. They reestablished this frontier town on the bank opposite Spain in only 5 months. Pombal's motivation was jealousy of Spain. Much has changed, but **Praça de Pombal** remains. An obelisk stands in the center of the square, which is paved with inlays of black-and-white tiles radiating like sunrays and is filled with orange trees. Separated from its Iberian neighbor by the Guadiana River, Vila Real de Santo António has car-ferry service between Portugal and Ayamonte, Spain.

Essentials
ARRIVING
BY TRAIN Most visitors from Lisbon take the train to Faro, then proceed by bus to Vila Real (see below).

BY BUS   From Faro to Vila Real, buses run each day to the Vila Real bus station on Avenida da República. They take 1¾ hours and cost 5.50€ one-way. For information and schedules, call ℂ **28/989-97-60.**

BY FERRY   In summer, ferries run between Ayamonte, Spain, and Vila Real daily from 9am to 7pm. The fare is 2.50€ per passenger or 6€ per car. Ferries depart from the station on Avenida da República; call ℂ **28/154-31-52** for more information.

VISITOR INFORMATION

The **tourist office** is on Avenida Infante D. Henrique, 8900 Monte Gordo (ℂ **28/ 154-44-95**). It's open Monday to Friday 9:30am to 5:30pm October to April, and Tuesday to Thursday 9:30am to 7pm and Friday to Monday 9:30am to 5:30pm May to September.

Exploring the Town

Vila Real de Santo António is a great example of 18th-century town planning. A long esplanade, Avenida da República, follows the river, and from its northern extremity you can view the Spanish town across the way. Gaily painted horse-drawn carriages take you sightseeing past the shipyards and the lighthouse.

A 5km (3-mile) drive north on the road to Mértola (N122) will take you to the gull-gray castle-fortress of **Castro Marim.** This formidable structure is a legacy of the border wars between Spain and Portugal. The ramparts and walls stand watch over the territory across the river. Afonso III, who expelled the Moors from this region, founded the original fortress, which was razed by the 1755 earthquake. Inside the walls are the ruins of the Igreja de São Tiago, dedicated to St. James.

Southwest of Vila Real is the emerging resort of **Monte Gordo,** which has the second-greatest concentration of hotels in the eastern Algarve (after Faro). Monte Gordo, 4km (2½ miles) southwest of Vila Real at the mouth of the Guadiana River, is the last in a long line of Algarvian resorts. Its wide, steep beach, **Praia de Monte Gordo,** is one of the finest on Portugal's southern coast. This beach, backed by pine-studded lowlands, has the highest average water temperature in Portugal.

Sadly, what was once a sleepy little fishing village has succumbed to high-rises. Nowadays the *varinas* (fishermen's wives) urge their sons to work in the hotels instead of the sea, fishing for tips instead of tuna.

Where to Stay

Although Vila Real has hotels, most visitors prefer to stay at the beach at Monte Gordo (see below).

VILA REAL

Hotel Apolo   This hotel on the western edge of town is not the classiest stopover on the Algarve, but it's certainly adequate for an overnight stay. Near the beach and the river, it attracts vacationers as well as travelers who don't want to cross the Spanish border at night. The hotel has a spacious marble-floored lobby leading into a large bar scattered with comfortable sofas and flooded with sunlight. Each small, simply furnished guest room has a private balcony and a good bathroom equipped with a tub/shower combination.

Av. dos Bombeiros Portugueses, 8900-209 Vila Real de Santo António. www.apolo-hotel.com. ℂ **28/151-24-48.** Fax 28/151-24-50. 45 units. 49€–105€ double. Rates include buffet breakfast. AE, DC, MC, V. Free parking. **Amenities:** Bar; bikes; outdoor freshwater pool. *In room:* A/C, TV, hair dryer.

MONTE GORDO

Casablanca Inn ★ 🎁   Casablanca Inn is not directly on the beach, but its location on a flower-dotted downtown park makes up for it. The owner designed it to look like something you might find in a wealthy part of Morocco. There's a lush flower garden and a series of recessed arched balconies, and the design might be suitable for an updated version of the film classic *Casablanca*. The lobby bar is called Rick's and is covered with movie photos. Each midsize guest room contains a terrace and well-kept bathrooms.

Rua 7, Monte Gordo, 8900-474 Vila Real de Santo António. www.casablancainn.pt. ✆ **28/151-14-44.** Fax 28/151-19-99. 42 units. 65€–130€ double. Rates include buffet breakfast. AE, DC, MC, V. Free parking. **Amenities:** Restaurant; bar; 2 pools (1 heated indoor). *In room:* A/C, TV.

Hotel Navegadores   The sign in front of this large hotel is so discreet that you might mistake it for an apartment house. The establishment is popular with vacationing Portuguese and British families, who congregate under the dome covering the atrium's swimming pool, near the reception desk. You'll find a bar that serves fruit-laden drinks, and semitropical plants throughout the public rooms. About three-quarters of the guest rooms have private balconies. The hotel remains a group tour favorite. Rooms are comfortable but standard, without any flair. The beach is a 5-minute walk away.

Av. De Catalunha, 8900-468 Vila Real de Santo António. www.navotel.pt. ✆ **28/151-08-60.** Fax 28/151-08-74. 347 units. 66€–110€ double; 72€–120€ suite. Rates include buffet breakfast. AE, DC, MC, V. **Amenities:** Restaurant; 3 bars; exercise room; indoor heated pool; room service; spa; Wi-Fi (free, in lobby). *In room:* A/C, TV, hair dryer, minibar (in some).

Vasco da Gama Hotel   The entrepreneurs here know what their northern guests seek: lots of sunbathing and swimming. Although the hotel sits on a long, wide sandy beach, it also offers an Olympic-size pool with a high-dive board and about .5 hectares (1¼ acres) of flagstone sun terrace. All of the spartan, rather small guest rooms are furnished conservatively and come equipped with balconies and neatly kept bathrooms.

Av. Infante Dom Henrique, Monte Gordo, 8900-412 Vila Real de Santo António. www.vascodagamahotel.com. ✆ **28/151-09-00.** Fax 28/151-09-01. 185 units. 70€–200€ person double. Rates include buffet breakfast. AE, DC, MC, V. Free parking. **Amenities:** Restaurant; bar; babysitting; bikes; children's center; exercise room; outdoor freshwater pool; room service; 2 outdoor tennis courts (lit). *In room:* A/C, TV, hair dryer, minibar.

Where to Dine

The Restaurant at the Hotel Alcazar/The 19th Hole INTERNATIONAL/ PORTUGUESE   This hotel restaurant is a magnet for local residents as well as for the guests in residence. Its evening buffet is copious and varied. Expect lavish spreads that focus on salads, fresh fish, meat, pastries, fruits, and cheeses, all of them laid out like a cornucopia. Views within this ground-floor restaurant overlook the hotel's swimming pool and garden area, and the beach lies only about 278m (912 ft.) away. Lunches are served within a separate dining room, "The 19th Hole," and are a la carte, mostly salads, sandwiches, platters of grilled fish, chicken, beef, and pasta.

Rua de Ceuta 9. ✆ **28/151-01-49.** www.hotelalcazaralgarve.com. Main courses 9€–17€. AE, DC, MC, V. Daily noon–2pm and 6:30–9pm.

ALENTEJO & RIBATEJO

The adjoining provinces of Alentejo and Ribatejo constitute the heartland of Portugal. Ribatejo is a land of bull-breeding pastures; Alentejo is a plain of fire and ice.

Ribatejo is river country; the Tagus, coming from Spain, overflows its banks in winter. The region is famed for bluegrass, Arabian horses, and black bulls. Its most striking feature, however, is human: *campinos,* the region's sturdy horsemen. They harness the Arabian pride of their horses and discover the intangible quality of bravery in the bulls. Whether visiting the château of the Templars, which rises smack in the middle of the Tagus at Almourol, or attending an exciting *festa brava,* when horses and bulls rumble through the streets of Vila Franca de Xira, you'll marvel at the passion of the people. Ribatejo's *fadistas* (fado singers) have long been noted for their remarkable intensity.

The cork-producing plains of Alentejo (which means "beyond the Tagus") make up the largest province in Portugal. It's so large that the government has divided it into the northern Alto Alentejo (the capital of which is Évora) and southern Baixo Alentejo (whose capital is Beja).

Locals in Alentejo insulate themselves in tiny-windowed, whitewashed houses—warm in the cold winters and cool during the scorching summers. This is the least populated of Portuguese provinces, with seemingly endless fields of wheat. It's the world's largest producer of cork, whose trees can be stripped only once every 9 years.

In winter, the men make a dramatic sight, outfitted in characteristic long brown coats with two short-tiered capes, often with red-fox collars. The women are more colorful, especially when they're working in the rice paddies or wheat fields. Their short skirts and patterned undergarments allow them to wade barefooted into the paddies. On top of knitted cowls, with mere slits for the eyes, women wear brimmed felt hats usually studded with flowers.

Although dusty Alentejo is mostly a region of inland plains, it also has an Atlantic coast. It stretches from the mouth of the Sado River all the way to the border of the Algarve, just south of Zambujeira do Mar Carvalhal. This stretch of beach is the least crowded and least developed in Portugal. Towering rock cliffs punctuate much of the coastline south of Lisbon, interrupted by the occasional sandy cove and tranquil bay. Regrettably, there isn't much protection from the often-fierce waves and winds that rush in from the Atlantic; the waters are generally too chilly for most tastes.

Alentejo & Ribatejo

Castelo Branco

N18

Tomar

Castelo de Vide

Marvão

N118

Abrantes

Portalegre

Leiria

Alburqueque

Santarém

Chouto

Ponte de Sor

N80

Almeirim

Cartaxo

E01

Rio Tejo
(Tagus River)

Montargil

**Badajoz
(Spain)**

Estremoz

Elvas

Vila Franca
de Xira

Coruche

E90

Borba

N10

Arraiolos

N18

Vila
Viçosa

Vendas
Novas

N4

Rio Guadiana

Évora

E90 E01

Reguengos de
Monsaraz

Setúbal

N5

Alcácer
do Sal

Alcáçovas

E01

Viana do Alentejo

Rio Sado

Vidigueira

Grândola

N18

Moura

*ATLANTIC
OCEAN*

Beja

Santiago do Cacém

Serpa

Sines

FRANCE

PORTUGAL

SPAIN

Lisbon area of
detail

Driving is the best way to see the region because there are numerous towns to see and excursions to take from the major cities. Public transportation exists, but often you'll have a long, tiresome wait between connections. Both provinces lie virtually on Lisbon's doorstep—in fact, suburbs of the capital lie on their edges.

If you've just explored the Algarve (see chapter 9), you'll find Alentejo within striking distance. The best route to take into Alentejo from the south is IP-1 from Albufeira.

TOMAR ★★

Divided by the Nabão River, historic Tomar was bound to the fate of the notorious quasi-religious order of the Knights Templar. In the 12th century, the powerful, wealthy monks established the beginnings of the Convento de Cristo on a tree-studded hill overlooking the town. Originally a monastery, it evolved into a kind of grand headquarters for the Templars. The knights, who swore a vow of chastity, had fought ferociously at Santarém against the Moors. As their military might grew, they built a massive walled castle at Tomar in 1160. The ruins—primarily the walls—can be seen today.

By 1314, the Templars had amassed both great riches and many enemies; the pope was urged to suppress their power. King Dinis allowed them to regroup their forces in Portugal under the new aegis of the Order of Christ in 1319. In the 15th century, Henry the Navigator became the most famous of the order's grand masters, using much of their money to subsidize his explorations.

Essentials

ARRIVING

BY TRAIN   The train station (✆ 80/820-82-08) is on Avenida Combatentes da Grande Guerra, at the southern edge of town. Five trains arrive daily from Lisbon; the trip takes 2 hours and costs 10€ one-way.

BY BUS   The bus station is on Avenida Combatentes da Grande Guerra. For information, call the bus company, **Rede Expressos** (✆ **70/722-33-44;** www.rede-expressos.pt). Four buses a day arrive from Lisbon. The 2-hour trip costs 9€ one-way.

BY CAR   From Santarém, continue northeast along Route 3 and then cut east at the junction of N110. When you reach Route 110, head north. To reach Santarém from Lisbon, go north on E1.

VISITOR INFORMATION

The **Tomar Tourist Office** is on Avenida Dr. Cândido Madureira (✆ **24/932-24-27**). October to April, it's open daily 10am to 1pm and 2 to 6pm; May to September hours are Monday to Friday 10am to 7pm and Saturday and Sunday 10am to 6pm.

Exploring the Town

Capela de Nossa Senhora da Conceição   On the way up the hill to see the monastery, you can stop off at this chapel, crowned by small cupolas and jutting out over the town. Reached through an avenue of trees, it was built in the Renaissance style in the mid–16th century. The interior is a forest of white Corinthian pillars.

Btw. the old town and the Convento da Ordem de Cristo. ✆ **24/932-24-27.** Free admission. Daily 9am–6pm.

Convento da Ordem de Cristo ★★ From its inception in 1160, the Convent of the Order of Christ monastery experienced 5 centuries of inspired builders, including Manuel I (the Fortunate). It also fell victim to destroyers, notably in 1810, when Napoleon's overzealous troops turned it into a barracks. What remains on the top of the hill is one of Portugal's most brilliant architectural accomplishments.

The portal of the Templars Church, in the Manueline style, depicts everything from leaves to chubby cherubs. Inside is an **octagonal church ★** with eight columns, said to have been modeled after the Temple of the Holy Sepulchre in Jerusalem. The mosquelike effect links Christian and Muslim cultures, as in the Mezquita in Córdoba, Spain. The author Howard La Fay called it "a muted echo of Byzantium in scarlet and dull gold." The damage the French troops inflicted is very evident. On the other side, the church is in the Manueline style with rosettes. Throughout, you'll see the Templars insignia.

The monastery's eight cloisters embrace a variety of styles. The most notable, a two-tiered structure dating from the 12th century, exhibits perfect symmetry, the almost severe academic use of the classical form that distinguishes the Palladian school. A guide will also take you on a brief tour of a dormitory where the monks lived in austere cells.

The monastery possesses some of the greatest Manueline stonework in Portugal. A fine example is the grotesque **west window ★★★** of the chapter house. At first the forms emanating from the window might confuse you, but closer inspection reveals a meticulous symbolic and literal depiction of Portugal's sea lore and power. Knots and ropes, mariners and the tools of their craft, silken sails wafting in stone and re-created coral seascapes—all are delicately interwoven in this *chef-d'oeuvre* of the whole movement.

Atop a hill overlooking the old town. ☎ **24/931-34-81.** www.conventocristo.pt. Admission 6€ adults, 3€ ages 14–25, free for children under 14. June–Sept daily 9am–6pm; Oct–May daily 9am–5pm.

Igreja de São João Baptista In the heart of town is this 15th-century church, built by Manuel I. It contains black-and-white diamond mosaics and a white-and-gold baroque altar; a chapel to the right is faced with antique tiles. In and around the church are the narrow cobblestone streets of Tomar, where shops sell dried codfish, and wrought-iron balconies are decorated with bird cages and flowerpots.

Praça da República. ☎ **24/932-24-27.** Free admission. Tues–Sun 10am–7pm.

Museu Luso-Hebraico This Portuguese-Hebrew museum lies in the heart of the old Jewish ghetto. The building was the Sinagoga de Tomar—the oldest Jewish house of worship in Portugal, dating from the mid-1400s. A Jewish community worshiped here until 1496, when the Catholic hierarchy ordered its members to convert or get out of town. In time, the synagogue assumed many roles: Christian chapel, prison, warehouse, even hayloft. Today it enjoys national monument status. Samuel Schwartz, a German who devoted part of his life to restoring it, bought the building in 1923. He donated it to the Portuguese state in 1939. In return, Schwartz and his wife were awarded citizenship and protection during World War II. The museum exhibits many 15th-century tombs with Hebrew inscriptions, along with Jewish artifacts donated from around the globe. An on-site excavation unearthed a mikvah, or ritual purification bath.

Rua Dr. Joaquim Jaquinto 73. ☎ **24/932-98-14.** Free admission; donations accepted. Daily 10am–1pm and 2–6pm.

Shopping

Shopkeepers in Tomar work hard to acquire premises on the town's main shopping thoroughfare, Rua Serpa Pinto, an avenue known locally as *Corre Doura,* which refers to a medieval horse race that used to take place along this street in the 12th century. You'll find lots of outlets for folkloric goods, pottery, copperware, and wrought iron.

Where to Stay

MODERATE

Estalagem de Santa Iria ★ 🛍 Although not as swanky as Hotel dos Templários, this charming inn is like a grand country villa, filled with architectural and decorative touches from the region. Hallways with arches lead to the small to midsize bedrooms, which are furnished with regional artifacts and wood furnishings, along with shiny and well-kept bathrooms. Decoration is minimalist, with plaster walls painted white. Families are also fond of the inn, and the staff provides extra beds in the rooms for children ages 4 to 12 years. In business since the mid–20th century, the colonial-style, two-story inn lies in the center. Its on-site restaurant is a popular place with locals and visitors alike, and it specializes in market-fresh regional produce.

Parque do Mouchão, 2300-586 Tomar. www.estalagemsantairia.com. Ⓒ **24/931-33-26.** Fax 24/932-12-38. 14 units. 58€–85€ double; 90€–125€ suite. Rates include continental breakfast. AE, DC, MC, V. Free parking. **Amenities:** Restaurant; bar; Wi-Fi (free, in lobby). *In room:* TV.

Hotel dos Templários ★★ This large government-rated four-star hotel on the banks of the Rio Nabão seems incongruous in such a small town—it was expanded in 1994 to make it the largest hotel in the district. Five local businessmen created the hotel in 1967, but they would hardly recognize the place today. The midsize guest rooms, although ordinary, are quite agreeable, especially those in the new wing. Many open onto views of the Convent of Christ. All are well furnished and equipped, with neatly kept bathrooms. The public areas, including the lounges and the terrace-view dining room, are spacious. The hotel has wide sun terraces and a greenhouse.

Largo Cândido dos Reis 1, 2300-909 Tomar. www.hoteldostemplarios.pt. Ⓒ **24/931-01-00.** Fax 24/932-21-91. 177 units. 78€–132€ double; 135€–180€ suite. Rates include buffet breakfast. AE, DC, MC, V. Free parking. **Amenities:** Restaurant; bar; babysitting; children's center; exercise room; 2 heated pools (1 indoor); room service; sauna; outdoor tennis court (lit). *In room:* A/C, TV, hair dryer, minibar, Wi-Fi (12€ per 24 hr.).

INEXPENSIVE

Hotel Residencial Trovador 🏅 Rooms here are clean and comfortable, with conservatively patterned wallpaper and good beds. All units come equipped with well-maintained bathrooms. Breakfast is the only meal served. The hotel is close to the bus station and the commercial center of town, in a drab neighborhood of apartment buildings.

Rua 10 d'Agosto, 2300-553 Tomar. www.residencialtrovador.com.sapo.pt. Ⓒ **24/932-25-67.** Fax 24/932-21-94. 30 units. 45€–75€ double. Rates include buffet breakfast. AE, DC, MC, V. **Amenities:** Exercise room; room service; spa. *In room:* A/C, TV, Wi-Fi (free).

A Place to Stay & Dine Nearby

Estalagem da Ilha do Lombo ★ 🛍 This country inn, opened in 1975 and renovated in 2011, is an idyllic retreat on the Ilha do Lombo. The location is some 15km (9⅓ miles) southeast of Tomar. Its terrace provides a view of Portugal's version of the

Certain towns in the region—such as Évora—are on the main tourist circuit, but both Alentejo and Ribatejo have an abundance of small towns and villages intriguing to the traveler with the time and desire to seek them out. Our favorites:

Serpa Still languishing in the Middle Ages, Serpa is a walled town with defensive towers. It was incorporated into the kingdom of Portugal in 1295, after having belonged to the Infante of Serpa, Dom Fernando, brother of Dom Sancho II. Overlooking the vast Alentejo plain, Serpa is a town of narrow streets and latticed windows, famous for the cheese that bears its name, for pork sausage, and for sweets. Silvery olive trees surround the approaches to the town, and the whiteness of the buildings contrasts with the red-brown of the plains. The wild beauties of the river Guadiana, endless fields of grain, and cork-oak groves mark the landscape. In the town, you can see unique painted furniture, an archaeological museum, and several ancient churches. Serpa has become a lunch stop or rest stop for travelers on the way to and from Spain; many motorists spend the night at the hilltop pousada.

Monsaraz The old fortified town of Monsaraz lies 51km (32 miles) east of Évora en route to Spain. It's a village of antique whitewashed houses, with cobblestone lanes and many reminders of the Moors who held out here until they were conquered in 1166. Some of the women still wear traditional garb: men's hats on shawl-covered heads and men's pants under their skirts. The custom derives from a need for protection from the sun. Monsaraz overlooks the Guadiana Valley, which forms the border between Spain and Portugal.

The walled town can easily be visited from Évora in an afternoon. As you scale the ramparts, you're rewarded with a view over what looks like a cross between a bullring and a Greek theater.

Hoover Dam. Bedrooms at the inn range from small to midsize, each attractively and comfortably furnished and equipped with a tiled bathroom. The hotel staff will help you arrange canoeing on the lake, and windsurfing and water-skiing are also an option. The hotel also operates a traditional restaurant, using market-fresh ingredients in its preparation of both regional dishes and international fare.

Serra de Tomar, 2300-909 Tomar. www.ilhadolombo.com. ✆ **24/937-11-08.** Fax 24/937-14-03. 17 units. 130€–150€ double. Rates include buffet breakfast. MC, V. **Amenities:** Restaurant; bar; exercise room; outdoor pool; outdoor tennis court (lit). *In room:* A/C, TV, hair dryer, minibar.

Where to Dine

Chico Elias ★★★ 🏠 PORTUGUESE This is the special dining discovery of the area, the domain of the chef/owner, Maria do Céu, who is justly acclaimed as the most creative in the region. If you wish a special dish or a rare specialty, always call in advance to give fair warning. That specialty might be rabbit in a pumpkin—we kid you not. It's delectable. Other good-tasting dishes include a fricassee of eels, roast kid, or roast cod with acorn-sweetened pork. Our favorite dish is duck with figs, followed by, of all things, snails with beans. *Bacalhau* (dried codfish) with corn bread sounds like real peasant fare, but it has won praise from the dozens of visiting journalists, diplomats, and politicians who have dined here. For dessert, we'd recommend the glorious "drunken pears."

The highlight of a visit is the main street, Rua Direita. It contains the town's most distinguished architecture, wrought-iron grilles, balconies, and outside staircases.

Borba   On the way to Borba, you'll pass quarries filled with black, white, and multicolored deposits. In the village, marble reigns: Many cottages have marble door trimmings and facings, and the women kneel to scrub their doorways, a source of special pride. On Rua São Bartolomeu sits a church dedicated to São Bartolomeu. It displays a groined ceiling; walls lined with blue, white, and gold *azulejos* (decorative tiles); and an altar in black-and-white marble. The richly decorated ceiling is painted with four major medallions. As Portuguese churches go, this one isn't remarkable. But there are eight nearby antiques shops (amazing for such a small town) filled with interesting items. Borba is also a big wine center, and you might want to sample the local brew at a cafe, or perhaps at the pousada at Elvas.

Marvão   This ancient walled hill town, close to Castelo de Vide, is well preserved and is visited chiefly for its spectacular views. Just less than 6.5km (4 miles) from the Spanish frontier, the once-fortified medieval stronghold retains a rich flavor of the Middle Ages. Those with limited time who can explore only one border town in Portugal should make it this one—it's that panoramic. You get to Marvão by following a road around the promontory on which the little town stands, past the Church of Our Lady of the Star, the curtain walls, watchtowers, and parapets. Arcaded passageways, balconied houses with wrought-iron grillwork and Manueline windows, and a number of churches can be seen along the hilly streets. The castle, built in the 13th century, stands at the western part of the rocky outcropping. From the parapet, you'll have a panoramic view of the surrounding country—all the way to the Spanish mountains in the east, and a vast sweep of Portuguese mountain ranges.

Rua Principal 70, Algarvias. ☏ **24/931-10-67.** Reservations required. Main courses 16€–32€. No credit cards. Wed-Mon noon-3:30pm and 6-10pm.

Tomar After Dark

Despite Tomar's small size and emphasis on folklore, gregarious locals have lots of outlets for drinking and barhopping. You'll find *tascas* (taverns) and bars scattered throughout the town's historic core. One of the most charming and convivial is the **Quinta Bar,** Quinta do Falcão 26 (☏ **24/938-17-67**). People between the ages of 20 and 45 hang out and listen to live music.

ESTREMOZ ★

46km (29 miles) NE of Évora; 174km (108 miles) E of Lisbon; 12km (7½ miles) W of Borba

Rising from the plain like a pyramid of salt set out to dry in the sun, fortified Estremoz is in the center of the marble-quarry region of Alentejo. Cottages and mansions alike use the abundant marble in their construction and trim.

Essentials

ARRIVING

BY TRAIN   There is no train service to Estremoz.

BY BUS   The bus station is at Rossio Marquês de Pombal. For information call the bus company, **Rede Expressos** (© **70/722-33-44;** www.rede-expressos.pt). Two buses arrive daily from Évora, 1 hour away; three buses a day arrive from Portalegre, 1½ hours away.

BY CAR   From Évora (p. 268), head northeast along Route 18.

Exploring the Town

With enough promenading soldiers to man a garrison, the open quadrangle in the center of the Lower Town is called the **Rossio Marquês de Pombal.** The **Town Hall,** with its twin bell towers, opens onto this square. It has a grand stairway whose walls are lined with antique blue-and-white tiles, depicting hunting, pastoral, and historical scenes.

In the 16th-century **Igreja de Santa Maria (Church of St. Mary),** you'll see pictures by Portuguese primitive painters. The church formed part of the ancient fortress. It is open Tuesday through Sunday from 9:30am to noon and 3 to 5pm. Admission is free.

Another church worth a stop is .6km (less than a half-mile) south of the town on the road to Bencatel. The **Igreja de Nossa Senhora dos Mártires (Church of Our Lady of the Martyrs)** has beautiful tiles and an entrance marked by a Manueline arch. Dating from 1844, the church has a nave chevet after the French Gothic style of architecture. Hours vary according to the season and demands on the church staff, but in most cases, it's open daily from 8am to 6pm. Admission is free, although donations are accepted.

Castelo da Rainha Santa Isabel   From the ramparts of the Castle of Queen Saint Isabel, which dates from the 13th-century reign of Dinis, the plains of Alentejo spread out before you. Although one 75-year-old British lady reportedly walked it, the route to the top is best covered by car. Drive to the top of the Upper Town and stop on Largo de Dom Dinis. The stones of the castle, the cradle of the town's past, were decaying so badly that the city leaders pressed for its restoration in 1970. It was turned into a luxurious pousada (see "Where to Stay," below), the best place in town to stay or dine.

The castle's imposing once-fortified tower, attached to a palace, dominates the central plaza. Dinis's wife, Isabella, died in the castle and was unofficially proclaimed a saint by her local followers. Also opening onto the marble-and-stone-paved Largo are two modest chapels and a church. As in medieval days, soldiers still walk the ramparts, guarding the fortress. Admission is free for all. Nonguests can visit Tuesday through Sunday 9am to 5pm.

Largo de Dom Dinis. No phone for sightseeing information. (See "Where to Stay," below, for hotel reservation information.)

Shopping

The town's most famous product is a type of traditional earthenware water jug. Known as a *moringue,* it has two spouts, one handle, and sometimes a decorative crest that's stamped into the wet clay before it's fired. At least half a dozen street merchants sell the jugs in the town's main square, **Rossio Marquês de Pombal.** Stylish reminders of Portugal's agrarian past, they're associated with love and marriage. (Housewives traditionally carried water in them to workers in the fields.) Some are simple; others are glazed in bright colors.

10

ALENTEJO & RIBATEJO | Estremoz

At **Artesanato,** Avenida de São António (no phone), you'll find hundreds of terra-cotta figurines, another of the town's specialties. Each represents an archetype from the Alentejo workforce, and the designs include artfully naive depictions of washerwomen, sausage makers, carpenters, priests, and broom makers. Artesanato also sells some of the region's other handicrafts, including metalwork, woodcarvings, and weavings.

Where to Stay

EXPENSIVE

Pousada de Estremoz, Rainha Santa Isabel ★★★ This historic property is one of the best-known and most prominent government-owned tourist inns of Portugal; reserve months in advance. The deluxe establishment is set in the old castle dominating the town and overlooking the battlements and the Estremoz plain. Gold leaf, marble, velvet, and satin mingle with 17th- and 18th-century reproductions of furniture and decorations in the guest rooms and corridors. The accommodations range from former monks' cells to sumptuous suites with canopied beds. Ten excellent rooms are in a modern addition, all with well-maintained bathrooms. Dom Manuel received Vasco da Gama in the salon of this castle before the explorer left for India. In 1698, a terrible explosion and fire destroyed the royal residence, which then underwent several alterations. It became an armory, then a barracks, and then an industrial school. Its transformation into a castle-pousada has restored it as a historic monument without sacrificing comfort and style.

Largo de Dom Dinis, 7100-509 Estremoz. www.pousadas.pt. © **26/833-20-75.** Fax 26/833-20-79. 29 units. 94€–240€ double; 140€–320€ suite. Rates include continental breakfast. AE, DC, MC, V. Free parking. **Amenities:** Restaurant; bar; bikes; outdoor pool; room service. *In room:* A/C, TV, hair dryer, minibar, Wi-Fi (in some; 12€ per day).

MODERATE

Convento de São Paulo ★★ 🏨 Motorists might want to retreat to a romantic hideaway in the environs, 27km (17 miles) from Estremoz or 34km (21 miles) from Évora. Once in the town of Redondo, follow the signs to Aldeia da Serra for 10km (6¼ miles) where you'll come upon this charming inn. The origins of this restored hotel actually go back to 1182, although the present buildings, of course, were built much later.

Some accommodations lie in the former convent's ancient cells; others are of more recent construction. Regardless of their date of origin, guest rooms are well scrubbed, comfortable, conservative, and severely dignified, with all-white walls, dark furniture, and in most cases, wrought-iron headboards. A beautiful restaurant, serving an excellent cuisine, O Ermita, has been installed as well, and diners enjoy their meals beneath 18th-century restored frescoes. Some of the best regional specialties are served, chefs using products grown in the province itself. Many of the recipes were passed down from monks who used to inhabit the place.

Aldeia da Serra, 7170-120 Redondo. www.hotelconventospaulo.com. © **26/698-91-60.** Fax 26/698-91-67. 39 units. 95€–140€ double; 180€–210€ suite. Rates include breakfast. MC, V. Free parking. **Amenities:** Restaurant; bar; room service. *In room:* A/C, TV, hair dryer, Wi-Fi (free).

Páteo dos Solares ★ 🏨 This is a good alternative to the pousada, if that's booked up—though it's not quite in the same class, the *estalagem* does boast an atmosphere that evokes old Portugal. The manor house is rather pristine architecturally on its exterior, but it warms considerably once you're inside because of its large collection of century-old Portuguese tiles. Each bedroom is comfortable, well maintained, and traditionally furnished, with some modern twists—for example, some have a fireplace and a hydromassage tub. The hotel is set in well-kept gardens with an outdoor pool and tennis court, and is just a 10-minute walk from the town center. The on-site restaurant is known for its regional specialties.

Rua Brito Capelo, Largo do Castelo, 7100-509 Estremoz. www.pateosolares.com. ℂ **26/833-84-00.** Fax 26/833-84-19. 42 units. 160€–200€ double. Rates include buffet breakfast. AE, DC, MC, V. **Amenities:** Restaurant; bar; babysitting; outdoor pool; room service; outdoor tennis court (lit); Wi-Fi (free, in lobby). *In room:* A/C, TV, hair dryer, minibar.

Where to Dine

Pousada de Estremoz, Rainha Santa Isabel Restaurante ★ PORTUGUESE

The finest cuisine in town is served at this classic restaurant with vaulted ceilings. The best regional foodstuffs from the countryside are incorporated into a menu of perfectly seasoned and well-prepared dishes. The traditional tomato soup, an Alentejo classic, is served along with another classic, fried pork flavored with bits of fresh clams. Local trout filets are grilled with mint that's grown along the riverbanks. Meat dishes, such as grilled lamb cutlets flavored with fresh rosemary, are another winning combination, as is the selection of regional smoked meats from Alentejo. In such a provincial capital, the extensive menu comes as a surprise, especially in its array of products, from Iranian caviar to foie gras from the Landes region of France.

Largo D. Diniz, Castelo de Estremoz. ℂ **26/833-20-75.** Reservations recommended. Main courses 12€–28€. AE, DC, MC, V. Daily 1–3pm and 7:30–10:30pm.

ELVAS ★★

11km (6¾ miles) W of Badajoz, Spain; 223km (139 miles) E of Lisbon

The "city of plums," Elvas is characterized by narrow cobblestone streets (pedestrians have to duck into doorways to allow automobiles to inch by) and crenellated fortifications. The Moors held the town until 1226. Later, Spanish troops frequently assaulted and besieged it. It finally fell in the 1801 War of the Oranges, which ended with a peace treaty signed at Badajoz. Elvas remained part of Portugal, but its neighbor, Olivença, became Spanish. The Elvas ramparts are an outstanding example of 17th-century fortifications, with gates, curtain walls, moats, bastions, and sloping banks around them.

Lining the steep, hilly streets are tightly packed gold- and oyster-colored cottages with tile roofs. Many of the house doors are just 1.5m (5 ft.) tall. In the tiny windows are numerous canary cages and flowering geraniums. The four-tier **Aqueduto da Amoreira,** built between 1498 and 1622, transports water into Elvas from about 8km (5 miles) southwest of the town.

Essentials

ARRIVING

BY TRAIN   The train station is at Fontainhas (ℂ **80/820-82-08**), about 3km (1¾ miles) north of the city. Local buses connect the station to Praça da República, in the center. Four trains a day make the 5½-hour trip from Lisbon, requiring a change of trains in Entroncamento. The one-way fare is 20€.

BY BUS   The bus station is at Praça 25 do Abril (ℂ **26/862-28-75**). Seven buses per day make the 4-hour trip from Lisbon. The one-way fare is 16€. Fourteen buses daily make the 2-hour trip from Évora. The one-way fare is 12€. From Badajoz, frequent buses run throughout the day. The ride takes 20 minutes.

BY CAR   From Estremoz (p. 263), continue east toward Spain along Route 4.

VISITOR INFORMATION

The **Elvas Tourist Office** is on Praça da República (📞 **26/862-22-36**). It's open Monday to Friday 9am to 6pm, Saturday and Sunday from 10am to 12:30pm and 2 to 5:30pm.

EXPLORING THE TOWN   In **Praça Dom Sancho II** stands the **Sé** (cathedral). Under a cone-shape dome, it's a forbidding fortresslike building decorated with gargoyles, turrets, and a florid Manueline portal. The cathedral opens onto a black-and-white diamond square. Admission is free, and it is open daily from 10am to noon and 2 to 6pm. A short walk up the hill to the right of the cathedral leads to **Largo de Santa Clara ★**, a small plaza that holds an odd Manueline pillory with four wrought-iron dragon heads.

On the south side of Largo de Santa Clara is the **Igreja de Nossa Senhora de Consolação (Church of Our Lady of Consolation) ★**, a 16th-century octagonal Renaissance building with a cupola lined in 17th-century *azulejos* (tiles). It's open daily 9am to 12:30pm and 2 to 5pm. Admission is free.

The **castelo** (castle), Praça da República, built by the Moors and strengthened by Christian rulers in the 14th and 16th centuries, offers a panoramic view of the town, its fortifications, and the surrounding countryside. It's open daily from 9:30am to 1pm and 2:30 to 5pm (till 5:30pm Oct 10–Apr 1.) Admission costs 1.50€.

SHOPPING   The abundant folklore of this small town might whet your appetite for souvenirs. Take a stroll along the town's best shopping streets, **Rua de Alchemin** and **Rua de Olivença,** where you'll find rustic handicrafts appearing on all sides. If you want to target your destinations in advance, consider the wares at **Alchemin,** Rua de Alchemin, or any of the merchandise at the town's leading clothier, **Rente,** Rua de Alchemin (📞 **26/862-64-71**).

Where to Stay

MODERATE

Estalagem Quinta de Santo António ★★ 📖   This once private *quinta,* dating from 1668, now welcomes paying guests. This is one of the finest examples of Alentejo architecture in the region, and the property is enveloped by a beautiful garden. The interior was faithfully restored and decorated with antique furniture. The bedrooms are generally spacious and exceedingly comfortable, with well-maintained bathrooms. The on-site restaurant, A Quinta, is known locally for its superb cuisine of the Alentejo school. Activities on-site or nearby include horseback riding, biking, and motorboat rides.

Estrada de Barbacena, Abdo. 206, 7350-903 Elvas. www.qsahotel.com. 📞 **26/863-64-60.** Fax 26/862-50-50. 30 units. 61€–100€ double; 90€–154€ suite. Rates include buffet breakfast. AE, DC, MC, V. 6.5km (4 miles) northeast of Elvas along Estrada de Portalegre. Free parking. **Amenities:** Restaurant; bar; babysitting; bikes; children's center; outdoor pool; Wi-Fi (free, in lobby). *In room:* A/C, TV.

Pousada de Elvas, Santa Luzia ★★   A major link in the government-inn circuit is this hacienda-style building just outside the city walls. It sits at the edge of a busy highway (Estrada N4), about a 5-minute walk east of the town center. Fully renovated, with typical Alentejo hand-painted furniture, it was built in 1942 as a private hotel (which failed). The bone-white stucco villa faces the fortifications. The ground floor holds a living room, an L-shape dining salon, and a bar, all opening through thick arches onto a Moorish courtyard with a fountain, a lily pond, and orange trees.

The upper floor has some great guest rooms, and you can also stay in the nearby annex, a villa with a two-story entrance hall and an ornate staircase. All rooms are comfortable and cozily furnished. Because the hotel is small, it may be difficult to get a room without a reservation.

Av. de Badajoz, 7350-097 Elvas. www.pousadas.pt. © **26/863-74-70.** Fax 26/862-21-27. 25 units. 77€–90€ double. Rates include buffet breakfast. AE, DC, MC, V. Free parking. **Amenities:** Restaurant; bar; bikes; outdoor pool; room service; outdoor tennis court (lit). *In room:* A/C, TV, hair dryer, minibar, Wi-Fi (12€ per 24 hr.).

INEXPENSIVE

Hotel D. Luís Elvas   This well-established favorite is not only the largest hotel in Elvas, but one of the most affordable. It is the choice of most commercial travelers because of its conference rooms, but also a favorite with vacationers who enjoy its central location close to all the major monuments. The bedrooms are spread over four floors, and are midsize, with comfortable furnishings, though some rooms show a bit of wear and tear. The hotel also operates a first-rate restaurant with the most popular bar in town.

Av. de Badajoz-Estrada N4, 7350-903 Elvas. www.hoteldluis-elvas.com. © **26/863-67-90.** Fax 26/862-07-33. 90 units. 60€ double. Rates include buffet breakfast. AE, DC, MC, V. Free parking. **Amenities:** Restaurant; bar; outdoor pool; room service. *In room:* A/C, TV, hair dryer, minibar.

Where to Dine

Restaurante Don Quixote ★ 🍴 FRENCH/PORTUGUESE   The most adventurous dining choice around Elvas lies about 2.5km (1½ miles) to the west. The isolated compound is the focus of many a culinary pilgrimage and is very busy on weekends, especially with Spaniards, who create a holiday feeling with lots of convivial chatter. You can order a drink in the leather-upholstered English-style bar near the entrance and then move on to the dining room, decorated in traditional Iberian style. Rows of fresh fish arranged on ice behind glass grace the entrance to the sprawling dining room. Specialties include shellfish rice, grilled sole, grilled swordfish, roast pork, beefsteak Alentejano, and at least five kinds of shellfish. The fare is interesting and skillfully prepared, although it never scales any gastronomic peaks. Service takes a nose dive when the place is full.

Estrada 4, Pedras Negras. © **26/862-20-14.** Reservations recommended. Main courses 14€–30€. AE, DC, MC, V. Mon–Sat noon–4pm and 7pm–midnight; Sun noon–4pm.

Elvas After Dark

Don't expect the diversions and distractions of Lisbon—sleepy Elvas simply doesn't have them. Instead, consider a stroll through the town's historic core, looking for likable *tascas* (bars). Or, head less than 1km (about ¾ mile) west of town to the **Albergaria Jardim,** Estrada Nacional 4 (© **26/862-10-50;** www.albergariajardim.com). Local residents who come to drink and socialize fill this handsome pub.

ÉVORA ★★★

102km (63 miles) SW of Badajoz, Spain; 155km (96 miles) E of Lisbon

The capital of Alto Alentejo, Évora, a designated UNESCO World Heritage Site, is a historical curio. Considering its size and location, it's also something of an architectural phenomenon. Its builders freely adapted whatever styles they desired, from

Mudéjar to Manueline to Roman to rococo. Évora, once enclosed behind medieval walls, lives up to its reputation as a living museum. Sixteenth- and 17th-century houses, many with tile patios, fill nearly every street. Cobblestones, labyrinthine streets, arcades, squares with bubbling fountains, whitewashed houses, and a profuse display of Moorish-inspired arches characterize the town.

Many conquerors passed through Évora, and several left behind architectural remains. The Romans at the time of Julius Caesar knew the town as Liberalitas Julia. Its heyday was during the 16th-century reign of João III, when it became the Montmartre of Portugal; avant-garde artists, including the playwright Gil Vicente, congregated under the aegis of royalty.

Évora today is a sleepy provincial capital, perhaps rather self-consciously aware of its attractions. One local historian recommended to an American couple that they see at least 59 monuments. Rest assured that you could capture the essence of the town by seeing only a fraction of that. Évora is a popular day trip from Lisbon, but it's a long trek, which doesn't leave enough time to enjoy the town. Because of its isolation amid some of the loveliest rural landscapes in Portugal, and because of the wealth of attractions within it, an overnight here is recommended.

Essentials

ARRIVING

BY BUS   **Rede Expressos,** Avenida Sâo Sebastiâo (© **70/722-33-44;** www.rede-expressos.pt), provides bus service for the area. Fifteen buses a day arrive from Lisbon; the trip takes 1 hour and 45 minutes and costs 12€ one-way. Three daily buses make the 5-hour trip from Faro, in the Algarve. The cost is 16€ one-way. Seven buses a day connect Beja with Évora; the trip takes 1¼ hours and costs 7.50€ one-way.

BY CAR   From Beja (p. 274), continue north along Route 18.

VISITOR INFORMATION

The **Évora Tourist Information Office** is at Praça do Giraldo 73 (© **26/677-70-71**). It's open daily 9am to 6pm (7pm in summer).

Special Events

Évora's major festival is the **Feira de São João,** a folkloric and musical extravaganza. All the handicrafts of the area, including fine ceramics, are on display, and hundreds of people from the Alentejo region come into the city. The event, which takes place over the last 10 days of June, celebrates the arrival of summer. Food stalls sell regional specialties, and regional dances are presented. The tourist office (see "Visitor Information," above) can supply more details.

Exploring the Town

Igreja de Nossa Senhora de Graça   The Church of Our Lady of Grace is notable chiefly for its baroque facade, with huge classical nudes over the pillars. Above each group of lazing stone giants is a sphere with a flame—pieces of sculpture often compared to works by Michelangelo. The church was built in Évora's heyday, during the reign of João III. Columns and large stone rosettes flank the central window shaft, and ponderous neoclassical columns support the lower level. The church can be viewed only from the outside.

Largo da Graça. No phone.

Igreja de São João Evangelista ★ This church deserves to be better known: Although it's one of Évora's undisputed gems, it's seemingly little visited. The Gothic-Mudéjar Church of St. John the Evangelist, facing the Temple of Diana and next door to the government-owned pousada, is connected to the palace built by the dukes of Cadaval. It contains a collection of 18th-century tiles, and a guide will show you a macabre sight—an old cistern filled with neatly stacked bones removed from tombs. In the chapel's sacristy are some paintings, including a ghastly rendition of Africans slaughtering a Christian missionary. One highlight is a painting of a pope that has moving eyes and moving feet. You can also see part of the wall that once encircled Évora here.

Largo do Conde de Vila Flor. ✆ **26/673-00-30.** Admission 3€. Tues–Sun 10am–noon and 2–6pm.

Igreja Real de São Francisco The Church of St. Francis contains a chapel that's probably unlike any you've seen: The chancel walls and central pillars of the ghoulish 16th-century Capela dos Ossos (Chapel of Bones) are lined with human skulls and other parts of skeletons. Legend has it that the bones came either from soldiers who died in a big battle or from plague victims. Over the door is a sign that addresses visitors' own mortality: OUR BONES THAT STAY HERE ARE WAITING FOR YOURS! The church was built in the Gothic style with Manueline influences between 1460 and 1510.

Praça 1 de Maio. ✆ **26/670-45-21.** Admission 1€. Daily 9am–1pm and 2:30–6pm.

Sé (Cathedral) ★★ The cathedral of Évora was built in the Roman-Gothic style between 1186 and 1204. The bulky structure was notably restored and redesigned over the centuries. Two square towers, both topped by cones, flank the stone facade; one is surrounded by satellite spires. The **interior ★** consists of a nave and two aisles. The 18th-century main altar, of pink, black, and white marble, is the finest in town. At the sculptured work *The Lady of Mothers,* young women pray for fertility.

The museum houses treasures from the church, the most notable of which is a 13th-century Virgin carved out of ivory. It opens to reveal a collection of scenes from her life. A reliquary is studded with 1,426 precious stones, including sapphires, rubies, diamonds, and emeralds. The most valuable item is a piece of wood said to have come from the True Cross.

Largo Marquês de Marialva (Largo de Sé). ✆ **26/675-93-30.** Admission to cathedral free; to museum 5€ adults, free for children under 12. June–Aug Tues–Sun 9am–5:30pm; Sept–May Tues–Sun 9am–noon and 2–5:30pm.

Templo de Diana ★ The major monument in Évora is the Temple of Diana, directly in front of the government-owned pousada (see "Where to Stay," below). Dating from the 1st or 2nd century A.D., it's a light, graceful structure with 14 granite Corinthian columns topped by marble capitals. Although it is said to have been dedicated to the goddess, no one has actually proved it. The temple withstood the 1755 earthquake, and there's evidence that it was once used as a slaughterhouse. Walk through the garden for a view of the Roman aqueduct and the surrounding countryside.

Largo do Conde de Vila Flor. No phone. Free admission. Daily 24 hr.

Universidade de Évora In 1559, during the town's cultural flowering, this university was constructed and placed under the tutelage of the Jesuits. It flourished until the Jesuit-hating Marquês de Pombal closed it in the 18th century. The compound wasn't used as a university again until 1975.

The double-tiered baroque main building here surrounds a large quadrangle. Marble pillars support the arches, and brazilwood makes up the ceilings. Blue-and-white tiles line the inner courtyard. Other *azulejos* (tiles) depict women, wild animals, angels, cherubs, and costumed men, and contrast with the austere elegance of the classrooms and the elongated refectory.

Largo do Colégio. ℂ **26/674-08-00.** www.uevora.pt. Free admission. Mon–Fri 8am–7pm (until 8pm in Aug and until 1am Oct–Dec) with permission from the tourist office.

Shopping

Most of the best shops in Évora are on **Rua do 5 de Outubro,** which leads from a point near the cathedral to the perimeter of the historic town. Beyond that, your best bet is wandering and window-shopping in the neighborhood around the cathedral.

Where to Stay
EXPENSIVE

Convento do Espinheiro Hotel & Spa ★★★ ☺   On the Estrada de Estremoz (N18) stands a national monument that has been turned into one of the most luxurious inns in the Alentejo. Dating from 1458, it is a converted monastery with some of the facilities of a resort, including pools, a tennis court, and a spa that's the best in Alentejo. You have a choice of rooms in the former monk cells or else in a series of modern units. Bedrooms are beautifully furnished, and they open onto panoramic views of the rolling green hills and Alentejo countryside. There is an opulence here rarely found in the province. Also on-site is a deluxe restaurant featuring a first-rate regional cuisine with international specialties as well. A chapel on the grounds is covered with a stunning collection of hand-painted *azulejos.*

Canaviais, 7002-502 Évora. www.conventodoespinheiro.com. ℂ **26/678-82-00.** Fax 26/678-82-29. 92 units. 144€–230€ double. AE, DC, MC, V. Free parking. **Amenities:** 2 restaurants; 2 bars; babysitting; children's center; exercise room; 2 pools (indoor and outdoor); room service; spa. *In room:* A/C, TV, hair dryer, minibar.

Hotel M'AR De AR Aqueduto ★★★ ☺   At long last Évora has a hotel that is even more luxurious than the local pousada (see below). Inside the old city walls, this government-rated five-star hotel is today the choice address in the city. It is installed on the site of a palace and convent from the 16th century.

From the original Sepulveda Palace that stood here, you can still see the lovely chapel, domed ceilings, and a cluster of post-Gothic "Manueline" windows studding the main façade.

Otherwise, the boutique hotel is imbued with a sleek and sophisticated contemporary styling in both design and architecture. Bedrooms are the ultimate in luxury for Évora, with arguably the best beds of any hotel in the province. Most of the rooms contain a private balcony or terrace. The most deluxe bedrooms are in the spa section and are equipped for treatments to couples who prefer the intimacy of their bedroom; showers in these units are also equipped with a hydromassage tub, as well as a deck terrace facing an orange grove.

One of the reasons to stay here is to patronize the on-site restaurant. You can sample the culinary achievements of award-winning Antonio Nobre, author of *Portuguese Chefs, The Best Recipes.*

Rua Cândido dos Reyis 72, 7000-582 Évora. www.mardearhotels.com. ℭ **26/674-07-00.** 64 units. 172€–192€ double; 257€–345€ suite. AE, DC, MC, V. **Amenities:** 2 restaurants; bar; bike rentals; children's programs; concierge; exercise room; outdoor pool; room service; spa. *In room:* A/C, TV, DVD player (in some), hair dryer, minibar, Wi-Fi (free).

Pousada de Évora, Lóios ★★★   The Pousada de Évora, Lóios, under UNESCO protection, occupies the Lóios Monastery, built in 1485 on the site of the old Évora Castle, which was destroyed during a riot in 1384. Official Inquisition reports were kept in the chapter room, which features 16th-century doorways in Moorish-Portuguese style. After the 1755 earthquake, extensive work was done to repair and preserve the structure. Over the years it was used as a telegraph station, a primary school, an army barracks, and offices. The 1965 opening of the pousada made possible the architectural restoration of the monastery. Its position in the center of Évora, between the cathedral and the ghostlike Roman Temple of Diana, is unrivaled.

The white-and-gold salon (once a private chapel) boasts an ornate Pompeii-style decor and frescoes and is decorated with antique furnishings, hand-woven draperies, crystal chandeliers and sconces, and painted medallion portraits. All the guest rooms are furnished in traditional provincial style, with antique reproductions. Because the rooms used to be monks' cells, they are rather small.

Largo Conde de Vila Flor, 7000-804 Évora. www.pousadas.pt. ℭ **26/673-00-70.** Fax 26/670-72-48. 32 units. 136€–264€ double; 184€–330€ suite. Rates include buffet breakfast. AE, DC, MC, V. Free parking. **Amenities:** Restaurant; bar; outdoor pool; room service. *In room:* A/C, TV, hair dryer, minibar, Wi-Fi (12€ per 24 hr.).

MODERATE

M'AR De AR Muralhas ★   This modern hotel lies between the Alconchel and Raimundo gates in the most ancient part of Évora. Although the two-story hotel is contemporary and up-to-date in all ways, it manages to evoke a warm, cozy, regional ambience. The inn has furnished its public rooms with antiques gathered from the province. The beautifully furnished bedrooms are well maintained, with neatly kept tiled bathrooms. The on-site restaurant serves a notable provincial cuisine, and a pool and garden are on-site.

Travessa da Palmeira 4, 7000-546 Évora. www.mardearhotels.com. ℭ **26/673-93-00.** Fax 26/673-93-05. 91 units. 132€–220€ double; 197€–300€ suite. AE, DC, MC, V. Parking 5€. **Amenities:** Restaurant; bar; babysitting; bikes; outdoor pool; room service; Wi-Fi (free, in lobby). *In room:* A/C, TV/DVD, CD player, hair dryer, minibar.

INEXPENSIVE

Albergaria do Calvário   This is a former olive-processing plant that was renovated and turned into this well-run little hotel in 1998. It's about a 5-minute walk from the historic center. Next to the Convento do Calvário (a convent that's closed to the public), the hotel is attractively furnished, with good beds and tidy appointments. Neoclassical and rustic reproductions of antiques are used extensively. Breakfast is served in your room or on the Esplanade Terraces.

Travessa dos Lagares 3, 7000-565 Évora. www.albergariadocalvario.com. ℭ **26/674-59-30.** Fax 26/674-59-39. 23 units. 90€–108€ double; 110€–150€ suite. Rates include buffet breakfast. AE, DC, MC, V. Free parking. **Amenities:** Bar; bikes; room service; Wi-Fi (free, in lobby). *In room:* A/C, TV, hair dryer, minibar.

Albergaria Solar de Monfalim ★ 🎒   The Albergaria Solar de Monfalim is a delightful guesthouse with a touch of grandeur: A stone staircase leads up to a plant-lined entrance decorated with tiles. The hosts, the Serrabulhos, have improved the building by making the small to midsize guest rooms more comfortable while keeping the original antique atmosphere. The rooms, all in the main building, are well maintained, traditional, and quite pleasant. You can sit on the terrace nursing a drink and peering through the cloisterlike mullioned veranda.

Largo da Misericórdia 1, 7000-646 Évora. www.monfalimtur.pt. © **26/675-00-00.** Fax 26/674-23-67. 26 units. 60€–70€ double. Rates include continental breakfast. AE, MC, V. Parking 5€. **Amenities:** Bar; Wi-Fi (free, in lobby). *In room:* A/C, TV, hair dryer, minibar.

Residencial Policarpo Inside the city walls, this guesthouse is somewhat like a hostel. Behind the cathedral, it lies in a tranquil part of town. The property was once the private manor house of the Counts of Lousã. On one side the pension opens onto a panoramic view of the Alentejan plain; on the other it fronts a tiny patio with a granite gateway. No two rooms are alike, but most of them lie under wooden beams and high ceilings and are furnished with hand-painted regional pieces. Room 202 opens onto a view of the cathedral, and Room 101 is the most atmospheric, lined with *azulejos* and a massive wooden bed. Breakfast is taken in a room decorated with local art. Only half of the rooms are air-conditioned and contain private bathrooms.

Rua da Freiria de Baixo 16, 7000-898 Évora. www.pensaopolicarpo.com. © **26/670-24-24.** 19 units (8 with bathroom). 30€–40€ double without bathroom; 52€–60€ double with bathroom. No credit cards. **Amenities:** Bar; bike rentals; children's programs (ages 3-12); room service (breakfast only); Wi-Fi (free). *In room:* A/C (in some).

Residencial Riviera This small inn sits beside the cobblestones of one of the most charming streets in town, about 2 blocks downhill from the cathedral. Designed as a private villa, it retains many handcrafted details from the original building, including stone window frames, ornate iron balustrades, and the blue-and-yellow tiles of its foyer. Its small guest rooms are quite comfortable, with good beds, but are not very tastefully decorated, with mismatched furniture.

Rua do 5 de Outubro 49, 7000 Évora. www.riviera-evora.com. © **26/673-72-10.** Fax 26/673-72-12. 21 units. 67€–86€ double. Rates include buffet breakfast. AE, DC, MC, V. Parking nearby 10€. *In room:* A/C, TV, minibar, Wi-Fi (free).

Where to Dine

Guião ★ TRADITIONAL PORTUGUESE Guião is a regional tavern that's widely considered one of Évora's top four restaurants. It lies just off the main square, Praça do Giraldo. It's charmingly decorated with antique blue-and-white tiles. The family-run tavern offers local wines and Portuguese specialties. The hearty, robust meals are filling, if not exceptional. A typical bill of fare includes grilled squid, grilled fish, swordfish steak, and clams with Alentejo-style pork. The kitchen also prepares partridge in season.

Rua da República 81. © **26/670-30-71.** Main courses 12€–18€. AE, DC, MC, V. Tues–Sat noon–3:30pm and 7–10:30pm; Sun noon–3:30pm.

Restaurante Fialho ★ TRADITIONAL PORTUGUESE Fialho, which has flourished on this site since the end of World War II, is Évora's most traditional restaurant. Its entrance is unprepossessing, but the interior is warmly decorated in the style of a Portuguese tavern. Although Évora is inland, Fialho serves good shellfish dishes, including *sopa de Cacão* (regional shark soup), along with such fare as succulent pork with baby clams in savory sauce, and partridge stew. In season, a whole partridge might be available. The air-conditioned restaurant seats 90. The staff is particularly proud of the lavish array of local wines—the restaurant has one of the most comprehensive cellars in the district.

Travessa dos Mascarenhas 14. ℭ **26/670-30-79.** www.restaurantefialho.com. Reservations recommended. Main courses 13€–28€. AE, DC, MC, V. Tues–Sun 12:30–4pm and 7pm–midnight. Closed Sept 1-21 and Dec 24-31.

Évora After Dark

The town's historic core contains a few sleepy-looking bars, any of which might strike your fancy as part of an after-dark pub-crawl. The bar of the **Pousada de Évora, Lóios,** Largo Conde de Vila Flor (ℭ **26/673-00-70**), is a dignified option for a drink in a historic setting.

If you want to mingle and dance with the city's high-energy Lisbon wannabes, head for **Praxis Discoteca,** Rua Valdevinos, 21A (ℭ 26/670-81-77; www.praxisclub. com), which attracts both young locals and visitors to its precincts off Rua 5 de Outubro. It imposes a 11€ cover, but entrance includes your first two beers. It's open Monday through Saturday from 10pm to 6am.

BEJA ★

187km (116 miles) SE of Lisbon; 76km (47 miles) S of Évora

Julius Caesar founded Beja, which was once known as Pax Julia. The capital of Baixo Alentejo, the town rises like a pyramid above the surrounding fields of swaying wheat.

Beja's fame rests on what many authorities believe to be a literary hoax. In the mid–17th century, in the Convent of the Conceição, a young nun named Sóror Mariana Alcoforado is said to have fallen in love with a French military officer. The officer, identified as the chevalier de Chamilly, reputedly seduced her and then left Beja forever. The girl's outpouring of grief and anguish found literary release in *Lettres Portugaises,* published in Paris in 1669. The letters created a sensation and endured as an epistolary classic. In 1926, F. C. Green wrote *Who Was the Author of the Lettres Portugaises?,* claiming that their true writer was the comte de Guilleragues. However, a modern Portuguese study has put forth evidence that the *Lettres Portugaises* were, in fact, written by a nun named Sister Alcoforado.

Essentials

ARRIVING

BY TRAIN   There are no direct trains from Lisbon to Beja. A change is required in Funcheira. The one-way fare from Lisbon to Beja is 19€ to 25€ depending on the class of service. For information, call ℭ **80/820-82-08.**

BY BUS   Seven *expressos* (express buses) per day make the 3-hour run between Lisbon and Beja; the one-way fare is 14€. Seven buses a day come from Évora. The 1-hour trip costs 7.50€ one-way. Three buses a day run from Faro; it's a 3½-hour trip and costs 14€ one-way. For schedules, call ℭ **70/722-33-44.**

BY CAR   From Albufeira in the Algarve, take IP-1 north to the junction with Route 263, which heads northeast into Beja.

VISITOR INFORMATION

The **Beja Tourist Office** is at Rua Capitão João Francisco de Sousa 25 (ℭ **28/431-19-13**). The office is open Monday to Saturday 10am to 1pm and 2 to 6pm.

Exploring the Town

Castelo de Beja Beja castle, which King Dinis built in the early 14th century on the ruins of a Roman fortress, crowns the town. Although some of its turreted walls have been restored, the defensive towers—save for a long marble keep—are gone. Traditionally the final stronghold in the castle's fortifications, the old keep appears to be battling the weather and gold fungi. The walls are overgrown with ivy, the final encroachment on its former glory. From the keep you can enjoy a view of the provincial capital and the outlying fields.

Largo Dr. Lima Faleiro ℭ **28/431-18-00.** Admission 3€ adults, 1.50€ children under 18. June–Sept Tues–Sun 10am–1pm and 2–6pm; Oct–May Tues–Sun 9am–noon and 1–4pm. From the center, walk along Rua de Aresta Branco, following signposts.

Museu Rainha D. Leonor ★ The Queen Leonor Museum (founded in 1927–28) occupies three buildings on a broad plaza in the center of Beja: the Convento da Conceição and the churches of Santo Amaro and São Sebastião. The main building was a convent founded in 1459 by the parents of the Portuguese king Manuel I. Favored by royal protection, it became one of the richest and most important convents of that time. The Convento da Conceição is famous throughout the world because of a single nun, Mariana Alcoforado. She is said to have written the *Lettres Portugaises,* love letters to the French chevalier de Chamilly, at the convent in the 17th century.

Some of the building's most important features are the surviving pieces of the ancient convent. They are the church, with its baroque decoration, and the cloister and chapter house, which house one of the area's most impressive collections of 15th- to 18th-century Spanish and Portuguese tiles. Also on display are statuary and silverwork belonging to the convent and a good collection of Spanish, Portuguese, and Dutch paintings from the 15th to 18th centuries. The *Escudela de Pero de Faria,* a piece of 1541 Chinese porcelain, is especially unique. The first-floor permanent archaeological exhibition features artifacts from the Beja region.

The Santo Amaro church is one of the oldest churches of Beja and rests on what could be an early Christian foundation. It houses the most important Visigothic collection (from Beja and its surroundings) in Portugal.

The Church of São Sebastião is a small temple of no great architectural interest. It houses part of the museum's collection of architectural goods from Roman to modern times. It's not open to the public; access is by special request.

Largo da Conceição. ℭ **28/432-33-51.** www.museuregionaldebeja.net. Admission 2€, 1€ students, free for children under 15. Free on Sun. Tues–Sun 9:30am–12:30pm and 2–5:15pm.

Shopping

Beja is known for handicrafts, including charming hammered copper, in the form of serving dishes and home accessories, as well as the many forms of pottery and woodcarvings you might see in other parts of Ribatejo and Alentejo. **Rua Capital João Francisco de Sousa,** in the town center, is lined with all manner of shops.

Where to Stay

MODERATE

Pousada de Beja, São Francisco ★★★ This government-owned conversion of a 13th-century Franciscan monastery opened in the early 1990s, and quickly filled a need for a good hotel in the historic heart of town. From the end of World War II until the 1980s, it had functioned as an army barracks and training camp. The architects attempted to retain some of the building's severe medieval lines, with limited success because of serious deterioration. Rooms are generally spacious and attractively furnished, with good beds and excellent bathrooms. There's a garden on the premises with a modest chapel.

Largo Dom Nuno Álvarez Pereira, 7801-901 Beja. www.pousadas.pt. ℂ **28/431-35-80.** Fax 28/432-91-43. 35 units. 94€–143€ double; 127€–189€ suite. Rates include buffet breakfast. AE, DC, MC, V. Free parking. **Amenities:** Restaurant; bar; outdoor pool; room service; outdoor tennis court (lit); Wi-Fi (5€ per 24-hr. day, in lobby). *In room:* A/C, TV, hair dryer, minibar.

INEXPENSIVE

Hotel Melius 🌂   This is the town's best-recommended independent hotel; it's a better choice than the nearby Residencial Santa Bárbara (see below) but not as good as the pousada (see above). Opened in 1995, it lies on the southern outskirts of town beside the main road to the Algarve. The government-rated three-star, four-story hotel provides amenities like a gym and sauna that had been sorely lacking. The midsize guest rooms, though bland, are comfortable and well maintained, with good beds.

Av. Fialho Almeida, 7800-395 Beja. ℂ **28/431-30-80.** Fax 28/432-18-25. 60 units. 55€–70€ double; 85€–90€ suite. Rates include buffet breakfast. AE, DC, MC, V. Parking 3€. **Amenities:** Bar; exercise room; room service; sauna; Wi-Fi (free, in lobby). *In room:* A/C, TV, hair dryer.

Residencial Santa Bárbara   The Santa Bárbara is a little oasis in a town that has few good-value accommodations. The hotel is a shiny-clean, well-kept bandbox building. It's small in scale, with only a whisper of a reception lobby and elevator. The smallish guest rooms are compact but adequate, with good beds and neatly kept bathrooms.

Rua de Mértola 56, 7800 Beja. www.residencialsantabarbara.pt. ℂ **28/431-22-80.** Fax 28/431-22-89. 26 units. 55€–60€ double. Rates include buffet breakfast. AE, MC, V. Free parking. **Amenities:** Bar; room service. *In room:* A/C, TV.

VILA NOVA DE MILFONTES

32km (20 miles) SW of Santiago do Cacém; 186km (116 miles) S of Lisbon

A good stopover in lower Alentejo as you're heading south to the Algarve is the little beach town of Vila Nova de Milfontes. At the wide mouth of the Mira River, the sleepy resort is attracting more visitors because of the soft white-sand beaches that line both sides of the river. There are no other attractions and nothing to do here but relax, or perhaps search for antiques.

The castle that once protected the area from Moroccan and Algerian pirates has been restored and is now an inn. After a day on the beach, you can head south to even more beaches.

Essentials

ARRIVING

BY BUS   Three express buses a day make the trip from Lisbon. It takes 3½ hours and costs 15€ one-way. For schedules, call ℂ **70/722-33-44** in Vila Nova de Milfontes.

BY CAR   Chances are, you'll drive south from Setúbal (p. 183). Continue along N261 in the direction of Sines, and then follow N120-1 until you see the cutoff heading west in Vila Nova de Milfontes.

VISITOR INFORMATION

The **tourist office** is on Rua António Mantas (© **28/399-65-99**). In winter, it's open Tuesday to Saturday 10am to 1pm and 2 to 6pm; in summer, hours are Tuesday to Thursday 10am to 8pm, Friday to Monday 11am to 1pm and 2 to 7pm.

Where to Stay

Casa dos Arcos   In the center of town, and just a 5-minute walk from the beach, is this simple yet comfortable pension. The small to midsize guest rooms were modernized with neatly kept bathrooms. There is no grandeur or pretense here—the place provides an adequate stopover for the night, nothing more.

Rua do Cais, 7645-236 Vila Nova de Milfontes. © **28/399-62-64.** Fax 28/399-71-56. 25 units. 45€–75€ double. Rates include buffet breakfast. No credit cards. *In room:* A/C, TV.

Where to Dine

Restaurante Marisqueira O Pescador ★ PORTUGUESE/SEAFOOD   O Moura, as it's known locally, is the best *marisqueira* (seafood restaurant) in town. Even the town residents, who certainly know their fish, swear by it. Monkfish with rice is a savory offering, as is the kettle of *caldeirada,* a succulent seafood stew. The place is air-conditioned, and the welcome is friendly. The owners, Mr. and Mrs. Moura, used to be fishmongers, and they know their product well. Don't expect much in the way of decor—people come here just for the fish.

Largo da Praça 18. © **28/399-63-38.** Reservations recommended. Main courses 12€–24€. No credit cards. Daily 9am–midnight. Closed 2 weeks in Oct or Nov.

COIMBRA & THE BEIRAS

ncompassing the university city of Coimbra, the three provinces of the Beiras are the quintessence of Portugal. Beira is Portuguese for "edge" or "border"; the provinces are Beira Litoral (coastal), Beira Baixa (low), and Beira Alta (high). The region embraces the Serra de Estrela, Portugal's highest mountains—a haven for skiers in winter and a cool retreat in summer. The granite soil produced by the great mountain ranges blankets the rocky slopes of the Dão and Mondego river valleys and is responsible for producing the region's wine, ruby-red or lemon-yellow Dão.

The famed resort of **Figueira da Foz** draws the most beach devotees and is overcrowded in summer. However, you can take your pick of other beaches, from **Praia de Leirosa** in the south all the way to the northern tip at **Praia de Espinho.** Unlike those in the Algarve, the beaches along the Atlantic coast have powerful surf and potentially dangerous undertows, plus much cooler water. Check local conditions before going into the water. A yellow or red flag indicates that the water isn't safe for swimming (sometimes because of pollution).

Anglers from all over the world fly in to fish the waters in the **Serra de Estrela National Park** and the Vouga River. Less competitive anglers cast their lines along the Beira Litoral beach strip, with its many rocky outcroppings. Bream, sole, and sea bass are the major catches. You don't need a permit to ocean fish, but you do need a permit to fish in freshwater streams and rivers. Regional tourist offices provide information about permits.

LEIRIA

32km (20 miles) N of Alcobaça; 129km (80 miles) N of Lisbon

On the road to Coimbra, Leiria rests on the banks of the Liz and spreads over the surrounding hills. Though the modern-day town is industrial, it's still an inviting stop, with its hilltop castle, old quarter, and cathedral. Leiria is also the center of an area rich in handicrafts, such as hand-blown glassware. Its folklore is comparable to that of neighboring Ribatejo. This city of 110,000 is an important transportation hub and a convenient point for exploring Nazaré or Fátima (see chapter 8) or the Atlantic coast beaches.

Guarda N18

N232

N16

Viseu

Serra da Estrela

Covilhã

N233

N18

Castelo Branco

Fundão

N112

N223

E3

Oliveira do Hospital

N238

N17

N2

Oleiros

N2

serra do Caramulo

N234

Caramulo

Lousã

N350

Figueiró dos Vinhos

N1

Mealhada

Luso

Buçaco

Cúria

N1

N17

Conímbriga

N237

N235

Mira

N109

Coimbra

Rio Mondego

N1

Pombal

Aveiro

N111

E01 E80

N109

Figueira da Foz

Marinha Grande

Leiria

15 mi

15 km

PORTUGAL

area of detail

Lisbon

Essentials

ARRIVING

BY TRAIN   There are no direct trains from Lisbon to Leiria.

BY BUS   A total of 23 express buses from Lisbon make the 1-hour run to Leiria. A one-way ticket costs 12€. You can also take 1 of 10 daily buses from Coimbra (p. 286); the 1-hour trip costs 8.50€ one-way. For information and schedules, call ✆ 70/722-33-44.

BY CAR   Head north from Lisbon on the express highway A1.

VISITOR INFORMATION

The **Leiria Tourist Office** is at Jardim Luís de Camões (✆ 24/484-87-71; www.rt-leiriafatima.pt). The office is open Monday to Friday 9am to 12:30pm and 2 to 5:30pm.

What to See & Do in Leiria

EXPLORING THE TOWN   From any point in town, you can see the great **Castelo de Leiria ★** (✆ 24/481-39-82), once occupied by Dinis, the poet-king, and his wife, known as Sta. Isabella. The imposing castle has been extensively restored. The castle church, like the palace, is Gothic. From an arched balcony there's a **panoramic view ★** of the city and its surroundings. The Moors had a stronghold on this hill while they were taking possession of the major part of the Iberian peninsula. Portugal's first king, Afonso Henríques, took the fortress in the 12th century and twice recovered it after the Moors had retaken it.

Admission to the fortress is 2€; the museum admission is 3.50€. It's open Tuesday to Sunday April to October 10am to 6:30pm, and November to March 9:30am to 5:30pm. For more information, ask at the tourist office (see above). You can drive right to the castle's front door. On the way, you might visit the **Igreja de São Pedro,** Largo de São Pedro, which dates from the 12th century.

Around Leiria is one of the oldest state forests in the world. In about 1300, Dinis began the systematic planting of the **Pinhal do Rei,** with trees brought from the Landes area in France. He hoped to curb the spread of sand dunes, which ocean gusts were extending deep into the heartland. The forest, still maintained today, provided timber used to build the caravels Portugal used for exploring.

OUTDOOR ACTIVITIES   If you'd like to combine sightseeing with some beach life, head to **São Pedro de Moel,** 23km (14 miles) west of Leiria and 135km (84 miles) north of Lisbon. Take N242 west of Leiria to the glass-manufacturing center of Marinha Grande, and then take N242 the rest of the way (9km/5⅔ miles) to the ocean. São Pedro de Moel, perched on a cliff above the Atlantic, is known for its bracing ocean breezes. New villas have sprung up, yet the old quarter retains its cobblestone streets. The white-sand beaches run up to the village's gray-walled ramparts, and the scattered rocks offshore create controlled conditions, rolling breakers, and rippling surf. On a palisade above the beach at the residential edge of the village is a good hotel, the **Hotel Mar e Sol,** Av. da Liberdade 1, 2430-501 São Pedro de Moel, Marinha Grande (✆ 24/459-00-00; fax 24/459-00-19; www.hotelmaresol.com). A double room is 60€ to 120€, including breakfast.

SHOPPING   For such a small town, Leiria has a large number of shopping centers, called *centros comerciales.* We usually prefer to wander the streets of the historic core, looking for bargains and unusual handicrafts on **Praça Rodrigues Lobo** and the many narrow medieval streets radiating from it.

Where to Stay

MODERATE

Hotel Eurosol Jardim ★ This is not only the best hotel in town, it also happens to be the town's social hub—locals come here to congregate in its rooftop lounge bar and dining room. The hotel itself consists of two contemporary midrise towers, which compete with the stone castle crowning the opposite hill to dominate the skyline. The midsize rooms, well liked by business travelers, are equivalent to those in any first-class hotel in the north. They're all smart yet simple, with views, built-in headboards, and wood-paneled wardrobe walls.

Rua Dom José Alves Correia da Silva, 2414-010 Leiria. www.eurosol.pt. ✆ **24/484-98-49.** Fax 24/484-98-40. 38 units. 70€–85€ double; 90€–125€ suite. AE, DC, MC, V. Free parking. **Amenities:** Restaurant; 2 bars; exercise room; outdoor pool; room service; sauna; Wi-Fi (free, in lobby). *In room:* A/C, TV, minibar.

INEXPENSIVE

Hotel São Luís 🏄 This is the best budget hotel in Leiria. Ranked two stars by the government, it's spotless, and some of the rooms are spacious. You don't get a lot of frills, but you do get comfort and convenience at a fair price. The hotel serves a good breakfast, which is the only meal available.

Rua Henrique Sommer, 2410-089 Leiria. www.saoluishotel.com. ✆ **24/484-83-70.** Fax 24/484-83-79. 48 units. 60€ double. Rates include continental breakfast. AE, DC, MC, V. Limited free parking on street. **Amenities:** Bar; babysitting. *In room:* A/C, TV.

Residencial S. Francisco This affordable inn sits on the top floor of a nine-story building on the north side of town, a short walk from the river. Some of the well-maintained but small rooms offer panoramic views of Leiria. All have patterned wallpaper, functional leatherette furniture, and well-kept bathrooms. Breakfast is the only meal served.

Rua de São Francisco 26, 2430 Leiria. www.residencialsaofrancisco.net. ✆ **24/482-31-10.** Fax 24/481-26-77. 18 units. 40€–45€ double. Rates include continental breakfast. AE, DC, MC, V. Limited free parking on street. *In room:* A/C, TV, hair dryer, minibar.

Where to Dine

O Casarão ★ 🍴 PORTUGUESE Those with discerning palates make the 5km (3-mile) drive south of Leiria to the village of Azóia to dine at O Casarão, where chef José Rodrigues prepares some of the finest regional fare in the area. Over the years, Rodrigues has gathered some once-secret and ancient recipes from monasteries in the region. Adapting them to modern standards, he prepares an unusual repertoire of dishes, including such specialties as *bolo pinão*, a cake made of ground pine nuts. Of course, he's also an expert at more common dishes and offers a wide selection of fish, depending on the catch of the day. Two local favorites are codfish cooked with potatoes and rice studded with bites of seafood. We've enjoyed the always-reliable sole with tiny roasted potatoes. Surrounded by gardens, the dining room is in a large rustic home decorated with regional artifacts in a style typical of the region.

Cruzamiento de Azóia. ✆ **24/487-10-80.** Reservations recommended. Main courses 14€–25€. AE, DC, MC, V. Tues–Sun noon–3pm and 7–10:30pm. Closed 1 week in July. At the signposted turnoff to the port of Nazaré.

Reis PORTUGUESE/SEAFOOD In spite of its simplicity, this is the best independent restaurant in Leiria. Its faithful devotees like its basic but good food and reasonable prices. The chef specializes in grills, along with such regional fare as hearty soups, excellent fresh fish, and well-seasoned meats. Portions are large. In winter, a fireplace makes the Reis more inviting.

Rua Wenceslau de Morais 17. ℭ **24/482-28-34.** Main courses 7.50€–12€. AE, DC, MC, V. Mon–Sat noon–3pm and 7–10pm.

Leiria After Dark

Despite its modest size, Leiria has plenty of nightlife, both high energy and laid-back. We usually begin with a promenade along **Largo Cândido dos Reis,** which is lined with small *tascas* (taverns). If you're looking for something more substantial, try the well-upholstered **Eurosol Bar ★**, in the Hotel Eurosol, Rua Dom José Alves Correia da Silva (ℭ **24/484-98-49**). In a setting lined with unusual art, you can drink or flirt (or both) to your heart's content.

FIGUEIRA DA FOZ ★

129km (80 miles) S of Porto; 201km (125 miles) N of Lisbon; 40km (25 miles) W of Coimbra

North of Cascais and Estoril, at the mouth of the Mondego River, Figueira da Foz is the best-known and oldest resort on Iberia's Atlantic coast. Its name means "Fig Tree at the Mouth of the River," but how it got that name is long forgotten. Aside from its sunny climate, the resort's most outstanding feature is the golden-sand beach that stretches for more than 3km (1¾ miles).

Essentials

ARRIVING

BY TRAIN   Trains arrive at Largo da Estação (ℭ **80/820-82-08**), near the bridge. Thirteen trains per day arrive from Coimbra (see below). The cost of the 1-hour trip is 2.20€ one-way.

BY BUS   The bus station is the **Terminal Rodoviária,** Rua Herois do Ultramar (ℭ **70/722-33-44**). Three buses a day arrive from Lisbon; the trip takes 3 hours and costs 13€ one-way.

BY CAR   From Leiria (see above), continue north along Route 109.

VISITOR INFORMATION

The **Figueira da Foz Tourist Office** is on Avenida do 25 de Abril (ℭ **23/342-26-10;** www.figueiraturismo.com) and is open daily 9am to 8pm. In summer, it's open until midnight.

What to See & Do in Figueira da Foz

EXPLORING THE TOWN   Most visitors don't come to Figueira to look at museums, but the **Casa do Paço ★**, Largo Prof. Vítor Guerra 4 (ℭ **23/340-13-20**) is exceptional. It contains one of the world's greatest collections of Delft tiles, numbering almost 7,000; most depict warriors with gaudy plumage. The *casa* was once the palace of Conde Bispo de Coimbra, Dom João de Melo, who came here in the 19th century when royalty frequented Figueira. It's at the head office of the Associação Comerciale e Industriale, a minute's walk from the main esplanade that runs along the beach. The museum is open Monday to Friday 9:30am to 12:30pm and 2 to 5pm. Admission is free.

The casino (see below) owns one of the sightseeing oddities of the resort, **Palácio Sotto Mayor,** Rua Joaquim Sotto Mayor (ℭ **23/342-21-21**), which was once one of the grandest private manors in town, for decades owned by one of Portugal's most prominent families. Local rumors claim the property was seized by the casino to pay off a massive gambling debt. Today a visit here will give you a rare look into a luxurious private villa filled with antiques and paintings. Admission is 2€. It is open Tuesday to Sunday 2 to 6pm. You don't have to pay an admission for the slot machine area.

About 3km (1¾ miles) north of Figueira da Foz, bypassed by new construction and sitting placidly on a ridge near the sea, is **Buarcos,** a fishing village far removed from casinos and overpopulated beaches. From its central square to its stone seawalls, it remains unspoiled. Take Avenida do Brasil north from Figueira da Foz to get to Buarcos.

OUTDOOR ACTIVITIES   Figueira da Foz is on a wide, sandy **beach,** on a site first occupied by the Lusitanians. In July and August, the beach is usually packed body to body. Those who don't like sand and surf can swim in a **pool** sandwiched between the Grande Hotel da Figueira and the Estalagem da Piscina on the main esplanade.

You can also trek into the **Serra da Boa Viagem,** a range of hills whose summit is a favorite vantage point for photographers and sightseers. **Bullfights** are popular in season; the old-style bullring operates from mid-July to September.

Near Figueira da Foz, the **Quiaios Lakes** are ideal for sailing and windsurfing. (For information, contact the tourist office in Figueira da Foz; see above.) Another good center for windsurfing is the bay at **Buarcos,** adjoining Figueira da Foz. You can rent most windsurfing equipment at kiosks right on the beaches.

SHOPPING   If you're looking for handicrafts, head for **Shangrila,** Rua Maestro David Sousa 99A (✆ **23/342-80-11**). The outlet carries terra cotta, glazed porcelain, and some carved wood, leatherwork, and incised or burnished copper and brass. Looking for gold or silver filigree? Try the **Ourivesaria Ouro Nobre,** Praceta Dr. Joaquin Lopez Feteira 11 (✆ **23/342-39-52**), for one of the town's most appealing selections.

Where to Stay

Ibis Figueira Da Foz 🏊   Just a 5-minute stroll from the sandy beach, this is a midsize, efficiently run, affordable hotel. It's dependable but hardly dramatic, with a chain format and streamlined but standard bedrooms. The structure itself has more character than most cookie-cutter Ibis hotels because it was created out of a vastly restored stone house that was erected during World War I. Bedrooms are medium in size and comfortably though blandly furnished, each with a small bathroom.

Rua da Liberdade 20, 3080-168 Figueira da Foz. www.accorhotels.com. ✆ **23/340-81-90.** Fax 23/340-81-95. 47 units. 45€–79€ double. AE, DC, MC, V. Free parking. **Amenities:** Bar; Wi-Fi (free, in lobby). *In room:* A/C, TV.

Mercure Figueira da Foz ★★   This renovated 1950s-era hotel, on the seafront promenade overlooking the ocean, is the leading choice in town, and it's a leading favorite with tour groups. The hotel's interior is a world of marble and glass, more like that of a big-city hotel than a resort. A few of the midsize rooms on the sea have glass-enclosed balconies; most have open balconies. The hotel is open all year, though it's sleepy here in January.

Av. do 25 de Abril 22, 3080-086 Figueira da Foz. www.mercure.com. ✆ **23/340-39-00.** Fax 23/340-39-01. 102 units. 59€–125€ double. AE, DC, MC, V. **Amenities:** Restaurant; bar; babysitting; room service. *In room:* A/C, TV, hair dryer, minibar, Wi-Fi (free).

Pensão Esplanada   Across from a sandy beach, this little boardinghouse is in a building that dates from the turn of the 20th century, although the establishment itself dates from the late '80s. This recommendation is strictly for the frugal traveler who wants a Portuguese seaside holiday on a slim purse. Frankly, the place has creaky joints, and the rooms are not at the peak of their glory, although they are scrubbed daily. Hallway bathrooms are generally adequate unless the hotel is operating at its peak capacity. At least no one complains when it comes time to pay the bill.

Rua Engenheiro Silva 86, 3080-086 Figueira da Foz. ✆ **23/342-21-15.** Fax 23/342-98-71. 16 units, 10 with bathroom. 50€–75€ double. Rates include buffet breakfast. No credit cards. *In room:* TV.

Sweet Atlantic ★★★   The top hotel in town is an elegant and sophisticated, government-rated four-star hotel, lying just minutes from the beach overlooking the waterfront. Most of its bedrooms are suites opening onto water views. Inside, in both the bedrooms and public areas, an attractive, modernist style prevails. Cheaper are the studio suites with balconies and a separate living room, plus small kitchenettes. One-bedroom suites are more spacious, also with balconies and separate living areas. Each accommodation is individually furnished and decorated. The hotel not only offers the best spa in town, but has a first-class restaurant serving both international and regional dishes, especially fresh fish. In summer the hotel's bar lounge fills with a coterie of international visitors who keep the joint jumping.

Av. 25 de 3 Abril 21, 3080-086 Figueira da Foz. www.sweet-atlantic-hotel.com. ✆ **23/340-89-00.** 68 units. 95€ double; 132€–175€ suite. V. **Amenities:** Restaurant; bar; concierge; exercise room; room service; spa. *In room:* A/C, TV, hair dryer, minibar, Wi-Fi (free).

Where to Dine

O Peleiro ★ 🍴 PORTUGUESE   Unless you're dining at your hotel, such as the Mercure, you'll find that Figueira da Foz is not known for its restaurants. In-the-know foodies journey to the tranquil little village of Paião, 10km (6¼ miles) from Figueira for some fine dining in a building that used to be a tannery. Here the proprietor, Henrique, will welcome you into his establishment, which has been winning customers for more than 2 decades. The decor is in the classic Portuguese style, with terracotta floors and dark-wood furnishings placed under low ceilings. The countryside vibe extends to the kitchen, where chefs draw on local ingredients to turn out palate-pleasing dishes, including the fresh fish of the day, which can be broiled, grilled, or fried. Other worthy specialties are roast *cabrito* or kid; a savory rice dish studded with prawns; mixed grill; as well as grilled veal and zesty herb-flavored pork.

Largo Alvideiro, Paião. ✆ **23/394-01-59.** Reservations recommended. Main courses 14€–22€. AE, MC, V. Mon–Sat noon–3pm and 7:30–10:30pm. Closed 2 weeks in May and 2 weeks in Sept.

Figueira da Foz After Dark

Built in 1886, the **Casino Figueira,** Rua Dr. Calado 1 (✆ **23/340-84-00;** www.casinofigueira.pt), features shows, dancing, a nightclub, and gambling salons. Games of chance include blackjack, American and Continental roulette, and an old Continental game known as French Table (played with three dice). It doesn't charge an admission fee; drinks start at 6€. An a la carte meal averages 30€; the food is standard nightclub chow. The casino show begins at 11pm, and the club is open daily from 3pm to 4am.

COIMBRA ★★

118km (73 miles) S of Porto; 198km (123 miles) N of Lisbon

Coimbra, known as Portugal's most romantic city, was the inspiration for the song "April in Portugal." On the weather-washed right bank of the muddy Mondego, this

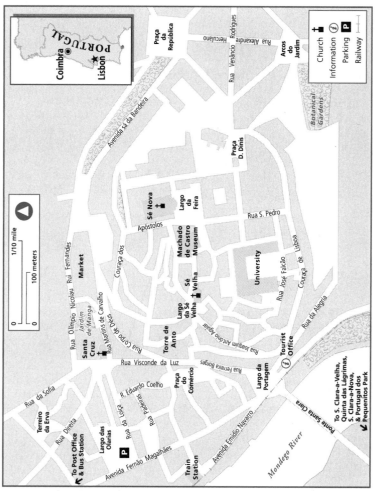

city of medieval churches is also the educational center of the country. Dinis I originally founded its university at Lisbon in 1290. Over the years, the university moved back and forth between Lisbon and Coimbra, but in 1537 it settled here for good. Many of the country's leaders were educated here, including Dr. António Salazar, dictator from 1932 to 1968.

Coimbra is at its best when the university is in session and the city radiates youthful energy. Noisy cafeterias, raucous bars, and such events as crew races lend a certain *joie de vivre* to the cityscape. You can make out who is a student because they wear black capes; their briefcases bear colored ribbons denoting the school they attend. (Yellow, for example, stands for medicine.)

Essentials

ARRIVING

BY TRAIN Coimbra has two train stations: **Estação Coimbra-A,** Largo das Ameias, and **Estação Coimbra-B,** 5km (3 miles) west of central Coimbra. For information, call (© **80/820-82-08**). Coimbra-B station is mainly for trains coming from cities outside the region, but regional trains serve both stations. Frequent shuttles connect the two. The train ride takes 5 minutes. Some 16 trains per day make the 3-hour run north from Lisbon. The one-way fare from Lisbon to Coimbra costs 17€ to 23€ depending on the train and the class of service. From Figueira da Foz, there's one train per hour. The trip takes 1 hour and costs 2.20€ one-way.

BY BUS The **bus station** is on Avenida Fernão de Magalhães (© **70/722-33-44**). Some two dozen buses a day arrive from Lisbon, after a 3-hour trip that costs 13€ one-way. Thirteen buses per day make the 6-hour trip from Porto (see chapter 12). The one-way fare is 18€.

BY CAR From Lisbon, take the express highway A1 north. The journey takes less than 2 hours, if there isn't too much traffic.

VISITOR INFORMATION

The **Coimbra Tourist Office** is on Largo da Portagem (© **23/948-81-20;** www.turismo-centro.pt). During the summer, the office is open Monday to Friday 9am to 8pm, and Saturday and Sunday 9am to 6pm. Winter hours are Monday to Friday 9am to 6pm, and Saturday and Sunday 9:30am to 12:30pm and 1:30 to 5:30pm.

What to See & Do in Coimbra

EXPLORING THE TOWN

Coimbra's charms and mysteries unfold as you walk up Rua Ferreira Borges, under the Gothic **Arco de Almedina** with its coat of arms. From that point, you can continue up the steep street, past antiques shops, to the old quarter.

Across from the National Museum is **Sé Nova (New Cathedral),** Largo da Sé Nova, which has a cold 17th-century neoclassical interior. Admission is free. It's open Tuesday through Friday from 9am to 12:30pm and 2 to 5:30pm. More interesting is **Sé Velha (Old Cathedral) ★★**, Largo da Sé Velha (© **23/982-31-38**), founded in 1170. The crenellated cathedral enjoys associations with St. Anthony of Padua. You enter by passing under a Romanesque portal. Usually a student is here, willing to show you (for a tip) the precincts, including the restored cloister. The pride of this monument is the gilded **Flemish retable ★** over the main altar, with a crucifix on top. To the left of the altar is a 16th-century chapel that contains the tomb of one of the bishops of Coimbra. Admission to the old cathedral is free; admission to the cloisters is 1.50€. The Sé Velha is open Monday to Saturday 10am to 6pm.

Igreja e Mosteiro da Santa Cruz ★ This former monastery was founded in the late 12th century during the reign of Afonso Henríques, Portugal's first king. Its original Romanesque style gave way to Manueline restorers in 1507. This is where the story of Pedro the Cruel and Inês de Castro reached its climax. Tiles decorate the lower part of the walls inside. Groined in the profuse Manueline manner, the interior houses the Gothic sarcophagi of Afonso Henríques, his feet resting on a lion, and on his son, Sancho I. The **pulpit ★**, carved by João de Ruão in the 16th century, is one of the noteworthy achievements of the Portuguese Renaissance. The **choir stalls ★** preserve, in carved configurations, the symbolism, mythology, and historic import of Portuguese exploration. With its twisted columns and 13th-century tombs, the two-tiered

Portugal's Romeo & Juliet

Coimbra's reputation for romance derives in part from the 14th-century story of Pedro the Cruel and Inês de Castro. The crown prince and the Spanish beauty, his wife's lady-in-waiting, fell in love at what's now the Hotel Quinta das Lágrimas, where Inês was then living. Unhappy with the influence Inês had over his son, Pedro's father, Afonso IV, eventually ordered her death. Three noblemen slit her throat in the *quinta's* garden. In the Igreja e Mosteiro da Santa Cruz (see above), Pedro forced his courtiers to pay homage to her corpse and kiss her hand. The lovers are buried together in Alcobaça's Mosteiro de Santa Maria (see chapter 8).

Gothic-Manueline **cloister** ★ is impressive. The facade is decorated like an architectural birthday cake, topped with finials and crosses.

Praça do 8 de Maio. ✆ **23/982-29-41.** Admission 2.50€. Mon–Sat 9am–noon and 2–7:30pm; Sun 4–7:30pm.

Universidade de Coimbra ★★   The focal point for most visitors to Coimbra is the University of Coimbra, established here in 1537 on orders of João III. Among its alumni are Luís Vas de Camões (the country's greatest poet, author of the national epic, *Os Lusíadas*), St. Anthony of Padua (also the patron saint of Lisbon), and the late Portuguese dictator, Dr. Salazar, once a professor of economics.

Ignore the cold statuary and architecture on Largo de Dom Dinis and pass under the 17th-century **Porta Férrea** into the inner core. The steps on the right take you along a cloistered arcade, **Via Latina,** to the **Sala dos Capelos,** the site of graduation ceremonies. Inside you'll find a twisted-rope ceiling, a portrait gallery of Portuguese kings, red-damask walls, and the inevitable *azulejos* (tiles). Afterward you can visit the **University Chapel,** decorated with an 18th-century organ, 16th-century candelabra, a painted ceiling, 17th-century tiles, and a fine Manueline portal.

The architectural gem of the entire town is the **Biblioteca Geral da Universidade (University Library)** ★★, also at Largo de Dom Dinis. Established between 1716 and 1723 and donated by João V, the library shelters more than a million volumes. The interior consists of a trio of high-ceilinged salons walled by two-story tiers of lacquer-decorated bookshelves. The pale jade and sedate lemon marble inlaid floors complement the baroque decorations of gilded wood. Chinese-style patterns have been painted on emerald, red, and gold lacquer work. The library tables are built of ebony and lustrous rosewood, imported from the former Portuguese colonies in India and Brazil. The three-dimensional ceilings and zooming telescopic effect of the room's structure focus on the large portrait of João V, set against imitation curtains in wood.

You might want to save the library for last; after viewing this masterpiece, other sights in town pale by comparison. To wind down after leaving the library, walk to the end of the belvedere for a panoramic view of the river and the rooftops of the old quarter. On the square you'll see a statue of João III and the famous curfew-signaling clock of Coimbra, known as *cabra* (goat).

Largo de Dom Dinis. ✆ **23/985-98-00.** www.uc.pt. Combined admission to Sala dos Capelos and Biblioteca 7€ adults, 3.50€ seniors, 4.10€ students and children 6–20; single admission to either Sala dos Capelos or Biblioteca 5€ adults, 2.75€ seniors, 3.25€ students and children 6–10. Mar–Oct daily 8:30am–7:30pm; Nov–Feb daily 9:30am–5:30pm.

NEARBY ATTRACTIONS

Convento de Santa Clara-a-Nova   Commanding a view of Coimbra's right bank, the New Convent of St. Clara contains the tomb of St. Isabella. Built during the reign of João IV, it's an incongruous blend of church and military garrison. The church is noted for a rich baroque interior and Renaissance cloister. In the rear, behind a grille, is the original tomb of the saint (closed except on special occasions). In 1677, her body was moved here from the Convent of St. Clara-a-Velha. Instead of regal robes, she preferred to be buried in the simplest habit of the order of the Poor Clares. At the main altar is the silver tomb (a sacristan will light it for you), which the ecclesiastical hierarchy considered more appropriate after her canonization.

Rua Santa Isabel. (ℭ **23/944-16-74.** Admission 1€. Daily 9am–noon and 2–5pm.

Portugal dos Pequenitos ☺   For children, this mixture of miniature houses—"Portugal for the Little Ones"—from every province of the country is Coimbra's main attraction. You'll feel like Gulliver strolling through a Lilliputian world. The re-creations include palaces, an Indian temple, a Brazilian pavilion (with photos of gauchos), a windmill, a castle, and the 16th-century House of Diamonds from Lisbon. You get there by crossing Ponte de Santa Clara and heading out Rua António Augusto Gonçalves.

Jardim do Portugal dos Pequenitos. (ℭ **23/980-11-70.** www.portugaldospequenitos.pt. Admission 9€ adults, 5.50€ children. Jan–Feb and Oct–Dec daily 10am–5pm; Mar–May and Sept 16–30 daily 10am–7pm; June–Sept 15 daily 9am–8pm.

Quinta das Lágrimas   Ever since the legendary poet Camões told the story of this "Garden of Tears," romantics from around the world have visited it. The gardens have been the property of the Osorio Cabral family since the 18th century, but before that they were owned by Inês de Castro, mistress of Pedro the Cruel, and their three illegitimate children. It's rumored that Dona Inês was killed by the spring fountain here, known as the *Fonte dos Amores.* Today, you can wander the gardens and also stay at the deluxe hotel on-site (see "Where to Stay," below).

Rua António Augusto Gonçalves. (ℭ **23/980-23-80.** Admission 3.50€. Daily 9am–7pm.

OUTDOOR ACTIVITIES

You will find tennis courts at the university stadium and at the **Clube Ténis de Coimbra,** Rua da Fonte do Castanheiro, Quinta da Estrela (ℭ **23/940-34-69**). All are open to the public and cost 10€ to 15€ per hour; call ahead to reserve a court. For horseback riding or excursions in the Beiras, contact **Centro Hípico de Coimbra,** Mata do Choupal (ℭ **23/983-76-95;** www.centrohipicocoimbra.com), open daily 10am to 1pm and 3 to 7pm. A 1½- to 2-hour excursion along country trails costs 18€ per person.

For swimming, head to the trio of pools at the **Piscina Municipal,** Rua Dom Manuel I (ℭ **23/979-66-20**). Take bus no. 5 or 7 from the center. Open daily from 9am to 7pm, it charges 7€ admission.

SHOPPING

Many of Coimbra's most interesting shops lie near the Sé Velha, on the narrow streets radiating from **Rua do Quebra Costas.** Because of its steep inclines, its name (The Street That Will Break Your Back) seems appropriate. Look for lots of outlets selling products manufactured in the surrounding region. The best bookstore, with a number of English editions, is **Livraria Bertrand,** Largo da Portagem 9 (ℭ **23/982-30-14**), a block from the tourist office.

Even the city's tourist authorities usually recommend short excursions into the suburbs and outlying villages for anyone seriously interested in shopping. Possibilities include the villages of **Lousã,** 21km (13 miles) southeast, and **Penacova,** 21km (13 miles) east, where unpretentious kiosks and stands beside the roads sell hand-woven baskets and ceramics. Contact the tourist office (see above) for directions.

A worthier destination is **Condeixa,** 17km (11 miles) south; its shops are better stocked, and the staff members are prepared for foreigners who don't speak Portuguese. To reach the village, take EN1 and follow signs toward Lisboa. Condeixa is home to nine independent ceramics factories, which are the source of most residents' income. The most appealing are **Ceramica Berardos,** Barreira, EN1, Condeixa (no phone); and **Filceramica,** Avenal, Condeixa (no phone). The merchants will usually agree (for a fee) to insure and ship your purchases. Because of the expense, it's usually a lot easier just to buy an extra suitcase, wrap your porcelain carefully, and haul it back with you on the plane.

Where to Stay

Note that the Pousada de Condeixa-a-Nova, Santa Cristina (reviewed at the end of this section) is nearby.

EXPENSIVE

Hotel Quinta das Lágrimas ★★★　The most luxurious place to stay in all the Beiras, the Estate of Tears gets its name from the story of Dom Pedro and Inês de Castro. Inês was murdered on the *quinta's* grounds, and her tears, it's said, were transformed into a pure, fresh stream of water. The red color of the rocks is said to be from her blood.

The duke of Wellington, the emperor of Brazil, and various kings of Portugal once occupied these rooms. They're now a hotel of great modern comfort that maintains the romanticism of its past. The midsize to spacious guest rooms are often sumptuous but not overly decorated, and everything is in traditional Portuguese style. You can find ample retreats in the drawing rooms and among the centenarian exotic trees, lovely fountains, and well-maintained gardens.

Rua António Augusto Gonçalves, Santa Clara, 3041-901 Coimbra. www.quintadaslagrimas.pt. ⓒ **23/980-23-80.** Fax 23/944-16-95. 35 units. 215€–335€ double; 389€–469€ suite. Rates include buffet breakfast. AE, DC, MC, V. Free parking. **Amenities:** Restaurant; bar; babysitting; exercise room; 9-hole golf course; 2 pools (1 heated indoor); room service; spa; Wi-Fi (free, in lobby). *In room:* A/C, TV, hair dryer, minibar.

Tivoli Coimbra ★　On a hillside above Coimbra's northern outskirts, a 15-minute walk from the town center, this is a favorite stop for bus tours. The midsize rooms are conservatively modern (too much so for some tastes) and filled with electronic gadgets such as bedside controls. Some rooms have views of the city or of the small garden behind the hotel.

Rua João Machado 4–5, 3000-226 Coimbra. www.tivolihotels.com. ⓒ **23/985-83-00.** Fax 23/985-83-45. 100 units. 83€–108€ double; 165€–188€ suite. Rates include buffet breakfast. AE, DC, MC, V. Free parking. **Amenities:** Restaurant; bar; babysitting; exercise room; Jacuzzi; indoor heated pool; room service; sauna. *In room:* A/C, TV, hair dryer, minibar.

MODERATE

Hotel Astória ★　The domed, triangular Astória has surrendered its role as market leader to the more glamorous Hotel Quinta das Lágrimas (see above), but the hotel is as inviting as ever. The comfortable hotel retains a faded grandeur. Its cupolas and wrought-iron balcony balustrades rise from a pie-shaped wedge of land in the city's congested heart. The guest rooms vary greatly in size, but all are comfortably furnished with well-maintained bathrooms.

Av. Emídio Navarro 21, 3000-150 Coimbra. ✆ **23/985-30-20.** Fax 23/982-65-57. 62 units. 92€–137€ double; 130€–155€ suite. Rates include buffet breakfast. AE, DC, MC, V. Parking 15€. **Amenities:** Restaurant; bar; babysitting; concierge; room service; Wi-Fi (free, in lobby). *In room:* A/C, TV, hair dryer.

Tryp Coimbra ★   This is the third-best hotel in this university city, coming in after the more luxurious Hotel Quinta das Lágrimas and Tivoli Coimbra (see above). The location is 100m (328 ft.) from Coimbra University Hospital and a 15-minute walk from the university grounds. All the midsize bedrooms are completely soundproof and are tastefully and comfortably furnished. Light wood furniture predominates, and beige and brown accents are used nicely. The atmosphere is so uncluttered that the hotel almost appears Japanese in its simplicity.

Av. Armando Gonçalves 20, 3000-059 Coimbra. www.solmelia.com. ✆ **23/948-08-00.** Fax 23/948-43-00. 133 units. 81€ double; from 122€ suite. Rates include buffet breakfast. AE, DC, MC, V. Parking 5.50€. **Amenities:** 2 restaurants; bar; babysitting; bikes; sauna. *In room:* A/C, TV, hair dryer, minibar, Wi-Fi (15€ per 24 hr.).

INEXPENSIVE

Best Western Hotel D. Luís ★   This is one of the most stylish hotels in the Coimbra area. Less than 1km (⅔ mile) south of the city, it lies on the road to Lisbon. The comfortable, well-maintained guest rooms, though a bit small, offer good beds and well-maintained bathrooms. The hotel has a pleasing modern design, brown-marble floors, and a restaurant that serves Portuguese and international food.

Rotunda Da Ponte Santa, 3040-091 Coimbra. www.bestwestern.com. ✆ **800/582-1234** in the U.S., or 23/980-21-20. Fax 23/944-51-96. 100 units. 59€–97€ double; 137€ suite. Rates include buffet breakfast. AE, DC, MC, V. Free parking. **Amenities:** Restaurant; bar; babysitting; bikes; room service. *In room:* A/C, TV, minibar, Wi-Fi (free).

Hotel Bragança   This bandbox hotel next to the train station is a possible choice if you arrive late at night by rail and other, better hotels are full. Primarily catering to businesspeople, it does a thriving trade in summer. The rooms vary in size—a few have balconies that overlook the main road; others are airless and often hot. The furnishings are utterly basic but adequate.

Largo das Ameias 10, 3000-024 Coimbra. www.hotel-braganca.com. ✆ **23/982-21-71.** Fax 23/983-61-35. 83 units. 60€–80€ double; 90€–110€ suite. Rates include buffet breakfast. AE, MC, V. **Amenities:** Restaurant; bar; babysitting; room service; Wi-Fi (free, in lobby). *In room:* A/C, TV.

Hotel Oslo   This hotel lies on one of the busiest streets in town and was built during the 1960s craze for Scandinavian design and decor. The small rooms are conservatively modern, unpretentious, and simple. Because of traffic noise, ask for a room at the rear, especially if you're a light sleeper.

Av. Fernão de Magalhães 25, 3000-175 Coimbra. www.hotel-oslo.web.pt. ✆ **23/982-90-71.** Fax 23/982-06-14. 36 units. 68€–100€ double. Rates include buffet breakfast. AE, DC, MC, V. Free parking. **Amenities:** Bar; babysitting; bikes; room service. *In room:* A/C, TV, hair dryer, Wi-Fi (free).

Residencial Domus   The Domus lies above an appliance store on a narrow commercial street. Machine-made golden-brown tiles cover its 1970s facade, and its rectangular windows are trimmed with slabs of marble. The reception desk is at the top of a flight of stairs, a floor above ground level. Rooms are usually large and well maintained. Many have contrasting patterns of carpeting and wallpaper, creating a haphazardly functional but cozy family atmosphere. Most guest rooms have shower-only bathrooms, but a handful have only showers and sinks with a shared bathroom down the hall. A stereo system plays in the TV lounge, which doubles as the breakfast room.

Rua Adelino Veiga 62, 3000-002 Coimbra. www.residencialdomus.com. ☏ **23/982-85-84.** Fax 23/983-88-18. 20 units, 15 with bathroom (shower only). 35€–60€ double with bathroom (shower only); 30€–35€ double without toilets. Rates include breakfast. AE, MC, V. **Amenities:** Wi-Fi (free, in lobby). *In room:* A/C, TV.

Where to Dine

EXPENSIVE

Arcadas da Capela ★★★ INTERNATIONAL   In the elegant and previously recommended Hotel Quinta das Lágrimas, you'll find the best restaurant in Coimbra and the only Michelin-starred one in the area. The repertoire of dishes is seductive to the palate. A meal here is like a voyage of discovery, depending on the inspiration of the chef for that day.

The market-fresh cuisine uses only the top-quality ingredients of the region when available. The chef claims, "I cook in tune with the rhythms of the season." Fresh vegetables and herbs are organically grown on the hotel's own grounds. The menu sometimes offers recipes from the 18th century, although adapted for modern tastes. You never know what will be on the menu at the time of your arrival—perhaps fresh raspberries from the garden or wild watercress harvested nearby for a salad. From the orchard emerge oranges and avocados. A main dish might include a delectable filet of salmon with a green risotto. Fish and meat dishes are sublime.

In the Hotel Quinta das Lágrimas, Rua António Augusto Gonçalves. ☏ **23/980-23-80.** www.quinta-daslagrimas.pt. Main courses 24€–42€; fixed-price menus 50€–80€. AE, DC, MC, V. Daily 7:30–10pm.

MODERATE

Dom Pedro CONTINENTAL/PORTUGUESE   Dom Pedro is across the river, near a congested part of town. After negotiating a vaulted hall, you'll find yourself in an attractive room with tables grouped around a splashing fountain. In winter, a corner fireplace throws welcome heat; in summer, the thick walls and terra-cotta floor provide a kind of air-conditioning. Full Portuguese and Continental meals might include codfish Dom Pedro, grilled squid, pepper steak, or pork cutlet Milanese. The food is basic; as our Portuguese host informed us at the end of the meal, "I didn't promise you a rose garden—only dinner."

Av. Emídio Navarro 58. ☏ **23/982-91-08.** Reservations recommended. Main courses 12€–24€. AE, DC, MC, V. Daily 8am–10:30pm.

O Alfredo PORTUGUESE   This unobtrusive pink-fronted building looks more like a snack bar than a formal restaurant. Though the ambience is simple, it's a pleasant place for a quiet meal—the restaurant is on the less populated side of the river, on the street that funnels into the Santa Clara Bridge. Full Portuguese meals might feature pork Alentejo-style, shellfish paella, Portuguese-style stew, several types of clam dishes, roast goat, and regional varieties of fish and meat. Although the wine is often better than the food, this is nonetheless a satisfying choice.

Av. João das Regras 32. ☏ **23/944-15-22.** Main courses 12€–22€. MC, V. Daily noon–3pm; Tues–Sun 7–10:30pm.

Restaurante A Taberna ★ PORTUGUESE   Out of a lackluster lot, this tavern ranks at the top of the independent eateries of this university city. Popular with students and local residents as well as visitors, its kitchen turns out a notable though typical cuisine set against a backdrop of regional decorations in two different dining rooms, one seating 20 patrons and another seating 50. The chef goes to the market himself to look for the best and freshest of ingredients. Back in the kitchen, he turns out such specialties as goat meat roasted tender in wine or oven-cooked veal with roast potatoes soaking up the juice. The typical fishermen's favorite, codfish with potatoes, is another good dish.

Rua Dos Combatentes da Grande Guerra 86. © **23/971-62-65.** www.restauranteataberna.com. Reservations recommended. Main courses 14€–18€. AE, MC, V. Mon 7:30–10:30pm; Tues–Sat 12:30–3pm and 7:30–10:30pm; Sun 12:30–3pm.

INEXPENSIVE

Café Santa Cruz ★★ CAFE   This is the most famous coffeehouse in Coimbra, perhaps in the whole of northern Portugal. In a former auxiliary chapel of the cathedral, it has a high ceiling supported by flamboyant stone ribbing and vaulting of fitted stone. The paneled waiters' station boasts a marble top handsome enough to serve as an altar. A favorite gathering place by day or night, it has a casual mood; cigarette butts are tossed on the floor. Scores of students and professors come here to read the newspaper. There's no bar to stand at, so everyone takes a seat on an intricately tooled leather chair at one of the marble-topped hexagonal tables. If you order cognac, the shot will overflow the glass.

Praça do 8 de Maio. © **23/983-36-17.** www.cafesantacruz.com. Sandwiches 3.50€–6€; coffee 1€. MC, V. Summer Mon–Sat 8am–2am; winter Mon–Sat 8am–midnight. Closed Sept 25–Oct 8.

Coimbra After Dark

The city's large student population guarantees an active, sometimes raucous nightlife. You'll find the bars around the Sé Velha and its square, **Largo da Sé Velha,** packed with students, professors, and locals, who drink, gossip, and discuss academic priorities. Our favorite experience is hopping randomly from bar to bar. For late-night fado, head for **À Capella,** Rua Corpo de Deus (© **23/983-39-85**) which was turned into a cafe from a chapel constructed back in 1364. Open daily 1pm to 3am, it offers nightly performances at 9:30, 10:30, and 11:30pm, with a 5€ cover charge.

Student celebrations in Coimbra include the **Queima das Fitas (Burning of the Ribbons),** a graduation ritual during the first or second week of May. Then loosely organized *serenatas* (troupes of students who re-create the music and aura of medieval troubadours) sing and wander through Coimbra's streets at unannounced intervals. It's impossible to predict when and where you're likely to find these spontaneous reminders of yesteryear.

A Place to Stay Near Coimbra

Pousada de Condeixa-a-Nova, Santa Cristina ★★   One of Portugal's finest pousadas, this inn, which opened in 1993, is a modern four-story hotel whose design was vaguely inspired by a 19th-century palace. It replaced a gone-to-seed mansion, and many of that building's embellishments, including moldings, were used in the reconstruction. Other furnishings were imported from the site of a tragic fire at the Palácio de Sotto Maior, near Lisbon. The guest rooms are generally spacious, light, and sunny. The furnishings are tasteful, with well-chosen fabrics and carpeting, plus a tiled bathroom with a tub and shower. Many guests visiting Coimbra, 15km (9⅓ miles) away, prefer to stay here.

Condeixa-a-Nova, 3150-142 Condeixa. www.pousadas.pt. © **23/994-40-25.** Fax 23/994-30-97. 45 units. 74€–144€ double. Rates include buffet breakfast. AE, DC, MC, V. Free parking. **Amenities:** Restaurant; bar; babysitting; outdoor pool; room service; outdoor tennis court (lit). *In room:* A/C, TV, hair dryer, Wi-Fi (12€ per 24 hr.).

AN excursion TO THE ROMAN TOWN OF CONÍMBRIGA

One of Europe's great Roman archaeological finds, **Conímbriga ★** is 16km (10 miles) southwest of Coimbra. If you don't have a car, you can take a bus from Coimbra to Condeixa, 1.8km (1 mile) from Conímbriga. The bus, AVIC MONDEGO, leaves Coimbra at 9am and returns at 1 and 6pm. From Condeixa, you reach Conímbriga by walking or hiring a taxi in the village.

The site of a Celtic settlement established in the Iron Age, the village was occupied by the Romans in the late 1st century A.D. From then until the 5th century, the town knew a peaceful life. The site lay near a Roman camp but never served as a military outpost, though it was on a Roman road connecting Lisbon (Roman Olisipo) and Braga (Roman Bracara Augusta).

You can walk from the small **Museu Monográfico** along the Roman road to enter the ruins. The museum contains artifacts from the ruins, including a bust of Augustus Caesar that originally stood in the town's Augustan temple. The **House of Cantaber ★** is a large residence, and in its remains you can trace the life of the Romans in Conímbriga. The house was occupied until intruders seized the family of Cantaber. The invaders also effectively put an end to the town in the mid–5th century.

Another point of interest is the **House of the Fountains ★★**, constructed before the 4th century, when it was partially destroyed by the building of the town wall. Much of the house has been excavated, and you can see remains of early Roman architecture as it was carried out in the provinces.

Roman mosaics in almost perfect condition have been unearthed in area diggings. The designs are executed in blood red, mustard, gray, sienna, and yellow; the motifs include beasts from North Africa and delicately wrought hunting scenes. In one of the houses you can see mosaics with mythological themes. The diggings attest to the ingenuity of Roman design. Columns form a peristyle around reflecting pools, and the remains of fountains stand in courtyards. There are ruins of temples, a forum, patrician houses, water conduits, and drains. Feeding the town's public and private bathrooms were special heating and steam installations with elaborate piping systems. The town even had its own aqueduct.

The ruins are open daily 9am to 8pm (until 6pm in winter). The museum is open Tuesday to Sunday 10am to 8pm. Admission is 4€ for adults and free for children under 14. For more information, call ℰ **23/994-11-77** or visit www.conimbriga.pt.

BUÇACO ★★

28km (17 miles) N of Coimbra; 232km (144 miles) N of Lisbon; 3.3km (2 miles) SE of Luso

The rich, tranquil beauty of Buçaco's forests was initially discovered by a humble order of barefoot Carmelite monks, following the dictates of seclusion prescribed by their founder. In 1628, they founded a monastery at Buçaco and built it with materials from the surrounding hills. Around the forest, they erected a wall to isolate themselves further and to keep women out.

The friars had a special love for plants and trees, and each year they cultivated the natural foliage and planted specimens sent to them from distant orders. Buçaco had always been a riot of growth: ferns, pines, cork, eucalyptus, and pink and blue clusters of hydrangea. The friars introduced such exotic flora as the monkey puzzle, a tall Chilean pine with convoluted branches. The pride of the forest, however, remains its stately cypresses and cedars.

Essentials

ARRIVING

BY BUS Buçaco is best explored by car. However, if you're depending on public transportation, you can visit the forest on a day trip from Coimbra. Buses from Coimbra to Viseu detour from Luso through the forest and stop at the Bussaco Palace Hotel. Five buses per day (three on Sun) make the 1-hour trip; a one-way ticket is 6€. For information and schedules, call © 70/722-33-44.

BY CAR From Coimbra, head northeast along Route 110 to the town of Penacova at the foot of the Serra do Buçaco. From there, continue north, following signposts along a small secondary road.

VISITOR INFORMATION

The nearest tourist office is at Luso (see below).

Exploring the Area

The forest created by the order of Carmelite monks who settled here in 1628 has been maintained through the ages. Such was the beauty of the preserve that a papal bull, issued in 1643, threatened excommunication to anyone who destroyed one of its trees. Though the monastery was abolished in 1834, the forest survived. Filled with natural spring waters, the earth bubbles with many cool fountains, the best known of which is **Fonte Fria (cold fountain).**

The Buçaco forest was the battleground where Wellington defeated the Napoleonic legions under Marshal André Massena. The Iron Duke slept in a simple cloister cell after the battle. A small **Museu Militar do Buçaco (Museum of the Peninsular War),** less than 1km (⅔ mile) from the Bussaco Palace Hotel (© 23/193-93-10), reconstructs much of the drama of this turning point in the Napoleonic invasion of Iberia. The small museum collection consists of engravings, plus a few guns. It's open Tuesday to Sunday 10am to 12:30pm and 2 to 5pm, and from 10am to 4pm in the off season. Admission is 2€.

In the early 20th century, a great deal of the Carmelite monastery was torn down to make way for the royal hunting lodge and palace of Carlos I and his wife, Amélia. He hardly had time to enjoy it before he was assassinated in 1908. The Italian architect Luigi Manini masterminded the neo-Manueline structure of parapets, buttresses, armillary spheres, galleries with flamboyant arches, towers, and turrets. After the fall of the Braganças and the transformation of the palace into a hotel, wealthy tourists took their afternoon tea by the pools underneath the trellis hung with blossoming wisteria.

One of the best ways to savor Buçaco is to drive the 550m (1,804 ft.) up to **Cruz Alta (high cross),** through the forests and past hermitages. The **view from the summit ★** is among the best in Portugal. Take Carretera Nacional No. 1 to get to the top.

Where to Stay & Dine

Bussaco Palace Hotel ★★★   This palace is an architectural fantasy, ringed with gardens and exotic trees imported from the far corners of the Portuguese empire. One of Europe's most grandiose smaller palaces, it's in the center of a 100-hectare (247-acre) forest.

Once a vacation retreat for Portuguese monarchs, it's where the deposed Queen Amélia decided to make her final visit to the country. (The government allowed the deposed Queen Amélia to return to Buçaco for one final visit in 1945. After that she left for France and her eventual death in 1951.) In 1910, the Swiss-born head of the kitchen, the former king's cook, persuaded the government to let him run the palace as a hotel, and it has served as one ever since.

Despite the wear and tear caused by thousands of guests, the structure is intact and impressive. Especially notable is the grand staircase with ornate marble balustrades, 4.5m-wide (15-ft.) bronze torchieres, and walls of blue-and-white tiles depicting important scenes from Portuguese history. Each richly furnished drawing room and salon is a potpourri of whimsical architecture. The most spectacular abode is the queen's suite, which has a private parlor, dressing room, sumptuous marble bathroom, and dining room. All rooms have a dignified, conservative decor.

Mata do Buçaco, Buçaco 3050-261 Luso. www.almeidahotels.com. ✆ **23/193-79-70.** Fax 23/193-05-09. 64 units. 100€–217€ double; 300€–1,125€ suite. Rates include continental breakfast. AE, DC, MC, V. Free parking. **Amenities:** Restaurant; bar; babysitting; concierge; room service; outdoor tennis court (lit). *In room:* A/C (in some), TV, hair dryer, minibar (in some), Wi-Fi (free).

LUSO

31km (19 miles) N of Coimbra; 230km (143 miles) N of Lisbon; 8km (5 miles) SE of Cúria

Luso, a little spa town on the northwestern side of the Buçaco mountains, boasts a mild climate and thermal waters for both drinking and bathing. The radioactive and hypotonic water is low in mineral content. It is said to treat kidney ailments, circulatory problems, and allergies of the respiratory tract and skin.

The old spa town, **Termas do Luso,** Rua Álvaro Castelões 9 (✆ **23/193-79-10;** www.termasdoluso.com), is open April 1 to September 30 Monday to Friday 8am to 7pm, Saturday and Sunday 9am to 8pm; from October 1 to March 31 Monday to Friday 8am to 6pm, Saturday and Sunday 9am to 7pm. The staff here specializes in treating urinary diseases, hypertension, diseases of the respiratory system, and skin diseases.

Besides the health-oriented aspects of the spa, Luso is a resort area that shares many of its facilities with Buçaco, 3.3km (2 miles) away. During the spa season, festivities and sports events are held at the casino, nightclub, and tennis courts, as well as on the lake and at the two pools, one of which is heated. Thermal spa enthusiasts flock here from June to October.

Essentials

ARRIVING

BY TRAIN   From Coimbra, line 110 extends west. Three trains a day run to Luso. The one-way fare is 2€. Call ✆ **80/820-82-08** for more information.

BY CAR   From Coimbra, head north along the Lisbon-Porto motorway—the most important highway in the country—until you come to the signposted turnoff for Luso. Head east for another 6km (3¾ miles).

VISITOR INFORMATION

The **Luso Tourist Office** is on Rua Emídio Navarro 136 (✆ **23/193-91-33;** www. jtluso-bucaco.pt). It's open June 10 to September 22 Monday to Friday 9am to 12:30pm and 2 to 5:30pm; September 23 to June 9 daily 9am to 12:30pm and 2 to 5:30pm.

Where to Stay

Grande Hotel de Luso ★★ Nestled in a valley of rolling forests, the sprawling Grande Hotel offers comfortable, well-proportioned rooms with matching furnishings. Some open onto private terraces with views of the tree-covered valley. Guests praise the thermal spa facilities here, though the hotel is also close to the town's main spa facility. You can lounge and sunbathe on the grassy terrace, or relax under the weeping willows and bougainvillea arbor.

Rua Dr. Kid Oliveira 86, 3050-210 Luso. www.hoteluso.com. 🕿 **23/193-79-37.** Fax 23/193-79-30. 143 units. 75€–136€ double; 105€–283€ suite. Rates include continental breakfast. AE, DC, MC, V. Free parking. **Amenities:** Restaurant; bar; babysitting; bikes; children's center; 2 pools (1 heated indoor); room service; spa; 2 outdoor tennis courts (lit); Wi-Fi (5€ per hour, in lobby). *In room:* A/C, TV, hair dryer, minibar.

Where to Dine

Restaurant O Cesteiro PORTUGUESE This unpretentious restaurant is near the train station, about a 5-minute walk from the center. It's on the road leading out of town toward Mealhada. The popular bar does a brisk business with local artisans and farmers. The fare is likely to include duck stew, roast goat, roast suckling pig with saffron sauce, and an array of fish dishes, including cod. The food is decently prepared and fresh. On weekends, Portuguese families fill the tables.

Rua José Duarte Figueiredo 78, 3050-235 Luso 🕿 **23/193-93-60.** Main courses 8€–15€. MC, V. Daily noon–3pm and 7–10pm.

CÚRIA

11km (6¾ miles) NW of Luso; 26km (16 miles) NW of Buçaco; 229km (142 miles) N of Lisbon; 19km (12 miles) N of Coimbra

Cúria, in the foothills of the Serra de Estrela, forms a well-known tourist triangle with Luso and Buçaco. Its spa has long been a draw for people seeking the curative properties of the medicinal waters, which are slightly saline and contain calcium sulfates and sodium and magnesium bicarbonates. In addition, the town has tennis courts, swimming pools, roller-skating rinks, a lake for boating, cinemas, and teahouses. The season for taking the waters is April to October; June sees the beginning of the largest influx.

Because it's in the Bairrada winegrowing district, Cúria offers some of the finest wines of the region. It's also the home to famous local cuisine, including roast suckling pig, roast kid, and sweets.

Essentials

ARRIVING

BY TRAIN Fifteen trains per day make the 25-minute trip between Coimbra and Cúria. If you're visiting Cúria by train from Lisbon, go first to Coimbra and change trains there.

BY BUS There is no bus service to Cúria.

BY CAR From Coimbra, head north along N1.

VISITOR INFORMATION

The **Cúria Tourist Office** is on Praça De Luís Navega, Largo da Rotunda (🕿 **23/150-44-42;** www.turismodocentro.pt). It's open daily 9am to 12:30pm and 2 to 6pm.

Where to Stay & Dine

Belver Grande Hotel da Cúria Golf & Spa ★★   This is a grand old spa hotel in the old-fashioned tradition. The Grande Hotel was an elegant hideaway for many of Europe's crowned heads after it opened in the 1880s, but then it saw years of neglect. Following massive renovations, it reopened in 1990 with a carefully trained staff. The most prominent structure in town, with a lavish Art Nouveau facade, the hotel reigns as the finest in the region. Decorative touches in the public rooms include marble floors and lavish upholstery and carpets. The midsize to spacious guest rooms come in two styles: Art Deco nostalgic and conservative modern. The hotel is a few steps west of the center of the village, less than a kilometer (⅔ mile) from the railway station.

Tamengos-Anadia, 3780-541 Anadia. www.grandehoteldacuria.com. ✆ **23/151-57-20.** Fax 23/151-53-17. 84 units. 75€–93€ double; 135€–170€ suite. Rates include buffet breakfast. DC, MC, V. Free parking. **Amenities:** Restaurant; bar; babysitting; exercise room; 2 pools (1 heated indoor); room service; spa; Wi-Fi (5€ per hour, in lobby). *In room:* A/C, TV.

Hotel das Termas ★   Simply getting to Hotel das Termas speaks to its get-away-from-it-all vibe—guests take a curving road through a parklike setting with lacy shade trees before arriving at the hotel itself. The whole operation exudes a British colonial atmosphere, with lots of brass and wicker. The guest rooms have a homey feeling, with lots of floral chintz, wooden beds, and walls of wardrobe space. Facilities for health and relaxation, including a park with trails leading around a lake, are on-site.

Cúria, 3780-541 Tamengos. www.termasdacuria.com. ✆ **23/151-98-00.** Fax 23/151-58-38. 104 units. 65€–100€ double; 105€–136€ suite. Rates include buffet breakfast. AE, DC, MC, V. Free parking. **Amenities:** Restaurant; bar; babysitting; bikes; exercise room; outdoor pool; room service; spa; outdoor tennis court (lit). *In room:* A/C, TV, hair dryer, Wi-Fi (free).

Pensão Lourenço ✆   Throughout this spa town, a series of signs points motorists to this simple inn, which you'll find in a tree-lined hollow away from the town center. It occupies a pair of buildings on either side of a narrow road. One of the buildings contains a ground-floor cafe whose tables sometimes spill into the road. Guest rooms are small, with timeworn but comfortable furnishings. Most of the guests are seniors; many are pensioners who come to Cúria season after season. They form a closely knit community of shared interests and needs.

Rua Dos Ulmeiros, Cúria, 3780-550 Anadia. ✆ **23/151-22-14.** 15 units. 25€–36€ double. Rates include buffet breakfast. AE, DC, MC, V. Free parking on street. Closed Oct–May. *In room:* TV.

Quinta de São Lourenço ★   In the village of São Laurenço do Barrio, 3km (1¾ miles) from the center of Cúria, stands this unexpected discovery. A manor house, built in the 1700s and enveloped by vineyards and a pine forest, has been converted to receive paying guests. The bathrooms are modern, with tubs, but much of the house, including the antiques and wooden floors, evokes another time. Bedrooms are well maintained and comfortably furnished, much like a typical Portuguese family house. The main house has a modern extension containing the bedrooms, and there is also an apartment to rent.

Visconde de Siabra 6, 3780-179 São Lourenço do Bairro. www.quinta-de-s-lourenco.pt. ✆ **23/152-81-68.** Fax 23/152-85-94. 6 units. 85€ double or apt. Rates include buffet breakfast. No credit cards. Free parking. **Amenities:** Outdoor pool. *In room:* TV, kitchenette in apt, no phone, Wi-Fi (free).

AVEIRO ★

56km (35 miles) N of Coimbra; 68km (42 miles) S of Porto

Myriad canals spanned by low-arched bridges crisscross Aveiro. At the mouth of the Vouga River, it's cut off from the sea by a long sandbar that protects clusters of islets. The architecture is almost Flemish, a good foil for a setting of low willow-reed flatlands, salt marshes, spray-misted dunes, and rice paddies.

On the lagoon, brightly painted swan-necked boats traverse the waters. Called *barcos moliceiros*, the flat-bottomed vessels carry fishers who harvest seaweed used for fertilizer. They're ever on the lookout for eels, a regional specialty, which they catch in the shoals studded with lotus and water lilies. Outside the town are extensive salt pits, lined with fog-white pyramids of drying salt.

Essentials

ARRIVING

BY TRAIN   The **rail station** is at Largo da Estação (✆ **80/820-82-08**). At least 30 trains per day make the 40-minute run from Porto (see chapter 12). The one-way fare from Porto to Aveiro is 2.50€ to 20€ depending on the train. Some 29 trains arrive daily from Coimbra; the trip takes an hour and costs 4.50€ to 20€ depending on the train. Twenty-six trains per day arrive from Lisbon; it's a 5-hour trip, and the fare from Lisbon to Aveiro is 18€ to 38€ depending on the train and the class of service.

BY BUS   **Rede Expressos** (which is the national express bus company) runs five buses a day from Lisbon to Aveiro. The trip takes 3 hours and 15 minutes and costs 16€. For information and schedules, call ✆ **70/722-33-44.** Rede Expressos has a website: www.rede-expressos.pt.

BY CAR   Continue north along A1 from Coimbra to the junction with N235, which leads west to Aveiro.

VISITOR INFORMATION

The **Aveiro Tourist Office** is at Rua João Mendonça 8 (✆ **23/442-07-60;** www. turismodocentro.pt) and is open in summer Monday to Friday 9am to 8pm, Saturday and Sunday 9am to 6pm; in winter Monday to Friday 9am to 6pm, Saturday and Sunday 9:30am to 12:30pm and 1:30 to 5:30pm.

What to See & Do in Aveiro

EXPLORING THE AREA

Aveiro is quite congested, and many readers have expressed disappointment with the incessant whine of Vespas and the foul-smelling canal water. Others, however, find it worth the journey.

The lagoons and many secret pools that dot the landscape around Aveiro make for a fine **boat excursion.** Inquire at the tourist office (see above).

Convento de Jesús ★, Avenida Santa Joana Princesa (✆ **23/442-32-97**), is hailed as the finest example of the baroque style in Portugal. The Infanta Santa Joana, sister of João II and daughter of Afonso V, took the veil here in 1472. Her tomb, an inlaid rectangle of marble quarried in Italy, attracts many pilgrims. Its delicate pale pinks and roses lend it the air of a cherub-topped confection.

The convent, owned by the state and now called the **Museu de Aveiro ★**, displays a lock of the saint's hair, her belt and rosary, and a complete pictorial study of her life. The **portrait ★** of her here is exceptional; painted in the late 15th century, it is attributed to Nuno Gonçalves. What's most noteworthy about the convent, though, is its carved gilt work, still lustrous despite the dust.

An assortment of 15th-century paintings, royal portraits of Carlos I and Manuel II (the last two Bragança kings), 16th-, 17th-, and 18th-century sculpture, and antique ceramics makes up the bulk of the collection here. There are also some well-preserved 18th- and 19th-century coaches and carriages. After viewing all this, you can walk through the cloisters, which have Doric columns. The museum is open Tuesday to Sunday 10am to 5:30pm. Admission is 4€ for adults and free for children under 15.

On Rua Santa Joana Princesa is the 15th-century **Igreja de São Domingo,** with blue-and-gold altarpieces and egg-shape windows flanking the upper nave. The facade, in Gothic-Manueline style, is decorated with four flame finials. To the right (facing) is a bell tower.

After a meal of stewed eels and a bottle of hearty Bairrada wine, you might want to explore some of the settlements along the lagoon. In **Ílhavo,** about 5km (3 miles) south of Aveiro on the IC1, you can stop at the **Museu Marítimo de Ílhavo,** Avenida Dr. Rocha Madahil (© **23/432-99-90;** www.museumaritimo.cm-ilhavo.pt). The unpretentious gallery offers an insight into the lives of people who live with the sea. It displays seascape paintings, fishing equipment, ship models, and other exhibits. The museum is open September to June Tuesday to Friday 9:30am to 6pm, Saturday and Sunday 2:30 to 5pm; and July and August Tuesday to Friday 10am to 7pm, Saturday and Sunday 2:30 to 7pm. Admission is 3.50€ for adults and 2.25€ for seniors and children 6 to 17.

From Ílhavo, you can drive less than 2km (1¼ miles) south to **Vista Alegre,** the famed village of the porcelain works. Britain's Elizabeth II and Spain's Juan Carlos have commissioned pieces of Vista Alegre porcelain. On a branch of the Aveiro estuary, the village is the site of an open market held on the 13th of every month, a tradition dating from the late 1600s. You'll find ceramics, fresh vegetables, a few antiques, and *ovos moles* (egg yolk sweets); it's worth attending if you're in town on market days. The market doesn't have any set hours but it's usually in operation by 8am and shuts down around 3pm.

Vista Alegre Museum, Fábrica Vista Alegre (© **23/432-06-00**), records the history of porcelain, starting in 1824 when the factory was founded here. It's open Tuesday to Friday 9am to 6pm; Saturday and Sunday 9am to 12:30pm and 2:30 to 5pm. Admission is 3€ and free for children under 12.

OUTDOOR ACTIVITIES

In the Rota da Luz area near Aveiro, you can go **windsurfing** in many places, including Ria de Aveiro and Pateira de Fermentelos. The long stretches of sand and the formation of waves also provide ideal conditions for **surfing;** particularly good Rota da Luz **beaches** are Esmoriz, Cortegaça, Furadouro, Torreira, São Jacinto, Barra, Costa-Nova, and Vagueira. The whole stretch of the Ria estuary is ideal for **water-skiing,** and many rivers, notably the Pateira and the Ria, are suited for **canoeing** and **rowing.**

There's good **fishing** along the Rota da Luz. The tourist office (see above) provides helpful information. The local waterways contain carp, lampreys, and barbels, along with gray mullet, bass, and eels. The best places for trout are the rivers Paiva, Arda, Antuã, Caima, Alfusqueiro, and Águeda.

Horseback riders head for the **Escola Equestre Aveiro,** Quinta Chão Agra, Vilarinho (© **23/491-21-08;** www.escolaequestreaveiro.com), 6.5km (4 miles) north of

Aveiro on N109. It offers trekking rides across the wetlands around Aveiro. The cost is 25€ per rider for 2 hours. Call for reservations and more information.

Many visitors to the area like to go **biking,** particularly along the traffic-free route between Aveiro and Ovar. You can get free bikes near the tourist office on Rua João Mendonça (📞 **23/440-63-00**).

SHOPPING

You'll find handicrafts and the sophisticated porcelain manufactured in the village of Vista Alegre, 6.5km (4 miles) south. To visit the **Vista Alegre factory outlet** (📞 **23/432-06-00**), follow the signs from Aveiro's town center. Free visits to the manufacturing facilities are conducted Monday to Friday from 9am to 12:30pm and 2 to 5pm. The factory outlet is open Tuesday to Friday 10am to noon and 2:30 to 5pm.

The town's most visible and best-stocked shopping venues are on the main boulevard bisecting the town, **Avenida Dr. Lourenço Peixinho.** The shops on this street sell virtually everything a local resident might need to pursue the good life in the Portuguese and international style.

Trendy shoppers head for the boutique-studded mall, **Association of Cultural Mercado Negro,** Rua João Mendonça 17, which is found on the second floor of a huge town house on the main canal that runs through town. The restored building from the 1800s also doubles as a cultural center. On weekends, you can enjoy live music in some of the bars here; the center is also the venue for an occasional film festival. This is the major gathering point on a Saturday afternoon for the youth of Aveiro.

Where to Stay

Hotel Afonso V ★ We think this is the best place in town, though many people prefer the Hotel Imperial (see below). If you're driving, signs will direct you to the hotel, in a residential, tree-lined neighborhood. Small sea-green tiles line the facade. A recent enlargement and renovation turned the original core into a contemporary structure. The midsize guest rooms are comfortably furnished.

Rua Dr. Manuel das Neves 65, 3810-101 Aveiro. www.hoteisafonsov.com.pt. 📞 **23/442-51-91.** Fax 23/438-11-11. 78 units. 74€–95€ double; 150€–185€ suite. Rates include buffet breakfast. AE, MC, V. Parking 5€. **Amenities:** Restaurant; bar; babysitting; Wi-Fi (5€ per hour, in lobby). *In room:* A/C, TV, hair dryer, minibar (in some).

Hotel Arcada ★ 🏵 The family-owned Arcada enjoys an enviable central position, with a view of the traffic in the canal out front. In summer, white pyramids of drying salt on the flats are visible from the guest rooms. The modernized hotel retains its classic beige-and-white 1930s facade and its rooftop decorated with ornate finials. The hotel occupies the second, third, and fourth floors of the old building. Many of the midsize guest rooms open onto balconies. Some are done up in the traditional Portuguese style; others evoke a bland international style, with blond furnishings. *Note:* All the units on the second floor are subject to noise; rooms on third and fourth floors are more tranquil. Breakfast is the only meal served.

Rua Viana do Castelo 4, 3800 Aveiro. www.hotelarcada.com. 📞 **23/442-30-01.** Fax 23/442-18-86. 49 units. 69€–89€ double. Rates include buffet breakfast. AE, DC, MC, V. No parking. **Amenities:** Bar; babysitting; room service. *In room:* A/C, TV.

Hotel Imperial ★ Unexceptional but efficient and modern, the Imperial is often cited as the best hotel in town by those who prefer it over the Hotel Afonso V (see above). It attracts local young people, who gravitate to the lounge for drinks or to the airy dining room (a favorite with tour groups). Many of the small, neutrally decorated guest rooms and all of the lounges overlook the Ria de Aveiro and the garden of the Aveiro museum, the old convent. From the summer terrace, a view sweeps over the arid expanse of the district's salt pans. All rooms are furnished in contemporary style, with many built-in features.

Rua Dr. Nascimento Leitão, 3810-108 Aveiro. www.hotelimperial.pt. ℂ **800/780-1234** in the U.S., or 23/438-01-50. Fax 23/438-01-59. 107 units. 55€–98€ double; from 70€ suite. Rates include buffet breakfast. AE, DC, MC, V. No parking. **Amenities:** Restaurant; bar; babysitting; exercise room; outdoor pool; room service; sauna. *In room:* A/C, TV, hair dryer, minibar, Wi-Fi (free).

Hotel João Padeiro ★ ▮▮   Beside the N109, 7km (4⅓ miles) north of Aveiro, João Padeiro is a sienna-colored building concealing an elegant hotel. It was a village cafe until the Simões family transformed it more than a decade ago. You enter a reception area filled with family antiques. Each unit is unique, and most contain an antique four-poster bed; all boast exuberantly flowered wallpaper, coved ceilings, and hand-crocheted bedspreads.

Rua da República 13, Cacia, 3800-533 Aveiro. ℂ **23/491-13-26.** Fax 23/491-27-51. 27 units. 64€ double; 89€ suite. Rates include buffet breakfast. AE, DC, MC, V. **Amenities:** Restaurant; bar; babysitting; room service. *In room:* TV.

Hotel Moliceiro ★   This stylish hotel is filled with atmosphere and with rooms opening onto a view of the river, an enclosed garden, or else the bustling Art Nouveau Mercado do Peixe where fishermen arrive early in the morning with the latest catch of grouper, sardines, whatever. Many guests who used to check into the Hotel Arcada are now deserting it to enjoy the more upscale comforts of Moliceiro, which takes its name from the centuries-old boats of Aveiro. The hotel was constructed on a bend of the canal in the old city. Its designer blended antique features with sleek "moderno," creating a cozy, intimate atmosphere in both the public rooms and private units.

Rua Barbosa de Magalhães 15-17, 3800-154 Aveiro. www.hotelmoliceiro.com. ℂ **23/437-74-00.** Fax 23/437-74-01. 49 units. 100€–200€ double. AE, DC, MC, V. No parking. **Amenities:** Bar; room service. *In room:* A/C, TV, hair dryer, minibar, Wi-Fi (free).

Veneza Hotel ★ ▮▮   This hotel occupies a Moorish-style building that was once an aristocratic private villa. An iron fence encloses the front courtyard, where trees, vines, and hand-painted tiles surround a fountain. The best rooms look out over the third-floor loggia onto a goldfish-filled basin in the garden. You'll find this well-preserved house (known in Portuguese as an *antiga moradia senhoria,* meaning "antique manor house") on a busy downtown street leading into the city from Porto. Breakfast is the only meal served.

Rua Luís Gomes de Carvalho 23, 3800-211 Aveiro. www.venezahotel.pt. ℂ **23/440-44-00.** Fax 23/440-44-01. 49 units. 58€–125€ double. AE, DC, MC, V. Parking 5€. **Amenities:** Bar; babysitting; room service. *In room:* A/C, TV, hair dryer, minibar, Wi-Fi (5€ per hour).

Where to Dine

A Cozinha do Rei ★ INTERNATIONAL/PORTUGUESE   A Cozinha do Rei is in the best hotel in town (see the Hotel Afonso V review, above) and its menu offerings tend to live up to the standards set by the hotel. The formal restaurant serves regional and international meals—the fresh fish is a good bet—in a modernized sunwashed room. Service is among the best in town.

In the Hotel Afonso V, Rua Dr. Manuel das Neves 66. ℂ **23/442-51-91.** Regular main courses 9.50€– 25€; seafood main courses 18€–54€. AE, MC, V. Tues–Sun noon–3pm and 7:30–11pm.

Restaurante Centenário PORTUGUESE Centenário stands at the side of Aveiro's version of Les Halles. From the front door you can see the teeming covered market; laborers often stream up to the elongated bar after unloading produce early in the morning. The high-ceilinged, modern room contains lots of polished wood and has a large window opening onto the street. The restaurant is also called *A Casa da Sopa do Mar,* and that shellfish-laden soup is the house specialty. In addition to a steaming bowl, you can order grilled pork or veal, fried or grilled sole, codfish *brasa* (cooked over charcoal), and an array of other tasty specials. This isn't gourmet fare, but it is satisfying.

Largo do Mercado 9-10. ⓒ **23/442-27-98.** www.restaurantecentenario.com. Main courses 9€–20€. MC, V. Tues–Sun noon–3pm and 7:30–11pm.

Where to Stay & Dine Nearby

Pousada da Torreira Murtosa, Ria de Aveiro ★★ The government operates this pousada, about 30km (19 miles) northwest from Aveiro on a promontory surrounded by water on three sides. Between the sea and the lagoon, the contemporary building makes good use of glass and has rows of balconies on its second floor. You can reach it by boat from Aveiro or by taking a long drive via Murtosa and Torreira. A waterside terrace opens onto views of fishing craft. The inn is popular with vacationing Portuguese families. The compact guest rooms are furnished with built-in pieces, including firm beds.

Bico do Muranzel, 3870-301 Torreira-Murtosa. www.pousadas.pt. ⓒ **23/486-01-80.** Fax 23/483-83-33. 20 units. 102€–204€ double. Rates include buffet breakfast. AE, DC, MC, V. Free parking. **Amenities:** Restaurant; bar; babysitting; outdoor pool; room service; outdoor tennis court (lit). *In room:* A/C, TV, hair dryer, minibar.

Aveiro After Dark

The core of the city's nightlife is the **Canal de São Roque,** near the Mercado de Peixe in the town center. Here you'll find a trio of 18th-century stone salt warehouses. They've been transformed into attractive, richly folkloric bars that draw loyal local patrons. One is **Sal Poente** (ⓒ **23/438-26-74;** www.salpoente.com), which functions from noon to 2:30pm and 7:30 to 10pm as a well-managed restaurant, and then Friday and Saturday from 10:30pm to around 2am as a venue for live concerts. Expect to hear lots of Brazilian samba and rock—everything except fado. Sal Poente is one of the few eateries in town with views that encompass both the lagoon and the town's age-old salt pans.

CARAMULO

81km (50 miles) NE of Coimbra; 280km (174 miles) N of Lisbon

Set against a background of mimosa and heather-laden mountains, this tiny resort between Aveiro and Viseu is a good place from which to view the surrounding country. About 3km (1¾ miles) north of town, at the end of a dirt road, is a watchtower that affords a panoramic view of the Serra do Caramulo.

Essentials

ARRIVING

BY TRAIN There is no train service to Caramulo.

BY BUS From Lisbon, you must go to Tondela and then make connections into Caramulo. You can also go from Lisbon to Viseu (see below) and then ride the bus to

Caramulo, though you'll have to allow at least 5 hours. Or you can take the train from Lisbon to Coimbra (see earlier in this chapter), a bus to Tondela, and another bus to Caramulo.

BY CAR The village is usually approached from Viseu (see below). Follow N2 south for some 24km (15 miles) to Tondela, and then take a right onto N230 and follow signs for Caramulo for about 19km (12 miles).

VISITOR INFORMATION

Caramulo doesn't have a tourist office. Before setting you, you might want to check with the tourist office in Coimbra (see earlier in this chapter) for information.

Exploring the Area

From the tip of the mountain, about 7km (4⅓ miles) from town at **Caramulinho,** you can see for miles. The panoramic sweep includes the Lapa, Estrela, Lousa, and Buçaco ranges; the Serras da Gralheira and de Montemuro; and the coastal plain. To reach the best viewing place on the 1,000m-high (3,281-ft.) peak, take Avenida Abel de Lacerda from Caramulo west to N230-3 and then go less than 1km (⅔ mile) on foot. Another panoramic vista spreads out from the summit of **Cabeça da Neve,** off the same road you'd take to go to Caramulinho.

Museu do Caramulo ★ (⚹ 23/286-12-70; www.museu-caramulo.net) houses at least 60 vintage cars, including a 1905 four-cylinder De Dion–Bouton, a 1909 Fiat, an 1899 Peugeot, a 1902 Oldsmobile, a 1911 Rolls-Royce, and a 1902 Darracq. The cars have been restored to perfect condition. A few early bicycles, one dating to 1865, and motorcycles are on exhibit as well. The museum is not just about transportation, though—it also contains Portuguese and foreign paintings and art by such diverse artists as Dalí, Picasso, and Grão Vasco. The museum is located on Avenida Abel de Lacerdo, and admission is 6€ for adults, 3€ for children 6 to 12, and free for children under 6. The museum is open daily 10am to 1pm and 2 to 6pm (until 5pm in winter).

Where to Stay & Dine

Estalagem do Caramulo ★★ 🎒　High as an eagle's nest, this inn sits near the crest of a mountain ridge. The well-designed inn resembles a spread-out chalet. You ascend to the reception, living, and dining rooms; one salon flows into another. In winter, guests sit by the copper-hooded fireplace. Beyond the wooden grille is a pleasant dining room, with a window wall that overlooks the hills. From there, you can see the impressive Estrela Mountains, 77km (48 miles) away.

The guest rooms are small but attractive, with Portuguese antiques and reproductions. Wide windows open onto private balconies. Lots of fishing opportunities are to be had; the nearby Águeda and Criz rivers teem with trout and *achigas*.

3475-031 Caramulo. www.estalagemdocaramulo.wrhotels.com. ⚹ **23/286-12-91.** Fax 23/286-16-40. 12 units. 56€–70€ double. Rates include continental breakfast. AE, DC, MC, V. Free parking. **Amenities:** Restaurant; bar; babysitting; outdoor pool; room service; Wi-Fi (free, in lobby). *In room:* A/C, TV, hair dryer, minibar.

VISEU ★

97km (60 miles) E of Aveiro; 92km (57 miles) NE of Coimbra; 291km (181 miles) NE of Lisbon

The capital of Beira Alta, Viseu is a thriving provincial city. It's also a city of art treasures, palaces, and churches. Its local hero is an ancient Lusitanian rebel leader, Viriatus. At the entrance of Viseu is the Cova de Viriato, where the rebel, a combination Spartacus and Robin Hood, made his camp and plotted the moves that turned back the Roman tide.

Some of the country's most gifted artisans ply their trades in and around Viseu. Busy weaver women create the unique quilts and carpets of Vil de Moinhos, local artisans of Molelos produce the region's provincial pottery, and women with nimble fingers embroider the town's feather-fine bone lace.

Essentials

ARRIVING

BY TRAIN The nearest rail station is at Nelas, about 24km (15 miles) south. For train information, call ✆ **80/820-82-08.** Buses run from Nelas to Viseu; the fare is 4€. The fare from Lisbon to Nelas is 16€.

BY BUS Eleven Rede Expressos buses per day make the trip from Coimbra in 1 hour and 15 minutes; fare is 8€. Fourteen buses per day come from Lisbon, the trip taking 3 hours, 30 minutes and costing 16€. For information, call ✆ **70/722-33-44.**

BY CAR Viseu lies near the center of the modern expressway, IP-5, which cuts across Portugal. IP-5 hooks up with the Lisbon-Porto motorway. Coming from Spain, motorists enter Portugal at the Vilar Formoso Customs station and then head west to Viseu.

VISITOR INFORMATION

The **Viseu Tourist Board** is on Avenida Gulbenkian (✆ **23/242-09-50;** www. turismodocentro.pt). Hours vary throughout the year, so call ahead.

What to See & Do in Viseu

EXPLORING THE TOWN

Viseu offers much to see and explore at random. Wander below the cubistic network of overlapping tiled rooftops, and through the narrow alleys and encroaching macadam streets. If your time is limited, make your first stop **Largo da Sé,** the showplace of Viseu. Here, on one of the most harmonious squares in Portugal, you'll find the town's two most important buildings.

Largo da Sé (Cathedral) ★ The severe Renaissance facade of this cathedral evokes a fortress. Two lofty bell towers, unadorned stone up to the summit of the balustrades, with crowning cupolas, are visible from almost any point in or around town. The second-story windows—two rectangular and one oval—are latticed and symmetrically surrounded by niches containing religious statuary.

On your right, you'll first find the two-story Renaissance cloister, adorned with classic pillars and arcades faced with tiles. The cathedral interior is essentially Gothic but infused with Manueline and baroque decorations. Plain, slender Romanesque columns line the nave, supporting the vaulted Manueline ceiling with nautically roped **groining** ★. The basic color scheme inside plays brilliant gilding against muted gold stone. The emphasis is on the Roman arched chancel, climaxed by an elegantly carved **retable** ★ above the main altar. The chancel makes ingenious use of color counterpoint, with copper, green gold, and brownish yellow complementing the gilt work. The ceiling continues in the sacristy.

Largo da Sé. ✆ **23/243-60-65.** Free admission. Daily 9am–noon and 2–6pm.

Museu de Grão Vasco ★★ This museum, next door to the cathedral, was named after the 16th-century painter, also known as Vasco Fernandes. The Portuguese master's major works are on display; especially notable is *La Pontecôte,* in which lance-like tongues of fire hurtle toward the saints, some devout, others apathetic. There's also an intriguing collection of sculpture from the 13th to the 18th centuries, with a stunning **Throne of Grace ★** from the 1300s.

Paço dos Três Escalões. (℃) **23/242-20-49.** www.ipmuseus.pt. Admission 4€, free for children under 15. Tues 2–6pm; Wed–Sun 10am–6pm.

SHOPPING

Viseu has many handicrafts shops. On **Rua Direita,** the main street, you'll find merchants selling pottery, wrought iron, and woodcarvings. The most comprehensive stock is at the **Casa da Ribeira,** Largo Nossa Senhora da Conceição, Praça da República ((℃) **23/242-97-61**), which carries selections from many of the region's best artisans.

Where to Stay

Hotel Avenida 🦅 Avenida is a small hotel right off Rossio, the town's main plaza. It's the domain of the personable Mario Abrantes da Motto Veiga, who has combined his collection of African and Chinese antiques with pieces of fine old Portuguese furniture. The small guest rooms vary in size and character. For example, room no. 210B boasts a high-coved bed and an old refectory table and chair; an adjoining chamber has a wooden spindle bed and a marble-topped chest.

Av. Alberto Sampaio 1, 3510-030 Viseu. www.hotelavenida.com.pt. (℃) **23/242-34-32.** Fax 23/243-56-43. 29 units. 45€ double. Rates include buffet breakfast. AE, DC, MC, V. Free parking. **Amenities:** Bar; babysitting. *In room:* TV, Wi-Fi (free).

Hotel Grão Vasco ★ After days of driving in the lodging-poor environs, you'll find it a pleasure to check in here. In the heart of town, near Praça da República, Hotel Grão Vasco is built like a motel and sits amid gardens and parks. The decor is colorful and contemporary, and the guest rooms are decorated with reproductions of traditional Portuguese furnishings. Most guest room are large, and all have well-maintained bathrooms and balconies overlooking an oval pool.

Rua Gaspar Barreiros, 3510-032 Viseu. www.hotelgraovasco.pt. (℃) **23/242-35-11.** Fax 23/242-64-44. 109 units. 76€–96€ double; 99€ suite. Rates include buffet breakfast. AE, DC, MC, V. Free parking. **Amenities:** Restaurant; bar; babysitting; outdoor pool; room service. *In room:* A/C, TV, hair dryer.

Montebelo Hotel & Spa ★★ This independent hotel is the best in town, with an enviable reputation based on the attentiveness of its multilingual staff. Less than .5km (⅓ mile) from the town center, on a rise providing a panorama over the countryside, it stands in a pleasant garden. The four floors incorporate hundreds of large windows. The midsize rooms are traditionally and comfortably furnished.

Urbanização Quinta do Bosque, 3510-020 Viseu. www.hotelmontebelo.pt. (℃) **23/242-00-00.** Fax 23/241-54-00. 172 units. 91€–160€ double; 210€–290€ suite. Rates include buffet breakfast. AE, DC, MC, V. Free parking. **Amenities:** Restaurant; 2 bars; exercise room; golf course; 2 heated pools (1 indoor); room service; spa; outdoor tennis court (lit); Wi-Fi (5€ per hour, in lobby). *In room:* A/C, TV, hair dryer, minibar.

Palácio dos Melos ★★ In the monumental zone, an old castle has been brought up-to-date, completely modernized, and turned into a boutique hotel of charm and grace. In the heart of the old city, close to the cathedral, the hotel stands next door to one of the ancient seven gateways that led into the heart of the old city. Spacious, well-designed bedrooms are either in the main building or in a wing alongside. The design successfully blends the traditional and modern. A special feature is an esplanade with a panoramic view. The bar is one of the meeting places of town, and the first-class restaurant on-site serves both regional and international dishes.

Rua Chão Mestre 4, 3510-103 Viseu. www.hotelpalaciodosmelos.pt. ✆ **23/243-92-90.** 27 units. 70€–116€. AE, MC, V. No parking. **Amenities:** Restaurant; bar; room service; Wi-Fi (free). *In room:* A/C, TV, hair dryer.

Pousada de Viseu ★★ A former hospital from 1842 was taken over and completely restored and turned into a lovely first-class hotel. The original three statues on the facade—Faith, Hope, and Charity—still look out over the old city. In 1799, Dona Maria I levied a taxi on everyone in the Viseu province to pay for the construction of the original building, which took nearly 4 decades to build. Bedrooms are furnished with contemporary sleek pieces, and doubles are either standard (still quite comfortable), or superior, more spacious and better appointed. Guests seeking more luxury can book one of the spacious suites. On-site is a first-rate restaurant, specializing in seafood dishes, mountain trout, and young goat.

Rua do Hospital, 3500-161 Viseu. www.pousadas.pt. ✆ **23/245-73-20.** 84 units. 95€–114€ double; 128€–143€ suite. AE, DC, MC, V. No parking. **Amenities:** Restaurant; bar; exercise room; 2 pools (indoor and outdoor); room service; spa. *In room:* A/C, TV, hair dryer, minibar, Wi-Fi (free).

Quinta de São Caetano ★ 🏠 Less than 1km (⅔ mile) north of the center of Viseu, this is one of the most renowned properties in the region. Built in the 17th century, with a chapel dating from 1638, it was the home for many years of the viscountess of St. Caetano. It was also the setting of the novel *Eugénia e Silvina,* by the prominent contemporary Portuguese novelist Agustina Bessa Luís.

Members of the Vieira de Matos family run the severely dignified hotel. On the premises are a garden with mature trees (including a century-old Atlantic cedar) and a greenhouse where flowers grow. Dark-grained, sometimes antique furnishings fill the thick-walled rooms. Guest rooms in various sizes and shapes are traditionally furnished, with excellent beds. With prior notice, lunch and dinner can be prepared for groups.

Rua Possa dos Feiticeiras 38, 3500-020 Viseu. www.solaresdeportugal.pt. ✆ **23/242-39-84.** Fax 23/243-78-27. 6 units. 90€ double. Rates include buffet breakfast. MC, V. Free parking. **Amenities:** Outdoor pool. *In room:* A/C, no phone.

Where to Dine

Restaurante Típico O Cortiço PORTUGUESE In the oldest part of Viseu's historic core, close to the cathedral and upstairs from the Museu de Grão Vasco, this is one of the most appealing restaurants in town. A team of articulate, English-speaking locals prepares winning versions of time-tested dishes. You can select from several tasty versions of codfish, roasted breast of duck, stewed or roasted partridge (when available), and rack of rabbit simmered in red wine. One of the most prized dishes is octopus, grilled or fried, with herbs and lemon. Many diners consider it the best in the region. The wines, from throughout Portugal, are reasonably priced.

Rua de Augusto Hilário. ✆ **23/242-38-53.** www.restaurantecortico.com. Main courses 10€–25€. AE, DC, MC, V. Daily noon–3pm and 7–11pm.

PORTO & ENVIRONS

Porto (Oporto in English) is Portugal's second-largest city and its capital of port wine. The 15th-century residence of the royal family, and a bastion of trade and mercantilism, the city is rich in the legacy of the past—art treasures, medieval cathedrals, famous museums, a fine library, and other attractions. Many old homes trace their beginnings to fortunes made in Portugal's overseas colonies and, in some cases, to events leading up to the Age of Discoveries.

Every year, port wine is brought from vineyards along either side of the Douro River to lodges at Vila Nova de Gaia, across the river from Porto, where it's aged, blended, and processed. In the past it was transported on flat-bottomed boats called *barcos rabelos.* With their long rudders and flapping sails, these boats with tails skirted down the Douro like swallows. Nowadays, they've nearly given way to the train and even the unglamorous truck.

The city, which is undergoing a major renovation and sprucing up, has never looked better. Some of its alleyways—especially those around the old port—look as if they haven't changed since the Middle Ages. Porto's labyrinth of steep streets, with their decorative *azulejos* (tiles) and wrought-iron balconies, often filled with potted flowers, is reason enough to visit the city.

Especially rewarding is the **Barredo** section, a UNESCO World Heritage Site. Architect Fernando Namora, a Porto citizen, is supervising the restoration of this old-fashioned district. The sectors of Miragaia and Ribeira are also being restored.

The city also boasts a lively arts and cultural scene. The **Serralves Foundation,** one of the country's most dramatic cultural centers, often sponsors events. Many art galleries have sprouted up in the hilly **Miragaia** district, near the river. Poetry readings, art exhibits, and live jazz and rock concerts characterize Porto today.

An underrated stretch of coastal resorts and fishing villages lies between Porto and the southern reaches of the **Minho** district. The Atlantic waters, however, are likely to be on the chilly side, even in July and August. In recent years, the resorts have grown tremendously; they're known more to European vacationers than to Americans, who still prefer the Algarve. Overall, however, Porto and the coast to its north and south are among the most rewarding places to visit in Portugal.

Flying from Lisbon is the speediest way to Porto, though the express train takes 2½ to 3 hours, and the motorway takes only 3½ hours. Once in Porto, the transportation hub of the area, you can explore the coastal towns by bus or car.

PORTO ★★★

314km (195 miles) N of Lisbon; 304km (189 miles) S of La Coruña, Spain; 589km (366 miles) W of Madrid, Spain

Port and other River Douro wines still dominate Portugal's second-largest city. One of the most underrated cities of Europe, Porto dazzles with its riverfront walks, stately bridges, art, architecture, and port wine lodges. This center of finance and fashion is moving up to the forefront of Iberian tourism as more and more travelers unlock its secrets. Use Porto as your base for a voyage of discovery through the vineyards along the banks of the Douro.

Essentials

ARRIVING

BY PLANE   Porto stretches along the last 5km (3 miles) of the river Douro and is the hub of northern Portugal's communication network. The quickest and easiest way to get there is by plane. **TAP,** the Portuguese airline, provides connections between Lisbon and Porto, and there are daily flights year-round. Flights arrive at the **Aeroporto Francisco de Sá Carneiro** (✆ 22/943-24-00; www.ana.pt/portal/page/portal/ANA/AEROPORTO_PORTO). The main office of TAP is at the airport (✆ 70/720-57-00).

A taxi, the most convenient way to get from the airport into the city center, costs 28€ to 35€ for up to four passengers with luggage. Far cheaper than a taxi is Metro E (violet line), taking you from the airport into the center in about half an hour and costing 1.40€ for a one-way trip. Buses 601, 602, and 604 pick up passengers on the sidewalk adjacent to the luggage-retrieval carousels at the airport. Buses run at 30-minute intervals every day between 5am and 1am, making stops at many of the city's major hotels and at strategic points within Porto. The fare costs 1.45€ per person each way. For more information, call ✆ 80/820-01-66, or go to www.stcp.pt.

BY TRAIN   Porto has two main rail stations. The **Estação de São Bento,** Praça Almeida Garrett (✆ 80/820-82-08), is in the city center, only a block from Praça de Liberdade. Trains from here serve the Douro Valley and destinations in the north, including Viana do Castelo and Braga. East of the center, but connected to São Bento by rail, is the busier and more modern **Estação de Campanhã,** Largo da Estação de Campanhã (✆ 80/820-82-08). It serves the south, including Lisbon, as well as international routes. For any other rail information, go to www.cp.pt.

Eighteen trains arrive per day from Lisbon; the trip takes 3 to 4 hours and costs 21€ one-way in second class and 31€ one-way in first class. Eleven trains a day make the 90-minute trip from Viana do Castelo; a one-way ticket costs 7€. Seventeen trains per day arrive from Coimbra; it's a 75-minute trip and costs 16€ one-way.

BY BUS   At least five buses a day make the trip from Lisbon to Porto. The trip takes 3 to 4 hours and costs 16€ one-way. It ends at the **bus station,** Rua Alexandre Herculano 366 (✆ 70/722-33-44). Nineteen buses per day arrive from Coimbra; the trip takes 1 hour and costs 12€ one-way.

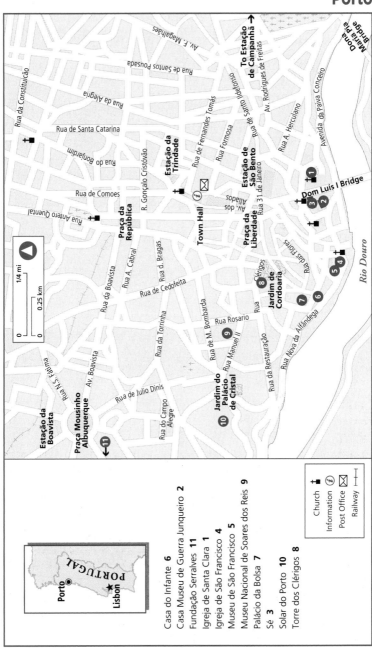

Casa do Infante **6**

Casa Museu de Guerra Junqueiro **2**

Fundação Serralves **11**

Igreja de Santa Clara **1**

Igreja de São Francisco **4**

Museu de São Francisco **5**

Museu Nacional de Soares dos Reis **9**

Palácio da Bolsa **7**

Sé **3**

Solar do Porto **10**

Torre dos Clérigos **8**

+■ Church
ⓘ Information
⊠ Post Office
+ Railway

PORTUGAL

Porto

Lisbon ★

BY CAR The Lisbon-Porto superhighway cuts driving time between Portugal's two leading cities to just over 3 hours. For motorists, Porto is the center of the universe— all major roads in the north fan out from here. From Spain, the nearest border crossing is at Tuy–Valença do Minho. After that, you can head south for some 125km (78 miles) to Porto on N13.

VISITOR INFORMATION

One of the most helpful tourist offices in Portugal is the **Porto Tourist Board,** Rua do Clube Fenianos 25 (✆ **22/339-34-72;** www.portoturismo.pt). The office is open July to September daily 9am to 7pm; in the off season, it's open daily 9am to 5:30pm. Another tourist office, at Rua de Infante Dom Henrique 63 (✆ **22/206-04-12**), keeps the same hours.

City Layout

Regardless of your method of transport, you'll need to acquaint yourself with the geography of this complicated city. It's probably best to start with the city's justly famous bridges. Connecting the right bank to the port-wine center of Vila Nova de Gaia and the lands south is the **Ponte de Dona Maria Pia,** an architectural feat of Alexandre-Gustave Eiffel (of Eiffel Tower fame). Another bridge spanning the Douro is the **Ponte de Dom Luís I.** An iron bridge of two roadways, it was completed in 1886 by Teófilo Seyrig, a Belgian engineer inspired by Eiffel. Another bridge, Edgar Cardoso's **Ponte de Arrábida,** which opened in 1963, is bright and contemporary. Totally Portuguese in concept and execution, it's one of the largest single-span reinforced-concrete arches in Europe.

The heart of Porto is **Avenida dos Aliados,** with its parklike center, where families sometimes go for a stroll. It's bounded on the south by **Praça General Humberto Delgado.** Two major shopping streets lie on either side of Praça de Liberdade: **Rua dos Clérigos** and **Rua 31 de Janeiro.** Rua Clérigos leads to the landmark **Torre dos Clérigos,** which some consider the symbol of Porto.

The verdant suburb of **Foz do Douro** stands adjacent to where the River Douro empties into the sea, about 5km (3 miles) to the northwest of Porto. Foz (that's the way its name is shortened by most residents of North Portugal) is scenic, calm, and mostly residential, a middle- and upper-class suburb whose income level is in distinct contrast to the grinding poverty of some neighborhoods in downtown Porto. Foz is known as a "green lung" for Porto, with a rather high percentage of nightclubs and restaurants.

Vila Nova de Gaia

For more than a century, the "other" bank of the Douro has sheltered representatives of the port-wine industry, many of which maintain a sales outlet and, in most cases, warehouses. It lies just across the river from Porto, within a very short walk from the Praça de Ribeira, but spiritually, it's a long way away. Poverty is a little more obvious on this side of the river, and the buildings are a bit less well maintained.

Hotels are extremely limited here, and only a few of the restaurants are oriented to the tourist trade. The port-wine lodges are by far the most visible entities on this side of the river. Despite occasional flashes of bravura from the local tourist board, the mostly residential district has far fewer monuments and attractions than Porto. To reach it from Porto, take bus no. 900 or 901.

Porto: Hometown of Port Wine

Porto (known also as the Port) gave its name not only to port wine but also to Portugal and its language. The name derives from the Roman settlement of Portus Cale. The Douro, which comes from Rio do Ouro (River of Gold), has always been Porto's lifeblood. The city perches on a rocky gorge that the Douro cut out of a great stone mass. According to the writer Ann Bridge, "The whole thing looks like a singularly dangerous spider's web flung across space."

Porto's most intriguing neighborhood is **Ribeira.** The steep, narrow streets and balconied houses evoke Lisbon's Alfama, though the quarter has its own distinctive character. Ribeira preserves the timeless quality of many of the old buildings and cobbled streets lining the riverbank.

Many visitors write off Porto as an industrial city with some spectacular bridges, but there's much to enjoy here. As the provincial capital and university seat, Porto has its own artistic treasures. The city beats with a sense of industriousness—it's not surprising that Henry the Navigator was born here in the late 14th century.

Matosinhos is set about 11km (6¾ miles) to the northwest of Porto, beyond Foz. It is metallic, industrial, intensely commercial, and dominated by the heavy machinery that's in place to unload some of the biggest transport ships in the world. Much of it is devoted to vast warehouses, unloading docks, and cranes.

Getting Around

Porto's Metro system is both aboveground and underground (more underground, of course) in the center of the city. The network consists of five different lines and serves the center of Porto but also reaches out to certain municipalities within the Greater Porto area, including Matosinhos, Vila Nova de Gaia, and Póvoa de Varzim. Service is daily from 6am to 1:30am. Waiting time for subway cars can range from 12 to 30 minutes. To ride the Metro, you must purchase a card for .50€. Depending on the distance, your ride will cost from 1€ to 2€. Machines, placed in all the subway stops, determine the cost of your ride. You press in your ultimate destination, and the machine indicates how much money you need to feed it. To validate your ticket, you have to put the amount of money owed into the machine. For more information, contact **Metro do Porto,** Avenida Fernão de Magalhães (© **22/508-10-00;** www. metrodoporto.pt).

Porto is also well serviced by a network of buses, trolleys, and trams; tickets begin at 1.50€. If you plan extensive touring in the area, a **Passe Turístico** is a good deal. It includes 3 days of transportation for 11€ or 1 day for 5€. Tobacco shops and kiosks around town sell the pass. For more information, contact the **Porto Tourist Board,** at Rua do Clube Fenianos 25 (© **22/339-34-72;** www.portoturismo.pt).

Taxis are available 24 hours a day. Call © **22/507-64-00** for radio taxis, or hail one on the street or at a taxi stand.

You can go from the center of Porto to the oceanfront of Foz do Douro on tram no. 1E. A Metro line also connects Porto to Foz; yet another line ("the yellow line") begins at Gaia, across the river from Porto, and carries you on a limited run to a few stops on the left bank.

[FastFACTS] PORTO

Banks Most banks and currency-exchange offices are open Monday through Friday from 8:30 to noon and 1 to 4:30pm. Two central ones are the **Banco Espírito Santo & Comercial de Lisboa,** Av. dos Aliados 45 (☎ **22/209-00-00;** www.bes.pt), and the **Banco de Portugal,** Praça Liberdade 92 (☎ **22/207-71-00**).

Consulates The United States and Canada don't maintain consulates in the north. There's a British Consulate at Travessa Barão de Forrester 86, Vila Nova de Gaia (☎ **80/820-35-37;** www.ukinportugal.fco.gov.uk/en). Vila Nova de Gaia is located in the Porto District, south of the city of Porto on the other side of the Douro River.

Drugstores Porto has many pharmacies. The

Farmácia Central do Porto, Rua Venezuela 117 (☎ **22/200-16-84**), is centrally located. If you don't speak Portuguese, ask someone at your hotel to call for you.

Emergencies Emergency numbers include police (☎ **112** or fire also at **112**), Red Cross (☎ **22/600-63-53**), and Hospital de Santo António, Largo Professor Abel Salazar (☎ **22/207-75-00**). You can also phone ☎ **112** for an ambulance.

Hospital The major one is **Hospital de Santo António,** along Largo Professor Abel Salazar (☎ **22/207-75-00**).

Internet Access Try **Laranja Mecânica,** at Rua de Santa Catarina 274. It's very centrally located in downtown Porto. It charges 1.30€ per hour and is open Monday to Saturday 10am

to 11pm, and Sunday 3 to 8pm.

Post Office The main post office is at Praça General Humberto Delgado (☎ **22/340-02-02**), near the tourist office. It sells stamps Monday to Friday 8am to 9pm, Saturday 9am to 6pm, and Sunday 9am to 12:30pm and 2 to 6pm. You can send telegrams and faxes during those hours as well.

Telephone It's possible to place long-distance calls at the post office (see above). Otherwise, go to the **phone office,** Praça de Liberdade 62. It's open Monday to Saturday 8am to 10pm, and Sunday 2 to 9pm. By placing your calls at these public institutions, you avoid hotel surcharges, which can be as much as 40%. Porto's city code is ☎ 022.

Exploring the City

Put on your walking shoes to explore the riverfront, especially the Ribeira sector, most of it looking like it's still in the Middle Ages. Spared from the great earthquake that struck Portugal in 1755, Porto is still riddled with magnificent baroque structures. Porto is ancient but also modern, as a visit to the Gulbenkian Foundation's National Museum of Contemporary Art reveals. River cruises on the Douro can top off any day.

Seeing all the worthwhile sights of Porto requires some legwork, but your discoveries will compensate you for the effort. The tourist office suggests that you take at least 3 days to explore Porto, but most visitors spend only a day.

For those on a short schedule, the most famous things to do are visiting a wine lodge at Vila Nova de Gaia; taking in the panorama from the Torre dos Clérigos, with its view of the Douro; visiting the Sé (cathedral); strolling through the most important museum, the Museu Nacional de Soares dos Reis; walking through Ribeira, the old quarter; and, if time remains, seeing the Church of São Francisco, with its stunning and richly gilded baroque interior.

CHURCHES

Igreja de Santa Clara ★ Completed in 1416, the interior of the Church of St. Clara was transformed by impassioned 17th-century artists, masters of woodwork and gilding. Nearly every square inch is covered with carved and gilded **woodwork** ★ depicting angels, saints, cherubs, and patterned designs in an architectural mélange of rococo and baroque. The clerestory windows permit the sun to flood in, making a golden crown of the upper regions. In deliberate contrast, the building's facade is squat and plain. If the keeper of the keys takes a liking to you, he'll lead you on a behind-the-scenes tour of the precincts. In the Tribute Room, for example, he'll point out a devil carved on the choir stalls.

Largo de 1 Dezembro. © **22/205-48-37.** Free admission. Mon–Fri 9:30–noon and 3–7pm; Sat 3–7pm; Sun 10am–noon. Funicular dos Guindais.

Igreja de São Francisco ★★ The Gothic Church of St. Francis, reached by steps leading up from the waterfront, was built between 1383 and 1410. In the 17th and 18th centuries, it underwent extensive **baroque decoration** ★★. The vault pillars and columns are lined with gilded woodwork: cherubs, rose garlands, fruit cornucopia, and frenzied animals, all of it entwined and dripping with gold. Many of the wide-ribbed Gothic arches are made of marble. Soaring overhead, the marble seems to fade and blend mysteriously with the gray granite columns and floors.

The Romanesque rosette dominates the facade, whose square portal is flanked by double twisted columns. Above the columns, a profusely ornamented niche contains a simple white statue of the patron saint. In the rose window, 12 mullions emanate from the central circle in apostolic symbolism, ending in a swaglike stone fringe. The steps spill fanlike into the square, along the base of the curved walls. Nearby, through a separate entrance, is the Museu de São Francisco (see below).

Rua do Infante Dom Henrique. © **22/206-21-00.** Admission (including church and museum) 3€. Daily 9am–6pm. Tram: 1.

Sé (Cathedral) ★ This cathedral grew and changed with the city—that is, until about the 18th century. Founded by a medieval queen and designed in a foreboding, basically Romanesque style, it's now a monument to changing architectural tastes. Part of the twin towers, the rose window, the naves, and the vestry are elements of the original 13th-century structure. Builders added the austere Gothic cloister at the end of the 14th century and later decorated it with *azulejos* (tiles) ★ depicting events from the Song of Solomon. Opening off the cloister is the Chapel of St. Vincent, built in the late 16th century.

The main chapel was erected in the 17th century, and in 1736 the baroque architect Nicolau Nasoni of Italy added the north facade and its attractive loggia. Twisted columns flank the monumental **altar** ★, and the nave is adorned with fading frescoes. In the small baroque Chapel of the Holy Sacrament (to the left of the main altar) is an altarpiece fashioned entirely of silver. The work is so elaborate that the whole piece gives the illusion of constant movement.

Rua de Dom Hugo. © **22/205-90-28.** Admission to Sé free; cloister 3€. Daily 9am–12:30pm and 2:30–6pm. Tram: 22.

MUSEUMS

Casa Museu de Guerra Junqueiro The famous Portuguese poet Guerra Junqueiro lived here between 1850 and 1923. The Italian architect Nicolau Nasoni (1691–1773) built the house. The room arrangements preserve Junqueiro's private art collection and memorabilia. The collection includes Georgian and Portuguese silver; Flemish chests; Italian, Oriental, Spanish, and Portuguese ceramics; and ecclesiastical wood and stone carvings.

Rua de Dom Hugo 32. ℂ **22/200-36-89.** Admission 2.10€, free for children under 10. Tues–Sat 10am–12:30pm and 2-5:30pm; Sun 2-5:30pm. Tram: 22.

Fundação Serralves (Museu Nacional de Arte Contemporânea) ★   Run by the Gulbenkian Foundation in Lisbon, the National Museum of Modern Art is the most visited museum in Portugal, and is an outpost of culture in western Porto. It occupies a new building in an 18-hectare (44-acre) **park ★** next to the sherbet-pink Art Deco mansion where the collection was formerly displayed. Pritzker Prize–winning architect Álvaro Siza, a native son, designed the stark granite-and-stucco new structure. The original building is Porto's finest example of 1930s Art Nouveau. The museum exhibits the work of an exemplary coterie of contemporary Portuguese painters, designers, and sculptors. Exhibits change constantly, but there's always something interesting on display. The descriptions of the works are in Portuguese, but you can ask to see an English-language video on the artists. It's also worth the time to wander through the sculptured gardens and see their fountains. There's even old farmland tumbling down toward the Douro.

Rua Don João de Castro 210. ℂ **22/615-65-00.** www.serralves.pt. Admission 5€. Tues–Fri 10am–5pm; Sat–Sun 10am–8pm. Bus: 3, 19, 21, 35, or 78. Tram: 18.

Museu de São Francisco   The sacristan at the Museum of St. Francis estimates that 30,000 human skulls have been interred in the cellars here. He could be exaggerating, but this dank building was once the burial ground for both the rich and poor. Nowadays it's a catacomb unique in Portugal. A section of it looks like an antiques shop. Paintings on display include one of St. Francis of Assisi worshiping Christ on the Cross. Curios include some of the first paper money printed in Portugal and an 18th-century ambulance that was really a sedan chair. The Sala das Sessões, built in rich baroque style, is now a meeting hall with a Louis XIV table and João V chairs. Wherever you go in the room, the painted eyes of framed bishops follow you.

Rua da Bolsa 44. ℂ **22/206-21-00.** Admission (including church and museum) 4€, free for children 9 and under. Mar–Oct daily 9am–7pm; Nov–Feb daily 9am–5pm. Tram: 1.

Museu Nacional de Soares dos Reis   Created in 1833 by the order of Dom Pedro IV, the Nacional was called the Museu Português when it opened in 1840. A hundred years later, it was declared a national museum and dedicated to Soares dos Reis (1847–89), the noted sculptor from Porto whose remarkable works include **Desterrado ★** and *Flor Agreste*. Portraits and allegorical figures can be seen in the same gallery.

In the foreign painters collection, you'll find Dutch, Flemish, Italian, and French works, including two portraits by François Clouet (1522–72), and landscapes by Jean Pillement (1727–1808). The most representative and unified display is that of the Portuguese 19th-century painters, particularly from the Porto School. Henrique Pousão (1859–87) and Silva Porto (1850–93) are represented by fine naturalistic work. Also on display are decorative arts—ceramics, glassware, gold and silver work, furniture, and other objects.

Rua de Dom Manuel II 56. ℂ **22/339-37-70.** http://mnsr.imc-ip.pt. Admission 5€, free for children under 10, and free for everyone on Sun. Tues 2-6pm; Wed–Sun 10am–6pm. Tram: 18.

MORE ATTRACTIONS

Casa do Infante   Tradition has it that Porto's fabled hometown boy, Prince Henry the Navigator, was born in this house—now appropriately called the House of the Prince—which dates from the 1300s. In the 1800s, the building was used as a Customs house. Today it contains a **Museu Histórico,** with documents, manuscripts, and various archives relating to the history of Porto.

Rua de Alfândega 10. © **22/206-04-00.** Admission 2.10€. Tues–Sat 10am–noon and 2–5pm; Sun 2–5:30pm. Tram: 1.

Palácio de Bolsa   Late in the 19th century, Porto's municipal council decided to build a stock exchange so ornate that it would earn the instant credibility of investors throughout Europe. The result is this echoing testimonial to the economic power and savvy of north Portugal during the late Industrial Revolution. The podiums, desks, benches, and lecterns were removed long ago; the place functions today purely as a municipal showplace, without stock-trading activities of any kind. Instead you'll be ushered through something that might remind you of an abandoned royal palace, complete with massive staircases, a library, a "president's room," a domed "hall of nations" (site of stock-trading activities of yesteryear), an intricately paneled General Assembly room, and a "portraits room" in the Louis XVI style, wherein six full-length portraits of the last six Portuguese monarchs are on permanent display. The architectural highlight is the **Arabian Hall ★**, a pastiche of the Alhambra in Granada. Oval in shape, it is adorned with arabesques, carved woodwork, and stained-glass windows, all evocative of the Moors of long ago. The garden in back is especially lovely.

Rua Ferreira Borges, 4050-253 Porto. © **22/339-90-00.** www.palaciodabolsa.pt. Admission (with guided 30-min. tour in English, French, and Spanish included) 7€ adults, 5€ children under 12. Nov–Mar daily 9am–1pm and 2–6pm; Apr–Oct daily 9am–7pm. Tram: 1.

Torre dos Clérigos   West of Praça de Liberdade, follow Rua dos Clérigos to the Clérigos Tower, which the Italian architect Nicolau Nasoni designed in 1754. The tower's six floors rise to a height of some 76m (249 ft.), which makes it one of the tallest structures in the north of Portugal. You can climb 225 steps to the top of the belfry, where you'll be rewarded with one of the city's finest views, of Porto and the river Douro. The Italianate baroque **Igreja dos Clérigos,** at the same site, was also built by Nasoni and predates the tower.

Rua São Filipe De Nery. © **22/200-17-29.** Admission to tower 2€; church free. Tower Nov–Mar daily 10am–noon and 2–5pm; Apr–July and Sept–Oct daily 9:30am–1pm and 2–7pm; Aug daily 10am–7pm. Church Mon–Sat 9am–noon and 3:30–7:30pm; Sun 10am–1pm. Tram: 18.

Sampling Port & Touring the Lodges ★★

No other city in Portugal is as devoted to port wine as Porto. The history of the city itself is largely dependent on this product, and hundreds of locals labor to promote the product in markets throughout the world.

The actual **port-wine lodges** (Taylor's Port, Sandeman, Ferreira, Porto Cálem, and Ramos Pinto) lie across the river from Porto at Vila Nova de Gaia. Like the sherry makers at Jerez de la Frontera, Spain, these places are hospitable and run free tours for visitors.

Ferreira   The legendary Ferreira is one of the biggest wine lodges in Porto. Dating from the early 1800s, it was launched by Dona Antónia Adelaide Ferreira. From a modest beginning, with only a handful of vineyards, her company rose in power and influence, gobbling up wine estate after wine estate. At its apex, its holdings stretched all the way to the border of Spain, making its owner the richest woman in the nation. The fabled entrepreneur (known as Ferreirinha, or "Little Ferreira") nearly drowned in the Douro in 1861, but her voluminous petticoats kept her buoyant. Her companion, an Englishman named Baron de Forrester, who did not wear petticoats, wasn't as lucky.

Tours take you through the caves displaying endless bottles of port and past fascinating modern and antique machinery. At the end of the tour, you can attend a tasting of one or two bottles and make purchases at the company store.

Av. Diogo Leite 70. ✆ **22/375-20-66** or 22/374-52-92. www.sogrape vinhos.eu. Daily 10:30am–12:30pm and 2–6pm. Bus: 900, 901, or 906.

Porto Cálem   Founded in 1959 by the Cálem family, this wine-production company was taken over by a bank based in Vigo, Spain, in 2001. Its tour is much less formal than one at Sandeman, next door (see below). A tour hostess guides you through the barrel-making process, leading you past 75-year-old oaken casks, each laid out in an antique stone-sided warehouse whose walls are marked with the high-water marks of each of the floods of the past 200 years. The tour eventually heads upstairs to an antique room whose displays of port evoke the great days of the wine trade at its best. The cellars are a bit newer than those at the more established firms, but the port, depending on the vintage, is just as good.

Av. Diogo Leite 344. ✆ **22/374-66-60.** www.calem.pt. May–Oct daily 10am–7pm (6:30pm last visit); Nov–Apr Mon–Sat 10am–6pm (5:30pm last visit). Bus: 900, 901, or 906.

Ramos Pinto ★★   This wine producer is usually acknowledged as the most interesting and best-preserved of any in Porto and Vila de Gaia. Owned since 1991 by the French champagne company Roederer, it showcases the creation in 1880 by Adriano Ramos Pinto of an outfit that placed enormous interest in the advertising campaigns of its era. You'll be given a guided tour of the cellars, with information about port and its manufacture, plus tastings at the end of the tour. But what you'll get in addition to the tour of the cellars is a visit to the corporate offices, each re-created in turn-of-the-20th-century style, complete with the artworks and furniture selected by the company founder or his cohorts. On the premises is one of the largest collections of posters ever assembled during the Belle Epoque, many of them works of art in their own right, each proclaiming the virtues of port as a defining factor of an elegant lifestyle. Tours are conducted in Portuguese, French, Spanish, and English, and because of the outfit's strong corporate links with France, you're likely to find goodly numbers of French tourists on board. Incidentally, one of the most celebrated and most frequently showcased products of this company is a 10-year-old tawny port named Quinta de Ervamoira. It's named after a particularly beautiful villa in the region, around which some of the company's grapes are produced. It might be a good idea to haul a bottle of it home with you, as it's not widely available elsewhere.

Av. Ramos Pinto 400. ✆ **22/370-70-00.** www.ramospinto.pt. Mar–Oct daily 10am–12:30pm and 2–6pm; Nov–Feb 9:30am–12:30pm and 2–5:30pm. Bus: 900, 901, or 906.

Sandeman ★   The most famous port-wine center is Sandeman, owned by Seagram's of Canada. In a former 16th-century convent, George Sandeman of Scotland established Sandeman in 1780. The company became notorious in the 1920s for its ad campaigns, which featured sex appeal in ways never before seen in the port-wine industry. (Satyrs carrying gleeful, scantily clad flappers off into the forest for a glass of port or whatever . . .) The Sandeman "Don," created in 1928, and inspired by the cape-clad troubadours of Coimbra, has been viewed as one of the most compelling and successful images in the world of advertising. The House of Sandeman also operates a museum that traces the history of port wine and of the company. You can purchase Sandeman products on the premises.

Largo Miguel Bombarda 3. ✆ **22/374-05-33.** www.sandeman.com. Admission 4€. Mar–Oct daily 10am–12:30pm and 2–6pm; Nov–Feb Mon–Fri 9:30am–12:30pm and 2–5:30pm. Bus: 900, 901, or 906.

Solar do Porto   Head here if you're looking for a relatively fair and unbiased presentation of all of the ports in the region. Within the Quinta de Macieirinha, an elegant 18th-century villa ringed with roses, you can sample glasses of every port produced in Portugal in a setting that evokes an upscale private home. Glasses of port cost 1.50€ to 25€ each; bottles go for 8€ to 200€ each. Don't expect anything approaching a nightclub or even a bona fide restaurant (it's more like an upscale cocktail bar where the only drinks happen to be port). A short list of simple foods (cheese, olives, breads, almonds, pistachios) that go well with port is served. The staff is prepared to offer educational insights into the port-making process.

While you're here, make it a point to drop into the **Museu Romântico** (✆ **22/605-70-33**), which occupies the same 18th-century villa as the Solar do Porto. It's open Tuesday to Saturday 10am to 12:30pm and 2 to 5:30pm, and Sunday 2 to 5:30pm. It charges 2€ for adults and is free for students and for persons under 18. Admission is free for everyone, regardless of age, every Saturday and Sunday. Inside you'll find a collection of 18th- and 19th-century furniture, paintings, porcelain, and portraits that evoke the monarchical history of Portugal.

Rua de Entre-Quintas 220. ✆ **22/609-47-49.** www.ivdp.pt. Mon–Sat 4pm–midnight. Bus: 200. Tram: 1.

 "PORTING" & dining

Much of the character, architecture, and history of Porto derive from its wine trade. As such, you'd be well advised to take a morning tour of two or three of the wine lodges of **Vila Nova de Gaia,** learning about the nuances of port and the vast amounts of time and labor that go into it. And if you happen to be on that side of the river already, consider a lunch at a restaurant that's richly permeated with the old-fashioned mystique of the port industry, **Barão de Fladgate,** Rua do Choupelo 250, Vila Nova de Gaia (✆ **22/374-28-00;** www.tresseculos.pt). Owned and operated by the Taylor Wine Company, and set within the walled compound the company maintains on a hillside high above the Douro, it's slow, graceful, and much more formal and old-world than any other restaurant in Vila Nova de Gaia. In some ways, it's a gastronomic showcase for the port wine industry, and the Taylor Wine Company, in particular.

If you arrive on foot, expect to be seriously winded by the time you reach the restaurant, thanks to the steep uphill climb past forbidding stone walls that line the narrow streets on either side. Once at a table, you'll be offered a glass of Taylor (white port) and then will be presented with a list of the company's other products by a formally dressed battalion of waiters. Menu items are strictly Portuguese, including dried cod with fresh cream sauce, pork medallions with caramelized pineapple, and old-fashioned specials including a *cozinhado* (stew) of the day. As you dine, views of Porto, just across the river, spread out across the panorama. Main courses cost 12€ to 21€ each. The opening hours of the restaurant all year-round are Monday to Saturday 12:30 to 3pm and 7:30 to 10:30pm, Sunday 12:30 to 4pm. Reservations are required.

Taylor's Port   The cellars of Taylor's Port are among the most interesting in Porto. The firm is the last of the original English port companies to remain family owned. Tours here are less rigidly orchestrated than those at the other wine lodges, and the atmosphere is less modernized. Known for its carefully selected grapes, Taylor's produces vintage ports, single Quinta wines, and even a rare 40-year-old tawny port. You'll be served a glass of wine on the terrace, which has a view of the city and the river.

Rua do Choupelo 250. ℂ **22/374-28-00.** www.taylor.pt. Mon–Fri 10am–6pm, Sat–Sun 10am–5pm. Metro: General Torres.

WALKING TOUR: THE HEART OF PORTO

START:	**Terreiro de Sé.**
FINISH:	**Estação de São Bento.**
TIME:	**2½ hours.**
BEST TIMES:	**Any day between 10am and 4pm.**
WORST TIMES:	**Monday through Friday from 8 to 10am and 4 to 6pm, because of heavy traffic.**

The only suitable way to explore the heart of the inner city is on foot. Nearly all the major monuments are in the old part of town, and the major sights are close together. The streets are often narrow and sometimes confusing to the first-time visitor; even armed with a good map, you're likely to get lost from time to time. Long accustomed to entertaining foreigners, the people of Porto are generally friendly and hospitable, and will point you in the right direction.

Begin your tour in the heart of the old town, at:

1 Terreiro de Sé

This square is dominated by the cathedral, founded as a fortress church in the 12th century and greatly altered in the 1600s and 1700s. Square-domed towers flank the main facade. "Cathedral Square" is also bordered by an 18th-century former Episcopal palace, now municipal offices. Noted for its granite-cased doors and windows, it contains an exceptional stairway. Also on the square are a Manueline-style pillory and a statue of Vímara Peres, the warrior of Afonso III of León, who captured ancient Portucale in A.D. 868.

To the rear of the cathedral is one of Porto's most charming streets:

2 Rua de Dom Hugo

If you continue along this street, you'll pass the Chapel of Our Lady of Truths. It's invariably closed, but you can peek through the grille at the gilded rococo altar, with a statue of the Virgin at the center.

Along this same street at no. 32 stands the:

3 Casa Museu de Guerra Junqueiro

This white mansion, now a museum, was the home of the poet Guerra Junqueiro (1850–1923). The Italian architect Nicolau Nasoni designed the building.

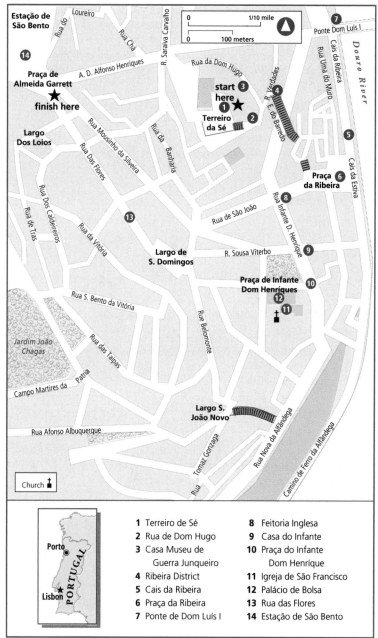

Estação de São Bento
Loureiro
Rua do
Rua Chá
R. Saraiva Carvalho
0 | 1/10 mile
0 | 100 meters
Ponte Dom Luís I
Cais da Ribeira
Rua Uma do Muro
Douro River

Praça de Almeida Garrett
A. D. Alfonso Henriques
Rua da Dom Hugo
start here ③
R. Verdades
④
R. E. do Barredo

finish here

① ★
Terreiro da Sé ②

Largo Dos Loios
Rua Mousinho da Silveira
Rua da Banharia
Cais da Estiva
⑤

Rua Das Flores
Praça ⑥ da Ribeira

Rua Dos Caldeireiros
Rua de Trás
Rua da Vitória
⑬
Rua de São João
Rua Infante D. Henrique
⑧

Largo de S. Domingos
R. Sousa Viterbo
⑨

Rua S. Bento da Vitória
Rue Belmonte
Praça de Infante Dom Henríques
⑫ ⑩
✝ ⑪

Jardim João Chagas
Rua das Taipas
Patria
Campo Martires da

Largo S. João Novo
Rua Nova da Alfândega
Camino de Ferro da Alfândega

Rua Afonso Albuquerque
Tomaz Gonzaga
Rua

Church ✝

Porto
PORTUGAL
Lisbon

1 Terreiro de Sé	**8** Feitoria Inglesa
2 Rua de Dom Hugo	**9** Casa do Infante
3 Casa Museu de Guerra Junqueiro	**10** Praça do Infante Dom Henríque
4 Ribeira District	**11** Igreja de São Francisco
5 Cais da Ribeira	**12** Palácio de Bolsa
6 Praça da Ribeira	**13** Rua das Flores
7 Ponte de Dom Luís I	**14** Estação de São Bento

Continue along Rua de Dom Hugo, a narrow street that curves around the eastern side of the Sé, until you come to some steep steps. These were carved through remaining sections of the town walls that existed in the Middle Ages. This brings you into one of the most colorful and poverty-stricken sections of Porto, the:

4 Ribeira District ★★

The back streets of this historic neighborhood have much charm. The area abounds with arcaded markets, churches, museums, monuments, and once-elegant buildings.

Regardless of which alley you take, everything eventually merges onto the:

5 Cais de Ribeira

The quayside section of the Ribeira district opens onto the Douro. Locals come here for the low-cost *tascas* (taverns) and seafood restaurants, which were constructed into the street-level arcade of the old buildings.

The center of the district is:

6 Praça de Ribeira

Locals sit in the sun here telling tall tales. From here, visitors can take in the port-wine lodges across the Douro at Vila Nova de Gaia.

Now head north to the:

7 Ponte de Dom Luís I

This is the middle of the trio of bridges over the river Douro. The iron bridge was designed by Seyrig, one of Gustave Eiffel's collaborators, in 1886. It has an upper and a lower span, both of which funnel traffic to Vila Nova de Gaia.

After viewing the bridge and the river, retrace your steps to Praça de Ribeira. At the west side of the square, walk up Rua de São João to the:

8 Feitoria Inglesa (Factory House of the British Association)

This is the headquarters of the Port Wine Shippers' Association. One of the most fabled buildings in the Ribeira district, it stands where Rua do Infante Dom Henrique crosses Rua de São João. British consul John Whitehead designed the "factory" in 1786.

Follow Rua do Infante Dom Henrique to the:

9 Casa do Infante

The Casa do Infante lies at the corner of Rua de Alfândega. Porto-born Henry the Navigator, who launched Portugal on the Age of Discovery, reputedly was born in this house.

Follow Rua do Infante Dom Henrique to:

10 Praça do Infante Dom Henrique

A statue of Prince Henry the Navigator graces this square. Here you can visit a big covered food market, where tripe is sold in great quantities. Although shunned by much of the Western world (except by Florentines), tripe is said to be the favorite food of the denizens of Porto.

The highlight of this square is the:

11 Igreja de São Francisco

Originally this was a Gothic church. Its adjacent museum once was the property of a Franciscan monastery. This church boasts the most lavish, spectacular church interior in Porto—and the competition is fierce.

Behind the church, facing the square, is Porto's:

12 Palácio de Bolsa (Stock Exchange)

It takes up a great deal of the site of what used to be a Franciscan monastery. It's known for an oval Arab Room whose stained glass and arabesques are said to imitate the style of the Alhambra in Granada, built by the Moors. The Stock Exchange stands at Rua de Bolsa and Rua Ferreira Borges.

Follow Rua Ferreira Borges west, veering north to Largo de São Domingos. At the top of this square, continue northwest along:

13 Rua das Flores (Street of Flowers)

Some visitors consider this the most romantic street in Porto. It has long been known for the quality of its silversmiths, but what makes the street so architecturally striking is its wrought-iron balconies.

This street eventually opens onto Praça de Almeida Garrett, named for the famed Portuguese writer. On this square is the:

14 Estação de São Bento

This is the most central of Porto's railway stations. Its grand main hall is decorated with large tiles tracing the history of transportation in Portugal.

Where to Stay

Porto provides the most interesting selection of superior accommodations north of Lisbon.

EXPENSIVE

HF Ipanema Park ★★   This elegant hotel is the blockbuster modern hotel in Porto. Rising 15 floors and filled with grand comfort, HF Ipanema Park is located a 15-minute taxi ride from the heart of town. Its good-size bedrooms open onto the ocean of the Douro estuary. Not to be confused with the cheaper HF Ipanema Porto (see below), this deluxe hotel is a study in good taste, with luxuriously furnished bedrooms and suites, each done in pastels with comfortable furnishings and marble-clad bathrooms. Extra amenities are everywhere, including phones in the bathrooms. Facing a winter garden, its on-site restaurant, Jardim d'Inverno, blends a Portuguese cuisine with international dishes. The facilities, such as an outdoor pool on the 15th floor, are the best in town.

Rua Serralves 124, 4150-702 Porto. www.ipanemaparkhotel.pt. ✆ **22/532-21-00.** Fax 22/610-28-09. 281 units. 68€–125€ double; 300€–325€ suite. Rates include buffet breakfast. AE, DC, MC, V. Parking 11€. Bus: 203. **Amenities:** Restaurant; bar; babysitting; concierge; exercise room; 2 outdoor pools; sauna; Wi-Fi (free, in lobby). *In room:* A/C, TV, hair dryer, minibar.

Hotel Infante Sagres ★★★   Plush, legendary, and elegant, this hotel is one of the most traditional luxe choices in Porto. It was built in 1951 by a wealthy textile manufacturer as a guesthouse for the clients of his firm. Later it evolved into a semiprivate address for executives of the wine and textile industries. Baronial and imposing, it boasts the most impressive public rooms of any hotel in the north of Portugal, thanks to stained glass, elaborate tile work, wrought iron, polished stone, acres of mahogany paneling, and brass. It's extremely comfortable—a high-caliber staple among Porto hotels, with a desirable location close to the commercial core of town. Other than the suites, which are spectacular, bedrooms are comfortable but somewhat conventional-looking, with dignified decors, high ceilings, quietly substantial furnishings, and marble-sheathed bathrooms.

Praça Filipa de Lencastre 62, 4050-259 Porto. www.hotelinfantesagres.pt. ⓒ **22/339-85-00.** Fax 22/339-85-99. 72 units. 214€–275€ double; 385€–825€ suite. Rates include buffet breakfast. AE, DC, MC, V. Limited free parking on street; 10€ in nearby garage. Metro: Aliados. **Amenities:** Restaurant; bar; babysitting; concierge; room service; spa. In room: A/C, TV, hair dryer, minibar, Wi-Fi (free).

Pestana Porto ★★ 🎒 The Pestana is located portside and is composed of 11 separate but interconnected buildings, each between 200 and 400 years old. Inside you'll find an intriguing blend of antique granite blocks and hypermodern minimalism. Expect an attentive and youthful staff, a sense of architectural zest and excitement, and rooms that are among the most comfortable and imaginative in Porto. Bathrooms are large and airy, combining glossy slabs of beige stone with hand-chiseled granite blocks. Decorative schemes incorporate lots of full-grained hardwoods, sophisticated lighting, and all the modern electronics you'd expect.

Praça de Ribeira 1, 4050-513 Porto. www.pestana.com. ⓒ **22/340-23-00.** Fax 22/340-24-00. 48 units. 175€–222€ double; 261€–318€ suite. Rates include buffet breakfast. AE, DC, MC, V. Parking (in nearby lot) 12€. Tram: 1. **Amenities:** Restaurant; bar; bikes; room service. In room: A/C, TV, hair dryer, minibar, Wi-Fi (free).

Porto Palácio ★ This 23-floor tower is one of Porto's most stylish and desirable modern hotels. Set back from a busy street in the Boavista section, a short distance from the city's commercial center, its exterior has bands of stone and reflecting bronze glass. Each good-size guest room has a well-kept bathroom.

The hotel's restaurants serve mainly regional fare, with some international choices.

Av. de Boavista 1269, 4100-130 Porto. www.hotelportopalacio.com. ⓒ **22/608-66-00.** Fax 22/609-14-67. 252 units. 260€–310€ double; 520€–850€ suite. AE, DC, MC, V. Parking 1.30€ per hour. Bus: 202. **Amenities:** 4 restaurants; bar; babysitting; exercise room; 2 indoor heated pools; room service; spa. In room: A/C, TV, hair dryer, minibar, Wi-Fi (free).

Sheraton Porto Hotel & Spa ★★★ This 12-floor hotel is the tops in modern luxury for Porto. In the center of the city, the sleek hotel of marble, wood, steel, and glass forms a new landmark on Porto's cityscape. Rooms come in a wide range, ranging from standard to club rooms (on the upper floors) and executive suites. But even the simplest doubles are roomy and airy, with contemporary, stylish furnishings and tiled bathrooms. Live music is a nightly feature in the New Yorker Bar. Guests in the club rooms enjoy a rooftop terrace with a panoramic view over Porto. The hotel spa, with its adjacent juice bar, is the finest in the city.

Rua de Tenente Valadim 146, 4100-476 Porto. www.starwoodhotels.com. ⓒ **22/040-40-00.** Fax 22/040-41-99. 266 units. 152€–285€ double; from 480€ suite. AE, DC, MC, V. Parking 18€. Bus: 902. **Amenities:** Restaurant; 2 bars; babysitting; concierge; health club & spa; indoor heated pool; room service). In room: A/C, TV, hair dryer, minibar, Wi-Fi (19€ per day).

Tiara Park Atlantic Porto ★★ One of the most dramatically modern hotels in town, this hotel offers three vertical rows of bay windows along its 13-floor concrete shell. The hotel, about 3km (1¼ miles) from the heart of the city, is a favorite of conventioneers. Though in the same price bracket, it's too big to offer the personalized service of Hotel Infante Sagres (see above). The well-furnished midsize guest rooms have well-kept bathrooms.

Av. de Boavista 1466, 4100-114 Porto. www.tiara-hotels.com. © **22/607-25-00.** Fax 22/600-20-31. 232 units. 130€–250€ double; 200€–898€ suite. AE, DC, MC, V. Parking 19€. Bus: 502. **Amenities:** Restaurant; bar; babysitting; concierge; exercise room; room service. *In room:* A/C, TV, hair dryer, minibar.

MODERATE

Grande Hotel do Porto ★ Charming and evocative of a long-gone way of life, this is a carefully renovated relic of a hotel that's set on an all-pedestrian street with the densest collection of shops in central Porto. It was originally built in 1891 in a five-story "Grand Hotel" format that's still visible in its late Victorian facade and elaborate exterior detailing. After radical renovations, today it boasts an appealing combination of 1950s and Belle Epoque decor. Some noise might filter up through the open windows into the bedrooms above. But that's overcome by the charm of very wide stairwells and hallways, high-ceilinged accommodations with more space than you might have expected, contemporary decor, and better-than-average service.

Rua Santa Catarina 197, 4000-450 Porto. www.grandehotelporto.com. © **22/207-66-90.** Fax 22/207-66-99. 97 units. 109€–148€ double; 170€–250€ suite. AE, DC, MC, V. Bus: 206. Parking 11€. **Amenities:** Restaurant; bar; room service. *In room:* A/C, TV, hair dryer, minibar, Wi-Fi (13€ per day).

Guest House Douro ★ ⛟ Arguably, this is the best guesthouse in Porto, lying in the historic Ribeira section, with views of the Douro River and the port lodges on the opposite bank. In spite of the antique neighborhood, the building has been totally renovated and modernized, offering much comfort. The individually decorated guest rooms are small, but each possesses big windows allowing guests to take in the panoramic view. Innkeepers Carmen and João have received many letters of praise from readers, citing their hospitality.

Rua Fonte Taurina 99-101, 4050-270 Porto. www.guesthousedouro.com. © **22/201-51-35.** Fax 22/201-51-36. 140€–175€. Rates include breakfast. MC, V. No parking. Bus: 1 or 57. **Amenities:** Breakfast room. *In room:* A/C, TV, hair dryer, Wi-Fi (free).

HF Fénix Porto ★ ♦ A rather stylish, government-rated four-star hotel, the Fénix avoids the dull bandbox style of many of its competitors and has a more dramatic facade and a striking lobby. A welcoming staff of professionals greet you at a location that's convenient to both the airport and the rail station. The bedrooms are midsize and are attractively decorated without any overadornment. Rooms come in a wide range, including some executive doubles, which are larger, as well as some premier doubles lying on the 12th and 13th floors with better views. A fashionable restaurant on-site uses fresh, seasonal ingredients, and the hotel bar is an ideal rendezvous to meet friends or else watch sporting events on the giant flatscreen TV. Most of the accommodations are priced at the lower end of the scale (see below).

Rua Gonçalo Sampaio 282, 4150-365 Porto. www.hfhotels.com. © **22/607-18-00.** Fax 22/607-18-10. 148 units. 59€–260€. AE, DC, MC, V. Parking 9€. Bus: 303. **Amenities:** Restaurant; bar; babysitting; room service. *In room:* A/C, TV, hair dryer, minibar, Wi-Fi (free).

HF Ipanema Porto ★ The government-rated four-star Ipanema Porto (don't confuse it with the five-star Ipanema Park, above) is one of the best hotels in Porto. A sleek 10-story modern structure, it's a prominent feature of the city's skyline, with elongated rows of smoked glass that are visible from the highway to Lisbon. In fact, one of this hotel's assets is that it's easy to find. Exit the highway at the signs indicating the direction of Porto, and you'll find it on a cobblestone road leading to the town center, less than 2km (1¼ miles) away. The handsomely furnished midsize guest rooms have cedar accents and views of Porto.

Rua do Campo Alegre 156–172, 4100-168 Porto. www.hfhotels.com. ☎ **22/607-50-59.** Fax 22/606-33-39. 150 units. 62€–125€ double; from 90€ suite. Rates include buffet breakfast. AE, DC, MC, V. Parking 9€. Metro: Casa de Música. Bus: 200 or 207. **Amenities:** Restaurant; bar; babysitting; concierge; room service. *In room:* A/C, TV, hair dryer, minibar, Wi-Fi (free).

Hotel da Bolsa ★ 🏛 This centrally located hotel occupies what was originally a private social club built in 1908. About 30 years later, after a disastrous fire, it was rebuilt in the Beaux Arts style into the headquarters of an insurance company. In 1994, after several years of being closed, it reopened as a well-managed and unpretentious government-rated three-star hotel. Bedrooms are compact but high-ceilinged, many with floor plans that were influenced by the building's former role as a private office. Each is comfortable and blandly decorated with Victorian prints, tiled bathrooms, and plain contemporary furniture.

Rua Ferreira Borges 101, 4050-253 Porto. www.hoteldabolsa.com. ☎ **22/202-67-68.** Fax 22/205-88-88. 36 units. 100€–151€ double. Rates include buffet breakfast. AE, DC, MC, V. Parking 10€. Tram: 18 or 22. **Amenities:** Bar. *In room:* A/C, TV, Wi-Fi (free).

Hotel Dom Henrique ★ Though designed for business travelers, Dom Henrique is equally accommodating to vacationers. In the city center, this restored hotel is in a 22-story tower, and boasts a 17th-floor bar that affords panoramic views. The bedrooms are among the most spacious in the city because the hotel was originally intended for offices before a switchover. The accommodations are attractively decorated in creams and reds, with tasteful, comfortable wood furnishings; the roomy bathrooms are luxurious and clad in marble and stocked with complimentary toiletries. The cuisine in the ground-floor restaurant is often refreshingly imaginative. Though most rooms are moderately priced, some extra-large, amenities-filled rooms here fall into the "expensive" category.

Rua Guedes de Azevedo 179, 4049-009 Porto. www.hoteldomhenrique.pt. ☎ **22/340-16-16.** Fax 22/340-16-66. 112 units. 70€–125€ double; 120€–170€ suite. Rates include buffet breakfast. AE, DC, MC, V. Parking nearby 10€. Metro: Trindade. **Amenities:** Restaurant; bar; babysitting; room service. *In room:* A/C, TV, hair dryer, minibar, Wi-Fi (13€ per day).

Mercure Porto Centro ★ This good-value hotel opens onto one of the busiest, most colorful squares of Porto, and is opposite the National Theater and about a 10-minute walk from the river. It's popular with international port-wine buyers, probably because of its convenient location.

The lobby sets the tone of combining the traditions of yesterday with the modern comforts of today, with old paintings, antique furniture, pillars, and cushioned seating. The guest rooms are also traditional but comfortable; while not grand, they're tastefully decorated, with coordinated fabrics, French windows, and tiled bathrooms. Note that, in spite of soundproofing, traffic noise is audible from some front rooms.

Porto Praça de Batalha 116, 4049-028 Porto. www.mercure.com. ☎ **22/204-33-00.** Fax 22/204-34-99. 149 units. 69€–110€ double; from 99€ suite. AE, DC, MC, V. Parking 10€. Tram: 22. **Amenities:** Restaurant; bar; room service. *In room:* A/C, TV, hair dryer, Wi-Fi (free).

Quality Inn Porto In the heart of the city, this six-story hotel lies in the Barredo section, which UNESCO has declared an historic heritage site. The hotel is severely modern and is not exciting in any way, but it's a practical, no-frills choice with affordable prices. The streamlined, functional guest rooms offer comfort, well-kept bathrooms, and deluxe toiletries.

Praça de Batalha 127–130, 4000-102 Porto. www.choicehotels.com. © **877/424-64-23** in the Canada, or 22/339-23-00. Fax 22/200-60-09. 113 units. 70€–125€ double. Rates include buffet fast. Parking 10€. Tram: 22. **Amenities:** Bar; Wi-Fi (5€ per hour, in lobby). *In room:* A/C, TV, hair dryer.

INEXPENSIVE

Albergaria Miradouro ★ 👬

Resembling an eagle's nest, Albergaria Miradouro is a slim 13-floor structure built atop a hill within a commercial and residential neighborhood not far from the heart of town. The rooms boast great vistas; from the windows, you can watch ships laden with port making their way to the open sea. The corner guest rooms are preferable; two walls have wardrobes and chests (with a built-in pair of beds), and the other walls are glass. Every unit has a vestibule, luggage storage, a valet stand, desks, a sitting room, and a well-maintained bathroom. The small-scale public rooms are tasteful. The lower bar is decorated with wall tiles from Japan and Portugal. The walls of the upper bar open onto a view. The Restaurante Portucale (see review below), which serves international cuisine, is the best in town.

Rua de Alegria 598, 4000-037 Porto. © **22/537-07-17.** Fax 22/537-02-06. 30 units. 60€–80€ double. Rates include continental breakfast. AE, DC, MC, V. Free parking. Metro: Marques. **Amenities:** Restaurant; bar; room service; Wi-Fi (free). *In room:* A/C, TV, hair dryer, minibar.

Castelo Santa Catarina ★ 👬

A former residential showplace, this hotel lies behind a high wall in a commercial neighborhood less than 2km (1¼ miles) from the center. In the 1920s, a Brazilian military officer returned to his native Porto determined to build the most flamboyant villa in town. He created a sprawling compound with greenhouses, terraced gardens, a chapel, and a sumptuous main house. Today the tile-covered exterior walls almost give an encapsulated history of Portugal.

After ringing the bell, you'll be ushered down a labyrinthine series of halls and narrow stairways. Each of the small guest rooms contains carved antique furniture, often of rosewood. The plumbing fixtures are designed with a florid Art Nouveau flair.

Rua de Santa Catarina 1347, 4000-457 Porto. www.castelosantacatarina.com.pt. © **22/509-55-99.** Fax 22/550-66-13. 26 units. 45€–60€ double; 70€ suite. Rates include continental breakfast. AE, DC, MC, V. Free parking. Metro: Marques. **Amenities:** Babysitting. *In room:* TV (in some).

Residencial Rex 🗝

The facade of this place fits in gracefully with its location on one of Porto's most beautiful squares. Its design, inspired by Art Nouveau, features sea-green tiles, cast-iron embellishments, and Roman-style window treatments. It was built by a Portuguese aristocrat around 1845 and transformed into a *pensão* (boardinghouse) in 1925. The present family-owners have been here since 1980. A majestic marble staircase leads from the street into the reception area. The lobby and small guest rooms are crowned with ornately molded plaster ceilings, and much of the furniture is antique. The bathrooms have been modernized.

Praça de República 117, 4050-497 Porto. © **22/207-45-90.** Fax 22/207-45-93. 21 units. 60€ double. Rates include breakfast. AE, MC, V. Free parking on adjacent driveway. Metro: Trindade. **Amenities:** Bar. *In room:* A/C, TV, hair dryer, Wi-Fi (free).

Tryp Porto Centro

In the center, near the famous Santa Catarina street, this well-run modern hotel is ideal for shoppers. Although Tryp Porto Centro looks dull on the outside, it is most welcoming, with public lounges and a bar furnished in streamlined modern style with subtle color schemes. Most often used by business travelers, who appreciate its efficiently run operations, this hotel can also comfortably accommodate vacationers. The bedrooms are small to midsize, but well equipped and comfortably furnished with beds that are frequently renewed. There's even a good little restaurant on-site if you don't want to go out at night.

Rua da Alegria 685, 4000-046 Porto. www.solmelia.com. ✆ **22/519-48-00.** Fax 22/519-48-19. 62 units. 54€–90€ double. AE, DC, MC, V. Parking 8.50€. Metro: Marques. **Amenities:** Restaurant; bar; babysitting; room service; Wi-Fi (free, in lobby). *In room:* A/C, TV, hair dryer, minibar.

IN FOZ DO DOURO

Hotel Boa-Vista 🛏️🍴 Set within an antique villa, a few steps from the São João do Foz fortress, this hotel evokes old Porto at its most nostalgic. It was originally built as a hotel around 1900, on the site of a ruined Franciscan monastery. In 2000, a team of architects added a modern wing and a rooftop swimming pool, enlarging the site from 39 rooms to today's total of 71. Guest rooms are very well maintained, attractive, and simple, usually with wood-grained furniture. Most of them offer views encompassing the mouth of the Douro. The more modern rooms have granite floors and a more streamlined look; the original ones have a slightly dated 1980s feel, with beige carpeting instead of granite floors, and somewhat nondescript but very comfortable decor.

Esplanada do Castelo 58, Foz do Douro, 4150-196 Porto. ✆ **22/532-00-20.** Fax 22/617-38-18. 71 units. 82€–100€ double. Rates include buffet breakfast. AE, DC, MC, V. Parking 4€ per day. Bus: 500. **Amenities:** Restaurant; bar; exercise room; outdoor pool. *In room:* TV, hair dryer, minibar, Wi-Fi (4€ per hour).

Where to Dine

When Prince Henry the Navigator was rounding up the cattle in the Douro Valley to feed his men aboard the legendary caravels, he shipped out the juicy steaks and left the tripe behind. The people of Porto responded bravely and began inventing recipes using tripe. To this day they carry the appellation *tripeiros* ("tripe eaters"), and it has become their favorite dish. To sample this specialty, the adventurous can order *tripas à moda do Porto* (tripe stewed with spicy sausage and string beans).

But chefs prepare so much more, turning the city into a showcase of the rich bounty of the north of Portugal—classics like *caldo verde* soup (potatoes and kale), and dozens of recipes for *bacalhau* (dried salt cod). Trout, eel-like lampreys, and pork dominate most menus, though you can also order tender veal and steak. Roast *cabrito* (kid) is also a local favorite. Everything is washed down with Douro wines.

VERY EXPENSIVE

DOP ★★★ PORTUGUESE Chef Rui Paula is the darling of the media in the north of Portugal, and a reservation at one of his elegant tables is considered one of the reasons to visit Porto, at least for foodies. Media have praised his inspired dishes, especially his "reinventions" of traditional dishes from the Portuguese recipe pantry. Lying in the historic Ribeiro district of the city, DOP is installed in the 14th-century Palácio das Artes. Although the outside is stately and traditional, the spacious restaurant with its high ceilings is stylish and sleekly contemporary.

Chef Paula divides his menu into three different tasting sensations, the Douro Menu, the Artes Menu, and the Sea Menu. The tripe is a winning dish even for diners who "hate" tripe. Codfish Gomes de Sá is bound for glory, as is the velvety terrine of foie gras. Some of the best vegetables grown in nearby fields appear in his vegetarian dishes, worthy meals unto themselves. The fish and seafood plates are sublime.

Palácio das Artes, Largo de São Domingoes. ✆ **22/201-43-13.** www.ruipaula.com. Reservations required. Tasting menus 65€–75€. AE, DC, MC, V. Tues–Sun 12:30–3:30pm and 7:30–11pm; Fri–Sat 7:30pm–midnight. Bus: 1 or 57.

EXPENSIVE

Aqua Douro ★ INTERNATIONAL/PORTUGUESE Set upstairs from the lobby level of the also-recommended Pestana Porto hotel (see above), but with direct access from the ramparts which flank its edges, this is an absolutely superb venue for gracious dining, thanks partly to a staff who really knows what it's doing. The setting is a high-ceilinged sparsely furnished room dotted with contemporary art, with a wall of windows overlooking the waters of the Douro. The chefs have excellent credentials, and their cuisine is well crafted. Many of the dishes are light yet full of flavor, and some are impertinently inventive. Sample the codfish flavored with fresh herbs and served with freshly baked corn bread or the filet of sea bass with garlic-coated prawns and quick "seared" potatoes. Rice with morsels of tender duck appears on your plate with green asparagus and horseradish cannelloni (you heard that right). The service is first-rate, as is the wine *carte*.

In the Pestana Porto. Praça de Ribeira 1. (🕐 **22/340-23-00.** Reservations recommended. Main courses 20€–38€. AE, DC, MC, V. Daily 12:30–3:30pm and 7:30–10:30pm. Tram: 1.

Churrascão do Mar ★ BRAZILIAN/PORTUGUESE   Porto's most elegant restaurant is housed in what locals call an *antiga moradia senhorial* (antique manor house), built in 1897 and beautifully restored to its Belle Epoque glory. The setting and elegance alone might justify a dinner here—and the cuisine matches the setting. Some of the town's finest chefs turn out excellent cuisine from South America. The staff seems determined not to let anyone leave unsatisfied. The best items are grilled fish and grilled seafood. Grilled meats are also superb. Everything is served with Brazilian spices or mild sauces to enhance the flavor. Service is in one of four rooms, all of which are quite charming. If you are staying outside of Porto, the restaurant will provide transportation by bus to the grounds.

Rua João Grave 134. (🕐 **22/609-63-82.** Reservations required. Main courses 21€–37€. AE, DC, MC, V. Mon–Sat noon–3:30pm and 7–11pm. Closed last 2 weeks of Aug. Bus: 502.

Restaurante Escondidinho ★ PORTUGUESE   Near the transportation hub of the Estação de São Bento, the Escondidinho (meaning "hidden" or "masked") restaurant is an 80-year-old regional tavern popular with port-wine merchants and English visitors. The intimate 31-table dining area contains time-blackened beams and timbers, a baronial stone fireplace, and a collection of antique Portuguese ceramics. The chairs, with intricate carving and brass studs, are just right for a cardinal—or at least a friar. The waiters serve with old-world charm and will candidly tell you the day's best dishes. The restaurant serves excellent steaks, but most people come here for fresh seafood. Working with turbot, sole, hake, sea bass, shellfish, and anything else that's fresh, the chef creates well-seasoned grills, skewers, and other excellent dishes. Shellfish soup and charbroiled sardines are always good choices. Specialties include hake in Madeira sauce and chateaubriand for two. For dessert, try a kirsch omelet or orange pudding.

Rua Passos Manuel 144. (🕐 **22/200-10-79.** www.escondidinho.com.pt. Reservations recommended. Main courses 14€–29€. MC, V. Daily noon–3pm and 7–11pm. Bus: Any with stops at Estação de São Bento.

MODERATE

Aquário Marisqueiro ★★ PORTUGUESE   In business for more than half a century, Aquário Marisqueiro is one of the finest seafood restaurants in Porto. Its dining rooms are interconnected through a central kitchen, and it's within sight of the city hall and close to the Hotel Infante Sagres. It's run by members of an extended family, who give the place a cozy and nurturing vibe. Seafood reigns supreme, from a starter soup made by boiling the shells of *mariscos* (shellfish) to main course options such as cod, sole, and trout with ham. Standout dishes are the Spanish-style clams and the grilled sea bass.

Rua Rodrigues Sampaio 179. ✆ **22/200-22-31.** www.aquariomarisqueiro.com. Reservations recommended. Main courses 10€–24€. MC, V. Mon–Sat noon–10pm. Metro: Aliados.

Boca do Lobo ★ CONTINENTAL/PORTUGUESE   For a reminder of just how formal and elegant Portugal can really be, come to this restaurant—the jewel of the also-recommended Hotel Infante Sagres (see above). It's positioned on the lobby level of a hotel that was originally conceived as a semiprivate club for wine-trade administrators, and as such, contains many aspects of a formal and very wealthy 19th-century private home—including the kind of service rituals that other dining rooms abandoned long ago. Ceilings are quite high, and the staff is very formally dressed. You have a choice of cold or hot starters, ranging from a carpaccio of salmon with arugula to lasagna of grilled octopus in garlic oil. The chef also makes one of the best fish soups we've ever enjoyed in Porto. For a main course, the kitchen turns out a delectable rib-eye steak with your choice of three sauces, or else you can order duck magret in a port-wine sauce with truffles, or perhaps a fish dish such as tuna steak in an onion marinade. The chocolate cake with chocolate ice cream and a red fruit sauce is sinfully wicked.

In the Hotel Infante Sagres. Praça Filipa de Lencastre 62. ✆ **22/339-85-00.** Reservations recommended. Main courses 17€–22€. AE, DC, MC, V. Daily 12:30–2:30pm and 7:30–10:30pm. Metro: Aliados.

Don Tonho ★★★ CONTINENTAL/PORTUGUESE   This consistently ranks as one of the most spectacular and relentlessly hip restaurants in Porto, with superb food and a physical layout that is a triumph of historical renovation. Opened in 1992 by a group of investors who included Portugal's most famous pop singer, Rui Veloso, it sits on the eastern edge of the town's medieval port. You'll wait for your table in a street-level bar, amid an intriguing collection of 18th-century stonework and latter-day poured concrete. The sprawling upstairs dining room contains a medley of different architectural styles.

   Menu items are savory and superb. Stellar examples include a soup of fresh green beans with herbs and tomatoes, at least four (and sometimes more) preparations of codfish, roasted kid in red-wine sauce, a wide selection of shellfish, and modernized versions of the kind of earthy rural food that many Portuguese remember fondly from their childhoods. The wine list is so comprehensive that some American gastronomy magazines have added it to their reference collection for research on the Portuguese wine industry.

Cais de Ribeira 13-15. ✆ **22/200-43-07.** www.dtonho.com. Reservations required. Main courses 16€–30€. AE, DC, MC, V. Daily 12:30–2:45pm and 7:30–11:15pm. Tram: 1.

Restaurante Portucale ★★★ INTERNATIONAL/PORTUGUESE   This restaurant, one of the most courtly in Porto, opened in 1969 on the 13th (uppermost) floor of the same building that contains the also-recommended hotel the Albergaria Miradouro (see above). Expect a combination of aristocratic Portugal with a slightly dated 1970s-era decor (including some tangerine-hued tile work). It offers panoramic views of the cityscape around it; tables that are elaborately set with fine silver, porcelain, and flowers; and absolutely superb food.

   Specialties usually include foie gras with truffles in puff pastry, wild boar in red-wine sauce, roast capon with walnut sauce, braised escalopes of fresh foie gras, and stewed kid in red wine. You can choose from two different preparations of partridge—

our favorite is stuffed with foie gras and stewed in port. The grilled sea bass with tartar sauce is also excellent, as is an old-fashioned and succulent dish, sole Walewski.

In the Albergaria Miradouro. Rua de Alegria 598. ℂ **22/537-07-17.** www.miradouro-portucale.com. Reservations required. Main courses 16€–30€. AE, DC, MC, V. Daily 12:30–2:30pm and 7:30–11pm. Metro: Marques.

INEXPENSIVE

Brasserie Irene Jardim PORTUGUESE   This dining room often does a thriving business with locals. The menu is made up of traditional recipes often given creative touches. Start perhaps with the fresh mushrooms stuffed with smoked ham, bacon, and cream cheese and follow with such mains as blackened swordfish filet in a spicy sauce on slices of sweet potato with a side of banana croquettes. Another specialty is loin of pork in a berry sauce with mashed chestnuts and wild mushrooms. For dessert, opt for the apple strudel with vanilla ice cream.

Praça Parada Leitão 17. ℂ **22/201-17-87.** www.irenejardim.izispot.com. Reservations recommended. Main courses 8€–17€. MC, V. Tues–Sun 12:30–3pm and 7:30–10:30pm. Metro: Aliados.

Cufra ★ PORTUGUESE/SHELLFISH   This is one of the oldest shellfish eateries in the city, long known for its quality food and produce from the Douro region. Dishes are rich, making imaginative use of local ingredients as reflected by their shellfish stew à la Cufra, one of the best concoctions in the city. The chefs also prepare a shellfish rice dish or a savory shellfish with kidney beans. The house specialty is steak à la Cufra, tender and full of flavor. A special pork steak is another savory delight. The *pudim flan* (egg custard) is a fine way to end any meal.

Av. da Boavista 2504. ℂ **22/617-27-15.** www.cufra.pt. Reservations recommended. Main courses 12€–26€. AE, MC, V. Tues–Sun noon–2am. Bus: 202.

Farol de Boa Nova ✦ PORTUGUESE   Set on the upper level of the two stone tiers overlooking the waterfront, this is an authentic staple on the Portuguese restaurant scene. A brightly lit service bar sits near the entrance, and the restaurant offers additional seating in the cellar and on a terrace. Menu items are simple but good, with many meals relying on the same recipes that the patrons' grandparents used. The finest examples include fried filets of sole, veal cutlets, and Portuguese sausages.

Muro dos Bacalhoeiros 115. ℂ **22/200-60-86.** Main courses 10€–18€. No credit cards. Daily noon–3pm and 7–11pm. Closed 3 weeks at Christmas. Tram: 1.

Guarany BRAZILIAN   Trading on romantic references to heroic Guarani Indians in faraway Brazil (once a Portuguese colony), this cafe opened in 1933, and still retains friezes and murals depicting Amazonia in all its romanticized glory. It's a popular cafe and brasserie, packing in diners at lunch and dinner, thanks to fair prices and uncomplicated food that, while not the top of its category, is nonetheless filling and flavorful. Examples include grilled codfish with eggs and potatoes and magret of duckling with port-wine sauce. Menu items also include sandwiches, soups, and salads.

Av. dos Aliados 85. ℂ **22/332-12-72.** www.cafeguarany.com. Reservations recommended. Main courses 12€–18€. AE, DC, MC, V. Cafe daily 9am–midnight; restaurant daily noon–11pm. Metro: Aliados.

La Merceria PORTUGUESE   This is an appealingly affordable middle-bracket restaurant set directly on the port. It's authentic enough to attract locals and has a long history of coping with the annual midwinter floods from the nearby Douro. Look for signs of water damage, including warped wine racks and paint peeling from the ground-floor doors. There's a cozy upstairs dining room that's accessible via a very steep wooden staircase, and the decor includes hanging hams and turn-of-the-20th-century accessories. The food is fresh and well prepared, although hardly imaginative: The restaurant's patrons come for the tried-and-true recipes familiar to them from their mothers' kitchen, including grilled octopus, several different preparations of codfish, and steaks.

Cais da Ribeira 32. ✆ **22/200-43-89.** Reservations recommended Fri–Sat nights. Main courses 10€–25€. DC, MC, V. Daily noon–4pm and 7–11:30pm. Closed Tues Oct–Mar. Tram: 1.

O Caçula PORTUGUESE   In the Boavista zone, this restaurant is tasteful and comfortable, offering a Portuguese cuisine that has been updated for modern tastes. It is both a cafe, with Internet access, and a formal restaurant. The chefs always prepare a fresh soup of the day, or else you can pick from such starters as bruschetta with melted goat cheese, or perhaps a salad of four different types of lettuce with cheese from the Azores, whipped together with a mustard and honey sauce dressing. Vegetarian courses include ratatouille with basmati rice served with grilled polenta. Among the best fish dishes are grilled tuna steak in a sage sauce or grilled codfish filet on a bed of fresh spinach. The chefs are equally skilled at turning out meat dishes, including grilled lamb steak with a Thai sauce or rump steak served with black beans.

Travessa do Bonjardim 20. ✆ **22/205-59-37.** www.ocacula.com. Reservations recommended. Main courses 9€–15€. MC, V. Mon–Sat noon–3pm and 7–10pm. Tram: 1E.

O Muro 🎁 PORTUGUESE   This is an earthy, rough-and-ready fish restaurant a short walk from the Praça de Ribeira. Don't expect grandeur: The decor is utilitarian and the staff is gruff. But there's a convivial amiability about the place, with a terrace that was built as part of the foundation buttresses for this medieval waterfront neighborhood. Owned by a once-professional soccer player and his Mozambique-born wife, it specializes in the type of hearty and straightforward cuisine that used to make the Portuguese Empire run. The best dishes include codfish- or octopus-studded rice; red snapper or turbot; fried codfish; and steak with mushrooms, milk, cream, herbs, and lemon-flavored butter. Most dishes are at the lower end of the price scale listed below.

Muro do Bacalhoeiros 87–88. ✆ **22/208-34-26.** Main courses 12€–25€. MC, V. Daily noon–2am. Tram: 1.

IN VILA NOVA DE GAIA

Adega & Presuntaria Transmontana II PORTUGUESE   Set within easy walking distance of most of the port-wine sales outlets, across the river from the medieval core of Porto, this rustic-looking restaurant showcases the rich and hearty cuisine of Portugal's most remote province, Trás-os-Montes. The venue resembles a stone *tasca* (tavern), where at least two dozen cured hams hang from the ceiling. The best-tasting menu items include platters of cured ham, green cabbage soup, shrimp in garlic sauce, octopus with green sauce, and stewed or grilled meat in the Minho style.

Av. Diogo Leite 80, Vila Nova de Gaia. ✆ **22/375-83-80.** Reservations recommended. Main courses 10€–22€. AE, DC, MC, V. Daily 11am–2am. Bus: 900, 901, or 906.

IN FOZ DO DOURO

Shis Restaurante ★ PORTUGUESE/CONTINENTAL/FUSION   The most interesting restaurant in town occupies a glass and aluminum cube built on pilings above the rocky shoreline of the Atlantic, close to the north bank of the mighty Douro. Ringed with outdoor decks whose tables are sheltered from the constant winds by transparent barricades, Shis is the kind of elegant and stylish place that would tempt a resident of Porto out to Foz for either a night on the town or a pre-seduction dinner. Owner and chef Antonio Vieira, within an avant-garde, mostly white décor, successfully renders very fresh Portuguese seafood into artful presentations of sushi, sashimi, and tempura. Meat eaters are usually presented with a short list of very fresh cutlets, casseroles, and stews, each prepared with style by a culinary team who knows what they're doing. *Note:* Although it's open daily throughout the summer, the restaurant's winter hours were still being concretized at press time, so advance reservations are important.

Priai do Ourigo, Esplanad do Castelo. © **22/618-95-93.** www.shisrestaurante.com Reservations recommended. Main courses 13€–22€. AE, MC, V. Daily 10am–3am.

ShiS JAPANESE/INTERNATIONAL   One of the most popular and appealing beachside restaurants in Porto lies in the residential suburb of Foz do Douro, at the bottom of a cement staircase that descends from the waterfront boulevard above. Its design might remind you of a giant glass-and-steel box. Windows take in views of a lighthouse and the jagged mouth of the Douro River as its waters merge with the sea. Whenever it's nice outside, dozens of wicker-topped tables sprawl along a wide terrace nearby, protected from the wind by a Plexiglas breakfront. Most of the time, however, diners huddle inside, seeking protection from the wind, rain, and fog. We savored the grilled monkfish with garlic butter, although a wide array of shellfish was featured as well, including a garlic-flavored lobster thermidor. The chef shows his considerable talent in such dishes as filet of sea bass with artichokes or filet of fish in a citrus sea foam. Another delight is a clam risotto with an avocado cream sauce. Sushi and sashimi are also on the menu, but the choice is limited, so it might be better to stick to the previously recommended dishes.

Esplanada do Castelo, Foz do Douro. © **22/618-95-93.** Reservations recommended. Main courses 15€–28€. AE, MC, V. Daily 10am–3am. Bus: 500.

Shopping

Porto is hardly the shopping mecca that Lisbon is, and you may want to save your major purchases for that city. The one exception is port wine, which is for sale everywhere, although you may prefer to make your purchases at the wine lodges across the river. Window shoppers stroll along on the shop-flanked streets branching off from Praça da Liberdade. Gold-plated filigree and silver attract shoppers to the Rua das Flores, where they can also find handicrafts from the north of Portugal.

In the past few years, many fashion designers have lived and created in and around Porto, as the area is a center for big textile and apparel industries. The latest fashions are sold mainly at the shopping malls, which dominate the local scene. The most elegant of these malls include the **Centro Comercial Peninsular,** Praça do Bom Sucesso, and the particularly charming **Centro Comercial Via Catarina.** It's in the pedestrian zone of the city's most vital shopping street, **Rua de Santa Catarina,** at the corner of Rua Fernandes Tomar. The storefronts inside duplicate the facades you'd see in a folkloric village of northern Portugal. If you're looking for the designer wares of noteworthy clothiers from France, Italy, and Spain, these malls have them.

Other shopping malls have a sometimes uneven distribution of upscale and workaday shops. They include the **Centro Comercial de Foz,** Rua Eugénio de Castro, which is adjacent to the sea and especially pleasant in midsummer, and the **Centro Comercial Aviz,** Avenida de Boavista, rather inconveniently located in the middle of the city's largest concentration of automobile dealerships. The big but seriously decayed **Centro Comercial Brasilia,** which is, to an increasing degree, being stocked with inexpensive manufactured goods from Asia, is on Praça Mouzinho de Albuquerque. More chic and upscale, with a greater emphasis on clothing, furniture, and housewares, is the **Centro Comercial Cidade de Porto,** Rua do Bom Sucesso, whose shops are interspersed with restaurants, bars, movie theaters, and cafes.

The city's many open-air markets make for romantic strolls. You can buy caged birds at the **Mercado dos Passaros ★**, Rua de Madeira (near the San Bento railway station), every Sunday from 7:30am to 1pm, and potted plants at Mercado das Flores, Praça de Liberdade, every day of the week between April and October from 9am to 5pm.

For a glimpse of the agrarian bounty of northern Portugal, head for the **Mercado de Bolão,** the city's most famous open-air market, where hundreds of merchants sell food, flowers, spices, and kitchen equipment. Open Monday to Friday 9am to 5pm, and Saturday 9am to 12:30pm, it sprawls for several blocks beside one of the great shopping arteries of Porto, Rua de Santa Catarina.

Porto has always sheltered a community of artisans crafting gold jewelry from stones brought in from all parts of the once-mighty Portuguese Empire. One of the city's leading jewelers is **David Rosas, Lda,** Av. de Boavista 1471 (✆ **22/606-10-60;** www. davidrosas.com) is stocked with wristwatches, gemstones, and miles of gold chains.

The local showcase for Portugal's fabled Arraiolos carpets—nubby, pure wool carpets that teams of women spend hours crafting—is **Casa dos Tapetes de Arraiolos ★**, Rua de Santa Catarina 570 (✆ **22/205-48-16**). Look for symmetrical patterns that make full use of the subtle palettes of grays, blues, greens, and soft reds that have attracted non-Portuguese homeowners to these carpets for many generations.

For high-quality leather ware, including suitcases, wallets, belts, briefcases, duffel bags, and handbags, go to **Haity,** Rua de Santa Catarina 212 (✆ **22/205-96-30;** www.haity.pt).

A bookstore that has been cited as the most beautiful in Iberia, stocking a small percentage of its titles in English, is the **Livraria Lello,** Rua das Carmelitas 144 (✆ **22/201-81-70**). Partly because of its inventories, but especially because of its lavish Art Nouveau design, this is the best-known and most prestigious bookstore in Porto. A fixture among readers in northern Portugal since around 1900, it has two floors of lavishly ornate iron and plasterwork, a small cafe on the second floor, and a staff that's congenial but impossibly slow.

If you're looking for any standard international perfumes, as well as more esoteric brands available for the most part only in Iberia, head for **Perfumaria Castilho,** Rua de Sá de Bandeira 80 (✆ **22/208-56-58**).

To stock up on traditional Portuguese handicrafts, begin at the **Regional Center of Traditional Arts (CRAT),** Rua da Reboleira 37 (✆ **22/332-02-01**). In an aristocratic 18th-century town house, it sells the best handicrafts from artisans throughout the country's northern tier. Lively competitors in the handicrafts trade include **Casa Lima,** Rua de Sá de Bandeira 83 (✆ **22/200-52-32**), where the inventories include large numbers of gloves, umbrellas, crystal, and embroideries, many of them laboriously crafted within the region. At **Casa dos Linhos ★**, Rua da Fernandes Tomás 660 (✆ **22/200-00-44**), you'll also find good linen and embroideries—many of them excellent examples of the exquisite handiwork that has traditionally been produced in the north of Portugal.

One of the finest names in Portuguese porcelain is **Vista Alegre,** Rua Cândido dos Reis 6 (✆ **22/200-45-54**). It carries a variety of items and can arrange shipping. Prices vary greatly, depending on the handwork involved, how many colors are used, and whether a piece is decorated in gold.

Porto After Dark

The greatest cultural center in the north of Portugal is Casa da Música (see below), but there is so much more. Many galleries stage nightly exhibitions—check the monthly *Time Out Porto* for listings. The early evening begins in the old-style cafes, especially those in Ribeira along the waterfront. Expect the usual dance and music clubs, but know in advance that Porto is not Paris on the Douro. It goes to bed when the clubs are getting going in Lisbon.

Casa da Música ★, Av. da Boavista 604–610 (© **22/012-02-20;** www.casada-musica.com; Bus 202), is the cultural center of Porto. Designed by Ellen van Loon and Rem Koolhaas, this house of music contains a 1,250-seat Grand Auditorium and a 315-seat Small Auditorium, plus a Cybermusic Arena, where musicians can install multimedia projects and composers can produce electronic works. The Casa da Música presents a complete range of classical and jazz events, with most tickets costing under 25€, although some performances are free. You can purchase tickets in advance on their website. The building's daringly avant-garde architecture, including an auditorium sheathed in plywood and dyed fire-engine red, has caused much controversy in this traditional city.

Many night owls simply walk through the commercial district, along streets radiating from Rua de Santa Catarina, and stop at any appealing tavern or cafe.

Boys 'R US, Rua Dr. Barbosa de Castro 63 (© **91/754-99-88;** Metro: Trindade or San Bento), is one of Porto's hottest dance clubs, a late-night celebration of loud house and garage-style music, flashing lights, and homosexuality. Set within the warren of narrow medieval streets near the San Bento railway station, it opens Wednesday and Friday to Sunday at 11pm, remaining open until between 2 and 4am, depending on business. There's no entrance fee, but everyone is expected to order a minimum of 6€ of drinks during their time inside.

Battered but hip, with hints of the psychedelic era of the 1960s, the **31 (Trintaeum) Bar,** Rua do Passeio Alegre 564, in Foz do Douro (© **22/618-57-21;** www.trintaeum.com; bus no. 500), occupies a compact town house on the cobble-covered, seafront main avenue in the residential suburb of Foz. Immediately adjacent and under the same ownership is the **Cerveja Viva,** where the bar list contains mostly beers, as opposed to the cocktails that are available in the more cutting-edge 31. Many first-timers make it a point to duck into both establishments, just as a comparison, for a quick nip and taste of local nightlife.

For the best view of the raging Atlantic to go with your drink, head for **Praia da Luz,** Avenida do Brasil (© **22/617-32-34;** bus no. 500), which occupies prime real estate on a rocky shoreline near the point where the Douro empties into the Atlantic. Watching waves from the ocean breaking and frothing from behind large windows is reason enough to visit—that and catching the live music. It's open daily 9am to 2am.

ESPINHO

18km (11 miles) S of Porto; 307km (191 miles) N of Lisbon

Espinho is a popular resort on the Costa Verde. It offers many activities for growing crowds of vacationers. The town has a range of shops, restaurants, hotels, and campsites in the pinewoods near the sandy beach. Sports enthusiasts will find tennis courts, a bullfighting ring, and an 18-hole golf course.

Essentials

ARRIVING

BY TRAIN   From Porto, trains depart from the **Estação de Campanhã** (✆ **80/820-82-08**) about every hour during the day. Trip time is 35 minutes. A one-way ticket to Porto-Espinho costs 1.50€.

BY BUS   Buses depart about once an hour from Porto's **Autovia Espinho,** Rua Alexandre Herculano, near Praça de Batalha (✆ **22/200-75-44**). Trip time is 30 minutes. A one-way ticket to Porto-Espinho costs 2€.

BY CAR   From Porto, head south along IC-1.

VISITOR INFORMATION

The **Espinho Tourist Office** is at Rua 23, 271 (✆ **22/733-58-72;** www.cm-espinho.pt). It's open Monday to Friday 9am to 6pm, Saturday and Sunday from 9:30am to 12:30pm and 2 to 5:30pm.

Exploring Espinho

DAYTIME ACTIVITIES   Sports-related activities in Espinho tend to revolve around the beach. At least four beaches are within an easy walk from the town center. Closest and most crowded is **Praia Baía;** most distant (though only .5km, or ⅓ mile, east of the center) and least crowded is **Praia do Costa Verde.** Between the two stretch the beige sands of **Praia Azula** and **Praia Pop,** both of which boast clean sunbathing areas and access to not particularly dangerous surf. If you prefer calmer waters, head for the town's largest swimming-pool complex, **Solar Atlântico,** adjacent to Praia Baía (✆ **22/734-41-79**). Fed with seawater, it has separate pools for diving and swimming, hundreds of devoted aficionados (only some of whom actually swim), and lots of options for voyeuristic intrigue. It's open from June to September.

Grass and hard tennis courts, soccer fields, and volleyball courts are in the **Nave Sportiva,** Rua da Nave (✆ **22/731-00-59**). The cluster of outdoor playing fields on the eastern outskirts of town opened in 1996.

The **Oporto Golf Club** is on Rua do Golf (✆ **22/734-20-08;** www.oportogolf club.com), about 2.5km (1½ miles) south of Espinho. The 18-hole course is the second oldest in continental Europe. Greens fees are 70€ per person.

SHOPPING   The three most interesting products produced in the surrounding region are carved-wood models of Portuguese fishing boats painted in bright colors, woven baskets, and dolls in regional dress whose bodies are carved from wood or fashioned from clay. Some shops operate only seasonally. Many sell items like suntan oil, sunglasses, and cheap souvenirs. The town's main shopping street is Rua 19.

If you happen to be in town on a Monday, Espinho is home to one of the largest outdoor markets in the region. Known as the **Feira de Espinho,** it takes place every Monday from 7am to 8pm along the entire length of Rua 24, Rua 23, and Rua 22. Look for carloads of produce and meats, plus some clothing and other trinkets you'd expect at a flea market.

Where to Stay & Dine

Hotel Solverde ★★★   Solverde is one of the most luxurious hotels in the north. It stands on the beach of Granja, about 16km (10 miles) south of Porto, less than 2km (1¼ miles) north of Espinho, and about 32km (20 miles) from the Porto airport. The rates are among the lowest in Portugal for a government-rated five-star hotel. The generally spacious guest rooms are well furnished, with excellent roomy bathrooms.

Av. de Liberdade 212, 4410-154 San Felix de Marinha. www.solverde.pt. ☎ **22/733-80-30.** Fax 22/731-32-00. 174 units. 104€–250€ double; 325€–450€ suite. Rates include buffet breakfast. AE, DC, MC, V. Free parking and heliport. **Amenities:** Restaurant; 2 bars; babysitting; concierge; health club & spa; 3 outdoor pools; room service; 3 tennis courts (lit); Wi-Fi (free, in lobby). *In room:* A/C, TV, hair dryer, minibar.

PraiaGolfe Hotel ★   This is the best among the generally unimpressive accommodations within Espinho proper. Offering many modern comforts and overlooking the sea, the streamlined hotel is located about 50m (164 ft.) from the railway station. The rooms are comfortable, with neatly kept bathrooms. Tennis courts and golf courses are nearby. In summer, the hotel is almost always booked, so reservations are essential.

Rua 6, 4500-357 Espinho. www.praiagolfe.com. ☎ **22/733-10-00.** Fax 22/733-10-01. 133 units. 78€–140€ double; 142€–160€ suite. Rates include continental or buffet breakfast. AE, DC, MC, V. Free parking. **Amenities:** 2 restaurants; 2 bars; babysitting; exercise room; indoor heated pool; room service; spa; Wi-Fi (free, in lobby). *In room:* A/C, TV, hair dryer, minibar.

Espinho After Dark

If you want to gamble, you're in luck. The big gray **Casino Espinho,** Rua 19 no. 85, 4501-858 Espinho (☎ **22/733-55-00;** www.solverde.pt), offers roulette, French banque, baccarat, and slot machines. Open all year, it has a restaurant and nightclub in addition to the gaming tables. Admission is free for bingo and slot machines; to gain access to the gaming tables, you must show proper ID (such as a passport). The nightclub stages international cabaret. Dinner and the show cost between 25€ and 50€ without drinks; the show alone is 15€, which includes one drink. The casino is open year-round (except Christmas) Sunday to Thursday from 3pm to 3am; Friday and Saturday, it's open from 4pm to 4am.

Espinho doesn't have any conventional dance clubs. The town does have eight or nine bars where somebody might actually get up and dance to recorded music, which includes healthy doses of Brazilian samba and whatever happens to be prevalent in London and Lisbon. If you're into nighttime prowling, head to the beachfront bars near the southern perimeter of the historic center and take your pick. Our favorites, each on Rua 2 and each immediately adjacent to the beach, include **Bombar, Bar Pasha, Surfing Bar,** and **Double "O" Bar.** Their busiest and most animated seasons are during the summer, with a breezy indoor-outdoor ambience that's conducive to chitchat. None of these has a listed phone number, and each has a terrace and a character that varies according to who's in town at the time of your visit.

VILA DO CONDE

27km (17 miles) N of Porto; 341km (212 miles) N of Lisbon; 42km (26 miles) S of Viana do Castelo; 3km (1¾ miles) S of Póvoa do Varzim

At the mouth of the river Ave, the charming little town of Vila do Conde has been discovered by summer vacationers who seek out its fortress-guarded sandy beaches and rocky reefs. Along the wharves, you might still see piles of rough hand-hewn timbers used in the building of the sardine fleet. Shipbuilding is a traditional industry here, and they still make a few wooden-hulled vessels, some for the local fishing fleet and others for use on the cod banks of Newfoundland.

The women of the town have long engaged in the making of lace using a shuttle, a craft handed down from generation to generation. So revered is this activity that the **Feast of St. John,** celebrated from June 14 to June 24, features processions by the *rendilheiras* (lace makers) and the *mordomas* (women who manage the cottage-industry homes), during which the latter wear magnificent chains and other ornaments of gold. Artisans from this area also make the region's famous hand-knit and hand-embroidered fishers' sweaters. The making of sweets (there's a famous confectionery that uses convent recipes) is another local occupation.

Essentials

ARRIVING

BY TRAIN   Trains run from Porto's Estação de Trindade, Rua Alferes Malheiro (☎ **22/508-10-00**), several times daily, taking 35 minutes each way, costing 3€ per person for a one-way ticket.

BY BUS Buses leave Porto from the **Auto Viação do Minho,** Rua Régulo Megauanha (℃ **22/200-61-21**). Three or four buses a day make the 40-minute trip daily. Tickets cost 4€.

BY CAR From Porto, head north along IC-1.

VISITOR INFORMATION

Vila do Conde Tourist Office is at Rua do 25 de Abril 103 (℃ **25/224-84-73;** www.cm-viladoconde.pt). It's open September to June Monday to Friday 9am to 6pm, Saturday and Sunday 9:30am to 1pm and 2:30 to 6pm; July and August Monday to Friday 9am to 7pm, Saturday and Sunday 9:30am to 1pm and 2:30 to 6pm.

Exploring the Resort

BEACHES OF VILA DO CONDE Both of the resort's beaches, **Praia do Forno** and **Praia da Senhora de Guia,** combine fine-textured white sand with smaller crowds—often much smaller—than at equivalent beaches on the Algarve or near Lisbon. A handful of kiosks and shops sell suntan lotion, sunglasses, and beachwear. Both beaches are within about a 3-minute walk from the resort's commercial center.

CHURCHES Sitting fortresslike on a hill, the large, squat **Convento de Santa Clara (Convent of St. Clare)** ★, on the north bank of Rio Ave Largo de D. Afonso Sanches (℃ **25/263-10-16**), was founded in the 14th century. The present monastery was built in the 1700s, accompanied by construction of a 999-arch aqueduct to bring water from nearby Póvoa do Varzim. Part of the water conduit is still visible.

In the upper rooms, you can see relics and paintings collected through the centuries by the nuns. The building is now a charity home. Simplicity and opulence play against each other in a combination of Gothic and Romanesque styles. The plain altar of its church offers contrast to the gilded stalls behind the communion grilles and the ornately decorated ceilings. A side chapel contains 14th-century sarcophagi. One is the elaborately carved tomb of Dom Afonso Sanches, founder of the convent; the feet of his effigy rest on a lion. Also here are the tomb of his wife, Dona Teresa Martins, topped by a figure dressed in the habit of a Franciscan Tertiary nun, and those of two of their children. The convent is open daily from 9am to 12:30pm and 2 to 6pm. Admission is free.

The 16th-century parish church, **Igreja Matriz** (℃ **25/263-13-27**), is also worth seeing. It stands in the center of town near the market. Another national monument is the **pillory,** opening onto Praça Vasco de Gama. Built from 1538 to 1540, it consists of a graceful column, slightly twisted, which recalls many creations from the Manueline art style.

LACE MAKING Visitors are welcomed free at the **Museu Escola de Rendas,** the lace-making school on Rua de São Bento (℃ **25/224-84-70**). Here you can purchase the finest examples of lace for which the town is known. Vila do Conde guards its lace-making and pastry-making traditions with fierce pride. The Rendas school is devoted to perpetuating the traditions of Portuguese lace making, and it's one of the largest technical schools in the country. Some students enroll as early as age 4 and tend to have completed their technical training before they turn 15. A handful of the matriarchs associated with the school, now in their 70s, remember its importance in their town when they were young girls. You can buy most of the lace made in the school at its on-site boutique. Admission is free. The Museu Escola de Rendas is open Monday to Friday 10am to noon and 2 to 6pm, Saturday to Sunday 3 to 6pm. For more information, contact the **tourist office** at ℃ **25/224-84-73.**

A nearby annex, **Centro de Artesanato,** Avenida Dr. João Canavarro, also stocks lace curtains and tablecloths, doilies, and trim. Most of the lace you'll see here is white, designed according to traditional patterns established long ago. In recent years, however, lace makers have experimented with colored thread.

PASTRIES & SWEETS   During the 18th and 19th centuries, the nuns of Vila do Conde developed recipes for pastries and sweets that their detractors claimed were thinly masked substitutes for their yearnings for love and affection. Examples of the sweets they invented are still sold in almost every cafe and about a dozen pastry shops in the village. The best known of these pastries are *papo de anjo* (angel's belly) and *doce de feijão* (bean sweets). The ones seemingly best appreciated by modern-day palates are the *Jesuitas* (Jesuits), concocted from lavish amounts of eggs, flour, and sugar. You'll see dozens of outlets for these confections.

Where to Stay

Estalagem do Brazão ★   This inn, in the center of the village, is styled like a gracious pousada. Its compact guest rooms are of contemporary design, with built-in headboards, comfortable armchairs, and firm beds. All units contain well-maintained bathrooms equipped with tub/shower combinations.

Av. Dr. João Canavarro, 4480-668 Vila do Conde. www.estalagemdobrazao.com. ✆ **25/264-20-16.** Fax 25/264-20-28. 30 units. 56€–82€ double; 82€–110€ suite. Rates include buffet breakfast. AE, DC, MC, V. Free parking. **Amenities:** Restaurant; bar; bikes; room service. *In room:* A/C, TV, hair dryer, minibar.

Where to Dine

Ramon PORTUGUESE   At the entrance to Vila do Conde stands this well-run restaurant decorated in a regional Portuguese style. It's small, with only 20 tables, but in summer it opens the terrace for overflow guests. Although many beachfront restaurants come and go seasonally, this is a reliable year-round choice. The fresh shellfish depends on daily market prices and can be quite expensive, but most dishes, including fish, are reasonably priced. The chefs make the best paella at the resort, and they also prepare a delicious array of grilled fish based on the catch of the day. A specialty is *tamboril à Ramon,* which is a white fish, known as "rape," served with potatoes and fresh garlic. The kitchen also seems to lavish special care on the soups.

Rua 5 do Outubro 176. ✆ **25/263-13-34.** Reservations recommended in summer. Main courses 13€–27€. AE, MC, V. Wed–Mon noon–3pm and 7:30–11pm. Closed for 3 weeks in mid-Sept and mid-Oct.

OFIR & FÃO

47km (29 miles) N of Porto; 364km (226 miles) N of Lisbon; 36km (22 miles) W of Braga

Ofir is the best beach resort between Porto and Viana do Castelo. The long white-sand beach here is dramatic at any time of the year but is exceptional during summer. The **White Horse Rocks,** according to legend, were formed when fiery steeds from the royal stock of King Solomon were wrecked on the beach.

While Ofir's hotels and restaurants offer every convenience in a secluded setting, more local color is at Fão, 2 to 3km (1¼–1¾ miles) inland on an estuary of the Cávado River. Framed by mountain ridges in the background and a river valley, the village, which dates from Roman times, is the sleepy gateway to Ofir. The *sargaceiros* (gatherers of sargasso), with their stout tunics, rake the offshore breakers for the seaweed used in making fertilizer. On the quays here, you can lunch on sardines cooked on grills or counteract your overdose of sunshine with a mellow glass of port wine.

Essentials

ARRIVING

BY TRAIN   There's no direct rail service to Fão or Ofir. Passengers go to Póvoa do Varzim, 15km (9⅓ miles) south, and continue by bus.

BY BUS   From Porto, buses depart from **Auto Viação do Minho,** Rua Régulo Megauanha (📞 **25/200-61-21**). Three or four buses per day service the area. Trip time is 65 minutes; tickets cost 5€.

BY CAR   From Póvoa do Varzim, continue north along Route 30 for 15km (9⅓ miles).

VISITOR INFORMATION

The nearest tourist office is the **Esposende Tourist Bureau,** Avenida Arantes de Oliveira, Esposende (📞 **25/396-13-54**; www.visitesposende.com). Esposende lies on the opposite bank of the Rio Cávado Estuary from Ofir and Fão. It's open in winter Monday to Saturday 9:30am to 12:30pm and 2 to 5:30pm; in summer daily 9am to 7pm.

Where to Stay & Dine

Axis Ofir Beach Resort Hotel ★   The Axis Ofir's older central core contains guest rooms furnished in traditional Portuguese fashion, with reproductions of regional furniture. The adjoining wings are modern and quite luxurious, built motel-style right along the dunes, with the beach in full view of the second-floor balconies.

The hotel is a resort unto itself, with a vast flagstone terrace bordering soft green lawns, including a golf course. Though the public rooms are appealing, most guests head to the wide oceanfront terrace for sunbathing.

Av. Raul de Sousa Martins, Ofir, 4740-405 Esposende. www.axishoteisegolfe.com/ofir. 📞 **25/398-98-00.** Fax 25/398-18-71. 191 units. 80€–100€ double; 100€–165€ suite. Rates include buffet breakfast. AE, DC, MC, V. Free parking. **Amenities:** Restaurant; cafe; 2 bars; babysitting; health club; outdoor pool; room service; spa; 2 outdoor tennis courts (lit); Wi-Fi (free, in lobby). *In room:* A/C, TV, minibar.

Estalagem Parque do Rio   This first-class modern inn on the Cávado River is in a pine-covered garden 5 minutes from the main beach. It has two excellent garden pools with surrounding lawns. The small guest rooms are well designed, with private balconies. All units come equipped with well-maintained bathrooms. The resort, planned for those who stay for more than a day, offers a full range of activities such as tennis and swimming. Less adventurous guests can simply congregate at the snug wood-paneled bar in the beamed dining room.

Abdo. 1, Ofir-Fão, 4740-405 Esposende. www.parquedorio.pt. 📞 **25/398-15-21.** Fax 25/398-15-24. 36 units. 55€–90€ double; 75€–125€ triple. Rates include continental breakfast. AE, MC, V. Free parking. **Amenities:** Restaurant; bar; bikes; outdoor pool; room service; outdoor tennis court (lit); Wi-Fi (free, in lobby). *In-room:* A/C, TV.

THE MINHO REGION & TRÁS-OS-MONTES

13

The Minho, in the verdant northwest corner of Portugal, is almost a land unto itself. The region begins some 40km (25 miles) north of Porto and stretches to the frontier of Galicia, in northwest Spain. In fact, Minho and Galicia and their people are strikingly similar. The regions share a Celtic background.

Granite plateaus undulate across the countryside, broken by the green valleys of the Minho, Ave, Cávado, and Lima rivers. For centuries, the region's bountiful granite quarries have been emptied to build everything from the great church facades in Braga and Guimarães to the humblest village cottages. Green pastures contrast sharply with forests filled with cedars and chestnuts.

The small size of the district and the proximity of the towns make it easy to hop from hamlet to hamlet. Even the biggest towns—Viana do Castelo, Guimarães, and Braga—are provincial in nature. You'll sometimes see wooden carts in the streets, drawn by pairs of dappled and chocolate-brown oxen. These noble beasts are depicted on the pottery and ceramics for which the Minho (especially Viana do Castelo) is known.

The Minho was the cradle of Portuguese independence. From here, Afonso Henríques, the first king, made his plans to capture the south from the Moors. Battlemented castles along the frontier are reminders of the region's former hostilities with Spain, and fortresses still loom above the coastal villages.

Porto (see chapter 12) is the air gateway to the Minho. A car is the best way to see the north if you have only a short time; if you depend on public transportation, you can visit some of the major centers by bus and rail.

The far northeast province of Portugal is a wild, rugged land—Trás-os-Montes, or "beyond the mountains." Extending from south of the Upper Douro at Lamego, the province stretches north to Spain. Vila Real is its capital. Rocky crests and deep valleys break up the high plateau, between the mountain ranges of Marão and Gerês. Most of the population lives in the valleys, usually in houses constructed from shale or granite. Much of the plateau is arid land, but swift rivers and their tributaries supply

Vigo

SPAIN

Valença Monção N202 Melgaço

Riba de Mouro

Sierra do Suajo

Rio Coura Vila Nova
de Cerveira

Caminha
Moledo do Minho N101

Vila Praia
de Âncora

Lindosa

N203

Soajo

Rio Lima Ponte da Barca

Ponte
de Lima *Sierra do Barroso*
N203 *Rio Homem*

Viana do Castelo Arcos de
Valdevez Gerêz

Rio Cávado N103

Vieira do Minho
Cerdeirinhas

Mar Póvoa de Lanhoso

Barcelos **Braga** Arosa

Esposende Cabeceiras
de Basto

Vila Nova
E01 de Famalicão
N13 **Guimarães**

N14 Fafe

Póvoa de Varzim

Vila do Conde Caldas de
Vizela Celorico
N101 de Basto

E82

*ATLANTIC
OCEAN*

N15

area of
detail FRANCE

Porto

SPAIN

0 10 mi
0 10 km Lisbon

COSTA VERDE

ample water, and some of the valleys have fertile farmland. The Tâmega River Valley is known for the thermal springs found there as far back as Roman days.

This land is rich in history and tradition, offering the visitor a new world to discover, from pre-Roman castles to pillories and interesting old churches. The inhabitants are of Celtic descent, and most speak a dialect of Galician.

You can reach Trás-os-Montes by train from Porto. Service is to Régua, not far from Lamego, which serves as a gateway into the province in the Pais do Vinho, where grapes from vineyards on the terraced hills provide the wines that are credited to Porto. Lamego is actually in the province of Beira Alta. You can drive through this land of splendid savagery, but don't expect superhighways.

GUIMARÃES ★★

48km (30 miles) NE of Porto; 69km (43 miles) SW of Viana do Castelo; 364km (226 miles) N of Lisbon

The cradle of Portugal, Guimarães suffers from a near embarrassment of riches. At the foot of a range of *serras* (mountains), this first capital of Portugal has preserved a medieval atmosphere in its core. The city was the birthplace of Afonso Henríques, the first king of Portugal and son of a French nobleman, Henri de Bourgogne, and his wife, Teresa, daughter of the king of León and Castile. For her dowry, Teresa brought the county of Portucale, whose name eventually became Portugal. Portucale consisted of the land between the Minho and the Douro, taking in what is now the city of Porto. Teresa and Henri chose Guimarães as their court, and Afonso Henríques was born here.

After Henri died, Teresa became regent for the baby king. She soon fell into disfavor with her subjects for having an affair with a count from Galicia and developing strong ties with her native Spain. As a young man, Afonso revolted against the regent's forces outside Guimarães in 1128. A major victory for Afonso came in 1139, when he routed the Moors near Santarém. He broke from León and Castile and proclaimed himself king of Portucale. In 1143, Spain recognized the newly emerged kingdom.

Guimarães had another famous son, Gil Vicente (1465–1537?). Founder of the Portuguese theater, he's often referred to as the Shakespeare of Portugal. Although trained as a goldsmith, Vicente entertained the courts of both João II and Manuel I with his farces and tragicomedies. He also penned religious dramas.

Today Guimarães is a busy little town with an eye toward commerce, especially in weaving, tanning, and kitchenware and cutlery manufacturing. It's also known for its craft industries, particularly pottery, silver- and goldsmithing, and embroidery.

Essentials

ARRIVING

BY TRAIN Fifteen trains daily make the 2-hour run between Porto and Guimarães. The fare from Porto to Guimarães is 2.50€ to 11€ depending on the train. Call ✆ 80/820-82-08 for schedules.

BY BUS Guimarães is easily accessible from Braga (p. 346); buses make the 1-hour trip frequently during the day. A one-way bus ticket from Braga to the Guimarães bus station, Quinta das Lameiras, is 5.50€. For information call ✆ 70/722-33-44.

BY CAR Drive northwest from Porto on N105-2 and N105.

VISITOR INFORMATION

The **Guimarães Tourist Office** is at Largo Cónego José Maria Gomes (☎ **25/351-83-94;** www.guimaraesturismo.com). It's open Monday to Friday 9am to 12:30pm and 2 to 5:30pm.

Exploring the Town

If you'd like to step into the Middle Ages for an hour or two, stroll down **Rua de Santa Maria ★**. It has remained essentially unchanged for centuries, except that nowadays you're likely to hear blaring music—in English, no less. Proud town houses, once the residences of the nobility, stand beside humble dwellings. The hand-carved balconies, aged by the years, are most often garnished with iron lanterns (not to mention laundry).

At the end, you'll come upon a charming square in the heart of the old town, **Largo da Oliveira (Olive Tree Square).** Seek out the odd chapelette in front of a church. Composed of four ogival arches, it's said to mark the spot where, in the 6th century, Wamba was asked to give up working his fields to become the king of the Goths. Thrusting his olive stick into the tilled soil, he declared that he would accept only if his stick sprouted leaves. So it did, and so he did—or so goes the tale.

The best excursion in the environs is to **Penha ★**, 5.5km (3½ miles) southeast of the center of town. At 620m (2,034 ft.), this is the loftiest point in the Serra de Santa Catarina. Penha can be reached from the end of Rua de Dr. José Sampaio by cable car for 4.20€ round-trip. The car runs from April to September Monday to Friday 10:30am to 7pm (Sat–Sun until 8pm). In the off season, it is open Friday to Sunday, and holidays the hours are from 10am to 6pm. Call the **Turinpenha** at Estação Inferior do Teleférico—Campo das Hortas 4800-026 Guimarães (☎ **25/351-50-85;** www.turipenha.pt).

Dominating the skyline of Guimarães itself is the 10th-century **Castle of Guimarães ★**, Rua Dona Teresa de Noronha, where Afonso Henríques, Portugal's first king, was born. High-pitched crenels top the strategically placed square towers and the looming keep. The view is panoramic. For more information, contact the staff at the Paço dos Duques (☎ **25/341-22-73** or 25/351-72-01). Almost in the shadow of the castle is the squat, rectangular 12th-century Romanesque **Igreja de São Miguel de Castelo,** where Afonso Henríques was baptized. Nearby is a heroic statue of the mustachioed, armor-clad Afonso, helmeted with sword and shield in hand. The church keeps irregular hours. The castle (no phone) is open Tuesday through Sunday from 9:30am to 12:30pm and 2 to 5:30pm (Aug until 7pm). Admission is free unless you visit the panoramic tower, **Torre de Menagem,** which costs 2€.

Igreja de São Francisco   The Church of St. Francis contains by far the most dramatic church **interior ★** in town. Entered through a Gothic portal, the spacious interior is faced with Delft blue-and-white *azulejos* (tiles) **★**. In the transept to the right of the main altar is a meticulously detailed miniature re-creation of the living room of a church prelate, from the burgundy cardinal's chapeau resting on a wall sconce to the miniature dog and cat. On the second altar to the right is a polychrome tree of life that represents 12 crowned kings and the Virgin, with her hands clasped and her feet resting on the heads of three cherubs. Entered through the south transept, the **sacristy ★** lies under a beautiful coffered ceiling decorated with grotesques. A stunning Arrábida marble table rests in the center of the floor.

Largo de São Francisco. ☎ **25/341-24-50.** Free admission. Tues–Sat 9:30am–noon and 3–5pm; Sun 9:30am–1pm.

Museu de Alberto Sampaio ★   The Alberto Sampaio Museum is in the Romanesque cloister and the buildings of the old monastery of the Collegiate Church of Our Lady of the Olive Branch. Besides a large silver collection, it displays the tunic worn by João I at the battle of Aljubarrota, which decided Portugal's fate. The museum also displays priestly garments as well as paintings, ceramics, and medieval sculpture. A fresco illustrates a gloating Salome, rapturous over the severed head of John the Baptist. In one of the rooms are pieces from a baroque chapel, with enormous wood-carved angels bearing torches.

Rua Alfredo Guimarães. (C) **25/342-39-10.** www.ipmuseus.pt. Admission 3€, free for children under 14, and free for all on Sun mornings. Tues–Sun 10am–6pm. Closed holidays.

Paço dos Duques ★   From the keep of the castle you can see the four-winged Palace of the Dukes of Bragança. Constructed in the 15th century, it has been heavily restored. Many critics have dismissed the rebuilt structure with contempt. If you're not a purist, however, you might find a guided tour interesting.

Perched on the slope of a hill, the palace possesses an assortment of treasures, including portraits of Catherine of Bragança, who married Charles II of England, the "Merrie Monarch" and lover of Nell Gwynne. You can also view copies of the large Pastrana tapestries depicting scenes from the Portuguese wars in North Africa, scabbards and helmets, Persian hangings, Indian urns, ceramics, and Chinese porcelains. The chapel opens onto the throne chairs of the duke and duchess; nearby are double-tiered cloisters.

Rua Conde Dom Henrique. (C) **25/341-22-73.** http://pduques.imc-ip.pt. Admission 5€, free for children under 15. Tues–Sun 10am–6pm.

Shopping

In the town's historic core, two streets are particularly noteworthy. The narrow medieval **Rua de Santa Maria** is the street long acknowledged by art historians as the most beautiful in town. Here you'll find some outlets for handicrafts and such souvenirs as ceramics, woodcarvings, handmade lace, and embroidered linen. More geared to the needs of residents is the main commercial thoroughfare, **Rua Gil Vicente.** For handicrafts, the best-stocked shop in town is **Artesanato de Guimarães,** Rua Paio Galvão ((C) **25/351-52-50**). Loosely affiliated with the municipal government, it functions as a showplace for the works of dozens of artisans from throughout the region, with an emphasis on textiles, woodcarvings, ceramics, and metalwork.

Where to Stay
EXPENSIVE
Pousada de Guimarães, Santa Marinhan   With foundations dating from the 12th century, this restored pousada is one of the most impressive in Portugal. Teresa, mother of Afonso Henríques, built it in 1154 as an Augustinian convent. It gained a baroque facade in the 18th century, when the soaring interior halls and spouting fountains were installed. The ornate Manueline church that occupies part of the building still offers Mass on Sunday. The property lies at the end of a winding road about 2km (1¼ miles) north of the town center on N101-2. Signs indicate the direction.

Take the time to explore both the upper halls and the gardens. One of the best rooms is a beautifully furnished large salon. At the end of one of the soaring halls, a fountain bubbles beneath an intricate wooden ceiling, surrounded by an open arcade that encompasses a view of the faraway mountains.

The guest rooms are a pleasing blend of old stonework, modern plasterwork, regional fabrics, and Portuguese lithographs. About half are in a relatively modern wing attached to the medieval core. The newer units, although modern, are decorated nonetheless in a traditional Portuguese style.

Costa, 4801-011 Guimarães. www.pousadas.pt. ✆ **25/351-12-49.** Fax 25/351-44-59. 51 units. 110€–215€ double; 149€–340€ suite. Rates include buffet breakfast. AE, DC, MC, V. Free parking. **Amenities:** Restaurant; bar; babysitting; children's center; outdoor pool; room service. *In room:* A/C, TV, hair dryer, minibar, Wi-Fi (in some; 12€ per 24 hr.).

MODERATE

Hotel de Guimarães ★★   We still prefer to stay at either of the pousadas we recommended, but this big, government-rated four-star hotel is a good alternative if you want lots of amenities. Favored by business clients and tour groups, it lies at the center of the historic core. The contemporary decor is tasteful, and the bedrooms are midsize to spacious, each with a good-size bathroom. The hotel also offers the best facilities at the resort, including a gym and an indoor swimming pool. If you don't demand character and charm from your hotel but like to be buffeted in comfort with many distractions, including bars and on-site dining, this is the best choice.

Rua Eduardo de Almeida, 4801-911 Guimarães. www.hotel-guimaraes.com. ✆ **25/342-48-00.** Fax 25/342-48-99. 116 units. 95€–125€ double; 125€–185€ suite. AE, DC, MC, V. Free parking. **Amenities:** Restaurant; bar; babysitting; exercise room; indoor heated pool; room service; spa. *In room:* A/C, TV, hair dryer, minibar, Wi-Fi (15€ per 24 hr.).

Pousada de Guimarães, Nossa Senhora de Oliveira ★★   The ambience at the second pousada in town differs from the atmosphere at the Pousada de Guimarães, Santa Marinha (see above), which is bigger and livelier. This establishment was created when a handful of 16th-century stone town houses were combined into a single rambling hotel. Many of their original features have been preserved. The pousada has a loyal clientele, a location on one of Portugal's most beautiful medieval squares, and a distinctive country-inn flavor. The street is so narrow that you'll have to park (free) in a well-marked lot about 31m (102 ft.) away.

The front rooms are of good size, but those on the side tend to be smaller. The accommodations contain twin beds, regional fabrics, and rug-covered tile floors. This place exudes intimate warmth, heightened by the wooden ceilings, tavern bar, and fireplace in the restaurant, whose windows look out over the square.

Rua de Santa Maria, 4801-910 Guimarães. www.pousadas.pt. ✆ **25/351-41-57.** Fax 25/351-42-04. 16 units. 90€–175€ double; 108€–185€ suite. Rates include buffet breakfast. AE, DC, MC, V. Free parking. **Amenities:** Restaurant; bar; room service. *In room:* A/C, TV, hair dryer, minibar, Wi-Fi (in some; 12€ per 24 hr.).

INEXPENSIVE

Hotel Fundador   This central hotel offers comfortable but small guest rooms in a medium high-rise. Though the pousadas are preferable, the Fundador is a decent place to spend the night. Rooms have piped-in music and well-kept bathrooms. The hotel isn't stylish, but it's functional and well kept, and boasts fine service. The penthouse bar serves snacks.

Av. Dom Afonso Henríques 740, 4810-431 Guimarães. www.hotelfundador.com. ✆ **25/342-26-40.** Fax 25/342-26-49. 72 units. 55€ double. Rates include buffet breakfast. AE, DC, MC, V. Free parking. **Amenities:** Bar; room service. *In room:* A/C, TV, hair dryer, minibar, Wi-Fi (free).

Where to Dine

MODERATE

Solar do Arco Restaurante ★ INTERNATIONAL/PORTUGUESE   The town's best restaurant, outside of hotel dining, is this winning spot, which is installed in an antique house in the historic center with a rustic decor featuring lots of wood. The chef fashions superb dishes based whenever possible on local market-fresh produce. "We are rustic but also noble," our waiter assured us. The shrimp with white beans was excellent, as was the roast veal with potatoes and greens so fresh they tasted like they were just picked. And what respectable Portuguese dining room would not offer a codfish specialty of the day? The chef prepares a savory codfish stew with onions, potatoes, and fresh greens. We launched our repast with a cream of shellfish soup and saved room for dessert, which was a tart of summer fruits.

Rua da Santa Maria 48-50. © **25/351-30-72.** www.solardoarco.com. Reservations recommended. Main courses 9€-28€. AE, DC, MC, V. Daily noon-3:30pm and 7pm-midnight.

INEXPENSIVE

El Rei Dom Afonso REGIONAL PORTUGUESE   In an enviable position in the heart of the medieval sector, this little restaurant opens onto the rear of the former town hall and the Pousada de Guimarães, Nossa Senhora de Oliveira. The patrons are mostly locals, joined by occasional foreigners. It offers good fish and tender meat dishes, including pork and codfish, plus country-fresh vegetables. Try hake filets or house-style steak. Service is efficient, albeit sometimes rushed.

Praça de São Tiago 20. © **25/341-90-96.** Main courses 12€-20€. AE, DC, MC, V. Mon-Sat 12:30-3pm and 7-11pm.

BRAGA ★

50km (31 miles) N of Porto; 367km (228 miles) N of Lisbon

Nearly everywhere you look in Braga there's a church, a palace, a garden, or a fountain. Known to the Romans as Bracara Augusta, the town has been called home by other conquerors, including the Suevi, the Visigoths, and the Moors. For centuries, it has been an archiepiscopal seat and pilgrimage site; the Visigoths are said to have renounced their heresies here. Braga is also a long-standing religious capital. It stages the country's most impressive observances of *Semana Santa* (Holy Week), when torch-lit processions of hooded participants, eerily evocative of the KKK, parade by.

Politically, Braga is Portugal's most conservative city. In 1926, a coup here paved the way for Salazar to begin his long dictatorship. Paradoxically, Braga is a hot place at night, primarily because of its young people. In fact, its lively streets have earned it a reputation for being "Lisbon in miniature."

Although aware of its rich history, the capital of Minho is very much a city of today. Its historic core and cathedral lie at the center, but the periphery bustles with commerce and industry, including a lot of manufacturing—brick making, soap making, textiles, smelting, engineering, and leather goods. Today 65,000 residents live with noisy streets, increasing numbers of ugly and uninspired apartment blocks, and traffic congestion on streets that not long ago contained a few cars and maybe a donkey or two.

Essentials

ARRIVING

BY TRAIN   The train station is on Largo da Estação (© **80/820-82-08**). Some 30 trains per day make the transit from Porto to Braga, taking between 45 minutes and

70 minutes. The fare from Porto to Braga is 2.50€ to 20€ depending on the train and the class of service. From Coimbra, 17 trains a day make the 4-hour trip. The direct trip from Coimbra to Braga takes 1 hour and 40 minutes and costs 20€.

BY BUS　　The bus station is at Central de Camionagem (☎ **25/320-94-00**), a few blocks north of the heart of town. Buses arrive every hour from Porto; the trip takes 1½ hours and costs 6€ one-way. From Guimarães, there is one bus daily; the trip takes an hour and costs 5.50€. From Lisbon, eleven daily buses make the 5½-hour trip. The fare is 19€ one-way.

BY CAR　　From Guimarães (see the preceding section), head northwest along N101.

VISITOR INFORMATION

The **Braga Tourist Office** is at Av. da Liberdade 1 (☎ **25/326-25-50;** www.cm-braga.pt). It's open October to May Monday to Friday 9am to 12:30pm and 2 to 6:30pm, Saturday and Sunday until 5:30pm; June to September Monday to Friday 9am to 7pm, Saturday and Sunday 9am to 12:30pm and 2 to 5:30pm.

What to See & Do in Braga

EXPLORING THE TOWN

Museu dos Biscainhos　　This museum is in Biscainhos Palace, a building from the 17th and 18th centuries that for about 300 years has served as the house of a noble family. The original gardens are still here. The museum has painted and ornamented ceilings and walls with panels of figurative and neoclassical tiles. Its exhibition rooms contain collections of Portuguese furniture and pottery, glassware, silverware, textiles, and Portuguese, Oriental, and Dutch Delft porcelain.

Rua dos Biscainhos ☎ **25/320-46-50.** www.ipmuseus.pt. Admission 2€, free for children under 15. Tues–Sun 10am–12:15pm and 2–5:30pm. Closed holidays.

Santuário Bom Jesús do Monte ★★　　Bom Jesús do Monte is a hilltop pilgrimage site; it's reached on foot, on a funicular (the ride costs 1€), or by car along a tree-lined roadway. The baroque granite double staircase dating from the 18th century might look daunting, but if it's any consolation, pilgrims often climb it on their knees. The stairway is less elaborate than the one at Remédios at Lamego but is equally impressive. On the numerous landings are gardens, grottoes, small chapels, sculptures, and allegorical stone figures set in fountains.

N103-3, 5km (3 miles) southeast of Braga. ☎ **25/367-66-36.** Free admission. Daily 7:30am–8pm.

Sé de Braga ★　　Inside the town, interest focuses on the Sé (cathedral), which was built in the 12th century by Henri de Bourgogne and Dona Teresa. After he died, she was chased out of town because of an illicit love affair, but in death Henri and Teresa were reunited in their tombs in the Chapel of Kings.

The Sé has undergone decorative and architectural changes. The north triple-arched facade is austere and dominating, with a large stone-laced Roman arch flanked by two smaller Gothic ones. What appear to be the skeletons of cupolas top the facade's dual bell towers, which flank a lofty rooftop niche containing a larger-than-life statue of the *Virgin and Child.* Under a carved baldachin in the apse is a statue of Our Lady of the Milk—that is, the Virgin breast-feeding the infant Jesus. The statue is in the heavily ornamental Manueline style but is somehow pious and restrained.

Inside you might think you've entered one of the darkest citadels of Christendom. If you can see them, the decorations, including a pair of huge 18th-century gilded organs, are profuse. In the 1330 **Capela da Glória** ★ is the sarcophagus of Archbishop Dom Gonçalo Pereira, with an unctuous expression on his face. It was carved by order of the prelate.

You can visit the **Treasury of the Cathedral** ★ and the **Museum of Sacred Art,** an upstairs repository of Braga's most precious works of art. On display are elaborately carved choir stalls from the 18th century, embroidered vestments from the 16th to the 18th centuries, a 14th-century statue of the Virgin, and a Gothic chalice from the same period. An 18th-century silver-and-gilt monstrance adorned with diamonds is by Dom Gaspar de Bragança. In the cloister is a Pietà.

Sé Primaz, Rua Dom Paio Mendez. © **25/326-33-17.** www.se-braga.pt. Free admission to Sé; museum and treasury 3€, free for children under 12. Summer daily 8:30am–6:30pm; winter daily 8:30am–5:30pm.

SHOPPING

The town's best outlet for gifts and handmade souvenirs is in the **tourist office** (see "Essentials," above). You'll find an impressive array of appealingly textured linens, pottery and ceramics, and woodcarvings that evoke the values and traditions of northern Portugal.

Nearby is a textile factory that transforms flax into linens; the factory outlet boasts a rich stock of houseware linens, some of them of heirloom quality. Head 4km (2½ miles) north of the city, following signs to Prado. In the hamlet of São Paio Merelim, you'll find the factories of **Edgar Duarte Abreu,** São Paio de Merelim (© **25/362-11-92**).

Where to Stay

EXPENSIVE

Meliá Braga ★★★   This northern city has long been overdue for a deluxe, stylish, and luxurious hotel, and Meliá has finally established one. Lying about a 30-minute walk from the historic center, the mammoth hotel and spa is suitable for vacationers as well as the commercial traveler. Its facilities are the finest in the area. The bedrooms contain an elegant contemporary decor, with sleek furnishings and the latest in bathroom design. Some of the suites come with kitchenettes. The designer of the hotel made use of various hues of brown when decorating the bedrooms.

El Olivo, the on-site restaurant, is far better when the hotel hasn't booked a tour group. The chefs are known for their varied themed buffets and their "show cooking" style. The indoor and outdoor pools are heated, and there is a separate pool for children. The exercise room is state of the art, as is the deluxe spa.

Av. General Carrilho de Silva Porto 8, 4715-380 Braga. www.meliabraga.com. © **25/314-40-00.** 161 units. 110€–232€ double; from 250€ suite. AE, DC, MC, V. Free outdoor parking; indoor parking 15€. **Amenities:** Restaurant; 2 bars; concierge; exercise room; 2 heated pools (1 indoor, 1 outdoor); room service. *In room:* A/C, TV, hair dryer, minibar, Wi-Fi (free).

MODERATE

Bracara Augusta ★★   In the historic district, Braga's most select boutique hotel is installed in a massively renovated building from the 14th century that still retains many of its original features, including stone walls. Two miles from the train station, it is for those who prefer a small, intimate hotel. For grander luxury and far more facilities, Meliá Braga (see above) is the first choice. The conversion was tasteful, and the furnishings are comfortable and well chosen. A welcoming basket of fruit and mineral water greet you upon arrival, and you can relax in an idyllic garden. Maintenance keeps

the place spotlessly clean. Other features include a good restaurant offering ↘
specialties and one of the best hotel breakfasts around. On a pedestrian-only stre↖
the location is one of the best in the area, close to museums, churches, and shops.

Av. Central 134, 4710-229 Braga. www.bracaraaugusta.com. ℂ **25/320-62-60.** 17 units. 69€–99€ double; 109€–149€ suite. AE, DC, MC, V. No parking. **Amenities:** Restaurant; bar; room service. *In room:* A/C, TV, hair dryer, minibar, Wi-Fi (free).

Hotel Turismo Braga ★   The Turismo's best asset is that it's convenient to lots of shops, restaurants, and cafes. You enter the hotel through a cafe-studded arcade, which opens onto a two-story lobby with a spacious wood-paneled lounge, bar, and restaurant. Each midsize guest room contains a spacious balcony opening onto traffic; the walls are covered with blue-and-white tiles. Furnishings are standardized but still comfortable, and the beds are firm. The hotel has a rooftop pool and an eighth-floor snack bar.

Praceta João XXI, 4715-036 Braga. www.hotelturismobraga.com. ℂ **25/320-60-00.** Fax 25/320-60-10. 132 units. 75€–85€ double; 90€–140€ suite. Rates include buffet breakfast. AE, DC, MC, V. Parking 6€. **Amenities:** Restaurant; bar; outdoor rooftop pool; room service; Wi-Fi (5€ per hour, in lobby). *In room:* A/C, TV, hair dryer.

Pousada de Braga, São Vicente ★   A 19th-century classical palace, once belonging to a Minho nobleman, has been carefully restored and turned into this inviting inn. You have a choice of standard rooms or better-equipped superior rooms, plus two suites. Regardless of the classification, each is tastefully and comfortably furnished with tiled bathrooms and generous space. The pousada also has a first-class restaurant on-site that serves regional specialties of the Minho.

Largo de Infias, 4710-299 Braga. www.pousadas.pt. ℂ **25/320-95-00.** Fax 25/320-95-09. 26 units. 90€–150€ double; from 122€ suite. Rates include buffet breakfast. AE, DC, MC, V. Parking 10€. **Amenities:** Restaurant; bar; babysitting; outdoor pool; room service; Wi-Fi (12€ per day, in lobby). *In room:* A/C, TV.

INEXPENSIVE

Albergaria Senhora-A-Branca ★ 💼   This good-value discovery lies on a historic square about a 7-minute walk from the exact center of town. Modern comforts have been installed throughout the restored four-story antique building. Bedrooms are small to midsize, but they are attractively and comfortably furnished, each with a small bathroom. The friendly owner used to be in the antique business, and he used part of his former merchandise to decorate the hotel, giving it added charm.

Largo da Senhora a Branca 58, 4710 Braga. www.albergariasrabranca.pt. ℂ **25/326-99-38.** Fax 25/326-99-37. 20 units. 55€ double; 60€ suite. Rates include buffet breakfast. AE, DC, MC, V. Free parking. **Amenities:** Room service. *In room:* A/C, TV, Wi-Fi (3€ per hour).

Hotel Residencial D. Sofia ⚓   The town's best bargain lies close to the cathedral, a business thriving for more than a decade in an antique but restored building. Bedrooms are midsize and traditionally furnished, often with handcrafted pieces. The place is basic and merely functional, but it's such good value and so tidily maintained that we have to highly recommend it. Although breakfast is the only meal served, you have several restaurant choices nearby.

Largo São João do Souto 131, 4700 Braga. www.hoteldonasofia.com. ℂ **25/326-31-60.** Fax 25/361-12-45. 34 units. 63€–77€ double; 78€–95€ suite. AE, MC, V. Free parking. **Amenities:** Bar. *In room:* A/C, TV, minibar.

AT BOM JESÚS DO MONTE

Hotel do Elevador ★ Near the Bom Jesús do Monte, this traditionally styled hotel was completely rebuilt in 1998 and named for a nearby and still-working water-powered elevator from the 1800s. The hotel is now mainly known for its 120-seat panoramic restaurant, opening onto the best views in Braga. But the midsize bedrooms offer much comfort and boast classic decor and tasteful furnishings.

Parque do Bom Jesús do Monte, 4700 Braga. www.hoteisbomjesus.pt. *C* **25/360-34-00.** Fax 25/360-34-09. 22 units. 60€–115€ double. Rates include buffet breakfast. AE, DC, MC, V. Free parking. The hotel is 3km (1¾ miles) outside of Braga on a wooded hillside. **Amenities:** Restaurant; bar; room service; Wi-Fi (free, in lobby). *In room:* A/C, TV, hair dryer, minibar.

Where to Dine

Centurium ★ REGIONAL PORTUGUESE This restaurant, in the Hotel Bracara Augusta, is the best in town. Both the hotel and restaurant lie to the west of the center of Braga. The chefs showcase the bounty of the rich agricultural province of the Minho, serving regional wines. You might start with *caldo verde*, the cabbage and potato soup so famous in the region. Meats are carefully selected, and the fish is market fresh. Succulent pastas are also a feature of the restaurant.

Av. Central 134, 4710-229 Braga. *C* **25/320-62-60.** Fax 25/320-62-69. www.bracaraaugusta.com. Reservations recommended. Main courses 9€–19€. AE, MC, V. Mon-Sat noon-3pm and 7:30-11pm.

O Alexandre PORTUGUESE Since the 1970s, this small eatery has attracted patrons from all walks of city life, including the mayor and church officials. It seems busiest at lunch, when businesspeople book most of the tables. Regional wines accompany most meals. You can order off the a la carte menu, but always ask about the daily specials. Portions are generous, and the cooking is rich. Roast *cabrito* (kid) is in season in June; the year-round favorite is *bacalhau* (dried salt cod), prepared in an infinite number of ways.

Campo das Hortas 10. *C* **25/361-40-03.** Reservations recommended. Main courses 18€–25€. DC, MC, V. Daily noon-3:30pm and 7-11pm.

O Inácio ★ REGIONAL PORTUGUESE In an old stone structure outside the Arco da Porta Nova (the town gate), O Inácio is the most popular restaurant in town. It has thrived as a restaurant since the 1930s for good reason: The owner has a well-stocked wine cellar and offers a finely crafted menu of usually fresh ingredients deftly handled in the kitchen.

The rustic decor features rugged walls and hand-hewn beams from the 1700s, regional pottery, and oxen yokes; in colder months, a fire burns in an open hearth. The Portuguese specialties usually include *bacalhau à Inácio* (codfish), *papas de sarrabulho* (a regional stew served in winter only), and *bife de caçarola* (pot roast). Roast kid is featured occasionally. Most fish dishes, which are fresh, are good picks, and the rum omelet soufflé is a must for dessert.

Campo das Hortas 4. *C* **25/361-32-35.** Reservations recommended. Main courses 16€–20€. AE, DC, MC, V. Wed-Mon 12:30-3:30pm and 7-10pm. Closed for 2 weeks in Sept.

Braga After Dark

As a university city with a population as young and hip as any comparable city in Europe, Braga has a lot of nightlife, most of it spinning around dozens of bars and low-rent dance clubs. The best bars lie almost adjacent to one another, near the corner of Avenida Central and Praça da República. Our favorite is **Café Vianna**

(☏ **25/326-23-36;** Mon–Sat 7am–2am; Sun 9am–midnight). It serves coffee, wine, and whiskey in settings redolent of local gossip and intrigue.

BARCELOS

23km (14 miles) W of Braga; 365km (227 miles) N of Lisbon

Barcelos is a sprawling river town that rests on a plateau ringed by green hills. The town doesn't feature any single major attraction—though its outdoor markets are famous—but it is responsible for why the Portuguese national icon is the rooster. According to legend, a pilgrim passed through Barcelos in the 16th century, only to be wrongfully accused of theft. The pilgrim swore his innocence, and then went on to say that the judge's dinner that night would declare him innocent, too. Sure enough, a rooster was cooked and about to be served as the main course in the magistrate's dinner, when it crowed. The pilgrim was consequently set free.

Essentials

ARRIVING

BY TRAIN   The station is on Avenida Alcaides de Faria (☏ **80/820-82-08**). To reach Barcelos from Braga, go by train to the town of Nine, from which there is a direct train link into Barcelos, costing 2.70€ one way. Fifteen trains a day make the 45-minute trip from Viana do Castelo that costs 2.70€.

BY BUS   The station is on Avenida Dr. Sidónio Pais (☏ **70/722-33-44**). One bus a day arrives from Braga. It's a 25-minute trip that costs 5.50€.

BY CAR   From Braga, follow N103 due west.

VISITOR INFORMATION

The **Barcelos Tourist Office** is at Largo Doutor José Novais 8 (☏ **25/381-18-82;** www.cm-barcelos.pt). Open in summer Monday to Friday 9:30am to 6pm, Saturday 10am to 1pm and 2 to 5pm, and Sunday 10am to 1pm and 2 to 4pm; in winter Monday to Friday 9:30am to 6pm, and Saturday 10am to 1pm and 2 to 5pm.

What to See & Do in Barcelos

EXPLORING THE TOWN   Try to visit Barcelos on Thursday, when the **market** (7am–6pm) takes over the **Campo da República,** almost 400 sq. m (4,306 sq. ft.), with a fountain at the center. You'll see local handicrafts—rugs, dyed pillows stuffed with chicken feathers, chandeliers, crochet work, pottery, and hand-painted earthenware cockerels, Portugal's most characteristic souvenirs.

Opening onto the tree-studded main square are some of the finest buildings in Barcelos. The 18th-century **Igreja de Nossa Senhora do Terco** resembles a palace more than a church, with a central-niche facade topped by finials and a cross. The tile work around the baroque altar depicts scenes of monks at labor and a moving rendition of the Last Supper. Also fronting the *campo* is the **Hospital da Misericórdia,** a long, formal 17th-century building behind a spiked fence.

Of more interest is the small, octagonal **Igreja do Bom Jesús da Cruz,** with a tile-faced cupola. An upper balustrade, punctuated by large stone finials and a latticed round window about the square portal, contrasts with the austerity of the walls. The interior is more sumptuous, with crystal, marble, and gilt. There are no set hours for visits, though generally one can enter daily from 9am to noon and 3 to 6pm. Don't count on always finding someone to admit you, however.

Overlooking the swirling Cávado River are the ruins of the 1786 **Palace of the Braganças.** The original palace site, as well as the town of Barcelos itself, was bestowed on Nuno Álvares by João I as a gift in gratitude for his bravery in the 1385 battle at Aljubarrota. Check out the representation of the palace on the facade, to see how it must have looked back then.

You can wander through the ruins, which have been turned into an archaeological museum called the **Museu Arqueológico** (☎ 25/382-47-41), filled with sarcophagi, heralded shields, and an 18th-century tile fountain. It's open daily 9am to noon and 2 to 6pm, and admission is free. The **Museu de Olaria** (☎ **25/382-47-41;** www.museuolaria.org), underneath the palace, has exhibits on pottery, including a blood-red ceramic oxen with lyre-shape horns. Enter on Rua Cónego Joaquim Gaiolas. It is open Tuesday to Friday 10am to 5:30pm, Saturday and Sunday from 10am to 12:30pm and 2 to 5:30pm. Admission is 2.20€ for adults, 1.10€ for students and children.

The adjoining Gothic **Igreja Matriz** (parish church) contains a baroque altar decorated with cherubs, grapes, gold leaf, and birds and an interior whose sides are faced with multicolored tiles.

SHOPPING   The unique **Centro do Artesanato de Barcelos ★★**, Torre de Porta Nova (☎ **25/381-21-35**), is a gem. It displays some of the best regional handicrafts at the best prices we've encountered in the north. The center has an age-old stone tower that rises opposite the Church of São da Cruz. A wide display of goods is for sale on its street level and upper floor.

One outstanding collection alone makes the trip to Barcelos worth it. It consists of witty, sophisticated ceramics from the heirs of Rosa Ramalho, who was known as the Grandma Moses of Portuguese ceramics. Some of these figures show the influence of Picasso. Ms. Ramalho created figures depicting eerie people. For example, she put the heads of wolves on nuns and gave goats six legs—all in muted forest green or butterscotch brown. In addition, there's a good selection of the ceramic red-combed Barcelos cockerels, with many variations on the traditional motif in red and black. Local wares include black ceramic candlesticks, earthenware bowls used for *caldo verde* (a fortifying soup of greens and vegetables), hand-knitted pillows, handmade rugs in bold stripes, and hand-loomed bedspreads.

If this place doesn't have what you're looking for, head for **Largo do Dom António Barroso** in the center of town, where a handful of other souvenir and handicrafts shops sell the products of local artisans.

Where to Stay

Bagoeira Hotel   The best hotel within the town itself, Bagoeira Hotel also contains the best restaurant (see below). The hotel's modern facade is graced with wrought-iron balconies. Located in the heart of the city in front of the Campo da Feira de Barcelos, the guest rooms are midsize, simply furnished, neatly maintained, and comfortable.

Av. Dr. Sidónio Pais 495, 4750-333 Barcelos. www.bagoeira.com. ☎ **25/380-95-00.** Fax 25/382-45-88. 54 units. 55€–75€ double; 75€–99€ suite. Rates include breakfast. MC, V. Free parking. **Amenities:** Restaurant; bar; room service. *In room:* A/C, TV, minibar.

Hotel Do Terco   Ranking just under the Bagoeira Hotel, this is a serviceable little hotel in the heart of Barcelos, near the shopping area. The functionally furnished guest rooms are spread over two floors, offering doubles, twin beds, or king-size beds. Rooms open onto balconies or terraces. The ground-floor bar is a gathering point at night.

Rua de Sao Bento, 4750-267 Barcelos. www.hoteldoterco.com. ✆ **25/380-83-80.** Fax 25/380-83-83. 37 units. 55€–65€ double; 85€ triple. Rates include continental breakfast. MC, V. Free parking. **Amenities:** Bar; room service; Wi-Fi (free, in lobby). *In room:* A/C, TV.

Where to Dine

Bagoeira Restaurante ★ PORTUGUESE   This is the most charming little restaurant in town. You'll find oceans of local color along with good-tasting regional food based on recipes handed down by grandmothers. The setting boasts fresh flowers, wrought-iron chandeliers, and patina-coated wood surfaces. Try *feijoada*, the national dish of northern Portugal, redolent with beans and beef, or else fresh vegetable soup made with a bountiful harvest from the countryside. The chef also specializes in freshly caught fish, which is then grilled to perfection. Chicken with rice is a local favorite, and on market day (Thurs) people from the countryside fill up the tables, often ordering stewed pork cooked with pig's blood. The restaurant also rents comfortable rooms (reviewed above) and has a dramatic panoramic bar, Pelouro.

Av. Dr. Sidónio Pais 495. ✆ **25/380-95-00.** www.bagoeira.com. Reservations required only for Thurs lunch. Main courses 9€–27€. AE, DC, MC, V. Daily noon–10:30pm.

Dom António PORTUGUESE   This local favorite, which opened in the mid-1980s, lies on the street level of an old town house in the town's historic heart. It has a rustic interior and a polite staff. The restaurant features hearty soups, *bacalhau Dom António* (a popular house specialty concocted from codfish, onions, and potatoes), superb shellfish rice, grilled salmon, grilled steaks, and grilled pork chops.

Rua Dom António Barroso 87. ✆ **25/381-22-85.** Main courses 10€–20€. AE, MC, V. Daily 9am–midnight.

ESPOSENDE

20km (12 miles) S of Viana do Castelo; 48km (30 miles) N of Porto; 367km (228 miles) N of Lisbon

Esposende is a beach resort town where Atlantic breezes sweep the pines and sand dunes, and cows graze in nearby pastures. The surrounding countryside is no longer unspoiled—the area has been extensively developed, and a wide new road runs along the seafront—though you'll still see an occasional ox cart in the street and men and women in broad-brimmed hats working the vineyards in the foothills. The beach, lining both sides of the Cávado estuary, is large and fine. Small fishing vessels plod along the river carrying anglers to the bass upstream. Archaeological digs have revealed the remains of a Roman city and necropolis, but that doesn't seem to have disturbed Esposende in the least.

Essentials

ARRIVING

BY TRAIN   There is no train service to Esposende.

BY BUS   A bus trip from Porto to Esposende takes about an hour and costs 7.50€ one-way. Call ✆ **70/722-33-44** for schedules.

BY CAR   From Porto, take IC-1 north.

VISITOR INFORMATION

The **Esposende Tourist Office** is on Avenida Arantes de Oliveira (✆ **25/396-13-54;** www.visitesposende.com). In winter, it's open Monday to Saturday 9:30am to 12:30pm and 2 to 5:30pm; in summer, it's open daily 9am to 7pm.

Where to Stay

Estalagem Zende ★★   Rated a luxury inn by the government, Estalagem Zende lies on the main road to Viana do Castelo, right outside Esposende. One-third of the well-maintained, midsize guest rooms have minibars. Furnishings are worn but comfortable, with good beds and well-kept bathrooms.

Estrada Nacional 13, 4740-203 Esposende. www.estalagemzende.com. ☏ **25/396-90-90.** Fax 25/396-90-91. 25 units. 40€–75€ double. Rates include buffet breakfast. AE, DC, MC, V. Free parking. **Amenities:** Restaurant; bar; room service. *In room:* A/C, TV, minibar (in some).

Hotel Suave Mar 🎣   A semimodern hotel on the river, Suave Mar attracts frugal travelers who don't want to pay for the first-class accommodations at neighboring Ofir and Fão (see chapter 12). The midsize rooms are pleasant and comfortable, with well-kept and equipped bathrooms. The restaurant serves some of the best food in town; its mix of Portuguese and international cuisine is a nod to the 20 years the owners spent in Brazil.

Av. Eng. Arantes e Oliveira, 4740-204 Esposende. www.suavemar.com. ☏ **25/396-94-00.** Fax 25/396-94-01. 84 units. 59€–113€ double; 76€–123€ junior suite; 123€–156€ suite. Rates include buffet breakfast. AE, DC, MC, V. Free parking. **Amenities:** Restaurant; 2 bars; exercise room; 2 outdoor pools; room service; outdoor tennis court (lit). *In room:* A/C, TV, hair dryer, minibar, Wi-Fi (5€ per hour).

Where to Dine

Restaurant Zende SEAFOOD/PORTUGUESE   In the previously recommended Estalagem Zende (see above), this restaurant serves an array of seafood recently caught off the coast. The fish is usually grilled and served with local garlic and herbs. The shellfish soup is the best bet to open your meal. Favorite dishes with the locals, and justifiably so, include grilled tiger shrimp, or grilled sea bass with fresh regional vegetables. Lamb from nearby meadows, served with fresh vegetables, is also a savory dish.

Estrada Nacional 13. ☏ **25/396-90-90.** Main courses 12€–28€. AE, DC, MC, V. Daily noon–3pm and 7–10:30pm.

VIANA DO CASTELO ★

71km (44 miles) N of Porto; 388km (241 miles) N of Lisbon; 25km (16 miles) N of Esposende

Viana do Castelo, between an estuary of the Lima River and a base of rolling hills, is one of the most folksy cities in northern Portugal. Though Viana is today a major center of deep-sea fishing and the site of such industries as pyrotechnics, wood manufacturing, ceramics, and boat building (after years of decline), it still exudes a traditional vibe. Its narrow streets are lined with Manueline manors and occasionally, you'll spot an ox cart with wooden wheels clacking along the stone streets.

The town is known for its pottery and regional handicrafts but it's even better known for its regional festivals, the most famous of which is the annual *Festa de Nossa Senhora de Agonia* (Festival of Our Lady of Agony), which takes place in late August. This festival gives women a chance to wear regional garb, such as strident orange, scarlet, and Prussian blue, and layers of golden necklaces with heart- and cross-shape pendants.

Essentials

ARRIVING

BY TRAIN   The station is on Avenida dos Combatentes da Grande Guerra (☏ **80/820-82-08** for information). Eleven trains per day arrive from Porto; the trip takes 2 hours and costs 7€ one-way.

BY BUS The station, **Central de Camionagem** (📞 **25/882-50-47**), is at the eastern edge of the city. Buses arrive every hour from Porto; the 1½-hour trip costs 7.60€ one-way. Seven buses make the trip from Lisbon each day; it takes 6 hours, and a one-way ticket costs 19€.

BY CAR From Porto or Esposende, continue north along IC-1.

VISITOR INFORMATION

The **Viana do Castelo Tourist Office** is on Rua do Hospital Velho (📞 **25/882-26-20**). It's open Monday to Saturday 9am to 12:30pm and 2:30 to 6pm, and Sunday 9:30am to 1pm.

What to See & Do in Viana do Castelo

EXPLORING THE TOWN The town center is **Praça da República ★**, one of Portugal's most handsome squares. At its heart is the much-photographed 16th-century **Chafariz Fountain,** with water spewing from the mouths of its figures. The most impressive building on the square is the dour, squat, three-story **Igreja da Misericórdia.** The lower level is an arcade of five austere Roman arches, and the two upper levels are ponderous Renaissance balconies. A rooftop crucifix crowns the structure. Each level's four supporting pillars are primitive caryatidlike figures. The church fronts Rua da Bandeira and adjoins the former charity hospice, Hospital da Misericórdia. Inside the church you'll find pictorial tiles made in 1714, ornate baroque altars, a painted ceiling, and woodcarvings.

The other building dominating the square is the 1502 **Paço do Concelho** (the former town hall), constructed over an arcade made up of three wide, low, Gothic arches. The crenel-topped facade displays a royal coat of arms and wrought-iron balcony windows above each arch.

The best views of both turf and surf are from the ramparts of the **Castelo de Santiago da Barra,** reached by following Rua General Luís do Rego. In 1589, Philip I of Spain ordered that the walls of the castelo be built—this is the reason "do Castelo" was added to Viana's name. It's open Monday to Friday 9am to 12:30pm and 2 to 5:30pm. Call 📞 **25/882-02-70** for more information.

To enjoy one of the great panoramas in the north of Portugal, you can visit the **Miradouro de Santa Luzia ★★**, a belvedere on the hill of Santa Luzia, where the view of Viana is especially stunning at night when all the lights go on. To the north of town, the belvedere is topped by the modern **Basilica de Santa Luzia** (📞 **25/882-31-73**), constructed in a neo-Byzantine style. A trio of rose windows illuminates its interior, and the chancel and apse are adorned with frescoes. For another **panoramic view ★★**, you can climb the 142 steps that begin in the sacristy. The basilica, reached along Estrada de Santa Luzia, is open daily from 8am to 8pm, and access to the dome is 1€. You can drive the 7km (4⅓ miles) to this Santa Luzia belvedere—signs from the center of town direct you to it—or else you can take a long, long flight of steps up the 200m (656-ft.) climb. The steps begin behind the rail station.

SHOPPING The wares sold here tend to be earthier, more rustic, and less influenced by fads than what's usually available closer to Lisbon. In addition to the ceramics and woodcarvings that are widely available in other regions, look for linens and embroideries, sometimes in bewitchingly subtle patterns. The main shopping streets, **Rua Manuel Espregueira** and **Rua da Bandeira,** contain shops selling virtually everything you'd need to dress yourself or accessorize a house.

If you're looking for handicrafts, try **Arte Regional,** Avenida dos Combatentes da Grande Guerra (✆ **25/882-90-45**), and **Arte Minho,** Rua de São Pedro 21–23 (✆ **25/882-10-52**).

Where to Stay

MODERATE TO EXPENSIVE

Casa Melo Alvim ★★★   This is the oldest urban mansion in Viana do Castelo and an inn of such antique charm and character that it has quickly become one of the most coveted stopovers in the north of Portugal. Except for views, it clearly outdistances the Pousada de Viana do Castelo, Monte de Santa Luzia (see below), which was the reigning hotel in town for many years. Built in the Manueline style in 1509, this inn had a long history before it was finally restored and turned into a luxurious place for overnight guests. In keeping with its original decor, the new inn still has an air of sobriety about it, a winning combination of natural light and natural materials. Access to the upper floors is along a baroque stairwell with banisters. The small to midsize bedrooms and suites are decorated in a sober but comfortable style, with excellent modern furnishings including a good-size bathroom. Furnishings in the rooms reflect various ages and styles of Portuguese design.

Av. Conde da Carreira 28, 4900-343 Viana do Castelo. www.meloalvimhouse.com. ✆ **25/880-82-00.** Fax 25/880-82-20. 24 units. 115€–175€ double; 150€–205€ suite. Rates include buffet breakfast. AE, DC, MC, V. Free parking. **Amenities:** Restaurant; bar; bikes; room service; Wi-Fi (free, in lobby). *In room:* A/C, TV, hair dryer, minibar.

Flôr de Sal ★★   Casa Melo Alvim has more charm and tranquillity, but in terms of facilities and comfort, Flôr de Sal is the town's leading hotel. It stands at the edge of the Atlantic's waters, and all of its rooms open onto uninterrupted views of the lashing waves. The hotel is one of the most avant-garde and modern in the north of Portugal. Bedrooms are elegant, tasteful, and supremely comfortable with state-of-the-art bathrooms. All the guest rooms are graced with large windows, and those facing the west also have private balconies or terraces. The less desirable rooms face east and the mountains in the distance.

The hotel offers some of the finest dining in town, including the best buffet lunch in the area, followed by a delectable medley of regional dishes and international specialties for dinner. When the weather is good, you can dine on a terrace overlooking the ocean. The facilities are wide ranging, including the best spa and health club in the area, along with two heated indoor saltwater swimming pools.

Av. de Cabo Verde, Praia Norte, 4900-350 Viana do Castelo. www.hotelflordesal.com. ✆ **25/880-01-00.** Fax 25/880-01-01. 57 units. 135€–190€ double; 155€–195€ junior suite. AE, DC, MC, V. Free parking. **Amenities:** Restaurant; 2 bars; health club & spa; 2 indoor heated saltwater pools; room service; Wi-Fi (5€ per hour, in lobby). *In room:* A/C, TV, hair dryer, minibar.

Pousada de Viana do Castelo, Monte de Santa Luzia ★★   Some 6km (3¾ miles) north of the town center, the government-owned Monte de Santa Luzia sits on a wooded hillside high above the most congested part of the city. It's just behind the illuminated dome of the neo-Byzantine Basilica of Santa Luzia. Built in 1895, the hotel has neoclassical details and granite balconies, giving it the appearance of a royal palace, especially when it's floodlit at night. Winding cobblestone roads run through a forest to the entrance. At the summit, you'll find the area's best view of the city and river.

Guest rooms are spacious, and some bathrooms have Jacuzzis. The high-ceilinged public rooms gained Art Deco sheen when the hotel was completely renovated. The pousada boasts long expanses of glistening marble, stylish Jazz Age accessories, a comfortable bar and restaurant, and enormous, echoing halls.

Monte de Santa Luzia, 4901-909 Viana do Castelo. www.pousadas.pt. ☏ **25/880-03-70.** Fax 25/882-88-92. 51 units. 110€–213€ double; 149€–230€ suite. Rates include buffet breakfast. AE, DC, MC, V. Free parking. **Amenities:** Restaurant; bar; babysitting; exercise room; outdoor freshwater pool; room service; outdoor tennis court (lit). *In room:* A/C, TV, minibar.

INEXPENSIVE

Hotel do Parque This hotel, at the base of the bridge crossing the Lima River on the edge of town, is the second-best choice within the town center. It feels like a small resort, with lounges overlooking two pools (one reserved for children). The main floor has a lounge and an interior winter garden. The midsize guest rooms are quite contemporary, with built-in furnishings, balconies, and neatly kept bathrooms.

Praça da Galiza, 4900-476 Viana do Castelo. www.hoteldoparque.com. ☏ **25/882-86-05.** Fax 25/882-86-12. 124 units. 48€–70€ double. Rates include buffet breakfast. AE, DC, MC, V. Free parking. **Amenities:** Bar; 2 outdoor freshwater pools; room service; Wi-Fi (5€ per hour, in lobby). *In room:* A/C, TV, hair dryer.

Hotel Viana Sol Residencial Behind a dignified granite-and-stucco facade, near a commemorative column and fountain in the town center, this well-designed hotel is 3 blocks south of Praça da República. In contrast to its elegantly severe exterior, its spacious public rooms are sheathed with white marble, capped with mirrored ceilings, and illuminated with a three-tiered atrium. The lobby bar is near a pagoda-shape fountain. The small to midsize guest rooms are sparsely furnished, and most don't have views.

Largo Vasco da Gama, 4900-322 Viana do Castelo. www.hotelvianasol.com. ☏ **25/882-89-95.** Fax 25/882-34-01. 65 units. 58€–75€ double. Rates include buffet breakfast. AE, DC, MC, V. Limited free parking on street. **Amenities:** Bar; exercise room; indoor heated pool; room service; sauna; outdoor tennis court (lit). *In room:* TV.

Where to Stay Nearby

The most romantic places to stay in and around Viana do Castelo are the antique *quintas.* In these restored manor houses, you can literally stay with the Portuguese aristocracy. You can make reservations through **Turismo de Habitação,** Praça da República, 4990-062 Ponte de Lima (☏ **25/874-16-72;** fax 25/874-14-44; www.solaresdeportugal.pt). You must send a check directly to the owners, with 50% prepayment required when your reservation is made. A minimum stay of 2 nights is required, and you must make reservations at least 3 days before arrival.

The Viana do Castelo area has some of the most elaborate and stylized *quintas* in Portugal. A random sampling follows.

Casa de Rodas ★ 👥 Constructed in typical *quinta* style, with a red-tile roof and stucco walls, this large guesthouse is between a wooded area and a farm that grows grapes for consumption in Santiago de Compostela. It's less than a kilometer (about ⅔ mile) from Monção, which is known for its *termas* (spa) treatments for rheumatism and respiratory ailments. Monção is 69km (43 miles) northeast of Viana do Castelo.

The house was built in the 16th century, destroyed by fire in 1658 during Portugal's battle for independence, and reconstructed soon afterward. Guest rooms come in a variety of shapes and sizes, but all are well maintained and traditionally furnished, with neatly kept bathrooms with shower stalls. The location along the border of Spain allows for day trips to the Spanish cities of Vigo and Santiago de Compostela, as well as the beach, about a 30-minute drive away.

4950-524 Monção. ☎ **25/165-21-05.** 10 units. 80€ double. Rates include continental breakfast. No credit cards. Free parking. **Amenities:** Outdoor pool. *In room:* No phone.

Quinta do Convento de Val de Pereiras This hotel occupies a 15-hectare (37-acre) site and has been famous since the Middle Ages for its freshwater springs. According to legend, St. Francis of Assisi, who performed many miracles here on his way to Santiago de Compostela, blessed them. In 1316, a stone building on the site functioned as a monastery. Some 200 years later, the monks were evicted, and a community of Franciscan nuns controlled the premises for another 300 years. Around 1890, everything except one of the towers of the original monastery was demolished, and a new Minho-style monastery, similar in design to a large manor house, was erected. It lies 1.8km (1 mile) from Ponte de Lima, across the Douro from the town center. Bedrooms are well furnished and maintained, each with a private bathroom. Don't expect any in-room amenities other than a phone. *Warning:* Always call to confirm a room before heading here because the inn is closed from time to time.

Lugar Val de Pereiras, 4990 Arcozelo, 4990-261 Ponte de Lima. ☎ **25/890-00-60.** Fax 25/890-00-69. 10 units. 77€ double; 100€ suite. Rates include buffet breakfast. No credit cards. Free parking. **Amenities:** Bar; outdoor pool; outdoor tennis court. *In room:* A/C, TV.

Where to Dine

A Ceia 🍴 PORTUGUESE This artfully rustic restaurant occupies a prime position in the heart of town. You enter through a prominent bar area, where you'll be tempted to linger with the many regulars who appreciate their wine and only rarely seem to want to rush to dinner. Portions are generous, and the food is flavored in traditional and time-tested (but not particularly innovative) ways. It seems universally popular among the extended families who sometimes conduct their once-a-week powwows at long connected tables. Menu items include steaming bowls of bean-and-meat stew, tripe, roast pork with clams, succulent roast goat, veal and beef dishes, and steaming bowls of such soups as *caldo verde* (made from greens and vegetables).

Rua do Raio 331. ☎ **25/326-39-32.** Reservations recommended Sat-Sun. Main courses 14€-20€. AE, MC, V. Tues-Sun noon-3pm and 7-10pm.

Os 3 Potes ★★ INTERNATIONAL/PORTUGUESE Off Praça da República, this restaurant was an old bakery before its conversion into one of the best regional dining rooms in Viana do Castelo. The atmosphere is rustic. On Saturday, folk dancing is featured and the place takes on a touristy feel. Fado music is featured every other Friday. Have someone at your hotel call for a reservation. We recommend *caldo verde* (a soup made from greens and vegetables) to begin, followed by such main dishes as codfish, lampreys (eels), or fondue bourguignon. The restaurant is somewhat hard to find but worth the search.

Beco dos Fornos 7-9. ☎ **25/882-99-28.** Reservations recommended in summer. Main courses 14€-23€. AE, DC, MC, V. Daily noon-3:30pm and 7-10:30pm. Closed Mon Oct-May. From Praça da República, take Rua de Sacadura Cabral.

Viana do Castelo After Dark

You won't lack for bars and cafes that serve alcohol and refreshments. If you're interested in music and energy, consider a visit to the town's most popular dance club: **Foz Café,** Praia do Cabedelo (☎ **25/833-24-85;** www.fozcaffe.com), open Tuesday to Sunday noon to 3pm and 7pm to 1am.

Upriver 213km (132 miles) from Viana do Castelo is **Ponte de Lima,** which is exactly what one hopes a Portuguese village will be like. Spread lazily along the tree-lined banks of the Lima River, it's named for the Roman bridge with 27 arches spanning the water. Jagged ramparts surround Ponte de Lima, and massive towers, narrow winding streets, and fortified doors decorate the houses.

The drive along the north side of the river takes you through grape arbors, pastoral villages, and forests of cedar, pine, and chestnut. Red-cheeked locals stand silhouetted against moss-green stone walls as they interrupt their toil in the cabbage fields to watch you pass by. We've never recommended cabbages as a sightseeing attraction, but they are here. Jade green and monstrous, they grow to wild heights of 2m (6½ ft.). They're most often used to make *caldo verde,* the fabled regional soup.

The town, founded on the site of a Celtic settlement, was developed by the Romans, who named it Forum Limicorum. It was important for both river trade and river defense. Thick stone walls still enclose the town, guarding the bridge across the Lima; though the Roman wall has been partially destroyed to make room for roads, you can walk along the top of what's left. Part of the Roman bridge is still in use, too. It has a buttressed extension, made under King Dom Pedro in 1355 because of changes in the river's course.

An 18th-century fountain graces the town's main square, and houses of that era are still occupied. Ruins of ramparts from the Middle Ages and a solitary keep can be seen, opposite the old bridge. Go up the stone steps of the keep to visit the **Biblioteca Pública Municipal,** founded in the early 18th century. Its archives are rich in historic documents.

The Ponte de Lima **market,** held on alternate Mondays, is known throughout Portugal. Its sellers show up in regional costumes. On the north side of the bridge is the cattle market where oxen and steers are sold; little bags are nestled between the horns of the animals, containing a "magic potion" said to ward off the evil eye. Below the bridge is a place reserved for eating such alfresco delights as roast sardines, accompanied by glasses of *vinho verde* (green wine). If you take a walk along the riverside, you can survey the stalls of various craftspeople, including cobblers, carpenters, and goldsmiths. Sometimes you'll see women wringing out their clothes along the riverbanks. At certain times of the year, the Lima is likely to be dry, but when it's full, anglers often catch trout here.

Ponte de Lima has a collection of beautiful antique properties, ranging from farms to manor houses—often, a stay at one of these unique accommodations is reason enough to visit the town. There are about 60 such properties in the region. Information about them is available through **Turismo de Habitação,** 4990-062 Ponte de Lima (📞 **25/874-16-72;** fax 25/874-14-44; www.solaresdeportugal.pt).

Another stellar property is the **Paço de Calheiros,** Calheiros, 4990-575 Ponte de Lima (📞 **25/894-71-64;** fax 25/894-72-94; www.pacodecalheiros.com). Perched on a hill overlooking the town, it's the best-known *solar* (country villa) in Ponte. The nine doubles and three apartments in converted stables go for 125€. Breakfast and parking are included. A first-rate dinner can be arranged on request. The *solar* has lush gardens and a pool.

Back in Ponte de Lima, you can dine at **Encanada,** Mercado Municipal 7 (📞 **25/894-11-89**), which serves the best regional cookery around. Try the special fried pork or homemade fish cakes. Eels with rice is a local specialty, but it's available only in winter. Meals are served Friday through Wednesday from noon to 3pm and 7 to 10:30pm; prices start at 13€.

VILA REAL

399km (248 miles) NE of Lisbon; 113km (70 miles) E of Porto

The capital of Trás-os-Montes is a lively little town built on a hilly plateau in the foothills of the Serra do Marão. Bridges across the ravines link some parts of town. Gorges cut by the Corgo and Cabril rivers, which flow together here, are visible from a terrace high above, where a castle once stood. You can reach the lookout by following a direct line from the cemetery. From this vicinity, you can also see houses overhanging the ravine of the Corgo.

You can spend a worthy 2 hours or so wandering through Vila Real's historic core and enjoy a glass of port in one of the cafes, which brim with youthful energy. The main sights and buildings of interest are along the Avenida Carvalho Araújo.

The agricultural town makes a good base for many beautiful trips into the area, including the **Parque Nacional do Alvão** to the northwest, with its waterfalls, flower-filled valleys, and ravines. The tourist office provides maps and suggests places to visit. To drive to the park, follow the IP-4 west for 10km (6¼ miles), turning onto N304 heading for Mondim de Bastro and Campeã. This stretch takes you through some of the most scenic areas of Trás-os-Montes—once you've passed through the dreary modern suburbs of Vila Real, which are in marked contrast to the mellow historic core.

Essentials

ARRIVING

BY TRAIN   There is no rail service.

BY BUS   Buses from Porto take only 1½ hours. Seven buses make the run each day, and the one-way fare is 8€. Eight buses a day make the 5-hour-and-50-minute trip from Lisbon. The cost is 19€ one-way. For information and schedules, call ✆ **25/932-26-74.**

BY CAR   From Porto, continue east along the express route, A4, following signs to Amarante, where you continue east along N15 into Vila Real.

VISITOR INFORMATION

The **Vila Real tourist office** is at Av. Carvalho Araújo 94 (✆ **25/932-28-19;** www. cm-vilareal.pt). It's open daily 9:30am to 12:30pm and 2 to 6pm.

What to See & Do in Vila Real

EXPLORING THE TOWN   You won't be dazzled by "must-see" monuments, although the historic core as a whole makes for an interesting walk. Vila Real is called a Royal Town because it contains many formerly aristocratic houses dating from the 16th to the 18th centuries. It's fun to poke your nose down the tiny offshoot streets, hoping to make discoveries. The main monuments are concentrated in and around Avenida Carvalho Araújo.

Chief among these is the **Capela Nova (New Chapel),** sometimes called the Capela dos Clérigos (Chapel of the Clergy) by the locals. It is the finest baroque monument in Vila Real. The architecture, with a floral facade, might have been the work of Nicolau Nasoni, the 18th-century master. The chapel lies 2 blocks east of the cathedral, Rua dos Combatentes da Grande Guerra, between Rua Direita and Rua 31 de Janeiro. It is open daily 10am to noon and 2 to 6pm. Admission is free.

Farther north is **Igreja São Pedro (St. Peter's Church),** at Largo de São Pedro, just off the main street. From 1528, though much altered over the ages, this church has an intriguing interior, with much baroque gilt carving and a chancel adorned with colorful tiles. Its main attraction, and reason enough for a visit, is the coffered ceiling of carved and gilded wood. It is open daily 8am to 8pm. Admission is free.

The **Câmara Municipal (Town Hall),** Avenida Carvalho Araújo (✆ **25/930-81-00**), also merits a look. It has an Italian Renaissance-style stone staircase constructed in the early 1800s. In front is a lantern pillory. It is open Monday to Friday 9am to 5:30pm. Admission is free.

Although it's not open to the public, you can stop to admire the **Casa de Diogo Cão,** Av. Carvalho Araújo 19. This is the reputed birthplace of the navigator who discovered the Congo River in 1482. The exterior of the house was altered, and it now reflects 16th-century Renaissance style. Although the explorer visited the legendary King Manicongo, and the powerful monarch reportedly was baptized as a Christian, little is known about Cão. Dom João II concealed all records in the Torre do Tombo in Lisbon to keep the discoveries from the Castilians. The earthquake of 1755 destroyed the archives.

The greatest attraction in the area lies not in Vila Real, but 4km (2½ miles) east of the city, on the N322 highway signposted to Sabrosa. The grapes of the original Mateus rosé wine were grown in vineyards here, and it is also home to the **Casa de Mateus ★★**—a perfect example of baroque architecture, with a stunning **facade ★★** preceded by a "mirror" of water. This is the building pictured on the Mateus wine label. Dating from the first half of the 18th century, the main section of the manor house has a stunning balustraded staircase and a high-emblazoned pediment surrounded by allegorical statues. Sacheverell Sitwell called it "the most typical and the most fantastic country home in Portugal." The twin wings of the manor advance "lobsterlike," in Sitwell's words.

An ornamental stone balustrade guards the main courtyard, and lovely pinnacles crown the roof cornices. The architect is unknown, although some authorities claim it was the work of Nicolau Nasoni, who might have designed the Capela Nova (see above).

The manor house and the gardens are open for tours (✆ **25/932-31-21;** www. casademateus.com). The house contains heavy silk hangings, high wooden ceilings, paintings of bucolic scenes, and a tiny museum. You'll see vestments, Sèvres vases, and an 1817 edition of the Portuguese classic *The Lusiads,* printed in Paris. The **gardens ★★** are among the most beautiful in Europe, with a tunnel of cypress trees shading the path.

Casa de Mateus is open June to September daily 9am to 7:30pm; October, March, April, and May daily 9am to 1pm and 2 to 6pm; November to February 10am to 1pm and 2 to 5pm. A full guided tour costs 7€ per person. It's 4.50€ just to tour the gardens.

SHOPPING   If you happen to be in Vila Real on June 28 and 29, you can purchase some of the region's fine black pottery, which is sold at St. Peter's Fair. At other times, you can find the pottery, made in the surrounding countryside, at little shops throughout the historic district. Many visitors also come here just to buy Mateus sparkling rosé wine (see above).

Where to Stay

Hotel Miracorgo ★   This is the city's best choice for lodging. It's in the commercial section, which makes it popular with businesspeople, but it has an impersonal aura. The hotel spreads across two buildings—one has five floors, and the other has 12 floors. The sterile quality recedes somewhat when you enter the midsize accommodations, most of which open onto views of a scenic valley. All are comfortably furnished, with well-maintained bathrooms.

Av. 1 de Maio 78, 5000-651 Vila Real. www.hotelmiracorgo.com.sapo.pt. © **25/932-50-01.** Fax 25/932-50-06. 166 units. 71€ double; 98€ suite. Rates include buffet breakfast. AE, DC, MC, V. Free parking. **Amenities:** Restaurant; bar; indoor heated pool; room service. *In room:* A/C, TV, hair dryer, minibar.

Pousada de Alijó, Barão de Forrester ★★ 👜   Our favorite retreat in Trás-os-Montes lies in the village of Alijó, some 29km (18 miles) southeast of the center of Vila Real; it's a lovely stop for motorists who don't mind the short drive. The inn takes its name from the Scotsman Baron Forrester, who in the 19th century plotted a map of the Douro River, opening it up to navigation. In time, the Forrester family became wealthy port vintners. The location of this retreat is in the heart of the Douro Wine Region, an area famous for its *quintas* (manor houses) surrounded by port-wine vineyards that grow on terraces. The hotel staff can arrange cruises on the Douro for guests. The inn is decorated in a warm traditional style, with beautifully maintained and comfortable bedrooms along with tidily organized bathrooms. The excellent on-site restaurant opens onto two terraces with views of the countryside, and on a chilly night you can retreat with a glass of port to a cozy nook in front of the fireplace.

Rua José Rufino, 5070-031 Alijó. www.pousadas.pt. © **25/995-94-67.** Fax 25/995-93-04. 21 units. 90€–180€ double. Rates include buffet breakfast. AE, DC, MC, V. Free parking. **Amenities:** Restaurant; bar; outdoor pool; room service; outdoor tennis court (lit). *In room:* A/C, TV, hair dryer, minibar, Wi-Fi (12€ per 24 hr.).

Where to Dine

Restaurante Espadeiro ★ PORTUGUESE   This is the finest independent restaurant in Vila Real. The name, which means "the swordsman," honors a brave Tramontane warrior, Lourenço Viegas. You'll need to climb a flight of stairs to enter the modern, rustically decorated restaurant, which has a large, sunny terrace, a bar with a panoramic view, and a dining room with a fireplace. The chefs are rightly proud of their region and its foods. One delicious specialty is trout stuffed with Parma-style ham; seafood rice is another. If you are leery of the meat byproducts used in the *feijoada* (bean stew), you can always opt for baked ham instead. Some dishes—including stewed tripe and roast kid—are fiercely regional and only for the adventurous palate.

Av. Almeida Lucena. © **25/932-23-02.** www.restauranteoespadeiro.com. Reservations recommended. Main courses 11€–23€. AE, MC, V. Tues–Sun noon–3pm and 7–10pm. Closed 2 weeks in Oct or Nov.

BRAGANÇA ★

139km (86 miles) NE of Vila Real; 522km (324 miles) NE of Lisbon

Bragança (Braganza in English) is the best-preserved medieval town in Portugal. It was under the aegis of the House of Bragança, which ruled Portugal from 1640 until its overthrow early in the 20th century. On a hilltop, a long, fortified wall still surrounds the medieval town, which overlooks the modern town in the northeastern reaches of the country on a rise of ground in the Serra da Nogueira, some 600m (1,969 ft.) above sea level.

Essentials

ARRIVING

BY TRAIN   There is no direct train service here. The nearest station is in the town of Mirandela, which is connected by bus to Bragança. For information and schedules, call ℂ **80/820-82-08.**

BY BUS   Rede Expressos (ℂ **27/330-01-083;** www.rede-expressos.pt) runs 6 buses a day from Porto to Bragança. The trip takes 3 hours and 30 minutes and costs 13€ one-way. The same company runs seven buses a day from Lisbon. The journey takes 7 hours and costs 19€ one-way.

BY CAR   From Vila Real, continue northeast on E82.

VISITOR INFORMATION

The **tourist office** is at Avenida Cidade de Zamora (ℂ **27/338-12-73;** www.cm-braganca.pt). In winter, it's open Monday to Friday 9am to 12:30pm and 2 to 5pm, Saturday 10am to 12:30pm; in summer, hours are Monday to Friday 10am to 12:30pm and 2 to 6:30pm, Saturday 9am to 12:30pm and 2 to 5pm, and Sunday 9am to 1pm.

What to See & Do in Bragança

EXPLORING THE TOWN   Bragança lies at the edge of the **Parque Natural de Montesinho (Montesinho Natural Park),** one of the wildest regions on the Continent. A walled citadel, or castle, on a hilltop crowns the town of Bragança. The **Upper Town** ★ grew up around this brooding old castle. In a small public garden within the citadel stands a Gothic pillory. A medieval shaft has been driven through the stone effigy of a boar, which has a depression carved in its snout. The boar is believed to date from the Iron Age, and it's possible that it was used in ancient pagan rituals.

A **Cidadela** (sometimes called O Castelo) dates from the 12th century. Dom João I reconstructed it in the 14th century. The heyday of this castle came under the fiefdom of the dukes of Bragança, the ruling family of Portugal from 1640 until the monarchy collapsed in 1910. The Upper Town was also a major silk center in the 1400s—in part because of a prosperous Jewish merchant community. The Inquisition dispersed most of the merchants. The citadel's tall, square keep, Torre de Menagem, today contains the **Museu Militar** (ℂ **27/332-23-78**), with displays that range from medieval suits of armor to a World War I machine gun used in trench warfare. Other exhibits display collections of African art, some from Angola, gathered by Portuguese soldiers. The museum is open Tuesday to Sunday 9am to noon and 2 to 5pm. Admission is 2€ for adults and free for children under 10.

Beside the castle, you can look at the **Torre da Princesa (Princess Tower).** Here the fourth duke of Bragança imprisoned his wife, Dona Leonor. She was said to be so beautiful that he didn't want other men to look at her. However, when he moved his court to Lisbon, he murdered her.

Also part of the castle complex in the Upper Town, the **Domus Municipalis (Town Hall)**—built over a cistern—dates from the 12th century. It is one of the few remaining Romanesque civic buildings in the country. The interior is a cavernous room lit by little round arches. It's open daily 9am to noon and 2 to 5pm. Admission is free.

A final building of note is the 16th-century **Igreja da Santa Maria** (**St. Mary's Church;** no phone). The interior is distinguished by a barrel-vaulted painted ceiling from the 18th century. The painting depicts the Assumption of the Virgin in many colors. Solomonic (twisted) columns frame the front door. Hours are daily 9am to noon and 2 to 5pm.

The citadel and Upper Town are the reasons to go to Bragança. If time remains, you can also explore the Lower Town, with its major boulevard and (in the summer) sidewalk cafes.

Museu Abade de Baçal, Rua Abílio Beça 27 (© **27/333-15-95;** www.ipmu-seus.pt), occupies a former bishop's palace. A local priest, Francisco Manuel Alves (1865–1947), created this bizarre assemblage. He collected everything from Iron Age depictions of pigs to ancient tombstones. He also collected antiques, ceramics, folkloric costumes, old coins, regional paintings, silver, archaeological artifacts—virtually anything that caught his eye, including church plates and vestments. The museum is open Tuesday to Friday 10am to 5pm and Saturday and Sunday 10am to 6pm. Admission is 2€.

After exploring Bragança, visit the **Parque Natural de Montesinho ★★.** (You can pick up a map at the tourist office; see above.) This forbidding but beautiful land of towering mountains and high plateaus stretches northwest and northeast of Bragança. Here you'll discover some of the most rugged—certainly the wildest—land in the country. It is still home to wolves, wild boars, and foxes, among other animals. In the little villages you'll see as you drive through the vast land, life is lived nearly the way it was a century ago, although modern intrusions have occurred.

At least until the outbreak of World War II, many pre-Christian rituals were still practiced here. The area stretches over 467 sq. km (180 sq. miles). In all, fewer than 9,000 people live in fewer than 100 villages. This is one of the best places in Portugal for trekking along well-worn mountain paths, most of which date from the fall of the Visigothic empire. Sometimes you can spot an endangered bird such as the black stork. Because trails are unmarked, the tourist office provides brochures, useful maps, and advice.

SHOPPING   Head for the shops around **Largo da Sé** (sometimes called Praça da Sé), the cathedral precinct, for local handicrafts. You'll find locally produced copper and leather goods, plus woven fabrics. The shops also carry ceramics from the surrounding area. Many similar shops also lie within the walls of the citadel.

Where to Stay

Hotel Turismo São Lázaro ★   This is the second-best place to stay in town, ranking under the pousada (see below). Modern and functional, it is short on style but fine on comfort. Bedrooms are of a good size, tastefully decorated, and comfortably furnished with sleek, modern tiled bathrooms. If you don't want to go out at night, you can dine on regional specialties at the on-site restaurant.

Av. Cidade de Zamora-Nordeste, 5300-111 Bragança. www.hoteis-arco.com. © **27/330-27-00.** Fax 27/330-27-01. 272 units. 81€ double; 122€ suite. AE, MC, V. Free parking. **Amenities:** Restaurant; bar; babysitting; concierge; room service; outdoor tennis court (lit); Wi-Fi (in lobby; 2.50€ per half-hour). *In room:* A/C, TV, hair dryer.

HR Residencial Classis   Although its accommodations fall far short of the more luxurious ones in the pousada (see below), this little hotel is reliable, inexpensive, well run, and immaculately kept. And because other local hotels might be fully booked in the summer, the HR Residencial Classis is worth considering—you'll still sleep well here. The midsize guest rooms are comfortably furnished, with well-maintained bathrooms. The hotel is convenient to the train and bus stations.

Av. João da Cruz 102, 5300-178 Bragança. www.bragancanet.pt/braganca/classis. © **27/333-16-31.** Fax 27/332-34-58. 20 units. 40€–48€ double. Rates include buffet breakfast. AE, DC, MC, V. Limited free parking on street. **Amenities:** Bar; room service. *In room:* A/C, TV, minibar.

Pousada de Bragança, São Bartolomeu ★★   On the heights of the Serra da Nogueira, with a panoramic view of the 12th-century castle of Bragança, this is the best place to stay in the area. The fairly spacious guest rooms are well furnished and maintained, with private balconies and neatly kept bathrooms.

The pousada makes an ideal stop for travelers entering the country from Spain at Alcanices-Quintanilha, about a 30-minute drive away. The view at night is the most spectacular in Bragança, taking in the crenellated fortifications of the old city. Guests enjoy the rustically decorated public rooms, especially the one with an open fireplace. The international and regional cuisine is the best in the area.

Estrada de Turismo, 5300-271 Bragança. www.pousadas.pt. © **27/333-14-93.** Fax 27/332-34-53. 28 units. 90€–175€ double. Rates include buffet breakfast. AE, DC, MC, V. Free parking. **Amenities:** Restaurant; bar; outdoor pool; room service. *In room:* A/C, TV, hair dryer, minibar, Wi-Fi (in some; 12€ per 24 hr.).

Where to Dine

La Em Casa ⚑ TRADITIONAL PORTUGUESE   With pine-paneled walls and a rustic atmosphere, this modern, airy restaurant is one of the town's most consistently reliable. In the center of the city, it attracts the rare foreign visitor but has a devoted local following. Diners are drawn by the kitchen's deft handling of local produce and fresh seafood. The rack or leg of lamb is aromatic and tender, and veal is served in the typical style of the province, grilled with potatoes and flavored with a sauce made with fresh garlic and vinegar. Octopus also appears on the menu, coated in egg batter and sautéed golden brown. Sometimes fado performances are staged here.

Rua Marquês de Pombal 7. © **27/332-21-11.** Reservations required. Main courses 10€–18€. AE, DC, MC, V. Daily 12:30–3pm and 7:30–11:30pm.

Pousada de Bragança, São Bartolomeu ★ INTERNATIONAL/PORTUGUESE   Though it might lack the local flavor of the town's various taverns, this is the most refined place to dine in the area, with many chefs who have worked in Continental kitchens. Dishes are perfectly prepared and filled with robust country flavor. Among the favorites are stewed rabbit with peppers, grilled trout with smoked ham, and a particularly excellent spit-roasted veal with small baked potatoes. Good starters include the French bean salad with fresh tuna fish or a codfish salad; the fish is served with fresh chopped onions and vine-ripened tomatoes. Every day a selection of fresh pastries appears on the "sweets buffet."

Estrada de Turismo. © **27/333-14-93.** Main courses 15€–22€. AE, DC, MC, V. Daily 12:30–3pm and 7:30–10pm.

Solar Bragançano ★★ PORTUGUESE   In a 3-centuries-old house on the main square of town, this old-fashioned restaurant is our all-time favorite in the area. It serves the best, most flavor-filled regional dishes. You'll get a true taste of Trás-os-Montes here and will likely have a good time, too. A tiled stairway leads to a formal dining room decorated in a typical style, with hand-woven regional rugs, chandeliers, and wood ceilings. You can also dine in an inside garden. The chef's local specialties include game dishes in autumn—perhaps pheasant with chestnuts or hare with rice. Spicy game sausages are another exciting choice, as is white Montesinho kid, perfectly roasted. You might conclude your meal with regional goat cheese; discerning locals do, and we always follow their example.

Praça da Sé (Largo da Sé). *©* **27/332-38-75.** Reservations recommended. Main courses 12€–26€. AE, DC, MC, V. Daily noon–3pm and 7–11pm.

MADEIRA & PORTO SANTO

The island of Madeira ★★★, 850km (528 miles) south-west of Portugal, is the mountain peak of an enormous volcanic mass. The island's craggy spires and precipices of umber-dark basalt end with a sheer drop into the blue water of the Atlantic Ocean, which is so deep near Madeira that large sperm whales often come close to the shore. If you stand on the sea-swept balcony of Cabo Girão, one of the world's highest ocean cliffs (590m/1,936 ft. above sea level), you'll easily realize the island's Edenlike quality, which inspired Luís Vaz de Camões, the Portuguese national poet, to say Madeira lies "at the end of the world."

The summit of the mostly undersea mountain is at Madeira's center, where **Pico Ruivo,** often snowcapped, rises to an altitude of 1,860m (6,102 ft.) above sea level. It is from this mountain peak that a series of deep, rock-strewn ravines cuts through the countryside and projects all the way to the edge of the sea. The island of Madeira is only 56km (35 miles) long and about 21km (13 miles) across at its widest point. It has nearly 160km (99 miles) of coastline, but no beaches. In Madeira's volcanic soil, plants and flowers blaze like creations from Gauguin's Tahitian palette. With jacaranda, masses of bougainvillea, orchids, geraniums, whortleberry, prickly pear, poinsettias, cannas, frangipani, birds of paradise, and wisteria, the land is a veritable botanical garden. Custard apples, avocados, mangoes, and bananas grow profusely throughout the island. Fragrances such as vanilla and wild fennel mingle with sea breezes and permeate the ravines that sweep down the rocky headlands.

In 1419, João Gonçalves Zarco and Tristão Vaz Teixeira of Portugal discovered Madeira after being diverted by a storm while exploring the west coast of Africa, some 564km (350 miles) east. Because the island was densely covered with impenetrable virgin forests, they named it Madeira (wood). Soon it was set afire to clear it for habitation. The blaze is said to have lasted 7 years, until all but a small northern section was reduced to ashes. Today the hillsides are so richly cultivated that you'd never know there had been such extensive fires. Many of the island's groves and vineyards, protected by buffers of sugar cane, grow on stone-wall ledges next to the cliff's edge. Carrying water from mountain springs, a complex network of man-made *levadas* (water channels) irrigates these terraced mountain slopes.

The uncovered *levadas*, originally constructed of stone by slaves and convicts (beginning at the time of the earliest colonization and slowly growing into a huge network), are most often .3 to .6m (1–2 ft.) wide and deep. By the turn of the 20th century, the network stretched for 1,000km (621 miles). In the past century, however, the network has grown to some 2,140km (1,330 miles), of which about 40km (25 miles) are covered tunnels dug into the mountains.

Madeira is both an island and the name of the autonomous archipelago to which it belongs. The island of Madeira has the largest landmass of the archipelago, some 460 sq. km (178 sq. miles). The only other inhabited island in the Madeira archipelago is **Porto Santo** ★ (about 26 sq. km/10 sq. miles), 40km (25 miles) to the northeast of the main island of Madeira. *Réalités* magazine called Porto Santo "another world, arid, desolate, and waterless." Unlike Madeira, Porto Santo has beaches and has built several hotels.

A series of other islands populate the archipelago, including the appropriately named *Ilhas Desertas,* or the Empty Islands, 19km (12 miles) southeast of Funchal (the capital of the island of Madeira), and even more remote islands, called *Selvagens,* or Wild Isles, lie near the Canary Islands and are a possession of Spain. None of these is inhabited.

Madeira can be a destination unto itself, and, in fact, many Britons fly here directly, avoiding Portugal altogether. Most North Americans, however, tie in a visit to Madeira with trips to Lisbon. It isn't really suited for a day trip from Lisbon—the island deserves a minimum of 3 days, if you can afford that much.

MADEIRA ESSENTIALS

853km (530 miles) SW of Portugal; 564km (350 miles) W of the African coastline

Essentials

ARRIVING

The quickest and most convenient way to reach Madeira from Lisbon is on a 90-minute **TAP** flight. The daily flights (9–13, depending on the season) stop at the Madeira airport then go on to Porto Santo.

Getting to Madeira's capital, Funchal, is easier and cheaper than you might think, especially if you fly aboard any TAP plane into Lisbon from anywhere outside of Portugal and then connect with a TAP commuter flight from Lisbon to Funchal. If you fly business class into Lisbon from virtually anywhere within TAP's overseas network (including flights to Portugal that originate in both the New York area and London), no additional funds are charged for passengers continuing on to Madeira. If you're flying coach class, however, with even the cheapest of APEX deals, the supplement you'll pay for the final round-trip leg into Funchal will rarely exceed $100 and, in many cases, might not even exceed $50. If you're going to Madeira, your best bet is to book all legs of your trip to Portugal as part of the same ticketing process.

In addition, TAP has five direct flights daily, and British Airways flies nonstop (Mon, Wed, Fri, and Sat) from London to Funchal. Trip time is 4 hours.

In Madeira, planes arrive at **Aeroporto de Madeira** (✆ 29/152-07-00; www. aeroportosdamadeira.pt), east of Funchal, at Santa Cruz. **Taxis** into Funchal's center can take from 15 to 20 minutes and cost 25€ for a typical fare. However, the taxis that wait at the airport take airline passengers anywhere they want to go on the island. If you're going to Funchal or from Funchal back to the airport, you can also take a **bus,** run by the Sociedad de Automobiles de Madeira (✆ 29/120-11-50; www.sam. pt), which can take from 40 minutes to 1 hour (depending on the number of stops)

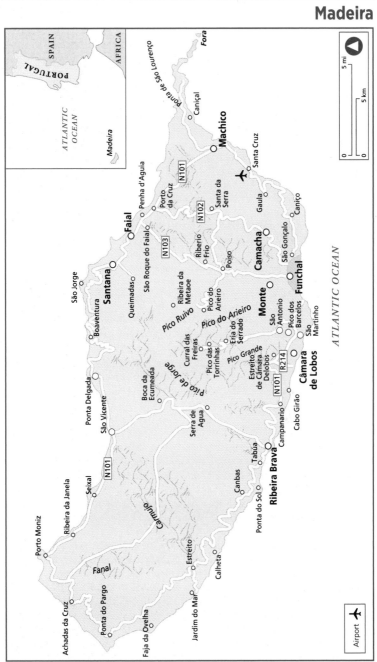

FROMMER'S favorite MADEIRA EXPERIENCES

Riding a Toboggan. Madeira's most fabled activity is taking a **carro de cesto** ride in a wicker-sided sled from the high-altitude suburb of Monte to Funchal. Two drivers run alongside the sled to control it as it careens across slippery cobblestones. It's a great joy ride that lasts 20 minutes.

Escaping to the Golden Beaches of Porto Santo. Pirates of the Atlantic once romped on the 6.5km (4 miles) of beaches in this relatively forgotten part of the world.

Spending a Morning at the Mercado dos Lavradores (Market of the Workers). Go early—between 7 and 8am, at the latest—to see this market come alive. Flower vendors, fishers, and local terrace farmers sell an array of local wares (produce, fish, clothing, flowers, baskets, ceramics, prepared food, crafts) not seen anywhere else in Madeira. Check out the fish, everything from tuna to eel, that you'll be served later in local restaurants. It's open Monday to Saturday 7am to 8pm.

Tasting the Local Wines. Go to any *taverna* (tavern) on the island and acquaint yourself with the array of local wines, all fortified with grape brandy. Before you leave the island, be sure to sample all the different selections: the world-renowned, light-colored **Sercial,** the driest of the Madeira wines; the golden-hued, slightly sweeter **Verdelho;** the decidedly sweet **Boal,** a dessert wine that's good with cheese; and the sweetest: rich, fragrant **Malmsey,** which is served with dessert.

Attending the End of the Year Festival. The most exciting (and most crowded) time to visit Funchal is during this festival, December 30 to January 1, when live music, food stalls, dancing, costumes, and parades fill the streets. At night, fireworks light up the bay, with the mountains in the background forming an amphitheater.

and costs only 5€ one-way. These buses run as needed and are timed to meet incoming and outgoing flights. They stop at three or four places in the town center as the need arises because there is no central bus station.

VISITOR INFORMATION

An English-speaking staff runs the desk at the **Madeira Tourist Office,** Av. Arriaga 16 (© **29/121-19-00;** www.turismomadeira.pt), in Funchal. It's open Monday to Friday 9am to 7pm, and Saturday and Sunday 9am to 3pm. The office distributes maps of the island, and the staff will make suggestions about the best ways to explore the beautiful landscape. They also have information about ferry connections to the neighboring island of Porto Santo.

TAP has an office in Funchal at Av. das Comunidades Madeirenses 8–10 (© **70/720-57-00** or 29/123-92-11). It's open Monday to Saturday 9am to 6pm.

Island Layout

The capital of Madeira, **Funchal,** is the focal point of the island and the gateway to its outlying villages. When Zarco landed in 1419, the sweet odor of wild fennel led him to name the town after the aromatic herb (*funcho* in Portuguese). Today this southern coastal city of hillside villas and narrow winding streets is the island's most luxuriant area, filled with fertile fields, hundreds of flowering gardens, and numerous exotic estates.

A long, often traffic-clogged street, **Avenida do Mar,** runs east-west along the waterfront. North of this is **Avenida Arriaga,** the "main street" of Funchal. At the eastern end of this thoroughfare is the Sé (cathedral), and at the western end is a large traffic circle that surrounds a fountain. As Avenida Arriaga, site of several hotels, heads west, it changes its name to **Avenida do Infante.** As it runs east, it becomes **Rua do Aljube.** Running north-south, the other important street, **Avenida Zarco,** links the waterfront area with the heart of the old city.

To explore and savor Madeira, adventurous visitors (definitely not for the queasy), with time to spend, go on foot across some of the trails strewn around the island. Hand-hewn stones and gravel-sided embankments lead you along precipitous ledges, down into lush ravines, and across flowering meadows. These dizzying paths are everywhere, from the hillsides of the wine-rich region of Estreito de Câmara de Lobos to the wicker-work center of Camacha. A much easier way to go, of course, is on an organized tour or on local buses, or you can rent a car and risk the hazardous driving on hairpin curves.

If you'd like to take a circular tour of the entire island, you can take N101 either east or west of Funchal, which traverses the coast of the entire island. Heading west from Funchal, you'll pass women doing their laundry on rocks, homes so tiny that they're almost like dollhouses, and banana groves growing right to the edge of the cliffs that overlook the sea. Less than 10km (6¼ miles) away is the coastal village of **Câmara de Lobos (Room of the Wolves),** the subject of several paintings by Sir Winston Churchill. A sheltered, tranquil cove, it's set amid rocks and towering cliffs, with hillside cottages, terraces, and date palms. The road north from Câmara de Lobos, through vineyards, leads to **Estreito de Câmara de Lobos** (popularly known as Estreito), the heart of the winegrowing region that produces Madeira's wine. Along the way you'll spot women sitting on mossy stone steps doing embroidery, and men wearing brown stocking caps with tasseled tops as they cultivate the ribbonlike terraces. (Incidentally, the islanders' blond locks were inherited from early Flemish settlers.)

Lying 16km (10 miles) west of Câmara de Lobos, **Cabo Girão** is one of the highest ocean-side cliffs in the world. You can stand here watching the sea crash 580m (1,903 ft.) below while also taking in a panoramic sweep of the Bay of Funchal.

From **Cabo Girão,** return to Funchal by veering off the coastal road past São Martinho to the belvedere at **Pico Dos Barcelos.** In one of the most idyllic spots on the island, you can see the ocean, mountains, orange and banana groves, bougainvillea, and poinsettias, as well as the capital.

By heading north from Funchal, you can visit some outstanding spots in the heart of the island. Past São António is **Curral das Freiras,** a village huddled around an old monastery at the bottom of an extinct volcanic crater. The site, whose name means Corral of the Nuns, was originally a secluded convent that protected the nuns from sea-weary, woman-hungry mariners and pirates.

If you go north in a different direction, one destination to visit is **Santana,** which many visitors have described as something out of Disney's *Fantasia*. Picture an alpine setting with waterfalls, cobblestone streets, green meadows sprinkled with multicolored blossoms, thatched cottages, swarms of roses, and plunging ravines. The novelist Paul Bowles wrote, "It is as if a 19th-century painter with a taste for the baroque had invented a countryside to suit his own personal fantasy."

Southwest of Santana, is **Queimadas,** rising to an altitude of 900 meters (2,953 ft.). From here, many people make the 3-hour trek to the apex of **Pico Ruivo**

(Purple Peak), the highest point on the island, 1,860m (6,102 ft.) above sea level. This is a difficult, long, hot climb and is recommended only for the hearty and those with no fear of heights. The best access to Pico Ruivo is from Pico do Arieiro (see "Pico do Arieiro," later) because the trail from there is the most scenic.

Southeast of Santana, heading for Faial, a colorful hamlet with tiny A-frame huts, the road descends in a series of sharp turns into a deep ravine. The lush terraces here are built for cows to graze on, not for produce.

In the east, about 30km (19 miles) from Funchal, is historic Machico, where Portuguese explorers first landed on Madeira. The town is now visited mainly because of the legend of "the lovers of Machico," an English couple who were running away to get married but whose ship is said to have sank here in 1346. In the main square of the town stands a Manueline church constructed at the end of the 15th century, supposedly over the tomb of the ill-fated pair. The facade contains a beautiful rose window. In the interior are white marble columns and a frescoed ceiling over the nave. Try to view the village from the belvedere of **Camões Pequeno.** You can walk uphill to the belvedere by following a signpost in the center of Machico.

On the way back from Machico, you can detour inland to the village of **Camacha,** perched in a setting of flowers and orchards. It's the island center of the wickerwork industry. You can shop here or just watch local craftspeople making chairs and other items. You'll find that though the stores in Funchal are amply supplied, some items are as much as 20% cheaper in Camacha.

GETTING AROUND MADEIRA

Remember that distances are short on Madeira, but you should allow plenty of time to cover them because of the winding roads.

BY BUS   The cheapest, albeit slowest, way to get around Madeira is by bus. If you want to tour on your own, you can make excursions on local buses that go all over the island at a fraction of the cost the tour companies charge, but you will miss the commentary of an organized tour, of course. A typical fare in Funchal is 1.15€ to 2.10€; rides in the countryside can cost 5€. Sometimes only one bus a day runs to the most distant points. Some of the rides into the mountains can be quite bouncy and uncomfortable. There is no bus station in Funchal, but you can buy tickets for anywhere on the island at any of the newsstands in the center of Funchal. For information about schedules, call © **29/170-55-55.**

Most buses depart from the large park at the eastern part of the Funchal waterfront bordering Avenida do Mar. Buses to Camacha or Caniço leave from a little square at the eastern sector of Rua da Alfândega, which runs parallel to Avenida do Mar near the marketplace.

BY TAXI   The going taxi rate is about 90€ per day, but three or four passengers can divide the cost. Always negotiate (many taxi drivers speak English) and agree on the rate in advance. Most taxis are Peugeots or Mercedes, so you'll ride in relative safety and comfort and won't have to worry about navigating the nightmarish roads. If you're in Funchal, you'll usually find a line of taxis across from the tourist office along Avenida Arriaga.

BY CAR   Unless you're a skilled driver used to narrow roads, reckless drivers, and hairpin turns, you should not rent a car on the island. If you need to, however, most hotels can make arrangements for car rentals.

Avis (© 800/331-1212 in the U.S.; www.avis.com) has offices at the Aeroporto da Madeira, in Santa Cruz (© 29/152-43-82), and in Funchal, at Largo António Nobre 164 (© 29/176-45-46). **Hertz** (© 800/654-3001 in the U.S.; www.hertz.com) has a kiosk at Aeroporto da Madeira, in Santa Cruz (© 29/152-30-40). **Budget Rent-a-Car** (© 800/527-0700 in the U.S.; www.budget.com) has an outlet at Estrada Monumental 182 (© 96/857-47-98). You can also rent vehicles at **Europcar,** Aeroporto da Madeira (© 29/152-46-33; www.europecar.com).

ORGANIZED TOURS   If you don't care to venture out on your own, you can take one of the many organized bus tours that cruise through the valleys and along the coast of Madeira. You can arrange to be picked up at your hotel or at the tourist office; if you're staying at a hotel outside of Funchal you usually must pay a small surcharge to be picked up. For more information, contact the tourist office (see "Essentials," above) or **Intertours,** Av. Arriaga 30, 3rd Floor (© **29/120-89-00;** www.intertours. com.pt), in Funchal.

The most popular excursion is Intertours' **full-day western island tour** that incorporates virtually every accessible point on Madeira, including the island's remote northwestern tip, **Porto Moniz,** and the lovely harbor of **Câmara de Lobos,** a few miles west of Funchal. The full-day tour, offered Tuesday, Thursday, and Saturday, is 44€ per person, including lunch; 33€ without lunch.

Another possibility (called the Eastern Island Tour), is usually offered Monday, Wednesday, and Friday and costs 44€ with lunch; it includes a visit to the **wickerworks at Camacha,** where thousands of pieces of locally crafted work, from small baskets to entire groupings of furniture, are on sale.

As a final tour, you can book an organized excursion called **"Madeira Nights"** whose staff will escort you to the Restaurant Relogio at Camacha. Here, patrons are served a typical island dinner and entertained by fado and folkloric dancing. After the dinner and show, members of the tour get back onto their bus and are escorted back to their hotels.

[FastFACTS] MADEIRA

Area Code   The country code for Portugal is © **351;** the area code for Madeira is **29.**

Automated Teller Machines (ATMs)   Most ATMs (available 24 hr. a day) are located in Funchal, but you can also find some ATMs in towns throughout the island.

Business Hours   **Shops** are usually open Monday to Friday 9am to 1pm and 3 to 7pm, and Saturday 9am to 1pm. They're closed Sunday. **Municipal buildings** are

open Monday to Friday 9am to 12:30pm and 2 to 5:30pm. All **banks** are open Monday to Friday 8:30am to 3pm.

Consulates   The Consulate of the **United States** is on Rua da Alfândega 10 (© **29/123-56-36**), off Avenida do Infante. The Consulate of the **United Kingdom** is on Rua da Alfândega 10, third floor (© **29/121-28-60**). All other consulates are located only in Lisbon.

Dentist   A good English-speaking dentist, **John de Sousa,** has an office in Marina Shopping on the third floor, office 304, Avenida Arriaga (© **29/123-12-77**), in Funchal.

Doctor   A good English-speaking doctor is **Francis Zino,** in the Edificio Zino, Avenida do Infante (© **29/174-22-27**), in Funchal.

Drugstores   Drugstores (chemists) are open Monday to Friday 9am to 1pm and 3 to 9pm. The rotation emergency, night service,

373

and Sunday schedules are posted on the doors of all drugstores. A reliable, centrally located chemist is **Farmácia Honorato,** Rua da Carreira 62 (☏ **29/120-38-80**).

Emergencies Call ☏ **112** for a general **emergency,** ☏ **29/120-84-00** for the **police,** ☏ **29/174-11-15** for the **Red Cross,** and ☏ **29/170-56-00** for a **hospital** emergency.

Hospital The island's largest hospital is the **Hospital Distrital do Funchal,** Cruz de Carvalho (☏ **29/170-56-00**).

Laundry & Dry Cleaning Try **Lavandaria Donini,** Rua das Pretas (☏ **29/122-44-06**), Funchal. Clothing can be laundered or dry-cleaned in 1 or 2 days. It's open Monday to Saturday 9am to 7pm.

Lost Property The Lost Property office is located at the airport in the police building, next to the passenger terminal (☏ **29/152-08-90**).

Newspapers & Magazines The island stocks a good selection of such English-language publications as *Newsweek, Time,* and the *International Herald Tribune,* as well as periodicals in French, German, and Spanish.

Police Dial ☏ **29/120-84-00.**

Post Office If you've had your mail sent *Poste Restante* (general delivery), you can pick it up at Funchal's **Zarco Post Office,** Av. Zarco 9, 9000-069 (☏ **29/120-28-30**), near the tourist office, as long as you bring your passport to identify yourself. From here, you can also place long-distance phone calls (without steep hotel surcharges) and send telegrams, faxes, and telexes. The office is open Monday to Friday 8:30am to 8pm, and Saturday from 9am to 1pm.

Other post offices offering the same services are **Calouste Gulbenkian,** Avenida Calouste Gulbenkian (Mon–Fri 9am–6:30pm), near the Monument of the Infante Dom Henrique; **Monumental,** on Estrada Monumental, near the Lido swimming pool (Mon–Fri 8:30am–6:30pm); and **Mercado,** Rua do Arcipreste, near the Municipal Market (Mon–Fri 8:30am–6:30pm). Signs in the center of Funchal that read CORREIOS point the way to the nearest post office.

Safety In terms of crime statistics, Madeira is safer than mainland Portugal, especially Lisbon. However, as in any area that attracts tourists, a criminal element preys on visitors. Pickpockets and purse-snatchers are the major villains. Protect your valuables, as you would at any resort.

Taxes Madeira imposes no special taxes other than the value-added tax (VAT) on all goods and services purchased in Portugal. Refer to "Fast Facts," in chapter 15, for more information.

WHERE TO STAY IN FUNCHAL

Madeira enjoys year-round popularity, though April through May and September through October are the most comfortable and, in many ways, the most beautiful times to visit. You might want to avoid visiting in August because that's when *capacete,* a shroud of cooling mist, tends to envelop the island. If you're visiting in the summer, air-conditioning might be vital to you—unless you're at a retreat in the mountains—because the island is often so hot.

Madeira's hotels range from some of the finest deluxe accommodations in Europe to attractively priced old-fashioned *quintas* (manor houses) for budget travelers. Chances are, you won't be staying in the center of Funchal, but on the outskirts, where many of the best hotels with pools and resort amenities are. However, these make travelers dependent upon transportation into town, and only the first-class and deluxe hotels lying outside of Funchal offer vans that take guests into town at frequent intervals. Staying in the center of town has its downfalls as well; because

Funchal

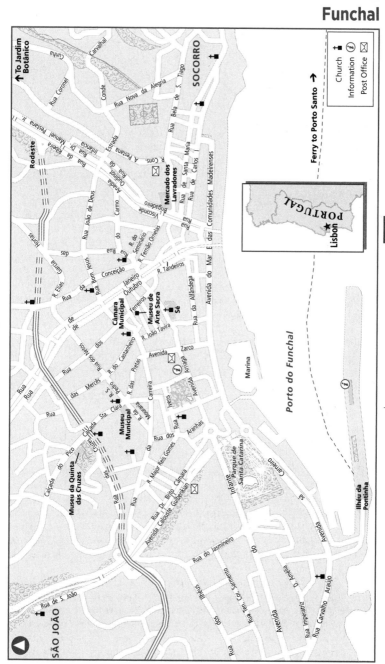

SÃO JOÃO

Rua de S. João

Museu da Quinta das Cruzes

Museu Municipal

Câmara Municipal

Museu de Arte Sacra

Sé

Mercado dos Lavradores

SOCORRO

Rodeste

To Jardim Botânico

Zarco

Avenida Arriaga

Avenida

Marina

Porto do Funchal

Parque de Santa Catarina

Ilhéu da Pontinha

Ferry to Porto Santo →

PORTUGAL

Lisbon

Church
Information
Post Office

heavy traffic fills the center of Funchal most of the day, hotels there tend to be noisy. Nevertheless, for shopping and the widest selection of restaurants, Funchal is your best bet.

Note: Street-side parking on the narrow streets of Funchal is notoriously difficult to find and if you do, it's almost never free, and requires returns virtually every hour to feed the meter. Even large hotels in the city center maintain very few parking spaces, directing their clients instead to the nearest of many covered or underground parking lots in the city center. Rates vary with the location and the time of day you opt to park, but you can expect to pay between 1€ and 1.30€ per hour. Two of the most central of the parking lots include the ones associated with the **Anadia Shopping Center,** Rua Anadia (no phone), and with the **Dolce Vita Shopping Center,** on the Rue Dr. Brito Camra (no phone) near the seafronting Ribera de São João. Parking at hotels and restaurants on the outskirts of town is plentiful and invariably free.

Very Expensive

Choupana Hills Resort & Spa ★★★   An oasis of charm, elegance, and tranquility, there is nothing like this resort and spa on Madeira. An elite retreat, it lies in the hills 4km (2½ miles) north of Funchal. Its public and private rooms are on top of a mountain just above the Botanical Gardens and stand in a well-landscaped 8-hectare (20-acre) plot of land opening onto views of the bay and the Atlantic Ocean. The choice way to stay here is in one of four unique suites set apart from the resort's other pavilions and designed as a total hideaway. But all the bedrooms exude understated luxury and are comfortable; units are spread across wooden bungalow-style buildings, each with a large terrace. The resort also boasts two bars and a first-class restaurant specializing in fusion cuisine. And there's the added attraction of one of the island's best spas.

Travessa do Largo da Choupana, 9060-348 Funchal, Madeira. www.choupanahills.com. ©**29/120-60-20.** Fax 29/120-60-21. 64 units. 305€–357€ double; 520€–750€ suite. AE, DC, MC, V. Bus: 29. **Amenities:** Restaurant; bar; babysitting; concierge; exercise room; 2 pools (1 heated indoor); room service; spa; Wi-Fi (free, in lobby). *In room:* A/C, TV/DVD, hair dryer, minibar.

The Cliff Bay ★★★ ☺   One of the island's top lodgings, rivaled and surpassed only by Reid's (see below), this nine-story hotel is dramatically located on a craggy bluff towering over wave-lashed rocks, 1.5km (1 mile) west of Funchal's center. A group favorite, the deluxe hotel stands on the site of a former banana plantation. All but a dozen or so rooms have great exposure to ocean or harbor views. Units are generally spacious, with such luxuries as sitting areas and roomy marble bathrooms with deluxe toiletries and tub/shower combos. The restaurants, from the Rose Garden to Il Gallo d'Oro to the Blue Lagoon (featuring Portuguese and international cuisine), are among the finest on the island, again surpassed only by the options at Reid's. Babysitting and children's programs make this place appealing to families with young children.

Estrada Monumental 147, 9004-532 Funchal, Madeira. www.cliffbay.com. © **29/170-77-00.** Fax 29/176-25-25. 201 units. 190€–395€ double; 400€–482€ junior suite; from 525€ suite. AE, DC, MC, V. Bus: 1 or 2. **Amenities:** 3 restaurants; 4 bars; airport transfers (29€); babysitting; children's programs; concierge; exercise room; 2 pools (1 indoor, 1 outdoor); room service; spa; outdoor tennis court (lit); watersports equipment/rentals. *In room:* A/C, TV/DVD, hair dryer, minibar, Wi-Fi (free).

Reid's Palace ★★★   The legendary place to stay in Funchal is Reid's, founded in 1891 by William Reid but now owned by the Orient Express. Its position is "smashing," as the British say, along the coastal road at the edge of Funchal, on 4 hectares

(10 acres) of terraced gardens that descend the hillside to the rocky ocean shores. The English who frequent the hotel in large numbers (Sir Winston Churchill stayed here) spend their days strolling the walks lined with hydrangeas, geraniums, gardenias, banana trees, ferns, and white yuccas.

The spacious guest rooms are conservative in the finest sense, with well-chosen furnishings (antiques or reproductions), sitting areas, desks, and plenty of storage space. The bathrooms have marble or tile walls and floors, plus tub/shower combinations, robes, and luxurious toiletries.

The gourmet restaurant, Les Faunes (see "Where to Dine in Funchal," later in this chapter), is on the sixth floor, in the garden wing.

Estrada Monumental 139, 9000-098 Funchal, Madeira. www.reidspalace.com. ✆ **800/223-6800** in the U.S., or 29/171-71-71. Fax 29/171-71-77. 163 units. 410€ classic double; 585€ superior double; 875€ junior suite; 1,130€ superior suite; 2,295€ executive suite. Rates include buffet breakfast. AE, DC, MC, V. Bus: 4, 6, 48, or 61. **Amenities:** 4 restaurants; 2 bars; airport transfers (57€); babysitting; children's programs; concierge; health club & spa; 3 outdoor pools; room service; 2 outdoor tennis courts (lit); watersports equipment/rentals. *In room:* A/C, TV, hair dryer, minibar, Wi-Fi (free).

Royal Savoy Madeira ★★★ ☺ Though lacking the tradition of Reid's Palace, this is nonetheless a pocket of posh for lovers of sleek contemporary styling with lots of facilities and amenities. The latest government-rated five-star luxury resort, it is a distinguished address for luxury living in the sun, lying a 10-minute walk north of the center. It's also a family favorite because of its children's programs and special facilities such as a kiddie pool. Rooms go from midsize to spacious and come in many varieties, ranging from junior suites to mammoth penthouse suites.

The stunning complex opens onto views of the Atlantic, and is peppered with pools, sun decks, terraces, tropical gardens, fountains, water cascades, and lush subtropical gardens, even a sea-walk promenade. The Royal Savoy has some of the best facilities for sports on the island; you can arrange everything from underwater adventures to horseback riding and boating. The on-site restaurants are also among the very best in Madeira, dishing out fresh, quality meals.

Rua Carvalho Araújo, 9000-022 Funchal, Madeira. www.madeiraroyalsavoy.com. ✆ **29/121-35-00.** Fax 29/121-35-30. 172 units. 197€–334€ double; 214€–334€ junior suite; from 557€ suite. Rates include continental breakfast. AE, DC, MC, V. Bus: 1. **Amenities:** Restaurant; 2 bars; airport transfers (32€); concierge; exercise room; 3 pools (1 heated indoor); room service; spa. *In room:* A/C, TV/DVD, hair dryer, kitchenette in junior suites, minibar, Wi-Fi (15€ per day).

Expensive

Eden Mar ★ ☺ This well-run hotel rises six floors from the swimming complex (the Lido). Though often booked by tour groups from England, it is still suitable for the individual traveler, especially families that like its rooms with kitchenettes. The midsize to spacious guest rooms open onto views of the sea. Decorated with textiles, the hotel has first-rate furnishings and excellent tiled bathrooms. The restaurant serves international and Portuguese cuisine.

Rua do Gorgulho 2, 9004-537 Funchal, Madeira. www.portobay.com. ✆ **29/170-97-00.** Fax 29/176-19-66. 146 units. 92€–107€ double; 137€–153€ junior suite. AE, DC, MC, V. Bus: 1, 2, 4, or 6. **Amenities:** Restaurant; 6 bars; airport transfers (29€); babysitting; children's center; exercise room; 3 pools (1 heated indoor); room service; spa; outdoor tennis court (lit); Wi-Fi (free, in lobby). *In room:* A/C, TV, kitchenette.

Estalagem Quinta da Casa Branca ★★★ 👜 This grand country manor, surrounded by its own manicured grounds, is the personification of estate living on the island. You'll be close to the city center, but vastly removed from the hectic activity of Funchal. An old manor house dominates the grounds, but the guest rooms are entirely modernized and up-to-date, complete with spacious bathrooms. You can expect the services and comfort of a first-rate hotel here. The dining room and bar area are in a restored outbuilding, and a swimming pool makes this a bit like a resort.

Rua da Casa Branca 7, 9000-088 Funchal, Madeira. www.quintacasabranca.pt. *(C)* **29/170-07-70.** Fax 29/176-50-33. 29 units. 205€–290€ double; from 385€ suite. Rates include buffet breakfast. AE, DC, MC, V. Bus: 6. Free parking. **Amenities:** Restaurant; 2 bars; babysitting; health club & spa; outdoor heated pool; room service. *In room:* A/C, TV, hair dryer, minibar, Wi-Fi (free).

Meliá Madeira Mar ★★ The Meliá opens onto the small pebble beach of Corgulho and is one of the most elegant resorts in Funchal, though not quite up there in the ranks of The Cliff Bay or Reid's (see above). Guest rooms are among the island's finest and come in a wide array of choices, including twin or superior accommodations, with private furnished verandas, some offering a sea view. Suites come with kitchenettes and spacious living areas. One floor is set aside for smokers. Room amenities range from safety boxes to beverage-making facilities.

You have two restaurant options: Mare Nostrum offers themed hot and cold buffets, often with live shows; Il Massimo serves deluxe Italian cuisine.

The spa is one of the finest on island, complete with sauna and Jacuzzi, along with various therapy treatments.

Rua de Leichlingen 2, 9000-003 Funchal, Madeira. www.meliahotels.com. *(C)* **29/172-41-40.** Fax 29/177-36-17. 220 units. 144€–230€; from 256€ suite. AE, DC, MC, V. **Amenities:** 2 restaurants; 3 bars; babysitting; concierge; exercise room; 2 pools (indoor and outdoor); room service; spa. *In room:* A/C, TV, hair dryer, minibar, Wi-Fi (free).

Pestana Carlton Madeira ★★ This is a luxurious 18-story structure near Madeira's only casino, with direct access to the sea via stairs that lead down from the hotel. The hotel lies on a promontory overlooking Funchal Bay in the fashionable Vale-Verde Garden district, next to Reid's Palace (see above). All of the spacious guest rooms, many furnished in provincial style, have private balconies and comfortable, tasteful furniture. The more expensive rates are for the deluxe sea-view rooms. The oceanfront (southern) exposure of these rooms means their balconies and patios receive dawn-to-dusk sunlight. The three restaurants serve fine cuisine, but be forewarned that at times they close to everyone but tour groups. The Atlântico features a show with dinner; Os Arcos has an international and regional menu; and the Taverna Grill specializes in pub fare such as steaks.

Largo António Nobre, 9004-531 Funchal, Madeira. www.pestana.com. *(C)* **29/123-95-00.** Fax 29/122-33-77. 285 units. 120€–239€ double; 210€–321€ suite. Rates include buffet breakfast. AE, DC, MC, V. Bus: 1, 2 4, 9, or 10. **Amenities:** 4 restaurants; 5 bars; babysitting; concierge; 2 golf courses; health club & spa; 3 pools (outdoor); spa; tennis court (lit). *In room:* A/C, TV, kitchenette.

Pestana Casino Park Hotel & Casino ★ Part of Madeira's Casino and Conference Centre, this deluxe citadel is a 7-minute walk from the town center, nestled in a subtropical garden overlooking the harbor. Designed by Oscar Niemeyer—one of the architects of Brasília, Brazil—the gray-concrete main building is low (only five stories) and undulating. The complex consists of the hotel as well as a conference center and a casino.

The small to midsize guest rooms—tastefully decorated in bright, sunny colors—have balconies with panoramic views over the harbor and town. Most rooms have only twin beds, but all boast first-class furnishings. Bathrooms have dual basins and bidets. Two comfortable lounge areas grace each floor. The luxurious dining room overlooks the port and town of Funchal, and the international Grill Room has an extensive wine cellar.

Rua Imperatriz Dona Amélia, 9004-513 Funchal, Madeira. www.pestana.com. © **29/120-91-00.** Fax 29/123-20-76. 379 units. 115€–163€ double; 189€–326€ suite. Rates include buffet breakfast. AE, DC, MC, V. Bus: 1, 2, 10, 12, or 16. **Amenities:** 3 restaurants; 3 bars; babysitting; exercise room; room service; spa; 2 outdoor tennis courts (lit). *In room:* A/C, TV/DVD, hair dryer, minibar.

Quinta da Bela Vista ★★ 🛎 The core of this government-rated five-star hotel, in the hills above Funchal, dates from 1844, when it was built as a private villa. Its owner has added two outlying annexes in the Portuguese colonial style. A verdant garden surrounds the annexes, which hold comfortable guest rooms that are slightly larger than the older accommodations in the main villa. Furnishings include high-quality mahogany reproductions and a scattering of English and Portuguese antiques. A well-staffed formal restaurant, Casa Mãe, is in the original villa. The more relaxed Avista Navios offers sweeping views and regional and international cuisine.

Caminho do Avista Navios 4, 9000-129 Funchal, Madeira. www.belavistamadeira.com. © **29/170-64-00.** Fax 29/170-64-01. 90 units. 172€–340€ double; from 480€ junior suite. Rates include buffet breakfast. AE, DC, MC, V. Bus: 3 or 8. **Amenities:** 2 restaurants; 3 bars; babysitting; concierge; exercise room; outdoor freshwater heated pool; room service; outdoor tennis court (lit). *In room:* A/C, TV, hair dryer, Wi-Fi (free).

Quinta das Vistas Palace Gardens ★★★ One of the grandest hotels to open in Funchal is this pocket of posh created from a landmark manor house that stands on the brow of a hill opening onto panoramic vistas of the Atlantic, the mountains in the distance, and the city itself. The public areas of this government-rated five-star hotel are decorated so elegantly and warmly that they evoke a wealthy private home. The stylish interior opens onto well-tended gardens studded with fountains, a pavilion, a pond filled with swans, and even a 9-hole minigolf course.

A favorite of honeymooners, the *quinta* offers luxuriously furnished and spacious guest rooms, decorated in Portuguese marble and wooden furnishings, each with a state-of-the-art private bathroom. The finest of carpeting, woods, and fabrics were used to enhance the rooms, which open onto private-view balconies.

One of the special features of the property is its south-facing pool complex: A heated indoor pool opens onto a passage that leads to an outdoor pool with a waterfall extending to a second heated outdoor pool and even an ice chamber—talk about a good place to cool off. La Belle Terrasse, with tables placed out for a view, is among the finest hotel dining rooms on the island, serving both lunch and dinner in a romantic atmosphere.

Caminho de Santo Antonio 52, 9000-187 Funchal, Madeira. www.quintadasvistasmadeira.com. © **29/175-00-07.** Fax 29/175-00-17. 71 units. 132€–222€ double; 250€–431€ suite. AE, DC, MC, V. Bus: 50. **Amenities:** Restaurant; 2 bars; airport transfers (32€); babysitting; exercise room; 3 pools (1 heated indoor; 1 heated outdoor; 1 unheated outdoor); room service; spa. *In room:* A/C, TV, hair dryer, minibar, Wi-Fi (free).

Moderate

Enotel Quinta do Sol ★ The government-rated four-star Quinta do Sol is among the best in its category on Madeira. In an attractive setting, it offers well-furnished guest rooms. Rooms are sun-flooded, with big windows and contemporary furniture; some have balconies with views of the sea. Units without balconies are both larger and less expensive. The hotel has a bar-restaurant, Magnolia, which offers Portuguese and international food and wine.

Rua Dr. Pita 6, 9000-089 Funchal, Madeira. www.enotelquintadosol.com. ✆ **29/170-70-10.** Fax 29/176-62-87. 156 units. 45€–61€ double; 61€–159€ triple. Rates include buffet breakfast. AE, DC, MC, V. Bus: 2, 8, or 12. **Amenities:** Restaurant; 2 bars; airport transfers (32€); babysitting; exercise room; Jacuzzi; 2 pools (outdoor, 1 for kids); room service; Wi-Fi (free, in lobby). *In room:* A/C, TV, fridge, hair dryer, minibar.

Hotel do Carmo   The Hotel do Carmo provides modern accommodations in the center of Funchal and is ideal for thrifty travelers who want to be in the heart of town. It's laid out in a honeycomb fashion, and most guest rooms open onto balconies overlooking the busy street scene below. Rates for rooms with and without balconies are the same. Guests gather at the rooftop pool, which affords a good view of the harbor. The rooms are simple, with contemporary but well-used furnishings. Meals are served in a spacious dining room or can be taken onto a terrace on the second floor. The chefs specialize in a Portuguese and international cuisine, making use of the rich produce of Madeira.

Travessa do Rego 10, 9054-502 Funchal, Madeira. www.hoteldocarmomadeira.com. ✆ **29/120-12-40.** Fax 29/122-39-19. 80 units. 50€–99€ double; 90€–130€ triple. Rates include buffet breakfast. AE, DC, MC, V. Bus: 1, 2, 4, 6, 8, 9, or 10. **Amenities:** Restaurant; bar; babysitting; outdoor pool; sauna; Wi-Fi (free, in lobby). *In room:* TV.

Hotel Girassol ☺   Hotel Girassol offers immaculate accommodations at reasonable rates. It's on the outskirts of Funchal, overlooking the Tourist Club (a small complex with a restaurant, pool, and platform for swimming in the sea), where guests can access the sea for a small charge. Most double rooms are actually suites, consisting of a bedroom, a small sitting room, and a veranda, which make them ideal for families looking for roomier accommodations. Each unit has a terrace or balcony overlooking the garden, the mountains, or the sea. One pool is set aside for children. The dining room, which serves regional and international cuisine, has sea views and, at dinner, live music.

Estrada Monumental 256, 9004-539 Funchal, Madeira. www.hotelgirassolmadeira.com. ✆ **29/170-15-70.** Fax 29/176-54-41. 136 units. 75€ double; 90€–120€ suite. Rates include buffet breakfast. AE, DC, MC, V. Bus: 1, 3, or 6. **Amenities:** Restaurant; 3 bars; babysitting; exercise room; 2 outdoor pools; room service. *In room:* A/C, TV, hair dryer, minibar, Wi-Fi (free).

Quinta da Penha de França ★★ ☺   This gracious old manor house is now a guesthouse, with an annex containing 33 sea-view rooms, a balcony, and a terrace. Rooms in the older section have high ceilings, thick walls, casement windows, and a scattering of old-fashioned furniture, including some family antiques. Rooms in the annex are more contemporary, with traditional country-house designs. Like a family home, the *quinta* is chock-full of antiques, paintings, and silver. Near the Royal Savoy (see above), it stands in a garden on a ledge almost hanging over the harbor. It's a short walk from Funchal's bazaars and is opposite an ancient chapel. Unlike most hotels on Madeira, many of this hotel's rooms have connecting doors, which can be opened and rented as two rooms, for families with one to three children.

Rua da Penha de França 2 and Rua Imperatriz da Amélia, 9050-014 Funchal, Madeira. www.penha franca.com. ✆ **29/120-46-50.** Fax 29/122-92-61. 109 units. 46€–116€ double; 85€–157€ triple. Rates include buffet breakfast. AE, DC, MC, V. Bus: 2, 12, or 16. **Amenities:** 2 restaurants; 2 bars; airport transfers (32€); babysitting; outdoor seawater heated pool; Wi-Fi (free, in lobby). *In room:* A/C, TV, hair dryer, minibar.

Inexpensive

Dorisol Estrelícia   This hotel lies on the upper floors of a high-rise building, constructed up a hill from the main hotel drag. The location is a bit inconvenient, so rates seem low considering the quality of the rooms. Most units are midsize. All are well appointed, with durable modern furniture, neatly kept bathrooms, and a view of the sea. The hotel minibus runs to the center of Funchal several times a day.

Caminho Velho da Ajuda and Rua Casa Branca, 9000-113 Funchal, Madeira. www.dorisol.com. © **29/ 170-66-00.** Fax 29/176-48-59. 148 units. 53€–120€ double. Rates include buffet breakfast. AE, DC, MC, V. Bus: 1, 2, 4, or 6. **Amenities:** Restaurant; 3 bars; airport transfers (32€); babysitting; children's center; health club with sauna and Jacuzzi; 2 pools (1 indoor); outdoor tennis court (lit); Wi-Fi (free, in lobby). *In room:* TV, hair dryer, minibar.

Hotel Madeira ★   This five-story hotel sits in the center of Funchal, behind the tranquil Park of San Francisco. The rooftop pool has an extraordinary panoramic view of the town, mountains, and sea, and there's a solarium area with a bar and snack services. The small to midsize guest rooms surround a plant-filled atrium. One of the nicest features is the sheltered sun window attached to each unit. Some rooms have balconies—the ones in the front overlook buildings and have no view, but those in the rear have views of the mountains above Funchal. All are comfortably furnished, with worn but durable furniture and tidily kept bathrooms.

Rua Ivens 21, 9000-049 Funchal, Madeira. www.hotelmadeira.com. © **29/123-00-71.** Fax 29/122-90-71. 53 units. 66€ double; 74€ junior suite. Rates include buffet breakfast. AE, MC, V. Bus: 2, 12, or 16. **Amenities:** Bar; outdoor pool. *In room:* A/C (in some), TV, hair dryer, Wi-Fi (free).

Hotel Windsor ★ 🍴   This is one of the most stylish hotels in Funchal. The government-rated four-star hotel consists of two buildings connected by an aerial passage above a sun-flooded enclosed courtyard. The marble-sheathed lobby is laden with plants, wicker chairs, and Art Deco accessories. The free parking garage is almost a necessity in this crowded commercial neighborhood. Guest rooms are not particularly large, and few have views, but they are comfortable and nicely decorated, with wall-to-wall carpeting and wooden furniture. The hotel has a cafe-bar designed to resemble a Jazz Age nightclub, as well as the more formal Windsor Restaurant. The latter serves reasonably good and moderately priced Portuguese and international cuisine, with local swordfish as a specialty.

Rua das Hortas 4C, 9050-024 Funchal, Madeira. www.hotelwindsorgroup.pt. © **29/123-30-81.** Fax 29/ 123-30-80. 67 units. 60€ double. Rates include buffet breakfast. No credit cards. Bus: 1, 12, or 16. **Amenities:** Restaurant; 2 bars; outdoor pool. *In room:* TV, hair dryer, Wi-Fi (free).

On the Outskirts of Funchal
EXPENSIVE

Casa Velha do Palheiro ★★★   This unique inn was constructed in 1804 as a hunting lodge for the first Count of Carvalhal and then was restored in 1996 to become Madeira's first government-rated five-star country-house hotel, a type of accommodations more common in England. The hotel, a member of the Relais & Châteaux chain, adjoins the par-71 championship Palheiro golf course, about a 15-minute drive from Funchal. It is the only hotel in Madeira on a golf course. Rooms vary in shape and size, but all are richly furnished in an old-fashioned but comfortable way, with first-class furnishings and neatly kept bathrooms. The restaurant and bar serve quality international and Portuguese cuisine.

Rua da Estalagem 23, São Gonçalo, 9060-415 Funchal, Madeira. www.casa-velha.com. ℂ **29/179-03-50.** Fax 29/179-49-25. 37 units. 198€–328€ double; 363€–419€ suite. Rates include buffet breakfast. AE, DC, MC, V. Bus: 33. **Amenities:** Restaurant; bar; babysitting; exercise room; golf course nearby; outdoor heated pool; room service; sauna; Wi-Fi (free, in lobby). *In room:* TV, hair dryer, minibar (in some).

Quinta Jardins do Lago ★★ 🏨   Set in beautiful botanical gardens, this luxury hotel lies in the Achada district of Funchal, one of the hills enveloping the city. A little over .5km (⅓ mile) from the center, its landscaped grounds open onto panoramic vistas of both the Atlantic and the mountains in the distance. The gardens alone are reason enough to stay here, containing 495 different species of plants on 2.5 hectares (6¼ acres) of landscaped beauty, including rare trees from Africa, China, Japan, and even a jacaranda from Argentina.

General Beresford, at the time of Britain's wars with France under Napoleon, commanded his country's forces on Madeira and selected this 1700s mansion as his private residence. Much of what he enjoyed remains to delight visitors today—a library, antiques, a billiard room, and a breakfast area with a rare ceramic wall panel handpainted and glazed in the 1500s. The guest rooms, annexed to the 1750 manor house, are spacious and beautifully furnished, offering traditional comfort but modern amenities as well. The Beresford restaurant offers formal service and refined Continental and Portuguese cuisine. Among the mango trees is a large semicovered heated pool with a bistro, Jacuzzi, sauna, and steam bath.

Rua Dr. João Lemos Gomes 29, 9000-158 São Pedro. www.jardinsdolago.com. ℂ **29/175-01-00.** Fax 29/175-01-50. 40 units. 91€–169€ per person double; 135€–328€ per person suite. AE, MC, V. Bus: 15. **Amenities:** 2 restaurants; bar; exercise room; Jacuzzi; outdoor freshwater heated pool; room service; sauna; outdoor tennis court. *In room:* A/C, TV, hair dryer, minibar.

MODERATE

Quinta Bela São Tiago ★ 🏨   A traditional Madeiran manor house from 1834 has been successfully converted into a government-rated four-star hotel of considerable charm. Until the early 20th century, this manor house was the private residence of Madeira's vice-governor. Surrounded by extensive gardens, the manor has expanded over the years from its original core. But the modern extension is in keeping with the original architectural plan. Rooms open onto the view of the mountains as a backdrop or the bay of Funchal in the distance. Bedrooms are suitably grand and tastefully restored, with a choice of suites or standard doubles; many have balconies with panoramic views.

Rua Bela de São Tiago, 9050-042 Funchal. www.quintabelasaotiago.com. ℂ **29/120-45-00.** Fax 29/291-20-45. 64 units. 84€–113€ double; 259€–310€ suite. AE, MC, V. Bus: 40. **Amenities:** Restaurant; bar; airport transfers (32€); exercise room; Jacuzzi; 2 outdoor pools (1 for kids); room service; sauna. *In room:* A/C, TV, hair dryer, minibar, Wi-Fi (free).

Quinta Perestrello Heritage House ★★   Standing in well-manicured gardens, this is a restored manor house with much of its traditional architecture, including high ceilings, remaining intact. To its original core, modern extensions have been added. The spacious bedrooms are tastefully and comfortably furnished, many of them opening onto panoramic views. All rooms have a terrace or balcony. Guests can take a dip in the heated swimming pool or simply soak up sun on the terrace. An onsite restaurant serves superb island meals for hotel guests.

Rua Dr. Pita 3, 9000-089 Funchal. www.quintaperestrellomadeira.com. ℂ **29/170-67-00.** Fax 29/170-67-06. 36 units. 74€–135€ double; 126€–189€ triple. AE, DC, MC, V. **Amenities:** Restaurant; bar; airport transfers (32€); health club & spa; outdoor pool; room service; Wi-Fi (free, in lobby). *In room:* A/C, TV, hair dryer.

Quintinha de São João ★ 👜 Dating from 1900, this *quinta* (manor house) is one of the best preserved in the Funchal area, surrounded by age-old trees and graced with classic architecture. Once an elegant private residence, it has been tastefully converted into a family inn. Most of the good-size, standard guest rooms contain twin beds; some suites are available. All rooms are handsomely decorated, often with traditional embroidery and Madeiran handiwork covering the beds. Old-style furnishings and antiques appear throughout, but modern luxuries include neatly kept bathrooms. The restaurant, A Morgadinha, offers a variety of regional and international dishes, and features unusual Goan specialties. The terrace bar, Vasco da Gama, overlooks the Bay of Funchal and is one of the most scenic places in town for a drink.

Rua da Levada de São João and Estalagem Quintinha São João 4, 9000-191 Funchal, Madeira. www. quintinhasaojoao.com. ☎ **29/174-09-20.** Fax 29/174-09-28. 43 units. 100€–150€ double; 145€–180€ junior suite; 179€–210€ suite. Rates include buffet breakfast. AE, DC, MC, V. Bus: 11. **Amenities:** Restaurant; bar; babysitting; exercise room; 2 heated pools (1 indoor); room service; outdoor tennis court (lit); Wi-Fi (free, in lobby). *In room:* A/C, TV/DVD, hair dryer, minibar.

INEXPENSIVE

Quinta da Fonte ★★ 👜 This is our favorite B&B on the island, a converted 1850 manor house lying midway between Monte and Funchal. Set in the midst of landscaped gardens and tropical fruit trees, the antique-filled house opens onto panoramic views of Funchal. Of all the accommodations on Madeira, this one comes closest to being a live-in museum. Staying here is like living in an old family home owned by Madeiran aristocrats of long ago.

The house is filled with art and artifacts, providing a warm, luxurious atmosphere. Of all the accommodations, we most prefer the Dona María bedroom, with an exquisite set of furniture, including not only the bed, but the dresser, commode, table, and chairs. Breakfast is offered on a family-style table built in 1854 of the preciously rare Madeira wood *pau santo,* or holy wood. A shared veranda and reading room are on the second floor, and a living and dining room are downstairs. Another, smaller, veranda is ideal for sunset watching.

Estrada dos Marmeleiros 89, 9050-209 Funchal, Madeira. www.madeira-island.com/hotels/quintas/ quintadafonte. ☎ **29/123-53-97.** 4 units. 50€–70€ double. No credit cards. Bus: 20, 21, 21C, 22, 23, or 26. **Amenities:** Wi-Fi (free, in lobby). *In room:* TV, no phone.

WHERE TO DINE IN FUNCHAL

Many visitors to Madeira dine at their hotels, but there's no reason you can't sneak away for a regional meal at one of the Funchal restaurants listed below. This list just happens to begin with the pick of the hotel restaurants.

Very Expensive

Il Gallo d'Or ★★★ MEDITERRANEAN/IBERIAN Not surprisingly, the island's finest restaurant is found at Madeira's best hotel. For the award-winning chef, Benoît Sinthon, the island's fresh produce plays a key role in his specialties, but he also draws on various regions throughout Iberia for high-quality ingredients. Tables are placed inside or outside opening onto views of the Atlantic.

The cuisine is celestially light and delicate, in perfect pitch between creativity and tradition. In an elegant setting, you can enjoy the chef's inspiration for the evening, backed up by an impressive wine list. The helpful staff will guide you through it. The freshly caught seafood is especially enticing.

You might start with a freshly made lobster salad with green asparagus, citrus, and an orange vinaigrette, or a pastille of scallops studded with truffles and served with foie gras. Main courses might include a tender Black Angus steak or the fresh catch of the day, perhaps a seafood medley. Finish with a jellied pyramid of passion fruit, or gooseberries with avocado foam. *Note:* Il Gallo d'Or hosts a weekly dinner dance.

In The Cliff Bay, Estrada Monumental 147. ⓒ **29/170-77-00.** Reservations required. Main courses 35€–48€; fixed-price menus 65€–85€. AE, DC, MC, V. Daily 7–10pm. Bus: 1, 2, or 35.

Expensive

Casa Velha ★ MEDITERRANEAN One of the top-ranking restaurants of Funchal for the past 20 years, the setting for this first-class dining choice is lovely, and so is the carefully prepared food using top-quality ingredients. On a cold day off-season you can enjoy the big log fire and drinks in the wood-paneled bar. In fair weather diners like to retreat to a table in the courtyard, catching the night's breeze.

The dishes change with the season, to take advantage of the best produce of any given month. Seafood and fish are always a feature, and the chefs work wonders with sea bass, fresh tuna, and a superb grilled scabbard fish. A vegetarian risotto is superbly prepared if you don't want fish or meat. For a starter, try the *d'amelia*, the freshly caught swordfish, which is a tantalizing opening. If you have room, the desserts are top-notch, especially the crêpes suzette prepared at your table. Wines are reasonable in price, and many in-the-know diners sip offerings from Madeira itself, especially the island's white wine, which pairs nicely with the fish dishes. The excellent service is an added plus.

Rua Imperatriz D. Amélia 69. ⓒ **29/120-56-00.** www.casavelharestaurant.com. Reservations required. Main courses 18€–32€. AE, DC, MC, V. Daily noon–2:30pm and 7–10pm. Bus: 1.

Les Faunes ★★ FRENCH Try to dine at least once at Les Faunes, the island's finest hotel dining room, which takes its name from the series of Picasso lithographs decorating the walls. Live piano music accompanies your meal, and winter guests often dress for dinner, the men in black tie.

The chef offers a variety of French specialties and some typical Portuguese dishes. To begin, you can try everything from Portuguese soup to the chef's own smoked fish. Favorite entrees are *caldeirada* (fish stew) and lobster (grilled or poached). The chef's special pride is swordfish with banana. You can select from the dessert cart or ask for a hot soufflé, preferably made of passion fruit or strawberries.

In Reid's Palace, Estrada Monumental 139. ⓒ **29/171-71-71.** www.reidspalace.com. Reservations required. Jacket and tie required for men. Main courses 17€–34€. AE, DC, MC, V. Mon, Wed–Fri, and Sun 7–10pm. Closed in summer. Bus: 4, 6, 48, or 61.

Moderate

Casa Madeirense ★ INTERNATIONAL/PORTUGUESE Owner Filipe Gouveia extends a hearty welcome and is delighted when guests enjoy his elegant regional decor of *azulejos* (tiles) and hand-painted murals. His lively bar evokes a thatched-roof house in the village of Santana. Fresh fish and shellfish dominate the menu, but the best dish is *cataplana de marisco* (savory shellfish stew). The tuna steak is grilled to perfection, and you can also enjoy tender, perfectly seasoned peppercorn steak or chateaubriand.

Estrada Monumental 153. ⓒ **29/176-67-00.** www.casamadeirense-funchal.com. Reservations recommended. Main courses 15€–30€. AE, DC, MC, V. Mon–Sat noon–3:30pm and 6–10:30pm. Closed Aug. Bus: 1, 2, or 4.

Inexpensive

Dos Combatentes ✔ TRADITIONAL PORTUGUESE   Dos Combatentes is a good choice for regional food. At the top of the Municipal Gardens, the simple restaurant serves well-prepared dishes, including rabbit stew, roast chicken, stewed squid, and swordfish with bananas. Most dinners begin with a bowl of the soup of the day. Portions are ample, and two vegetables and a green salad come with the main dish. Desserts are likely to be simple, such as caramel custard, chocolate mousse, and fresh fruit. The waiters are efficient but not adept in English.

Rua Ivens 1. ℂ **29/122-13-88.** Main courses 6€–18€. AE, DC, MC, V. Mon–Sat 11:45am–3pm and 6:30–10:30pm. Bus: 2, 12, or 16.

O Celeiro ★ 🏠 TRADITIONAL PORTUGUESE   This rustic restaurant serves some of the most authentic and best regional dishes in the capital. O Celeiro attracts visitors and businesspeople with reasonable prices and big helpings of delicious fare. Freshly caught swordfish is cooked with bananas, a longtime island favorite. Tuna steak is marinated in wine and garlic sauce and served with fresh mushrooms. Our longtime favorite is *cataplana de marisco,* a kettle of seafood stew that tastes different every time we sample it. You might also opt for a tender steak in peppercorn sauce. With *espetada* (skewered beef on a spit), you'll want crusty bread for soaking up the juices.

Rua das Aranhas 22. ℂ **29/123-06-22.** www.restauranteoceleiro.com. Reservations recommended. Main courses 12€–28€. AE, DC, MC, V. Mon–Sat noon–3pm and 6–11pm. Bus: 2, 12, or 16.

On the Outskirts of Funchal

A Seta ★ TRADITIONAL PORTUGUESE   A Seta (The Arrow) specializes in supreme regional cuisine. It's almost midway between Funchal and Monte, 4km (2½ miles) from either, along winding roads. The mountainside restaurant, a favorite with tour groups, is a tavern where you can order inexpensive yet tasty meals. The rustic decor incorporates burned-wood trim, walls covered with pine cones, and crude pine tables.

All meals start with a plate of homemade coarse brown bread still warm from the oven. Above each table is a hook with long skewers *(espetadas)* of charbroiled meat, usually beef or chicken, seasoned with olive oil, herbs, garlic, and bay leaves. You slip off chunks while mopping up juices with the crusty bread. Other specialties served on platters (not skewers) include grilled steaks and several kinds of fish, including cod. Fried potatoes are always done well here (ask for some hot sauce).

Estrada do Livramento 80, Monte. ℂ **29/174-36-43.** Reservations recommended. Main courses 14€–24€. AE, DC, MC, V. Thurs–Tues noon–3pm and 6–11pm. Bus: 19 or 23.

EXPLORING MADEIRA

Seeing the Sights in Funchal

Funchal's stately, beautiful **Praça do Município (Municipal Square)** is a study in light and dark; its plaza is paved with hundreds of black-and-white half-moons made from lava. (Masonry is a well-rehearsed Madeiran art form; and in Funchal, many of the sidewalks are paved with cobblestones that are arranged into repetitive patterns defined by contrasting colors.) The whitewashed buildings surrounding it have black-stone trim and ocher-tile roofs. On the south side of the square is a former archbishopric now devoted to a museum of religious art (see Museu de Arte Sacra, below). Rising to the east is the **Câmara Municipal** (city hall), once the 18th-century palace of a rich Portuguese nobleman. It's noted for its distinctive palace tower rising over the surrounding rooftops.

Jardim Botânico ★ On the road to Camacha, about 4km (2½ miles) from Funchal, this botanical garden is one of the best in Portugal, with **faraway views ★** of the bay. Opened by the government in 1960 on the grounds of the old Quinta do Bom Sucesso plantation, the garden includes virtually every tree or plant growing on Madeira. Some of the subtropical plants were imported from around the world, including anthuriums and birds of paradise from Africa and South America. A heather tree, discovered near Curral das Freiras, is said to be 10 million years old. The gardens open onto panoramic views of Funchal and its port.

Caminho do Meio. ℂ **29/121-12-00.** Admission 4€ adults, 2€ children under 14. Daily 9am–6pm. Bus: 29, 30, or 31.

Museu da Quinta das Cruzes ★★ This museum is the former residence of João Gonçalves Zarco, who discovered Madeira in 1419. The surrounding park is of botanical interest and contains a noteworthy collection of orchids. The museum houses many fine examples of English furniture and China-trade porcelains brought to Madeira by expatriate Englishmen in the 18th century. You'll see rare Indo-Portuguese cabinets and the unique chests native to Madeira, fashioned from *caixas de açúcar* (sugar boxes, dating from the 17th c.). Also worth noting is a superb collection of antique Portuguese silver.

Calçada do Pico 1. ℂ **29/174-06-70.** www.museuquintadascruzes.com. Admission 2.50€. Tues–Sun 10am–12:30pm and 2–5:30pm. Bus: 1, 2, 4, or 6.

Museu de Arte Sacra The Museum of Sacred Art occupies an old bishop's house in the center of town. Many of its exhibitions came from island churches, some of which are no longer standing. Its most interesting collections are a series of paintings from the Portuguese and Flemish schools of the 15th and 16th centuries. The paintings are on wood (often oak); an outstanding example is the 1518 *Adoration of the Magi*. A rich merchant commissioned it and paid for it with sugar. A triptych depicts St. Philip and St. James, and there's an exceptional painting called *Descent from the Cross*. Ivory sculpture, gold and silver plate, and gilded wood ornamentations round out the collection.

Rua do Bispo 21. ℂ **29/122-89-00.** www.museuartesacrafunchal.org. Admission 3€. Tues–Sat 10am–12:30pm and 2:30–6pm; Sun 10am–1pm. Bus: 1, 2, 4, or 6.

Museu Municipal do Funchal ☺ The Municipal Museum displays land and aquatic animal life of the archipelago. Specimens include moray eels, eagle rays, scorpion fish, sea cucumbers, sea zephyrs, sharp-nosed puffers, and loggerhead turtles. Also on display are many of the beautifully plumed birds seen around Madeira, although the most interesting exhibit to us is the collection of ferocious-looking stuffed killer sharks, evocative of the film *Jaws*. This museum is a favorite with families, although the curator says that very small children are sometimes afraid of the exhibitions. The museum, a minor attraction, need not take up much more than 30 minutes of your time, not counting the time it takes to get here. The buses listed below will take you to a stop where you get off and follow the signs to the museum grounds. It's a pleasant 10-minute walk to the entrance.

Rua da Mouraria 31. ℂ **29/122-97-61.** Admission 3€ adults, free for children under 12. Tues–Fri 10am–6pm; Sat–Sun noon–6pm. Bus: 1, 2, 4, or 6.

Quinta Palmeira Gardens ★★★ Lying only a 5-minute ride from the center of Funchal, these carefully restored gardens are one of the botanical highlights of Madeira. The gardens were once owned by the well-known sugar industrialist Harry Hinton, and most of the gardens were designed at the beginning of the 20th century. They have undergone an extensive restoration and are more gorgeous than ever, featuring a large collection of exotic plants, some unique to Madeira. The gardens are filled with curiosities, including a stone window salvaged from the house where Columbus once lived on the island.

Rua da Levada de Santa Luzia, Funchal. ℂ **29/122-10-91.** Mon–Fri 9am–noon and 2–5pm. Bus: 26.

Sé (Cathedral) ★ The most intriguing of Funchal's churches is the rustic 15th-century Sé, with its Moorish carved cedar ceiling, stone floors, Gothic arches, stained-glass windows, and baroque altars. The cathedral is at the junction of four busy streets in the historic heart of town. Note that open hours are subject to change depending on church activities.

Rua do Aljube, Funchal. ℂ **29/122-81-55.** Free admission; donation suggested. Mon–Sat 7am–1pm and 4–7pm; Sun 8am–8:30pm. Bus: 1, 2, 4, or 6.

Exploring the Rest of the Island

Funchal is an excellent launching pad for exploring the island's mountainous interior and lush coastlines. During your exploration of Madeira, you're likely to see many banana, date, and fruit trees. Please remember that local farmers rely on these trees to make a living, and the fruity bounty should not be "harvested" for a picnic while touring the island.

THE OUTSKIRTS OF FUNCHAL

Immediately east of Funchal, the **Quinta do Palheiro Ferreiro ★★** is a beautiful spot for a stroll. The mansion is the private property of the Blandy wine family, former owners of Reid's Palace. The 12-hectare (30-acre) estate, with some 3,000 plant species, is like a pleasure garden. The camellia blooms that burst into full flower from Christmas until early spring are reason enough to visit. You'll also see many rare flowers (several from Africa) and exotic trees.

The estate is open Monday to Friday 9am to 4:30pm. Admission is 10€. You must get permission to picnic on the grounds: Ask at the gate upon your arrival. Bus no. 36 from Funchal runs here. By car, drive 5km (3 miles) northeast of Funchal, following N101 toward the airport. Fork left onto N102 and follow signposts toward Camacha until you see the turnoff to the *quinta*.

The grandest *miradouro* (or belvedere) in Madeira is **Eira do Serrado ★★★**, at 1,175m (3,855 ft.). This belvedere looks out over the Grande Curral, which is the deep crater (nicknamed "the belly button" of the island) of a long extinct volcano in the center of Madeira. You can look down into this awesome crater, viewing farms built on terraces inside the crater itself. The panorama takes in all the craggy mountain summits of Madeira if the day is clear. You can drive all the way to the lookout point, where you can park your car and get out to take in the view. The location is 16km (10 miles) northwest of Funchal. To reach the lookout point, head west out of Funchal on Rua Dr. João Brito Câmara, which leads to a little road signposted to Pico

Dos Barcelos. Follow the sign to Eira do Serrado until you reach the parking lot for the belvedere.

After taking in the view at the belvedere, head north along N107, which is signposted, to the stunningly situated village of **Curral das Freiras ★**, 6.5km (4 miles) north of Eira do Serrado. Meaning "Corral of the Nuns," the village used to be the center of the **Convento de Santa Clara,** where the sisters retreated for safety whenever Moorish pirates attacked Funchal. On the way to the village, the road goes through two tunnels cut through the mountains. Curral das Freiras sits in almost the exact geographic center of Madeira, lying in a valley of former volcanoes (all now extinct). The volcanoes surrounding Curral das Freiras were said to have been responsible for pushing up the landmass that is now Madeira from the sea. The village of whitewashed houses is centered on a small main square with a church of only passing interest. Most visitors stroll around the village, take in views of the enveloping mountains, have a cup of coffee at one of the cafes, and then head back to Funchal. Allow about 2 hours to make the 36km (22-mile) circuit of Eira do Serrado and Curral das Freiras.

WESTERN MADEIRA

If time is limited, head for the western part of Madeira, where you'll find panoramic views along the coastlines, dramatic waterfalls, and cliffs towering over the ocean. Leave Funchal on the coastal road, N101, heading west for 19km (12 miles) to the village of Câmara de Lobos, beloved by Sir Winston Churchill.

Câmara de Lobos

You approach Câmara de Lobos, meaning "Room of the Wolves," after passing terraces planted with bananas. The little fishing village of whitewashed red-tile-roofed cottages surrounds a cliff-sheltered harbor and rocky beach. If you come here around 7 or 8am, you can see fishers unloading their boats after a night at sea. You won't have a lot to do here beyond walking along the harbor to take in the view or perhaps following Churchill's example and becoming a Sunday painter.

The village also makes a good spot for lunch. The best place to eat is **Santo Antonio** (*✆* **29/191-03-60**), some 5km (3 miles) from Câmara de Lobos, in the tiny village of **Estreito de Câmara de Lobos** (popularly known as Estreito). Near the little village church, owner Manuel Silvestro offers mostly grills, including golden chicken, cooked over an open hearth. A specialty is *espetada,* Madeira's most famous dish—delicately flavored skewered beef on a spit. Don't expect elegance—you dine at simple paper-covered tables and mop up juices with crusty bread. Santo Antonio is open daily from noon to midnight; main courses cost 7€ to 18€. Major credit cards are accepted, and no reservations are needed.

Cabo Girão ★

The cliffs you might have seen from Câmara de Lobos lie 16km (10 miles) west of the village. To get to Cabo Girão, take R214 up a hill studded with pine and eucalyptus. From the 570m (1,870-ft.) belvedere, the panorama down the almost-sheer drop to the pounding ocean is thrilling. The terraced farms you'll see clinging to the cliff edges are cultivated entirely by hand because the plots are too small for either animal or machine.

Ribeira Brava

Continuing on the coast road west, you'll come to Ribeira Brava, which lies 15km (9⅓ miles) west of Cabo Girão and 48km (30 miles) west of Funchal. Meaning "Wide

River," Ribeira Brava is a lovely little Madeiran village (founded in 1440) and the sunniest spot on the island. It even has what locals refer to as a "beach," although you might view it as a strip of pebbles along the water.

We like to visit the village for its bustling seafront fruit market, which is active every morning except Sunday. Even if you don't buy anything, it's worth a stroll through the market to take in the amazing bounty grown in the mountains of Madeira. It also provides a great photo opportunity. As you stroll through the village, you'll encounter locals selling island handicrafts, and you can visit a little 16th-century church in the center of the village. It has absolutely no artistic treasures, but locals are fond of pointing it out to visitors anyway. There is one more sight, the ruins of the 17th-century **Forte de São Bento.** This towered fort once protected the fishing village against pirates from the African coast to the east. From Ribeira Brava, head north along N104 to the center of the island, toward Serra de Água.

Serra de Água

You reach Serra de Água, a little village 6.5km (4 miles) north of Ribeira Brava, by traversing a sheer canyon. One of the best centers for exploring Madeira's lush interior, it's also the site of one of the island's best pousadas (government-sponsored inns). Surrounded by abundant crops, jade-green fields, ferns, bamboo, weeping willows, and plenty of waterfalls, the village enjoys one of the loveliest settings in Madeira. Come here not for attractions, but for pure scenic beauty, though you should be warned that mist and clouds often shroud the town.

For dining and lodging, seek out the **Dorisol Pousada dos Vinháticos ★**, Estrada de São Vicente Serra de Água, 9350 Ribeira Brava (© **29/195-23-44;** fax 29/195-25-40; www.pousadadosvinhaticos.com), near the top of a pass on the winding road to São Vicente. The solid stone pousada, a tavern-style building with a brick terrace, opened in 1940. The tasty food is hearty and unpretentious, often depending on the catch of the day. Specialties include *espetada* (a swordfish version), ox tongue with Madeira sauce, and local beef flavored with regional wines. Main courses cost 10€ to 22€; hours are daily from noon to 6pm and 7 to 9pm. Reservations are recommended.

Most of the immaculate guest rooms are done in Portuguese modern style; a few contain antiques. All have good views. The price of a double is 48€ to 80€, including breakfast. Major credit cards are accepted, and parking is free.

From Serra de Água, the route climbs to the 990m (3,248-ft.) **Boca da Encumeada ★**, or Encumeada Pass, 6.5km (4 miles) north of Serra de Água. It's one of the island's best centers for hiking (information about hiking is available from the tourist office in Funchal), and a belvedere affords great panoramas over both sides of Madeira.

Following the route northwest of Boca da Encumeada, you reach the village of São Vicente, 14km (8⅔ miles) northwest of Boca da Encumeada and 56km (35 miles) northwest of Funchal.

São Vicente

One of the best-known towns on the north coast lies where the São Vicente River meets the ocean. Again, you come here for the sweeping views, some of the most dramatic on the island. Part of the fun of going to São Vicente is taking the one-lane north-coast route. In a miraculous and costly feat of engineering, it was chiseled out of pure cliff face. It's a nightmare if you encounter one of the bloated tour buses taking this highway. You'll often have to back up because the drivers rarely give way.

Constructed in 1950 and nicknamed the "gold road," the drive offers views of water cascading down the slopes. Many locals have planted vineyards in this seemingly inhospitable terrain.

In such a remote outpost, an inn comes as a welcome relief. You'll find good food and lodging at **Estalagem do Mar,** Juncos, Fajã da Areia, 9240 São Vicente (② **29/184-00-10;** fax 29/184-00-19; www.estalagemdomar.com). Most visitors pass through here only to dine on the excellent regional and international cuisine. Specialties include swordfish prepared in almost any style. Many versions of sea bass are served, and the meat dishes—especially perfectly grilled veal chop and beef filet in mushroom cream sauce—are also good. Main courses cost 10€ to 25€; it's open daily noon to 3pm and 7 to 10pm. Reservations are recommended.

If you decide to spend the night, the 91-room inn offers rather simply furnished accommodations opening onto views of the ocean. The inn has a provincial look, with flowery curtains and spreads, but rooms are modern, with tiled bathrooms, TVs, and phones. On the premises are an indoor and outdoor pool, a tennis court, a Jacuzzi, a sauna, a gym, and a game room. Limited room service is available. The three-floor hotel was built in the early 1990s. A double costs 45€ and a suite costs 66€, including breakfast. Parking is free. Major credit cards are accepted, and reservations are recommended.

From São Vicente, you can continue west along N101 to the town of Porto Moniz, 16km (10 miles) away in one of the remotest parts of Madeira.

Porto Muniz ★

This portion of the "gold road" is one of the most difficult but dramatic drives in Portugal, requiring nerves of steel. The road is boldly cut into the side of a towering cliff that plunges vertically into the ocean below. Eventually you arrive at Porto Moniz, a fishing village of great charm built at the site of a sheltered anchorage shaped by a slender peninsula jutting out toward an islet, Ilhéu Mole. This is the only sheltered harbor on the north coast of Madeira. Porto Moniz boasts no major sights other than the old village itself, with its fishermen's cottages and cobbled lanes. The adventure is surviving the trip.

For the best food in the area, head for **Restaurante Orca,** Vila do Porto Moniz, Porto Moniz 9270 (② **29/185-00-00;** fax 29/185-00-19). Tasty options include swordfish in mushroom and cream sauce, filet of beef served with dates, and fresh tuna steak breaded in corn flour and then sautéed and served with country cabbage and potatoes. Main courses cost 12€ to 33€. Food is served daily from noon to 4pm and 6:30 to 9pm. Major credit cards are accepted, and reservations are recommended.

After leaving Porto Moniz, you can continue southwest along N101, going back along a winding road via Ribeira Brava and Câmara de Lobos until you finally make the full circuit back into Funchal.

SANTANA & CENTRAL MADEIRA

For a final look at Madeira, you can cut through the center of the island, heading north from Funchal. This route takes you to such scenic highlights as Pico do Arieiro and Santana, and is one of the finest parts of Madeira for mountain hiking.

Pico do Arieiro ★★

This mountain and the settlement built on its side, 36km (22 miles) north of Funchal, really evoke the island's volcanic nature. When the 1,780m (5,840-ft.) peak is not covered by clouds (it's likely to be obscured Dec–Mar), the panoramic views are stunning. Pico do Arieiro is the third-tallest mountain on the island. To reach it, follow Rua 31 de Janeiro out of Funchal, and take N103 as it climbs to Monte. When you reach the pass at Poiso, some 10km (6¼ miles) north of Monte, take a left and continue to follow the signposts into Pico do Arieiro.

Once at the **miradouro** (belvedere) ★ at Pico do Arieiro, you'll have a panoramic sweep of the central mountains of Madeira. To the southeast is the village of Curral das Freiras (see above). To the immediate northeast you can take in a panorama of Penha d'Águia (Eagle's Rock), a rocky spike that is one of the most photographed sites in Madeira. You will also have a view of Pico Ruivo to the northwest (Madeira's highest point, at 1,860m/6,102 ft.), which can be accessed from Pico do Arieiro by a difficult 8km (5-mile) hill walk that takes approximately 4 hours.

Ribeiro Frio ★

Instead of taking the left fork at Poiso and heading for Pico do Arieiro (see above), you can go straight to reach Ribeiro Frio, an enchanting spot 11km (6¾ miles) north of Poiso.

Ribeiro Frio (Cold River) is a little village in the Madeira Forest Park (a protected area of trees and mountains in the center of Madeira that is spared from development) that occupies a dramatic setting in view of waterfalls, jagged peaks, and sleepy valleys.

You can take one of the most dramatic walks in Madeira from Ribeiro Frio. Just follow the signposts from Ribeiro Frio directing you to the **Balcões ★★**. This walk passes along Levada do Furado and takes you on footpaths cut out of basalt rock until you reach the belvedere, whose dizzying perch overlooks the jagged peaks of the Pico do Arieiro, Pico das Torres, and Pico Ruivo. This 40-minute walk is of only moderate difficulty and is suitable for the average visitor with no special hiking skills.

If the mountain air gives you an appetite, head south from Balcões for a 5-minute drive to **Victor's,** on N103 in Ribeiro Frio (✆ **29/157-58-98**), a chaletlike mountain restaurant known for afternoon tea and good regional food and wine. Trout from the area hatchery (prepared in a variety of ways) is a specialty; we prefer it grilled golden brown. You'll also find typical Madeiran cuisine, including lamb stew with potatoes, and swordfish with bananas. Main courses cost 12€ to 18€. The restaurant is open daily 9am to 9pm; reservations are recommended. Major credit cards are accepted.

Follow N103 out of Ribeiro Frio, heading north toward the coast. In the village of Faial, you'll find a connecting route, signposted west, to the village of Santana.

Santana ★

Eighteen kilometers (11 miles) northwest of Ribeiro Frio and 40km (25 miles) north of Funchal, Santana is the most famous village in Madeira and certainly the prettiest. It is noted for its A-framed, thatched-roof cottages called *palheiros*. Painted in bright, often flamboyant colors, they are the most-photographed private residences on the island. On a coastal plateau, Santana lies at an altitude of 742m (2,434 ft.).

Outside Santana is the **Madeira Theme Park ★**, at Estrada Regional 101, Fonte da Pedra (✆ **29/157-04-10;** www.parquetematicodamadeira.pt), set on 2.8 hectares (7 acres). This immense park and garden explores island history, culture, and tradition and is filled with various exhibits, including typical Santana houses. It is riddled with amusements, everything from a lake to a watermill to a kiddie playground. Staff provide you with a map of the park when you pay your admission. You can plan to have lunch here, as there are various eating places—including a cafeteria, two theme restaurants, and even a self-service dining spot for the frugal traveler—showcasing the gastronomy of Madeira. The park is open daily 10am to 7pm (closed Mon in winter) and charges 10€ for adults and 8€ for seniors and children ages 5 to 14; children ages 4 and under are admitted for free.

You can find food and lodging at one of the most frequented establishments on the north coast, **Quinta do Furão ★**, Achada do Gramacho, 9230 Santana (© **29/157-01-00;** fax 29/157-35-60; www.quintadofurao.com). The 43-unit inn lies in a vineyard on a clifftop setting that opens onto a panorama of the ocean. Most visitors stay just for the day to sample the cuisine, which is the finest on the north coast. The rustic dining room serves Madeiran, Portuguese, and international cuisine. Dishes include swordfish cooked with banana, grilled T-bone steak in garlic butter, and filet of beef baked in a pastry case and served with Roquefort sauce. You must try the local goat cheese. Main courses cost 10€ to 25€. Open hours are daily from noon to 3:30pm and 7 to 9:30pm. Reservations are recommended.

The inn is also a delightful place to stay. The ample guest rooms are well furnished in the regional style, with excellent mattresses, TVs, phones, and small to midsize bathrooms that are tiled and neatly kept. Some accommodations open onto sea views, and others face the mountains. The inn has a swimming pool, gym, Jacuzzi, and pub. Doubles with half-board cost 140€; a suite costs 190€, including breakfast. Parking is free. Major credit cards are accepted at the hotel and the restaurant.

SPORTS & OUTDOOR ACTIVITIES ON MADEIRA

Madeira's often pleasant climate invites visitors to enjoy outdoor activities, even if they consist mainly of strolling through Funchal and along park pathways and lanes.

DEEP-SEA FISHING   This is a popular sport on Madeira. The catch is mainly longtail tuna, blue marlin, swordfish, and several varieties of shark. Most boat rentals are moderately priced. The tourist office (see "Essentials," earlier in this chapter) can supply information about boat rentals and rates.

GOLF   The island maintains two 18-hole courses, both open to the public and accustomed to foreigners. The easier and better established is the **Clube de Golf do Santo da Serra,** in the hamlet of Santo da Serra (© **29/155-01-00;** www.santo daserragolf.com), on the island's northeastern side, about 24km (15 miles) from Funchal. Greens fees are 100€ for 18 holes. On rocky, steep terrain that some golfers find annoying is the **Palheiro Golf Course,** in the hamlet of **São Gonçalo,** 9050 Funchal (© **29/179-01-20;** www.palheirogolf.com), about 5km (3 miles) north of Funchal. It charges 100€ for 18 holes. Both establishments rent clubs and carts and provide local caddies; both also feature a clubhouse with a bar and restaurant, abundantly accented with mimosas, pines, and eucalyptus trees.

SWIMMING   Madeira doesn't have beaches. If your hotel doesn't have swimming facilities, you can use those of the **Complexo Balnear do Lido (Lido Swimming Pool Complex),** Rua do Gorgulho (© **29/176-22-17**), which has an outdoor

Olympic-size pool as well as a spacious outdoor pool for children. It's open daily in summer from 8:30am to 9pm, and off-season from 8:30am to 7pm. Adults pay 7€. Children under 10 swim free with parents; otherwise, they pay 4€ to use the pool. You can rent lounge chairs or umbrellas for 4€ each. The complex has a cafe, a restaurant, an ice-cream parlor, bars, and facilities for exercising in the water. To get there from Funchal, take N101 west for 5 minutes until you see the turnoff for Rua do Gorgulho, at which point you head south along this road to the Lido complex. The Lido is signposted from N101—you shouldn't have any trouble finding it. By public transit, take bus no. 6.

TOBOGGAN RIDES   By far the most entertaining rides on the island are on the two- or three-passenger toboggans, which resemble big wicker baskets resting on wooden runners. You get into one of the cushioned passenger seats for a ride down the slippery-smooth cobblestones, which takes about 20 minutes to reach Funchal. Runners are greased with suet to make them go smoother. Trained sled drivers run alongside the sled. If the sled starts to go too fast, they can hop on the back of it and slow it down. Originally, these sleds were used to transport produce from Monte to Funchal, but over the years tourists began to request rides in them, and an island attraction was born. When you pass Terreiro da Luta, a point along the way of your ride (at a height of 875m/2,871 ft.), you'll enjoy a panoramic view of Funchal and see monuments to Zarco and Our Lady of Peace.

Before you begin your descent, visit the **Church of Nossa Senhora do Monte,** which contains the iron tomb of the last of the Habsburgs, Emperor Charles, who died of pneumonia on Madeira in 1922. From a belvedere nearby, you can look down on the whole of Funchal.

Toboggan rides from Monte to Funchal cost 25€ for 2 and end up at Estrada do Livramento, in Funchal. For more information, contact **Carreiros dos Montes** (© 29/178-39-19).

WATERSPORTS   The activities desks of several major hotels, including **Reid's Palace** (see "Where to Stay in Funchal," earlier in this chapter), can arrange waterskiing, windsurfing, and rental of boats or sailing dinghies for guests and nonguests. If you want to go snorkeling or scuba diving, check with the **Madeira Carlton Hotel,** Largo António Nobre 9004-531 (© 29/123-95-00; www.pestanacarlton madeira.com).

SHOPPING IN MADEIRA

Crafts are rather expensive on the island, but collectors might want to seek out exquisite Madeira embroidery or needlework. Check to see that merchandise has a lead seal attached to it, certifying that it was made on Madeira and not imported. The businesses listed in this section are all in Funchal.

At the factory **Patricio & Gouveia ★**, Rua do Visconde de Anadia 33 (© 29/122-29-28), you can see employees making stencil patterns on embroidery and checking for quality of materials, though the actual embroidery is done in private homes and this process is not likely to be of great interest to anyone not seriously interested in embroidery. Of the several embroidery factories of Funchal, this is not only the most famous but also the best place to buy embroidery. Many of the routine souvenir shops scattered throughout the island sell embroidery from Taiwan and other places, but the embroidery at Patricio & Gouveia is the real thing—every item is guaranteed to be handmade on the island. **Bordal-Bordados da Madeira,** Rua Doctor Fernão Ornelas 77 (⌀ **29/122-29-65**), also carries an outstanding selection of completed embroidery.

Craft Shops & Factories

Casa do Turista ★   Near the waterfront in Funchal, this is the best place on the island for Madeira handicrafts. On the patio, with a fountain and semitropical greenery, is a miniature village, with small-scale typical rooms furnished in the local style. The merchandise includes handmade embroideries in linen or cotton (the fabric is often imported from Switzerland and Ireland), tapestries, wickerwork, Portuguese pottery and ceramics, Madeiran wines, fruit, and flowers. You'll find all types of embroidery and appliqués, as well as "shadow work" (a technique in which stitching takes place on the reverse of a transparent fabric, with the design showing through to the front in a very subtle manner). Prices are determined by the number of stitches. Rua do Conselheiro José Silvestre Ribeiro 2. ⌀ **29/122-49-07.**

Casa Oliveira   There's an embroidery factory on the premises of this shop. The store is primarily a retail outlet for one of the largest embroidery manufacturers in town, and everything sold in the shop is handmade on the island. It turns out everything from embroidered towels to delicate negligees to elegant "heirloom" tablecloths. The outlet is also known for its handmade and hand-painted ceramics. If you're seeking island souvenirs such as T-shirts, you'll find a large selection here, too. Rua da Alfândega 11. ⌀ **29/122-93-40.**

Madeira Wine

Funchal is the center of Madeira's **wine industry.** Grapes have grown in the region since the early 15th century, when Henry the Navigator introduced vines and sugar cane to the island's slopes. Every Madeira wine is fortified, brought up to full strength with high-proof grape brandy. The distinctive flavor of Madeira comes from being kept for months in special rooms called *estufas*. These *estufas* have high temperatures instead of the cool chambers where most bottles of wine are stored. *Madeira* refers to a whole body of wines that ranges from very sweet to very dry. Even the cheapest Madeira is quite remarkable, and the French, among others, use the least expensive Madeira for cooking, which adds more flavor than sherry or Marsala.

The light-colored Sercial, with a very dry taste, is gently scented. This wine is often compared to a Fino Sherry, although Sercial has its own special bouquet and character. Bual (sometimes known as Boal) is more golden in color and is a medium sweet wine, sometimes served as a dessert wine. It is velvety in content, its color ranging from a dark gold to a brown. Mainly a dessert wine, Malmsey is a sweet, chestnut-brown Madeira. The grapes that today produce Malmsey were the first ever shipped to the island.

Madeira Wine Company ★, Av. Arriaga 28 (⌀ **29/174-01-00;** www.madeira winecompany.com), a well-stocked wine shop next to the tourist office, offers samples from the diverse stock, which covers virtually every vintage produced on the island for the past 35 years. The shop is housed in a former convent dating from 1790. The building contains murals depicting the wine pressing and harvesting processes, which proceed according to the traditions established hundreds of years ago. You can savor a wide range of Madeira wines in a setting of old wine kegs and time-mellowed chairs and tables made from kegs. Admission is free; it's open Monday to

Friday 9:30am to 6:30pm, and Saturday from 10am to 1pm. **Guided tours** cost 5€. Tours last 1 hour and take visitors into a museum of antique winemaking equipment and past displays of some of the oldest bottles of Madeira wine. The highlight of the tour, however, is when visitors are taken into a cellar bodega for an actual wine tasting. Visitors are escorted through the premises Monday to Friday at 10:30am and 3:30pm, and again on Saturday at 11am.

Markets and Bazaars

The Workers' Market, **Mercado dos Lavradores** ★, at Rua Hospital Velho, is held Monday through Saturday from 7am to 8pm but is liveliest in the morning. Flower vendors dressed in typical Madeiran garb of corselets, leather boots, and striped skirts will generally let you photograph them if you ask them—especially if you buy some flowers. The market is filled with stalls selling island baskets, crafts, fruits, and vegetables, and offers Madeira's largest array of that day's fish catch.

In Funchal's **bazaars,** found throughout the center of town, you can purchase needlepoint tapestries, Madeiran wines, laces, and embroidery on Swiss organdy or Irish linen, as well as local craft items such as goat-skin boots, Camacha basketry, and other eclectic merchandise. The colorful **City Market,** at Praça do Comércio, Monday through Saturday, offers everything from yams to papaws to a wide array of handicrafts, including products in wicker and leather.

At these bazaars, you can find good deals on handmade shoes and tooled leather. However, prices on other items (embroidery, needlework, table linens, and tropical flowers) can be high, so have an idea of what you want to pay for certain items and sharpen your bargaining skills before going. Madeira is an excellent place to buy tropical (though expensive) flowers such as orchids and birds of paradise, all of which can be shipped to the United States. U.S. Customs allows flowers from Madeira into the United States, as long as they are inspected at any American airport upon arrival.

MADEIRA AFTER DARK

The glittering **Entertainment Complex at the Pestana Casino Park Hotel & Casino** ★★, Avenida do Infante, Funchal (✆ 29/120-91-00; www.casinoda madeira.com), is the most obvious entertainment venue for first-time visitors. The complex offers an array of options. Foremost is a **casino,** the only one on Madeira, which offers roulette, French banque, craps, blackjack, and slot machines. To be admitted, you must be 21, present a passport or other form of identification, and pay a 5€ government tax. The casino is open daily from 4pm to 3am.

Nearby, on Avenida do Infante, is a dance club, **Copacabana** ★ (✆ 92/751-64-32), that's at its liveliest after 11pm Thursday through Saturday; it charges a cover (including one drink) of 7€. On Sunday at 9pm, the hotel offers a Las Vegas–style cabaret show. For the show only, there's a minimum bar tab of 15€ per person; dinner, two drinks, and a view of the show costs 55€. In addition, the complex contains bars, kiosks, and boutiques. You must be 18 or older to enter.

Options outside the casino complex are limited, although some hotels present dinner shows. Funchal isn't the best place in Portugal to hear fado, but you can sample the music at **Arsenios Restaurant,** Rua de Santa Maria 169 (✆ 29/122-40-07), which serves dinners ranging in price from 15€ to 30€. It's open daily from 8 to 10pm.

Teatro Municipal Baltazar Dias, Avenida Arriaga (✆ **29/123-35-69**), in the center of Funchal, presents plays (in Portuguese only) and occasional classical music concerts. The tourist office has information, and you can purchase tickets at the box office.

The town's dance club action is fairly limited. **Vespas,** Av. Sá Carneiro 7 (✆ **29/123-48-00;** www.discotecavespas.com), a warehouselike club near the docks, attracts a young crowd. It's open Thursday through Saturday from 10pm to either 2 or 3am (depending on business). If you're over 35, you might head for the spacious **Taverna Bar,** Largo António Nobre 9007 (✆ **29/123-95-00**), in the Madeira Carlton Hotel. It features modern dance music and hits from the 1970s and 1980s. Hours are Thursday to Saturday 10:30pm to 2am. Neither club has a cover charge.

Prince Albert, Rua da Imperatriz Dona Amélia (✆ **29/123-57-93**), is a Victorian pub complete with plush cut-velvet walls, tufted banquettes, and English pub memorabilia. Next to the Savoy, it serves English spirits and oversize mugs of beer at the curved bar and at tables under Edwardian fringed lamps. It's open daily 11am to midnight.

You also might try the restaurant/*taverna* **A Seta,** where you can sample the local wine until 11pm. (See "On the Outskirts of Funchal," earlier in chapter.)

PORTO SANTO ★

39km (24 miles) NE of Madeira

The second major island of the Madeira archipelago is Porto Santo, an arid landmass that presents a marked contrast to the lushness of the main island. It is 14km (8⅔ miles) long and 5km (3 miles) wide, with a 6.5km (4-mile) strip of fine sandy beach along the southern shore. The island is not as hilly as Madeira: Its highest elevation is about 509m (1,670 ft.) above sea level, at **Pico do Facho.**

João Gonçalves Zarco and Tristão Vaz Teixeira, who discovered Madeira, landed on Porto Santo in 1418 when they took refuge from a storm. To express gratitude for their survival, they named the island Porto Santo (Holy Port). It was not until 1419 that the men were able to sail on and make landfall on the main island. Prince Henry the Navigator gave Teixeira and Zarco authority to run Madeira, but he placed Porto Santo in the hands of Bartolomeu Perestrello.

The island gets very dry in the summer, which makes it popular with beachgoers but not good for crops. The foodstuffs grown on Porto Santo in the winter include grain, tomatoes, figs, and melons, as well as grapes, from which sweet wines are made. A few remaining unusual windmills crown the island's low hills.

The water of Porto Santo supposedly has therapeutic value. It's a popular drink not only on the island, but also in Madeira and Portugal. The water-bottling plants, fish canneries, and a limekiln make up the island's industries.

Essentials
ARRIVING
BY PLANE The flight from Madeira to the little **Campo de Cima** airport (✆ **29/198-01-20;** www.aeroportosdamadeira.pt), Estrada Regional 101, at Porto Santo, takes only 15 minutes and offers spectacular views. Always reserve well in advance for July and August, when beach lovers descend en masse. Flights generally

cost 77€ one-way and 100€ round-trip. In peak season, count on eight flights per day; frequency diminishes in the off season. For ticket reservations and information, call ☏ 70/722-72-82. (See "Essentials," earlier in this chapter, for information on arriving from Lisbon or international destinations.) The airport lies right outside of town, a 30-minute walk from the center. Taxis (☏ 29/198-23-34) meet all arriving flights, and a fare into town typically costs 10€. There is no bus service from the airport to the center of town.

BY BOAT   Regularly scheduled ferry service connects Madeira and Porto Santo. The Lobo Marinho departs Funchal Harbor daily. Tickets cost 43€ to 53€ round-trip, depending on the season.

Saturday to Thursday, the ferry usually departs Madeira at 8am and arrives in Porto Santo at 10:15am. The departure from Madeira on Friday isn't until 7pm. During the month of August, a ferry departs Madeira at 8am daily. Always check the schedules for return trips from Porto Santo, which vary. You can purchase tickets at the **Lobo Marinho** office, Rua da Praia, Funchal (☏ 29/121-03-00; www.portosantoline.pt), Monday to Friday from 9am to 12:30pm and 2:30 to 6pm. On weekends, you can buy a ticket at any travel agency in Funchal.

The boats arrive at a little port about a 30-minute walk from the center of town. Taxis await arriving boats and will take you into the center or to one of the nearby hotels for 5€. There is also bus service into the center, which costs 1€ per passenger.

VISITOR INFORMATION

The **tourist office** is at Avenida Henrique Vieira e Castro, Porto Santo (☏ 29/198-23-61; www.madeiratourism.org). It's open Monday to Friday 9am to 5:30pm and Saturday from 10am to 12:30pm.

Getting Around

Most visitors get around on foot or rely on a **taxi** (☏ 29/198-23-34) for excursions. In town, you can usually pick up a taxi along Rua Doctor Nuno Teixeira. Car rentals can be arranged at **Moinho,** at Porto Santo Airport (☏ 29/198-31-60).

Exploring the Island

Most visitors come here strictly for the wide beach of golden sand along the southern coast. It's ideal for swimming in unpolluted waters or for long strolls. If you tear yourself from the beach for a day, you will find some minor attractions. **Vila Baleira,** a sleepy town of whitewashed stucco houses, merits an hour of your time. You'll be following in the footsteps of Christopher Columbus as you make your way along its cobblestone streets.

Locals call the town Vila, and it lies at the center of the 6.5km-long (4-mile) beach. Stop for a drink at Café Ballena on **Largo do Pelourinho ★**, the main square. Shaded by palm trees, it is the center of life on the island. To the right of the Church of Our Lady of Piedad, follow a sign along the alley to the **Casa de Cristovão Colombo,** Travessa da Sacristia 4 (☏ 29/198-34-05; www.museucolombo-portosanto.com). The explorer is said to have lived here with his wife, Isobel Moniz. Documentation about the Columbus visit to Porto Santo is skimpy, but it appears that he did live here for a short time. In an annex, you can view maps and engravings depicting major events in his life. The museum is open Monday to Friday from 10am to noon and 2 to 5:30pm, Saturday and Sunday from 10am to 1pm. Admission is 1.50€.

THE AZORES: LOST CONTINENT OF atlantis

One of the most offbeat travel experiences in Europe is a trip to the nine Portuguese islands off the Azores. Mythologists believe the remote Portuguese islands in the mid-Atlantic are the only remnants of the lost continent of Atlantis. For hundreds of years these islands were considered the end of the earth, the outer limits of the European sphere of influence beyond which ships could not sail. Even today, they're a verdant but lonely archipelago in the middle of the ocean, seemingly more tuned to Boston than Lisbon. The cluster of islands is the place where the winds of the Atlantic meet; cyclones call on each other, and visiting urbanites can lose themselves in the often fog-bound volcanic islands occupied by 240,000 hearty people.

When the first explorers directed their ships' prows into the Atlantic, the volcanic slopes of the Azores were the westernmost-known points of land. Phoenicians, Vikings, and Genoese were among the early explorers who dared sail west from Europe across the uncharted Atlantic.

The autonomous archipelago spans a distance of more than 805km (500 miles) from the southeastern tip of Santa Maria to the northwestern extremity at Corvo. The main island of **São Miguel** lies about 1,223km (760 miles) west of Portugal (3,396km/2,110 miles east of New York), making the Azores the most isolated islands in the entire Atlantic.

Completely uninhabited when discovered, the Azores were named by Diogo de Silves (a captain of Henry the Navigator) after the hook-beaked *açor* (compared to both a hawk and an eagle), which sailed on the air currents over the coast. The date: 1427 (give or take a year or two). It wasn't long before settlements sprang up. Besides the Portuguese settlers, Flemish immigrants came to the central Azores, and today's place and family names show this influence.

Eventually it was learned that the entire island group was actually composed of three distinct archipelagos: the eastern section of **Santa Maria** and **São Miguel;** the central section with **Terceira** (the scene of bullfighting in the streets),

Later you can follow Rua Infante Dom Henrique, off Largo do Pelourinho, to a beach-surrounded, flower-filled **park** with a statue dedicated to Columbus. This is one of the most restful and scenic spots on the island.

After seeing the town and its meager attractions, you can visit some of the island's scenic highlights. They include **Pico do Castelo,** north of Vila Baleira, on a small and difficult road. It affords a perspective on the whole island and endless views of the sea. Pick up picnic provisions at one of the little shops in Vila Baleira. A fortified castle once stood here to guard Vila Baleira from attacks by pirates. Only four cannons remain—islanders removed most of the castle's stone for building materials. The island government has planted pine trees to keep the air moist, but they never grow beyond 3m (9¾ ft.), so as not to obscure the view. From Pico do Castelo, you can follow signs to **Pico do Facho,** the tallest point on the island.

At the southwestern tip of the island, **Ponta da Calheta** is another scenic destination. To get there, take the road west out of Vila Baleira. It has a view of the little offshore island of Baixo, across a dangerous channel riddled with reefs. The beach is made of black basalt rocks, so it's not suitable for swimming.

Graciosa, cigar-shaped **São Jorge** (Raul Brandão's ethereal island of dust and dream), **Pico** (with a cloud-capped mountain), and **Faial** (vulnerable to earthquakes and known for the eerie crater of the extinct volcano, Caldeira); and the western group made up of **Flores** (flowers), where the vegetation runs riot in a setting of lakes, waterfalls, and valleys, and **Corvo** (the smallest member—everybody knows everybody else—and a visit by a foreigner is an occasion).

The Azores are a study in color. The unknown writer who once made the much-publicized characterization the "Gray Azores" must have been color-blind. Much of the color of the archipelago comes from the flowers that grow rampantly in its volcanic soil: azaleas, camellias, heather, agapanthus, and rhododendrons. Although occasionally lashed by violent storms, the enchanted islands enjoy a mild climate: The temperature averages around 58°F (14°C) in winter, only 75°F (24°C) in the summer.

Even though one might expect these isolated islanders to be insular, the rugged people here, who contend with the elements of nature daily, are hospitable to strangers. Coming back from a walk in the São Miguel hills, we were stopped by a boy riding a mule. Under a straw hat with a hoe slung over his shoulder, the boy smiled as he bid us *boa tarde.* The world YALE was written across his sweatshirt. It seemed that his uncle had attended Yale. "Do you know him?" the boy asked. "He now lives in Boston."

Every man, woman, and child in the island chain seemingly has relatives living in the United States. Many settled in New Bedford, Massachusetts (of *Moby-Dick* fame), during the whaling heyday of that port, taking jobs as sailors, fishermen, whalers, and caulkers. Many of the immigrants returned to the Azores, however, after earning their fortunes across the sea.

Space is too tight for more details here, but information is available by contacting the **Azores Tourist Board,** Rua Ernesto Rebelo 14-P 9900-112 Horta, Faial (🕿 **29/220-05-00;** www. visitazores.com). A division of SATA Airlines, **Azores Express** (www.sata.pt) has direct flights from Boston to the Azores.

Directly north lies another of the island's great lookout points, **Pico dos Flores.** Access is over a pothole-riddled dirt road. The cliffs here also have a panoramic view of the islet of Baixo, to your left. The tiny islet to your right is Ferro.

While in the southwestern part of the island, you can also follow the signs to **A Pedreira ★,** on the slopes of Pico de Ana Ferreira. The amazing basalt rock formation brings to mind organ pipes stretching toward the sky.

Where to Stay
MODERATE
Porto Santo Hotel & Spa ★   Right on the beach, a 15-minute walk from the center of town, this government-rated four-star hotel is one of the leading hotels on the island. The two-story building is decorated in contemporary style and is set in a peaceful garden setting. The midsize rooms are standard but well furnished. Make reservations far in advance if you plan to visit in August. The restaurant serves regional and international cuisine; in the summer, the lavish Wednesday night buffet

is the hottest ticket on the island. The hotel has two bars, one in the restaurant and the other on the beach.

Campo Baixo, 9400-015 Porto Santo. www.hotelportosanto.com. © **29/198-01-40.** Fax 29/198-01-49. 97 units. 118€–266€ double. Rates include buffet breakfast. AE, DC, MC, V. **Amenities:** Restaurant; 2 bars; babysitting; exercise room; 3 pools (1 heated indoor); spa; 2 outdoor tennis courts (lit). *In room:* A/C, TV, hair dryer, minibar.

Torre Praia Hotel ★★   The island's second leading hotel is on the outskirts of Vila Baleira, adjacent to its own beach. Rated four stars by the government, it offers midsize to spacious guest rooms. Spread over three stories, they're well furnished, with excellent beds and state-of-the-art plumbing. Most have water views. The restaurant, constructed around an old watchtower, is one of the island's best. Head to the bar on top of the hotel for great views.

Rua Goulart Medeiros, 9400-164 Porto Santo. www.hoteltorrepraiaportosanto.com. © **29/198-04-50.** Fax 29/198-24-87. 66 units. 100€–235€ double; 130€–400€ suite. Rates include buffet breakfast. AE, DC, MC, V. **Amenities:** 2 restaurants; 3 bars; babysitting; exercise room; Jacuzzi; outdoor pool; room service; sauna; Wi-Fi (free, in lobby). *In room:* A/C, TV, hair dryer, minibar.

Vila Baleira Thalassa ★★ ☺   The island's premier hotel lies 4km (2½ miles) from the center of Vila Baleira, opening onto a long, sandy beach with a playground and beach room. The largest on Porto Santo, the hotel is linked by an underground tunnel to an outdoor leisure area with pool and various drinking and eating facilities, as well as beach equipment, a spa, a gym, and a diving center.

The hotel itself contains restaurants, bars, shops, public lounges, and an indoor pool connected to a kiddie pool. The guest rooms, often furnished in wicker, are midsize and the best on the island (32 of the units are junior suites). Most of the airy bedrooms open onto private balconies overlooking the water.

The on-site Atlantic Restaurant in the main building serves only buffets, which are wide-ranging in scope and cuisine, with a variety of regional and international specialties.

Cabeço da Ponta-Apartado 243, 9400-909 Porto Santo. www.vilabaleira.com. © **29/198-08-00.** Fax 29/198-08-01. 256 units. 85€–187€ double; 120€–290€ suite. AE, MC, V. **Amenities:** 2 restaurants; 2 bars; babysitting; bikes; children's center; concierge; exercise room; 2 seawater pools (1 heated indoor); room service; spa; Wi-Fi (free, in lobby). *In room:* A/C, TV, hair dryer, minibar.

INEXPENSIVE

Praia Dourada Hotel   This affordable hotel lies within the center of Vila Baleira. It opened in 1980 and was last renovated in 1998. Its three floors contain standard, motel-like rooms. Rooms are light, airy, and well furnished, though they lack any particular luster. Many units have private balconies. The hotel, about a 5-minute walk from a beach, attracts many frugal Madeirans in the summer. Breakfast is the only meal served.

Rua D. Estêvão de Alencastre, 9400-161 Porto Santo. www.booking.com/hotel/pt/praia-dourada. © **29/198-04-50.** Fax 29/198-24-84. 100 units. 70€–125€ double. Rates include buffet breakfast. AE, DC, MC, V. **Amenities:** Bar; outdoor pool; Wi-Fi (free, in lobby). *In room:* TV.

Where to Dine

Most guests dine at their hotels, which are also open to nonguests (see "Where to Stay" above). Some little eateries around the island specialize in fresh fish.

Baiana PORTUGUESE   Near the town hall in the center of Vila Baleira, this is a regular rendezvous, popular with visitors and locals alike. In fair weather, guests select a table on the sidewalk and order drinks, sandwiches, or full regional meals. The tasty dishes include filet of beef cooked at your table and served with a selection of sauces. Instead of beef, *espetada* comes with skewered squid and shrimp, delicately flavored and served with fresh lemon. Pork in wine and garlic marinade is another tasty offering.

Rua Dr. Nuno S. Teixeira. ✆ **29/198-46-49.** Reservations recommended. Main courses 12€-18€. AE, DC, MC, V. Daily noon–3:30pm and 6:30–11pm.

PLANNING YOUR TRIP TO PORTUGAL

This chapter addresses the where, when, and how of visiting Portugal—all the logistics of putting your trip together and taking it on the road.

GETTING THERE

By Plane

Flying from New York to Lisbon typically costs less than from New York to Paris, Amsterdam, or Frankfurt. The key to snagging bargain airfares is to shop around.

Flying time from New York to Lisbon is about 6½ hours; from Atlanta to Lisbon (with a stopover), it's 12 hours; from Los Angeles to Lisbon (with a stopover), it's 15 hours; and from Montreal or Toronto, it's 8 hours.

MAJOR AIRLINES **TAP Air Portugal** (© 800/221-7370; www. tap-airportugal.us), the country's national airline, flies to four continents aboard one of the youngest fleets in the airline industry. From North America, it maintains nonstop flights to Lisbon—sometimes with direct ongoing service to Porto—from Newark, New Jersey (once or twice a day, depending on the season) and from Miami (two to three times a week, depending on the season).

Thanks to TAP's membership in the Star Alliance, the airline's flights from Newark and Miami are timed to coincide with transfer of flights operated by, among others, United and US Airways, thereby making for convenient connections and sharing of mileage bonus awards among the various members

Within Portugal, TAP flies to nine destinations, the most popular of which include Lisbon (airport code: LIS), Porto (OPO), and Faro (FAO).

Continental Airlines (© 800/231-0856 in the U.S.; www.continental. com) began flying to Lisbon from Newark International Airport in 1997. The increased capacity comes as a welcome addition to existing air service, particularly during heavy travel periods in summer.

Air Canada (© 888/247-2262 in the U.S. or Canada; www.aircanada. com) no longer offers direct flights to Lisbon, but it does offer daily flights from Toronto and Montreal to Paris, where you can transfer to another carrier to reach Lisbon.

Avoiding "Economy-Class Syndrome"

Deep-vein thrombosis, or as it's known in the world of flying, "economy-class syndrome," is a blood clot that develops in a deep vein. It's a potentially deadly condition that can be caused by sitting in cramped conditions—such as an airplane cabin—for too long. During a flight (especially a long-haul flight), get up, walk around, and stretch your legs every 60 to 90 minutes to keep your blood flowing. Other preventive measures include frequent flexing of the legs while sitting, drinking lots of water, and avoiding alcohol and sleeping pills. If you have a history of deep-vein thrombosis, heart disease, or another condition that puts you at high risk, some experts recommend wearing compression stockings or taking anticoagulants when you fly; always ask your physician about the best course for you. Symptoms of deep-vein thrombosis include leg pain or swelling, or even shortness of breath.

For flights from the U.K., contact **British Airways** (℡ 0844/493-0787; www.britishairways.com) or **TAP** (℡ 0845/601-0932; www.tap-airportugal.com). Or contact the budget carriers **easyJet** (℡ 0843/104-5000; www.easyjet.com), which flies daily to Lisbon from both Gatwick and Luton airports in the U.K., or **Ryanair** (℡ 0871/246-0000; www.ryanair.com) which flies from London's Stansted Airport to Porto, Portugal's second city.

TAP also has frequent flights on popular routes from major cities in western Europe. Its flights to Lisbon from London are an especially good deal; sometimes they're priced so attractively that one might combine a sojourn in England with an inexpensive side excursion to Portugal. TAP gives passengers the option of stopping midway across the Atlantic in the Azores, and it makes baggage transfers and seat reservations on connecting flights within Portugal much easier.

REGULAR FARES All airlines divide their calendar year into three seasons—basic, shoulder, and peak—whose dates might vary slightly from airline to airline. TAP's basic season, when fares are typically least expensive, is November 1 to December 14 and December 25 to March 31. The most expensive season is its peak season from June 1 to September 15, when passengers tend to solidly book most transatlantic flights. Other dates are shoulder season.

DISCOUNTED FARES For families, one strong attraction of TAP is that infants under 2 years pay 10% of the adult fare. (About a half-dozen bassinets are available on transatlantic flights, allowing parents to lift infants off their laps onto specially designed brackets during certain segments of the flight.) Children under 12 pay 75% of the adult price for most categories of tickets.

TAP offers a winter senior citizen fare from its three U.S. gateways to anywhere in Portugal. The discount is 10% off published fares. The discount applies for seniors (travelers 62 years of age or older) plus a companion of any age (spouse, grandchild, or friend). The maximum stay abroad with this type of ticket is 2 months. You must purchase tickets at least 14 days before departure.

Subject to change, TAP offers a one-way youth fare. It's 50% off the regular fare, depending on the season, between New York or Boston and Lisbon. Tickets of this type can be purchased only at the last minute because they can be booked only within

72 hours of departure. Youth fares are offered only to travelers ages 12 to 24 and only if space is available. They cannot be mailed; you must purchase them in person at a travel agent or any TAP counter.

None of the above options takes into account promotional fares airlines might initiate while you're planning your trip. These are usually particularly attractive during the basic season.

By Car

Portugal is crisscrossed by a network of modern highways, with most highways leading to either Lisbon or Porto, the country's two largest cities. Direct access between the two cities is via at least three highways, the largest and fastest of which is the A1 Autoroute. The main route south from Lisbon to the Algarve is the A2.

With the exception of the A1 and A2, using route numbers to identify highways in Portugal is sometimes confusing, since many are designated only with signs indicating their final destinations or to important cities en route. Central, historic cores of every city in Portugal are signposted "Centro," a clue that helps keep motorists headed in the right direction in their search for a city's medieval center.

Travel time between Lisbon and some major cities is as follows: Porto, 3½ hours; Faro (capital of the Algarve), 3 hours; Coimbra 3½ hours; and Fátima 1½ hours.

When crossing the border between Spain and Portugal, cars and their passengers usually pass unchallenged, unless there's a security alert in effect at the time of your crossing.

For information on car rentals and gasoline (petrol) in Portugal, see "Getting Around," later in this section.

By Train

Thousands of traveling Brits (and foreigners visiting the U.K.) cross France and Spain by rail to begin their Portuguese holiday. If you opt for this option, expect lots of worthwhile scenery, and be aware that you'll have to change trains in Paris.

Trains from London originate in Waterloo Station, pass through the Channel Tunnel, and arrive in Paris at Gare du Nord. Don't expect to merely cross over a railway platform to change trains: You'll have to traverse urban Paris, moving from Gare du Nord to Gare Montparnasse. You can do this for the cost of a Métro ticket, but if you have luggage, hiring a taxi makes the transit a lot easier. (Taxis line up near your point of arrival.) From Gare Montparnasse, the train continues through France but requires a change of equipment in Hendaye, on the Spanish-French border. It continues to Lisbon's Santa Apolónia station. Total travel time for this itinerary is 22 hours, so we strongly recommend reserving a couchette (sleeping car). Budgeteers can save about 10% off fares by taking a slower, less convenient ferry across the English Channel. However, this option adds at least 5 hours, additional transfers, and many hassles at the docks on either side of the water, and will involve you in imbroglios that probably aren't worth the savings.

From Paris, the most luxurious way to reach Portugal is by the overnight Paris-Madrid Talgo express train. It leaves from Gare d'Austerlitz and arrives in Madrid's Chamartín Station, where you transfer to the Lisboa Express.

In Madrid, the Lusitania Express leaves the Atocha Station at 10:45pm and arrives in Lisbon at 8:15am; the 11pm train arrives in Lisbon at 8:40am.

For more complete information about rail connections, contact **Caminhos de Ferro Portuguêses,** Calçada do Duque 20, 1249 Lisboa (**℡ 21/102-30-00;** www. cp.pt).

If you plan much travel on European railroads, get the latest copy of the *Thomas Cook European Timetable of Railroads*. This 500-plus-page book documents all of Europe's main passenger rail services with detail and accuracy. It's available online at www.thomascookpublishing.com.

EURAILPASSES   The Eurailpass is one of Europe's greatest bargains, permitting unlimited first-class rail travel through 17 countries in Europe, including Portugal. Passes are for periods as short as 15 days or as long as 3 months and are strictly non-transferable.

The **Eurail Global Pass** allows you unlimited travel in 18 Eurail-affiliated countries. You can travel on any of the days within the validity period, which is available for 15 days, 21 days, 1 month, 2 months, 3 months, and some other possibilities as well. Prices for first-class adult travel are 529€ for 15 days, 683€ for 21 days, 841€ for 1 month, 1,188€ for 2 months, and 1,464€ for 3 months. Children 4 to 11 pay half-fare; those 3 and under travel for free.

A **Eurail Global Youth Pass** for those ages 12 to 25 allows second-class travel in 22 countries. This pass costs 345€ for 15 days, 445€ for 21 days, 547€ for 1 month, 772€ for 2 months, and 952€ for 3 months.

The **Eurail Selectpass** offers unlimited travel on the national rail networks of any three, four, or five bordering countries out of the 22 Eurail nations linked by train or ship. Two or more passengers can travel together for big discounts, getting 5, 6, 8, 10, or 15 days of rail travel within any 2-month period. A sample fare: For 5 days in 2 months you pay 334€ for three countries.

Other passes include **Eurail Global Flexi Pass,** allowing you to choose either 10 or 15 days of unlimited travel in 18 European countries, including Portugal, within a 2-month period. In first class, 625€ gets you 10 days of travel in 2 months, rising to 820€ for 15 days in 2 months. Children 4 to 11 pay half the adult fare.

If you're under 26, you can avail yourself of a **Eurail Global Flexi Pass Youth.** In second class, you get 10 days of travel in 2 months for 407€, or 15 days in 2 months for 534€. For that you get to travel in 22 European countries, including Portugal.

Portuguese Railpass offers any 3 days in a month for 155€, or 4 days in a month for 199€. This pass is good for unlimited first-class travel within Portugal.

Travel agents in all towns and railway agents in major North American cities sell all these Eurail tickets, but the biggest supplier is **Rail Europe** (**℡ 877/272-RAIL** [7245] in the U.S. for information; **℡ 0870/584-8848** for reservations from the U.K.; www.raileurope.com). Your best deal is to book with the 0870 number in England. If you reserve at least 7 days in advance, you get various reductions.

Many different rail passes are available in the United Kingdom for travel in Britain and continental Europe. Stop in at the **International Rail Centre,** Victoria Station, London SW1V 1JY (**℡ 0870/584-8848** in the U.K.). Some of the most popular passes, including Inter-Rail and Euro Youth, are offered only to travelers under 26 years of age; these allow unlimited second-class travel through most European countries, including Portugal.

By Bus

There is no convenient bus service from other parts of Europe to Portugal. Flying, driving, and traveling by rail are the preferred transport methods. However, the buses that do make the trip—say, from London or France—offer somewhat lower prices (and less comfort) than equivalent journeys by rail.

The largest bus line in Europe, **Eurolines Ltd.,** 52 Grosvenor Gardens, London SW1W 0UA (✆ **0871/781-8177;** www.eurolines.com), operates bus routes to Portugal that stop at several places in France (including Paris) and Spain along the way. Buses leave from London's Victoria Coach Station daily, travel by ferry across the English Channel, and arrive in Lisbon 37 hours later. Tickets from London to Lisbon cost £83 to £110 one-way and £188 round-trip.

Eurolines also offers service from London's Victoria Coach Station to Faro, in southern Portugal, every Monday, Wednesday, and Friday at 10pm. Arrival is 2 days later, after multiple stops and delays.

By Boat

Brittany Ferries operates from Plymouth, England, to Santander, Spain. From March through November, crossing time is 23 to 24 hours. Between October and April, the trip takes 30 to 33 hours. Contact Brittany Ferries, Millbay Docks, Plymouth, England PL1 3EW (✆ **0871/244-0744;** www.brittany-ferries.co.uk), for exact schedules and more information. From Santander, you can drive west to Galicia, in Spain, and then head south toward Portugal, entering through the Minho district.

GETTING AROUND

By Car

Many scenic parts of Portugal are isolated from train or bus stations, so you need a private car to do serious touring. That way, at least in terms of transport, you'll be relatively self-sufficient, unhindered by the somewhat fickle train and bus timetables, which often limit your excursions to places close to the beaten track.

Portugal has fewer superhighways than you might expect, and they're often interspersed with lengthy stretches of traffic-clogged single-lane thoroughfares. The roads, however, provide access to hard-to-reach gems and undiscovered villages.

RENTALS Three of North America's major car-rental companies maintain dozens of branches at each of Portugal's most popular commercial and tourist centers, at rates that are usually competitive.

Budget (✆ **800/472-3325** in the U.S.; www.budget.com) has offices in more than a dozen locations in Portugal. The most central and most used are in Lisbon, Faro (the heart of the Algarve), Porto, Praia da Rocha (also a popular Algarve destination), and Madeira. Because Portugal has one of the highest accident rates in Europe, you should seriously think about buying the optional CDW (collision-damage waiver) insurance.

Note that some North American credit card issuers, especially American Express, sometimes agree to pay any financial obligations incurred after an accident involving a client's rented car, but only if the imprint of the card is on the original rental contract. Because of this agreement, some clients opt to decline the extra insurance coverage offered by the car-rental company. To be sure that you qualify for this free insurance, check in advance with your card issuer. Know that even though the card's issuer might eventually reimburse you, you'll still have to fill out some complicated paperwork and usually advance either cash or a credit card deposit to cover the repair cost.

Avis (☎ **800/331-1084** in the U.S.; www.avis.com) maintains offices in downtown Lisbon and at the airport, and at 17 other locations throughout Portugal. One office is at Avenida Praia Da Victoria, Lisbon (☎ **21/351-45-60**).

Hertz (☎ **800/654-3001** in the U.S.; www.hertz.com) has about two dozen locations in Portugal and requires a 3-day advance booking for its lowest rates. Hertz's main office is at Rua Castilho 72, Lisbon (☎ **21/942-63-00**).

Kemwel Drive Group (☎ **877/820-0668**; www.kemwel.com), sometimes offers a viable alternative to more traditional car-rental companies. Kemwel leases entire blocks of cars a year in advance at locations throughout Portugal and then rents them back out to qualified customers who pay the entire price in advance. In Portugal, you can retrieve Kemwel cars in Lisbon.

Auto Europe (☎ **888/223-5555**; www.autoeurope.com) leases cars on an as-needed basis from larger car-rental companies throughout Europe. Its rates sometimes are lower than those at Hertz and Avis.

Note: In most cases, you must be between 21 and 75 years old to rent a car in Portugal.

GASOLINE Gasoline (petrol, to the British) stations are plentiful throughout Portugal. However, if you wander far off the beaten track, it's always wise to have a full tank and to get a refill whenever it's available, even if your tank is still more than half full. The government clamps price controls on gas, and it should cost the same everywhere. Credit cards are frequently accepted at gas stations, at least along the principal express routes. You should note that ever-changing gas prices are much higher than you're probably used to paying, and gas is measured in liters.

DRIVER'S LICENSES U.S. and Canadian driver's licenses are valid in Portugal. But if you're at least 18 and touring other destinations in Europe by car, you should probably invest in an international driver's permit. In the United States, apply through any local branch of the **American Automobile Association (AAA);** for a list of local branches, contact the national headquarters, 1000 AAA Dr., Heathrow, FL 32746-5063 (☎ **800/222-1134**; www.aaa.com). Include two 2×2-inch photographs, a $10 fee, and a photocopy of your state driver's license. In Canada, you pay C$10 and apply to the **Canadian Automobile Association (CAA),** 2525 Carling Ave., Ottawa, ON K2B 7Z2 (☎ **613/820-1890**; www.caa.ca).

Note that your international driver's license is valid only if it's accompanied by an authorized license from your home state or province.

In Portugal, as elsewhere in Europe, to drive a car legally you must have in your possession an international insurance certificate, known as a **Green Card** (Carte Verte or Carte Verde). The car-rental agency will provide you with one as part of your rental contract.

DRIVING RULES Continental driving rules apply in Portugal, and international road symbols and signs are used. Wearing safety belts is compulsory. Speed limits are 90kmph (56 mph) on main roads, and 60kmph (37 mph) in heavily populated or built-up sections. On the limited number of express highways, the speed limit is 120kmph (75 mph).

ROAD MAPS   Michelin publishes the best Portugal road maps, and they're available at many stores and map shops throughout Europe and in the U.S. and Canada. Or you can order them from Michelin, P.O. Box 19008, Greenville, SC 29602-9008 (© **866/866-6605** in the U.S.) The maps are updated every year; always try to obtain the latest copy because Portugal's roads are undergoing tremendous changes. One of the best Michelin maps to Portugal is no. 440 (on a scale of 1:400,000, or 1 inch = 9.8km/6 miles).

BREAKDOWNS   If you rent your car from one of the large companies, such as Avis or Hertz, 24-hour breakdown service is available in Portugal. If you're a member of a major automobile club, such as AA, CAA, or AAA, you can get aid from the **Automóvel Club de Portugal** (**ACP;** © **70/750-95-10;** www.acp.pt).

HITCHHIKING   Portugal doesn't have any laws against hitchhiking, but it isn't commonly practiced. If you decide to hitchhike, do so with discretion. Usually Portuguese auto insurance doesn't cover hitchhikers. Considering the potential danger to both the passenger and the driver, hitchhiking is not recommended.

By Plane

Portugal is a small country, and flying from one place to another is relatively easy. Though most people still take trains to get around, **TAP Air Portugal** flies four times a day to Faro, in the Algarve, and Porto, the main city of the north. Service to Faro is likely to be more frequent in July and August. Four flights a day depart for Funchal, capital of Madeira, plus limited service to the Azores.

For more information, contact TAP Air Portugal, Gare Do Oriente, 1200 Lisboa (© **70/720-57-00;** www.tap-airportugal.pt).

By Train

The Portuguese railway system is underdeveloped compared to those of the more industrialized nations of western Europe. Still, trains do connect the capital and more than 20 major towns. Express trains run from Lisbon, Coimbra (the university city), and Porto. Electric trains, which leave from the Lisbon waterfront, travel along the Costa do Sol (Estoril and Cascais) and on to Queluz and Sintra.

At Lisbon's Santa Apolónia Station, you can make connections for international service and the Northern and Eastern lines. The Rossio Station serves Sintra and the Western line; the Cais do Sodré Station handles service for the Costa do Sol resorts of Estoril and Cascais. Finally, trains leave from the Sul e Sueste Station for the Alentejo and the Algarve.

In summer, express trains depart Lisbon for the Algarve Monday through Saturday. They leave from the Barreiro Station (across the Tagus—take one of the frequently departing ferries). Off-season service runs four times weekly. For information about rail travel in Portugal, phone © **80/820-82-08** in Lisbon, or check the Portuguese Railways website at www.cp.pt.

Railroad information and tickets for travel between almost any two stations in Europe, including stations throughout Portugal, are available from the representatives of the **Portuguese National Railway,** Rail Europe, Inc. (© **800/848-7245** in the U.S.; www.raileurope.com). The telephone representatives sell one-way and round-trip tickets into or out of Portugal, tickets for travel within Portugal, and rail passes for travel within Portugal and the rest of Europe. Couchettes (sleeping cars) can be arranged. See "Getting There," earlier, for more information on rail passes.

Getting Around

PLANNING YOUR TRIP TO PORTUGAL

SENIOR DISCOUNTS   The Portuguese National Railway's 50% discount policy applies for people 65 and older. These tickets are good all year.

By Bus

Buses are a cheap means of transportation in Portugal. A network of buses links almost all the major towns and cities. Many routes originate in Lisbon. The former national bus company, **Rodoviária Nacional** (✆ 70/722-33-44; www. rede-expressos.pt), has been privatized but essentially offers the same service as before. In addition, Portugal has many local and private regional bus links.

Express coaches between major cities are called *expressos.* Once in most cities and towns, you can take cheap bus rides to nearby villages or sights. Of course, in many towns and all cities, you can use buses to get around within the city.

TIPS ON ACCOMMODATIONS

The government rates hotels in Portugal from five stars to one. The difference between a five-star hotel and a four-star hotel will not always be apparent to the casual visitor. Often the distinction is based on square footage of bathrooms and other technicalities. When you go below this level, you enter the realm of the second- and third-class hotel. Some can be decent and even excellent places to stay. Third-class hotels are bare-bones accommodations in Portugal.

When you check into a hotel, you'll see the official rates posted in the main lobby and somewhere in your room, perhaps at the bottom of the closet. These rates, dictated by the Directorate of Tourism, are regulated and really are a form of rent control. They include the 13% service charge and 18% value-added tax (VAT).

Coastal hotels, especially those in the Algarve, are required to grant off-season (Nov–Feb) visitors a 15% discount. To attract more off-season business, a number of establishments offer this discount from mid-October through March.

If an infraction such as overcharging occurs, you can demand to be given the **Official Complaints Book,** in which you can write your allegations. The hotel manager is obligated to turn your comments over to the Directorate of Tourism. The directorate staff reviews them to see if punitive action should be taken.

Prices & Ratings in This Guide

Unless otherwise indicated, prices in this guide include the 13% service charge and all taxes. Breakfast might or might not be included; individual write-ups reflect various hotel policies about breakfast. All references in Portugal to "including breakfast" refer to a continental breakfast of juice, coffee, or tea and croissants, butter, and jam. If you stay at a hotel and order bacon and eggs or other extras, you'll likely be billed for them as a la carte items. Parking rates are per day.

Pousadas

When traveling through the countryside, plot your trips so you'll stop over at the government-owned pousadas (tourist inns). The Portuguese government has established these inns in historic buildings, such as convents, palaces, and castles, including Henry the Navigator's Sagres and a feudal castle in the walled city of Óbidos. Often pousadas occupy beautiful physical settings, and they are generally (but not always) in regions that don't have many suitable hotels. Although the rates are not low, for the quality and services offered pousadas represent a moderate value. A guest can't stay more than 5 days because there's usually a waiting list. If you're on your honeymoon, ask about special terms that may be available. For our recommendations, see "The Best Pousadas," in chapter 1.

Travel agents can make reservations at pousadas, or you can contact **Pousadas de Portugal,** Av. Sta. Joana Princesa 10, 1749 Lisboa (© **21/844-20-01;** www.pousadas.pt).

Country Homes

Far more exciting—at least to us—than pousadas is the chain of farm estates, country homes, and restored manor houses that have opened to the public here. These properties are the most highly recommended in this guide, and they offer grand comfort and lots of charm, often in a historic setting.

The best and most extensive network is in the region of Viana do Castelo, where you can sometimes board with the poor but proud Portuguese aristocracy. Many of these manors and farms are called *quintas*. All of these properties are privately run, and breakfast is always included. For more information, contact **Solares de Portugal,** Praça da República, 4990 Ponte de Lima (© **25/874-16-72;** www.solaresdeportugal.pt). Local tourist offices also provide directories that include color photographs and maps with directions.

Other Special Accommodations

Tourist inns not run by the government are known as *estalagems.* Often these offer some of the finest accommodations in Portugal; many are decorated in the traditional Portuguese, or *típico,* style and represent top-notch bargains.

The *pensão* is a boardinghouse that charges the lowest rates in the country. The "deluxe" *pensão* is a misnomer; the term simply means that the *pensão* enjoys the highest rating in its category. The accommodations are decidedly not luxurious and are generally the equivalent of a second-class hotel. The boardinghouses are finds for the budget hunter. Many prepare generous portions of good local cuisine. There are both first- and second-class boardinghouses. The *residência* is a form of boardinghouse, without board; these establishments offer a room and breakfast only.

Another addition to the accommodations scene is the *solare.* Most are spacious country-manor houses, formerly property of the Portuguese aristocracy, that are now being restored and opened as guesthouses. Many date from the Age of Exploration, when navigators brought riches back from all over the world and established lavish homes that were passed down to their heirs. The inns are all over the country, but most are along the Costa Verde, between Ponte de Lima and Viana do Castelo.

Information on the *solares* program is available from the **Portuguese National Tourist Office,** 590 Fifth Ave., 4th Floor, New York, NY 10036 (© **800/PORTUGAL** [767-8842] or 646/723-0200; www.portugal.com).

One of the best associations for arranging stays in private homes is **Privetur** (© **+44 20/3287-1839;** www.privetur.co.uk). It represents manor houses and country homes in all the major tourist districts. Privetur can arrange accommodations in circumstances that are sometimes more personalized than stays in large hotels.

Reservations

Reservations are essential for peak-season summer travel in Portugal, when many hotels fill with vacationing Europeans. Unless you're incurably spontaneous, you'll probably be better off with some idea of where you'll spend each night, even in low season.

Most hotels require at least a day's deposit before they'll reserve a room. You can usually cancel a room reservation a week ahead of time and get a full refund, but check your hotel's policy when you book. It's important that you enclose a prepaid International Reply Coupon with your payment, especially if you're writing to a budget hotel. Better yet, call and speak to a staff member, or send an e-mail.

[FastFACTS]

Addresses In Portugal, the ground floor is not called the first floor as in the United States; what Americans would call the fourth floor is actually the third floor. "ESP" after a floor number indicates that you should go left, and "DIR" means turn right.

American Express **Travel Store** is the entity representing American Express, although operating independently under license from American Express. You can find locations in Lisbon, at Rua Rodrigues Sampaio 97 (✆ **21/356-53-00**); and at Aeroporto de Lisboa (✆ **91/200-05-13**).

Area Codes See the "Fast Facts" sections for individual cities for info on telephone area codes.

Babysitters Check with your hotel's staff for arrangements. Most first-class hotels can provide babysitters from lists that the concierge keeps. Remember to request a babysitter no later than the morning if you're going out that evening. Also, if you and your children do not speak Portuguese, request a sitter with at least a minimum knowledge of English.

Business Hours Hours vary throughout the country, but there is a set pattern. Banks generally are open Monday through Friday from 8:30am to 3pm. Currency-exchange offices at airports and rail terminals are open longer hours, and the office at Portela airport outside Lisbon is open 24 hours a day. Most museums open at 10am, close at 5pm, and often close for lunch between 12:30 and 2pm. Larger museums with bigger staffs remain open at midday. Shops are open, in general, Monday through Friday from 9am to 1pm and from 3 to 7pm, and Saturday from 9am to 1pm. Most restaurants serve lunch from noon until 3pm and dinner from 7:30 to 11pm; many close on Sunday. Many nightclubs open at 10pm, but the action doesn't really begin until after midnight and often lasts until between 3 and 5am.

Car Rental See "Getting There" earlier in this chapter.

Cellphones See "Mobile Phones," later in this section.

Crime See "Safety" later in this section.

Customs You can take into Portugal most personal effects and the following items duty-free, provided that they show signs of use: a portable typewriter and one video camera or two still cameras with 10 rolls of film each; a portable radio, a tape recorder, and a laptop PC per person; 200 cigarettes, or 50 cigars, or 250 grams of tobacco; 2 liters of wine or 1 liter of liquor per person over 17 years old; and sports equipment, including fishing gear, one bicycle, skis, tennis or squash racquets, and golf clubs. Returning U.S. citizens who have been away for 48 hours or more are allowed to bring back, once every 30 days, $800 worth of merchandise duty-free. You'll be charged a flat rate of duty on the next $1,000 worth of purchases. Any dollar amount beyond that is subject to duty at whatever rates apply. On mailed gifts, the duty-free limit is $200. Be sure to have your receipts or purchases handy to expedite the declaration process. **Note:** If you owe duty, you are required to pay on your arrival in the United States, using cash, personal check, government or traveler's check, or money order; some locations also accept Visa or MasterCard.

To avoid having to pay duty on foreign-made personal items you owned before your trip, bring along a bill of sale, insurance policy, jeweler's appraisal, or receipt of purchase. Or you can register items that can be readily identified by a permanently affixed serial number or marking—think laptop computers, cameras, and CD players—with Customs before you leave. Take the items to the nearest Customs office, or register them with Customs at the airport from which you're departing. You'll receive, at no cost, a Certificate of Registration, which allows duty-free entry for the life of the item.

With some exceptions, you cannot bring fresh fruits and vegetables into the U.S. For specifics on what you can bring back, download the invaluable free pamphlet "Know Before You Go" online at www.cbp.gov. (Click on "Travel," then click on "Know Before You Go! Online Brochure.") Or contact U.S. Customs & Border Protection (CBP), 1300 Pennsylvania Ave. NW, Washington, DC 20229 (© **877/CBP-5511** [227-5511]) and request the pamphlet.

For a clear summary of Canadian rules, request the booklet "I Declare," issued by the Canada Border Services Agency (© **800/461-9999** in Canada, or 204/983-3500; www.cbsa-asfc.gc.ca). Canada allows its citizens a C$750 exemption, and you're allowed to bring back duty-free one carton of cigarettes, one can of tobacco, 40 imperial ounces of liquor, and 50 cigars. In addition, you're allowed to mail gifts to Canada from abroad valued at less than C$60 a day, provided they're unsolicited and don't contain alcohol or tobacco (write on the package "Unsolicited gift, under $60 value"). All valuables, including serial numbers of valuables you already own, such as expensive foreign cameras, should be declared on the Y-38 form before departure from Canada. **Note:** The C$750 exemption can only be used once a year and only after an absence of 7 days.

The duty-free allowance in Australia is A$900 or, for those under 18, A$450. Citizens can bring in 250 cigarettes or 250 grams of loose tobacco, and 1,125 milliliters of alcohol. If you're returning with valuables you already own, such as foreign-made cameras, you should file form B263. A helpful brochure available from Australian consulates or Customs offices is "Know Before You Go." For more information, call the Australian Customs Service at © **1300/363-263,** or log on to www.customs.gov.au.

U.K. citizens returning from a non-E.U. country have a Customs allowance of 200 cigarettes; 50 cigars; 250 grams of smoking tobacco; 2 liters of still table wine; 1 liter of spirits or strong liqueurs (over 22% volume); 2 liters of fortified wine, sparkling wine or other liqueurs; 60cc (ml) perfume; 250cc (ml) of toilet water; and £145 worth of all other goods, including gifts and souvenirs. People under 17 cannot have the tobacco or alcohol allowance. For more information, contact HM Revenue & Customs at © **0845/010-9000** (from outside the U.K., 020/8929-0152), or consult their website at www.hmrc.gov.uk.

The duty-free allowance for New Zealand is NZ$700. Citizens over 17 can bring in 200 cigarettes, 50 cigars, or 250 grams of tobacco (or a mixture of all three if their combined weight doesn't exceed 250g), plus 4.5 liters of wine and beer, or 1.125 liters of liquor. New Zealand currency does not carry import or export restrictions. Fill out a certificate of export listing the valuables you are taking out of the country; that way, you can bring them back without paying duty. Most questions are answered in a free pamphlet available at New Zealand consulates and Customs offices: "New Zealand Customs Guide for Travelers, Notice no. 4." For more information, contact New Zealand Customs Service, The

Customhouse, 17–21 Whitmore St., Box 2218, Wellington (℗ **64/9927-8036** or 0800/428-786 in New Zealand; www.customs.govt.nz).

Disabled Travelers Because of Portugal's many hills and endless flights of stairs, visitors with disabilities might have difficulty getting around the country, but conditions are slowly improving. Newer hotels are more sensitive to the needs of those with disabilities, and the more expensive restaurants, in general, are wheelchair-accessible. However, since most places have limited, if any, facilities for people with disabilities, you might consider taking an organized tour specifically designed to accommodate travelers with disabilities.

In general, facilities for persons with disabilities lag behind what is available in the United States or even in Spain. Of course, you'll fare better in big cities such as Lisbon and do less well in rural areas. Many modern museums. especially in Lisbon, are equipped to handle persons with disabilities.

The preferred mode of transportation in Portugal for those with disabilities is the train. More and more stations have ramps, and many trains are equipped with wheelchair lifts, specially equipped toilets, and even separate seating areas. All Eurostar trains are wheelchair accessible and most InterCity (IC) trains and some EuroCity (EC) trains are as well. If a person with disabilities can drive a car, Hertz and Avis seem to offer the best selection of hand-controlled vehicles.

There is no local agency to help travelers with disabilities, so you should secure special arrangements and advice before you go, most often from international organizations which can provide specific information or in some cases make arrangements in Portugal.

Doctors The reception desks of all hotels keep a list of local doctors to call. Of course, you should request an English-speaking one. Also, see "Hospitals" below.

Drinking You must be 18 to drink in Portugal. In Lisbon, bars are open until dawn. You can purchase beer, wine, and liquor in most markets, cafes, restaurants, and liquor stores. There are no restrictions on when you can purchase alcohol.

Driving Rules See "Getting Around," earlier in this chapter.

Drugs Illegal drugs are plentiful in Portugal, although penalties can be severe if you're caught possessing or selling illegal narcotics. Judges tend to throw the book at foreigners caught selling illegal narcotics. Courts rarely allow foreigners out on bail, and local prosecutors have a high conviction rate. All the U.S., British, and Canadian consulates can do is provide you with a list of local attorneys.

Electricity Voltage is 200 volts AC (50 cycles), and you need a converter if you bring any electronics from the United States or Canada. Many hardware stores in North America sell the appropriate converters. The concierge desks of most hotels will lend you a transformer and plug adapters, or tell you where you can buy them nearby. If you have any doubt about whether you have the appropriate transformer, ask at your hotel desk before you try to plug in anything.

Embassies & Consulates If you lose your passport or have some other pressing problem, you'll need to get in touch with your embassy.

The Embassy of the United States, on Avenida das Forças Armadas (Sete Rios), 1600 Lisboa (℗ **21/727-33-00;** http://portugal.usembassy.gov), is open Monday through Friday from 8am to 12:30pm and from 1:30 to 5pm. If you've lost a passport, the embassy can take photographs for you and help you to obtain the proof of citizenship needed to get a replacement.

The Embassy of Canada is at Av. da Liberdade 198–200, EDIT Victoria 3rd Floor, 1269 Lisboa (℗ **21/316-46-00;** www.canadainternational.gc.ca). It's open Monday through Friday from 9am to noon and from 2 to 4pm (till 1pm Fri July–Aug).

Traveling with Minors

It's always wise to have plenty of documentation when traveling with children in today's world. For changing details on entry requirements for children traveling abroad, keep up-to-date by going to the U.S. Department of State website: www.travel.state.gov.

To prevent international child abduction, E.U. governments have initiated procedures at entry and exit points. These often (but not always) include requiring documentary evidence of relationship and permission for the child's travel from the parent or legal guardian not present. Having such documentation on hand, even if not required, facilitates entries and exits. All children must have their own passport. To obtain a passport, the child *must* be present—that is, in person—at the center issuing the passport. Both parents must be present as well. If not, then a notarized statement from the parents is required.

The Embassy of the United Kingdom, Rua São Bernardo 33, 1249 Lisboa (📞 **21/392-40-00;** www.ukinportugal.fco.gov.uk), is open Monday to Friday 9am to 1pm and 2:30 to 5:30pm.

The Embassy of the Republic of Ireland, Av. da Liberdade 200, 1250 Lisboa (📞 **21/330-82-00**), is open Monday through Friday from 9:30am to 12:30pm.

The Embassy of Australia, on Av. da Liberdade 200, 2nd Floor, 1250 Lisboa (📞 **21/310-15-00;** www.portugal.embassy.gov.au), is open Monday through Friday from 9am to 5pm.

New Zealanders should go to the Embassy of the United Kingdom (see above).

Emergencies For the **police** (or an ambulance) in Lisbon, telephone 📞 **112.** In case of **fire,** call 📞 **112.** For the **Portuguese Red Cross,** call 📞 **21/391-39-00.** The **national emergency** number in Portugal is 📞 **112.**

Family Travel On Portuguese airlines, you must request a special menu for children at least 24 hours in advance. If baby food is required, however, bring your own and ask a flight attendant to warm it to the right temperature.

Arrange ahead of time with your hotel for such necessities as a crib, a bottle warmer, and a car seat.

Most museums in Portugal grant half-price admission for kids under 12.

Look also for our "Kids" icon, indicating attractions, restaurants, or hotels and resorts that are especially family-friendly throughout the country.

Gasoline Please see "Getting There," earlier in this chapter.

Health You should encounter few health problems traveling in Portugal. The tap water is generally safe to drink, the milk is pasteurized, and health services are good. Occasionally, the change in diet can cause some minor diarrhea, so you might want to take along some anti-diarrheal medicine.

In large cities such as Lisbon and Porto, it is relatively easy to get over-the-counter medicine, and generic equivalents of common, noncontrolled prescription drugs are often available over-the-counter as well. If you find yourself suddenly missing a medication for which a prescription is required, a local doctor will usually do his or her best, pending legalities, to provide you with the prescription a local pharmacy would need to fill it. (Explain your problem to the pharmacist, and he or she will usually do whatever is necessary to help.) To save yourself time and paperwork, especially if you plan on traveling to remote villages and towns in the Portuguese countryside, it is always wise to stock up, in advance of your departure from home, on any special medications you might need, bringing enough medication from home to last for the duration of your trip.

Medical facilities are generally available in Portugal but, in many cases, might not meet U.S. standards. If a medical emergency arises, your hotel staff can usually put you in touch with a reliable doctor. If not, contact your embassy or a consulate; each one maintains a list of English-speaking doctors. We list hospitals under "Hospitals," below.

Portugal does not offer free medical treatment to visitors, except for citizens of certain countries, such as Great Britain, which have reciprocal health agreements. Nationals from such countries as Canada and the United States have to pay for medical services rendered.

In most cases, your existing health plan will provide the coverage you need. But double-check; you might want to buy **travel medical insurance** instead. Bring your insurance ID card with you when you travel.

Hospitals   A prime choice for medical aid is the **Hospital S. Francisco Xavier, SA** (Estrada Forte do Alto do Duque, Lisboa; ✆ **21/043-10-00;** www.hsfxavier.min-saude.pt). An alternative is **Hospital de Egas Moniz, SA** (Rua da Junqueira 126, Lisboa; ✆ **21/043-10-00;** www.hegasmoniz.min-saude.pt).

Insurance   For information on traveler's insurance, trip cancellation insurance, and medical insurance while traveling, please visit www.frommers.com/planning.

Internet & Wi-Fi   Although the availability of high-speed Internet access lags just a bit behind the better-funded Internet obsessions rampant in, say, the U.S. and northern Europe, Internet access is rapidly improving in Portugal despite the current economic crisis. Many of the country's politicians have expressed their hopes of providing every resident in Portugal free, or at least inexpensive, access to both the Internet and multimedia technology. Although that goal is a long way from completion, the country presently boasts more than 1,000 centers, each identified as an *Espaço Internet,* tucked away within universities, cybercafes (most of which are in urban areas and resorts frequented by tourists), airports, and hotel lobbies.

If you opt to bring your own wireless-access laptop, at least some of your e-accessibility issues will be solved, since hundreds of hotels have added wireless technologies to their entire premises or at least to designated "hotspots," usually within their lobbies. And many resort hotels, recognizing the perceived need on the part of their guests to stay in e-touch with their business and personal affairs while abroad, maintain computer terminals, screens, and keyboards within their public areas, allowing guests to sign on, usually for free.

Language   English is often spoken in the major resorts and at first-class and deluxe hotels; in smaller places, you'll often need the help of a phrase book or dictionary. One of the most helpful is the *Portuguese Phrase Book* (Berlitz).

Legal Aid   Contact your local consulate for a list of English-speaking lawyers if you run into trouble with the law. After that, you're at the mercy of the local courts.

Healthy Travels to You

The following government websites offer up-to-date health-related travel advice.

- **Australia:** www.smartraveller.gov.au
- **Canada:** www.hc-sc.gc.ca/index_e.html
- **U.S.:** www.cdc.gov/travel

---

frommers.com: THE COMPLETE TRAVEL RESOURCE

Planning a trip or just returned? Head to **Frommers.com**, voted Best Travel Site by *PC Magazine.* We think you'll find our site indispensable before, during, and after your travels—with expert advice and tips; independent reviews of hotels, restaurants, attractions, and preferred shopping and nightlife venues; vacation giveaways; and an online booking tool. We publish the complete contents of over 135 travel guides in our **Destinations** section, covering over 4,000 places worldwide. Each weekday, we publish original articles that report on **Deals and News** via our free **Frommers.com Newsletters.** What's more, **Arthur**

Frommer himself blogs five days a week, with cutting opinions about the state of travel in the modern world. We're betting you'll find our **Events** listings an invaluable resource; it's an up-to-the-minute roster of what's happening in cities everywhere—including concerts, festivals, lectures, and more. We've also added weekly **podcasts, interactive maps,** and hundreds of new images across the site. Finally, don't forget to visit our **Message Boards,** where you can join in conversations with thousands of fellow Frommer's travelers and post your trip report once you return.

15

LGBT Travelers Following the example set by neighboring Spain, Portugal has legalized same-sex marriage in spite of violent opposition. Nonetheless, attitudes toward homosexuality vary by region, with Lisbon being the center of gay male life (less so for lesbians). The country has a strong Catholic heritage, and public displays of same-sex affection, especially in rural areas, might bring disapproval. Even so, overt homophobia is rare in Portugal. Nearly all hotels in Portugal are savvy about checking in same-sex couples, even if a double bed is requested.

Mail While in Portugal, you can have your mail directed to your hotel (or hotels), to the American Express representative, or to *Poste Restante* (General Delivery) in Lisbon. You must present your passport to pick up mail. The general post office in Lisbon is on Praça do Comércio, 1100 Lisbon (© **21/322-09-20**); it's open daily from 8:30am to 6pm.

Sending either a postcard or letter from Portugal to anywhere else in Europe costs .85€. Sending either a postcard or letter from Portugal to anywhere else in the world costs 1€.

Mobile Phones With an increasing focus on being able to whip out a cellphone whenever a traveler needs it, some visitors prioritize getting a mobile/cellphone as one of their first tasks upon arrival.

In Portugal, whoever makes the cellphone call pays the charges, whether it's to or from either a landline or mobile phone; the receiving phone is not charged. Whoever inaugurates the call generally is charged both for the call connection and for the time spent talking on the phone. This rate is charged per second. Most published rates don't include IVA (VAT), which is extra.

Since sending a text message is usually cheaper than dialing a phone number, sending text messages is extremely popular in Portugal, mainly as a means of communicating informally with friends.

You'll likely not be able to use a North American cellphone in Portugal unless it's GSM/GPRS compatible and unless it operates with a SIM card. Virtually all mobile phones in Iberia, the U.K. and other parts of Europe operate with this system, as do AT&T and

T-Mobile cellphones from North America; North American cellphones tied into to smaller, regional carriers sometimes aren't.

But even if your phone is compatible with the system that operates in Portugal, you'll very likely need to have it unlocked. This means taking your mobile or cellphone to a mobile phone shop that offer this service, where a staff member will remove whatever it is that made your mobile or cellphone work exclusively on your previous provider's network. And then be very alert to the fact that roaming charges for U.S.-based phones, even if you successfully convert them, are more expensive (and sometimes roaringly more expensive) than for local cellphone users tied into local (i.e., Portuguese) cellphone plans.

Considering the technical complications of converting a U.S.-based cellphone for use in Portugal (and the hassle of reconverting it back to the North American system after your return), many travelers opt to simply buy a prepaid cellphone when they arrive in the country.

If you're buying a mobile or cellphone in Portugal, you can choose to have a contract (not a good idea unless you're opting to remain for many months) or opt for a pay-as-you-go phone. When you sign a contract, it's assumed that you'll be on location for payment of a monthly bill, that you're a resident with a local bank account, and that you'll be within Portugal for several months or more. If that's indeed the case, you'll usually qualify for cheaper rates and, depending on special promotions in effect at the time of your purchase, a free or cheap mobile phone.

But even with generally higher rates, if you don't make many calls or send many text messages in any given month, a pay-as-you-go phone may end up being cheaper. As you would expect, you only pay for what you use.

You can "recharge" your prepaid phone with additional credit, usually through the use of a precoded certificate you can buy at newspaper kiosks or markets.

In general, call quality, coverage, and customer service tends to be relatively consistent among the range of carriers. If a rural backwater within Portugal tends to have spotty coverage, that spotty coverage will be roughly equivalent among all the carriers.

Vodafone (www.vodafone.pt), **WiFiPT** (www.ptwifi.pt), and **ArTelecom** (www.artelecom. pt) are three of the largest and most reliable mobile phone service providers in Portugal. Each maintains a website describing efficient ways of signing up for cellphone purchase and use either before or after your arrival in Portugal, and each employs some English-language speakers as part of their customer-service staffs.

As a means of keeping things straightforward and simple, we usually recommend that you opt for the cheapest phone, purchased outright, and the simplest plan that's suitable for the time you plan to spend in Europe. Special promotions and features change fairly often.

You'll be able to buy a cell/mobile phone in Portugal in department stores or through any of the dozens of dealers scattered in locations throughout the country. Smaller cell/mobile phone stores are numerous. Beware of any "used" phones, available from street vendors, selling for bargain-basement prices.

Generally, the prices for new mobile phones in Portugal start at 22€ for the cheapest models and up to 500€ for the latest models with all the bells and whistles you'd expect.

A Word About SKYPE: Unless you've invested in a cellphone with wireless connectivity to the Internet within Iberia, and unless you've taken the steps to make it compatible with the phone networks of Portugal, it's usually assumed that for compatibility with SKYPE, you'll have to carry a laptop computer with wireless Internet connectivity. If that's the case, and if your laptop is SKYPE-compatible, we applaud your sense of computer savvy. Just be alert to the dangers of banging up your laptop during the rigors of travel, and retain a sense of humor about nonconnectivity issues, which will vary widely according to your equipment and the local e-scene.

Money & Costs Portugal is no longer the bargain basement of Europe that it was in the '60s and '70s. Prices have moved more into alignment with the other European Union countries, but it's cheaper than neighboring Spain and much less expensive than the countries of the north, especially Scandinavia.

In its role as a member of the European Union, establishments such as hotels and restaurants accept cash, credit cards (usually American Express, Diners Club, MasterCard, and Visa) and travelers checks, the latter increasingly rare these days. Banks will exchange foreign currencies, such as British pounds or U.S. dollars, into euros.

Portugal doesn't impose limits on the amount of foreign currency you can bring into the country, but you are advised to declare the amount carried to prove to the Portuguese Customs Office that the currency came from outside the country. Visitors are allowed to take out the same amount (or less) of foreign currency that they brought in with them.

The euro, the single European currency, became the official currency of Portugal on January 1, 1999. The symbol of the euro is €; its official abbreviation is EUR.

It's a good idea to exchange at least some money—just enough to cover airport incidentals and transportation to your hotel—before you leave home (though don't expect the exchange rate to be ideal), so you can avoid lines at airport ATMs.

Frommer's lists exact prices in the local currency. The currency conversions quoted below were correct at press time. However, rates fluctuate, so before departing consult a currency exchange website such as www.oanda.com/convert/classic to check up-to-the-minute rates.

THE VALUE OF THE EURO VS. OTHER POPULAR CURRENCIES

Euro (€)	US$	UK£	C$	AUS$	NZ$
1	1.45	0.90	1.40	1.335	1.75

Beware of hidden credit card fees while traveling. Check with your credit or debit card issuer to see what fees, if any, will be charged for overseas transactions. Recent reform legislation in the U.S., for example, has curbed some exploitative lending practices. But many banks have responded by increasing fees in other areas, including fees for customers who use credit and debit cards while out of the country—even if those charges were made in U.S. dollars. Fees can amount to 3% or more of the purchase price. Check with your bank before departing to avoid any surprise charges on your statement.

WHAT THINGS COST IN LISBON	EURO €
Taxi from the airport to central Lisbon	12.00
Double room (moderate)	145.00
Double room (inexpensive)	85.00
Three-course dinner for one, without wine (moderate)	35.00
Bottle of beer	3.00–5.00
Cup of coffee	2.25
Admission to most museums	5.00
Average theater ticket	7.50–16.00

MAJOR CHANGE IN credit cards

More and more places in Portugal are moving from the magnetic-strip credit card to the new Chip and PIN system. The program is designed to cut down on the fraudulent use of credit cards by requiring users to enter a four-digit personal identification number, or PIN, in a keypad near the cash register. More and more banks are issuing customers Chip and PIN versions of their debit or credit cards. In some cases, a waiter will bring a hand-held model to your table to verify your credit card.

In the changeover in technology, some retailers have falsely concluded that they can no longer take swipe cards, or can't take signature cards that don't have PINs anymore.

For the time being you should be able to use both the new and old cards in shops, hotels, and restaurants regardless of whether the businesses have the old credit and debit cards machines or the new Chip and PIN machines

installed. But expect a lot of confusion before you arrive in Portugal or elsewhere.

In the transition period between traditional swipe credit cards and those with an embedded computer chip, here's what you can do to protect yourself:

○ Call the number on the back of each card and ask for a four-digit PIN before leaving home.

○ Keep an eye out for the right logo displayed in a retailer's window. You want Visa or MasterCard, not Maestro, Visa Electron, or Carte Bleue.

○ Know that your Amex card will work where an Amex logo is displayed, but the card is not as widely accepted as Visa and MasterCard.

○ As a last resort, make sure you have enough cash to cover your purchase.

For help with currency conversions, tip calculations, and more, download Frommer's convenient Travel Tools app for your mobile device. Go to www.frommers.com/go/mobile and click on the Travel Tools icon.

ATM cards are plentiful in Portugal, even in small towns, but especially in Lisbon and Porto. There is a typical surcharge of $1 to $5 per withdrawal.

Newspapers & Magazines No major English-language newspapers or magazines are published within Portugal. In larger cities such as Lisbon or Porto, you can purchase many British newspapers (including the *Daily Mail,* the *Mail on Sunday,* and *The Times* [London]) at local street kiosks.

Packing For helpful information on packing for your trip, download our convenient Travel Tools from your mobile device. Go to www.Frommers.com/go/mobile and click on the Travel Tools icon.

Passports For visits of less than 3 months, U.S., Canadian, Irish, Australian, New Zealand, or British citizens need only a valid passport to enter Portugal.

For details on obtaining a passport, contact the passport office in your country:

○ **Australia** Australian Passport Information Service (☏ 131-232, or visit www.passports.gov.au).

○ **Canada** Passport Office, Department of Foreign Affairs and International Trade, Ottawa, ON K1A 0G3 (☏ 800/567-6868; www.ppt.gc.ca).

Dear Visa: I'm Off to Portugal!

Some credit card companies recommend that you notify them of any impending trip abroad so that they don't become suspicious when the card is used numerous times in a foreign destination and block your charges. Even if you don't call your credit card company in advance, you can always call the card company if a charge is refused. Keep in mind that toll-free numbers listed on the back of the card can't be dialed from Portugal—a good reason to find out the company's standard toll number. Perhaps the most important lesson here is to carry more than one card with you on your trip; a card might not work for any number of reasons, so having a backup is the smart way to go.

○ **Ireland** Passport Office, Setanta Centre, Molesworth Street, Dublin 2 (℃ 01/671-1633; www.foreignaffairs.gov.ie).

○ **New Zealand** Passports Office, Department of Internal Affairs, 47 Boulcott St., Wellington, 6011 (℃ 0800/225-050 in New Zealand, or 04/474-8100; www.passports.govt.nz).

○ **United Kingdom** Visit your nearest passport office, major post office, or travel agency or contact the Identity and Passport Service (IPS), 89 Eccleston Sq., London, SW1V 1PN (℃ 0300/222-0000; www.ips.gov.uk).

○ **United States** To find your regional passport office, check the U.S. State Department website (www.travel.state.gov/passport) or call the **National Passport Information Center** (℃ **877/487-2778**) for automated information.

Petrol See "Getting Around," earlier in this chapter.

Pharmacies The Portuguese government requires selected pharmacies, *farmácias de serviço* in Portugal, to stay open at all times of the day and night. They do so under a rotation system. Check with your concierge for the locations and hours of the nearest drugstores. In general, pharmacies in Portugal are open Monday through Friday from 9am to 1pm and from 3 to 7pm, and Saturday from 9am to 1pm.

Police If you need a police officer anywhere in Portugal, dial ℃ **112,** and you'll be routed to the individual precinct responsible for your location and your situation. If for any reason you want to bypass that deeply entrenched system, you can always opt to phone the local precinct if you know the number—the staff at many of the nation's hotels can provide you with that number. In Lisbon, the phone number for the Metropolitan Police Command is ℃ **21/765-42-42;** in Porto, it's ℃ **22/209-20-00.**

Some police forces in Portugal maintain subsections which are specifically charged with protecting order and addressing issues associated with tourists, and where, presumably, law enforcement officers command a working knowledge of English and/or languages other than Portuguese. In Lisbon, for access to the "tourist police," call ℃ **21/342-16-23;** in Porto, dial ℃ **22/208-18-33.** Frankly, "tourist police" officers have only limited authority and are usually called on for minor infractions, and spend at least some portion of their time dealing with rowdy behavior and/or disorderly conduct, sometimes alcohol-induced, with the understanding that any genuinely serious breach of legality will be handled by the conventional local police anyway. If you're faced with any significant legal or health-related emergency, you should dial ℃ **112.**

Safety Though Portugal has a relatively low rate of violent crime, petty crime against tourists is on the rise in continental Portugal. Travelers can become targets of pickpockets and purse-snatchers, particularly at popular sites, in restaurants, and on public transportation.

Rental cars and vehicles with nonlocal license plates are targets for break-ins, and travelers should remove all luggage from vehicles upon parking. Drivers in Portugal should keep car doors locked when stopped at intersections.

In general, visitors to Portugal should carry limited cash and credit cards and should leave extra cash, credit cards, and personal documents at home or in a hotel safe. Travelers should also avoid using ATMs in isolated or poorly lit areas. While thieves can operate anywhere, the U.S. Embassy receives frequent reports of theft from the following areas:

Lisbon Area: Pickpocketing and purse-snatching in the Lisbon area occur in buses, restaurants, the airport, trains, train stations, and trams, especially tram no. 28 to the Castle of São Jorge. Gangs of youths have robbed passengers on the Lisbon-Cascais train. At restaurants, thieves snatch items hung over the backs of chairs or placed on the floor. There have been reports of theft of unattended luggage from the Lisbon Airport. Special care should be taken at the Santa Apolónia and Rossio train stations, the Alfama and Bairro Alto districts, the Castle of São Jorge, and Belém.

Other Areas: Thefts have been reported in Sintra, Cascais, Mafra, and Fátima. Automobile break-ins occur in parking areas at attractions and near restaurants. Special care should be taken in parking at the Moorish Castle and Pena Palace in Sintra, and at the beachfront areas of Guincho, Cabo da Roca, and Boca do Inferno.

Senior Travel Mention the fact that you're a senior when you make your travel reservations. Although all of the major U.S. airlines have canceled their senior discount and coupon book programs, many hotels still offer discounts for seniors. In most cities, people over the age of 60 qualify for reduced admission to theaters, museums, and other attractions, as well as discounted fares on public transportation.

Members of **AARP,** 601 E St. NW, Washington, DC 20049 (© **888/687-2277** in the U.S.; www.aarp.org), get discounts on hotels, airfares, and car rentals. AARP offers members a wide range of benefits, including *AARP The Magazine* and a monthly newsletter. Anyone over 50 can join. Some places in Portugal honor AARP discounts, and it always pays to ask.

Road Scholar (© **800/454-5768** in the U.S.; www.roadscholar.org) arranges study programs in Portugal for those ages 55 and over (and a spouse or companion of any age). Most courses last 2 to 4 weeks, and many include airfare, accommodations in university dormitories or modest inns, meals, and tuition.

Smoking The government of Portugal imposes a ban on smoking in enclosed public places and in commercial establishments. Owners of large spaces—that is, more than 100m (328 ft.)—can decide whether or not to allow smoking. However, they have to display a sign to that effect and provide designated smoking areas.

Single Travelers Many people prefer traveling alone—except for the relatively steep cost of booking a single room, which is usually well over half the price of a double.

Many British agents are keenly aware of the needs of the single traveler. One tour operator whose groups are usually at least half singles is **Explore Worldwide Ltd.,** Nelson House, 55 Victoria Rd., Hampshire, England GU14 7PA (© **+44 845/867-9493;** www. explore.co.uk). It has a well-justified reputation for offering offbeat tours, including 14-day expeditions to five islands of the Azores, and motorcoach tours through the highlights of "Unknown Spain and Portugal." Groups rarely include more than 16 participants; children under 14 are not allowed.

TravelChums (www.travelchums.com) is an Internet-only travel-companion matching service with elements of an online personals-type site, hosted by the respected New York–based Shaw Guides travel service. They periodically offer trips to Portugal.

Student Travel   The **International Student Travel Confederation** (**ISTC;** www.aboutistc.org) was formed in 1949 to make travel around the world more affordable for students. Check out its website for comprehensive travel services information and details on how to get an **International Student Identity Card (ISIC),** which qualifies students for substantial savings on rail passes, plane tickets, entrance fees, and more. It also provides students with basic health and life insurance and a 24-hour helpline. The card is valid for a maximum of 18 months. You can apply for the card online or in person at **STA Travel** (✆ **800/781-4040** in North America; www.statravel.com), the biggest student travel agency in the world; check out the website to locate STA Travel offices worldwide. If you're no longer a student but are still under 26, you can get an **International Youth Travel Card (IYTC)** from the same people, which entitles you to some discounts. **Travel CUTS** (✆ **800/667-2887;** www.travelcuts.com) offers similar services for both Canadians and U.S. residents. Irish students may prefer to turn to **USIT** (✆ **01/602-1906;** www.usit.ie), an Ireland-based specialist in student, youth, and independent travel.

Taxes   Because Portugal and neighboring Spain simultaneously joined the Common Market (now the European Union) on January 1, 1986, Portugal imposed a value-added tax (VAT; known within Portugal as the IVA) of between 6% and 23%, depending on the product, on most purchases made within its borders.

At this writing, however, faced with a debt crisis and pressure from other member nations of the European Union, Portugal will probably redefine the percentages charged for IVA (VAT) impositions on hotels, restaurants, services, and luxury goods during the lifetime of this edition. In the words of one high-placed official, "not even the country's top fiscal authorities can predict what percentages will be in effect for subcategories at the time of your visit," other than the assurance that IVA rates within mainland Portugal might be escalated upward from the present range of between 6% to 23%, with increasing numbers of goods and services assessed with higher rates within that range. Note the possibility of slight variations on those assessments within the semi-autonomous regions of Madeira and the Azores.

One trend is probably certain: Such deluxe goods as jewelry, furs, oceangoing yachts, and expensive imported liquors will be assessed at the upper regions of the above-noted range. Because a scotch and soda in a Portuguese bar is defined as a luxury good, thereby carrying this high tax, many people have changed their alcohol preferences from imported scotch to Portuguese brandy and soda or, more prosaically, beer.

To get a VAT refund on purchases that qualify (ask the shopkeeper), present your passport to the salesperson and ask for the special stamped form. Present the form with your purchases at the booth marked for IVA tax refunds at the airport. You'll get your money refunded right at the booth. For VAT refunds, you can also apply to **Global Blue** (www.global-blue.com).

Telephones   To call Portugal, follow these steps:

1. Dial the international access code: 011 from the U.S.; 00 from the U.K., Ireland, or New Zealand; or 0011 from Australia.

2. Dial the country code 351.

3. Dial the city code (don't include the 0), and then the number.

To make international calls: To make international calls from Portugal, first dial 00 and then the country code (U.S. or Canada 1, U.K. 44, Ireland 353, Australia 61, New Zealand 64). Next you dial the area code and number. For example, if you wanted to call the British Embassy in Washington, D.C., you would dial 00-1-202-588-7800.

For directory assistance: Dial 📞 **118** if you're looking for a number inside Portugal, and dial 📞 **177** for numbers to all other countries.

For operator assistance: If you need operator assistance in making a call, dial 📞 **171.**

Toll-free numbers: Calling a 1-800 number in the States from Portugal is not toll-free. In fact, it costs the same as an overseas call.

Time Portugal is 5 hours ahead of Eastern Standard Time in the United States. Like most European countries, Portugal has daylight saving time. It moves its clocks ahead an hour in late spring and an hour back in the fall, corresponding roughly to daylight saving time in the United States; exact dates vary.

Tipping Most service personnel in Portugal expect a good tip rather than a small one, as in the past. Hotels add a service charge (known as *serviço*), which is divided among the entire staff, but individual tipping is also the rule. Tip 1€ to the bellhop for running an errand, 1€ to the doorman who hails you a cab, 1€ to the porter for each piece of luggage carried, 2.50€ to the wine steward if you've dined often at your hotel, and 1.50€ to the chambermaid.

In first-class or deluxe hotels, the concierge will present you with a separate bill for extras, such as charges for bullfight tickets. A gratuity is expected in addition to the charge. The amount will depend on the number of requests you've made.

Figure on tipping about 20% of your taxi fare for short runs. For longer treks—for example, from the airport to Cascais—15% is adequate.

Restaurants and nightclubs include a service charge and government taxes of 18%. As in hotels, this money is distributed among the entire staff, so extra tipping is customary. Add about 5% to the bill in a moderately priced restaurant, and up to 10% in a deluxe or first-class establishment. For hatcheck in fado houses, restaurants, and nightclubs, tip at least 1€. Washroom attendants get .50€.

Toilets Major cities have public toilets. If not, cafes provide facilities, but owners expect you to make some small purchase, so you'll be viewed as a paying customer.

Vat See "Taxes" earlier in this section.

Visas Visas are not needed by U.S., Canadian, Irish, Australian, New Zealand, or British citizens for visits of less than 3 months.

Visitor Information Before you go, contact one of the overseas branches of the **Portuguese National Tourist Office.** The main office in the **United States** is at 590 Fifth Ave., 4th Floor, New York, NY 10036-4702 (📞 **646/723-0200**). In **Canada,** the office is at 60 Bloor St. W., Ste. 1005, Toronto, ON M4W 3B8 (📞 **416/921-98-70**). In the **United Kingdom,** contact the Portuguese Tourist Office, 11 Belgrave Sq., London SW1X 8PP (📞 **0845/355-1212;** www.visitportugal.com).

The following websites are helpful:

○ www.portugal.com: Investments, Trade, and Tourism of Portugal, a government agency, maintains this site. It is a general information resource, providing data about tourism and attractions, among other information.

○ www.portugal-info.net: This site provides an encyclopedic range of information about accommodations, restaurants and cuisine, events, entertainment, and sports. The focus is on Lisbon and the Algarve, and it's of special use to visitors from the United Kingdom.

○ www.pousadas.pt: This site provides the best details on pousadas (government-sponsored inns scattered throughout the country). It offers geographic details, current rates, information on online bookings, and even photographs.

○ www.tap-airportugal.us: This site provides data about TAP's (Portuguese Air Transportation) flights in Portugal and online reservations. New features include all published fares and data about how to change reservations.

Water Tap water is generally potable throughout Portugal, but bottled water is always safer. Even if the water in Portugal isn't bad, you won't be used to the microbes and can become ill. In rural areas, the water supply might not be purified. Under no circumstances should you swim in or drink from freshwater rivers or streams, as the water might be polluted by sewage or you can pick up parasites.

Wi-Fi See "Internet & Wi-Fi," earlier in this section.

Index